Because It's Just and Right

The Untold Back-Story of the US Recognition of Jerusalem as the Capital of Israel and Moving the US Embassy to Jerusalem

Farley Weiss

and

Leonard Grunstein

Printed by:
Geviyah Publishing Company, LLC
Israel Heritage Foundation
(geviyahpublishingcompanyllc@gmail.com)

Printed in the United States of America

TESTIMONIALS FROM NOTABLES

Ambassador David Friedman

On May 14, 2018, I presided over the opening of the United States Embassy to Israel in its holy capital, Jerusalem -- the proudest day of my life. The opening of America's embassy in Jerusalem was the culmination of decades of efforts by American heroes who courageously stood for the undeniable truth that Jerusalem has always been, and always will be, the center of Jewish spiritual, intellectual and political life. In Because It's Just and Right: The Untold Back-Story of the US Recognition of Jerusalem as the Capital of Israel and Moving the US Embassy to Jerusalem, Farley Weiss and Leonard Grunstein tell the story of these heroes, and, in so doing, recount the legal, political and social headwinds which they encountered and overcame on their "right and just" journey. This book is essential reading for a complete understanding of why Jerusalem is, and must always remain, the undivided eternal capital of the Jewish State.

David Friedman, US Ambassador to Israel 2017-2021

Senator Joe Lieberman

"In this book, Farley Weiss and Len Grunstein tell the dramatic story of how the United States Congress enacted legislation to move our Embassy in Israel to Jerusalem in 1995, and how twenty-three years later in 2018, it was finally moved there because, as the book's title says, it was "Just and Right."

I was privileged to work with a bipartisan group of Senate co-sponsors of the 1995 legislation – Senators Bob Dole, Pat Moynihan, and Jon Kyl, and to be there in Jerusalem when our Embassy opened on May 14, 2018. I remember speaking to Farley on that historic day, viewing the text of the Jerusalem Embassy bill which was displayed, and expressing our shared gratitude that the move was as good for the United States as it was for Israel."

Governor Mike Huckabee

Both Democrat and Republican Presidents promised to carry out the law and rightfully recognize Jerusalem as the legitimate capital of Israel and the Jewish people. But they all found excuses to deny Israel the respect of its own seat of government until President Trump did it. I was in the White House shortly after he announced he would do it and I asked him why did HE do it when all those before him declined due to international pressure and fear within the State Department. He simply said to me: "Because I said I would, and it was the RIGHT thing to do." Refreshingly straightforward and exactly what we should have done!

Alan Dershowitz
Professor emeritus Harvard

I was privileged to be at the opening of the U.S. embassy in Jerusalem. It was the culmination of many years of efforts, promises and delays. Finally, the truth has begun to be recognized: that Jerusalem is the eternal capital of the nation state of the Jewish people. Now other nations must join in acknowledging this truth through their actions. This book should promote that important development.

Stuart Force

"Since the loss of our son, Taylor Allen Force, on March 8, 2016, in a stabbing attack committed by a 22 year old Palestinian Arab smuggled into Israel, I have been trying to understand the dynamics at play in the Israeli/Palestinian conflict. Until Farley and Len's scholarly work, there hasn't been a source that addresses its many complex facets. This book should be on every reference shelf covering Israel and the Mideast.

I wish that Farley and Len's book had been available as we worked for passage of the Taylor Force Act that stops United States financial aid to the Palestinian Authority until it ends its Pay For Slay policy paying terrorists for attacks on innocent civilians in Israel. It would have greatly aided my efforts to understand both the generalities and specifics of the subject. The extensive inclusion of quotes from the principals involved helps separate the fiction of the widespread biased reporting favoring Palestinian Arab propaganda from the reality of their stated goal of erasing the State of Israel, and is an important accomplishment of this book."

Jeanine Esperne

As the senior staffer in Senator Jon Kyl's office assigned to the bill to relocate the Embassy of the United States to Jerusalem, I can say Farley's and Leonard's book tells the true story behind the long, hard fought effort to pass the legislation jointly proposed by Jon and Senator Joe Lieberman. The bill met fierce resistance from all quarters, especially the Clinton Administration.

If not for the perseverance, courage and faith of Senators Kyl and Lieberman, we would not today celebrate our embassy in Jerusalem. It's no easy feat to turn back fifty years of passions, prejudices, and the threats of violence to rectify an unjust historical mistake. In a time when most Americans believe their elected officials are corrupted by personal gain and blinded by partisanship, the US Embassy in Jerusalem stands as a testament to what principled leadership on Capitol Hill can accomplish.

Jeanine V. Esperne, Former National Security Advisor, U.S.
Senator Jon Kyl (R-AZ)

Rabbi Efrem Goldberg, Senior Rabbi at the Boca Raton Synagogue

The prophet Ezekiel stated (5:5), "This is Jerusalem, I have set her in the midst of nations and countries are around her." The Talmud (Derech Eretz Zuta 9) teaches that Jerusalem is the eye of the universe. Indeed, throughout history, disproportionate focus and attention has always been placed on the sovereignty of Jerusalem.

In their outstanding book, *Because It's Just and Right: The Untold Back-Story of the US Embassy in Jerusalem,* Farley Weiss and Leonard Grunstein, have provided a compelling and irrefutable survey of the legal, historic and religious evidence that Jerusalem was, is and will always be, the undivided, eternal capital of the Jewish people and of the State of Israel. The 2018 opening of the United States Embassy in Jerusalem was the fulfillment of legislation passed twenty-three years earlier recognizing Jerusalem as Israel's capital, but much more than that, it was a reflection and recognition of a truth that dates back thousands of years earlier.

Farley and Leonard don't just tell the remarkable story of the US Embassy Opening in Jerusalem against great odds, they lived it, contributed towards it, and now, in this book they invite us to celebrate it with them.

Rabbi Steven Pruzansky JD

The authors narrate and analyze the torturous path that led to US recognition of Jerusalem as Israel's capital and the relocation there of the American embassy. Along the way, we encounter political commitment and double talk, good intentions and malice, fecklessness and courage. The facts - some of them new to me but all well sourced - reveal the story of modern Israel and modern Jerusalem. The authors are obviously lovers of Jerusalem - and all lovers of Jerusalem will love this book.

Mark I. Lichbach
Emeritus Professor and Former Chair
Department of Government and Politics
University of Maryland

Using biblical sources as its starting point, Farley Weiss and Leonard Grunstein motivate a comprehensive documentary history of the struggle over the US embassy in Jerusalem. A unique contribution to US foreign policy and US-Israeli relations, this book will interest scholars and practitioners who wish to connect norms of Jewish theology with empirics of contemporary world affairs.

Arnold Roth

My daughter Malki was one of fifteen people murdered in the bombing of the Sbarro pizzeria in Jerusalem, Israel on August 9, 2001. The pain of her loss is felt every day by our family and many other families as two Americans were murdered in the attack - Malki and a young woman from New Jersey pregnant with her first child - while a third, a young mother, was in a coma for 22 years and has since passed away.

Fifteen innocents were murdered that day, seven of them children, and 130 others suffered injuries. Four Americans were among the latter.

"Because it is Just and Right", the book by Farley Weiss and Len Grunstein deals, as its title proclaims, with the idea of a Middle East policy based on moral principles.. The authors relate how the terrorist who masterminded the Sbarro atrocity brought the human bomb - a man with an explosives-filled guitar case slung across his back and a fierce zeal to kill and be killed - to the pizzeria's entrance in the bustling center of Israel's capital.

The mastermind's name is Ahlam Ahmad Al-Tamimi. She lives free as a celebrity and hero in Jordan today. A treaty between Jordan and the United States made in 1995 requires that Jordan take her into custody and hand her to the American authorities who have been waiting for this to happen since the charges became public in March 2017.

But she remains free in Jordan. She has been an FBI Most Wanted Terrorist since 2017 with a State Department reward of $5 million on her head. And yet, as the book makes clear, Jordan appears to pay no price for breaching the extradition treaty and failing to extradite her to Washington.

The book makes it clear that policies are needed that are based on justice and moral clarity. And unsurprisingly, as with the US Embassy move to Jerusalem which is where my family lives, a policy based on morality and justice is also a policy that will succeed.

-- Arnold Roth, an attorney and technology business manager, serves as honorary chair of the Malki Foundation which he and his wife Frimet established in 2001. Its work honors the memory of their daughter Malki, murdered in a terrorist attack on the Sbarro pizza shop in the center of Jerusalem.

Rabbi Dr. Joseph Frager

The move of the American Embassy from Tel Aviv to Jerusalem on May 14th, 2018 by President Trump was one of the greatest achievements that a Pro-Israel Activist could wish for. "Because It's Just and Right" details the foundations and underpinnings of the Embassy Move. Nothing happens in a vacuum. Senator Jon Kyl of Arizona who was the keystone in the process was introduced to me by Farley Weiss at a National Council of Young Israel Dinner at the time he was putting forward his "Jerusalem Embassy Act of 1995". This legislation paved the way for the eventual relocation of America's Embassy to the rightful, never to be divided, and eternal capital of Israel-Jerusalem. Yerushalayim (Hebrew for Jerusalem) is mentioned over 600 times in Tanakh. It is not mentioned once in the Koran. It is the heart and soul of the Jewish People. Farley Weiss and Leonard

Grunstein have made the Jewish People proud. Rabbi Dr. Joseph Frager is the Chairman of the Executive Board of American Friends of Ateret Cohanim And the Executive Vice President of the Israel Heritage Foundation. He is a lifelong Activist and Physician.

TABLE OF CONTENTS

ACKNOWLEDGEMENTS
Leonard Grunstein

It is with a profound sense of gratitude that I humbly thank G-d for inspiring, empowering, and enabling me to be a part of this sacred mission with Farley Weiss to bring to light the story of how the US recognized Jerusalem as the capital of Israel and moved the US Embassy to Jerusalem, as well as, why it was just and right to do so.

Experience has taught me that life is not random. Coming to Florida and meeting Farley, who became a dear friend, was not just some chance occurrence. Farley told me about his involvement with Senator Kyl and then Governor DeSantis concerning Jerusalem and other Israel-related matters. We began what developed into a series of deep and factual discussions about history and the US-Israel relationship. When he asked me to work with him on writing a book about recognizing Jerusalem and moving the Embassy there, I immediately responded in the affirmative.

Farley is a brilliant, forthright, and very talented individual, and it is my privilege to be his friend and collaborator on this book. As I researched the story and we continued our discussions and analysis, the book began to evolve into its present form, which not only recounts the story of the US recognition of Jerusalem as the capital of Israel but, just as importantly, why it is just and right.

Chanie encouraged me to pursue this book project, graciously read the early drafts, and offered her thoughts and advice. My son was an amazing resource, and he graciously provided me with his brilliant and cogent insights and comments. He and the others noted below, with whom I had discussions about any of the matters covered in the book, of course, bear no responsibility for the content of the book. The approaches taken, opinions expressed, or any errors in the book are those of the authors.

All my children and grandchildren were an invaluable source of encouragement and a wellspring of support for this undertaking. Their excitement was infectious and helped sustain me during the tireless hours of research and writing of this book.

Thanks to everyone on the publishing team. Your efforts are much appreciated.

Ethics of our Fathers (Avot 1:1) records the Members of the Great Assembly counseled us to deliberate before rendering judgment. My teacher, Rabbi Asher Weiss, explained that this means a person should not be so sure of himself or herself since we no longer have the benefit of prophecy. Better to discuss matters with other experts before reaching a conclusion. I am most grateful to the many fine scholars and other experts, as well as talented writers, with whom I had occasion to discuss and bounce around ideas concerning particular matters covered in this book. I will always treasure their marvelous insights and those incisive conversations.

Thank you to all the extraordinary individuals who graciously furnished their thoughts about the book for publication in the book. You are amazing.

ACKNOWLEDGMENTS

Farley Weiss

I am most grateful for the opportunity I had, thank G-d, to play a small part in the effort to get the United States to recognize Jerusalem as Israel's capital and to move the U.S. Embassy to Jerusalem.

It was a privilege to work with Senator Jon Kyl and his staff who were deeply involved in leading the process. They rightly believed the cause was just and right and that it was in the U.S.' national interest that it come to fruition.

Thank G-d, I also found Leonard Grunstein to work with on this book and to tell this story. I am so grateful to Len for all his efforts in writing this book with me. He is an extraordinary writer, researcher, scholar, and. an exceptional person that I am proud to call my dear friend.

I could not have done this without my amazing and supportive wife, Jessica, who gave me time to work on this book. She has also been so helpful from the inception of this endeavor, reading an early version of this book and providing us her thoughtful insights throughout this process. Our children have been excited for the publication of this book and have encouraged all our efforts.

I also feel it is important to mention the role played by my beloved parents, of blessed memory. They firmly supported my involvement in the effort to move the US Embassy to Jerusalem. I greatly appreciated that they participated in the dinner in which we honored Senator Kyl shortly after the passage of the Jerusalem Embassy Act in 1995, as well as the dinner the next year, in which Jerusalem Mayor Ehud Olmert attended specifically to thank Senator Kyl.

I was fortunate to work with my father, who was an esteemed patent attorney. He taught me so much including to fight for what is right, and his wisdom has guided me throughout my life. My mother was honored as a top Immigration Judge in America. She had a well-earned reputation for fairness. Her love, insight, and sound judgment were an integral part of my upbringing. I marveled at how she was able to do this all while raising a family of seven kids. I now know from being married to Jessica and seeing her excel at being a consummate immigration attorney, extraordinary mother of six children, and a wonderful wife that she, like my mom, is one of those rare individuals we sing about at the Sabbath meal each Friday night. It is a paean celebrating women of accomplishment like my beloved Jessica, who are somehow able to accomplish all that they do with aplomb.

My siblings have also inspired me. They are all very accomplished individuals, with several having written books and appeared in film documentaries.

I am truly grateful to Senator Kyl for his friendship and the seminal leadership role he assumed in conceiving and then causing the Jerusalem Embassy Act to be passed into law. In the process, I gained a much greater understanding of politics and how things actually got done. He is a paradigm of how an extremely talented person with impeccable ethics can still manage to get good things done in a difficult environment with the President opposing his efforts. Knowing and working with him was an invaluable lesson in life.

I was also honored to work with Congressman Matt Salmon and his Chief of Staff and my friend Glenn Hamer on the passage of the first Congressional Resolution requiring Palestinian Arab terrorists who wounded or murdered Americans to be brought to justice. I had previously worked closely with Glenn on the Jerusalem Embassy Act when he, together with Jeanine Esperne, were on Senator Kyl's staff. Thank you, Glenn and Jeanine, and kudos to you for your tremendous work on the legislation and for including me in assisting your extraordinary efforts.

Thank you as well to Governor (then Congressman) Ron DeSantis and his staff, who enabled me to play a part with them to push for the U.S. recognition of Jerusalem and moving the Embassy there. Governor DeSantis has shown an extraordinary understanding of the challenges Israel faces and how both the US and Israel benefit from strengthening the US-Israel relationship. As described in detail in the book, Governor DeSantis played a significant role in making recognition of Jerusalem as the capital of Israel and moving the Embassy there a reality, as well as in connection with other Israel-related matters.

I know I speak for Len, too, in expressing how we both very much appreciate Senator Jon Kyl's kind words in his Foreword to this book.

We also both humbly appreciate the important comments from Senator Joe Lieberman, Ambassador David Friedman, Governor Mike Huckabee, and Professor Alan Dershowitz and the heartfelt words of Stuart Force and Arnold Roth as well as the gracious statements from Rabbi Efrem Goldberg, Rabbi Steven Pruzansky, Rabbi Dr. Joseph Frager and Dr. Mark Lichbach. We also appreciate all those who have been kind enough to provide us with their thoughts for inclusion in this book. I was spurred to work on and care about these issues because of the influence of my Hebrew High teacher and friend Meir Jolovitz, and I thank him and appreciate the fact that my life became more meaningful and purposeful as a result of his entertaining, impactful lectures.

FOREWORD

Senator Jon Kyl

This book tells the story of the rationale for conception of and efforts to pass the legislation requiring relocation of the US embassy in Israel to Jerusalem and the Trump administration's eventual implementation of the requirement after many years of dithering by three previous administrations.

In retrospect, the large margins of Congressional support for the Jerusalem Embassy Act and the relative ease in its implementation more than two decades later should not have been surprising. History is replete with examples of rapid collapse of shibboleths of conventional wisdom once actually challenged.

Led by the US State Department, opposition to the Act in 1995 reflected long-standing bias against Israel and a fear that recognition of Jerusalem as Israel's capital would complicate US diplomatic efforts in the Middle East. Every year after passage of the Act, successive presidents employed the Presidential Waiver provision of the law to avoid igniting predicted anti-US sentiment on the "Arab street". Both reactions misjudged the political realities of the situation and, at the same time, ignored the moral imperative for the US to rectify an egregious slight to a friend and ally.

The authors correctly incorporate my rationales for the Act in their title—first because it was just and right and second because it was my belief that, until it was clear to Israel's enemies that the status of Jerusalem was settled and that the US would back Israel's claim, a negotiated settlement of issues would not be possible. Judging by the somewhat muted reaction to President

Trump's long overdue action, at least by some of Israel's former Arab enemies, it appears a positive and more realistic view of the situation indeed has taken hold.

The legislative history of the Act is well told in this book. My staff, led by Jeanine Esperne and assisted by Glenn Hamer, was instrumental to the success of a freshman Senator naive enough to think he could get such a bill passed. At least I understood that support from Republican leadership was crucial; Majority Leader Bob Dole agreed to be a lead sponsor of the bill and was indispensable to its passage in the Senate, and Speaker of the House, Newt Gingrich, saw to its passage in the House. I also knew Democratic support would be important, given opposition by the Clinton administration. Senators Joseph Lieberman, Daniel Inouye, and Daniel Patrick Moynihan were obvious choices, and they were helpful throughout the effort.

Finally, advisors outside the Senate acted at critical moments to support the cause. My friend, Doug Feith, a noted expert on Israel, authored an important op-ed in the New York Times and provided critical counsel to me. Farley Weiss helped orchestrate events before and after passage, including a dinner featuring then mayor of Jerusalem, Ehud Olmert. I am grateful for all of this support.

Today, it may seem that US recognition of Jerusalem as Israel's capital was obvious and inevitable; but it wasn't in 1995. The importance of this historical account is to remind us of how passage of the Jerusalem Embassy Act was accomplished against political odds and why it was so necessary. Perhaps it also illustrates that, sometimes, there is more support for doing what is "just and right" than conventional wisdom would suggest.

PREFACE

On May 14, 1948, the reestablished State of Israel was declared. US President Harry S. Truman was the first to recognize the State of Israel that same day.

The next morning, on May 15, 1948, Israel faced an invasion by five Arab countries in what became known as the 1948 War of Independence. Israel beat back the invasion, and Armistice Agreements were signed with Egypt, Syria, Lebanon, and Jordan in 1949. Only Iraq refused to sign an Armistice, preferring to withdraw its troops and hand over the sector it occupied to the Jordanian Arab Legion.

Israel declared Jerusalem as its capital on January 23, 1950. However, unlike its recognition of Israel, the US did not formally recognize Jerusalem as Israel's capital until Congress first passed the 1995 Jerusalem Embassy Act and, then pursuant to the provisions thereof, only after US President Donald J. Trump finally did so on December 6, 2017.

For almost seventy years, the US did not locate its Embassy in Israel's capital of Jerusalem. This was the only capital chosen by a recognized sovereign nation desiring that the US Embassy be located there, where the US State Department singularly refused and placed the Embassy elsewhere. To put this in perspective, consider that the US established an embassy in East Berlin, despite asserting the East German Government was 'without any legal validity' and had no sovereignty over East Berlin, as more fully discussed in Chapter V below.

It was frankly illogical to treat Israel's actual legal right to sovereignty over Jerusalem (including West Jerusalem) worse than the illegitimate assertion of control over East Berlin, by a puppet of the Soviet Union, based on temporary occupation zones created in the aftermath of World War II. Indeed, there were ample reasons to support treating Israel more favorably, as an ally, and morally, and yet, it wasn't. After all, the historical and legal right of the Jewish people to Jerusalem dates back more than 3,000 years and has been recognized under International Law in the 1920 San Remo Resolution, as unanimously confirmed by the League of Nations in 1922, as well as the US, in the 1924 Anglo-American Treaty, as more fully discussed in Chapters I and II, below. In addition, Israel is an ally and friend of the US, with shared values and interests, unlike the erstwhile East German Government, which was an enemy of the US and its ally West Germany in the Cold War.

This begs the question of why Israel was treated so shabbily by the US. This historical wrong is not explainable in terms of precedent, nor did it arise in a vacuum. Why this was so, who acted to remedy the situation, and the process of accomplishing the same, as well as why it took so long to rectify this historical wrong, are among the subjects taken up in this book.

The path to recognition of Jerusalem as the capital of Israel was not a short, direct route. It was, instead, a long and tortuous process. There were, however, critical inflection points that weren't so obvious at the time, as well as the collective contributions of a few good people who genuinely cared to do what was right. The cumulative effect, though, of the combination of all these efforts did make a real difference, and that's why this story is so important to tell.

We began to write this book to tell the untold story of how this all came about. However, as we poured through the papers Farley Weiss had collected working with Senator Jon Kyl and his staff on the Jerusalem Embassy Act, we began to appreciate it was not enough just to recount what had happened factually. There was an underlying ethos that permeated the thinking of Senator Jon Kyl, then-Congressman Ron DeSantis, President Trump, and many others, who devotedly worked so hard to make this a reality. It is summarized in the title of this book Because It's Just and Right. We determined to explain why it was just and right for Jerusalem to be the capital of Israel.

Along the way, we faced a number of questions, and we hopefully adequately answered them in this book. These include the following:

1. Why does the subject of Jerusalem ignite such passion?

2. Why is it just and right that undivided Jerusalem remain the capital of Israel?

3. Why is it legally improper to take Jerusalem away from Israel, as some purport to demand?

4. Why didn't the US immediately recognize Jerusalem after Israel declared it to be its capital, and why did it take so long for the US finally to do so?

We also dealt with a number of ancillary issues like the pompous, hyperbolic, absurd, and slanderous statements made by detractors of Israel falsely labeling Israel an apartheid state, occupier, committer of genocide, ethnic cleanser, and violator of International Law. This toxic propaganda-driven war of words is a prominent feature of social media and public discourse. These and other antisemitic tropes are hopefully shattered and wholly debunked in this book.

As we researched this book, we learned much about the history of Jerusalem, its legal status, and the arguments asserted in an effort to delay or prevent recognition. The makeup of the coalition of those arrayed against recognition in the US State Department and foreign policy establishment may have changed over time, and the nature of their biases, prejudices, and conflicts of interest may have evolved, but the predispositions embedded in the corporate culture militating against change has not been fundamentally altered. What began as a mix of prejudices favoring the oil-producing Arab nations, policies fostering an aversion to taking any risk with regard to Israel (even when only a calculated risk and far outweighed by the benefits that might reasonably be achieved), ideological imperatives and ingrained religious and other biases (including latent and patent antisemitism) has morphed into an almost obsessive fixation with not changing or challenging the established corporate tradition that singles out Israel for what amounts to a negative version of special treatment.

The individuals who caused the US to recognize Jerusalem were consummate realists who objectively viewed the world differently than those constrained by the mores and traditions of the corporate culture within the foreign policy establishment. They took calculated risks, and their investment in doing what was just and right continues to yield enormous dividends. This includes the Abraham Accords and the continuing process of peace and prosperity it engendered.

If we are passionate, it is because we have come to know why it is just and right that undivided Jerusalem is and must remain the capital of Israel.

Our hope is that the reader will also come to a similar conclusion and, in addition, will confidently and unhesitatingly know how and what to answer when someone makes an honest inquiry about the subject or even when confronted with bombastic pious, sounding pronouncements of the variety noted above.

We sincerely hope that our unabashed message of the triumph of what is just and right will resonate and that the blessings of genuine peace will radiate from Jerusalem.

INTRODUCTION

On Monday, May 14, 2018, the world witnessed an extraordinary and historic event. The United States, under the leadership of President Trump, moved its Embassy in Israel from Tel Aviv to Jerusalem, and on that day, it was formally dedicated and officially opened.

It was a glorious day. US Secretary of Treasury Steve Mnuchin was in attendance, as well as Ivanka and Jared Kushner, who were there as the personal representatives of Ivanka's father, US President Donald J. Trump. Prime Minister Benjamin Netanyahu of Israel spoke at the event. So did US Ambassador to Israel, David Friedman, who personally led the charge that finally won the day on the matter of recognizing Jerusalem that had bedeviled so many prior US administrations. The speakers also included religious leaders like Pastor John Hagee, and his powerful speech added to the significance of the occasion.

Also attending was Congressman (now Governor) Ron DeSantis. Few knew of the seminal role Governor DeSantis played in bringing this moment to fruition. Senator Jon Kyl, one of the foremost, albeit unheralded, proponents of the recognition of Jerusalem and the Embassy move there and who did so much to enable this day to occur, was not there in person. However, Farley Weiss (Farley) was present in his capacity as the President of the National Council of Young Israel and a member of the Conference of Presidents of Major Jewish Organizations, and he was in electronic communication with Senator Kyl. Farley had worked assiduously behind the scenes with Senator Kyl and his staff and thereafter with Congressman DeSantis and his team, helping to make this day possible. Senator Kyl was later honored by Israel's Ambassador to the US, Ron Dermer, who traveled to

Phoenix, bringing a personal letter from Israel Prime Minister Netanyahu thanking and commending him for his leadership.

As Farley sat there among the guests and dignitaries cheerfully greeting one another, he could not escape an awareness of the insistent opinions of others, who desperately tried to prevent or mar this celebratory occasion. There were the voices in Europe, in the Middle East, and even in Washington, which struck an entirely different and ominous tone. Some made dire predictions of massive outbreaks of violent protests in the streets of Israel and Muslim countries, Jihadist terror attacks against US targets, destabilization of the broader region, and a breakdown in US relations with Arab countries. Some declared it was the final nail in the coffin ending the possibility of any Arab-Israel accord and that President Trump would have blood on his hands. Farley even received an unexpected call from an individual he respected, warning him that this was all folly and if he pursued the matter, then he would be responsible for the loss of lives. In the moment, no one could have been faulted for feeling some trepidation.

The common denominator was the breathless use of hyperbole to express concerns and risks that had already been fully considered and vetted. Despite all the anxiety, there was no actionable intelligence concerning any real threat posed of imminent mortal danger. The flawless dedication of the new Embassy and its continuing and secure presence in Jerusalem is a testament to those with the courage, foresight, and determination to make it a reality. It all turned out well, and US prestige and national security interests were not damaged but rather enhanced by the recognition of Jerusalem and the Embassy move there.

It was President Trump, who courageously made the momentous decision finally to move the US Embassy to Jerusalem, the capital of Israel, where the Embassy rightly belonged. President Trump overcame enormous pressures opposing the move and the recognition of Jerusalem as Israel's capital. US Ambassador to Israel David Friedman was one of the main driving forces within the administration pushing for President Trump to make this decision. However, he had many vocal and powerful opponents both inside and outside the administration. Fortunately, though, there were also some, like Vice President Mike Pence, who stood up in favor of the decision or played other roles in support thereof.

The story of how this all came about, including first the recognition of Jerusalem as the capital of Israel and then the moving of the Embassy there, is riveting. Contrary to the predictions of the naysayers, it did not result in calamitous consequences. Instead, it led to the wonderful Abraham Accords, which effectively and finally ended the more than a half-century-long Arab-Israel war that had plagued the region. The change in attitude is even evident in the rhetoric used to describe the relationship between Israel and its neighbors. The once common refrain referring to the Arab-Israel conflict is no longer in vogue because it is no longer relevant.

With the benefit of twenty-twenty hindsight, we can now see that the process leading to President Trump's decision was not the product of the vagaries of chance. It was the culmination of a historical process stretching over nearly four millennia and, most recently, somewhat more than two decades. No one could be faulted for believing that this amazing accomplishment was the culmination of a process of intermediate steps and achievements unobtrusively guided by divine providence. Principal players included Senator Jon Kyl in 1995 and, later, in 2017, then-Congressman Ron DeSantis, as more fully discussed below.

On the walkway to the gathering to view the Embassy opening was the text of the Jerusalem Embassy Act of 1995. Senator Jon Kyl of Arizona had originated this legislation. At the time, he was a freshman Senator. Farley was then the President of the Young

Israel of Phoenix, an Orthodox Jewish Synagogue. Little did Farley know that his invitation to then-Senate Candidate Jon Kyl to speak to his Synagogue just before his election to the Senate would lead to an enduring relationship with the Senator, as well as his staff, including Glenn Hamer. It would inspire Farley's involvement with Senator Kyl's staff in promulgating the historic legislation that Senator Kyl originated and was ultimately passed, known as the Jerusalem Embassy Act of 1995.

This was no mean achievement. Senator Kyl's vision, untiring efforts, and wise and skillful ability to negotiate and compromise were essential to achieving this phenomenal result. One of the major roadblocks Senator Kyl encountered in the Senate was the Clinton administration's opposition to the passage of a law recognizing Jerusalem as the capital of Israel and requiring the Embassy to be moved there. Obtaining overwhelming bi-partisan support was crucial. This was accomplished by negotiating a presidential waiver provision that was added to the text of the draft Law. Few could have predicted at the time how fortuitous it would be that the Jerusalem Embassy Act of 1995 contained this provision, as noted below.

The Law was overwhelmingly passed in the Senate (95-5) and in the House (374-37). However, the willingness to add this provision frustrated some of the more inflexible idealists, who had previously supported Senator Kyl in promoting the passage of the Law. As a result, they, unfortunately, withdrew their support because of the waiver. However, as detailed below in this book, it was that very waiver provision that likely saved the Law from a perhaps, fatal, Constitutional challenge. The Law also continues to protect the results it enabled, and President Trump achieved, as more fully discussed below.

Senator Kyl worked with Senate Majority Leader Robert Dole, who became the lead sponsor of the bill and helped assure overwhelming support for the passage of the Act. This included orchestrating the meeting that led to the compromise presidential waiver language added to the bill prior to passage. This did not diminish Senator Kyl's contribution; it only served to enhance it. Senator Kyl continued to play a seminal role, leading the fight to negotiate the strongest acceptable language and accomplish the timely passage of the Act so as to achieve the intended and remarkable result. He epitomized Ronald Reagan's famous dictum: "There is no limit to the amount of good you can do if you don't care who gets the credit."

Not long after Senator Kyl's initial retirement from the Senate in 2012, Farley moved to Florida and soon began a relationship with then-Congressman (now Governor) Ron DeSantis. Congressman DeSantis saw an opportunity, as a result of the election of President Trump, to bring to fruition the relocation of the US Embassy to Jerusalem. He appointed Jason Lyons to lead an Advisory Council on Jerusalem, and Jason added Farley to this Council. Congressman DeSantis was one of the few members of Congress actively to press for the Embassy move to Jerusalem, and yet his vital role is generally not well known to this day.

Who could have imagined when the concept of passing a law about Jerusalem and the Embassy was first conceived, the result would be this magnificent day? Yet, like so many tales of the Biblical Prophets and Writings, what seemed like almost random occurrences came together over a period of years to achieve what, retrospectively, some might describe as an almost inevitable outcome. Nevertheless, at the time, this was not apparent, nor was there even a consensus that this objective was desirable, let alone achievable. So many obstacles had to be overcome, and there were so many naysayers who spoke of grave risks, none of which ever truly came to pass.

The lessons learnt along the way were legion. They included standing for what's right and doing your best. It's not for us to shirk from a task because we can't reasonably complete it on our own. As Ethics of the Father's[1] counsels, it is not our duty to

---

[1] Avot 2:16.

complete the task; but neither are we at liberty to neglect it. Ultimately, whether it's because of trust in G-d[2] to do the rest or not, one of the profound mysteries of life is by acting to set a course of action in motion; sometimes, things do work out. Hence, the compelling need to step up and take a leadership role, especially where there is no one else present willing to do so. Thus, as the Ethics of the Fathers[3] notes, in a pithy aphorism, in a place where there is no one to take a leadership role, try your best to act like a leader. The intuitive and practical application of these ethics, as well as the commitment, energy, and determination to do what was right, were integral to the impressive results achieved.

These may sound like quaint platitudes, but they're not. They are real-life lessons acquired and refined in the heat of the iron cauldron of politics, as will become apparent from the events described in this book. Many of the facts and circumstances have not heretofore been published. It is with a sense of humility and awe that they are disclosed in the hope that they will be appreciated, much as Farley experienced them at the time.

 There were many who, over a number of years, strove mightily to accomplish this outstanding achievement. The roles they each played with aplomb are reminiscent of another Biblical tale, depicted in the Scroll of Esther[4]. As Mordecai advised Queen Esther, perhaps all these strange and otherwise unexplainable events and circumstances occurred so that she would be in a position to act and accomplish a mission as a part of G-d's master plan. He cautioned if she didn't choose to be a part of the unfolding real-life drama, then someone else would take up the part. It was, however, much better not to miss the opportunity to

---

[2] Some might wonder why the name of 'G-d' is not fully spelled out. It's a religious custom designed to show reverence and respect by avoiding the use of G-d's name in vain (Third Commandment- Exodus 20:7) and also thereby preventing it from being erased. See, for example, Why Write "G-d" Instead of "G-o-d"?, by Yehuda Shurpin, at Chabad.org.

[3] Avot 2:5.

[4] Book (Megillat-Scroll) of Esther 4:14.

do good. Well, as the Scroll recounts, she didn't miss her chance and acted decisively to avoid an impending disaster and succeeded mightily. She was, however, aided in her mission by supporting actors, who similarly played their part[5].

One of the remarkable aspects of this story is that the three main protagonists, who heroically led the charge to accomplish this amazing result, namely Senator Kyl, Congressman DeSantis, and President Trump, are all not Jewish. Despite their varied backgrounds and personalities, they were all motivated to take the lead because they believed it was the just and right thing to do. This theme resonated among many of those who took part in this valiant effort over the years. It also inspired us to write this book so that everyone, no matter their religion, personal beliefs, philosophy, or absence thereof, might come to know why it is just and right that undivided Jerusalem is the capital of Israel and the US Embassy is located there.

These and other facets of the back story behind the passage of the Jerusalem Embassy Act, as well as critical details about its terms and conditions, are the subject of this book.

The story of the behind-the-scenes machinations and deal-making, which led to these outstanding achievements, is a veritable treasure trove of information that can inform and guide future work in this area. In that sense, it is not only a history of what occurred; it's also a handbook for those interested in playing a part in achieving good and making history.

Remember, too, that no matter how large or small a role, everyone can make a difference, especially as a part of a team effort. This principle was epitomized by Senator Kyl and his staff, which was superbly led by Jeanine Esperne and assisted by Glenn

---

[5] Most famous, of course, was Mordechai; but, there were others too, like Charvona (see, for example, Esther 7:9), who is also recognized in the Purim song known as Shoshanat Yaakov. There was also Hathach (see, for example, Esther 4:10), the intermediary between Esther and Mordechai, who the Talmud, in Babylonian Talmud (BT) Tractates Megillah 15a and Bava Batra 4a, reports was Daniel.

Hamer. Lest there be any doubt, just reflect on this story and how improbable it was for all these events and circumstances to come together to achieve the marvelous result of a US Embassy in Jerusalem and the recognition of Jerusalem as the capital of Israel. Such recognition ended an anomalous situation in which Israel was the only country in the world in which the U.S. did not have its Embassy in the capital of the foreign country, as desired by the host country.

Jerusalem is an extraordinary place. So many who have visited it have felt its unique welcoming presence. Jerusalem is also a state of mind. Thus, as the popular saying goes, my heart is in Jerusalem or, as the renowned King David and superlative Psalmist observed, forgetting Jerusalem would be like losing our motivating life force and joy of life[6]. Is it any wonder that reference is made to Jerusalem many hundreds of times in the Old Testament? In striking contrast, there is no explicit mention of Jerusalem even once in the Quran. Our recognition of the special qualities of Jerusalem began with our Patriarch Abraham, who, together with his son, the Patriarch Isaac, perceived[7] its hidden splendor from afar[8].

To some, Jerusalem is just a political football to be kicked around as a diversion. There are also those who appreciate that it has great significance to others and, therefore, it's a great bargaining chip to achieve some political end. Still, others desire to possess it, even if they can't appreciate its sublime qualities because they recognize it has inestimable value. Then there are a few, like the Jewish people, the actual and spiritual descendants of the Patriarchs, Abraham, Isaac, and Jacob, and Matriarchs, Sarah, Rebecca, Rachel, and Leah, who, through the ages, have so

---

[6] Psalms 137:5-6.

[7] However, not everyone does; as was the case with the other two individuals, Ishmael and Eliezer, who accompanied Abraham and Isaac, but just did not share their vision. See, Genesis 22:5 and see Meshech Chochma (by R' Meir Simcha HaKohen of Dvinsk, an 18th century commentator on the Bible), Vayera 43, as well as, R' Don Isaac Abarbanel's commentary on the Biblical verse.

[8] Genesis 22:4.

yearned to be a part of Jerusalem that they almost can't live without it. The miracle of having sovereignty over Jerusalem again, after more than two thousand years, is an undeniable and inspirational affirmation that life does have meaning and G-d controls the world. It's no wonder, then that the Jewish people treat this as a sacred trust and permit people of all religions to worship freely in this special place of Jerusalem.

Retention of undivided Jerusalem as the capital of Israel is an essential truth embraced by an overwhelming majority of the people of Israel on a non-partisan basis. Israeli Prime Minister Golda Meir, an iconic figure in Israel and the world, was a revered exponent of the Labor Party in the Knesset. Her position on Jerusalem, like so many other Prime Ministers and leading figures spanning the political spectrum from left to right in the Knesset, was that undivided Jerusalem must remain the capital of Israel[9].

The moving of the US Embassy to Jerusalem was only the beginning of what promises to be a new era of peaceful, harmonious, and prosperous relations between Israel and many nations that were once implacable enemies. The story continues to evolve, anchored on the firm bond and strength of the US-

---

[9] See, for example, Israel/Golda Meir Interview/Prime Minister Interview, on Thames TV, in 1970, on YouTube, as well as, Israel: Golda Meir Interview, on 4/19/1972, by AP (RR7216A), on YouTube. Golda Meir also spoke about the need for secure borders. Among other things, she noted how unrealistic it was for people to say that if only Israel returned to the pre-67 borders then there would be peace. After all, it did not work for all those years prior to 1967. A better plan was to have secure borders that would deter war instead of insecure borders that, in effect, irresponsibly attracted enemies to attack. Moreover, the quarrel was not about land; it was about Israel's very existence. She went on to discuss how there was no distinct Palestinian people. There were Arabs who lived west and east of the Jordan River. In this regard, she viewed herself as a Palestinian Jew, who actually held Mandatory Palestine papers. In the period prior to 1967, the Arab people living west of the Jordan River did not form their own state; rather they became Jordanian citizens, like their brethren living on the east side of the Jordan. She then rhetorically questioned why don't the Jews have a right to self-determination. The point, of course, is that they do and the effort to deny Israel's right to exist is the heart of the problem; not the artifice of raising contrived issues about the status of Jerusalem as the capital of Israel.

Israel relationship, which is tangibly expressed by the presence of the US Embassy in Jerusalem.

The next chapter began almost immediately thereafter with the advent of the miraculous Abraham Accords with the UAE under the sponsorship of the United States. Indeed, as Ambassador David Friedman recounted[10] so well, the road to peace led through Jerusalem. He noted that Isaiah's famous prophecy about how the nations of the world would beat their swords into plowshares and spears into pruning hooks[11] and never again know war[12] is preceded by verses regarding Judea and Jerusalem[13] and how peace would emanate from Jerusalem. The imagery is extraordinary. It depicts how Jerusalem[14] would be rightly established. Many countries would then come to Jerusalem and benefit from it being a center of knowledge, justice, and peace[15].

The Abraham Accords initiated a profound change between Israel and Arab nations in the Middle East. The wonderful effects of the good and fateful decision by President Trump to recognize Jerusalem as the capital of Israel and move the US Embassy continue to resonate. Where once, there was either no public recognition of Israel or what amounts to a cold peace with Israel, warm relations emerged, with genuine business and investment partnerships, cultural exchanges, and tourism[16].

---

[10] In a discussion with the authors.

[11] Displayed on the Isaiah Wall facing the UN headquarters in New York City.

[12] Isaiah 2:4.

[13] Isaiah 2:1-3.

[14] The place where the Holy Temple stood (Isaiah 2:2).

[15] Isaiah 2:3-4.

[16] Today, at least 167 of the 193 UN member states officially recognize Israel, including UAE, Bahrain, Sudan, Morocco and Bhutan. In addition there are also the non-UN member states of Vatican City, Kosovo, Cook Islands, among others, which officially recognize Israel. Only North Korea, Cuba and Venezuela, as well as, 23 Arab/Muslim states do not officially recognize Israel, although there are reports that Saudi Arabia and Indonesia are considering normalizing relations with Israel. (See, for example, Israel International Relations: International Recognition of Israel, at Jewish Virtual Library. org.)

The Abraham Accords have continued to grow and now also encompass Bahrain, Sudan, and Morocco. They have also yielded dividends in the burgeoning relations with other countries that had previously avoided any public connections with Israel, such as Saudi Arabia. The circle of peace and prosperity the Abraham Accords engendered continues to grow and exceed expectations. We hope and pray for peace and prosperity for the US and Israel and all who join in this glorious circle of peace.

The promise of lasting peaceful and mutually beneficial relations between Israel and its neighbors, once only a dream, is being translated into a tangible reality by genuine, albeit unsung, heroes. They are undaunted by the inertia and emotional concerns that seem to burden less creative and clear-thinking individuals, who somehow miss the win/win potential inherent in having good relations with Israel. They are also not overwhelmed by the ideological baggage that has historically frustrated so many attempts at establishing peaceful relations.

To all the faithful supporters of a strong US-Israel relationship, it's particularly important to realize that it's a long game. Progress is often measured not in large leaps but in small steps. No matter how de minimis the accomplishment may seem, treasure it because it's another point in what will hopefully be a winning game.

This book not only celebrates Jerusalem, it is also devoted to combating the propaganda-generated falsehoods of those who seek to delegitimize Israel and undermine its ancient and enduring connection to the Jewish people. In this regard, it is important to appreciate that the slogan *'From the river to the sea, Palestine shall be free'* is a euphemism. It calls, G-d forbid, for Israel not to exist and to eliminate the Jews from the entire area between the Jordan River and the Mediterranean Sea. In essence, it declares that the entire area, inclusive of the existing State of Israel, should be virtually Judenrein. This is the express goal of Hamas, which governs Gaza. It also continues to be the goal of the Palestinian Liberation Organization (PLO)[17], which, directly or indirectly, controls the Palestinian Authority (PA) and governs areas within Judea and Samaria under the Oslo Accords. This goal is espoused and pursued, despite the express provisions of the Oslo Accords prohibiting the same.

In furtherance of this malign purpose, the PA and Hamas promote terrorism and engage in disinformation campaigns designed to disassociate Jews from Israel, including Jerusalem. This includes brazenly asserting invented and false claims of indigeneity from time immemorial. The object of this contrived false narrative is to undermine and supplant any legal right for Jews to live in Israel and deny Israel's right to exist. Thus, the PA and Hamas prohibit land sales to Jews, with extremely strict penalties against violators, in any of the areas under their control.

Imagine being barred from buying a house anywhere in the US or Europe because you are a Muslim, Christian, or Jew. Yet, regarding Jews, this is the law under the PA and Hamas, and it is vigorously and brutally enforced, both judicially and extra-judicially. It is also the policy being actively promoted by the so-called Boycott, Divestment, and Sanctions (BDS) movement and defended by some in government in the US and European nations. Astoundingly, BDS and its proponents have sought to punish economically those doing what amounts to mutually beneficial trade, investment, and cross-border business among parties in the PA areas and Israel.

How can anyone justify frustrating bridge-building and business relations that are the most effective tools for promoting peaceful and prosperous relations among neighbors? Perhaps, this is the intended purpose; to create and enforce an environment of permanent discord and prevent people from getting along and

---

[17] Its Charter, expressly calls for the elimination of Israel, which has never actually formally been amended to delete the same, despite solemn commitments and agreements to do so, as more fully discussed below.

forming enduring and mutually beneficial bonds that might one day yield peace.

In stark contrast, Israel protects the rights of Muslims, Christians, and Jews, including, without limitation, to buy, sell, and own real estate, and promotes mutually beneficial business and other relationships so as to create an environment conducive to yielding peace and prosperity for all parties concerned. Moreover, despite Israel having clear title to and right of sovereignty over the land of Israel, including Jerusalem, as more fully discussed below, Israel does not seek to eliminate the PA or banish the Arab residents in the PA and Hamas controlled areas. Ironically, the ruthless and malign regimes of the PA and Hamas and their affiliates and supporters project onto Israel their evil intent and falsely accuse Israel of their very own malignant goals and malevolent plans. This might be amusing as the theme of some satirical parody, but in real life, it is outrageous and patently antisemitic.

We must, therefore, continue to persevere and separate fact from fiction. We live in times when, as the Talmud[18] predicted, truth is absent. Rather than deter us, though, this should embolden us because the Talmudic prognostication is about the period ushering in the ultimate redemption. We, therefore, must redouble our efforts to dispel the false and misleading myths created by the enemies of Israel and the Jewish people.

Consider, for example, the misuse of the term "West Bank" when referring to the parts of Judea and Samaria, including eastern portions of Jerusalem (where the Temple Mount, Western Wall, and Church of the Holy Sepulchre are located). Jordan illegally conquered these areas in its war of aggression against the fledgling reestablished State of Israel in 1948. Jordan subsequently illegally annexed them and used the term West Bank to describe them, in contra-distinction to Jordan proper, located on the East Bank of the Jordan River. This was a clever

---

[18] BT Sota 49b and Sanhedrin 97a.

artifice employed to create the fiction that Jordan was comprised of both sides of the Jordan River. In this regard, consider the use of the term West Bank in the Charter of the Palestinian Liberation Organization (PLO) of 1964, which, in Article 24, disclaims any sovereignty over the area of the West Bank (including Jerusalem), by the so-called Palestinian Arab people, asserting instead that it belongs to the Hashemite Kingdom of Jordan[19]. As with most fiction, they do not age well. However, the new breed of propagandists at the PA and Hamas and their cohorts are undaunted. They just blithely create new fictions, now called narratives, albeit false ones, even if they contradict the old tales that were also untrue.

Historically, the area was not called the West Bank, and it had no relationship to Jordan, either before its illegal conquest in 1948 or after the area was liberated by Israel in the defensive war of 1967, known as the Six Day War. Indeed, the famous United Nations General Assembly (UNGA) Resolution 181, popularly known as the Partition Resolution, correctly refers to these areas as Judea and Samaria. There is no mention of a West Bank, which not only did not exist; it would have been antithetical to the original intent and purpose of the Resolution.

We have endeavored to include in this book a serious discussion and analysis of source materials that challenge the false assumptions and deceptive pronouncements about Jerusalem that have made their way into the popular rhetoric of the charlatans and propagandists who deny any Jewish connection to Jerusalem.

As detailed below, the connection of the Jewish people to Jerusalem is undeniable. It dates back to ancient times, as evidenced by a plethora of historical (including Muslim, Christian, Jewish, and other) sources and archeological findings.

---

[19] Article 24 of the PLO Charter also disclaims any right to sovereignty over the Gaza Strip.

Thank G-d and all those who worked so hard to make US recognition of Jerusalem as the capital of Israel a reality. They did so, not because it was politically expedient but because they truly believed it was just and right. This book discusses why it is indeed just and right that Jerusalem was, is, and must remain the capital of Israel.

FARLEY WEISS
AND
LEONARD GRUNSTEIN

Because it's Just and Right

I.

THE BIBLICAL TITLE REPORT - AN INVALUABLE RECORD OF TITLE

The Bible is reputedly the oldest written record of title in the world. Most other written title records are relatively newly minted by comparison[20]. It is thus an incomparable documentary source that has stood the test of time.

The Bible records[21] that King David established Jerusalem as the capital of the Kingdom of Judea and Israel in the ancient Land of Israel more than three thousand years ago. He insisted on buying the land set aside for the First and Second Temples for cash and refused it as a gift. The transaction is recorded in the Book of Samuel[22] and in Chronicles[23]. The Midrash[24] explains that recording of this title[25] was critical so that the nations of the world could not defraud Israel and say that this was stolen property in Israel's hands. Amazingly, this statement, attributed

---

[20] See, for example, The History and Value of Land Records, by Amanda Farrell, at PropLogix, tracing recording of title back to 13th Century Scotland. There is also William the Conqueror's 11th century Doomsday Book (National Archives.gov.UK).

[21] II Samuel 5:5-7.

[22] II Samuel 24:24

[23] I Chronicles 21:25. The Talmud (BT Zevachim 116b) reconciles the apparent contradiction between the price described in the Book of Samuel (II Samuel 24:24) of 50 Shekels and the one in Chronicles, noted above of 600 Shekels. The total price King David paid was 600 Shekels. He then divided it 12 ways so that each of the Twelve Tribes would have a share in title to the land. See also Sifre, Numbers 42:3 and Deuteronomy 352:13.

[24] Genesis Rabbah 79:7.

[25] As well as the title to the Cave of the Patriarchs (Meorat HaMachpelah) in Hebron, which is recorded in Genesis 23:16 and the Grave of Joseph (Kever Yosef) in Nablus, which is recorded in Genesis 33:19.

to Rabbi Yudan bar Simon, was likely made almost two thousand years ago.

This book relies on a variety of documentary and archeological resources, as well as scriptural references and historical accounts. Some might scoff at the use of the Bible, as a relevant source, in the analysis contained in this book. Others might carp about the use of Talmudic and Midrashic literary sources, which codified the oral law and traditions attendant to the Bible[26].

---

[26] The Torah is comprised of the written text of the Bible and an oral explanation, which G-d gave to Moses. Thus, there are many details not expressly provided in the Bible, which are alluded to by the Biblical text or are otherwise an integral part of the oral tradition, which were eventually recorded in the Mishna, Talmud and/or Midrash. For example, the Bible states in Deuteronomy 12:21, the requirement that cattle be slaughtered as G-d commanded in order to eat the meat thereof; but does not specify the intricate details of how ritual slaughter is accomplished. Similarly the commandments to wear Tefillin (Deuteronomy 6:8), which are referred to as signs to be donned on the forehead between the eyes and on the arm, as well as, Tzizit (Numbers 15:38) that are strings to be attached to a four cornered garment and worn. The details of how these objects are constructed or formed, the way they look and when and how to wear them are a part of the oral law. Another aspect of the oral law and tradition embodied in the Talmud involves the proper deciphering of the coded language of Biblical texts to yield their true import and meaning. Thus, the Bible in describing the law of torts, sets forth the legal maxim, 'an eye for an eye...' (Leviticus 24:19-21). However, as the Talmud (BT Bava Kamma 83b-84a and Ketubot 32b) points out, the phrase is not to be taken literally. Rather, it provides for a standard of compensatory monetary damages. This body of oral explanation, laws and traditions was eventually set down in writing and codified first in the Mishna and then in the Talmud. The Talmud also set forth authoritative Rabbinical enactments, as well as, aggadic and some historical materials. There are also collections of legal, aggadic and some historical materials from this Tannaic period, which are generically known as Midrash, as well as, works from later periods that are also referred to as Midrash. The term Midrash is derived from the Hebrew root Doresh, meaning textual interpretation. The Tannaic Midrash Halacha, such as the Sifra and Sifre, are typically considered more authoritative from a legal precedent perspective than Midrash Aggadah from this period, such as the Midrash Rabbah, as well as, those from later periods. The first effort at formal codification was the Mishna, which was completed under the tutelage of Rabbi Yehuda HaNasi by the beginning of the 3rd century. The next step in the process of recording the oral law and traditions was the Talmud. There are two versions of the Talmud. The first in time was the Jerusalem Talmud, which was compiled and edited by the end of the 4th century. The Babylonian Talmud was compiled, edited and completed by the beginning of the 6th century, under the tutelage of Ravina and Rav Ashi. There are also other Tannaic and Amoraic works from this period and earlier, which are known collectively as the Midrash, as noted above. The Talmud is an authoritative

These encyclopedic works not only compiled the oral law and traditions, they also analyzed their provenance, as well as, recording the life, times and practices of the period they cover. However, whether or not the reader believes in the divine origin of the Bible, divine nature of the Prophets and Writings[27] , and divine inspiration for these other works does not detract from their use as invaluable source materials on the subject matter of this book.

It is undeniable that the Bible is ancient in origin, with verifiable texts dating back more than two thousand years[28] and other evidentiary support dating back more than three thousand years[29]. The mere fact that the Bible, including the Five Books of Moses, Prophets and Writings, were uttered at the time is

---

encyclopedic work that sets forth, in outline form, the oral law and traditions of the Torah, as well as, rules and methodologies for interpreting the law to apply to the vagaries of life and varying circumstances. A testament to its utility and authenticity is the fact that it has stood the test of time, in good stead, over the ages, since its completion. A great deal of attention is paid, in the Babylonian Talmud, to the provenance of statements of law and custom and to reconcile what appear to be variant versions. The result is an extraordinary and marvelous compilation that reports not only majority opinions but also dissenting opinions. The text also contains a variety of Aggadic materials, including, among other things, much profound wisdom and many deep insights into human nature. The work is so treasured that there is a beautiful custom embraced by many to study the Babylonian Talmud, in its entirety, in approximately seven-year cycles. At the conclusion of each such cycle there is a great celebration, in various locales, which the authors have attended. Len was a part of the celebration at Madison Square Garden and then again at the end of a later cycle in Met Life Stadium.

[27] Collectively, known as the Tanakh, an acronym for Torah (5 Books of Moses), Nevi'im (Prophets) and Ketuvim (Writings, including Psalms, Proverbs and Megillot, such as Esther), representing the canonical collection of the Hebrew scripture. For purposes of brevity, the term Bible is used in this book as a convenient all-inclusive reference to any or all of the texts included in the Tanakh.

[28] See, for example, The Dead Sea Scrolls, at Israel Museum, Shrine of the Book, (IMJ.org), which includes fragments of Biblical texts dating back to the 3rd century B.C.E.

[29] See, for example, The Three Oldest Biblical Texts, by Bryan Windle, in Biblical Archeology Report, dated 2/6/2019, 3,000–year-old inscription bearing name of biblical judge found in Israel, by Rossella Tercotin, in the Jerusalem Post, dated 7/13/2021 and An Early Israelite Curse Inscription From Mt. Ebal?, by Nathan Steinmeyer, in Bible History Daily, dated 4/25/2022.

probative. The chronicles of history and other statements of fact they contain cannot be summarily discounted. So too, the marvelous wisdom, knowledge, and cogent insights, as well as prescient perceptions provided in these texts, should not be categorically dismissed because of some pejorative preconceived opinion about authorship. Like any other ancient source, the Bible should, at the very least, be accorded scholarly respect for what it says. So too, the authoritative commentators, who have recorded their profound understanding of these works, including the meaning of sometimes abstruse passages. Taken together, this body of literature is matchless, and the provenance is unparalleled. It would be foolhardy to ignore or disdain it just because of some bias against those who treasure it as sacrosanct. The New Testament and Quran are also cited as appropriate.

One of the most famous Biblical commentators is Rashi[30], who lived in the eleventh century. He begins the story of the Land of Israel, including Jerusalem, with the first verse of Genesis[31], in the Bible. He explains that from a strictly textual point of view, there was no reason for the Bible to begin with a statement about G-d creating the world. After all, the Bible is dedicated to reciting the commandments, and the first is not set forth until later in Exodus[32]. He asks, why then not begin there?

Rashi's answer is prescient and most instructive. He posits that the nations of the world would question Israel's title to the Land of Israel. They would assert that the Children of Israel were robbers because they took the land of the seven nations of Canaan by force. The purpose of the extended recitation in the Bible of the provenance of the world was to establish that the entire world belonged to G-d, who created it. G-d could give all

---

[30] Rabbi Shlomo Yitzchaki, an 11th century sage and one of the preeminent commentators on the Bible.
[31] Genesis 1:1.
[32] Exodus, Chapter 12.

4

or any part to whomever G-d pleased, and G-d chose to give the land of Israel, including Jerusalem, to the Jewish people[33].

The Bible is a record of title. Thus, as a careful reader of the title record would note, the Canaanites had no legitimate claim to the Land of Israel. As Chizkuni[34] explains, the Land of Israel was a part of the inheritance Noah bequeathed to his son Shem[35]. Interestingly, the Bible reports, Malchi-Tzedek, who the Talmud and Midrash consider to be Shem[36], lived in and was the king of the city of Salem[37], or, as we know it, Jerusalem.

Abraham is a descendant of Shem[38], and as the Bible records, he and his descendants were vested with title to the Land of Israel as their inheritance[39]. As an aside, as descendants of Shem, the Children of Israel or Jewish people are categorized as Semites.

Title then passed to his son Isaac[40] and then to his son Jacob[41] (also known as Israel). Jacob then vested title in his progeny, known as the Children of Israel.

---

[33] Midrash Tanchuma Masei 10:1 and Genesis Rabbah 1:2, as well as, Yalkut Shimoni Remez 187. See also BT Sanhedrin 91a. Interestingly, Rashi interprets the word dimusana'ei (typically translated as usurpers), as used in the Talmudic text, to mean 'Ba'alei Hamas' (violent robbers), who wanted to steal a share in Judea and Jerusalem. The use of the term 'Hamas' is also curiously prescient given its modern usage by the contemporary terrorist organization seeking, G-d forbid, to accomplish the same malign goal. See further Megillat Taanit, Sivan 6, for a parallel report of the same incident.

[34] Rabbi Hezekiah ben Manoah, a 13th century Bible commentator.

[35] Chizkuni, Genesis 1:1. See also Tur HaAruch, Genesis 10:5.

[36] See Rashi commentary on Genesis 14:18, as well as, BT Nedarim 32b, Genesis Rabbah 56:10, Midrash Tehillim 76:2 and Pirkei D'Rabbi Eliezer 8:4. See also Zohar Chadash, Noah 128 and Midrash Tehillim 76:2.

[37] Genesis 14:18.

[38] Genesis 11:10-27. Shem was one of Noah's sons (Genesis 10:1). Abraham's lineage is traced from Shem (as noted in Genesis 11:10-27), as follows: Shem to Arpachshad, to Shelah, to Ever, to Peleg, to Reu, to Serug, to Nahor, to Terach, and then to Abraham.

[39] Genesis 12:7. The Bible uses the terms 'Achuzah' or 'Nachalah' meaning, inheritance, in describing the Nation of Israel's vested title to the Land of Israel, numerous times. See, for example, Genesis 17:8 and Deuteronomy 26:1.

[40] Genesis 26:3-4.

[41] Genesis 28:13.

Therefore, as the Bible declares[42], when the Children of Israel enter the Land, then known as Canaan, it is the land that was vested to them as a part of their inheritance. This is no passive statement or optional prerogative; it is an obligation vested in and binding on the descendants of Jacob, the Children of Israel. Indeed, Nachmanides, in his version of Sefer HaMitzvot (Book of the Biblical Commandments), lists and describes the obligation to inherit and take possession of the Land of Israel as the fourth of the Positive Commandments[43]. He also notes the Land of Israel should not be forlorn or left barren and desolate. In this regard, the accounts of Mark Twain[44] of his visit to Jerusalem and other parts of the Holy Land in 1867 and others over the years and photographs of Jerusalem, including even during the Jordanian occupation until the liberation of Jerusalem in 1967, are revealing and most compelling. They depict a forlorn and near desolate land.

It is noteworthy that little had changed in the six hundred years since Nachmanides' arrival in Jerusalem in 1267 and Twain's visit in 1867. He also describes the barrenness of the land he encountered[45]. However, Nachmanides goes on to explain this is a part of the miraculous quality of the Land of Israel, which resists cultivation by all who seek to settle it other than the Jewish people. As Isaiah[46] prophesized, "For G-d has comforted Zion, comforted all its ruins; and has made its wilderness like Eden and its desert like the garden of G-d". The evidence supporting Nachmanides' dictum and the fulfillment of Isaiah's prophecy is overwhelming. The Jewish people have made the desert bloom and developed the Land of Israel as no one else did in the history of the Land; it's irrefutable. Who can compare the

---

[42] Numbers 34:2 and see also Deuteronomy 17:14.
[43] Nachmanides, Hasogot HaRamban on Maimonides' Sefer HaMitzvot, Positive Commandments 4.
[44] The Innocents Abroad, by Samuel Clemens (aka Mark Twain).
[45] In a letter to his son, Nachman, from Jerusalem in 1267.
[46] Isaiah 51:3.

majesty of Jerusalem today to the abysmal conditions prior to the retaking of the City, in 1967, by the modern, reestablished State of Israel?

The survey description of the Land granted as an inheritance to the Jewish people is set forth in the contractual commitment G-d originally made to Abraham, as recorded in the Bible[47]. Abraham even did a walkthrough[48].

Title to the Land of Israel was reconfirmed again to Moses and the Jewish people[49], including in a more detailed description in the Book of Numbers in the Bible[50]. Indeed, as a part of Moses' penultimate testament in the Bible, he called upon the Heavens and the Earth to bear witness[51] to, among other things, that the Land of Israel was the inheritance of the Jewish people[52]. The Bible also reconfirms that it is the inheritance of Jacob[53] to the exclusion of any other progeny of his forbearers, Abraham or Isaac[54]. Interestingly, the Bible makes use of the term Chevel (measuring rope[55]) in connection with the recording of Jacob's inheritance of the Land. This unusual reference is cogent because the Chevel was used to measure out a metes and bounds description of a parcel of land. Moses is then allowed visually to

---

[47] Genesis 15:18-21.

[48] Genesis 13:17. See also Targum Jonathan thereon, which describes how Abraham thereby exercised his dominion and control over the length and breadth of the Land of Israel.

[49] Exodus 23:31.

[50] Numbers 34:1-13

[51] Deuteronomy 32:1 and see Rashi and Kli Yakar commentaries thereon.

[52] Deuteronomy 32:8-9 and see the Rashi, Ibn Ezra, Rashbam, Bechor Shor, Rosh and Chizkuni commentaries thereon.

[53] This reference is made to negate any unfounded claim by Esau, Jacob's twin brother, who received the Land of Edom, as his inheritance, as well as, Abraham's son Ishmael or the children Abraham fathered with Keturah. Abraham vested title to the Land of Israel solely in his son Isaac. Isaac had two sons Jacob and Esau. Isaac similarly vested title to the Land of Israel solely in Jacob. Abraham's other children received other gifts from Abraham. This subject is more fully discussed below in this book.

[54] See the (authoritative Tannaic Midrash Halacha) Sifre (Deuteronomy 312:1).

[55] See, for example, Bechor Shor and Ibn Ezra commentaries on Deuteronomy 32:9.

survey the Land, and, as the Bible records[56], this is the inheritance of the Children of Israel.

The Canaanites were the descendants of Noah's son Cham[57] and were actually illegally occupying the Land of Israel[58]. As the Bible notes[59], when Abraham came to Israel, the Canaanites, at the time, were also in the Land. The otherwise superfluous reference to 'at the time' is not casual or coincidental. The Maharal[60] explains it was meant to allude to the fact that the Canaanites were not there before because it was not their land, and they were not entitled to be there. Rather, they came to rob the Children of Israel of their heritage[61]. Rashi[62] notes that the Canaanites were gradually conquering the Land of Israel from the descendants of Shem. It had been allotted to Shem when Noah apportioned the Earth among his sons. Hence, the Bible[63] makes reference to Malchi-Tzedek (also known as Shem, as

---

[56] Deuteronomy 32:49 and see the Aderet Eliyahu commentary of the Vilna Gaon thereon.

[57] Genesis 10:6.

[58] The Bible (Genesis 10:19) explicitly describes the boundaries of Canaanite territory as extending only as far as Sidon in the north, the approaches to Gaza in the south, and as far as the approaches to Sodom, Gomorrah, etc. in the east; but not extending into the Land of Israel proper. See also Rashi commentary thereon. To the west of the Land of Israel is, of course, the Mediterranean Sea and, hence, not a concern in delineating the boundaries of Canaanite territory in terms of not encroaching on the Land of Israel. It is bracing to appreciate how timeless these survey and boundary considerations are in delineating a title description with landmarks and markers. In this regard, it should also be noted that the Bible sets forth the commandment (Deuteronomy 19:14) "not to move a neighbor's boundary landmarks (markers), set up by previous generations, in the inherited property vested in you, in the land that G-d has given you as an inheritance".

[59] Genesis 12:6 and see Rashi commentary thereon.

[60] Rabbi Judah Loew ben Bezalel, a 16th century sage, known as the Maharal of Prague or Maharal, in his Gur Aryeh commentary on Genesis 1:1.

[61] The HaEmek Davar (by Rabbi Naftali Zvi Yehudah Berlin) notes the term 'Makom' HaCanaani (place of the Canaanites), as opposed to HaAretz (land), is used in Exodus 3:8, to emphasize that it was truly not their land from the beginning of creation, rather it was just a place they were occupying at the time.

[62] Rashi commentary on Genesis 12:6.

[63] Genesis 14:18.

noted above) as the king of Salem (Jerusalem)[64]. Therefore, G-d assures Abraham that in the future, the Land of Israel would be returned to his descendants, the Children of Israel, who, as noted above, are also lineal descendants of Shem[65] and the rightful inheritors of title to the Land of Israel.

The Bible is, thus, the record of title that shows from the beginning of the world, through Israel's miraculous retaking of the land from the illegal occupiers and since, the Jewish people's legal title to the Land of Israel, as a fully vested inheritance, is just and right[66], as G-d intended. There is no comparable source of record legal title to the Land of Israel.

The Bible[67] also reports the basis for Jerusalem becoming the capital of Israel. It records that Jerusalem is the city G-d chose to establish the House bearing G-d's name under the stewardship of David, leader of the Nation of Israel. This striking endorsement has endured the test of time. Indeed, no nation has ever actually situated its capital in Jerusalem other than the Nation of Israel. In this regard, it should be noted that during the entire period of the Muslim occupation of Jerusalem, beginning with Caliph Omar and throughout the Ottoman period, Jerusalem was not a capital city. Even when Jordan occupied a portion of Jerusalem from 1948-1967, it did not move its capital to Jerusalem; but rather maintained its capital in Amman.

Despite being conquered a number of times by foreign empires and invaders, the Jewish connection to and presence in Jerusalem continued throughout the vicissitudes of thousands of years of history, a miracle in its own right. Moreover, the Jewish

---

[64] BT Nedarim 32b notes Abraham, a descendant of Shem, was also invested with the hereditary priesthood originally conferred on Shem.
[65] Both patrilineally and matrilineally. This includes Rachel and Leah, as well as, Bilhah and Zilpah (Pirke D'Rabbi Eliezer 36), who were all daughters of Laban. It should also be noted that Judah's wife Tamar was also a descendant of Shem (Genesis Rabbah 85:11).
[66] Kli Yakar (by Rabbi Shlomo Ephraim ben Aaron Luntschitz, a 17th century Biblical commentator) on Genesis 1:1.
[67] II Chronicles 6:5-6.

people never ceded or voluntarily gave up their right to the land of Israel. There are no treaties extant where the Jewish people legally surrendered their rights[68].

Yet, as the Midrash and Rashi predicted, there were those who continued to challenge Israel's title to Jerusalem. Nevertheless, time and again, including by the Supreme Council of Allied Powers at San Remo in 1920, it was recognized that the Land of Israel belonged to the Jewish people, as more fully described below in this book.

In 1948, when the modern independent State of Israel was reestablished, it was immediately attacked by Arab armies from a number of Arab countries, including Egypt, Jordan, and Syria[69], as well as many of their Arab brethren living in Israel[70]. This was despite UN General Assembly Resolution 181, which called for the end of the British Mandate and the re-emergence of the Jewish State. Israel miraculously won the war, overcoming

---

[68] See, for example, The Rape of Palestine, by William B. Ziff (Martino Publishing-2009), at pages 23-24.

[69] This was not the first time Arabs reportedly invaded Palestine. Here's an example reported by The New York Times on September 1, 1929, under the headline: Arabs Invade Palestine From Three Directions; Fight Reported at Haifa. The article also notes that a force of Syrian Arabs had crossed the border to march on Jerusalem.

[70] It is interesting to reflect on the headlines in newspapers at the time, which are most telling. Here are some examples: The Boston Globe (5/1/1948)-Arabs Invade Palestine; The Raleigh Times (5/1/1948)-Palestine Invaded by Arabs; The New York Times (AP-4/23/1948)-50,000 Arabs Will Invade Palestine, Cairo Suggests and (5/16/1948)-Arab Armies Invade Palestine; Reach Gaza, Bomb Tel Aviv Again; US Considers Lifting Arms Ban; UPI (5/15/1948)-Arab Nations Attack Israel; and L'intransigeant (5/15/1948)- Les Arabes Envahissent La Palestine. Palestine was clearly viewed as the Jewish state being invaded by Arabs. Otherwise, these headlines make no sense. If Palestine was believed to be an Arab state, then, in essence, they would just be absurdly proclaiming Arabs invade Arabs, which is wholly inconsistent with the actual news reported. The headlines are only plausible in the context of Palestine being the Jewish state (that was renamed Israel). Similarly, the reference in The New York Times headline in 1929, noted above. Query: if Israel had kept the name Palestine and Jews living there were known as Palestinians, as had been the case prior to 1948, then what would the Arabs living in Judea and Samaria call themselves? In the period 1949-1967, they called themselves Jordanian, as discussed below. Citizens of Israel, no matter whether they are Muslim, Christian, Jewish or any other religion or none, are all called Israeli's.

overwhelming odds against it. However, Jordan did illegally conquer and occupy the eastern portion of Jerusalem, including the Old City and its Jewish Quarter, as well as Judea and Samaria. These areas were ethnically cleansed of Jews, and many Jews were massacred, including in Gush Etzion. An armistice was eventually achieved under the auspices of Ralph Bunche, the UN Mediator, but the war waged by the Arabs against Israel did not end, with formal peace agreements entered into by any of the parties. The Arab nations refused to recognize Israel's existence, and years of terrorist attacks against Israel ensued that sometimes exploded into short and violent confrontations. This uneasy situation continued until 1967, when Egypt, in concert with Syria and Jordan, precipitated a war with Israel on three fronts, in the South, on the border with Gaza, in the North, in the Galilee and Golan Heights and in the East, including in Jerusalem.

Despite Israel's pleas to stay out of the war, Jordan decided to attack the western part of Jerusalem from the eastern part of Jerusalem during the 1967 Six-Day War. Israel launched a counterattack, and as a result, for the first time in almost 2,000 years, Jewish sovereignty was restored to all of Jerusalem. This included the holiest site in Judaism, the Temple Mount, which was the site of the Beit HaMikdash (both the First and the Second Temples) and the remnant of the retaining wall for the site, known as the Western or Wailing Wall, as well as, the Old City of Jerusalem and its renowned Jewish Quarter. Jordan had ethnically cleansed the Old City of Jerusalem and the other areas in Judea and Samaria that it illegally conquered of the Jews. It also denied access by Jews to the Holy Places under its control, despite agreeing to free access[71].

---

[71] Article VIII, Section 2, of the Israel and Jordan General Armistice Agreement, signed at Rhodes, on April 3, 1949. The provision also included use of the Mount of Olives Cemetery, which Jordan not only prevented while it was in control, but also despoiled, as noted below.

Indeed, the right to pray at many holy sites sacred to or cherished by various religions other than the Muslim one was severely restricted or even prohibited, as was the case with Jews. This all changed in the aftermath of the liberation of Jerusalem by Israel in June of 1967, when freedom of religion and worship, a basic right in Israel, was extended to all of Jerusalem. However, despite the foregoing, Jews are still restricted from praying on the Temple Mount because of PA and Jordanian resistance to Jews having access to the site for prayer.

On July 30, 1980, Israel's Knesset enacted the Jerusalem Basic Law, extending sovereignty over all of Jerusalem, including so-called East Jerusalem, and providing for the protection of the Holy Sites. The UN Security Council responded on August 20, 1980, by adopting Resolution 478 (1980), which censured Israel's adoption of the Jerusalem Law and the actions taken by Israel to change the status quo of Jerusalem. It called on member states to accept this decision and withdraw their diplomatic missions from Jerusalem. This was not a binding and enforceable resolution. It did not demand action be taken, nor was it promulgated under Chapter VII of the UN Charter. It was just another one of the many statements issued by the UN General Assembly, Security Council, or some other UN Committee or forum over the years that singled out Israel. There is clearly a bias or nefarious agenda shared by a number of malign actors in the power blocs comprising the UN membership. Through the force of their numbers within regional power groupings at the UN, as well as alignments with others of their ilk, they managed to control what amounts to a propaganda-generating function at the UN, in concert with their own homegrown malevolent and anti-Israel programs. However, when it came to the actual implementation of their anti-Israel rhetoric, they were usually blocked by veto, when it mattered, in the Security Council.

The United States formally abstained in the vote on this inappropriate, gratuitously negative, and impotent resolution, filled as it was with precatory and not mandatory language. It also did not remove its diplomatic presence in Jerusalem, which dates back to 1857. As detailed in this book, the liberation, and reunification of Jerusalem, as a result of the 1967 war, was consistent with International Law.

The US Congress' passage of the Jerusalem Embassy Act in 1995 added the power and prestige of US law to Israel's position that it was legally and justly entitled to sovereignty over Jerusalem. It was a solid rebuke to the UN's misguided assumptions and propagation of outright falsehoods about the nature of Israel's right to Jerusalem.

While, for a time, the United States did continue to maintain its Embassy in Tel Aviv (and only a consulate in Jerusalem), all this formally changed on Monday, May 14, 2018, when the US Embassy in Jerusalem was formally dedicated and officially opened in Jerusalem.

As noted above and more fully discussed below, others have made claim to Israel and Jerusalem over the years, and the PA baselessly continues to insist they have a claim[72]. However, none can present a record of title comparable to the Biblical one summarized above or offer any legitimate legal basis to repudiate the authoritative decisions that have unqualifiedly affirmed title to Israel, including Jerusalem, in the Jewish people.

As more fully discussed below, Israel's sovereignty over undivided Jerusalem is consistent with and not against International Law. The decision to recognize Jerusalem as the capital of Israel and move the US Embassy there was and is just and right.

---

[72] Although, as noted above, the PLO expressly abandoned any claim to Judea, Samaria and Gaza (including Jerusalem) and the so-called Palestinian Arabs effectively ceded any such claim to Jordan when they agreed to the illegal annexation by Jordan, as more fully discussed below.

II.

THE MATTER OF TITLE TO AND SOVEREIGNTY OVER JERUSALEM HAS LONG BEEN RESOLVED

Before discussing the specific background of the US recognition of Jerusalem as the capital of Israel and the move of the US Embassy to Jerusalem, it is important to analyze why that decision was legally correct and just. The fact of the matter is that the issue of Jewish sovereignty over Jerusalem has been litigated and decided in favor of the Jewish people on more than one occasion since David declared it the capital of Israel over 3,000 years ago. It is not some novel question of first impression, and the propaganda efforts directed at disassociating Jews from Jerusalem are absurd.

One of the first such legal actions[73] was brought approximately 2,350 years ago by descendants of the Canaanites[74], who, as noted above, were ancient occupiers of the Land of Israel. The Judge was no less a personage than Alexander the Great.

The question arose as to who would represent the Jewish people in defense of this momentous and extremely risky case. After all, the fate of the Jewish people hung in the balance. An adverse

---

[73] Megillat Ta'anit, Sivan 25; BT Tractate Sanhedrin, at page 91a; and Bereishit Rabbah 61.

[74] See Jerusalem Talmud (JT) Tractate Sheviit 6:1, at page 18a of the Zhitomir edition, as well as, the Maharsha, in his commentary on the BT Sanhedrin (page 91a) text noted above. The plaintiffs were descendants of the Girgashites, who left the land of Canaan, as Joshua and the Jewish people entered it. They resettled in a country, known as Afrikiya (see the Jerusalem Talmud Sheviit text, noted above). They are referred to as the children of Afrikiya in the Sanhedrin text noted above and as Canaanites in the Megillat Ta'anit (Sivan 25) and Bereishit Rabbah (61) texts noted above.

verdict would have meant the dispossession of the Jewish people from the land of their ancestors, the Land of Israel.

Geviyah[75] presented himself to the Sages and suggested he could handle the case. He counseled that sending him might afford the Sages some downside risk protection. Since he was not a recognized member of the presiding body of the Sages, therefore, his role might be disavowed if things went sideways. He was just an ordinary proverbial country lawyer taking his chances against a world-class prestigious law firm on the other side. Therefore, the credibility of the Sages would not be on the line.

At the trial, Geviyah examined the plaintiffs and asked what proof they had to support their claim to title to Israel. They testified the Bible[76] was their proof of record title. Well, Geviyah handily countered that assertion. He cited the very same Bible[77] to defeat the Canaanites' claim. As noted above, the Bible reports title to the Land of Israel was vested in the Children of Israel as an inheritance. The Canaanites had no legitimate claim to title to the Land. Moreover, the Canaanites had compounded their illegal occupation of the Land by sinning mightily, and G-d assured the Jewish people the Canaanites would be dislodged[78].

Geviyah moved for summary judgment dismissing their claims. He also asserted a counterclaim[79]. Alexander turned to the

---

[75] He is referred to as Geviyah ben Pesisa in the BT Sanhedrin (page 91a) and Megillat Ta'anit (Sivan 25) texts noted above and Geviyah ben Kosem in the parallel account in the Bereishit Rabbah (61) text noted above.

[76] Numbers 34:2. It is interesting to note that this Biblical verse cited by the Canaanite plaintiffs actually defeats their claim. It describes how the land of Canaan, according to its borders, is the land that shall belong to the people of Israel.

[77] Genesis 9:25. The Maharsha, in his commentary on the Sanhedrin (91a) text noted above, also explains there are other verses in the Bible evidencing the Jewish people's title to the Land of Israel. Some examples are cited below. He also refers to the Rashi commentary on Genesis 1:1, summarized below.

[78] See, for example, Deuteronomy 7:1 and 20:16.

[79] For all the many years of services they failed to provide to the Nation of Israel. See, for example, the Gibeonites, who as a part of their peace arrangement with Israel, agreed to perform certain services for the community and in support of the Temple services (Joshua 9 and see also JT Kiddushin 4:1 and Sanhedrin 6:7).

Canaanite plaintiffs and said he was granting the motion and ruling in favor of the Jewish people, including on Geviyah's counterclaim unless they could provide a compelling and convincing answer to the case presented by Geviyah. The Canaanite plaintiffs had no response, and so they asked for an adjournment of three days. It just delayed the inevitable because they could not formulate any answer since they had none. The fact was the very same Bible they relied on as evidence actually proved the title was properly vested in the Jewish people. It also supported the counterclaim asserted by Geviyah against them for the non-performance of services. Thus, judgment was rendered in favor of the Jewish people, both dismissing the Canaanite claim and on Geviyah's counterclaim. It would appear that the Canaanites used the three-day adjournment as a subterfuge. It permitted them time to flee the jurisdiction. Perhaps, this was in order to avoid the enforcement of the counterclaim.

If, as some so-called Palestinians claim[80], they are descendants of the Canaanites, then the matter of title to the land of Canaan, including Jerusalem, has already been resolved in favor of the Jewish people. Their purported ancestors were parties to the lawsuit before Alexander the Great noted above. The matter was adjudicated; they lost, and the Jewish people won. One can't help but wonder if these pretenders to the mantle of the Canaanites realize they are also thereby assuming the status of being among the most notorious sinners[81] in the Bible.

Others argue they are descendants of the Philistines. It's a clever, albeit contrived, subterfuge. It attempts culturally to appropriate the history of the Philistines, which is the source of the name Palestine given to the land of Israel by the Romans in an attempt

---

[80] See Camera, February 19, 2014, Saeb Erekat's Fabrication Exposes 'Palestinian Narrative'. See also, Abbas disavows Jewish ties to Temple Mount, compares Israel to Nazis, by Tovah Lazaroff, in the Jerusalem Post, dated 5/15/2023.
[81] See, for example, Deuteronomy 9:5, Leviticus 18:24-25 and Deuteronomy 18:9 and 12.

to erase its identity as a Jewish country. However, this claim fares no better. As the Bible records, the Philistines invaded the Land of Israel and illegally occupied portions. The Jewish people were forced to defend themselves against the Philistine invasion. In a series of climactic battles[82], David, first as a young warrior in King Saul's army and then, as the King of Israel, defeated the Philistine invaders and re-conquered the Land. It should also be noted that the Philistines were of Greek origin and not Arabs[83].

The descendants of Ishmael and Keturah, as plaintiffs, also brought legal action[84] against the people of Israel. Once again, Alexander the Great was the judge, and Geviyah was the attorney for the Jewish people. The plaintiffs argued that they, too, were children of Abraham like Isaac and cited the Bible[85] in support of their position. Therefore, they asserted they, too, were entitled to a share of the Land of Israel as an inheritance from their father, Abraham. Indeed, the children of Ishmael argued they were entitled to a double portion as the first-born[86].

At trial, Geviyah also adduced evidence from the Bible[87]. In essence, it records that Abraham gifted all his property during his lifetime. He gave Isaac all he owned. He gave his other children gifts of money[88] and/or ancestral property[89] in the land of the East. He also sent them there, far away from Isaac and the Land of Israel, because he wanted to avoid any disputes or

---

[82] See, for example, Samuel I-17:26 and 19:8, as well as, Samuel II-8:1.

[83] See, for example, The Philistines Were Likely of Greek Origin, According to DNA, by Philip Chrysopoulos, in the Greek Reporter, dated 5/18/2022 and Ancient DNA may reveal origin of the Philistines-Historical accounts and archaeology agree that the biggest villains of the Hebrew Bible were 'different'—but how different were they really? by Kristin Romey, in National Geographic, dated 7/3/2019. The Bible (Amos 9:7) records the Philistines came from Caphtor.

[84] Megillat Ta'anit, Sivan 25; BT Sanhedrin, at page 91a; and Bereishit Rabbah 61.

[85] Genesis 25:12 and 19.

[86] Deuteronomy 21:17.

[87] Genesis 25:5-6.

[88] See Ibn Ezra, as well as, Rashbam commentaries on Genesis 25:6.

[89] See Chizkuni commentary on Genesis 25:6

quarrels about inheritance among his sons after he passed on[90]. Hence, he settled all matters relating to his property during his lifetime, preferring not to rely on a will and someone else having to carry out his instructions[91]. Thus, Geviyah asserted, as the Bible records, title to the Land of Israel belonged wholly to Isaac and his progeny, the Children of Israel. Once again, Geviyah won the lawsuit.

If, as many Palestinian Arabs claim, they are descendants of Ishmael[92], then the matter of title to the land of Canaan, including Jerusalem, has already been resolved in favor of the Jewish people. Their ancestors were parties to the lawsuit before Alexander the Great. The matter was adjudicated; once again, they lost, and the Jewish people won. In this regard, it should also be noted the Qur'an[93] itself recognizes that the Land of Israel belongs to the Jewish people.

Yet, the matter of title to Jerusalem and the Land of Israel continues to be re-litigated. As noted above, Rashi predicted this would be the case. Rashi's answer is reminiscent of a land title legend involving an opinion of title issued by a Louisiana attorney to a bureaucrat at the FHA. It seems that the federal official did not accept title being traced back only 194 years; he wanted it traced back to its origin. In a somewhat sarcastic reply, the attorney reportedly proceeded to discuss the origin of title to the land, for the edification of the uninformed FHA bureaucrat, in the manner paraphrased below. He noted, as most schoolchildren know, the United States acquired ownership of Louisiana from France, in 1803, in what is commonly known as the Louisiana Purchase. France acquired the land by Right of Conquest from Spain. It, in turn, was acquired by Right of

---

[90] See Radak and Sforno commentaries on Genesis 25:6.

[91] Ibid, Sforno

[92] See The Arab Claim to Palestine because they are descendants of Ishmael, by Robert Morey.

[93] Quran 5:21, 17:104, 7:137, 26:59 and 10:93.

Discovery in the year 1492 through the efforts of a sea captain named Columbus. He did this in the course of his mission, seeking a new route to India, as authorized by Queen Isabella of Spain. Before the Queen granted this authority, she obtained the sanction of the Pope. In essence, his sanction, as the supreme religious authority in Europe, was deemed to represent approval of G-d for the expedition. Of course, the Louisiana attorney declared it is commonly accepted that G-d created the world, and it is safe to assume that Louisiana was a part of the world. The attorney concluded that G-d would, therefore, be the owner of origin. He said he hoped to (expletive deleted), the FHA bureaucrat would find this original claim to be satisfactory, and his client could now have his (expletive deleted) loan.

Whether this legendary tale was true or not, it provides a real-world context for Rashi's remarks at the very beginning of Genesis and those of the other Biblical commentators, summarized above. It also adds contemporary color to the deep understanding and amazing insights Rashi possessed so long ago. Frankly, saying Rashi is a profoundly respected Biblical commentator and authority is an understatement. His pithy comments continue to resonate through the ages.

In modern terms, the Bible provides a title abstract, which traces the chain of title to the Land of Israel and shows that it is properly vested in the Jewish people. Many things have changed since Rashi's times. He lived in the period of the Crusades when European Christian powers fought with Islamic ones over control of the Land of Israel. Jews were living there at the time and, thereafter, to date. They also lived there for thousands of years before that, as noted above. This is despite all the hardships they have endured. Empires rose and fell. A good portion of the Middle East, including the Land of Israel, was conquered and controlled by the Ottoman Empire during the period 1517-1917. The Ottoman Empire was on the losing side of World War I. This set the stage for the establishment of new or reconstituted

19

sovereign states out of the portions of its former empire, which it ceded to the victorious allies, as summarized below.

Today, the Jewish State of Israel governs the Land of Israel. However, some things have not changed. As Rashi anticipated, there are still those who continue to rehash the same old bogus claims that they and not the Jewish people are the rightful owners of the Land of Israel.

Having summarized how these title claims were adjudicated in ancient times, we now come to the early 20th century version. This time the context was the end of World War I. Representatives of the victorious allies, including the United States, Britain, Italy, France, and Japan, met in Paris in 1919. They had triumphed over the central powers, Germany, the Austrian-Hungarian Empire, and the Ottoman Empire, and they received presentations by various delegations of all sorts of claims to lands previously comprising a part of the German, Ottoman, and Austrian-Hungarian Empires. Thus, for example, in Europe, Poland was reborn, the borders of Czechoslovakia and Romania were fixed and recognized, and the country of Yugoslavia was created.

The Jewish people also presented their claim to an area that had been a part of the Ottoman Empire, which was referred to as Palestine at the time. The Jewish delegations included Dr. Chaim Weizmann, the future first president of the State of Israel. The Arab people also presented their claims. Emir Feisal led the Arab delegation.

Thereafter, in 1920, the Supreme Council of Allied Powers met in San Remo, Italy, in order to resolve many of these claims. The context is important. The Central Powers ceded control of portions of their Empires to the Allied Powers under the Peace Treaties signed with them. This included the area referred to as Palestine (now the country of Israel), as well as the areas that would become Turkey, Armenia, Iraq, Syria, Lebanon, and Saudi Arabia.

Under International Law, the Supreme Council had the power to dispose of these various territories that were formerly a part of the Ottoman Empire. It was in this capacity that the Supreme Council dealt with the claim of the Jewish people to an area referred to as Palestine (now the country of Israel). The claim was based on their historic title to the Land of Israel. The Jewish people sought to reconstitute their national home in Palestine as an autonomous commonwealth. The Arab people also presented their claims.

The Minutes of the Meeting of the Supreme Council[94] on the matter of Palestine are most illuminating. They reflect that representatives of the United States, British Empire, France, Italy, and Japan were present. The meeting also considered the matter of determining the borders of Turkey and Armenia, as well as issues related to Syria and Mesopotamia (current-day Iraq).

The Supreme Council Minutes record the discussions regarding the area denominated as Palestine and it being a national home for the Jews. In this regard, it is important to appreciate that presentations were made by Jewish as well as Arab delegations asserting claims as to Palestine. Members of the Syrian Delegation[95] met with the Supreme Council on February 13, 1919[96]. They argued that Palestine should be a part of Syria. On February 6, 1919, Emir Feisal, as head of the Hedjaz Delegation,

---

[94] Minutes of Palestine Meeting of the Supreme Council of The Allied Powers Held in San Remo at the Villa Devachan-April 24,1920.
[95] The Syrian Delegation included Chekri Ganem, an Arab Maronite Christian and Jamil Mardam Bey, an Arab Muslim, who help organize the Arab Congress of 1913 in Paris and eventually became a Prime Minister of Syria.
[96] See, America and Palestine: the attitude of official America and of the American people toward the rebuilding of Palestine as a free and democratic Jewish commonwealth, prepared and edited by Reuben Fink, New York: American Zionist Emergency Council (1944), at pages 445-446.

is reported to have said Palestine should be left on the side for the mutual consideration of all parties concerned[97].

Reference was made to the new projected State in the area denominated as Palestine and its borders. Consideration was also given to the civil and religious rights of the non-Jewish communities residing in Palestine.

The Supreme Council considered the claims of the various parties, deliberated, and decided title to Palestine was vested in the Jewish people[98].

In furtherance of the foregoing, the Supreme Council determined that Palestine would be reestablished as a national home for the Jews and a mandatory would be entrusted with implementing the foregoing under Article 22 of the Covenant of the League of Nations. The terms of the mandate were to be formulated by the Principal Allied Powers, who constituted the Supreme Council and submitted to the Council of the League of Nations for approval. This occurred, and the terms of the mandate were approved, as noted below. The effect was to confirm, as a matter of International Law, the reestablishment of Palestine as a national home for the Jewish People.

The Council of the League of Nations[99] unanimously adopted the San Remo[100] Resolution[101] on Palestine[102]. It thereby became an

---

[97] Ibid, at page 442.

[98] See Sovereignty Over the Old City of Jerusalem: A Study of the Historical, Religious, Political and Legal Aspects of the Question of the Old City, by Jacques Paul Gauthier (2007).

[99] By Resolution, dated July 24, 1922.

[100] Interestingly, Rabbi Meir Simcha of Dvinsk (known for his seminal work, the Meshech Chochma) referenced San Remo and the League of Nations reaffirmation of San Remo in a letter, citing it for the proposition that it represented the legal sanction of the nations of the world to reestablish the Jewish State of Israel and vitiating any concerns under BT Ketubot 111a. (The letter is reproduced in HaTekufah HaGedolah, by Rav Menachem Kasher, Volume I, at page 207, et seq.)

[101] Adopted on April 25, 1920.

[102] The very same resolution provided for the establishment of Syria and Mesopotamia (Iraq).

international agreement, binding on all of the member countries, which, in effect, confirmed title to Palestine (Israel) in the people of Israel, under International Law. It recited that recognition had been given to "the historical connection of the Jewish people with Palestine and to the grounds for reconstituting their national home in that country"[103]. There are a number of very important legal concepts embodied in this provision of the Council resolution. It effectively confirmed the Jewish people as the recognized indigenous people of Palestine for over three thousand five hundred years and, as noted above, rejected the claims of others. This absolutely demolishes the fallacious claim that Jews are just modern-day colonialists.

The Council resolution also did not purport to grant the Jewish people a newly minted right to Palestine; rather, it recorded that recognition had been given to the "grounds for" reconstituting their national home in that country. Thus, it was a pre-existing legal right that was recognized and acknowledged. Consistent with this principle, it called for "reconstituting" the Jewish people's national home in their homeland of Palestine, not building a new national home there, which had no prior existence.

The use of the term 'country' in the Council resolution is also cogent. It was no longer referred to as a geographical territory in the former Ottoman Empire; rather, Palestine was now referred to as a country. The sovereignty and legal title to the country of Palestine was vested in the Jewish people.

Article 4 of the resolution provided for a Jewish agency to be recognized as a public body and putative government to assist in the reestablishment of the Jewish national home, including taking part in the development of the country.

---

[103] In the Preamble to the Resolution unanimously adopted by the Council of the League of Nations.

Article 6 of the resolution provided for the settlement of Jews on the land, including State lands.

Article 11 of the resolution provided for the Jewish Agency to be able to construct or operate public works, services, and utilities and develop any of the natural resources of the country.

The Council entrusted a Mandate to Britain to implement the resolution of the League of Nations. Of course, the civil and religious rights of existing non-Jewish communities in the country were not to be prejudiced, and the granting instrument so provides.

Thus, Article 2 of the resolution provided for the Mandatory to place the country under such 'political', administrative, and economic conditions as shall enable the re-establishment of the Jewish National Home and the development of self-governing institutions. Political rights were reserved only for the Jewish people. As to all the inhabitants of Israel, their civil and religious rights were to be safeguarded, but only the Jewish people were granted political rights.

Article 7 of the resolution expressly provided that the administration of Palestine be responsible for enacting a nationality law, which shall include provisions framed so as to facilitate the acquisition of Palestinian citizenship by Jews who take up their permanent residence in Palestine. In essence, International Law expressly provided for a law of return for Jews to their native homeland of Palestine [Israel]. No similar provision was made for anyone else.

As Eugene Rostow[104] makes clear[105]:

---

[104] Eugene V. Rostow, Sterling Professor of Law and Public Affairs Emeritus, Yale University; Distinguished Research Professor of Law and Diplomacy, National Defense University; Adjunct Fellow, American Enterprise Institute, and Honorary Fellow of the Hebrew University of Jerusalem.
[105] The Future of Palestine, by Eugene V. Rostow, McNair Paper 24, November 1993, Institute for National Strategic Studies, National Defense University, Washington, D.C.

By protecting Arab "civil and religious rights", the mandate implicitly denies Arab claims to national political rights in the area in favor of the Jews; the mandated territory was, in effect, reserved to the Jewish people for their self-determination and political development, in acknowledgment of the historic connection of the Jewish people to the land. Lord Curzon, who was then the British Foreign Minister, made this reading of the mandate explicit.

Lest there be any doubt, Article 5 of the Council's resolution provided that "no Palestine territory shall be ceded or leased to or in any way placed under the control of the Government of any foreign Power". In essence, the title to the country of Palestine granted to the Jewish people at San Remo could not be revoked or granted to another by the Mandatory authority or the League. This legally includes the UN as the successor to the League. Palestine belonged to the Jewish people.

The San Remo Resolution was also a part of the Treaty of Sevres[106] with the Ottoman Empire and, in effect[107], ratified by the Treaty of Lausanne of 1923 with Turkey.

The Resolution of the Supreme Council of Allied Powers at San Remo was also endorsed in the Anglo-American Treaty on Palestine[108]. It actually incorporated the text of the resolution of the Council of the League of Nations, referred to above. It should be noted that the Anglo-American Treaty, among other things, provides as follows:

Whereas the Principal Allied Powers have agreed, for the purpose of giving effect to the provisions of article 22 of the Covenant of the League of Nations, to entrust to a

---

[106] Article 95.

[107] Article 16.

[108] It was also known as the Anglo-American Convention. It was signed on December 3, 1924 and ratified by the U.S. Senate on February 20, 1925, as noted below.

Mandatory selected by the said Powers the administration of the territory of Palestine, which formerly belonged to the Turkish Empire, within such boundaries as may be fixed by them;

Whereas recognition has thereby been given to the historical connection of the Jewish people with Palestine and to the grounds for reconstituting their national home in that country;

Article 5. The Mandatory shall be responsible for seeing that no Palestine territory shall be ceded or leased to, or in any way placed under the control of, the Government of any foreign Power.

Article 6. The Administration of Palestine, while ensuring that the rights and position of other sections of the population are not prejudiced, shall facilitate Jewish immigration under suitable conditions and shall encourage, in co-operation with the Jewish agency referred to in article 4, close settlement by Jews on the land, including State lands and waste lands not required for public purposes.

Article 7. The Administration of Palestine shall be responsible for enacting a nationality law. There shall be included in this law provisions framed so as to facilitate the acquisition of Palestinian citizenship by Jews who take up their permanent residence in Palestine[109].

---

[109] Query, how might the Supreme Court's decision in the Zivotofsky case (summarized in Chapter XIII, below) have been influenced, had the Treaty, including this provision, been raised? It might have been argued that, by virtue of the Treaty, US Law assured Jews the right to reside anywhere within the area of the Mandate (including perforce Jerusalem) and to have their nationality status recognized, as set forth in the very nationality law the President provided for in the Treaty. This included citizenship in the

The Treaty was concluded and signed by the respective representatives of the US and UK in London on December 3, 1924. The US Senate ratified it, under its power to advise and consent, on February 20, 1925, and President Calvin Coolidge approved it on March 2, 1925. It was formally ratified by Great Britain on March 18, 1925. The respective ratifications were exchanged, and the Treaty was formally proclaimed on December 5, 1925.

The Treaty, thus, formally and legally recognized the right of the Jewish people to sovereignty over all of Palestine, between the Jordan River on the East and the Mediterranean Sea on the West[110], including, of course, Jerusalem. Notwithstanding that

---

Jewish State then putatively named Palestine, which was renamed Israel. The State Department policy, until 2020 (when Zivotofsky received the first passport recording his birth in Jerusalem, as being in Israel), denied this possibility. The Government in the Zivotofsky case argued it was pursuing the more than 60 year old policy of not recognizing any state's sovereignty over Jerusalem because of the unique sensitivity surrounding the issue (page 41 of Brief for the Respondent, on the Writ of Certiorari to the Supreme Court of the United States-no. 10-699, submitted by Donald B. Verrilli, Jr. Solicitor-General, et al, dated September 2011). In essence, the State Department was artificially preserving the internationalization (corpus separatum) scheme for Jerusalem, hatched by the UN in 1948 (which, in point of fact and law, was nothing more than a suggestion that was not legally binding), to negate any formal Israeli status for those born in Jerusalem. However, the Government's presentation ignored the even longer-standing Presidential policy originated at San Remo and embodied in the 1924 Treaty and by virtue thereof US Law. Moreover, it appears that this later policy urged by the State Department contravened the substantive import of this prior existing US Law. Furthermore, the Governmental assurances regarding the history of Presidential policy regarding Jerusalem should, at the very least, have been seriously qualified by virtue of the Treaty and the rights it granted, which survive and have the force of US Law. There are also the policy statements made by Presidents since President Wilson, as summarized in this book, in support of a Jewish commonwealth in all of Israel, which make no exception for Jerusalem. Thus, the 60-year old policy reference noted above is more fairly viewed as a change in prior policy that was made contrary to applicable law and established policy. It would appear that the Supreme Court was not fully apprised of these facts and circumstances. Fortunately, while this might make an interesting subject of academic speculation, the matter is now moot, ever since Jerusalem was recognized as the capital of Israel, by President Trump and as provided by Congress, in the Jerusalem Embassy Act of 1995, as discussed below.

[110] See Article 25 of the Treaty, which only allows some flexibility as to the areas, which are a part of the Mandate that are east of the Jordan River; not west, which is all set aside for the reestablishment of the then nascent modern State of Israel.

the British Mandate over Palestine was terminated[111], nevertheless, the rights granted under the Treaty to the Jewish people survive, as confirmed by the Vienna Convention on the Law of Treaties[112]. Therefore, it is respectfully submitted, it was and still is US Law that Jews have the right to settle in Judea and Samaria, including, without limitation, Jerusalem. This right was recognized by the President and is embodied in US law. In this regard, it is also submitted that the US may not promote a so-called Palestinian state that prohibits Jewish settlement in any part of the area of the original Mandate[113], which perforce includes Jerusalem.

The United States Constitution provides that the President "shall have Power, by and with the Advice and Consent of the Senate, to make Treaties, provided two-thirds of the Senators present concur"[114]. Treaties are binding agreements between nations and become part of international law. Treaties to which the United States is a party that are approved by the Senate also become the 'supreme Law of the Land' under the Constitution[115], and those that are self-executing automatically have the force of federal legislation[116].

---

[111] After the UNGA adopted Resolution 181, on 29 November 1947, Britain announced the termination of its Mandate for Palestine, which became effective on May 15, 1948. At midnight on May 14, 1948, the State of Israel declared its independence.

[112] Article 70, Consequences of the termination of a treaty, Section 1(b), of the Vienna Convention on the Law of Treaties (1969).

[113] See, Chapters I and II above, as well as, Legal Rights and Title of Sovereignty of the Jewish People to the Land of Israel and Palestine under International Law, by Howard Grief, at Nativ online, A Journal of Politics and the Arts, Vol. 2 of 2004 (acpr.org.il).

[114] US Constitution, Article II, Section 2.

[115] US Constitution, Article VI, Section 2.

[116] See, United State Senate-About Treaties, at senate.gov. and Treaties and Other International Agreements: The Role of the United States Senate, A Study Prepared for the Committee On Foreign Relations, United States Senate, by the Congressional Research Service, Library of Congress, January 2001. Self-executing treaties are those that do not require implementing legislation. They automatically become effective as domestic law immediately upon entry into force. Other treaties do not become effective as domestic law until implementing legislation is enacted and then technically it is the legislation, not the treaty unless incorporated into the legislation, which is the law of

In ratifying the Treaty, the US legally recognized the terms of the Palestine Mandate, pursuant to the San Remo Resolution, and the historical connection of the Jewish people with Palestine, as well as the reconstitution of their national home there. In this sense, this was the first US law that recognized the Jewish people's right to Jerusalem[117].

Interestingly, when the British illegally adopted the White Paper in 1939, restricting immigration by Jews to then Mandatory Palestine, a bipartisan group of fifteen[118] (out of the twenty-five) members of the House Foreign Affairs Committee urged the State Department to protest the British White Paper[119] and advise the British Government that it would be regarded as a violation of the 1924 Anglo-American Treaty. The group declared that the British plan to limit Jewish immigration to the Holy Land and attempt to fix the Jews as a permanent minority was a clear repudiation of the Treaty. They also said it was the duty of the American Government to see to it that the treaty was carried out in good faith.

---

the land.

[117] The Jewish People never gave up their title to the Land of Israel, including, of course, Jerusalem. There is no recorded treaty of surrender or abandonment of the Land of Israel by the Jewish People. Not only did the Jewish People never renounce their claim to Jerusalem, the references to Jerusalem in the Jewish prayer rituals are, in effect, a continuing protest that disputes the occupation of the Land of Israel by others. See, Zionism, Palestinian Nationalism and the Law 1938-1948, by Steven E. Zipperstein (Routledge-2021). It should also be noted that the Arabs living in Judea and Samaria, who now call themselves Palestinians, did in fact renounce any claims to sovereignty over the areas of Judea and Samaria, including Jerusalem, which were illegally annexed by Jordan, as more fully discussed below, in this book.

[118] Seven Republican and Eight Democrat Congressmen, including Sol Bloom, New York;
Luther A. Johnson, Texas; John Kee, West Virginia; James P. Richards, South Carolina; James A. Shanley, Connecticut; Ed. V. Izac, California; Robert G. Allen, Pennsylvania; W. O. Burgin, North Carolina; Hamilton Fish, New York; George Holden Tinkham, Massachusetts;
Edith Nourse Rogers, Massachusetts; Bruce Barton, New York; Robert J. Corbett, Pennsylvania;
John M. Vorys, Ohio; and Andrew C. Schifiler, West Virginia.

[119] See, Congressional Record, May 25, 1939, at page 6167 and 15 of House Foreign Affairs Body Hold White Paper Breaks Anglo-American Pact, at JTA, dated 5/28/1939.

President Franklin D. Roosevelt also later noted[120] that the US had never given its approval to the White Paper and reaffirmed support for the recreation of the Jewish commonwealth in Israel.

This was consistent with US policy as expressed by Presidents Wilson, Harding, Coolidge, and Hoover before him[121]. President Teddy Roosevelt, when he was a private citizen in 1918, wrote[122]: "it seems to me that it is entirely proper to start a Zionist state around Jerusalem". He also wrote a letter[123] outlining how he believed it was critical that the Jews be given control of Palestine.

Jerusalem was an integral part of Palestine, and it is, therefore, fully a part of the Land of Israel. There was no carve-out for Jerusalem in any of the foregoing sources of International Law confirming title to the country of Palestine in the Jewish people. To be clear, there were provisions made regarding respecting the rights of worship at the Holy Places. These, though, are indicative of sovereignty over Jerusalem, like the rest of Palestine, being fully vested in the Jewish people. Otherwise, why speak of respecting only certain rights? Indeed, the fact remains, it is only under Jewish sovereignty and control that these rights were and continue to be respected.

The UN Charter[124] did not change the legal status of Jerusalem as being a part of the Land of Israel, nor did the invasion by Jordan of the State of Israel in 1948. Jordan illegally occupied the

---

[120] See, Roosevelt Receives Zionist Leaders; Says U.S. Never Approved White Paper, in JTA, dated 3/10/1944.
[121] See, America and Palestine: the attitude of official America and of the American people toward the rebuilding of Palestine as a free and democratic Jewish commonwealth, prepared and edited by Reuben Fink, New York: American Zionist Emergency Council (1944), at pages 87-88. See also, Letter by Congressman Dingell (Michigan) to Secretary of State Hull, dated 5/20/1939, reproduced on page 283.
[122] Cited by Michael Oren, in his book, Power, Faith, and Fantasy: America in the Middle East 1776-the Present (W.W. Norton-2007), at page 359.
[123] Letter from Theodore Roosevelt to Lioubomir Michailovitch, the Serbian Minister, dated July 11, 1918, which can be found in the Theodore Roosevelt Center.org, digital library.
[124] Article 80.

eastern portion of Jerusalem, including the Old City, containing the Temple Mount and Western Wall, as well as other areas of what was known as Mandatory Palestine. This state of affairs continued until June of 1967, when, during the Six-Day War, Jordan attacked Israel. In this defensive war with Jordan, Israel re-captured the eastern portion of Jerusalem and the other areas west of the Jordan River, which had been unlawfully occupied by Jordan since 1948.

Thereafter, the Knesset of Israel adopted Laws[125] enabling the application of Israeli law and administration to Jerusalem and other areas recaptured and the extension of municipal boundaries, consistent with the foregoing. The Knesset later adopted a Basic Law: Jerusalem[126], which declared that the complete and united Jerusalem was the capital of Israel.

In passing the Jerusalem Embassy Act of 1995[127], the United States recognized that Israel had the right, under International Law and custom, to designate its own capital. The US Law also recognized that the City of Jerusalem had been the capital of the State of Israel since 1950. It also found that Jerusalem was a divided city from 1948-1967, and Israeli citizens of all faiths, as well as Jewish citizens of all states, had been denied access to the holy sites in the area controlled by Jordan. The Law went on to find Jerusalem had been re-united during the Six Day War of 1967 and that since then, persons of all religious faiths had been protected, respected, and guaranteed full access to the holy sites within the city.

---

[125] Volumes 1-2 of Laws, 1947-1974, Part IV. Jerusalem and the Holy Places, Section 13. Law-1967 and Administration Ordinance (Amendment 11) Law-1967, which were adopted on June 27, 1967. Also adopted, was Municipalities Ordinance (Amendment 6) Law-1967, which added after Section 8, new subsections 8a-b, which, among other things, enabled enlargement of the area of the municipality.

[126] On July 30, 1980, published in Sefer Ha-Chukkim No. 980 (1980)

[127] Public Law 104-45, dated November 8, 1995 and known as the Jerusalem Embassy Act of 1995.

There have been a number of cases before the Supreme Court of Israel that have dealt with the legal status of Jerusalem and other areas recaptured from Jordan in 1967. Israel has a much respected and admired independent judiciary with a well-deserved reputation for genuinely dispensing justice impartially. The cases summarized below are no exception. They are a testament to the independence of the Israeli judiciary and their dedication to the rule of law and the highest standards of justice, without bias or deference, no matter who appears before the court.

One example is the case of Temple Mount Faithful et al. vs. Attorney General et al[128]. In that case, the Supreme Court of Israel, in a well-reasoned opinion issued in 1993, held that Jerusalem, including the area of the Temple Mount, was a part of the State of Israel. It also held that the laws, jurisdiction, and administration of the State of Israel applied to Jerusalem[129].

Lest anyone incorrectly presume that the Supreme Court of Israel is biased in favor of Jews and against Arabs[130], here's

---

[128] Temple Mount Faithful-Amutah, et al vs. Attorney General, Inspector General of the Police, Mayor of Jerusalem, Minister of Education and Culture Director of the Antiquities Division, Muslim WAQF (H.C. 4195/90). The Supreme Court, sitting as the High Court of Justice (highest court of the State of Israel) on this case, was comprised of Justices Menachem Elon, Aharon Barak and Gavriel Bach. Their decision was dated September 23, 1993. An English translation of the decision was published in 45 Cath. U. L. Rev. 866 (1996).

[129] Interestingly, Farley worked as a volunteer law clerk for Justice Menachem Elon, the Deputy President of the Israeli Supreme Court, in the summer of 1988. Although he had no involvement in the case noted above, he did witness, first hand, Justice Elon's erudition, professionalism and impartiality, as well as, his absolute dedication to the pursuit of justice.

[130] Indeed, to the contrary, it might be argued that the Israeli Supreme Court bends over backwards in favor of Arabs. Take for example the case of Bishara v Attorney General decided on Februray 1, 2006 (HCJ 11225/03). As a member of the Knesset, Bishara, in two speeches, expressed support and approval for Hezbollah, which Israel had declared a terrorist organization. Bishara was indicted for supporting a terrorist organization and sought to dismiss the case on the grounds that he had substantive immunity under the law for the two speeches, since he made them while he was a member of the Knesset. However, the Israeli Immunity Law had an express exclusion for expressions of support for "an armed struggle of a terrorist organization against the State of Israel", which

another example which demonstrates, in no uncertain terms, the impartial and unbiased character of the Israeli Supreme Court. In the case of Hamad vs. Minister of Defense et al.[131], the Court found that homes illegally constructed in Amona, on private land owned by Arab residents in the adjacent town of Silwad, had to be demolished and vacated.

An independent judiciary making impartial decisions based solely on the facts and applicable law and respect for the rule of law[132] are the hallmark of a true democratic republic, and Israel is a shining example of these immutable principles in practice. Whether it is the Sheikh Jarrah case[133] or any other property dispute, the Israeli Supreme Court is devoted to rendering impartial justice. It also counts among its number Justice Khaled

---

were not protected under the Immunity Law. The Majority (President Barak and Justice Rivlin) held the exclusion should be interpreted strictly. Thus, while Bishara expressed support for Hezbollah, a terrorist organization, the Majority found that technically he did not explicitly support Hezbollah's armed struggle against the State of Israel, in the two speeches at issue. Consequently, the Majority ruled the exclusion from immunity did not apply. The Majority appears to have recognized it was straining to do so because, as it noted, there was a body of precedent, known as the 'margin of natural risk test'. It likely should have been applied to determine that Bishara was supporting Hezbollah's armed struggle. However, the Majority concluded that the statements were close to the line, beyond which it would not be possible to treat them as immune; but did not cross it. The Minority opinion was delivered by Justice Esther Hayut, who dissented and found that Bishara's two speeches were not protected by substantive immunity, because they did express support for the armed struggle of a terrorist organization against the State of Israel. The sordid tale of Bishara didn't end there. He later reportedly fled Israel in 2007, after being accused of spying for Hezbollah (see, Azmi Bishara, from Knesset black sheep to Qatar Insider, by Shatha Yaish, in The Times of Israel, dated 6/5/2018).

[131] Supreme Court of Israel, sitting as the High Court of Justice, decided on December 12, 2014 (HCJ 9949/08).

[132] This includes Constitutional protections in the US and Basic Law protections in Israel (which, like Britain and New Zealand, does not have a single written document known as the constitution; but rather a combination of written laws and precedents).

[133] See, for example, The Sheikh Jarrah property dispute and the false claim of Israeli land discrimination, by Avi Bell, at JNS, dated 5/21/2021 and Court freezes eviction of Palestinian family from Sheikh Jarrah home, by Aaron Boxerman, in The Times of Israel, dated 2/22/2022.

Kabub, of the Muslim faith[134], as well as previous Arab jurists who happened to be of the Christian faith.

The legal status of Jerusalem was also considered by the French Court of Appeals of Versailles in the case of PLO et ano vs. Societe Alstom Transport SA et al[135]. Mahmoud Abbas appeared for the PLO as President of the Executive Committee. The decision the Court issued in 2013 once again confirmed that the State of Israel was vested with sovereignty and title to Jerusalem under International Law. The defendant was involved with the tramway in Jerusalem. The PLO alleged the State of Israel was occupying so-called Palestinian territory illegally and was continuing with illegal settlement through the building of the Jerusalem tramway. It claimed a breach of Article 49 of the Fourth Geneva Convention, which provides that an Occupying Power shall not forcibly transfer parts of its own civilian population into the territory it occupies. It also claimed a violation of Article 53, which prohibits an Occupying Power from destroying real or personal property belonging to individuals, the state, or other public authorities, except when rendered necessary by military operations. It was claimed that work done on the public road for the construction of the light rail violated this provision.

The French Court of Appeals rejected these, as well as the other claims of the plaintiffs. The Palestinians had no legal right to Jerusalem, protected by International Law, and Israel was legally entitled to build the light rail in the area. It also held that the PLO and Palestinian Authority were not states, nor were they contracting parties to the Geneva Convention. Therefore, the provisions of the Geneva Convention cited by them did not apply. The Court also challenged the baseless assumptions

---

[134] See, Khaled Kabub sworn in as Israeli Supreme Court's first Muslim justice, at The Times of Israel, dated 5/9/2022.

[135] France-Palestine Solidarite, et ano vs. Societe Alstom Transport SA, Cour D'Appel De Versaille, Code nac: 59a (R.G. No. 11/05331), decided March 22, 2013.

asserted by the PLO. It held that the PLO's individual assessment as to a political or social situation is not determinative for purposes of legally establishing the purpose or lawfulness of a party's actions. While these kinds of vocal assertions may make for good propaganda on the lecture circuit, they do not constitute legal arguments. The Court was interested in law and real facts established by probative evidence, not speculations or mere assertions. Thus, the Court would not ascribe a nefarious political motive to the actions of the State of Israel just because the plaintiffs said so. The Court also caustically noted that Article 53 is about bombing, and Jerusalem was not being bombed by building a tramway. The Court held the State of Israel had a legal right to build the light rail. Indeed, in point of fact, it was constructed for the good purpose of bettering Jerusalem, which it lawfully governed.

It should also be noted the unfounded assertion that Section 49 somehow applies to Israel and Jerusalem is a particularly cruel and ironic canard. This provision was intended[136] to prevent a recurrence of such abhorrent actions as Nazi Germany's forcible: a) expulsion from Germany of its Jewish citizens and resettlement in concentration and death camps in occupied Poland; and b) impress of citizens of the countries it conquered as slave laborers in Nazi Germany. Thus, Section 49 expressly requires a "forcible" transfer of an Occupying Power's civilian population to a territory that it occupies. It is just specious to suggest that the citizens of Israel, who have moved to the united city of Jerusalem, are doing so because the State of Israel forcibly expelled them and transferred them to Jerusalem. Moreover,

---

[136] See Eugene V. Rostow Letter to the Editor, in the American Journal of International Law, Volume 84, pages 717-719 (1990), as well as, his letter to the New York Times, published April 1, 1992. He was Dean of Yale Law School and served as Under Secretary of State for Political Affairs under President Lyndon B. Johnson. See also International Committee of the Red Cross (ICRC) Commentary to the Fourth Geneva Convention of August 12, 1949 (edited by Jean S. Pictet), at pages 278-279 (1958), as well as, International humanitarian law, ICRC and Israel's status in the Territories, by Alan Baker, International Review of the Red Cross, Volume 94, Number 888 (2012).

Jerusalem is not an occupied territory, nor is Israel an Occupying Power. It was Jordan that had unlawfully taken and occupied the eastern portion of Jerusalem, including the Old City and other areas. Israel fought a lawful defensive war against Jordan and recaptured territory which had originally been vested in the Jewish people of Israel, as detailed above[137].

What has happened to our appreciation of genuine law and true facts? Does it really no longer matter? Despite all the pious-sounding pronouncements accusing Israel of violating International Law or being in illegal occupation of Judea and Samaria and even Gaza, this is just not the case. Indeed, as summarized above, courts of competent jurisdiction have ruled in favor of Israel, denying the validity of these baseless accusations and validating Israel's right to sovereignty over Judea and Samaria. As to Gaza, Israel neither occupies it as a matter of fact nor law, as more fully discussed below and in Chapter XIV.

Yes, the State of Israel can negotiate and, in the context of a genuine mutual agreement, with real sign-on by both sides, voluntarily agree to the creation of a new state, living side by side with it in peace[138]. However, there is no legal or moral imperative requiring Israel to cede some of its land for this purpose; nor is it just or right unilaterally to impose a divestiture of land from Israel against its will. Neither force of arms nor UN resolution

---

[137] See, Historical Approach to the Issue of Legality of Jewish Settlement Activity, by Eugene W. Rostow, in New Republic, on April 23, 1990.

[138] It also takes two to tango. Indeed, as Prince Bander of Saudi Arabia so well said, Arafat committed a crime against the Palestinian people in not accepting Ehud Barak's exceedingly generous offer, under the Clinton initiative in Camp David, in 2000. See, Israel's Liaison to Its Neighbors: Saudi Prince Bandar, by Aluf Benn, dated March 2, 2007, in Haaretz. See also Yasser Arafat's widow admits Palestinian terror campaign in 2000 was premeditated, by Jamie Weinstein, dated December 28, 2012, in the Daily Caller.

can legally accomplish this; it requires Israel's voluntary acceptance.

There's an old lawyer's adage that seems to animate the anti-Israel community that continues to make a lot of noise but says little or nothing of substance when it comes to Jerusalem. It suggests when an attorney has the law on his or her side, argue the law, when he or she has the facts, argue the facts and when he or she has neither, pound the table or ask for an adjournment. Having no law or probative factual evidence to support a legitimate claim, the propaganda mills of Hamas, the PA, and their sponsors, allies, and useful dupes loudly proclaim all sorts of baseless and dubious assertions. The noise is often deafening, but it must not be allowed to distract from the central, immutable conclusion that the historical and legal right of the Jewish people to Jerusalem is unchallengeable. Some also choose to proceed extra-judicially by threatening and actually committing violent acts of terrorism, invoking BDS, or attempting to control public opinion through Soviet-style propaganda and an apparatus of so-called NGOs. However, this is not justice; nor is howling slogans like justice for Palestine. They may be designed to signal virtue, but their goal is not virtuous. Rather, they seek the destruction of the State of Israel and are nothing more than a new veiled and sometimes overt expression of antisemitism.

Disinformation campaigns are not something new. We lived through it in the Cold War with the Soviet Union and its proxies, including the period of the 1960s-1980s. It lives on in the rhetoric of the PLO, an original proxy of the former Soviet Union, and in its new incarnation, as the Palestinian Authority (PA). We might have thought that many of these lessons of the Cold War would have been assimilated and taught to the new generation in school. However, it appears that for many, the opposite is true. They are being fed a false narrative about recent history. This includes Israel's 1967 defensive war for survival. Many of us are still around to remember firsthand what happened. It's time for those with genuine knowledge to speak out. We can't allow the apparatchiks to have free reign. We cannot afford to be complacent or allow misleading statements, canards, and flat-out untruths to go unchallenged. We must challenge them with the truth. It's a mission we must undertake with energy and determination.

Formally recognizing Jerusalem as the capital of Israel and finally deciding to move the U.S. Embassy there should not have been controversial. It effectuated the provisions of the 1995 Law that was adopted by an overwhelming majority of the Senate and House. It also finally brought the US in line with the historical and legal reality that Israel was justly and properly seized of title to and sovereignty over Jerusalem. Yet, there were still naysayers, including some reputed foreign policy experts, who predicted dire consequences. Not only were there no enduring negative results, the opposite occurred. The US' recognition of Jerusalem ended up being a catalyst that eventually helped lead to the Abraham Accords and the improvement of the prospects for peace in the Middle East.

As Senator Jon Kyl urged when he first proposed the concept of the Jerusalem Embassy Act, rather than frustrate the potential for peace, it would enhance it; but more on that below.

III.

SENATOR JON KYL AND HIS SEMINAL ROLE IN ORIGINATING THE JERUSALEM EMBASSY ACT OF 1995

In November of 1994, Jon Kyl was elected to the US Senate from Arizona. There was little in his background that augured the pivotal role he would play in causing the recognition of Jerusalem as the capital of Israel and relocating the US Embassy there.

As a Presbyterian Christian, Jerusalem being recognized as the capital of the reestablished modern State of Israel was not an integral part of his creed, nor was his constituency composed of many Jews, who considered this an important issue. He did have some Christian Evangelical backers and close Jewish friends, which might have accounted for his early exposure to the matter. However, as more fully discussed below, this could not explain his dogged determination to make recognition of Jerusalem and moving the Embassy there a reality.

This was not a decision Jon Kyl made based on the rigors of political calculus and poll testing. It was a personal one, based on his innate good sense and sound judgment on what was right and wrong, which was a fundamental part of his strong character. He was motivated by a moral imperative to do what was right and just. As he said in his own words, with reference to the Jerusalem Embassy Act of 1995 that recognized Jerusalem as the capital of Israel, which he had initiated and had been passed by Congress, nearly unanimously in the US Senate and by an overwhelming majority in the House of Representatives[139]:

> The most frequent question I get asked from folks is: what inspired me to go to Senator Dole with this initiative and press for its passage? Really, the answer is quite simple: it was the morally right thing to do. I've never questioned whether Jerusalem is the capital of Israel.

Harking back to an earlier time, in 1948, when President Harry S. Truman recognized the fledging and newly reestablished State of Israel, despite most of his top advisors urging him not to do so, he noted:

> President Truman was a man of plain good sense and sound moral judgment. What he lacked in sophistication, he made up in decency and clarity of thought. As Truman saw it, a state for the Jews in their ancient homeland might not be diplomatically convenient, but it was just... Truman understood that recognition of Israel was more than a matter of policy—it was a choice between right and wrong.

Senator Kyl also expressed the frustration that he and other members of Congress, such as Senator Lieberman, felt because of the reluctance of officials in the Clinton administration to implement the Law or acknowledge the responsibility of the United States to align itself clearly as a friend of Israel. This reticence would continue until President Trump finally made the

---

[139] Excerpts from speech delivered by Senator Kyl at the National Council of Young Israel dinner in New York City, on Sunday, March 22, 1998, where he was honored with the Defender of Jerusalem Award. Among other things, Senator Kyl also offered special thanks to Farley Weiss for being so helpful to him and his staff. It was Farley who had been instrumental in obtaining the invitation for Senator Kyl to speak at the National Council dinner. He was also privileged to sit with Senator Kyl at the dinner. Years later, Farley was elected the President of the National Council of Young Israel (comprised of over 100 Synagogues and with approximately 20,000 members). He also became a member of the Conference of Presidents of Major Jewish Organizations.

decision to implement the Law and recognize Jerusalem as the capital of Israel and move the US Embassy there.

Perhaps, it took someone with real estate savvy and real-life business experience to understand what was truly at stake, as well as the dynamics of how a good deal could be crafted and consummated by the parties. All too often, the prideful technocratic bureaucrats and academic pundits, who seemed to be an almost permanent part of the diplomatic establishment at the Department of State, were married to concepts of process devoid of practical results. It might be argued that the experience they so touted was, in reality, a collection of bad experiences, not good ones. Instead of learning from those bad experiences and not repeating the same mistakes, they seemed incapable of breaking their patterns of ineffective behavior. As Senator Kyl observed:

> In the case of the Middle East, the negotiating process is not constructive if it creates unrealistic expectations, for example, that the Arab side can redivide Jerusalem. Nor is it constructive if it results in bitter recriminations by Washington against Jerusalem's efforts to preserve Israeli security. A process that damages the US-Israeli relationship does not encourage Arab compromise and is not conducive to peace. Rather it rewards Arab inflexibility and signals Arab rejectionists that they may ultimately prevail if they work hard enough to weaken Israel by fraying its ties to the United States.

It's a brilliant summation of why the State Department's posture on how to foster peace in the region was fundamentally flawed. Senator Kyl did not end his analysis there. He went on to assess what was the essence of the issue that had to be overcome by the PA to enable negotiations to yield a sustainable peace:

> The key question in the Arab-Israeli negotiating process is whether the Palestinian Authority intends to end the

conflict or, instead, to obtain concessions that can be exploited against Israel in the future.

Senator Kyl then wisely noted:

> US officials often talk and act as if the mere fact of Arafat's participation in the process establishes that his intentions are peaceful. This is unwise and ignores the history of our century in which Lenin, Stalin, Hitler, Brezhnev, Ho Chi Min, Saddam Hussein, and Slobodan Milosevic have all participated in peace processes.

This devotion to pure process, as almost an end in and of itself, was so reflexive that it appeared mindless. Senator Kyl verily noted all too often, there was a tendency to get hung up on the negotiating process, but as he went on to say, "...the negotiating process is not an end in itself. It is valuable only if it moves the parties in the proper direction." In this regard, Senator Kyl pointed out, the Oslo Accords do not reflect a profound transformation of the Arab stance, which is still focused on Israel's right to exist.

Senator Kyl's observation went to the very heart of the problem. All the assumptions made on the basis that Israel's very existence and legitimacy are no longer at issue to the PA and Hamas are either dangerously naïve, misguided, or worse. The conflict is not about discrete issues like boundaries, arms control, and security arrangements. It's not about Arabs having rights to worship in the holy places in Jerusalem; that's already the case, and there is no issue reaffirming them.

The fundamental issue in negotiating and concluding any arrangement with the PA and Hamas was and continues to be their unwillingness to recognize and accept Israel's legitimacy and right to exist. This is a threshold requirement to any productive negotiations, and the recognition and acceptance must be genuine and unqualified to be meaningful. To better understand the cogency of Senator Kyl's insightful perception and how it relates to the Jerusalem Embassy Act he championed requires some background.

Jerusalem was never the capital of any Arab or other nation. It has only ever been the capital of the ancient Nation of Israel and now, once again, the modern reestablished State of Israel. Ramallah is currently the seat of self-government of the PA. When Jordan conquered a portion of Jerusalem in 1948 and illegally annexed it, Jordan did not move its capital there; but rather retained Amman as its capital. There was no clamoring by the Arabs living in the areas of Judea and Samaria (including the portion of Jerusalem) conquered by Jordan in 1948 to establish a capital there. The demand that Jerusalem be the capital and a part of any new Palestinian state is just a subterfuge.

As to Gaza, which today is a de-facto Palestinian state under the firm control of Hamas, some history might help illuminate the paucity of any support for their specious claim to Jerusalem. When Israel declared independence in May of 1948, Egypt and four other Arab countries invaded it. The Gaza Strip was conquered by Egypt, and its Jewish community of Kfar Darom[140] was destroyed. Egypt continued to control Gaza, even after the 1949 Armistice Agreement with Israel. Egypt only lost control of Gaza as a result of the Six-Day War, which it precipitated in June of 1967.

A peace treaty was signed with Egypt in March of 1979. Egypt demanded and received the return of all of the Sinai under the treaty. It did not, however, require control of Gaza.

Israel administered Gaza until it transferred governmental authority over Gaza to the Palestinian Authority in 1994, pursuant to the Gaza-Jericho Agreement[141]. It entirely withdrew

---

[140] See Jewish Communities Lost in War of Independence, on Israel Ministry of Foreign Affairs website.
[141] The Gaza-Jericho Agreement, signed in Cairo, on May 4, 1994.

from Gaza, including removing any military presence and all Israeli residents, in September of 2005.

Under the Oslo II Agreement[142] and the subsequent Disengagement Agreement of 2005[143] with the Palestinian Authority, Israel negotiated and obtained certain rights to patrol Gaza's coastal waters and air space. This was intended to enable Israel to interdict illegal weapons deliveries to Gaza, which are expressly prohibited under the Agreements noted above. These agreed-upon rights do not constitute effective governmental control[144] over Gaza.

Hamas won an election victory in Gaza over the PA in 2006[145]. Although there was a unity government with the PA in place for a short time, Hamas seized sole control of Gaza in 2007[146]. It remains the governing authority in Gaza to this day. Israel does not occupy Gaza. Indeed, in reflecting on these circumstances in 2008, the Supreme Court of Israel, in the Al-Bassiouni case[147], held that there was no occupation by Israel of Gaza under

---

[142] The Israeli-Palestinian Interim Agreement on the West Bank and Gaza Strip, dated September 28, 1995 (Oslo II). It follows up the original Oslo accord, embodied in the Israel-PLO: Declaration of Principles on Interim Self Government Arrangements, signed in Washington, D.C., on September 13, 1993. By its terms, it supersedes the Gaza-Jericho Agreement, dated May 4, 1994, The Agreement on the Preparatory Transfer of Powers and Responsibilities, signed in Erez, on August 29, 1994 and the Protocol on Further Transfer of Powers and Responsibilities, signed in Cairo, on August 27, 1995.

[143] Israel-Palestinian Authority Agreement on Movement and Access and Agreed Principles for Rafah Crossing, signed on November 15, 2005.

[144] See, Israel and the Struggle over the International Laws of War, by Peter Berkowitz, Hoover Institution Press-2012; Occupation and other forms of Administration of Foreign Territory, Report of Expert Meeting, by Tristan Ferraro, of the ICRC, dated March 2012; and Is Gaza Occupied?: Redefining the Status of Gaza Under International Law, by Elizabeth Samson, in the American University International Law Review, Volume 25, Issue 5, Article 4 (2010). See also the 2015 Judgments of the European Court of Human Rights, discussed below.

[145] Hamas celebrates election victory, by Simon Jeffery and agencies, in the Guardian, dated June 26, 2006.

[146] See, Hamas Seizes Broad Control in Gaza Strip, by Steven Erlanger, in the New York Times, dated June 14, 2007.

[147] Jaber Al-Bassiouni Ahmed and others v Prime Minister and Minister of Defense (HCJ 9132/07), Judgment dated January 27, 2008.

FARLEY WEISS AND
LEONARD GRUNSTEIN

International Law. It found that Israel did not have effective control over Gaza, and Israeli soldiers were no longer stationed in Gaza. Military rule had ended, and Israel had fully withdrawn from Gaza. It was, therefore, not in a position to enforce order and govern civilian life in Gaza. The Court was well aware of the security and other rights and obligations Israel had under the Oslo II Agreement and the Disengagement Agreement of 2005. Indeed, the very subject matter of the case was the arrangement under which Israel supplied Gaza with a portion of its electrical power requirements.

Hamas and the people of Gaza have no right to sovereignty over Jerusalem, and any claim they may assert is patently absurd. They live in another country that has no real connection to Jerusalem at all. Hamas' declarations that their continuing attacks on Israel and its citizenry are somehow justified because Israel exercises its sovereign rights in Jerusalem are ludicrous and nothing more than another cynical excuse and pretext for their terrorist aggression. It is nauseating to hear Hamas' allies and useful dupes mindlessly shout this baseless and malevolent propaganda as if doing so repeatedly and with greater volume and fervor could miraculously transform these false claims into anything approximating the truth.

Imagine if members of the First Nations in Vancouver, Canada, which as an aside, is located on unceded traditional First Nations' territory[148], were to attack the US with rockets, incendiary devices, and armed incursions. Imagine further if the attackers asserted they were justified, because of an eviction order granted by a New York court in Manhattan against a native-American, for non-payment of rent. After all, they might argue that the US was not the legitimate sovereign authority because the native-Americans, from the Canarsie tribe of Brooklyn, who purportedly sold it to Peter Minuit, at best only

---

[148] City of Vancouver formally declares city is on unceded Aboriginal territory, by Peter Meiszner, in Global News, dated June 25, 2014.

occupied the southern tip of Manhattan[149]. Most of Manhattan Island was then occupied by an entirely different tribe, the Weckquaesgeeks.

The US would surely defend itself with its armed forces, including eliminating the source and potential for further attacks. It would be fully within its rights to do so. The contrived justification for the attack would be summarily rejected as nonsensical.

Consider that as silly as the hypothetical situation described above sounds, an analogous argument was advanced by Hamas in an attempt to justify its attack on Israel with over four thousand missiles and rockets, indiscriminately targeting civilian areas in Israel in May of 2021[150]. Hamas, among other things, said it began the attack against Israel to force Israel's government to stop a pending court process[151]. It involved what amounts to a landlord and tenant dispute, which could be settled by the mere payment of rent, in the Sheik Jarrah (Shimon HaTzadik) neighborhood of Jerusalem[152]. This cynically contrived excuse was pure propaganda. Yet, it was dutifully repeated by a number of politicos in the US without even an attempt at serious inquiry and, of course, by a host of media acolytes, Israel haters, and cadres of misguided useful dupes.

Besides being nothing more than a preposterous pretense offered by terrorist Hamas, it should also be appreciated that the Arab people living in Gaza, Samaria, and Judea, including Jerusalem, unlike the First Nations in Vancouver, are relatively

---

[149] The $24 Swindle, by Nathaniel Benchley, in American Heritage, December 1959, Volume II, Issue 1.

[150] LIVEBLOG: At least 4000 Gaza rockets fired at Israel since May 10, I 24 News, May 16, 2021.

[151] Israeli-Hamas Ceasefire Threatened by Tensions Over Contested Jerusalem Neighborhood, by Dov Lieber, in the Wall Street Journal, dated May 27, 2021.

[152] Almost Nothing You've Heard About Evictions in Jerusalem Is True, by Avi Bell and Eugene Kontorovich, in the Wall Street Journal, dated May 14, 2021.

recent arrivals and not, in fact,, indigenous[153], as more fully discussed below. The sole extant people who have any legitimate claim to being indigenous to the area are the Jewish people for nearly four thousand years.

In this regard, it is important to appreciate that the demand for a so-called right of return is just a new contrived way of saying no Jewish State of Israel[154] and to displace the Jewish people from their homeland. To this day, PA law prohibits land sales to Jews. Those breaking the law are subject to harsh penalties that the PA does not shirk from imposing. The PA and Hamas also spew classical antisemitism, incite and glorify terrorism and call for Israel's destruction. This includes promoting hateful antisemitic rhetoric in the media, as well as teaching their children in school to hate Jews.

The Palestinian National Charter describes the entire Land of Israel, including the land within the ceasefire lines of 1948, as "an Arab homeland bound by strong national ties to the rest of the Arab Countries and which together form the large Arab homeland"[155]. It calls for liberation through armed struggle. Despite assurances that it would be amended to recognize the State of Israel, this, in fact, never actually occurred[156].

---

[153] See, for example, Debunking the claim that "Palestinians" are the indigenous people of Israel, by Daniel Grynglas, in the Jerusalem Post, dated 5/12/2015 and Were the Arabs Indigenous to Mandatory Palestine, by Sheree Roth, in Middle East Quarterly, Fall-2016, at meforum.org. See also, From Time Immemorial, by Joan Peters (HarperCollins-1984); The Year the Arabs Discovered Palestine, by Daniel Pipes, in Middle East Review, dated Summer 1989; a review of Joan Peters' book From Time Immemorial, by Daniel Pipes, in Commentary, dated July 1984; and The Rape of Palestine, by William B. Ziff (originally published by Longmans, Green and Co.-1938 and in paperback by Martino Publishing-2009).

[154] See, for example, The War of Return, by Adi Schwartz and Einat Wilf (All Points Books-2020), as well as, the discussion below about UN Security Council Resolution 242.

[155] Article 1.

[156] As more fully discussed in Chapter VIII below, despite assurances that the PLO Charter would be amended to recognize the existence and legitimacy of the State of Israel, this never in fact occurred.

The Hamas Covenant is overtly antisemitic. It compares Jews to Nazis[157], asserts Jews were behind World Wars I and II, and finds Jewish conspiracies everywhere[158]. Here's an example of the notorious antisemitic tropes and slanders it ruthlessly and shamelessly propagates in its Covenant:

> With their money, they took control of the world media, news agencies, the press, publishing houses, broadcasting stations, and others. With their money, they stirred revolutions in various parts of the world with the purpose of achieving their interests and reaping the fruit therein. They were behind the French Revolution, the Communist revolution, and most of the revolutions we heard and hear about here and there. With their money, they formed secret societies, such as Freemasons, Rotary Clubs, the Lions, and others in different parts of the world, for the purpose of sabotaging societies and achieving Zionist interests. With their money, they were able to control imperialistic countries and instigate them to colonize many countries in order to enable them to exploit their resources and spread corruption there.

> You may speak as much as you want about regional and world wars. They were behind World War I when they were able to destroy the Islamic Caliphate, making financial gains and controlling resources. They obtained the Balfour Declaration, formed the League of Nations through which they could rule the world. They were behind World War II, through which they made huge financial gains by trading in armaments and paved the way for the establishment of their state. It was they who instigated the replacement of the League of Nations with the United Nations and the Security Council to enable them to rule the world through

---

[157] Hamas Covenant, Article XX.
[158] Hamas Covenant, Article XXII.

them. There is no war going on anywhere without having their finger in it...

The imperialistic forces in the Capitalist West and Communist East support the enemy with all their might, in money, and in men. These forces take turns in doing that. The day Islam appears, the forces of infidelity would unite to challenge it, for the infidels are of one nation.

The undeniable falsehood of these outrageous accusations speaks volumes about the obnoxious Jew-hatred that is at the heart of Hamas' psyche. There can be no misunderstanding that this is about Jews because the Hamas Covenant makes no bones about blatantly and clearly speaking about Jews. It does not obfuscate its intent by concealing it behind contrived euphemisms and coded expressions, like Israelis or Zionists. It flat-out says Jews. Neither does it hide its goal of eliminating Israel.

The Hamas Covenant requires an armed Jihad against Israel to eliminate it and the Jews, generally. Thus, the preamble declares:

'Israel will exist and will continue to exist until Islam will obliterate it, just as it obliterated others before it.'

Article II provides:

'The land of Palestine is an Islamic Waqf consecrated for future Moslem generations until Judgment Day. No one can renounce it or any part, or abandon it or any part of it.'

Furthermore, Article XIII goes on to say:

'Palestine is an Islamic land... Since this is the case, the Liberation of Palestine is an individual duty for every Moslem, wherever he may be.'

Article XV then calls for Jihad by every Muslim, as follows:

'The day the enemies usurp part of Moslem land, Jihad becomes the individual duty of every Moslem. In the face of the Jews' usurpation, it is compulsory that the banner of Jihad be raised.'

Notice that the reference is blatantly made to "Jews". The usual transparent artifice of modern antisemites of referring to Zionists or Israelis as a euphemism for Jews is dispensed with in this document[159]. Similarly, Article XXVIII, which states:

'Israel, Judaism, and Jews challenge Islam and the Moslem people.'

These express provisions negate any misguided notions seeking nuanced distinctions between anti-Israel or anti-Zionist[160], on the one hand, and Jew-hatred, on the other hand. Indeed, it is not only delusional to pander to Jihadist terrorists in this fashion; it is foolhardy and puts the lives of others in mortal danger. How about just taking terrorists at their word, a much safer and more reasonable approach.

Lest there be any misunderstanding about the lurid antisemitic intent of Hamas, Article VII declares:

'The Day of Judgment will not come about until Moslems fight Jews and kill them. Then, the Jews will hide behind rocks and trees, and the rocks and trees will cry out: 'O Moslem, there is a Jew hiding behind me, come and kill him.'

Hamas also explicitly rules out the possibility of making peace with Israel and openly excoriates Egypt for doing so in Article

---

[159] See also Hamas Covenant, Article XXXII.
[160] It should also be noted that an overwhelming majority of Jews favor Israel (see, for example, Stop Being Shocked, by Bari Weiss, at Tablet, dated 10/14/2020 and AJC poll: American Jewish millennials care about Israel and are largely unworried about how it is perceived, by Ron Kampeas, at JTA, dated 4/26/2022). Israel's Jewish population is nearly half the total number of Jews in the world (see, for example, World Jewish population totals 15.2 million – with nearly half in Israel, by Judy Maltz, in the Forward, dated 4/26/2022). Thus, not only is being against the existence of the Jewish State of Israel definitionally antisemitic, as described in the IHRA definition, more fully discussed below; it is also factually and functionally antisemitic as well.

XXXII. It then goes on to accuse anyone making peace with Israel of treason and curse the peacemaker for doing so.

Isn't it about time that the world took Hamas at its word? Why engage in word games with a determined predator intent on realizing its own genocidal fantasies? The only real answer to Hamas is to stop it from doing harm. In this regard, it is important to recognize that the inaction or cover-up by the intersectional media, many NGOs, and even governmental authorities within the EU and the US is not limited to the persecution of Jews, Christians[161], the LGBT community, and women are also persecuted by Hamas and the PA, as discussed below. Yet, the prevailing false narrative perpetuated by many is it's not about ideology and antisemitism; it is just about land for peace. There are also those who wistfully and irresponsibly posture if only Israel would agree to some hair-brained scheme or another and, while it's at it, reopen its borders and drop its security safeguards, then all would be well. This fatuous plea might better be understood as a call for Israel and the Jewish people to finally solve what the Nazis euphemistically referred to as the Jewish Question with the Final Solution by voluntary assisted suicide; no, thank you!

It's manifestly obvious why the PA and Hamas so disdain peace and the peacemakers. Their whole raison d'etre is perpetuating a meaningless struggle against Israel and the Jewish people. They have no program tangibly to benefit the people under their ruthless control. The peace treaties between Egypt and Israel, Jordan and Israel, and now the glorious Abraham Accords and the ever-growing circle of peace and prosperity are a sharp and decisive rebuke to their ideology of hate and death cult.

Unless and until the Arab people living in the areas controlled by the PA and Hamas and their leadership (i) truly accept the existence of Israel, as a Jewish state, with secure and defensible

---

[161] See also Hamas Covenant, Article XIII.

borders; (ii) genuinely renounce any plan to destroy Israel and murder or displace the Jews; (iii) reform their educational system to teach respect for Israel and the Jews, not hate; and (iv) the leadership publicly acknowledges and engages in an education and publicity campaign among the people so as to make it absolutely clear that this recognition is not just a matter of expediency but rather a confirmation of what is truly just and right, in Arabic to the Arabic people and not just in English to the Western media (with the usual two-faced posture of one message to the home audience and another disparate one solely for Western consumption); there truly is no basis for any negotiations.

Most successful negotiations are based on narrowing the issues to the point where they are susceptible to some resolution or trade-off of one against another issue. Continuing to talk about such threshold matters as to whether, philosophically, a buyer should even buy or not, let alone whether the seller is the real owner and empowered to sell, are inconsistent with there being any real progress in a genuine negotiation. By analogy, the continuing attacks on Israel's legitimacy and constant questioning of whether it even has a right to exist are inconsistent with there being what purport to be final peace talks pending. That this continues to be the case after many decades of discussions and interim arrangements puts into question whether there were ever any truly meaningful negotiations and viable agreements. It appears, as some of the PA interlocutors claim, as noted below, this was all just an elaborate subterfuge.

It's ironic that it is a non-country, the PA, adhering to the terms of a Charter, which in effect denies it's a distinct nation or people separate and apart from the Arab people generally[162] and with

---

[162] Article 1 of the Palestinian National Charter states, 'Palestine is the homeland of the Arab Palestinian people; it is an indivisible part of the Arab homeland, and the Palestinian people are an integral part of the Arab nation'. Article 5 defines the Palestinians as 'those Arab nationals who, until 1947, normally resided in Palestine…'.

only a relatively recent and tenuous connection to the land, raising these issues about Israel. Moreover, whatever claims, if any, Arab residents of Judea and Samaria, including Jerusalem, may have had were surrendered to Jordan and, thus, they have effectively been extinguished, as more fully discussed below.

Remember, too, the PA has not demonstrated any genuine interest in statehood side by side with Israel. If it did, then that could have been accomplished many years ago by just saying yes to one of the many offers of peace extended by Israel. However, the raison d'être of the PA is not peace; it and its predecessor, the PLO, exist for the nefarious purpose of being against the existence of Israel. The PA has no positive program, only a negative one.

In striking contrast, it is Israel, a country with a Jewish majority that has significantly more than a three thousand year history in the Land and has been recognized as a reestablished country and sovereign state, by the world community, for more than seventy years, which is willing to discuss living side by side with a demilitarized so-called Palestinian state to be created where there was none before, on terms and conditions to be negotiated. The graciousness of the Israeli position and the unearned respect it offers to the PA in a thus far unrequited and unrewarded search for peace cannot be overstated. The response by the corrupt, disrespectful, and venomous PA and its erstwhile cohort terrorist Hamas is incongruous. It is not susceptible to the dictates of polite discourse; calling it out as evil would be an understatement.

The almost perverse fascination with and adulation of the PA and Hamas by radical leftists, self-identified as progressives, is bewildering[163]. After all, there is virtually no doubt that, unless

---

[163] See, for example, The Perverse and Perplexing Paradox of Palestine, by Martin Silverman, in Israel Opinion Today, at JNS, dated 1/13/2023 and What Would a Palestinian State Look Like?, by Daniel Doron, in The Weekly Standard and at Middle East Forum, dated 9/26/2016.

there is a fundamental change in the leadership and ethos of the PA and Hamas governed areas, any future Palestinian state would likely be the embodiment of values that are antithetical to progressive ones. The PA and Hamas are currently homophobic[164], misogynist, and tyrannical regimes. Gender and sexual orientation discrimination are rampant and sanctioned by law, and even harassment is tolerated[165]. Religious intolerance and antisemitism are endemic, and other forms of racism are condoned[166]. The PA is presently a virtually autocratic regime[167]. Abbas was last elected to a four-year term sixteen years ago. Both the PA and Hamas severely oppress political dissidents[168].

It is no wonder that the majority of Israeli Arabs polled said they preferred to live in Israel and not be a part of any Palestinian State[169]. It is perplexing that some in the US and EU, who purportedly cherish diversity, religious freedom, and individual liberty, favor the PA and Hamas regimes, which promote the very opposite agenda, as well as fostering and rewarding terrorism[170]. It would appear that the neo-Marxist view of the world that seems to have taken hold among some, which reflexively deems the more powerful (in this case Israel) evil (despite

---

[164] See, For Example, Palestinians: LGBTQ+ Not Welcome Here, By Emily Schrader, In The Jerusalem Post, Dated 6/20/2022.

[165] See, Facts and Figures UN Women-Palestine: Ending Violence Against Women and Jerusalem Institute of Justice, April 2016 Report on the Implementation of the Convention on the Elimination of All Forms of Discrimination Against Women under the PA and Hamas. See also, Facts and Figures: Ending Violence against Women, at UN Women.org-Palestine (which cites UN reports from 2017 and 2018).

[166] See, Anti-semitism and situation of Roma and people of African descent raised by experts as the Committee on Racial Discrimination examines the report of the State of Palestine, at UN Human Rights (OHCHR), dated 8/19/2014.

[167] See, for example, Report: Abbas creating dictatorship in Palestinian Authority, by Ariel Kahana, at Israel Hayom, dated 7/25/2022.

[168] See, for example, Palestine: Authorities Crush Dissent, at Human Rights Watch. org, dated 10/23/2018.

[169] See, for example, The Real Reason Arabs in Israel Do Not Want to Live in 'Palestine', by Khaled Abu Toameh, at the Gatestone Institute. Org, dated 2/4/2020.

[170] See, for example, Clear and Convincing: The Links between the PFLP and the European Government-funded NGO Network, dated 2/1/2023, at the NGO Monitor.org.

overwhelming evidence to the contrary) and less powerful (in this case the PA and Hamas) noble victims (despite overwhelming evidence to the contrary) requires a serious re-evaluation in light of the reality of life under the PA and Hamas.

Consider the depravity of rewarding terrorists and their families with stipends or pensions for killing Jews under what has been denominated as the 'Pay to Slay' (also known as the 'Pay for Slay') program[171]. Congress passed the Taylor Force Act[172] to address this odious practice[173]. The Act received overwhelming bi-partisan support and was signed into law by President Trump on March 23, 2018[174].

Taylor Force was an American veteran who was murdered by a Palestinian terrorist while visiting Israel. The PA awarded the terrorist's family a stipend for his homicidal efforts. The Act, in summary, provides for assistance that benefits the PA, for the West Bank and Gaza to be cut, with limited exceptions[175], so long as this abhorrent practice continues, as detailed below. Pursuant

---

[171] See, for example, The Department of Pay-for-Slay, by Douglas J. Feith & Sander Gerber, in Commentary, April-2017.

[172] Passed on March 23, 2018 as part of the Consolidated Appropriations Act, 2018, cuts American aid to the Palestinian Authority unless it ceases to pay stipends to the terrorists and their families, including the families of successful suicide bombers.

[173] A few weeks before the passage of the Taylor Force Act, Farley arranged for Taylor's father Dr. Stuart Force and, his ally in advocating for the legislation, Sander Gerber to speak at the National Council of Young Israel dinner in New York. Also attending the dinner and speaking was the future Mayor of New York Eric Adams. Dr. Force made an impassioned plea for the legislation and Gerber called out a specific member of Congress for holding up the legislation. Gerber told Farley that the specific member of Congress he mentioned in his speech was upset by his remarks. However, ultimately this helped convince the member to drop his opposition. The Taylor Force legislation soon became law shortly after the dinner.

[174] 22 USC 2378c-1. Limitation on Assistance to West Bank and Gaza.

[175] Under and in accordance with the terms and conditions of paragraph (b) of the Act, A) payments made to the East Jerusalem Hospital Network; (B) assistance for wastewater projects not exceeding $5,000,000 in any one fiscal year; and (C) assistance for any other program, project, or activity that provides vaccinations to children not exceeding $500,000 in any one fiscal year.

to this law, the Trump administration did, in fact, make cuts to aid payments.

However, as more fully discussed below, the PA, nevertheless, continues its despicable Pay to Slay program. In light of the foregoing, it is unfathomable why the Biden administration would decide simply to restore the aid cuts by the prior Trump administration[176]. After all, the PA continues flagrantly to violate the express conditions to funding provided under the Taylor Force Act. The PA did not correct its offensive conduct in the brief period between the end of the Trump administration and the decision to restart funding at the beginning of the Biden administration. Why reward the miscreant behavior of the PA? If anything, the penalties should have been redoubled, including enlisting the EU and others to cease directly or indirectly funding the PA until the Pay to Slay program was finally and truly ended.

It would also appear that the PA was emboldened by the Biden administration's decision to restore the aid cuts, so much so that it even raised the amounts it pays[177]. This is shocking, in light of the State Department's own reported findings in a non-public report of May 10, 2022, issued to Congress[178], as follows:

> The PA has not terminated payments for acts of terrorism against Israeli and U.S. citizens to any individual, after being fairly tried, who has been imprisoned for such acts of terrorism and to any individual who died committing such

---

[176] See, for example, Biden administration to restore $235m in US aid to Palestinians, at the BBC, dated 4/7/2021; Blinken: Biden will push $75m in Palestinian aid; reopen Jerusalem consulate, by Mark Moore, in the NY Post, dated 5/25/2021; and The Palestinian Authority Is Still Paying Terrorists, by Sean Durn, in Newsweek, dated 1/21/2021.

[177] See, for example, PA raises salary for terrorist who killed 9 at Hebrew U, By Lahav Harkov, in the Jerusalem Post, dated 8/1/2022 and Biden Meets with Abbas Despite Terrorists' Salary Raises, by Maurice Hirsch, Adv., at unitedwithisrael.org, dated 7/14/2022.

[178] How the Palestinians Pay Terrorists as Biden Pumps Millions of Aid Dollars Into Their Government, by Adam Kredo, in Washington Free Beacon, dated 5/16/2022.

acts of terrorism, including to a family member of such individuals.

The State Department reportedly concluded:

> The PA makes these payments in cash as part of an effort to obfuscate its actions and stop the international community from holding it accountable for awarding terrorists and their families, according to the State Department's findings.

Is it any wonder that the PA impudently continues to allocate hundreds of millions of dollars to terrorists and their families[179], given that there are no consequences or accountability for its wrongful conduct? Astonishingly, despite the State Department's report, noted above, detailing how the PA violates the Taylor Force Law that bars it from receiving US aid dollars until these pay-to-slay payments are stopped, the Biden administration pushed to increase U.S. aid dollars to the PA. More than three hundred and sixty million dollars of such U.S. funding was reportedly provided in 2021 alone[180].

While the Biden administration maintained it did not violate the law, this bare assertion hardly seems credible. There was no presentation about any new safeguards being put in place to prevent the continuing diversion of aid monies by the PA to fund Pay to Slay. The only lame explanation offered was, "The Biden administration is strongly opposed to the prisoner payment system and has consistently engaged the Palestinian Authority to end this practice."[181] What was clear, though, was the State Department's unabashed and unqualified confirmation that no

---

[179] See, for example, Palestinians Tell Truth About Terror Payments to Terrorist Murderers, by Nan Jacques Zilberdik, in the Algemeiner, dated 11/21/2021.
[180] U.S. Assistance for the Palestinian People, Press Statement, by Anthony J. Blinken, Secretary of State, dated 5/26/2021, at state.gov.
[181] Ibid.

"economic support funds" were withheld as a result of restrictions in the Taylor Force Act.

Astoundingly, it is reported[182] that in October of 2022, the State Department, in another non-public report to Congress, revealed that the PA had been given approximately half a billion dollars by the Biden administration even though it was still making payments to imprisoned terrorists, as well as, to the families of those who died while committing acts of terrorism. The report also found that Palestinian social media accounts and media organizations were broadcasting or publishing content praising or celebrating acts of violence. This was despite the PA's commitment to stop doing so as a condition of receiving US aid money.

A State Department spokesman is reported to have said the administration opposes the PA Pay to Slay program and has repeatedly pressed the PA to stop it. The fact that the State Department admitted that the PA has not done so, as most everyone else can readily recognize, nevertheless did not result in a suspension of any further payments of aid money. Incredibly, the official then blithely went on to say all US aid is allocated consistent with law, a mystifying conclusion.

This does not seem to be some inadvertent oversight or error. Rather, it appears to be a conscious policy to flout the intent and likely the letter of the Taylor Force Act. Frankly speaking, it is inexcusable and immoral. It is tantamount to condonation of and perhaps even complicity with this notorious program.

It is also clear that notwithstanding the 2018 Taylor Force Law, the PA, in 2019, allocated over $150 million to convicted terrorists. Another $191 million was paid to the families of

---

[182] See, for example, Palestinian Government Still Pay Terrorists as US Aid Dollars Flow, by Adam Kredo, in the Free Beacon, dated 10/18/2022 and House Republicans investigate Biden admin's funding of Palestinian government, by Gabe Kaminsky, in the Washington Examiner, dated 11/4/2022.

terrorists who were neutralized while conducting attacks against Israelis and Americans. Not only is there no sign these payments will end, PA leaders brazenly voice their support of their abhorrent Pay to Slay program on the international stage. PA President Abbas even declared, "Why should we have to clarify and justify providing assistance to families of prisoners and martyrs who are the victims of the occupation and its oppressive policies?", in his speech at the UNGA, on September 24, 2021. These are not the contrite words of a penitent vowing to end a murderous program; they are the defiant expression of an unrepentant killer who was one of the PLO leaders responsible for the Munich Massacre[183].

Lest there be any misunderstanding or ambiguity about the matter of responsibility for the senseless and horrific mass murder of Israeli Jewish athletes and their trainers at the Olympics in Munich, it was perpetrated by the so-called Black September Organization (BSO), a front for the PLO. The State Department confirmed BSO was just a cover for Fatah (the PLO) under the leadership of Yasser (sometimes spelled Yasir) Arafat and Mahmoud Abbas. This was disclosed in a Secret Telegram (since declassified) dated March 13, 1973. The gist of it, based on an intelligence brief prepared by the CIA and the State Department, is as follows:

> The Black September Organization (BSO) is a cover term for Fatah's [PLO's] terrorist operations executed by Fatah's intelligence organization Jihaz Al-Rasd. The collapse of Fatah's guerrilla efforts led Fatah to clandestine terrorism against Israel and countries friendly to it. Fatah funds, facilities, and personnel are used in these operations. There is evidence that the "BSO" operation in Khartoum

---

[183] See, for example, Abbas' other scandal is his refusal to apologize for Munich Massacre, by Michael Starr, in the Jerusalem Post, dated 8/21/2022.

was carried out with substantial help from Fatah's Khartoum office and applauded by Fatah radio...

For all intents and purposes, no significant distinction can be made between the BSO and Fatah.

The Telegram went on to describe how, although Arafat professed to disavow publicly any connection between Fatah and terrorist operations, nonetheless, the Fatah leadership, including Arafat, was clearly committed to terrorism.

The PLO's deadly operation in Khartoum, the capital of Sudan, occurred on March 1, 1973, at the Saudi Arabian Embassy going away party for US Deputy Chief of Mission George Curtis Moore. The party was reportedly[184] stormed by a gang of eight terrorists, who identified themselves as members of the Black September Organization. Of course, as noted above, this was merely a convenient cover for the PLO.

Curiously, at the end of February of 1973, the National Security Agency (NSA) had picked up radio traffic, including from Arafat and Salah Kalaf, another leader of the PLO, concerning a PLO

---

[184] See, for example, How Arafat Got Away with Murder, by Scott W. Johnson, in the Weekly Standard, dated 1/29/2007, which reports other details of the PLO's murderous Khartoum operation summarized above; Partners in Capital Crime, by Alan Berlind, in American Diplomacy, dated October 2012; and The Terrorist Attack on the Saudi Embassy in Khartoum, 1973, 2/20/2013, at the Association for Diplomatic Studies and Training. See also, 217. Intelligence Memorandum dated June 1993, at Foreign Relations of the United States, 1969-1976, Volume E-6, Documents on Africa, 1973-1976, at history.state.gov. It reports: "Initially, the main objective of the attack appeared to be to secure the release of Fatah/BSO leader Muhammed Awadh (Abu Da'ud) from Jordanian captivity."
It then notes:
" Information acquired subsequently reveals that the Fatah/BSO leaders did not expect Awadh to be freed, and indicates that one of the primary goals of the operation was to strike at the United States because of its efforts to achieve a Middle East peace settlement which many Arabs believe would be inimical to Palestinian interests."
The Memorandum goes on to report:
"The open participation of Fatah representatives in Khartoum in the attack provides further evidence of the Fatah/BSO relationship. The emergence of the United States as a primary fedayeen target indicates a serious threat of further incidents similar to that which occurred in Khartoum."

operation that was about to be conducted in Khartoum. However, shockingly, even though a message was drafted warning the US Embassy in Khartoum of the imminent PLO operation, it was not transmitted immediately. This was despite the message being labeled a 'flash' (highest priority) one. Instead, mysteriously, the State Department watch officer inexplicably downgraded the message to a routine communication. As a result, it arrived several days late.

The American Ambassador to Sudan, Cleo Noel Jr., and his Deputy Chief of Mission, George Moore, as well as Guy Eid, the Belgian Charge D'Affaires, were seized by the terrorists and held hostage. Other diplomats were also seized and were eventually released. There were several demands issued by the terrorists. They included the release of Sirhan Sirhan, the Palestinian Arab assassin of then-presidential candidate Robert F. Kennedy Jr.[185],

---

[185] Sirhan admitted that he killed Robert Kennedy because of his support for Israel. See, for example, Sirhan Says He Killed Kennedy to Protect Palestinians, by Gary Langer, at AP News, dated 2/19/1989 and For Sirhan Sirhan, no remorse, no release, by Charles Lane, in the Washington Post, dated 9/14/2021. Robert Kennedy visited Israel, towards the end of the British Mandate period, in 1948, before Israel declared independence. He wrote a series of reports describing what he saw, for the Boston Post. They have been assembled by Lenny Ben-David and are reproduced at jcpa.org, under the title, Robert Kennedy's 1948 Reports from Palestine. They are candid and illuminating. Interestingly, he thoroughly rebutted many of the misguided assumptions of the State Department, at the time, which would have done much better to rely on Kennedy's fresh, first hand and real-time reporting and analysis than their own biased, so-called experts. This includes debunking the absurd conspiracy theory about communist infiltration that was raised by the State Department in the meeting with Truman and Clifford, as well as, the treachery of the British, who didn't desire for the Jewish State to be reestablished and tried to abort it. He also vividly described the enormous contribution the Jewish people were making to development of the area and the prosperity it generated, which included attracting many Arab migrants to settle there. On the other hand, he also encountered the many disgruntled factions among the Arabs, who were otherwise at each other's throats and united only in their jealousy and hate for the Jewish people and their success. He was also impressed by the capability, esprit and courage of the Haganah and felt that Israel would be a stabilizing factor in the region. His analysis and evaluation were not only compelling, in many respects like the later statement about Israel noted above, they were even prescient.

BSO operatives held in Jordan, and several members of the Baader-Meinhoff gang held in Germany.

The demands were not met, and President Nixon and representatives of the other two governments, Jordan and Germany, announced they would not negotiate with terrorists. Kalaf directed the murder of the three hostages, and Arafat separately confirmed the instructions. The PLO terrorists then brutally murdered Cleo Noel Jr., George Moore, and Guy Eid by firing forty Kalashnikov rounds, beginning from the feet and up to the head, in order to inflict maximum suffering on the victims.

The eight terrorists then surrendered to authorities. Two were quickly released. The remaining six were tried and convicted and then turned over to their PLO handlers. At trial, the leader brazenly admitted that they acted under the orders of the PLO. In November of 1974, when Arafat made his infamous appearance at the UNGA, sporting his pistol, he was accompanied by Ali Hassan Salameh, the chief planner of the Khartoum murderous operation, and several other key participants.

The impudence of Arafat, a homicidal and maniacal demagogue, knew no bounds. Instead of hunting him down, together with his band of murderous thugs, arresting them and trying them for murder, Arafat was rewarded. It truly boggles the mind to appreciate the insouciance and even callous depraved indifference of those at the State Department, who somehow ignored the brutal murder of their colleagues and orchestrated the resurrection of the evil Arafat in the transparent guise of an erstwhile peace partner. They proceeded to lavish public praise on this newly created false messiah and paraded him around in a carefully staged Kabuki-like theater performance, which masked his sordid and malevolent character. The predisposition of State Department actors to appease at almost any cost was pervasive and obsessive. This institutional cultural phenomenon colors State Department thinking to this day. How else to explain the continuing courting of Arafat's right-hand man, Mahmoud Abbas, who financed the Munich Massacre[186]?

The US Ambassador to Saudi Arabia reported in a Telegram, dated March 14, 1973, from Jidda[187], that he informed King Faisal he had additional convincing evidence of the close links between BSO and Fatah and urged cutting off aid from Arab governments to Fatah, as a means of reducing its resources and administering a psychological blow. Otherwise, he cautioned, terrorists would be emboldened to ask more and more of moderate Arab governments. It was excellent advice, and the formula seems to have been followed by the Trump administration to good effect. However, it appears that the State Department nevertheless remains cynically averse to following the good counsel it offered to others.

It should also be noted that a hearing was held by the Subcommittee on Security and Terrorism of the Senate Judiciary Committee, chaired by Senator Jeremiah Denton, on April 23, 1986, on Legal Mechanisms to Combat Terrorism[188].

The object of the hearing was to explore the possibility of bringing Arafat and the PLO to justice for a long list of crimes, including the murders of Noel and Moore, among others.

Substantial evidence was adduced of pervasive criminal activity over a number of years, but the Justice Department was non-committal about the possibility of bringing a successful criminal prosecution, raising issues about the admissibility of the evidence. Remember, our criminal justice system requires proof beyond a reasonable doubt and has rules against hearsay and

---

[186] See, for example, 'Monstrous Lie': Mahmoud Abbas Harshly Condemned After Claiming Israel Had Committed '50 Holocausts', By Hank Berrien, at the Daily Wire, dated 8/17/2022.

[187] 81. Telegram From the Embassy in Saudi Arabia to the Department of State, Jidda, March 14, 1973, 1130Z, Foreign Relations of the United States, 1969-1976, Volume E-9, Documents on the Middle East Region, 1973-1976, at history.state.gov.

[188] Serial No. J-99-99, at ojp.gov.

other procedural requirements, which do not burden the intelligence community when gathering actionable intelligence. It was designed to protect the defendant, presumed to be innocent, from prosecutorial abuse. Be that as it may, this is not how governments function when determining how to engage with unfriendly parties and whether to trust, reward, and honor them.

It is respectfully suggested that a reasonable person reading the information collected by the Subcommittee from a variety of credible sources, which detail a sordid history of criminal activities intimately linked to Arafat and his circle of leadership, would balk at dealing with Arafat and the PLO. There are hundreds of pages of detailed descriptions in the record of the hearing. This includes materials regarding Arafat's responsibility for the murder, wounding, and kidnapping of numerous Americans, as well as his hostile positions against America, deeming both the US and Israel as the enemy, calling for the destruction of Israel through terrorism, and his promoting of terrorism internationally. Other documents include details about the BSO, such as it is merely a front for Arafat and the PLO. The documentation is extensive, detailed, and compelling. There are also submissions describing the continuing, extensive, and intimate relationship between Arafat and the PLO and their patron, the USSR, as well as other terrorist groups around the world. This includes the USSR training of PLO terrorists, supplying the PLO with weapons and money, and sharing intelligence through extensive contacts with the KGB and GRU. The documents also describe a variety of efforts by the PLO in concert with the USSR to undermine US interests in the Middle East, including US-sponsored peace efforts.

When all is said and done, it is incomprehensible that any serious player would just trust a commitment by Arafat and the PLO to make genuine peace with Israel and truly disavow terrorism. In point of fact, he and his successors have done neither and continue to promote terrorism and disclaim peace with Israel. Despite a fervent desire by many in the State Department to believe there is a difference between Arafat and his deputy and successor, Abbas, this is a dubious and frankly dangerous assumption. There really is little, if any, distinction between them, as a practical matter, when it comes to their commitment to continuing terrorism and seeking to eliminate Israel, as well as antipathy to the US. It was ludicrous to award Arafat a Nobel Peace Prize for the Oslo Accords, which he only honored in the breach. It is also immoral knowingly to continue benefiting the PA and enable it to fund the PA's evil Pay to Slay program.

It is also important to note that the heinous Pay to Slay program is not a matter of executive fiat; it is actually embodied in PA law[189]. These provisions are flagrant and egregious violations of the Oslo Accords[190], which explicitly provide, "Both sides shall take all measures necessary in order to prevent acts of terrorism, crime, and hostilities directed against each other, against individuals falling under the other's authority and against their property, and shall take legal measures against offenders." In essence, not only is the PA not preventing these horrendous acts, it is actually encouraging and rewarding them. This includes honoring the murderous terrorists[191].

---

[189] Law No. 14 (2004) on Aid for Prisoners in Israeli Prisons; Amended Palestinian Prisoners Law No. 19 (2004); and Decree No. 1 (2013) on the Amendment of Prisoners and Released Prisoners Law No. 19 (2004). In addition, there is PA Government Resolution of 2010, numbers 21 and 23, signed and published in the official Palestinian Authority Registry in April 2011, which puts all Palestinians and Israeli Arabs imprisoned in Israel for terror crimes on the PA payroll to receive a monthly salary from the PA (Official PA daily Al-Hayat Al-Jadida, April 15, 2011).

[190] Article XV of the Israeli-Palestinian Interim Agreement on the West Bank and the Gaza Strip, signed in Washington D.C., on September 28, 1995.

[191] See, for example, Palestinian Authority Paying Salaries to Terrorists with U.S. Money, by Itamar Marcus and Nan Jacques Zilberdik, dated July 28, 2011, at the gatestoneinstitute.org. and Incentivizing Terrorism: Palestinian Authority Allocations to Terrorists and their Families, by Brig.-Gen. (res.) Yossi Kuperwasser, at jcpa.org. (2016).

The Taylor Force Act requires cutting off U.S. aid to the PA until the Pay to Slay program is ended. Congress made factual findings under the Act, including as follows:

(1) The Palestinian Authority's practice of paying salaries to terrorists serving in Israeli prisons, as well as to the families of deceased terrorists, is an incentive to commit acts of terror.

(2) The United States does not provide direct budgetary support to the Palestinian Authority. The United States does pay certain debts held by the Palestinian Authority and funds programs for which the Palestinian Authority would otherwise be responsible.

The logic of the Act is exquisitely simple; money is fungible. Thus, aid that supplants the governance responsibilities of the PA frees up money for the PA to reward terrorists.

The operative provisions of the Act require that in order for the PA to receive funding, the Secretary of State must certify, in writing to Congress every 180 days, that the PA, the Palestine Liberation Organization (PLO), and any successor or affiliated organizations:

(A) are taking credible steps to end acts of violence against Israeli citizens and United States citizens that are perpetrated or materially assisted by individuals under their jurisdictional control, such as the March 2016 attack that killed former United States Army officer Taylor Force, a veteran of the wars in Iraq and Afghanistan;

(B) have terminated payments for acts of terrorism against Israeli citizens and United States citizens to any individual, after being fairly tried, who has been imprisoned for such acts of terrorism and to any individual who died committing such acts of terrorism, including to a family member of such individuals;

(C) have revoked any law, decree, regulation, or document authorizing or implementing a system of compensation for imprisoned individuals that uses the sentence or period of incarceration of an individual imprisoned for an act of terrorism to determine the level of compensation paid or have taken comparable action that has the effect of invalidating any such law, decree, regulation, or document; and

(D) are publicly condemning such acts of violence and are taking steps to investigate or are cooperating in investigations of such acts to bring the perpetrators to justice.

The Taylor Force Act remedies the profoundly immoral circumstance where American taxpayer funds are, in effect, benefitting the PA to enable it to incentivize the murder and maiming of people, including American citizens[192]. The PA must not be allowed to circumvent the plain meaning of the Taylor Force Act by the use of some subterfuge and other evasive tactics. This includes substituting a so-called 'needs-based' model for the one that bases compensation awarded on the amount of harm done by the terrorist. So too, funneling dollars through entities, like so-called NGOs, which are nothing more than conduits to evade compliance with the Act. Whatever the compensation formula used, it is premised on the individual committing terrorist acts and harming American and/or Israeli citizens being paid by the PA, PLO, or any successor or affiliated organization.

It is galling to realize that the US, as well as the EU[193], blithely and immorally, continue, in effect, to fund PA terrorism and murder by continuing aid payments that offset other PA

---

[192] See, for example, Five Americans among injured in Jerusalem shooting attack, by Amir Tal and Hadas Gold, at CNN, dated 8/14/2022.
[193] See, for example, A textbook case of EU funding, by Ruth Blum, in the Jerusalem Post, dated 6/16/2022.

obligations, freeing up cash used to fund the Pay to Slay program. This is nothing less than the condoning of evil terrorism and the vicious murder of innocents. Some might fairly argue it is tantamount to tacit approval of these miscreant actions[194].

This is not an indictment of all of the Arab people who live in Judea and Samaria, many of whom work and thrive in joint enterprises with Israel and others, who would welcome peace for the benefit of all people. It's a restrained commentary on the oppressive and terrorist leadership of the PA and Hamas, who not only seek to destroy Israel but also oppress their own people. For example, in Hamas-controlled Gaza and the PA-controlled areas, it is reported[195] domestic physical and mental abuse against women in the home is rampant; honor killings regularly occur; there is systemic discrimination against women, both civilly and criminally; women are blatantly mistreated and exploited, including in matters of economic access and inheritance; and there is no equal protection for women under the law.

Yet, there are still some in the US who seek to court the PA and Hamas. This alone should be reviled as immoral and a travesty, but consider the callous indifference of doing so at the expense of Israel; it's maddening. Perhaps, the humiliating exit of the US from Afghanistan will be an object lesson to those who just don't understand how proclaiming to have the PA and Hamas as purported allies or friends is demeaning and detracts from the prestige and credibility of the US. On the other hand, as the

[194] Is the Biden Administration Planning on Violating the Taylor Force Act, as the PA Continues Its Despicable Anti-Israel, Anti-America Pay-for-Slay Policy, by Sander Gerber, Mike Pompeo and Stuart Force, at jinsa.org, dated 3/10/2021 and Is 'Pay For Slay' Biden's Idea of Social Justice?, by Michael Lumish, at White Rose Magazine, dated 4/7/2022.
[195] See, Facts and Figures UN Women-Palestine: Ending Violence Against Women and Jerusalem Institute of Justice, April 2016 Report on the Implementation of the Convention on the Elimination of All Forms of Discrimination Against Women under the PA and Hamas.

Abraham Accords have demonstrated in no uncertain terms, being a loyal ally and friend to Israel adds luster to US prestige and can be leveraged into a genuine circle of peace and prosperity among the US, Israel, and a host of friendly countries in the Middle East and beyond.

Senator Kyl well understood the reality of the US' position in the world and how important it was to be loyal and reliable to allies and friends and project power. He had previously been a four-term member of the US House of Representatives and served on the House Armed Services Committee. In that capacity, he had received significant exposure to foreign affairs and was a vocal supporter of a strong American foreign policy.

In December of 1994, newly elected Senator Kyl made his first major foreign policy speech[196]. Amazingly, the subject he chose for this address was the matter of Jerusalem. He wanted to make clear his belief that the US should recognize the undivided Jerusalem as the capital of Israel and move the US embassy there. He declared his intention to offer legislation to achieve this result. His dedication was not about doing what was politically expedient or just appearing to be virtuous, even if it lacked any substance. His goal was to do what was right and not just to talk about it. Hence, his focus on enshrining Jerusalem's status as the capital of Israel in US law, not just sending another letter or passing another non-binding resolution.

He explained that this would send a clear signal to the rest of the world, including Israel's Arab negotiating partners, that the US considered Jerusalem the capital of Israel. It was a bold initiative, especially given the non-committal temperament of much of official Washington, which was content to stay on the sidelines when it came to the Israeli-Palestinian peace process. The concept of so-called evenhandedness, which resulted in aid appropriations to both sides, was pervasive. Never mind that it,

---

[196] A Capital Decision, by Edward Miller, in the RJC Newsletter of March-April 1996.

in effect, rewarded the Palestinians for their intransigence and misbehavior. The Clinton administration sought to be a mediator in any peace talks and not weigh in on either side of what it perceived to be a contentious issue like Jerusalem.

However, this was not acceptable to Senator Kyl and others. He was thus able to enlist the support of Senator Jesse Helms, the Chairman of the Foreign Relations Committee, and Senator Hank Brown, the Chairman of the Near Eastern and South Asian Sub-Committee. Armed with this backing, Senator Kyl approached Senate Majority Leader Bob Dole, who signed on and began actively working with Kyl to accomplish the passage of this measure.

One of the key themes to Senator Kyl's Weltanschauung, when it came to matters of foreign policy and peace, was that, in the real world, peace must be pursued through strength. This meant not only having a strong defense establishment capable of deterring threats to security but also recognition of legitimacy.

In the Middle East, Israel's legitimacy was at stake because its enemies challenged its very existence. There could be no legitimate peace unless Israel's existence was no longer an issue and, by extension, its legitimacy was unqualifiedly accepted. He reasoned if Israel did not have the right to declare its own capital, then why should its neighbors or enemies respect its rights on any other front? Moreover, if the US, Israel's trusted ally and friend, did not recognize this essential facet of legitimacy, then why should Israel's enemies? On the other hand, by recognizing undivided Jerusalem as Israel's capital, the US would be using its power and prestige to reinforce Israel's legitimacy. US recognition of Jerusalem as the capital of Israel was, therefore, critically important to enable peace. It would also compel everyone involved in the peace process to have realistic expectations of Jerusalem, which was essential to enduring peace.

Doug Feith, a Middle East specialist who had been on the National Security Council staff and a Deputy Assistant Secretary of Defense in the Reagan administration, acted as an informal advisor to Senator Kyl. When he heard about the speech referenced above, it is reported[197] he asked Senator Kyl whether he was seriously committed to the program he outlined in his speech. He expressed his concern that passing legislation into law would require a much greater effort than just mentioning support for such an idea in a speech, as many others had done before and since. Senator Kyl responded that moving the Embassy to Jerusalem would be his highest legislative priority for his first year in office in the Senate, and true to his word, he got it done.

Doug Feith echoed Senator Kyl's themes in May 1995 op-ed in the New York Times[198]after the bill originated by Senator Kyl was introduced by Senate Majority Leader Bob Dole in the Senate. Among other things, he addressed why the bill was sensible policy and was not, as some hopelessly cynical wags suggested, just an exercise in Presidential politics by Senator Dole, who was intent on running for President.

Doug Feith, like Senator Kyl, unequivocally concluded that leaving American support for Israel's sovereignty over Jerusalem an open question did not help promote peace. He averred that the position taken by Senators Dole and Kyl in the bill, which was endorsed by the Speaker of the House, Newt Gingrich, was logical. The US, by taking a firm and unqualified stance in favor of Israel having sovereignty over Jerusalem and enshrining it in US law, would make it likelier that Israel's Arab interlocutors would make the philosophical adjustments and political concessions necessary for peace.

---

[197] Ibid.

[198] To Promote Peace, Move the Embassy, by Douglas J. Feith, in the New York Times, dated May 29, 1995.

On the other hand, the Clinton administration's view that it was better not to decide firmly in favor of Israel and instead to continue to leave the question of its support on this critical issue open was illogical. It ignored the fact that the fundamental issue in the Arab-Jewish conflict was a fight over the legitimacy of a Jewish state in any part of what had been delineated as the area of the Palestine Mandate. The Arab anti-Jewish establishment wanted it all and insisted the Jews had no right to a state there.

Doug Feith noted, over the years since the beginning of the twentieth century, well before there was a State of Israel and since there were periods of violence. Even the Oslo Accords did not alter the basic reality that the PA and Hamas had not changed their hearts and minds and continued, irresponsibly and malevolently, to deny the legitimacy of Israel. It is laughable to believe that causing Israel to appear vulnerable will facilitate a change in the hearts and minds of Israel's enemies. Historically, that kind of weakened condition did not help achieve peace or even peace talks. He went on to assert it was only after being forced to acknowledge the strength of Israel's military power, its enduring ties to the US, and, since the end of the Cold War, the US' unchallenged global dominance, did some Arab powers abandon rejectionist positions and start negotiating.

True peace requires unqualified acceptance of Israel's legitimacy. As both Senator Kyl and Feith emphasized, the essence of the issue of legitimacy is embodied in Israel's sovereignty over Jerusalem. As Doug Feith put it:

> In as much as the essence of the Arab-Israeli conflict is legitimacy, the essence of the legitimacy issue is Jerusalem's right to sovereignty on Jerusalem. If Israelis do not have the right to sovereignty there, they can hardly justify sovereignty anywhere.

Jerusalem has been central to Jewish nationhood for 3,000 years. The Jew's national movement, after all, is Zionism,

Zion being Jerusalem. The Arabs understand this, too, which is why the importance of Jerusalem in Arab politics, diplomacy, philosophy, and literature increased as the struggle against Zionism intensified.

By relocating our embassy to Jerusalem, we would end our anomalous policy of refusing to recognize Israel's sovereignty in its own capital. We would proclaim that Israel's legitimacy in Zion is not an open question for us. This would signal that we expect all parties - not just Israel - to pursue peace on the basis of realism.

It is most disappointing and unfathomable to hear some vehemently advocate a separate state for the Arab residents of Judea and Samaria and, at the same time, deny that the Jews in Israel should have one. The abject hypocrisy of such an illogical position is mind-boggling. Why should Jews be the only group in the world not entitled to their own state and patrimony? The demand that Israel leave Jerusalem is also most disturbing and perplexing. After all, the Jewish people have undeniable historical and legal links to Jerusalem, and the Arabs don't; why then seek to legitimize the baseless pretensions of the PA and Hamas and deny the legitimacy of Israel's right to sovereignty over Jerusalem? It makes no sense at all to reward the sheer rapaciousness and abhorrent efforts of the PA and Hamas.

Doug Feith also provided an insider's perspective on how Senator Kyl's initiative was viewed in certain quarters. He noted, "Like all American pro-Israel initiatives, the bill to move the embassy is being deprecated in certain quarters as a cynical play for political points with American Jews". However, as Doug Feith then pointed out, "Such criticism is itself deeply cynical". In essence, this kind of reflexive and flawed supposition ignores the realities of how business is conducted in Congress. In fairness, almost every Congressional action pleases some constituencies and displeases others. Some politicians support any given action for political reasons, others for substantive reasons, and many for both reasons. More importantly, though, is the objective reality that Israel is not only a friend and ally of the US, it shares the values we in the US treasure so much. Hence, as Doug Feith said:

> But support for Israel as a fellow democracy and strategic ally has been sustained by a long line of Democratic and Republican administrations and Congresses. It reflects the nation's strong sympathy for Israel as evinced in public opinion polls decade after decade since 1948.

> The automatic assumption that a pro-Israel initiative is nothing more than pandering is unfair and at odds with America's national interest as most Americans see it.

The Clinton administration and the old hands at the State Department didn't share this worldview. They rejected the kind of approach that Senator Kyl was espousing. They thought they knew better. Yet, as history teaches us, their policies and understanding of the dynamics of how to bring the parties together and promote a sustainable peace deal did not actually produce salutary results. The fact remains that there were no new peace deals between Israel and other Arab states since the deal with Jordan until the assumptions of past administrations were challenged in the Trump administration, which produced the Abraham Accords.

It would also appear that anyone who suggested trying something new or adapting proven methods from the business world of deal-making was disdained as a parvenu, incapable of perceiving the unique demands, principles, and nuances of international diplomacy among high contracting parties. Nations and their diplomatic relations, they urged, were a breed apart. They did not act or react like other entities representing collections of ordinary people. It was, therefore, baselessly asserted that the art of negotiating international agreements among nations required incomparable skills of a class and quality distinguished from those used in the negotiation of prosaic business deals. In their quest to immortalize their own positions and stature, they seem to have forgotten that they and all the people they dealt with were, at their essence, mere mortals. All were subject to the same rules of human nature that govern regular business affairs and relations among ordinary people.

It did not require a new class of pretentious pseudo-nobility to represent a nation in its dealings with other nations. Perhaps, that was a part of the reason President Truman bucked at the pronouncements of what he called the 'stripped pants' boys of the State Department of his time. He was no fan of those who perceived themselves to be high born and a cut above and thus more capable than he of dealing with international relations. Unfortunately, there are still those who perceive themselves to be a part of an American bureaucratic version of the nobility. They seem to believe they have an exclusive and nearly prophetic understanding of what will and won't work in international affairs. However, whether it is the failures in Iraq, Iran, and Afghanistan or the missed opportunities prior to the Trump administration to accomplish peace deals like the Abraham Accords, it would appear the only real experience some of these pseudo-experts had was a failure. This, coupled with a willful determination not to learn from their bad experiences but rather to keep repeating them, assured continuing failures and no prospect of remediation. The definition of insanity, often attributed to Albert Einstein, of doing the same thing over and over again and expecting different results, seems to be the prevailing ethic, and it appears it still infects many State Department policy-makers to this day. Yet, they continue to press their case that their way was the only way and repeat failed policies, strategies, and tactics.

Similarly, their almost reflexive insistence that the only proactive policy Israel should pursue in defending its security is a diplomatic one as if diplomacy standing alone is the only prudent solution. As many appreciate, when confronted with a murderous, violent terrorist or armed attack, diplomacy can do little to prevent harm. This is especially so when the perpetrator makes no demands and is only intent on causing death, like a homicide/suicide bomber. The first order of business is to subdue or otherwise eliminate the threat of violent injury or death. Even if demands are made, they may only be a pretext. Moreover, giving into extortionate demands under the threat of bodily harm typically only engenders more such demands. The Mishna[199] records that, as a matter of public policy[200], they should not pay extortionate ransoms for captives. The Talmud[201] explains this is because if they do, it will only result in even more excessive demands or more kidnappings. Evil must not be reinforced and emboldened by being rewarded; rather, the wrongdoer must be held accountable.

Constructive discussions can occur when there is no longer a threat of imminent harm. Diplomacy does not offer a universal cure to all of the world's problems. The fact of the matter is diplomacy is most effective when it is backed up by credible force; words alone are usually not effective against an aggressor or predator. Consider an experience Leonard Grunstein (Len) had in the Old City of Jerusalem. There was a knifing, committed by an Arab terrorist, of a student at a Yeshiva[202] that was located in the Old City. The Yeshiva was somewhat unique because its mission was dedicated to providing a Torah education to penitent ex-cons. The Yeshiva of ex-cons responded by rumbling through the Old City in search of the assailant. They were a burly bunch, and the news of their foray echoed throughout the Old City. A few days later, there was a dinner scheduled between

---

[199] Mishna Gittin 4:6.
[200] Tikkun HaOlam.
[201] BT Gittin 45a.
[202] An institute of higher learning of Jewish Law and other Jewish studies. Some Yeshiva programs offer a course of studies, which may lead to the granting of Rabbinical ordination.

Ateret Cohanim[203] and leaders of the Arab community to restore peaceful relations. A representative of Ateret Cohanim approached Len at the make peace dinner and mentioned how this was how Ateret Cohanim functioned, as distinguished from how the ex-con Yeshiva rolled. Len responded that was fine, but absent the muscle shown by the ex-con Yeshiva students, it is unlikely there would have been a make-peace dinner. Diplomacy works best when there is power behind it.

There is another extremely important aspect of diplomacy. It is establishing and retaining true and reliable relationships with allies and friends. This is also a force multiplier of the highest order in the perception of those dealing with the US. To have loyal and reliable allies and friends, the US must be loyal and reliable. Even the perception that the US might be induced to pursue a separate agenda from the one agreed to with its friends and allies in a coalition of forces diminishes the aura of power the US wields. Thus, it is self-defeating and only serves to undermine its diplomatic muscle. Imagine then how much worse it is when the US advertises to enemies its willingness to do so.

When representatives of the US unilaterally insist the US is a so-called honest broker and, therefore, not a loyal and reliable ally and friend, that is how the US is regarded. Proclaiming that this posture is only intended to serve the goal of making peace between a terrorist regime and a friend and ally is as insouciant as it sounds. How could anyone be expected to trust the US if it is willing to pursue such a reckless course of action, with callous indifference to its friends and allies? The answer is that this tactic doesn't work in practice. It has proven a failure time and time again because it is truly antithetical to one of the most critical requirements for a functional peace agreement, a

---

[203] Ateret Cohanim is an organization that, among other things, works to redeem properties once owned by Jews in Israel's capital of Jerusalem, including reestablishing Jewish neighborhoods in the heart of the Old City of Jerusalem (see, ateretcohanim.org).

semblance of trust. Contrary to what might be the objective of those ostensibly wily US representatives virtuously insisting they are honest brokers, they are creating a condition of distrust instead of fostering trust. The perception created is that the US can be manipulated to abandon its ally Israel and submit to extortion by the PA merely to keep alive the charade that there is an ongoing peace process. The tactic is futile.

The peace process would be better served by the US acting as a trusted sponsor and genuine ally and friend of Israel, who could be counted on to confirm, in no uncertain terms, that undivided Jerusalem remaining the capital of Israel is non-negotiable. Narrowing the issues and establishing what is and is not negotiable is a much more efficacious means of reaching a workable agreement. It would also signal that having the US as a friend and ally means something tangible. Furthermore, being an enemy of the US and its allies must also have consequences. The failure to hold the PA and Hamas accountable for their malfeasance and instead even, in effect, reward it only serves to reinforce it. It makes a mockery of the sacred nature of agreements if they can be violated with impunity.

As Senator Kyl intuitively understood, it was time to shake up the establishment at the State Department and dispel the myths and false narratives which perpetuated the state of non-peace in the Middle East. A fresh approach was required, which rewarded friends and reinforced good behavior, rather than disdaining friends and rewarding the misbehavior of their enemies. Just pursuing policies based on a utopian vision of a world where people and nations don't act in their own self-interest has usually resulted in a dystopian nightmare because it is unsustainable and ultimately fails. Human nature does not fundamentally change, although behavior can be regulated by disdaining and punishing bad behavior and especially by rewarding and otherwise positively reinforcing good behavior[204]. A practical approach is to recognize self-interest and to broaden its application to become a form of enlightened self-interest, as discussed below:

The world is not a zero-sum game. People and nations working together can expand the pie so there is more to share. Thus, a party can earn more by enlisting the efforts of others in a shared vision with mutually beneficial interests. It's true in business and in international trade. This permits everyone participating to earn more than they might otherwise have, had they not participated in the joint venture. This recognition that others can benefit too and success is not defined by reaping benefits to the exclusion of anyone else is an important step in the maturation process of a person and a nation.

This enlightened view of self-interest and the kind of mutually beneficial bonds achieved as a result of applying this notion in practice are building blocks in the establishment of an enduring relationship. The deeper and more extensive such bonds are among a variety and greater number of people within two or more nations, the more difficult it becomes to sever the relationship. If post-war Europe demonstrates anything, it is the veracity of this principle of human relations. The success of NATO is not only in the mutual defense arrangements but also, importantly, in the economic unions it spawned. War, once a regular occurrence between Germany and France, is now virtually unthinkable.

Ultimately, negotiating and consummating a deal or relationship between two high contracting parties differs little more than in

---

[204] As the Talmud (BT Shabbos 156a) notes and Maimonides (Mishne Torah, Hilchot Deot) explains, our inborn character traits are neutral; they may be sublimated in pursuance of a higher purpose or misused. Thus, a person who has an otherwise ruthless killer instinct can, with the right motivation, become a gifted surgeon, excellent butcher or talented mohel.

degree from negotiating and concluding a deal or joint venture between two large multinational public companies. In the end, it's all about dealing with people, understanding their needs (individually, in a representative capacity, and collectively), negotiating compromises, and fashioning an alignment of interests that is often referred to as a win/win situation, as well as, communicating this ethos, so as to achieve sign-on at all levels within both of the contracting parties.

It is not always the case that a deal can be consummated. In this regard, it is critical to appreciate that the only thing worse than no deal is a bad deal. Indeed, a party may have to experience changed circumstances before it is amenable to entering into serious negotiations. Merely pursuing negotiations for negotiation's sake (i.e., process) can actually spoil the prospects for a deal. Other factors can also intervene to frustrate the ability to consummate a deal. Among the most persistent problems are non-substantive considerations like egos, ideology, or other non-productive non-business concerns that are antithetical to sound and meaningful business judgments. This includes the plethora of characters and so-called experts that may become involved in a large complex deal, who sometimes shield the actual decision-makers from coming together to reach a resolution that may involve some level of risk-taking.

Making a deal usually requires some level of trust between the parties and almost always involves some degree of risk. To overcome the challenge, trusted and credible intermediaries are often employed, who can vouch for the bona fides of a party and help orchestrate and facilitate a deal happening. In essence, they are able to bridge matters of trust by substituting their own credibility and acting, in a sense, as the moral guarantor of performance by a party. Of course, this means putting their own reputation on the line, and there are typically real-world consequences, including loss of prestige and business, if their fidelity or reliability is put into question.

A good, reliable, and effective intermediary is not a so-called 'honest broker', as that term is employed by the State Department, as a euphemism for the US distancing itself from its friend and ally Israel. Indeed, for the US to insist it's an honest broker diminishes its prestige and the useful role it might otherwise play in facilitating a deal being made by the parties. In essence, as noted above, it signals that the US cannot be trusted because it is prepared to be disloyal to its actual friends and allies.

The US' reputation is also not enhanced by the farcical pursuit of the PA, a kleptocratic regime that oppresses its own people and has proven to be wholly untrustworthy. The PA even touts its aversion to the US, flirting with actual enemies of the US, such as Iran and others[205]. It is disconcerting that the US continues to fall prey to the PA's manipulations and fund it despite not ending its Pay to Slay program, continuing to promote terrorism and antisemitism, as well as persecution of Christians. Doing this at the expense of Israel, a genuine ally and friend of the US with shared values and interests, compounds the pernicious nature of this nebulous quest.

The US' affectation to be a so-called honest broker does not magically transform it into a genuine impartial 'arbiter' or 'mediator'. In order to be impartial, the mediator or arbiter may not have a conflict or even an appearance of conflict, including by reason of any affiliation, relationship, or pecuniary or other interest in or in relation to any of the parties. Furthermore, to be effective, the mediator or arbiter must be voluntarily selected by the parties in a genuine attempt amicably to mediate and

---

[205] This included Saddam Hussein in the 1990 Gulf War (see, for example, In Bad Company: Yasser Arafat and Saddam Hussein, at the Washington Institute.org, dated 5/2/2002). It also includes Russia. Abbas even went so far as to declare support for Russia in its war with Ukraine (see, for example, PA President Abbas Expresses Support for Putin Over Ukraine Invasion as Russia Slams Israeli 'Illegal Occupation', by Ben Cohen, at the Algemeiner, dated 4/18/2022).

facilitate the resolution of a dispute. None of these standards have been met.

The US has its own interests in the region, as well as relationships with Israel and Arab states. The parties have not voluntarily asked the US to be a mediator or arbiter and have not agreed to be bound by the US' judgments. The US also continues to insist that it is not imposing an agreement on the parties, and any agreement must voluntarily be reached between the parties themselves. Purporting to play the role of what amounts to a pseudo-mediator by self-identifying as a so-called honest broker is little more than a charade and makes a mockery of the process. A true arbiter or mediator would likely consider this role unethical and demeaning. A more honest description might be a semi-disloyal ally and friend, seeking (albeit failing) to win new friends and influence. The ardor of some pursuing this misguided approach is emotionally driven by an ideological vision that is devoid of reality, which mischaracterizes PA and Hamas terrorists as victims instead of predators; ignores the stated goals of the PA and Hamas to eliminate Israel; and excuses their violations of agreements and commitments, as well as, other wrongdoing, as discussed in this book. Others may so blindly believe in the righteousness of their cause that sacrificing objective truth and friends and allies in pursuit of that goal is somehow justified. Never mind that the proverbial end hardly ever justifies using inappropriate means; if the means to be used are no good, then the end, too, should be re-evaluated. Yet others may think they're right to pursue such a misguided strategy, notwithstanding that it has failed repeatedly.

Whatever the motivation, disloyalty is poisonous. It challenges the very essence of reliability and credibility that is essential to anyone performing a productive role in fostering a deal[206]. After

---

[206] A party might compromise, make concessions or take some risks to make a deal, because of the moral, financial or other backing provided by a loyal ally and friend sponsoring the deal. The other side might also take the offer of a party more seriously,

all, it is foolhardy to trust and rely on anyone who has proven to be disloyal and unreliable. Fortunately, the US is not entirely run by those in the State Department advocating this non-productive role for the US. As described in this book, there are some who have acted to rein in this negative impulse and pursue a more enlightened policy that led to the recognition of Jerusalem, moving the Embassy there, and the Abraham Accords.

However, the mixed messaging and reversion to many of the old discredited policies by the current Biden administration, and the undoing of a good deal of the prior Trump administration's policies that proved so effective in promoting the Abraham Accords have taken a toll, as evidenced by the dramatic upsurge in murderous terrorist activity ever since funding was restored to the PA[207]. Why would the PA compromise when there's little or no downside to being intransigent because the conditioned response of the EU and US is to keep funding.

A win/win solution engages the enlightened self-interest of the parties. Neither side is obtaining all the advantages they may seek, but in the context of making a deal, both benefit. Identifying the benefits each will achieve only by consummating a deal together elevates self-interest into the enlightened variety. This is because only by both parties doing their part can each party benefit. This serves to make each party's commitment more credible. Parties to a mutually beneficial arrangement often seek to do more together, and with every successful outcome, the bonds become stronger and more enduring. It is a

---

because it is promoted and sponsored by the party's credible and reliable loyal friend and ally. On the other hand, when the putative sponsor is avowedly disloyal and unreliable, it only serves to frustrate the process and make it less likely a deal can be consummated. Why would anyone trust any assurances secured from such a disloyal source?

[207] See, for example, After Biden sent $1B to Palestinians, Israeli deaths from terror attacks rose 900%, by Daniel Greenfield, at World Israel News, dated 2/15/2023 and IDF: Terrorism in Israel, Judea and Samaria rose by over 300 percent in 2022, at JNS, dated 11/29/2022.

proven paradigm for consummating a deal and continuing to deepen the mutually beneficial relationship in the world of domestic and international business.

Loyalty to allies and friends is not some abstract concept or meaningless platitude. In actual practice, it creates strong bonds, especially when premised on shared values, interests, and goals. A nucleus of like-minded parties creates centrifugal forces that attract others to join the circle of friendship. On the other hand, disloyalty creates centripetal forces that ultimately drive friends and allies away. As Len's dad, of blessed memory, pithily put it, never trade old friends for new ones; it not only is wrong, it also doesn't work. This is because it engenders distrust and concerns about the individual's fidelity and reliability.

These principles of how good interpersonal and business relationships can be successfully established and retained should inform how we establish and maintain good relations among nations. Yet it appears these rules are only followed in the breach when it comes to the PA and Hamas and their enablers.

Senator Kyl sought to change the administration's blind devotion to a failed paradigm. His goal was for the US to pursue a wiser course of action, which made sense and had the real potential of bringing peace to the Middle East, as well as better assuring the security of Israel and the US. The story of how he and others successfully pursued this just and right goal is a most compelling one worthy of emulation. It formally begins with the introduction of a bill in the Senate known as the Jerusalem Embassy Act of 1995, which is more fully discussed below. The results of Senator Kyl's efforts to do what was just and right are now manifest. With the benefit of hindsight, we can see just how his prescient plan unfolded and how its promise of bringing lasting peace to Israel and its neighbors is being achieved in a step-by-step, sometimes grueling, and excruciatingly painful process. The evil forces of terrorism and antisemitism don't easily surrender or just readily fade away.

However, it's very clear now that the Arab-Israel conflict is over. What's left is a propaganda war of words seeking to demonize the one and only Jewish State of Israel and furtive efforts that sometimes erupt into overt battles seeking the destruction of Israel. This includes Iranian proxies, such as Hamas and Palestinian Islamic Jihad (PIJ); the machinations of European antisemites and their intersectional cohorts in the US and elsewhere; and the terrorist acts of neo-Marxist and pseudo-Islamists, such as the PA and Hamas[208], as well as, other front groups, affiliated organizations and the like. The Arabs living in the areas under the control of the PA and Hamas, known as the so-called Palestinian people, are mere pawns of the PA and Hamas in this struggle.

This is quite a change from the existential threats Israel faced from the coalition of Arab Nations that sought its destruction in a number of wars during the period 1948-1973. Hopefully, the Abraham Accords and the historical process it set in motion will continue to develop positively and bring true peace to the region. Imagine a time when the Iranian people shake off their dictatorial overlords and join the circle of peace with Israel. As the bonds of peace become unbreakable through the era of peace and prosperity they usher in, there may come a time when Hamas and the PA wither and are replaced by genuine democratic representatives who are interested in conferring on their people the extraordinary benefits of peace and prosperity through making an enduring peace agreement with Israel.

It all began with strengthening the US-Israel relationship forming an unbreakable bond based on shared values and mutual interests. The US then finally demonstrated, in a very public and tangible way, that it was a loyal, worthy, and reliable ally by

---

[208] See, for example, In groundbreaking ruling, Middle Eastern council declares 'fatwa' against Hamas, by Ruth Marks Eglash, at Fox News, dated 3/12/2023 and Hamas conduct 'violates laws of Koran' Islamic Fatwa Council rules, at the Jerusalem Post, dated 3/24/2023.

recognizing Jerusalem as the capital of its friend and ally Israel and moving its Embassy there.

This created an enduring axis of trust and reliability, which attracted others. Senator Kyl began the process that enabled and led to that extraordinary moment, and President Trump actually finally made it happen. In between, there were a number of other heroes who facilitated the process, as more fully detailed below.

To Arab nations faced with the threat of Iranian hegemony and the failure of the flawed JCPOA[209], the US' renewed and invigorated relationship with its friend and ally Israel, unburdened by the mixed signals of courting its enemies like the Iranian regime, Hamas, and the PA, provided a ray of hope that the US could indeed be counted on to be a loyal and reliable ally, even in difficult circumstances. The result was the nearly miraculous Abraham Accords.

The story of the reunification of Jerusalem and its recognition as the undivided capital of Israel is veritably Biblical in its implications. The Prophet Zechariah[210], one of the last of the prophets in the Bible and a member of the Great Assembly more than twenty-five hundred years ago, provided a description of the sequence of events that would occur, albeit not the precise dates. It is amazingly prescient.

Zechariah first predicted a world war where all the nations would gather in Jerusalem. It is respectfully suggested that this occurred in World War I. Interestingly, the Talmud[211] describes how, just like the army of Sennacherib, the bad guys would have one hundred and eighty-five thousand soldiers under arms, including various types of infantry and cavalry. Coincidently, the

---

[209] JCPOA is an acronym, meaning: Joint Comprehensive Plan of Action. As its title implies, it is not an actual agreement; rather it is a plan. The intent was to prevent Iran from pursuing its nuclear bomb-making program, which the JCPOA failed to accomplish. The subject is more fully discussed below in this book.
[210] Book of Zechariah, Chapter 14.
[211] BT Sanhedrin 95b.

Turkish and German forces under German command also had approximately one hundred eighty-five thousand troops, ranging from units of infantry to cavalry, as well as German aerodromes[212]. They faced an international army under British command, comprised of soldiers from the British Empire, including the UK, Australia, New Zealand, and India, as well as members of the Jewish Legion. The climactic battle of the WW I campaign in Israel was known as the Battle of Megiddo[213]. By the way, the term Armageddon is derived from this place's name. Coincidence? It is suggested that the combination of all these facts and circumstances and those noted below are hardly coincidental. After all, World War I and the climactic battle of international forces at Megiddo did set the stage for the restoration of the Jewish State of Israel, which, thank G-d, did, in fact, occur.

General Edmund Allenby, who led the British and other forces to victory, insisted on personally accepting the formal surrender of the City of Jerusalem. It appears he, too, felt the majesty and sanctity of the moment. On December 11, 1917, he reportedly rode up to the gates of the Old City and dismounted. He deliberately chose to walk into the Old City because, he said, only the Messiah should ride into the Holy City[214].

Also noteworthy is that Zechariah records that Jewish sovereignty over all of Jerusalem would be interrupted for a time. He prophesized that half the city would be exiled, but the rest of the population would not be uprooted from the city. It is all too reminiscent of what occurred when Jordan conquered the eastern portions of Jerusalem, including the Old City and its

---

[212] See, The World Crises, 1916-1918, Volume II, by Winston S. Churchill (Scribner-1927), at pages 47-48; The First World War, by Martin Gilbert (Holt-1994), at pages 370, 372, 376, 388, 391, 420, and 429; and Bavarian Air Force WWI Aerial Reconnaissance, at 101 Israel.com.

[213] The Battle of Megiddo, at the National Army Museum (nam.ac.uk).

[214] 1917 and the liberation of Jerusalem, by Barry Shaw, in the Jerusalem Post, dated 11/19/2017.

Jewish Quarter, in 1948. Zechariah also prophesized that thereafter Jerusalem would become whole again, and undivided Jerusalem would be inhabited by and under the sovereign authority of the Jewish people, as occurred in 1967 and thereafter.

Zechariah goes on to say that never again would destruction be decreed, and the Jewish people would dwell in Jerusalem securely. May the blessings of peace prevail.

IV.

SECURING PASSAGE OF THE JERUSALEM EMBASSY ACT-A STUDY IN THE DYNAMICS OF THE LAW-MAKING PROCESS

Freshman Senator Kyl began the process of seeking to pass a law that would recognize undivided Jerusalem as the capital of Israel and cause the US Embassy to Israel to be moved there from Tel Aviv by conferring with Senate Majority Leader Bob Dole shortly after he was sworn in January of 1995.

By February 17, 1995, he had sent a letter to Secretary of State Warren Christopher, which, among other things, stated that Jerusalem was an integral part of Israel and "The fact is, the status of Jerusalem is not, never was and would never be negotiable". He went on to note that the reluctance to do the right thing on Jerusalem, lest it interfere with the U.S.' ability to serve as an 'honest broker' regarding Arab and Israeli claims, was counter-productive. He opined that the U.S. was more likely to influence a settlement if Arab countries understood they couldn't play off the U.S. against Israel. He concluded the letter with a firm declaration:

> The United States is not neutral about Jewish rights in the ancient Jewish homeland or in Jerusalem. I believe the key to our diplomatic effectiveness is not our neutrality, but our power and loyalty to our friends and principles.

These are stirring and world-wise words to live by and proved true in practice. This is unlike the weak and two-faced policies espoused by the State Department, which only fostered a lack of trust in the bonafides of the U.S. as a reliable friend and ally.

They irresponsibly engendered an aura of uncertainty about U.S. intentions, which promoted enemies to seek advantage by deceptively manipulating and pitting the U.S. against its allies. As Senator Kyl so well pointed out, the US could more effectively promote peace by recognizing Jerusalem.

Secretary Christopher was not pleased with Senator Kyl's initiative, to say the least. Indeed, the Clinton administration sought to rebuff the effort to pass such a law. However, Senator Kyl was undeterred, and he joined with Senator Dole and then others to accomplish his goal.

Passing a law is not simple. It is particularly complicated in the area of foreign affairs, especially when the President and Executive Branch are against it and determined to frustrate the effort.

Senator Kyl's remarks[215], on May 9, 1995, upon introducing what became known as the Jerusalem Embassy Act of 1995, are a cogent, informative, and incisive analysis of why it was right and necessary to recognize undivided Jerusalem as the capital of Israel and to move the US Embassy there. He began by addressing the President of the Senate and humbly acknowledging that he was pleased to join the Majority Leader, Senator Dole, in introducing the legislation. He went on to say as follows:

> It is historic and important that the majority leader and the Speaker of the House are the primary sponsors of this legislation in the Senate and House.

> For three millennia—since King David established Jerusalem as the capital of the Jewish people—Jerusalem has been the center of Jewish liturgy. Twice a year, for the

---

[215] Congressional Record-Senate 141 Cong. Rec. (Bound) - Volume 141, Part 9 (May 4, 1995 to May 17, 1995), pages 12106 et seq.

last 2,000 years, Jews from around the world have offered a simple prayer: "Next Year in Jerusalem."

And throughout the Jewish people's long exile from the land of Israel, through the Holocaust, pogroms, and countless expulsions the "City Upon a Hill" served as the focal point of their aspiration to rebuild Israel.

In addition to Israel's undisputable historical and biblical claim to Jerusalem, upon regaining control over East Jerusalem in 1967, Israel has restored the holy city as a place open to all for worship.

Memories may be short, but it is important to remember that while Jordan occupied East Jerusalem—1948–1967—Jews were expelled and many Christians, feeling persecuted, emigrated. During this period, proper respect was not given to the spiritual importance of the city. A highway was even built on ancient burial grounds and religious sites desecrated.

Yet, successive United States administrations since 1948—for fear of interfering with the ability of the United States to serve as an honest broker for Arab and Israeli claims—have refused to recognize Israeli sovereignty over Jerusalem, and have refused to locate the United States Embassy in the capital of Israel. While there is superficial logic to that concern, I believe it bases United States policy on a disingenuous position—that if Arab leaders hold out long enough, the United States might abandon our ally and force it to do the one thing Israel has made clear it will never do—abandon its claim to Jerusalem as its eternal and undivided capital.

The fact is, the United States will not do that. Better that all parties understand that at the outset, rather than learning it at the unsuccessful conclusions of negotiations.

United States Middle East diplomacy should be based on honesty and on the power and loyalty to our friends and our principles. Moving the Embassy to Jerusalem should aid in any peace between Israel and her neighbors by sending a clear, unambiguous message that the status of Jerusalem is not and never will be negotiable.

Israel cannot under any circumstances negotiate this issue anymore than Americans would negotiate over Washington being our Capital.

Moving the United States Embassy to Jerusalem does no injustice to the Arab people, nor is it intended, in any way, to be disrespectful to them. During the hundreds of years in which Jerusalem was under Arab or Moslem rule, Jerusalem never served as a capital city for the rulers. And while East Jerusalem was under Jordanian control, Jordan's capital remained in Amman and was never moved to Jerusalem. Islam's holiest text, the Koran, does not mention Jerusalem a single time.

Even Moslems who pray at the Al-Aksa Mosque in Jerusalem face Mecca when they pray. No one can dispute, however, the historical and spiritual vitality of Jerusalem to Israel.

It is time for the United States to locate its embassy in the capital city of Israel, as is the case for every other country that the United States recognizes, whether it be ally or enemy.

Those who have expressed support for United States recognition of Jerusalem as the capital of Israel now have a way to convert words to action, by supporting the Dole-Kyl-Inouye resolution, so that construction of the United States Embassy in Jerusalem will commence in time for the city's 3,000-year anniversary as the capital of the people of Israel. "Next Year in Jerusalem."

The need for actual legislation to deal with the recalcitrance of the State Department to recognize Jerusalem as the capital of Israel and move the Embassy there had become apparent to most of the Senate, who joined in co-sponsoring the bill. As Senator D'Amato noted that day[216]:

> It is outrageous that the United States has diplomatic relations with 184 countries throughout the world and in every one, but Israel, our Embassy is in the functioning capital. In Israel, our Embassy is in Tel Aviv. I see no reason why this should be the case. It is wrong and it must end now. Jerusalem should not be thrown around like a bone to Yasir Arafat.

> Israel has endured much throughout her history and for her to have to suffer the indignity of her main ally refusing to place its Embassy in her functioning capital is an insult... Jerusalem, the holy city and ancient capital of Israel, must never again become divided.

> It was for this reason that Senator Moynihan, myself, and 91 other Members of the Senate sent a joint letter to the Secretary of State urging him to begin planning now for the relocation of the Embassy to Jerusalem by no later than May 1999. This letter was sent in March of this year. To date, there has been no reply. This is unfortunate.

> The matter is simple. Jerusalem is and will remain the permanent and un-divided capital of a sovereign Israel. I'm not going to let the State Department bureaucrats forget that.

> I call on the President to recognize this and to begin the process toward moving the U.S. Embassy to Jerusalem. It is shameful that the United States continues to bend to

---

[216] Ibid.

pressure to place the American Embassy in Tel Aviv and not in Jerusalem.

Mr. President, while I understand that the present negotiations are delicate, I do not want this administration to be under the impression that Jerusalem is some prize to be claimed by the Palestinians or anyone else. Let the message be clear: A united Jerusalem is off limits for negotiation. Jerusalem belongs to Israel, and our Embassy belongs in Jerusalem.

Senator Helms directly addressed the chimerical concern, continually raised by the State Department, about timing, in an effort to derail the legislative initiative. He noted, as follows, that day[217]:

There has been some murmuring during the past few days by those who oppose moving the United States Embassy from Tel Aviv to Jerusalem. Their contention is that this is a sensitive time in the peace process. Fair enough, but I need to be informed as to when no sensitive time in the peace process exists.

I remember well a time in 1988 when I offered legislation to move the United States Embassy to Jerusalem. After extensive negotiations with the Department of State—that also was a sensitive time in the peace process—we ended with what I understood to be an agreement to acquire land for an Embassy in Jerusalem. I am sorry to hear that my efforts of 1988 are being used today as an argument against passage of the legislation before us today...

Jerusalem, the Holy City, was divided by barbed wire for almost two decades. Worshippers were denied access to the Holy places under Jordanian rule in East Jerusalem. In the 28 years during which Israel has presided over a united

---

[217] Ibid.

city of Jerusalem, the rights of Christians, Jews and Moslems have been fully respected. Time and again, the Senate has voted overwhelmingly in favor of recognizing United Jerusalem as the Capital of Israel. I commend Senator Dole for his leadership in this and other matters.

The State Department was true to form in responding in opposition to the proposed legislation, by letter[218] from Warren Christopher, the Secretary of State in the Clinton administration. He asserted: "There is no issue related to the Arab-Israeli negotiations that is more sensitive than Jerusalem. It is precisely for this reason that any effort by Congress to bring it to the forefront is ill-advised and potentially very damaging to the success of the peace process."

His reference to 'Arab-Israeli' negotiations is revealing. In his letter, he uses the term 'Arab' in the context of achieving peace in the Middle East and in reference to Israel's neighbors. He goes on to use the now classic trope that "there are few other issues that are more likely to undermine negotiations and complicate the chances for peace than premature focus on Jerusalem".

We now know, in no uncertain terms, since President Trump's decision to recognize Jerusalem as the capital of Israel and move the Embassy there and the ensuing flourishing of the Abraham Accords that this seemingly defining principle in US Foreign affairs in the Middle East, of avoiding any commitment on the matter of Jerusalem as urged by Christopher, was just plain wrong. Not content to rest with the question of timing, he even raises the profile of the matter of Jerusalem further by arguing that it was: "perhaps the most sensitive and emotional issue for Arabs and Israelis, Muslims and Christians alike". He goes on to offer: "The enemies of peace would use the Jerusalem issue to inflame passions further and attack those who want to see the

---

[218] Letter from Warren Christopher, the Secretary of State to Senator Robert Dole, the Majority Leader, dated June 20, 1995.

negotiations succeed. Jerusalem is a powerful symbol of the hopes and aspirations of all sides. As such it has the potential to divide, to polarize, and to divert attention from the critical issues now being negotiated."

It is only after this discussion of peace in the broader frame of reference of the Middle East, generally, that Secretary of State Christopher first referenced the 'Palestinians'. He did this in the narrow context of how: 'The Palestinians and Israelis both understood this reality when they agreed in the Declaration of Principles that Jerusalem would be covered in the permanent status negotiations", which he noted was slated to begin as early as May 1996. He went on to note: "Safeguarding the negotiations is more vital than ever. This process is now entering an especially delicate period. Israelis and Palestinians have set a July 1 date for an agreement on the second phase of the Oslo accords, including an agreement on elections for the Palestinian Council." So much for his discussion of Palestinian matters; Secretary Christopher then immediately referenced the talks scheduled to occur between Israeli and Syrian Chiefs of Staff, on security issues, on June 27.

It should be noted that Secretary Christopher does not present the matter of the status of Jerusalem as central to the Palestinians in their relations with Israel; rather, it is a peripheral concern that is being preserved for the benefit of the Arab nations and even Christians of the world; and, hence, the reference to the hopes and aspirations of 'all sides', not just 'both' sides. Amazingly, he goes so far as to state that not only the Palestinians but also the Israelis are keeping the issue of Jerusalem open for this reason.

As to the Palestinians, this approach is understandable, given the position espoused in the original Palestinian National Charter that they had no claim to Jerusalem. It was a part of what was referred to as the West Bank of Jordan. As Article 24 of the Charter provides: "This Organization does not exercise any regional sovereignty over the West Bank in the Hashemite Kingdom of Jordan, on the Gaza Strip or the Himmah Area." Indeed, the Arab inhabitants of Judea and Samaria, including the portion of Jerusalem occupied by Jordan between 1948 and 1967, opted to accept Jordan's putative annexation of these areas in 1950[219] and voted for their representatives in the Jordanian legislature in Amman.

There was also the infamous speech Yasser Arafat gave in a Johannesburg Mosque when he attended the inauguration of Nelson Mandela as President of South Africa on May 10, 1994. He stated that the Jihad (Islamic Holy War) would continue and Jerusalem was not for the Palestinian people, it was for the entire Muslim nation.

Israel, though, is another matter entirely. To insinuate that somehow Israel was not vitally interested in retaining sovereignty over undivided Jerusalem as its capital is misleading. To suggest that the matter of the status of Jerusalem was left open is specious. After all, Israel had extended its sovereignty to the portions of Jerusalem liberated in the defensive war of 1967[220]. As to the western portion of Jerusalem that Israel had managed to retain in the 1948 War of Independence, it had been an integral part of Israel from its inception and in 1950[221], it was formally declared the capital of Israel. As a part of the Basic Law

---

[219] See discussion in Chapter IX, below.

[220] On June 27, 1967, the Knesset adopted an amendment to the Law and Administration Ordinance, stipulating in Article 11B that "the law, jurisdiction and administration of the state shall apply to all the area of the land of Israel which the government has determined by order." The next day, June 28, 1967, the Israeli government instituted the Law and Administration Order that applied the "law, jurisdiction and administration of the state" to the portions of Jerusalem that had been liberated in the 1967 war. The Knesset then authorized the minister of the interior to extend the boundaries of any municipality to include any area designated by government order. Accordingly, the minister of the interior expanded the borders of what had been so-called west Jerusalem to include the newly liberated portions. Israel then, by proclamation under the Municipalities Ordinance, stipulated that the annexed territory was included within the boundaries of the Jerusalem Municipality.

[221] On January 23, 1950, the Knesset declared Jerusalem the Capital of Israel.

of Jerusalem passed in 1980[222], the portions of Jerusalem that were liberated in 1967 were officially annexed and the entire and unified Jerusalem was reaffirmed as the undivided and eternal capital of Israel.

It is interesting to note how the representatives of Israel and the Palestinians thought about the matter. They bear little resemblance to the theme evoked by Secretary Christopher in his letter. Arafat, in that same 1994 infamous speech in Johannesburg noted above, declared that the Oslo Agreement of 1993 was nothing more than a temporary truce, and his goal was to take all of Israel, starting with Jerusalem. He even said he was in need of the Moslems in the Mosque audience to join as warriors of Jihad.

Israel's Prime Minister Yitzchak Rabin, who together with Arafat, signed the 1993 Oslo Agreement, was steadfast in his determination to maintain undivided Jerusalem as the capital of Israel. On October 25, 1995, he was in Washington and celebrated the passage of the Jerusalem Embassy Act the previous evening. In his speech, he said in no uncertain terms as follows:

> We differ in our opinions, left and right. We disagree on the means and the objective. In Israel, we all agree on one issue: the wholeness of Jerusalem, the continuation of its existence as capital of the State of Israel. There are no two Jerusalems. There is only one Jerusalem. For us, Jerusalem is not subject to compromise, and there is no peace without Jerusalem.

It was a beautiful heartfelt speech. Here it is reproduced[223] in full:

---

[222] On July 30, 1980, the Israeli Knesset ratified the Basic Law on Jerusalem, officially annexing the portions of the city of Jerusalem liberated in the 1967 war and declared it the eternal undivided capital of Israel, over which it exercised exclusive sovereignty.
[223] Israel Ministry of Foreign Affairs website, http://mfa.gov.il/MFA/MFA-Archive/1995/Pages/PM Rabin- Inauguration Jerusalem 3000 in Washington.aspx

Jerusalem is the heart of the Jewish people and a deep source of our pride. On this festive occasion, thousands of miles from home, here and now, we once again are raising Jerusalem above our highest joy, just like our fathers and our fathers' fathers did.

Jerusalem has a thousand faces — -- and each one of us has his own Jerusalem.

My Jerusalem is Dr. Moshe Wallach of Germany, the doctor of the sick of Israel and Jerusalem, who built Sha'arei Zedek hospital and had his home in its courtyard so as to be close to his patients day and night. I was born in his hospital. I am a Jerusalemite.

My Jerusalem is the focus of the Jewish people's yearnings, the city of its visions, the cradle of its prayers. It is the dream of the return to Zion. It is the name millions murmur, even on their deathbed. It is the place where eyes are raised and prayers are uttered.

My Jerusalem is the jerrycan of water measured out to the besieged in 1948, the faces of its anxious citizens quietly waiting in line for bread, the sky whose blackness was torn by flares.

My Jerusalem is Bab el-Wad —-- the road to the city — -- which cries out "Remember our names forever.". It is the ashen faces of dead comrades from the War of Independence, and the searing cold of the rusting armored cars among the pines on the side of the road.

My Jerusalem is the great mountain, the military cemetery on Mount Herzl, the city of silence whose earth holds the treasured thousands of those who went to bitter battle —-- and did not return.

My Jerusalem is the tears of the paratroopers at the Western Wall in 1967 and the flag which once more waved above the remnant of the Temple.

My Jerusalem is the changing colors of its walls, the smells of its markets and the faces of the members of every community and every faith, where all have freedom of thought and freedom of worship in the city where holiness envelops every stone, every word, every glance.

And my Jerusalem is the City of Peace, which will bear great tidings to all faiths, to all nations: "For the Torah shall come forth from Zion and the word of the Lord from Jerusalem... Peace be within thy walls and prosperity within thy palaces."

We differ in our opinions, left and right. We disagree on the means and the objective. In Israel, we all agree on one issue: the wholeness of Jerusalem, the continuation of its existence as capital of the State of Israel. There are no two Jerusalems. There is only one Jerusalem. For us, Jerusalem is not subject to compromise, and there is no peace without Jerusalem.

Jerusalem, which was destroyed eight times, where for years we had no access to the remnants of our Temple, was ours, is ours, and will be ours — -- forever.

"Here tears do not weaken eyes," wrote the Jerusalem poet Yehuda Amichai. "They only polish and shine the hardness of faces like stone."

Jerusalem is that stone.

It is suggested that many Christians and Muslims would also differ materially with Secretary Christopher's presumptions about the nature and extent of their concerns about Jerusalem, but more on this below.

Secretary Christopher then concluded his discussion of policy concerns before taking up his constitutional arguments with a warning that: "Few actions would be more explosive and harmful to these efforts than for the United States—as the key sponsor of this process—to be pushing the Jerusalem issue forward... The last thing we should want is for the U.S. at this very moment to put the focus back on Jerusalem."

The charade promulgated by the State Department concerning the status of Jerusalem has been going on since before Israel was reestablished in 1948, as noted above. The letter is a more nuanced albeit farcical version. The pretentious concerns about the explosive and sensitive nature of the subject are overblown and frankly have been superseded by events that belie the pronouncements.

The absurdity of the State Department's position and clarity of those like Senator Kyl and the other members of Congress, who, on a non-partisan basis, overwhelmingly approved the bill and voted it into law, is amply evidenced by what has ensued since passage of the Jerusalem Embassy Law of 1995.

Consider the concern about inappropriate timing was wholly misplaced; no real progress was made in the three years then under discussion or the almost three decades since Oslo. Jerusalem is not the essence of the issue with the Arab people living under the control of the PA and Hamas, nor is any land for peace formulation. As Charles Krauthammer, of blessed memory, wrote[224], "The issue is, and has always been, Israel's existence. That is what is at stake."

Consider, too, the entering into of the Abraham Accords and the circle of peace that it enabled, which continues to expand.

---

[224] See, Why They Fight, by Charles Krauthammer, of blessed memory, in the Washington Post, on July 14, 2006.

Whether it's former Secretary of State Kerry[225] or so many other State Department officials, few, if any, predicted this kind of extraordinary achievement. Indeed, most, like Kerry, predicted it could never occur until the PA and Hamas made peace with Israel, which they mistakenly offered was the heart of the problem in the Middle East. Their strident insistence is mystifying; it's almost as if they are addicted to this toxic and invented narrative that is belied by the reality of the situation. After all, what material interest does a resident of Gaza have in Jerusalem? In all likelihood, few, if any, ever visited there, let alone lived or owned property there and, similarly, the residents of Nablus and Hebron.

The fascination about Jerusalem is more likely premised on the nefarious attitude of denying it to the Jews, and even that affectation is beginning to wear thin among the Arab residents of Jerusalem. Indeed, a recent poll[226] found that ninety-three percent of the Arabs residing in Jerusalem polled favored continued governance by Israel over the PA, and even as to the remaining seven percent, most would not surrender their Israeli identity cards[227].

Given these indisputable factual data points, why would anyone, other than sinister PA or Hamas apparatchiks or their intersectional cohorts, antisemites, cynical or willfully ignorant dilettantes or useful dupes, cavalierly and without qualification, insist otherwise? In this regard, it is difficult to understand how

---

[225] See, for example, Why John Kerry and others were wrong about peace and Israel- analysis, by Seth Frantzman, in the Jerusalem Post, dated 9/17/2020.

[226] See, الإسرائيلي الحكم بقاء يفضلون القدس في العرب من 93% : رأي إستطلاع, at SHFA Palestinian News, dated 12/13/2021. (The title of the article translated by Google translate into English is: An opinion poll: 93% of the Arabs in Jerusalem prefer the continuation of Israeli rule).

[227] As an aside, a recent poll conducted in Gaza was also most instructive. It concluded that eighty percent of those polled blamed Hamas and the PA for the problems in Gaza, not Israel. See, Hamas, PA responsible for crises, say Gazans-poll, by Khaled Abu Toameh, in the Jerusalem Post, dated 12/23/2021.

a Brookings bi-partisan study in 2017[228] could debunk so many false myths about Israel being the source of the problems in the Middle East and yet, without coherent explanation, just cavalierly cite Jerusalem as one anomalous exception; a non sequitur, but more on this below.

The complex of biases, prejudices, false assumptions and presumptions regarding Jerusalem might fairly be categorized as a veritable syndrome. The most prevalent manifestation appears to be a fear of committing one way or the other when it comes to the sovereign status of Jerusalem. Sometimes, though, it is symptomatic of a deeper psychosis that is just another expression of Jew-hatred by denying any historical claim Jews and, by extension, Israel has to Jerusalem. The effort may be clothed in baseless assertions of non-historical false narratives or seemingly virtuous expressions of irrelevant abstract principles; however, we cannot be naïve or misled. Similarly, pious pronouncements and sentiments that bear no reasonable relationship to the actual facts and circumstances at play in Jerusalem have no probative value. The barrage of calumny is just another subterfuge to disguise or distract from what is, at its heart, just another lame attempt at denying Jerusalem or any part thereof to Israel and the Jewish people. The resort to this rubric, including the arrogant posturing, word salad of contemptible remarks and inexplicable rationales, as well as the seemingly mindless repetition of shouted slogans and unwillingness politely to debate and engage in civil discourse, is characteristic of this malaise. It may stem from a visceral dislike, deeper prejudice and even hatred of Israel and Jews. Whatever the case, it's all just a pretense that does not legally support

---

[228] Building "Situations of Strength" A National Security Strategy for the United States, Foreign Policy by Brookings, dated February 2017. Interestingly, the Bi-partisan team included Jake Sullivan, the National Security Advisor to President Biden and Martin Indyk, who served as Ambassador to Israel during the Clinton Administration and President Obama's special envoy for Israeli-Palestinian negotiations from July 2013 to June 2014.

taking Jerusalem, the capital of Israel, away from Israel, which is vested with the legal right to and actually exercises sovereignty over Jerusalem.

The Jerusalem Embassy Act of 1995 was designed to set the record straight and align the US with Israel in reaffirming Israel's sovereignty over an undivided Jerusalem and its status as Israel's capital. It did encounter resistance from the State Department from its inception. It would appear that some in power there did suffer from at least the residual effects of the Jerusalem syndrome, which had infected the State Department with the advent of the re-establishment of the State of Israel and became endemic to its institutional ethos. As more fully discussed below, the malady persists in some form even today. Being mindful of the problem is critical to dealing with it; just ignoring it does not make it disappear. One recent manifestation of the syndrome was the misguided effort to establish what amounts to a symbolic consulate in Jerusalem to the PA, but more on this below.

It is interesting to note that Senator Kyl, in a press release issued on October 13, 1995, upon formal introduction of the Bill he had originated and co-authored for passage in the Senate, addressed one of the pesky issues that continued to infect the State Department's thinking process. He declared:

> The United States is not neutral about Jewish rights in the ancient Jewish homeland or in Jerusalem. I believe the key to our diplomatic effectiveness is not our neutrality, but our power and loyalty to our friends and principles.

Secretary Christopher did raise one critically important issue in his letter regarding whether the Act, as then drafted, was constitutional. While the basis he asserted in the letter for challenging the constitutionality of the law, claiming exclusive Presidential authority in the field of foreign affairs, was not persuasive, nevertheless, as it turned out, absent the Presidential waiver, there was a real risk that it may not have passed constitutional muster, as more fully discussed below. The sponsors of the law had no way of truly knowing this at the time. It was before the Supreme Court decision in the Zivotofsky case, discussed below.

However, Christopher did not stop there. Astonishingly, Secretary Christopher ended his letter with a threat to recommend the President veto the legislation unless it satisfactorily addressed both the policy and constitutional concerns he set forth in his letter. This set in motion a series of events, which resulted in the crafting of a curative provision known as the Presidential waiver, which was embodied in the law as passed.

The concept of a Presidential waiver provision arose in a meeting among Senators Dole and Kyl, together with Senators Feinstein, Lautenberg and Levin. Dennis Ross also attended the meeting as the representative of the Clinton administration. At the time, Senators Kyl, Dole and Helms (Chairman of the Senate Foreign Relations Committee) had gathered many co-sponsors of the Bill. However, this did not assure a veto-proof majority in favor of the Bill. At the same time, the Feinstein group, who were carrying water for fellow Democrat President Clinton, sought to emasculate the bill, because the Clinton administration was against its passage and, hence, Secretary Christopher's letter.

Glenn Hamer described the highlights of the pivotal meeting to Farley shortly after it occurred. He also mentioned that coincidently on the way to the meeting, Senator Kyl saw Senator Inouye on the Senate subway. He asked him to assist with the Jerusalem Embassy legislation, and Inouye agreed to help with securing its passage. Amazingly, Senator Inouye showed up at the meeting and made an impassioned speech about the importance of the legislation to recognize Jerusalem as Israel's capital and then took his leave.

At the meeting, Glenn listened as Senator Kyl was pushing for the strongest language in the legislation, with Senator Feinstein and Lautenberg trying to water down the bill. Senator Dole, at first, was somewhat non-committal on the precise details of the bill because his primary interest was in securing a bill that would pass. Senator Lieberman ably helped fashion workable compromises between Senators Feinstein and Lautenberg, on the one hand, and Senator Kyl, on the other hand, which ultimately enabled passage of the Bill[229]. Dennis Ross, on behalf of the Clinton administration, opposed the entire legislation[230].

---

[229] It should be noted that in response to a New York Times, March 2, 1997 Week in Review article, reporting the US had not recognized Jerusalem and another article on March 4, 1997, reporting President Clinton did not believe that the US should take a position on the status of Jerusalem, Senators Jon Kyl and Joe Lieberman penned a letter to the Editor of the New York Times, dated March 5, 1997 and printed on March 9, 1997, noting a critical fact was omitted in the Times reporting, to wit: that United States Law recognized Jerusalem as the capital of Israel. They went on to write The Jerusalem Embassy Act, which passed the Senate, by a vote of 93 to 5 and passed the House, by a vote of 374 to 37, becoming law on November 8, 1995, expressly stated it is "the policy of the United States" that "Jerusalem should remain an undivided city...recognized as the capital of Israel".

[230] When it became clear that President Clinton would exercise the Waiver to delay moving the Embassy to Jerusalem beyond the original May 31, 1999 deadline specified in the Jerusalem Embassy Act, 84 Senators, on a bi-partisan basis, signed a letter, dated April 28, 1999, urging the President not to invoke the Waiver. They noted in the letter that "the establishment of the US Embassy in Jerusalem would demonstrate US support for Israel and, in particular, for Israel's national rights under international law..." They went on to write about how the conflict between Israel and its Arab antagonists was a fight over Israel's right to exist and the attacks on Israel's rights in Jerusalem were a means of trying to delegitimize Israel, generally. They noted that the US would promote the US's interests in security and peace in the region if the US rejected, without equivocation, any effort to redivide Jerusalem or to divide the US from Israel regarding Jerusalem. They further noted that unrealistic expectations on the Palestinian side about Jerusalem were harmful to the prospects for peace and the Administration's refusal to comply with the Jerusalem Embassy Act tended to feed such unconstructive expectations. The letter went on to discuss how the Act provided the President with only limited flexibility to exercise the Waiver, so as not to harm the US' national security interests; not because the President simply felt is was better not to move the Embassy or delay the move. The bi-partisan leadership of the House also wrote a letter to President Clinton, dated July 20, 1999, expressing disappointment with the President's exercise of the Waiver and noting that the Waiver provision was limited to the move of the Embassy and did not apply to the other provisions of the Act. The explicit statement of US policy contained in the Act regarding Jerusalem that Jerusalem

Eventually, Senator Dole intervened and asked Senators Feinstein and Lautenberg whether they would vote in favor of the legislation if he gave in on the waiver presidential waiver provision. Feinstein and Lautenberg agreed to support the legislation if the waiver was put in.

Senator Kyl reluctantly agreed to it because it meant the legislation would have a veto-proof majority. Kyl did clarify that the waiver was to be a narrow one[231], used only for national security purposes. It was not to be employed, as it ultimately was, as tantamount to an automatic default option. The requirement that the waiver be used only for reasons of national security was embodied in the Law, as passed, as follows:

SEC. 7. PRESIDENTIAL WAIVER.

(a) WAIVER AUTHORITY.—(1) Beginning on October 1, 1998, the President may suspend the limitation set forth in section 3(b) for a period of six months if he determines and reports to Congress in advance that such suspension is necessary to protect the national security interests of the United States.

(2) The President may suspend such limitation for an additional six month period at the end of any period during which the suspension is in effect under this subsection if

---

should remain united and recognized as Israel's capital was the law of the land and could not be waived. They urged the Administration to make a clear statement acknowledging this policy as the law of the land and vigorously to pursue this approach in relation to Jerusalem. Interestingly, First Lady Hillary Rodham Clinton, in a departure from her husband the President's non-committal position reportedly said she considered Jerusalem to be the "eternal and indivisible capital of Israel" and would actively advocate for the U.S. embassy move to Jerusalem, if elected to the Senate. (See First lady supports Jerusalem as capital of Israel, a report, contributed to by Bruce Morton and Sharona Schwartz, at CNN.com, dated 7/9/1999.)

[231] Kyl also reportedly discussed how the waiver provision was only to apply to moving the Embassy, but not to recognizing Jerusalem as Israel's capital. It would appear this fine distinction was ignored. As more fully discussed below, given the Constitutional concerns, this may have turned out to be for the best.

the President determines and reports to Congress in advance of the additional suspension that the additional suspension is necessary to protect the national security interests of the United States.

(3) A report under paragraph (1) or (2) shall include—(A) a statement of the interests affected by the limitation that the President seeks to suspend; and (B) a discussion of the manner in which the limitation affects the interests.

While past Presidents paid lip service to compliance with the letter of the Law by invoking what amounted to formulaic recitations of national security concerns, there was no serious effort made fully to re-analyze those concerns, from time to time, to see whether they truly still necessitated not moving the Embassy. In practice, the waiver provision was used as a means of evading the effectuation of the spirit and intent of the Law, that is, until President Trump was elected.

Ironically, the Presidential waiver provision likely saved the law from being challenged and held to be unconstitutional. In this regard, it should be noted that the reason urged by the Secretary of State for opposing the proposed law as originally drafted, on constitutional grounds, was rejected by the Court in the Zivotofsky case, as more fully discussed below. The Court applied a different and much more limited standard in that case, and the issue it raised was cured by the Presidential waiver provision.

As to the policy concerns Christopher raised, they were, in effect, rejected because the substantive provisions of the law otherwise remained unchanged. It was only the interposition of the Presidential waiver that temporarily prevented the execution of the law for national security reasons, as more fully outlined below.

This is a classic example of how man proposes, but G-d disposes[232]. The Clinton administration and their Senate cohorts thought that they had effectively killed the legislation by neutering it with the Presidential waiver provision. However, they could not have predicted that President Trump would be elected and would put together a team of talented and world-wise realists, like Ambassador David Friedman and Special Envoy Jason Dov Greenblatt. They would challenge the misbegotten institutional ethos of the State Department. The result was the President elected not to exercise the Presidential waiver, and an extraordinary outcome was achieved. This occurred despite the dreadful predictions of the old guard State Department cadres, who continued to hold on to their institutional myths that had proven false.

Bewilderingly, Senator Feinstein also stridently objected to President Trump's election not to exercise the waiver[233] and urged him not to recognize Jerusalem as the capital of Israel. She argued that doing so would spark violence and further alienate the United States, and undermine the prospects for a two-state solution. These were the same old arguments and predictions of dire consequences that had been asserted by the State Department doyens over the years. She did reference a newer trope about Sharon's visit to the Temple Mount sparking the Second Intifada, but that was discredited. As the Palestinian Communications Minister, Imad Al-Faluji, said[234]:

> Whoever thinks that the Intifada broke out because of the despised Sharon's visit to the Al-Aqsa Mosque[235] is wrong... The Intifada was planned in advance, ever since President Arafat's return from the Camp David

---

[232] Proverbs 19:21.
[233] Letter from Senator Dianne Feinstein to President Donald Trump, dated December 1, 2017.
[234] Al-Safir on 3/2/201, as translated by MEMRI.
[235] It should be noted that while Sharon visited the Temple Mount, he did not visit the Al-Aqsa Mosque.

negotiations, where he turned the table upside down on President Clinton.

The Mitchell Report[236] also concluded that the Sharon visit did not cause the Second Intifada. The visit may have been the excuse offered, but it had been planned well in advance.

Senator Feinstein then perplexingly argued that for fifty years, Democratic and Republican Presidents alike had chosen not to recognize Jerusalem as Israel's capital in order to remain impartial. It was almost as if she had a virulent case of amnesia, forgetting her bi-partisan role in passage of the Jerusalem Embassy Act, which stood at loggerheads with the obtuse position she was now espousing. It is astonishing that she warned President Trump against breaking a long tradition of bi-partisan foreign policy when it was she who was doing so by urging President Trump not to follow the plain meaning of the bi-partisan Jerusalem Embassy Act she had helped pass more than two decades before.

It was also presumptuous to speak of eroding American credibility as an unbiased mediator, inasmuch as it insinuates that the United States is a neutral third party that doesn't have its own personal interest in the matter or a relationship with any of the disputants. This is clearly not the case, and the very premise was, in effect, contradicted by another concern Senator Feinstein raised in her letter about how it would alienate the US's international partners such as Jordan. The concern turned out to be baseless. It wholly discounted the fact that Arab nations in the

---

[236] Sharm El-Sheikh Fact-Finding Committee Report- "Mitchell Report", dated April 30, 2001, addressed to President George W. Bush, which examined the causes of the outbreak and long and sustained period of violence by Palestinians that began at the end of September of 2000 and became known as the Second Intifada. The Intifada occurred in the wake of the failure of the July 2000 Camp David Summit, due to the refusal of Arafat to accede to the generous peace offer made by Israel and reach a permanent settlement with Israel. As noted below, President Clinton correctly blamed Arafat for the failure (See, Clinton to Arafat: It's All Your Fault, by Michael Hirsh, in Newsweek, dated 6/26/2001).

region need the US as an ally and friend, especially because of the threat posed by the Iranian regime and its proxies.

This whole approach also ignores the reality that posturing as an unbiased mediator when everyone knows this is not the case does much to harm US prestige and credibility. The charade and mixed messaging it engenders also undermine trust in the US as an ally, a much more serious concern. It calls into question the reliability of the US and its commitments, where credibility is essential. It also misapprehends one of the most important and meaningful predicates to serving any effective role in resolving a dispute involving a friend and ally, which is first to be a faithful and dependable friend and ally. If that threshold condition is not satisfied, then there is little hope any of the parties will truly trust the US.

Flirting with enemies of Israel and the US, like the PA and Hamas, and insinuating that the US/Israel alliance is malleable does not enhance the US' prestige and national security. It only makes the U.S. more prone to manipulation by ruthless enemies, who perceive the US to be a dilettante, not pursuing its vital interests; but rather flitting about trying to endear itself to everyone, including actual enemies devoted to programs antithetical to the US and its ally Israel.

The US' penchant for making friends with erstwhile enemies was easily abused and often misunderstood. Some continued to be real enemies and perceived the US' generous overture as an enhanced opportunity for deception and artifice. Others misinterpreted the offer of friendship as a ruse, and it only served to deepen their suspicions that the US had some hidden agenda. After all, why pursue such an irrational course of action given the reality of the ideological and actual antipathy of the PA and Hamas to the US and Israel?

The President had a choice; he could act like a serious player genuinely concerned about the fate of a friend and ally and doing what was just and right, as the Jerusalem Embassy Act intended or not. The President could easily have given in to shameless pressure. He could have continued to miscast the US in the role it had for so long played as a duplicitous and frankly dishonest broker. The US would then have continued to be susceptible to being manipulated by nefarious forces who sought to undermine what was just and proper and in the US' own interests.

President Trump did not take the bait and revert to the kind of impotent policies of the past borne of weakness and reactive leadership. Instead, President Trump boldly embraced the tenets of the Jerusalem Embassy Act of 1995 and pursued a focused, purposeful and affirmative program, which demonstrated in no uncertain terms that being a friend and ally of the US meant something.

Building on the tangible recognition of undivided Jerusalem as the capital of Israel and moving the embassy there, that had for so long unreasonably been denied to Israel, President Trump and his team went on to construct a circle of trust and peace with other Middle Eastern nations premised on that new reality. The timing was impeccable because the strengthened nexus of the US and Israel promised to be a genuine bulwark of defense, to which other nations could and did latch unto, against the very real threat the terrorist regime ruling Iran and its proxies posed to the Middle East. The relationships that emerged under the Abraham Accords are a testament to the wisdom of those policies and the paucity of the prior flawed ones advocated by Feinstein and her old State Department cronies.

Interestingly, even Dan Shapiro, Ambassador to Israel in the Obama administration and Senator Feinstein's foreign policy advisor at the time of the Jerusalem Embassy Act of 1995, involved in negotiating the Presidential waiver, sensed a positive change had occurred and had another take on the matter. In an article in Foreign Policy[237] magazine, he outlined his blueprint for how President Trump might move the Embassy to Jerusalem without, as he wrote, wrecking hopes for Israeli-Palestinian peace.

He began the article by noting that in his five years serving as U.S. Ambassador to Israel, whenever he spoke before an Israeli audience, the first or second question was always about when the U.S. would move its embassy to Jerusalem. In answer, Shapiro explained the Jerusalem Embassy Act of 1995 required it; but there was a Presidential waiver feature that permitted the President to delay the move of the Embassy if the President determined that it was in the national security interest of the US.

Shapiro wrote that he 'supported all three presidents' use of their national security waiver authority to delay the move in the interest of pursuing Middle East peace'. However, he said that he "never believed that arguments for moving the embassy were groundless, or that it must await a final Israeli-Palestinian peace agreement". Shapiro then went on to explain:

> I'm influenced by my love of Jerusalem — an emotional attachment born of decades studying its history — and sense of justice for Jewish claims to the city that are far too often called into question. The presence of a U.S. Embassy in parts of Jerusalem no one disputes are Israeli territory is one way of acknowledging the centuries of history that link the Jewish people to the city, the questioning of which is closely linked to the denial of Israel's very legitimacy.

As to the details, Shapiro could not bring himself to adopt the clean break with the past failed policies, which President Trump's lead-from-strength plan envisioned. Be that as it may, President Trump's plan worked. It is a testament to the prescience and wisdom of Senator Kyl and others, who

---

[237] So You Want to Move the U.S. Embassy to Jerusalem? Here's How, by Daniel B. Shapiro, in Foreign Policy, dated January 31, 2017.

challenged the almost mindless adherence by the State Department to false myths and ideological presumptions. They worked so tirelessly to bring their genuine appreciation of reality and program of what was just and right to fruition and were rewarded with success.

This is a rare tale of manifest karma in action, where the group trying to spike the ball, as proponents of the Presidential waiver provision, likely helped get it across the goal line. They first, in effect, saved the Act from a constitutional challenge and possible veto. Then the provision enabled the Act to continue to operate, as successive administrations casually exercised the veto. This assured an opportunity for the day that would finally come when President Trump recognized Jerusalem as the capital of Israel and caused the Embassy to be moved there.

Along the way, there were those, like Congressman Ron DeSantis, who would shine light on the law to determine whether there was full compliance with its provisions. However, for the most part, it just lay dormant, waiting patiently for the right moment when it could be fully activated under President Trump. Once that occurred, it became the indisputable law of the land that could no longer be changed by Presidential fiat, as more fully discussed below.

To Senator Feinstein's credit, when the Senate voted decisively that the Embassy could not be moved from Jerusalem at the beginning of the Biden administration, she was one of those who did vote in favor. The Resolution passed the Senate nearly unanimously[238].

On October 23, 1995, Senator Dole proposed the Amendment[239] to the bill[240], which included the Presidential waiver provision.

---

[238] By vote of the Senate 97-3 on February 5, 2021.
[239] Congressional Record-Senate Volume 141, Issue 164 (Monday October 23, 1995), pages S15494-S15495.
[240] Which also changed the name from the 'Jerusalem Embassy Relocation

Senator Kyl, in his introductory remarks upon presentation of the final version of the legislation that day for formal discussion and final passage in the Senate, alluded to the sausage-making process involved as a prelude to this historical moment. It was a most worthy effort. The legislation was ultimately passed by the Senate and the House the next day, on October 24, 1995, with a resounding near-unanimous vote of 93-5 in the Senate and 374-37 in the House. The Act became law, without presidential signature, on November 8, 1995.

Senator Kyl's speech[241] on October 23, 1995, upon beginning the formal consideration of the Bill, is a treasure trove that includes findings of material facts, cogent analysis and reasoned conclusions. He began by noting:

> This is historic legislation. It is important legislation for a variety of reasons that affect everyone in this body and, frankly, most of the people in this country. It is a strong statement of foreign policy implications. It is a strong statement in support of our longstanding relationship with the State of Israel.

> I want to begin by describing briefly what the legislation would do and what the rationale for the legislation is. The bill begins by making a series of findings which report on the history of the status of Jerusalem, leading up to some conclusions of policy by the U.S. Government. Let me state those conclusions of policy first.

The bill provides that:

> It is the policy of the United States that-Jerusalem should remain an undivided city in which the rights of every ethnic religious group are protected; Jerusalem should be recognized as the capital of the State of Israel; and the

---

Implementation Act of 1995' to its enduring name, the 'Jerusalem Embassy Act of 1995'.

[241] Congressional Record-Senate, October 23, 1995, at pages 28961-28963.

United States Embassy in Israel should be relocated to Jerusalem no later than May 31, 1999.

The bill then goes on to provide a mechanism for the President to establish, to relocate the U.S. Embassy in Jerusalem, and that that process would be completed by May 31, 1999. The bill originally provided for a beginning date in 1996, but out of deference to concerns expressed by the State Department and the President and others, that particular provision was taken out of the bill, primarily because, of course, the key is the date that the Embassy is opened, not the date that we begin construction on a new Embassy or the conversion of the existing consulate into a new Embassy.

Senator Kyl then turned to the findings that are stated in the legislation, as follows:

1. Each sovereign nation, under international law and custom, may designate its own capital and since 1950, the city of Jerusalem has been the capital of the State of Israel.

2. The city of Jerusalem is the seat of Israel's President, Parliament, and Supreme Court

3. The city of Jerusalem is also the site of numerous government ministries and social and cultural institutions of Israel.

4. The city of Jerusalem is the spiritual center of Judaism, and is also considered a holy city by the members of other religious faiths.

5. From 1948-1967, Jerusalem was a divided city and Israeli citizens of all faiths as well as Jewish citizens of all states were denied access to holy sites in the area controlled [then] by Jordan.

6. In 1967, the city of Jerusalem was reunited during the conflict known as the Six Day War.

7. Since 1967, Jerusalem has been a united city administered by Israel, and persons of all religious faiths have been guaranteed full access to holy sites within the city.

8. This year marks the 28th consecutive year that Jerusalem has been administered as a unified city in which the rights of all faiths have been respected and protected.

9. In 1990 the Congress unanimously adopted Senate Concurrent Resolution 106, which declares that the Congress, [and I am quoting from the resolution now] "strongly believes that Jerusalem must remain an undivided city in which the rights of every ethnic religious group are protected."

10. In 1992, the United States Senate and House of Representatives unanimously adopted Senate Concurrent Resolution 113 of the One Hundred Second Congress to commemorate the 25th anniversary of the reunification of Jerusalem, and reaffirming congressional sentiment that Jerusalem must remain an undivided city.

11. The September 13, 1993, Declaration of Principles on Interim Self-Government Arrangements lays out a timetable for the resolution of "final status" issues, including Jerusalem.

12. The agreement on the Gaza Strip and the Jericho Area was signed on May 4, 1994, beginning the five-year transitional period laid out in the Declaration of Principles.

13. In March of 1995, 93 members of the United States Senate signed a letter to the Secretary of State Warren Christopher encouraging "planning to begin now" for relocation of the United States Embassy to the city of Jerusalem[242].

14. The United States maintains its embassy in the functioning capital of every country in the world except in the case of our democratic friend and strategic ally, the State of Israel.

15. The United States conducts official meetings and other business in the city of Jerusalem in de facto recognition of its status as the capital of Israel.

16. In 1996, the State of Israel will celebrate the 3,000th anniversary of the Jewish presence in Jerusalem since King David's entry.

He then noted that the legislation, as a result of these findings, therefore, declared it to be the policy of the United States that:

1. Jerusalem should remain an undivided city;

2. Jerusalem should be recognized as the capital of the State of Israel; and

3. The United States Embassy in Israel should be relocated to Jerusalem no later than May 31, 1999.

As the mechanism for ensuring that this policy is adhered to, and that the Embassy is in fact opened on that date or before then, the Congress ensures that: Not more than 50 percent of the funds appropriated to the Department of State for fiscal year 1999 for

---

[242] The Act also refers to the fact that, in June of 1993, 257 members of the U.S. House of Representatives signed a letter to Secretary of State Warren Christopher stating that the relocation of the U.S. Embassy to Jerusalem should take place no later than 1999.

"Acquisition and Maintenance of Buildings Abroad" may be obligated until the Secretary of State determines and reports to the Congress that the United States Embassy in Jerusalem has officially opened.

Senator Kyl then summarized some of the history of Jerusalem and the US Government's position on the matter so as he said to assure everyone of the reasons why it is so important to recognize Israel's sovereignty over an undivided Jerusalem as its capital, to move the US Embassy there and to do all this now. He noted that:

> The United States Government had refused official recognition of Israeli sovereignty in Jerusalem for various reasons since Israel's inception, at first in line with the never implemented 1947 U.N. General Assembly partition recommendation for western Palestine. U.S. policy supported a special international status, corpus separatum, as it was called, for the city of Jerusalem. The impractical notion actually appealed to neither the Jews nor the Arabs, and in 1948, the Arab Legion conquered east Jerusalem, including the old city, as part of the general Arab military offensive to prevent Israel from coming in to being. Israel retained control over west Jerusalem.

> When east Jerusalem was under Arab rule, many Jews were prohibited from visiting their holy places and the synagogues in the old city were razed and Jewish burial places were desecrated.

> In 1967, as Egypt and Syria moved again toward war with Israel, the Israel Government urged King Hussein of Jordan to sit out the fighting and promised the territories he controlled would be left alone if he did so. The King failed to heed the warning. He attacked Israel and, as we all know, in the ensuing fighting he lost east Jerusalem and the West Bank.

Israel, under the Labor Party leadership at the time, declared that Jerusalem will remain undivided forever, as Israel's capital, and all people will have free access to their holy places.

Since 1967, the policy and practice of the U.S. Government regarding Jerusalem has, unfortunately, been somewhat inconsistent.

United States officials have often explained our Government's unwillingness to recognize Israeli sovereignty over any of Jerusalem on the grounds that the city status should be resolved through Arab-Israeli negotiations, or at that particular moment in time it was difficult, if not a good thing to do, in view of the relationships existing between the parties at those times.

On the other hand, our Government has repeatedly said that we do not favor redivision of the city. Yet, the State Department makes a point of prohibiting United States officials from visiting east Jerusalem under Israeli auspices. In other words, for purposes of official visits of Jerusalem, the United States Government distinguishes between east and west Jerusalem. But as proposals have been made over the years to move the United States Embassy to west Jerusalem — I note west Jerusalem and not east Jerusalem — the State Department refused on the grounds that we do not distinguish between east and west Jerusalem, and do not recognize anyone's sovereign claims to any of Jerusalem.

The only thing consistent about United States policy on Jerusalem, unfortunately, is its antagonism to Israel's claim there. In my view, this policy is unprincipled, notwithstanding the fact that on many occasions it was urged in support of positions on which we were supporting the Government of Israel. But I still believe, and I think one of the reasons for this legislation is, that the policy has not been viewed as principled, but rather entirely too pragmatic depending upon the circumstances of the time, and that view, in my personal opinion, is unworthy of the United States, and, frankly, as I will explain later, I believe unhelpful to the cause of peace.

Notwithstanding the several peace agreements that Israel has signed with its neighbors, Arab enemies of the Jewish state continue to insist that Israel is not legitimate, that it has no right to exist on what they deem to be Arab land. The international community, acting through the League of Nations and in the United Nations, based its acknowledgement of Jewish people's national rights in Palestine on the historical connection of the Jewish people with Palestine.

Though the long war against Zionism and Israel is now checked on the military level, it continues on the battlefield of ideas. That is why the actions of the United States with regard to a very tangible matter, the location of our Embassy, is so very, very important. It matters what position the United States takes in this battleground of ideas. And in this particular war, Israel's enemies have worked to not legitimize Israel, to deny the significance of the historical connection that I referred to before between the Jews and Zion, and to foster hope that someday Israel, perhaps then abandoned by its friends and exhausted by the unremitting hostility and violence of its foes, can be made to disappear, first as the Christian Crusaders of the Middle Ages wore worn down and ultimately expelled from the Holy Land.

The belief that Israel's friends are unreliable and Israel's resolve is weak is a major impediment to true Arab-Israeli peace. Unrealistic expectations on the part of Arab parties about Jerusalem make peace harder to achieve.

The Jerusalem Embassy relocation bill aims to close the question of United States support for Israel's rights in its own capital. I want to restate the point, Mr. President, because it is the critical reason why this legislation is brought before the U.S. Senate and the House of Representatives at this time. This bill, the Jerusalem Embassy relocation bill, aims to close the question of United States support for Israel's rights in its own capital. It aims at the heart of the legitimacy issue, for Jerusalem is the essence of the historical connection of the Jewish people with Palestine. The interest of peace, in my view, is not served by anyone thinking that Israel can be divided from the United States over the Jerusalem issue. It is an error to suppose the United States is more effective diplomatically when we pose as a neutral, honest broker between the Israelis and the Arabs seeking peace in the region.

U.S. influence does not derive from any claim of neutrality on our part in this particular conflict, although it is important that Arabs interested in peace understand the important bona fides of the United States in this question of peace. Rather, U.S. influence, I submit, derives from our status as a great power, the intensity of our worthy convictions, and our loyalty to our friends. And, if all three of those circumstances are well understood by all of the parties, it will be much easier for a true and lasting peace to be achieved, a peace which is so fragile that it can be jeopardized by the question of whether the United States should relocate its Embassy to west Jerusalem, a peace which is bound to fail on other grounds and, therefore, a peace not worth having. We want a lasting peace. The Israelis want a lasting peace. And I know that Arabs of good will want a lasting peace. And a lasting peace is based upon a bedrock of good faith and principles that are not inconsistent between the peace-making parties.

If there are fundamental-fundamental-differences between the peace-making parties, then the peace becomes too fragile to be sustained. And after thousands of years of conflict in this region, Mr. President, the people of this region deserve to have the opportunity to live in peace with each other as friends and under circumstances in which there is not always the cloud of uncertainty and even war and when there is not the cloud of danger in the streets which exists as it does today.

The many, many people of this body and the House of Representatives which support this legislation do so because we believe it will send a principled and constructive signal to all of the parties in the Arab-Israeli negotiations and establish the United States position in support of the State of Israel in clear and unmistakable terms.

Mr. President, before I turn the podium over, I want to acknowledge a couple of other points of view and some people who have been very instrumental in bringing this legislation forward.

The majority leader, Senator Dole, has made stirring speeches in support of this legislation and believes in his heart that it is the best way to proceed in order to make the kind of statement that I spoke of a moment ago. And he is joined by all of the original cosponsors with that idea in mind.

There are other Members of this body who have worked very hard to develop the language that would be most satisfactory to the Members of this body as well as to the President and to his Cabinet. Senator Lieberman from Connecticut is one of the people who has worked very long and hard to bring these ideas together and to try to achieve a very broad consensus so that when this legislation passes, it is with a broad bipartisan degree of support and, hopefully, the support of the administration as well.

Senator Dianne Feinstein, who is here, the Senator from California, and Senator Lautenberg from New Jersey have been engaged in meetings. They have to some degree a somewhat different point of view as to how this legislation will work out in terms of the negotiations that are currently pending between the Israelis and the Arabs in the region. But it is their desire, no less than mine and the other cosponsors, that we work toward the day when we can achieve the situation that this bill would achieve-namely, the relocation of the Embassy in Jerusalem.

So let there be no doubt that, though some Members of this body may have somewhat different views as to how best to achieve this objective, we are united in the objective, and we are determined to reach a point where the legislation can move forward with a strong bipartisan degree of consensus and eventually the support of the administration.

Senator Feinstein spoke next that day and, true to form, she voiced the administration's concerns about timing and the peace process with Israel's neighbors, as well as the threats of a veto and constitutional challenge[243]. Her sensitivity about the need to avoid the possibility of having "a divisive vote on an issue around which there has always been a consensus and to go through the unpleasantness of a veto confrontation, even with a successful override vote, would not be to anyone's benefit" is understandable and even laudatory. So too, was the basis she

---

[243] Lest there be any doubt about who and what informed Senator Feinstein's position, she noted the expertise of Dennis Ross and her being present at Martin Indyk's confirmation hearing, who echoed many of these concerns. She also introduced into the record a Department of Justice legal memo to Abner J. Mikva, counsel to the President in opposition to the bill, as well as, the Secretary Christopher Letter to Senator Robert Dole, discussed above.

gave for the Presidential waiver provision, which had been inserted in the bill, as noted above, so as to cure any constitutional infirmity and avoid a veto. As she well stated, "The concern expressed then that the original bill might precipitate a difficult situation I think has been remedied".

Senator Feinstein's opinion as to what might constitute a national security interest, a required predicate for exercising the Presidential waiver, is another matter. It did not conform to the definition that Senators Dole and Kyl outlined in their colloquy on the subject, as outlined below. She offered that she and perhaps some other Senators would agree that the conclusion of a comprehensive peace process between Israel and its neighbors came within the definition of a U.S. national interest sufficient to permit the President to exercise the Presidential waiver. Senators Kyl and Dole and at least the sixty other co-sponsors of the Act, who had signed on prior to insertion of the Presidential waiver provision, as well as many others, as Senator Feinstein recognized, likely disagreed with the substance of this broader interpretation suggested by Senator Feinstein. Their understanding was the meaning of what constituted a national security interest was much more limited. She did, however, agree:

> So Jerusalem's status as Israel's capital has never been in question here. The debate is, instead, focused on a side debate to the central issue, the placement of the Embassy, and I, like my colleagues, believe there is basic agreement in this body, and I share the view of my colleagues, that the United States Embassy in Israel does, indeed, belong in Jerusalem. It is elementary that a sovereign nation, as I have pointed out, has that right to place an Embassy at the site of a nation's capital with whom it enjoys diplomatic relations.

She went on to say:

125

So I am looking for a way that we can indicate the rights of the sovereign nation by saying that we should place our Embassy in Jerusalem, that it should be the policy of the Congress that Jerusalem is the capital and that Jerusalem should remain undivided, without presenting a provocation in what I think is the most important process for peace ongoing, certainly, in the history of the Middle East.

Senator Kyl then responded to the substance of Senator Feinstein's remarks and made a very insightful and compelling presentation, as follows:

Mr. President, let me make a couple of very brief comments before I take my place in the chair. I respect the views presented by the Senator from California. I will make additional comments with respect to the issue of the waiver as follows:

One of the problems that we have had with this issue, generally, and one of the reasons why Senator Moynihan brought his letter to the Senate, and why all of us have been pursuing legislation now to actually bring a close to the issue and make it clear that we will move our Embassy to Jerusalem, is that the United States has always found a reason not to do it. At the time, those seemed like valid positions. Obviously, we would not want a waiver to provide a mechanism for continued lip service to the concept without actually moving toward the actual relocation of the Embassy. That is why there has been some question about how waiver language should be inserted into the bill.

Also, there is some oddity, I think, in the matter that locating our Embassy in a country's capital would actually be deemed to be contrary to the national security interest of the United States. It seems to me that one has to stretch it a little bit to find that to be the case. Yet, I know there are those who believe that, even at this point in time, that is exactly the case. I think it is important that if there is to be some kind of waiver, it not be a waiver that the President can exercise because he has a policy dispute with the Congress on when and under what circumstances the Embassy should be moved. Such a waiver should be exercised by the President only because he finds that the national security interests of the United States require that. And the security of the United States is not necessarily the same as peace in the Middle East, which is not necessarily the same as a controversy between Arabs and Israelis over the status of peace discussions. So simply because it makes some Arabs anxious or angry, or gives them a political issue, is not, I think, a reason why such a waiver would ever be exercised.

I also think it is important that the whole world understand one point very clearly and I think, on this, we are united that when we talk about the final status of Jerusalem, which is subject to negotiation between the parties there, no one should suffer under any illusion that the United States feels itself bound not to locate our Embassy in West Jerusalem pending the outcome of those negotiations. The State of Israel's rights with respect to west Jerusalem, and our obligations and entitlements to put our Embassy in west Jerusalem, are in no way dependent on those final negotiations which do not go to the political status of west Jerusalem insofar as the Israelis are concerned.

To the point of the constitutional concerns alluded to by the Senator from California, there are differing opinions on this. I am a very strong advocate of the power of the President in this regard. I do not come lightly to the point of view that Congress has a prerogative in this case to require the relocation of the Embassy. I think it is good that the Record contain both the arguments in support of the Presidential and congressional power in that regard. I am delighted to see them both included in the Record at the conclusion of this debate.

I think it is important that the understanding be with all parties that whatever kind of waiver language may or may not be included in this bill, it is a temporary waiver only. We are not talking about the ability of the President to simply continue year after year after year, saying, gee, I am really with you on this, but I think I find a reason why we do not want to do it right now. That is the intent of any waiver. I know that is not what the Senator from California was saying.

Should there by any waiver language included, I want it to be crystal clear on the record that nobody is talking about a waiver which, however open-ended it may or may not be, would allow a President, every 6 months, to simply say that because he has a different point of view than Congress on this, he is going to refuse to implement what the Congress has directed him to do, finding that there is somehow a national security interest of the United States involved.

Mr. President, I conclude by making this point. I think the importance of this issue is illustrated by the fact that we have had difficulty in arriving at the exact language because everybody is concerned about what the impact of it will be. Those are very legitimate concerns. I am going to conclude by addressing myself to those concerns. This is not a tangential issue. It is symbolic in one respect, but sometimes symbolism is extraordinarily important. In this case it is, regardless of how you come down on this issue. If you are an Arab, for example, one can argue that this would make you very anxious and concerned. Therefore, the symbolism of it is very important. There are those, in fact, who believe that it would be so distressing to certain

Arabs if the United States exercises its legitimate right to put our Embassy where we want to, particularly since it is the capital of the host country, and that should not be considered to be a policy matter with respect to our position in these negotiations. But the fact of the matter is that some people will see it as that. Nobody should be allowed to use in a political campaign or in the conduct of terrorism, or in negotiations-the fact that a country like the United States exercises its right to put its Embassy in the capital of the host country. That is not a legitimate concern.

So while I understand the politics of it, that is different from the legitimacy of the issue.

The final point is this: Some people have said, well, even though it is an irrational and illegitimate argument, people will make it. As a result, it could bring a halt to the peace negotiations even. People might stop talking peace. There may be more demonstrations over this, even though it is not a legitimate position to be taken.

I will respond to that in this fashion because it goes to the heart of the debate. No one knows for sure. That is a very legitimate concern among those of us who are very, very supportive of the peace process and want it to succeed. Certainly, the people in the region feel that much more even than any of us in this body can.

I think it is also important to reflect upon the history of U.S. foreign policy and to note that every time the United States has been firm, fair, resolute, principled, consistent in its investigation of friendships and positions in the world, the world has been better off for that firm, principled expression.

It did not always suit nervous nellies during the cold war, that Presidents like President Reagan made firm statements about our commitments, calling the Soviet Union what at that time it was and many Russians since have confirmed. Sure, in many respects it was an evil empire. It made people very nervous when President Reagan said it. Many people say had the United States not taken firm positions, had President Reagan not spoken so clearly, that evil empire would still exist today. Had we not made it crystal clear to the Chinese that they could not invade Quemoy and Matsu Islands back in the 1960s, they might have done so. Had we made it clearer to Hitler that he would not get away with an attack on Poland, perhaps he would not have done so.

Mr. President, our history is replete with examples of situations in which history has shown that the world frequently was thrown into conflict in which great human suffering and loss resulted because leaders at the time were not firm enough and clear enough in the expression of the principles that stood behind their country's positions. In this case, I think a firm, clear statement of something as simple as the United States exercising its right to put its Embassy in the capital of a country as we have with every other country in the world except Jerusalem, I think to the extent that the United States makes that statement very clearly, we advance the ultimate cause of fundamental peace, a peace that is lasting. To that extent, I think it is important that we do that prior to the time that those negotiations are to be concluded.

I think that deals generally with the waiver issue however that issue is ultimately resolved[244].

A number of Senators spoke in support of the legislation and offered many cogent insights. Set forth below are just a few of

[244] Senator Kyl introduced into the Record, the Doug Feith's editorial, entitled, To Promote Peace, Move the Embassy, in the New York Times, dated May 29, 1995, summarized above.

their remarks. What is especially noteworthy is the strong bipartisan consensus and support for the bill and its objectives.

Senator Helms, for example, noted:

> The Government of Israel has asserted that Jerusalem is and will remain the capital of Israel. The dire warnings being heard that the peace process will be endangered are, in fact, threats. The peace process will be dismantled only if and when Yasir Arafat wants to dismantle it.

He went on to say:

> Like many of my colleagues, I have had the privilege of visiting Jerusalem on many occasions. I have seen the many holy sites which make Jerusalem the cradle of three of the world's largest religions-Judaism, Christianity, and Islam-and an inspiration to us all.

> I have also seen the bombed out buildings in West Jerusalem that stand just outside the wall of the Old City-buildings which were shelled during the time of the Jordanian occupation of East Jerusalem. Those buildings serve as a constant reminder of the sacrifices endured by the Jewish people from 1947 to 1967 when Jews were denied access to the holy sites in East Jerusalem; and a reminder that the world must never allow the citizens of Israel-and indeed Jews around the world-to be subjected to such suffering again.

> Mr. President, Israel is our strong friend and ally in the Middle East. As the only democracy in the region, this brave nation stands as a symbol of hope for millions. The people of Israel claim Jerusalem as their capital. This is their right. Their choice should be honored. America should recognize that Jerusalem is, and will remain, the undivided and permanent capital of the State of Israel.

Senator Snow reflected on the issue of timing. He noted:

Some may argue that now is not the time for us to establish a firm policy on the eventual location of the U.S. Embassy in Jerusalem. The irony, of course, is that it appears that for 47 straight years the State Department has never yet found precisely the right moment to take this commonsense action. All we are saying in this legislation is that we are giving State 4 years in which they certainly can find an appropriate time.

She went on to analyze the source of the problem as follows:

Only in the sometimes fantastic politics of the Middle East could this issue even be considered remarkable. It is a simple fact that Jerusalem — or at least some part of Jerusalem-has been Israel's capital city ever since Israel's 1948 war for independence. Observing this fact is no different than observing that the sun rises in the east. And trying to deny the act does not make it any less true.

This takes us to a potentially troubling aspect of the State Department's consistent refusal to recognize Jerusalem as Israel's capital. This policy originated from the days of the U.N. partition plan ending Britain's colonial mandate over the region. That plan envisioned the establishment of Jerusalem as an international city not under the sovereignty of any nation. The U .N. partition plan of 1947, however, was never implemented due to its total rejection by the Arab countries because it would have split the British protectorate into a Jewish and Arab state. Thus, the State Department continues to cling to a formal position refusing to acknowledge Israel's sovereignty over any part of Jerusalem.

The only, and I repeat only possible justification for such a position would be if the State Department believed that Israeli sovereignty over even west Jerusalem was illegitimate, and that Israel must cede the entire city to an Arab state or to international control.

If our country does not take this position, we have no more right maintaining our Embassy in Tel Aviv than we do insisting on maintaining our Embassy in Alexandria, Egypt, which was that country's capital until the military overthrow of its monarchy by Col. Gamel Abdel Nasser in 1952.

Mr. President, I believe it is long past time for our country to begin treating our closest ally in the Middle East-Israel-in the same way that we treat every Arab country, and indeed, every other country in the world with whom we maintain diplomatic relations. It is time for us to locate our Embassy in Israel's capital city, and stop making excuses why any particular moment never seems to be exactly the right moment. Sometime in the next 4 years that moment will arrive, and that is all this bill is saying.

Senator Gramm put the concerns about the peace process in prospective. He offered:

Mr. President, the Arab-Israel peace process must be judged by one question, and one question only: Will Israel be stronger and more secure at the end of the process than it was at the beginning? To achieve that end, I support this legislation to move the U.S. Embassy to Jerusalem...

The Clinton administration argues that moving the Embassy will destroy the peace process. I believe that the peace process can continue only if Israelis believe that their nation's vital interests will not be compromised. Moving our Embassy to Jerusalem will strengthen that conviction, and it will be a clear demonstration of the fact that no wedge will be driven between Israel and the United States over the status of Jerusalem...

It is outrageous that we have diplomatic relations with 184 countries throughout the world and in every one, except Israel, our Embassy is in the functioning capital.

Israel has endured much throughout her history and for her to have to suffer the indignity of her main ally refusing to place its embassy in her capital is an insult.

We would never allow another country to tell us where to locate our capital. Why are we dictating this to Israel?

In a time when the Palestinians are placing more and more demands on Israel and when the United States is providing $500 million to the PLO, only to find Yasir Arafat unable to deliver on his end of the peace agreement, we must make it clear that some things are not negotiable. Jerusalem for one is not a topic for negotiation. Jerusalem belongs to Israel.

If we delay moving our Embassy any longer, we will be raising unrealistic hopes about the future of this holy city.

Senator D'Amato emphatically reminded the State Department about the non-negotiable status of Jerusalem as the undivided capital of Israel. He declared in no uncertain terms:

Israel is and will remain the permanent and undivided capital of Israel. I am not going to let the State Department bureaucrats forget that.

The Clinton administration must recognize this and begin the process of moving the United States Embassy to Jerusalem. It is shameful that the United States continues to bend to pressure to keep its Embassy outside of Jerusalem.

While I understand that the present Middle East peace negotiations are both complicated and delicate, I do not want this administration to be under the impression that Jerusalem will belong to anyone other than Israel.

Further delay in moving the United States Embassy to Jerusalem will only embolden the Palestinians who believe that they have a justified claim to the city.

While some worry that such a move will damage the peace process, delay can only hurt it. If the future of Jerusalem remains unclear in the minds of the Palestinians then they will increase their demands and this will further complicate the already tense negotiations.

Let the message be clear: A united Jerusalem is off limits to negotiation. Jerusalem belongs to Israel and our Embassy belongs in Jerusalem.

Senator Lieberman reviewed the history of the U.S.-Israel relationship and highlighted many of the positive benefits it yielded to the U.S., as follows:

Jerusalem, city of peace, the holy city, was entered almost 3,000 years ago by King David. Mr. President, 47 years ago, in 1948, the modern State of Israel was established. The Prime Minister at that time, David Ben-Gurion, declared Israel a state and declared also that its capital would be Jerusalem, although at that time, after the war for independence, Jerusalem was a divided city: the western part Israeli; the old city and the eastern part, Jordanian.

In the normal course of diplomatic relations, every nation in the world would have established their embassy in the city, Jerusalem, designated as the capital by the new state of Israel, the state having been recognized by the United States, having been accepted as a member of the United Nations. But, for reasons that need not be spelled out in detail here, because of controversy that surrounded the State of Israel and its creation, the modern state, the United States did not move its Embassy to the capital of the State of Israel.

When you think about it, it is nothing short of outrageous. We have gone through 47 years of the history of this country, 47 years of extraordinary friendship between the United States and Israel based on common values, common history, our common commitment to what is appropriately described as the Judea-Christian tradition, our common commitment to democratic values. Through most of that time, the 47 years, Israel was the only country in the Middle East that was a democracy. It was 47 years in which our strategic relationships have grown ever closer, with joint military exercises and joint work on research and development, even, in this time, as we in the Senate have recently considered the priority threat that ballistic missiles represent to our country, the United States and Israel have been working jointly on a ballistic missile defense.

I remember once years ago hearing the then Prime Minister of Israel, Golda Meir, say, and I believe it is true today, that there is one country in the Middle East where the United States will always know — not just today, not just 10 years from now or 50 years from now or 100 years from now-as long as Israel exists, because the ties between these countries are so deep and so strong-there is one country in the Middle East where the United States will always know that in a time of need, in a time of conflict, in a time of danger, the United States can always land its planes, can always keep its equipment, can always bring its ships into Israeli docks. As she said, hopefully there will be a time-and, of course, we echo that here in this Chamber, and there is such a time now-where there are other countries in the Middle East where that is so, where U.S. troops, U.S. personnel, are welcome. But it will always be so in Israel.

Yet, in spite of all these points of common value, common interest, common strategic purpose, shared strategic developments, nonetheless the United States continued to be frozen into this inconsistent, illogical and in some senses insulting position of not moving its Embassy to the city of Jerusalem, which Israel has designated as its capital. There have been succeeding generations of American politicians — of both parties —who somehow manage to be committed to the movement of the embassy to Jerusalem during campaigns, but then when it comes time that they hold office, it does not happen.

I think we are about to change all that, and I think we are about to change it in a truly bipartisan way. It is, though a long overdue moment, nonetheless a critically important moment when we are in reach of a strong, bipartisan majority in this Chamber and in the other body in support of this legislation.

Would that the legislation were not necessary. But, it is. In some senses it may be unfortunate that it is, but in other senses it is fortunate that we bring this legislation to the Senate because the effect will be to show the world, to show the people of Israel, to show all concerned parties in the Middle East, that the representatives here in the Senate and in the House, both parties, from every section of the country, agree that this is a matter of principle, a matter of common sense, a matter in which the United States, a strong nation — the strongest nation in the world- acts like a strong nation and does what is consistent with its principles.

As to the Presidential waiver provision, he was adamant that it be narrowly drawn and limited. As he said:

I know there are concerns about constitutional questions. I know there is a discussion of a possible waiver going on;

that is to say, to give the President the authority under some circumstances to waive the ultimate penalties associated with not moving the Embassy by May 31, 1999. I understand those questions, and I am involved in the discussions of those questions.

But it seems to me, as my friend and colleague from Michigan, Senator Levin, said, it is critically important that any waiver be narrowly drawn in that it not be a waiver that will go on forever, but that if the President determines- first, the President must be required to find a genuine threat to America's national security to stop the forward movement of the Embassy to Jerusalem, a threat to our national security. Second, that the waiver ought to be limited in time to perhaps 6-month periods so that the President will have to make that decision each time those 6 months are over.

Senator Grams dismissed the false claims that the bill was political pandering and emphasized the need for a clear and unambiguous message that the U.S. supports Israel's right to Jerusalem. Set forth below are some of his remarks:

As the peace process continues, moving the United States Embassy to Jerusalem again will send a clear message that America supports Israel's claim to Jerusalem. It is far better that all parties in the Middle East peace process understand America's position and know that it is a clear position. By allowing our position to remain ambiguous throughout the peace talks, we would risk creating false and unrealistic expectations about the status and the destiny of Jerusalem.

Critics out there, including some in the administration, try to dismiss this bill as political pandering, but during his 1992 campaign it was President Clinton who deplored the fact that "George Bush has repeatedly challenged Israel's sovereignty over the united Jerusalem and groups Jerusalem with the West Bank and Gaza as up for negotiation. Bill Clinton and Al Gore will... support Jerusalem as the capital of the State of Israel."

S. 1322 has strong bipartisan support with 67 cosponsors. This bill has already been modified to provide the administration with more flexibility in trying to determine the construction timetable for a new Embassy in Jerusalem, and as a member of the Foreign Relations Committee, I hope the administration will drop any of its remaining opposition to this important symbolic legislation.

Mr. President, S. 1322 would rectify a half-century-old wrong, contribute to the ongoing peace process, implement the wishes of the American people, and it would fulfill the hopes of the Israeli people. I close by urging my colleagues to show that Congress overwhelmingly supports this effort.

Senator Lautenberg discussed some of the horrendous terrorist attacks, including the kidnapping and brutal murder of Nachshon Waxman, of blessed memory, and the murder of his own constituent, Alisa Flatow, of blessed memory, killed in a Hamas bus bombing. He also noted the need for a clear and unequivocal message to be sent regarding Israel's right to Jerusalem, as follows:

There is no doubt that Jerusalem will remain the undivided capital of Israel. What we are discussing today, frankly, is not whether or not the United States Embassy belongs in Jerusalem, our Ambassador to Israel should be stationed there; we are talking about something that is, frankly, I believe, a matter of timing more than a matter of principle...

Now, I, for one, have advocated the establishment of the American Embassy in Jerusalem from the day that Israel was declared a State, a country. I have said so as well in my many visits there-the first one being 1969 after the city had been united, when I saw what happened to holy Jerusalem during the years of occupation when there was total disregard for artifacts, for archeological treasures, for custom, for religion, for culture. I was stunned and glad to see the city undivided, and declared then, in 1969, that as long as I live and could do anything about it, that city would never be divided again, that it was essential that the world recognize that Jerusalem is the capital of Israel.

Senator Moynihan provided a sweeping and erudite analysis of why Jerusalem unquestionably was and must remain the undivided capital of Jerusalem. Set forth below are excerpts of his cogent remarks:

The Senate stands ready to correct an absurdity which has endured for nearly half a century. We propose to respect Israel's sovereign right to choose her capital. We do this by providing for the relocation of our embassy to the city which contains the Parliament of that State.

The bill which the distinguished majority leader has proposed will ensure that the United States Embassy in Israel is moved to Jerusalem, the undivided capital of that State, no later than May 31, 1999.

I have been involved with this particular issue in some measure since my tenure as Permanent Representative to the United Nations in 1975. By the early 1970's, the United States was faced with a General Assembly where a Soviet-led coalition wielded enormous power and used it in an assault against the democracies of the world. In that regard, I cite an editorial in the New Republic which recently said of the United Nations in that time that

"During the cold war, the U.N. became a chamber of hypocrisy and proxy aggression."

Proxy aggression, Mr. President, and in particular directed to the State of Israel, which became a metaphor for democracy under virtual siege at the United Nations.

Those who had failed to destroy Israel on the field of battle joined those who wished to discredit all Western democratic governments in an unprecedented, sustained attack on the very right of a U.N. member state to exist within the family of nations.

The efforts in the 1970's to delegitimize Israel came in many forms, none more insidious than the twin campaigns to declare Zionism to be a form of racism and to deny Israel's ties to Jerusalem. Those who ranted against the "racist Tel Aviv regime" were spewing two ugly lies. Both had at their heart a denial of Israel's right to exist.

The first lie, the infamous Resolution 3379, was finally repealed on December 16, 1991, after the cold war had ended and the Soviet Union dissolved.

Today, we take an important step to refute the second lie, the absurd suggestion that Israel did not have a right to select its own capital city.

Israel expects attempts by her enemies to undermine her, but it is more difficult to fathom our own refusal to recognize Israel's chosen capital and to locate our Embassy in Jerusalem. In so doing, we have given and continue to give unintended encouragement to those enemies of Israel who hope one day to be able to divide the United States and that nation, the only democratic state in the Middle East. For as long as Israel's most important friend in the world refuses to acknowledge that Israel's capital city is not its own, we lend credibility and dangerous strength to the lie that Israel is some-how a misbegotten, an illegitimate, or transient state.

This suggestion is all the more untenable when you consider that no other people on this planet have been identified as closely with any city as the people of Israel are with Jerusalem — a city which this year celebrates the 3000th anniversary of King David declaring it his capital. No Jewish religious ceremony is complete without mention of the Holy City. And twice a year, at the conclusion of the Passover Seder and the Day of Atonement services, all assembled repeat one of mankind's shortest and oldest prayers "Next year in Jerusalem."

Throughout the centuries Jews kept this pledge, often sacrificing their very lives to travel to, and live in, their holiest city. It should be noted that the first authoritative Turkish census of 1839 reported that Jews were by far the largest ethnic group in Jerusalem-and this long before there was a West Jerusalem, or even any settlements outside the ancient walled city.

When the modern State of Israel declared independence on May 14, 1948, Jerusalem was the only logical choice for the new nation's capital -even if it was only a portion of Jerusalem, the Jordanian Arab Legion having occupied the eastern half of the city and expelled the Jewish population of the Old City-Jerusalem was sundered by barbed wire and cinder block and Israelis of all faiths and Jews of all citizenship were barred from even visiting the section under Jordanian occupation.

The world was silent while the historic Jewish Quarter of the city was sacked and razed to the ground, 127 synagogues were destroyed, and 3,000 years of history were denied. This bizarre anomaly only ended on June 5, 1967, when Israel faced renewed aggression from Egypt and Syria, both then close friends of, and dependents of the Soviet Union. As hostilities commenced, Israeli Prime Minister Levi Eshkol sent a message to King Hussein of Jordan promising that, if Jordan refrained from entering the war, Israel would not take action against it. Jordan, however, attacked Israel that same day. Within the week, Israeli forces had captured all of Jerusalem, as well as other territories west of the Jordan River. The City of David was once again united, and has been since 1967. Under Israeli rule Jerusalem has flourished as it did not under Jordanian occupation, and the religious shrines of all faiths have been meticulously protected.

Israel has found itself repeatedly attacked, boycotted, and spurned by its neighbors. But slowly Israel has worked to secure a less hostile environment. First, the historic Camp David Accords brought peace between Israel and Egypt. All Senators are aware of the unprecedented accomplishments of the last 2 years. Jordan is at peace with Israel and a peace process is well underway with the Palestinians. In fact, Mr. Arafat gave voice at the United Nations just yesterday.

The United Nations is celebrating its 50th anniversary. Even Yasir Arafat, who 21 years ago addressed the General Assembly wearing a gun holster, spoke yesterday of the tremendous achievements in Israeli-Palestinian relations. The New York Times characterizes Mr. Arafat's remarks as "a far more conciliatory tone than during his last visit." And contrasts his earlier calls for the destruction of Israel with yesterday's General Assembly pledge to "turn over the leaf of killing and destruction once and for all so that the Palestinian people and Israeli people may live side by side."

There are those who might criticize our proposal, saying that we have no business taking such action while the peace process continues. On the contrary-or such is my view. This is our Embassy and congressional sentiment should be made known. In this I am reminded of a message from Prime Minister Yitzhak Rabin to the American-Israel Friendship League on November 28, 1993 in which he wrote:

In 1990, Senator Moynihan sponsored Senate Resolution 106, which recognized Jerusalem as Israel's united Capital, never to be divided again, and called upon Israel and the Palestinians to undertake negotiations to re-solve their differences. The resolution, which passed both houses of Congress, expressed the sentiments of the United States toward Israel, and, I believe, helped our neighbors reach the negotiating table.

The negotiators will soon turn to final status issues, as defined by the Declaration of Principles signed on September 13, 1993, by Israel and the Palestinians. The status of Jerusalem is one of the agenda items to be settled during this final stage of the peace process. It is inconceivable that Israel would agree to any proposal in which Jerusalem did not remain the capital of Israel. Since Jerusalem will continue to be the capital of Israel, it is time to begin planning to move the United States Embassy to ensure that at the end of the process, it will be where it belongs.

Our Embassy should have been moved long ago, but we recognize the momentous achievements taking place in the Middle East, and they temper our actions. Our intentions are clear. When the peace process is completed, which according to the Declaration of Principles, is scheduled for May 1999, our Embassy will be located in Jerusalem.

On March 20th of this year, Senator D'Amato and I sent a letter to Secretary Christopher with the support of 91 other Senators. That letter made it clear that the overwhelming majority of Senators agree with the proposition that "Jerusalem is and shall remain the undivided capital of the State of Israel." We also wrote that our embassy belongs in Jerusalem, and we asked the

Secretary to inform us of the steps being taken to make a relocation of our Embassy to Jerusalem possible.

Today we have before us legislation that reflects the spirit of our letter to Secretary Christopher. I am hopeful that the President will be able to sign this legislation. Prime Minister Begin once advised me that the ""battle for Jerusalem should never be fought in the halls of Congress." " I agree and am pleased that the majority leader worked with those of us on our side of the aisle to produce a draft that reflects the bipartisan consensus of the Senate. I would also like to commend my friend, the Senator from Connecticut, Senator Lieberman, for his considerable contribution to the formulation of this bill.

This administration has been effective in the Middle East peace process. Secretary Christopher has personally flown to the region numerous times and has clearly committed himself to active participation in the peace process. On the issue of our Embassy, I would respectfully suggest that the administration direct its attention to the comments of Prime Minister Rabin, as our letter to the Secretary of State noted:

> There can be little doubt that Jerusalem is a sensitive issue in the current peace process. While the Declaration of Principles stipulates that Jerusalem is a "final status" issue to be negotiated between the parties, we share Prime Minister Rabin's view which be expressed to the Knesset that: On Jerusalem, we said:

> "This Government, like all its predecessors, believes there is no disagreement in this House concerning Jerusalem as the eternal capital of Israel. United Jerusalem will not be open to negotiation. It has been and will forever be the capital of the Jewish people, under Israeli sovereignty, a focus of the dream and longing of every Jew."

> It continues: United States policy should be equally clear and unequivocal. The search for peace can only be

hindered by raising utterly unrealistic hopes about the future status of Jerusalem among the Palestinians and understandable fears among the Israeli population that their capital city may once again be divided by cinder block and barbed wire.

Charles Krauthammer adopted a similar line of argument in a column in the Washington Post on May 19, 1995, when he wrote:

True, the embassy move does endorse the proposition that Jerusalem is the capital of Israel. What possibly could be wrong with that? Is it the PLO position that even after a final peace, Jerusalem may not be the capital of Israel?

That is the simple proposition for the Senate today, Mr. President. This bill would provide for the relocation of our Embassy to Jerusalem where it has always belonged. It does not interfere with the peace process, because there is no scenario in which Israel would agree to relinquish Jerusalem as its capital.

Senator Moynihan also reviewed some of the absurd practices at the State Department, such as listing Jerusalem as a separate country in its phone directory, which he noted was finally corrected by Secretary Christopher, who listed Jerusalem under the Israel heading. He also mused about the real-world consequences of these misguided policies and practices, as follows:

That simple refusal by the United States Government to associate our consulate in Jerusalem with Israel carried much greater weight with the nonaligned countries than we realized.

They would not have acted as they had done in 1983 if they did not think at some measure we were not in disagreement. Our documents have so implied.

No doubt, we wounded the Israelis more than we intended as well, while sending a dangerous message to Israeli enemies.

Clarifying the status of Jerusalem began to gain momentum in the Senate in 1990 when I submitted S. Con. Res. 106, which States simply: "Jerusalem is and should remain the capital of the State of Israel." A simple declarative sentence which gained 85 cosponsors and was adopted unanimously by the Senate and by an overwhelming majority in the House.

Two years later, Senator Packwood and I submitted Senate Concurrent Resolution 113 to commemorate the 25th anniversary of the reunification of Jerusalem.

The measure stated that, "Congress strongly believes that Jerusalem must remain an undivided city." That, too, was agreed to unanimously, both in the Senate and the House.

Last year, in the wake of the massacre in Hebron, the United Nations Security Council adopted a measure which referred to Jerusalem as "occupied territory." Senator Mack and I sent a letter to the President, with the signature of 81 other Senators, calling on the administration to veto any U.N. Security Council resolution which states or implies that Jerusalem is occupied territory.

To his credit, President Clinton responded with a forceful promise to veto any future U.N. resolution which raised questions about the status of Jerusalem. A promise that he kept on May 17, 1995, when Ambassador Albright cast such a long overdue veto in the Security Council.

In the winter of 1981, I wrote an article in Commentary entitled "Joining The Jackals" in response to the Carter administration's disastrous support for a resolution challenging Israel's rights in Jerusalem. Almost 15 years later, we find that the jackals are in retreat. Israelis and

Palestinians are negotiating the details of their future. And today we have an opportunity to make a simple but important contribution to this process by unequivocally recognizing Israel's chosen capital.

Senator Lieberman thanked Senator Moynihan for his characteristically learned and principled statement. He went on to note:

The history of our Government's policy on this question of the location of the American Embassy in Israel is a tawdry history. It is not the history of a great and principled nation. It is a history of a nation that has, I think, in the words of a musical, "bowed and kowtowed" too often and too low, when it was not necessary, on a matter as fundamental as respecting a country-not just any country but a country that is a dear and cherished, valued ally-in its own decision about where its capital is. It is a sovereign nation, a member of the United Nations.

Senator Boxer addressed some misplaced concerns of opponents of the bill, including as follows:

A number of concerns have been expressed about the wisdom of moving the Embassy at this time. I want to address each of these concerns specifically.

Opponents have said that this bill could trigger anger and terrorism on the part of Israel's opponents. Indeed, when the bill was first being circulated, opponents said the peace process would fall apart. They said the peace process would fall apart if we even introduced this bill. But the peace process did not fall apart. As a matter of fact, the peace process moved forward. That is because this bill is not directly related to the peace process. As a matter of fact, this bill, as recently modified-and I support the modifications-shows great deference to the peace process. By removing the requirement for an early construction start date, this bill shows complete respect for the peace process. Opponents of this bill have also argued we should wait to move our Embassy until the so-called final status negotiations are complete. I would argue that, although the final status of Jerusalem may be an issue in the peace talks, the location of our Embassy is not. The location of an American Embassy is entirely an American decision.

In any case, our Embassy will be located within the pre-1967 West Jerusalem border, not in the more controversial eastern section. It is this fact that leads me to conclude that moving our Embassy would in no way prejudice the outcome of the final status negotiations. It is not as if we are breaking new ground in a new area that has not been under Israeli control.

Finally, and perhaps the most important point I wish to make for my colleagues today, is that when I was in Israel in November, I sensed an undeniable fear and concern about the future. Terrorist attacks were escalating. Support for peace was falling. As a matter of fact, there was not one person, whether it was a cab driver or a student, that I met who did not indicate to me the fears that they had.

Israel, of course, is taking a risk for peace, and, therefore, the people are taking a risk for peace. As a matter of fact, all the good people who come to the table, whatever side they are on, are taking a risk for peace. So, when I left Israel, I thought, we need to do something here to just show that we support the peace process, and that we support our close ally, Israel. I think this is something we can do that demonstrates a high level of respect for the good people of the State of Israel, and for the peace process as a whole.

I have a very balanced view of this issue. I believe that Yasir
Arafat must have what he needs to build confidence among
Palestinians for the peace process so that extremist groups
like Hamas renounce violence and go to the ballot box as
their way. I think this is very important. And that is why I
supported the Middle East Peace Facilitation Act, which
authorized continuing aid to the Palestinian authority so
long as they continued to meet their commitments to work
for peace. So, Mr. President, I support the Palestinians who
are working for peace, and I support the Israelis who are
working for peace. Just as we show support for the
Palestinians through the Peace Facilitation Act, we must
also show support for the people of Israel who have taken
some very serious risks for peace. I think that this bill sends
a very important message.

On the next day, October 24, 1995, consideration of the bill
continued. Senator Robb made a number of cogent remarks. He
offered:

I recognize the city of Jerusalem as the united, undivided,
eternal, and sovereign capital of Israel, and where the
United States Embassy is located should reflect that
reality. While some have urged caution about relocating
our mission in the midst of the peace process, it is my sense
that such a move, as envisioned by the Jerusalem Embassy
Relocation Act, will not create a detour on the road to
achieving a comprehensive Arab-Israeli peace.

Jerusalem stands today as an international city, where the
rights of all ethnic religious groups are protected and
freedom of worship is guaranteed. Diverse religious faiths
coexist peacefully. This week we are seeing a hopeful spirit
of internationalism expressed by many world leaders
celebrating the founding of the United Nations 50 years
ago. Like the community of nations joining together in
support of the United Nations many religious faiths and

sects engender a collective spirit of interdenominational harmony in Jerusalem.

Madam President, Prime Minister Rabin has told the Israeli people that ``I assure you that Jerusalem will remain united under Israel's sovereignty, and our capital forever.'' That expression leads me to the conclusion that the final status talks on the city should not focus on issues of overall sovereignty. Rather, making permanent each denomination's jurisdiction over its respective holy sites and collateral issues of autonomy should be the subject of the negotiations next year.

Even President Clinton has stated that ``I recognize Jerusalem as an undivided city, the capital of Israel-- whatever the outcome of the negotiations, Jerusalem is still the capital of Israel and must remain an undivided city, accessible to all.'' That statement represents a consensus that our Embassy belongs in the functional capital of Israel.

Among the 184 countries we maintain diplomatic relations with, Israel is the single exception to the rule of locating the United States chancery in the designated capital of each foreign nation. We have a responsibility to respect the decisions of where all countries locate their seat of government, and Israel should not be viewed in a different light.

Thus far in the peace talks, Israel has sacrificed the tangible--land--for the intangible--the security of its people. As we continue down the road of peace, Israel will cede valuable territory, natural resources, and political authority, while Palestinians will enjoy broader political and economic freedoms. There are no long-term guarantees for Israel. A single Hamas-sponsored terrorist attack can disrupt any sense of peace achieved at the negotiating table.

Madam President, that is why I endorse this move to demonstrate our long-term commitment to having our Embassy in Jerusalem which will symbolize the united and undivided character of this city. Such a move will not stand in the way of achieving a comprehensive peace. It will simply lay to rest doubts about the U.S. position on the status of our Embassy.

Senator Cohen amplified those sentiments in his remarks, as follows:

It has been over a decade since a majority of the Members of Congress, and I was proud to be among this group, called for the movement of our Embassy to where it belongs--in the capital of Israel. Since then, as Senator Moynihan has recited in detail, the Senate and the other body have repeatedly adopted by overwhelming and frequently unanimous votes legislation calling on the United States to affirm Jerusalem as Israel's undivided capital.

Most recently, nearly every Member of the Senate signed a letter to the President urging that the relocation take place no later than May 1999. This letter clearly rejected the assertion of some that declaring our intent to move our Embassy would endanger the peace process, noting that:

United States policy should be clear and unequivocal. The search for peace can only be hindered by raising utterly unrealistic hopes about the future status of Jerusalem among the Palestinians and understandable fears among the Israeli population that their capital city may once again be divided by cinder block and barbed wire.

We also endorsed in that letter Prime Minister Rabin's declaration that ``United Jerusalem will not be open to

negotiation. It has been and will forever be the capital of
the Jewish people, under Israeli sovereignty, a focus of the
dreams and longings of every Jew."

The bill we have before us, of which I am proud to be an
original cosponsor, brings this legislative process to
fruition by establishing in law United States policy that
Jerusalem should be recognized as the capital of Israel and
that our Embassy should be relocated there no later than
May 31, 1999, and by authorizing funding beginning this
year for construction of a United States Embassy in
Jerusalem.

To help that ensure the executive branch implements this
policy faithfully, the bill requires semiannual reports from
the Secretary of State, beginning in January, on the
progress made toward opening our Embassy in Jerusalem.
It also would give the State Department a strong financial
incentive by limiting the availability of its construction
funding after 1999 until the Embassy opens in Israel's
capital. As a practical matter, this limitation would not
actually take effect until the middle of the year 2000, given
the historical spend-out rates for the State Department's
construction budget. But it emphasizes the importance
Congress places on this matter.

Even with this inherent flexibility, however, the
administration has shown resistance to this legislation. In
response, Senator Dole has now added a broad waiver
authority that would allow the President to suspend this
limitation on State Department construction if he believes
it is necessary to protect the national security interests of
the United States.

I should also note that the bill carefully states that the
rights of every ethnic and religion group should be
protected in the undivided capital of Jerusalem. Three

major faiths revere Jerusalem as a holy city. The best way to protect the religious interests of members of all these faiths is to ensure that Jerusalem never again is divided, which would only threaten to reignite religious conflict...

Madam President, many of us in the Senate have had the opportunity to help cultivate America's special relationship with the State of Israel. As a strategic ally and an island of stability and democracy in an important but troubled region, Israel steadfastly supported American interests during the cold war. During the gulf war, when Saddam Hussein sought to gain control over Middle Eastern energy resources, Israel stood firmly with America, enduring savage attacks on its civilian population that were designed to split Israeli policy from United States policy.

Having protected U.S. interests in a hostile region for decades, the American-Israeli strategic alliance today is the foundation for the Middle East peace process. Without steadfast United States support for Israel, those among Israel's neighbors who have accepted the necessity for a negotiated peace settlement would not have done so. And without our continued steadfast support, the peace process will not be successful. Nowhere is this need greater than on the question of the status of Jerusalem.

Jerusalem is and will remain the undivided capital of the State of Israel, and we must not miss the opportunity to underline that fact--particularly today on the eve of the inauguration of the celebration of the 3,000th anniversary of Jerusalem's establishment as the capital of Israel. This legislation will help to ensure that the fourth millennium of this holy city will begin with an era of peace.

Senator Lott spoke about how the bill was all about the U.S.' national interest and not about domestic politics. He noted:

I am a cosponsor of this legislation, along with 63 other Senators. In a year some characterize as a very partisan year, you have a bipartisan consensus on this issue. Senators have come together for the national interest, something which is above politics.

This is what this bill is all about: The national interest. I have heard that this bill is solely about politics of the Presidential kind. That is not true--the proof is in the list of cosponsors: This list is bipartisan and balanced.

I have heard the argument against this bill, that moving our Embassy ahead of schedule would endanger the Middle East peace process. I am not persuaded by this argument. The United States has consistently recognized Jerusalem as Israel's capital. If we want to be an honest broker in peace talks between Israelis and Palestinians, we should be honest about our view of Israel's sovereignty over Jerusalem.

This bill would allow us to break ground in 1996 for the new Embassy. Next year will be the 3,000th anniversary year of Jerusalem. King David relocated his throne from Hebron to Jerusalem 3 millennia ago. Next year, America should move its Embassy to the city of David.

This bill is not a statement of animosity against any religion. Almost all Senators are on record supporting Israel's administration of Jerusalem as a unified and universal city, open to all followers of the three great world religions. This it has done for 28 years, and that will not be jeopardized.

This bill is not a statement against any country. This bill is for the official recognition on our part that our ally Israel has its governmental seat in Jerusalem. The peace negotiations can and should continue. We should facilitate such negotiations. Relocating our Embassy does not and should not have anything to do with ongoing peace talks.

So I think we should pass this bill, and I think the President should sign it. Jerusalem has always been at the crossroads of history and faith. We should begin next year to place our presence there.

I am reminded that people of the Jewish faith say at the end of the Passover and Yom Kippur services, ``Next year, in Jerusalem.'' This expresses their hope of return and the centrality of Jerusalem in the Jewish faith.

I say something similar, Madam President: That I hope this bill passes, and next year, we will be in Jerusalem breaking ground for a new Embassy in the Holy City.

Senator Mikulski echoed many of these sentiments and amplified them as follows:

Jerusalem is and always will be the capital of Israel. For thousands of years the Jewish people prayed, ``next year in Jerusalem.'' This prayer helped to sustain Jews even through the darkest days of the diaspora.

Even after Israeli independence, the holy sites of Jerusalem were closed to Christians and Jews. The Jewish quarter of the old city was destroyed. But since Jerusalem was unified in 1967, Jerusalem is open to all religions for the first time in its history.

I have visited Israel with Jews who were there for the first time. When we visited the Western Wall, I saw what it meant for them to touch the stones that their ancestors could only dream of. I saw that Jerusalem is not just a city or a capital. It is the religious and historic homeland of the Jewish people.

Why is Israel the only nation with which we have diplomatic relations that is not allowed to choose its own capital? The sight for the U.S. Embassy is in west Jerusalem, which has been part of Israel since its independence. We should have moved our Embassy long ago.

So over the years, I have supported every effort of Congress to call upon the executive branch to move our Embassy to Jerusalem. And each successive administration has ignored us.

But now, as Israel takes courageous steps toward peace, we are raising this issue again...

Madam President, this year we celebrate the 3,000 anniversary of Jerusalem. Let us mark this great event by reaffirming that Jerusalem is and always will be the capital of the State of Israel.

Senator Hatch noted the U.S. must not be ambivalent in its support of Jerusalem being the undivided capital of Israel; it would only muddle and frustrate the negotiations. He said:

Next year will begin the ``Final Status'' negotiations. There has been much positioning by certain parties over the future of Jerusalem. But Israeli governments have not vacillated over this issue, and their position has always been clear: Jerusalem is the seat of the Israeli Government, and Jerusalem shall remain the united capital of Israel. This is the conviction of the Israeli Government, the only democratic state and our most valuable ally in the region.

This should be our conviction now. Our ambivalence beyond this point will only muddle, and I believe frustrate, the final status negotiations. The parties must set the terms, and we must not confound expectations by perpetuating the anomaly of the U.S. Embassy in Tel Aviv. If we wish to continue supporting the peace process, and I firmly believe we should, then we must make clear that it is the policy of the U.S. Government to have its Embassy in

Jerusalem by the conclusion of the peace negotiations at the end of this century.

Senator Moseley-Braun drew an analogy to how the U.S. might react if some country chose not to locate their Embassy in the U.S. capital of Washington D.C. to make her compelling point, as follows:

> Imagine, Madam President, the huge outcry, within and outside of government, if any foreign nation refused to locate its embassy in our capital or insisted that it would maintain relations with us, but not in the location we designated as our capital city. That kind of refusal would create serious and unnecessary tensions between the United States and that country. After all, the question of where to locate the capital of the United States is for the United States to decide--and no one else.

> That same logic applies in this case to the capital of Israel. The question of where to locate its capital is for Israel to decide and no other nation or power to frustrate. And Israel decided long ago that Jerusalem would be its capital.

> If the argument is made that Middle East peace negotiations are at a delicate stage, and that this is not the time for this legislation, my response to that is: Peace negotiations are always at a delicate stage. The pendency of discussions should not force an untenable discrimination against one of the negotiators. Jerusalem has been the capital of Israel since 1950. The time for waiting is over. Forty-five years is a long enough period for closure of what should be a matter of simple fairness.

> Critics of this legislation also argue that the passage--even the discussion--of this legislation will undermine the peace process, thereby harming Israel's security and strategic interests. However, the Government of Israel and its citizens, the ultimate authorities on Israel's security

and strategic interests, do not share that view. They enthusiastically support the relocation of the American Embassy to the capital city, Jerusalem.

Others argue that the relocation of the American Embassy to Jerusalem would prejudge and prejudice the final status of Jerusalem negotiations under the Oslo agreement. I do not agree. The site the United States is considering for a future Embassy is in an area that has been part of Israel since its founding in 1948. Moreover, Israel's right to this section of Jerusalem is uncontested, even by the Palestine Liberation Organization.

Madam President, I understand and appreciate the uniqueness of the city of Jerusalem. It is unique in the world as a holy place. The hilltop city is sacred to Jews as the site of their ancient temple, to Christians as the birthplace of Christianity, and to Moslems as the site from which Muhammad ascended into heaven. It is all of these things--and it is also the capital of Israel.

Each and every U.S. Embassy abroad exists to represent our Government to the government of the country in which it is located. The Government of Israel is in Jerusalem. Jerusalem, therefore, is the only place our Embassy should be.

The logic of locating our Embassy in Israel's capital city is overwhelming and compelling, which is why this legislation enjoys such widespread, bipartisan support in both the Senate and the House of Representatives. I urge the prompt passage of this legislation, and I look forward to the day in the near future when the United States Embassy opens in Israel's capital--Jerusalem.

Senator Feingold spoke next and focused on the religious attachments to Jerusalem, as follows.

Like almost all of my colleagues, I believe that an undivided Jerusalem is the legitimate capital of the State of Israel, and that United States policy should clearly reflect that. Accordingly, the United States Embassy should be housed in Israel's capital, just like it is in every other country, and not in the country's economic center.

Of course, the Jerusalem issue is practically unique in world politics. The ancient city is holy for Jews, Christians, and Moslems...

Jews pray at the Kotel, the Western Wall, the last remaining wall of the ancient synagogues, as well as the scores of other holy sites nestled in so many quarters.

Named as the City of Peace, Jerusalem has unfortunately been split by war. Throughout history, Arabs and Jews and Christians have locked each other out, and have often accused each other of desanctifying religious monuments, and barring access to each other's holy places...

My own memory is seared by the defacing of meaningful and historic synagogues in the Old City's Jewish Quarter in 1947-67, when the city was not controlled by Israel. I remember with pain the laundry that hung on the Wailing Wall, a place of immensely spiritual and sacred value for Jews. I cannot forget the pictures of Jewish tombstones thrown around the Mount of Olives cemetery just at the foot of the walls of the Old City.

Though the international community has tried to split Jerusalem under the political solution of corpus separatum, to my mind, the spirituality and emotion of the city make division impossible. Given the 3,000 years of the history of Jerusalem, it will always be the heart of the Jewish people and the capital of the Jewish state. Indeed, it is the capital of the sovereign nation of Israel--a sovereignty the United States has heavily invested in and fiercely supported for 45 years. If our support for Jewish sovereignty over the land of Israel is to mean anything, then the United States should recognize Israel's capital appropriately...

I am very sensitive to concerns that such a move by the United States at this time would undermine the peace process. I understand the risk that perhaps the United States would compromise its important position as an honest broker in the peace process: To that, I respond that America's position is nonnegotiable since Israel's claim to Jerusalem is nonnegotiable. Already, there should be no doubt of what the United States position is; hiding our Embassy in Tel Aviv does not change that.

I am also troubled by suggestions that such a move would predetermine the outcome of the final status talks between Israel and the Palestine Liberation Organization, and tie the chairman's hands in other critical negotiations. I am not persuaded, however, that the move of the U.S. Embassy from Tel Aviv to Jerusalem would have such a devastating effect. It is important to keep this proposal in perspective, and not underestimate the power of the commitment of the parties themselves to the peace process--wherever the U.S. Embassy is housed. Further, I believe that Prime Minister Rabin's own assertions that Israel will not cede Jerusalem are just as important to the process, and can guide United States actions on the issue.

The stationing of the United States Embassy in Jerusalem has been a widely supported proposal. The Democratic Party has included it as a plank in our platform since 1967. Sweeping majorities in Congress have urged it for years. It has not been a partisan issue; it has not been a personal crusade for just a few Members of Congress. Indeed, it is when we have broad-based and bipartisan support such as this that coherent and successful policies emerge. Israel has always been a beneficiary of such unity. For that reason, I appreciate Senator Dole working with the administration to craft a bill that can have near-unanimous support, and to avoid the nonsense of division on an issue like Jerusalem.

Senator Kohl also addressed the religious connections to Jerusalem. As set forth below, he pointed out Israel has a proven record of ensuring access to the holy sites, which was not the case prior to its stewardship as the sovereign authority over Jerusalem:

> Jerusalem has emotional resonance that reaches far beyond the Middle East as the religious capital for all Jews and as an important religious site for many other faiths. The Israeli Government has earned our praise in its valiant efforts to ensure that people of all faiths have unhindered access to their holy sites. Unfortunately, Jerusalem has not always been so accessible, as Senator Lautenberg detailed for the Senate yesterday.

Senator Mack also addressed the danger of ambivalence, when it came to the U.S. firmly and unequivocally recognizing the sovereignty of Israel over undivided Jerusalem, as follows:

> The United States failure to recognize Jerusalem as the capital of Israel has only served to embolden the enemies of Israel, leading them to think perhaps the United States, Israel's closest ally, was ambivalent about the status of Jerusalem. We are not. And it is long past time for us to demonstrate our steadfast commitment to an undivided Jerusalem as the historic, governmental, and spiritual capital of Israel.

> Much of the discussion on this bill has addressed concerns that relocation of the U.S. Embassy to Jerusalem would have a detrimental effect on the peace process. The opposite is true. An essential part of the peace process

involves a clear understanding between the parties on a number of issues, an undivided Jerusalem as the capital of Israel is one. PLO compliance is another. On both counts, I want to be absolutely clear: both are essential to a lasting peace in the Middle East. Both are good for Israel and both are good for the Palestinian people. Both are fundamental prerequisites for moving forward into a phase of good relations between Israel and its neighbors. Both are necessary for stability, economic development, good government, and the rule of law for the Palestinian people.

Senator Pressler also weighed in on the fact that recognizing undivided Jerusalem as the capital of Israel would help, not impair, the peace process, as follows:

Madam President, I strongly disagree with those who claim that this legislation could threaten the Middle East peace process. There is no rational basis to question the Senate's commitment to achieving a lasting peace in the Middle East. All want to see the peace process succeed. The safety and security of all the people of Israel is critical to attaining a stable environment in the Middle East.

Clearly, a number of issues in the peace process remain to be worked out. However, there are a few facts that are not in dispute: Jerusalem is an undivided city. Jerusalem is a city open to all people of all nationalities and faiths. Jerusalem is the true capital of Israel. By relocating our Embassy in this historic city, we simply reinforce these facts--facts that reinforce U.S. policy. Nothing more. Nothing less.

Senator Dodd also spoke and said:

Let me say at the outset that I share the fundamental premise of the sponsors of this legislation, namely that Jerusalem is and should remain the undivided capital of the State of Israel. I also agree that the logical extension of that premise is that the U.S. Embassy should therefore appropriately be located in that city...

We must also be mindful of actions we might take here in this body that could further complicate efforts to reach a final agreement. It is within that context that the administration's opposition to legislatively mandating the relocation of the U.S. Embassy to Jerusalem by a date certain should be understood. Having said that, I believe that at this point not to vote in support of this legislation would send the wrong signal to those who would prefer to see the Middle East remain in turmoil. It would send the wrong signal to those who may hold some allusion that our views about the undivided nature of the capital of Israel will somehow change.

Of those who spoke on the record that day, only Senators Byrd and Chafee spoke in opposition to the bill.

Senate Majority Leader Dole noted:

This legislation is not about the peace process, it is about recognizing Israel's capital. Israel's capital is not on the table in the peace process, and moving the United States Embassy to Jerusalem does nothing to prejudge the outcome of any future negotiations.

Years ago, I expressed some concern about the impact of Jerusalem and related issues could have on the prospects for peace. But we live in a very different world today. The Soviet empire is gone, and Arab States can no longer use cold war rivalries in their differences with Israel. Iraqi aggression against Kuwait has been reversed with American forces fighting shoulder to shoulder with Arab allies. American military forces remain in the Persian Gulf region. Jordan has joined Egypt in making genuine peace with Israel. The second phase of the Declaration of Principles is being implemented, Gaza is under Palestinian control, and Israeli withdrawal from West Bank towns has begun.

Even yesterday Arafat met with a group of 100 some Jewish leaders in New York City. I never thought it would happen. It happened.

No one can fail to see that the Middle East has changed dramatically. In my view, now is the time to set the deadline for moving the American Embassy to Jerusalem.

In the more than 5 months since this legislation was introduced, there was not one single overture from the Clinton administration. There were veto threats and legal arguments, but no effort to even discuss our differences. Despite the administration's refusal to talk, the sponsors of the legislation remained willing to address concerns about the bill.

I had no doubt we can work it out and move forward on this legislation.

I want to thank my colleagues, Senator Lautenberg, Senator Feinstein, and others for their willingness to cooperate and work out some of the differences we had, along, of course, with Senator Kyl, Senator Lieberman, Senator Moynihan, and Senator Inouye.

The administration raised concerns over the lack of a waiver provision in the bill. Last Friday, they proposed a national interest waiver with no limits. In the interest of getting the broadest possible support--we hope, even including the support of the White House--the substitute adopted last night included a national security interest waiver. If the waiver is exercised, funding withholding would take place in the next fiscal year. This should take care of any possibly unforseen impact of the legislation. Despite having the votes to prevail, we have demonstrated our willingness to meet the concerns raised. We did not want a confrontation with the White House. In sum, we have gone the extra mile, and now is the time for the Senate to speak.

Some have said the Israeli Government is opposed to this legislation. Nothing could be further from the truth. The architect of the Oslo accord, Deputy Foreign Minister Yossi Beilin recently made Israeli Government views very clear:

Any timing for transferring any embassy to Jerusalem, is good timing. The earlier the better. Israel is the only nation in the world that doesn't have a recognized capital.

As I said when introducing this legislation, the time has come to move beyond letters, expressions of support, and sense-of-the-Congress resolutions. The time has come to enact legislation that will get the job done.

Madam President, we have a very sound piece of legislation before us today. I would particularly like to thank the lead sponsors and those who have been helpful in the process.

I am pleased that Senator Feinstein and Senator Lautenberg agreed to cosponsor the legislation after the substitute was worked out last night.

It would seem to me we ought to have unanimous or near unanimous support for this legislation.

It was then that Senators Kyl and Dole had their famous colloquy on the floor of the Senate concerning the nature and extent of the Presidential waiver provision, which had to be premised on U.S. national security interests, as specified in the Act, as follows:

Mr. KYL. The waiver provision in S. 1322 will be examined by many people. I would like to join with the distinguished majority leader in clarifying on the Record the meaning and purpose of the waiver language.

Mr. DOLE. I agree with my friend from Arizona, that it is important to address the scope and meaning of the waiver provision. It is important that no one think that this provision would allow the President to ignore the requirements of S. 1322 simply because he disagrees with the policy this legislation is promulgating. The President cannot lawfully invoke this waiver simply because he thinks it would be better not to move our Embassy to Jerusalem or simply because he thinks it would be better to move it at a later time. The waiver is designed to be read and interpreted narrowly. It was included to give the President limited flexibility--flexibility to ensure that this legislation will not harm U.S. national security interests in the event of an emergency or unforeseen change in circumstances.

Mr. KYL. What is the significance of the phrase ``national security interests'' as opposed to ``national interest''?

Mr. DOLE. This is the way we are ensuring that the waiver will not permit the President to negate the legislation simply on the grounds that he disagrees with the policy. ``National security interests'' in much narrower than the term ``national interest''--and it is a higher standard than national interest. The key word is security. No President should or could make a decision to exercise this waiver lightly.

Mr. KYL. Is it fair to say that the intention of the waiver is to address constitutional concerns that have been raised about S. 1322?

Mr. DOLE. It is fair to say the waiver is intended to address unusual or unforeseen circumstances. We believe S. 1322 is constitutional even without the waiver, but the constitutional questions that have been raised about it deal with issues so important that we think it is best to offer the President the limited flexibility of the waiver. It is within the constitutional appropriations power of Congress to withhold funds from the executive branch if it does not act in accordance with congressional mandates.

Mr. KYL. Although in drafting the legislation Senators did not limit the number of times the President could invoke the waiver authority, is it correct to say that the intent of the drafters is not to grant the President the right to invoke the waiver in perpetuity?

Mr. DOLE. The waiver authority should not be interpreted to mean that the President may infinitely push off the establishment of the American Embassy in Jerusalem. Our intent is that the Embassy be established in Jerusalem by May 1999. If a waiver were to be repeatedly and routinely exercised by a President, I would expect Congress to act by removing the waiver authority.

Senator Levin commended Senator Dole and the bi-partisan effort that led to this day, which he summed up as follows:

This is a meaningful day. It is a day where we finally acknowledge the reality, which is that Jerusalem is the capital of Israel and that at the end of the peace process will be the capital of Israel.

It will not help the peace process for there to be any ambiguity about where Israel's capital is. Our action today will help to eliminate any such ambiguity and to make it clear to all concerned that this country is finally going to do in Israel what we have done in every single country in the world, which is to place our Embassy in the capital city.

Senator Hutchinson also spoke in favor and said:

I thank the distinguished majority leader for bringing this to a head. It has not been easy. We have talked about this for years. The people of Israel have fought repeatedly to hold the State of Israel intact. They have designated their capital. The capital is Jerusalem. This historic, important religious city is their capital. I think it is most unusual for the United States to go to another city to establish its Embassy when the country where we are being hosted has established a different city for its capital.

The time has come long since for America to recognize the capital city of Israel. It is Jerusalem. It is time for us to move in a responsible way to have our Embassy also in the capital city of Jerusalem.

I commend the majority leader and the Senator from Arizona for their leadership in this area. I appreciate the fact that all factions have come together. Clearly, there must be some leeway for the President to make this move in a timely way. I think that leeway has been granted. This is quite a reasonable resolution. The time has come for us to have our Embassy in the capital of Israel. The capital is Jerusalem.

Senator Daschle then spoke and provided his own summary, as follows:

I think it is fair to say we all agree on three shared goals. The first is the most obvious: moving the Embassy to Jerusalem. We recognize that Jerusalem is the spiritual center and the capital of Israel, as well as a special city for those all over the world. Each country, as so many have already indicated, has the right to designate its capital, and certainly our Embassy should be there. Second, we want to ensure that Jerusalem remains an undivided city in which the rights of every ethnic and religious group are protected. That has been a goal articulated officially by this Senate since we adopted Senate Concurrent Resolution 106 in 1990. Third, and perhaps most important in the context of this debate and the negotiations that have taken place, we want to ensure that the peace process moves forward.

Then Senator Biden, now President, made a very strong presentation in support of the passage of the bill, as follows:

Madam President, thank you very much. I would like to thank my colleague from California for her leadership in bringing about what I think is a workable piece of legislation.

I would like to thank Senator Moynihan, who is not here. In 1983, he started this process. He argued we should be doing this, and we are finally getting there.

With regard to the last point made by my colleague from Connecticut about the peace process, I have had the view for the past 24 years that the only way there will be peace in the Middle East is for the Arabs to know there is no division between the United States and Israel--none, zero, none.

I argue that is why we are where we are today, because we did not relent under the leadership of this President and others. We made it clear that no wedge would be put between us, thereby leaving no alternative but the pursuit, in an equitable manner, for peace.

Those familiar, and all are on this floor, with the Jewish people know the central meaning that the ancient city of Jerusalem has for Jews everywhere. Time and again, empires have tried to sever the umbilical cord that unites Jews with their capital.

They have destroyed the temple. They have banished the Jews from living in Jerusalem. They have limited the number of Jews allowed to immigrate to that city. And, finally, in this century, they tried simply to eliminate Jews.

(Mr. KYL assumed the chair.)

They may have succeeded, Mr. President, in destroying physical structures and lives. But they have never succeeded in wholly eliminating Jewish presence in Jerusalem, or in cutting the spiritual bond between Jews and their cherished capital.

After the horrific events of the Holocaust, the Jewish people returned to claim what many rulers have tried to deny them for centuries: The right to peaceful existence in their own country in their own capital.

How many of us can forget that poignant photograph of an unnamed Israeli soldier breaking down in tears and prayer as he reached the Western Wall after his army liberated the eastern half of the city in the Six Day War?

Those tears told a story. A story of a people long denied their rightful place among nations. A people denied access to their most hallowed religious sites. A people who had finally, after long tribulation, come home.

Mr. President, it is unconscionable for us to refuse to recognize the right of the Jewish people to choose their own capital. What gives us the right to second-guess their decision? For 47 years, we, and much of the rest of the international community, have been living a lie.

For 47 years, Israel has had its government offices, its Parliament, and its national monuments in Jerusalem, not in Tel Aviv. And yet, nearly all embassies are located in Tel Aviv. I think this is a denial of fundamental reality.

Mr. President, are we, through the continued sham of maintaining our Embassy in Tel Aviv, to refuse to acknowledge what the Jewish people know in their hearts to be true? Regardless of what others may think, Jerusalem is the capital of Israel.

And Israel is not just any old country. It is a vital strategic ally.

As the Israelis and Palestinians begin the final status negotiations in May 1996--negotiations, I might add, that were made possible through the leadership of President Clinton--it should be clear to all that the United States stands squarely behind Israel, our close friend and ally.

Moving the U.S. Embassy to Jerusalem will send the right signal, not a destructive signal. To do less would be to play into the hands of those who will try their hardest to deny Israel the full attributes of statehood.

I urge my colleagues to support this legislation.

Senator Kyl concluded the debate on the bill with the following remarks:

I am pleased and honored to close this debate on this important and historic legislation which will finally cause the United States Embassy to be relocated in Jerusalem, the capital of Israel, by the year 1999.

We all know that diplomacy is filled with subtleties but that some things are fundamental. One of those fundamental things is the relationship between the United States and Israel.

Key to that relationship is an underlying principle. The principle is that Jerusalem is the essence of the historical connection of the Jewish people for Palestine. That is why Jerusalem is the capital of Israel.

This legislation, which is a bipartisan presentation of congressional intent that finally actions replace words, that deeds replace words, and expressing that historical connection, as I said, is supported in a bipartisan way by the overwhelming majority of both sides of the aisle.

There are approximately 50 Republicans which have cosponsored this legislation, and it is strongly supported as well by the many Democrats who have spoken on it.

I think the key here is for the American people to finally express, as I said, in deeds rather than words, their support for Israel through the acknowledgment that Jerusalem is the capital by the relocation of the United States Embassy in the capital city of Jerusalem.

As Senator Lieberman from Connecticut so ably pointed out, and Senator Dole did as well, this is not about the peace process, which we all support. Rather, it is an expression on the part of the United States that no longer will there be any doubt about our position relative to Jerusalem. It is an honest position, as Senator Lieberman said.

That is why, Madam President, it is so important for this body, in an overwhelming way, to express its support for the United States-Israel relationship by supporting this legislation to relocate the Embassy of the United States to the capital of Israel, Jerusalem.

The bill was read a third time, voted on, and overwhelmingly approved by the Senate, with 93 in favor[245], only 5 against[246] and 1 absent and not voting[247].

The bill was also voted on in the House of Representatives[248] that day under the leadership of Speaker Newt Gingrich.

Congressman Benjamin Gilman spoke first as an original co-sponsor of the bill in the House and said:

> Mr. Speaker, the legislation pending before us today, S. 1322 would move the United States Embassy in Israel from Tel Aviv to Jerusalem. This has been a priority of many in Congress for decades. Each time the issue was raised, successive administrations maintained that Congress was infringing on the Executive's power to conduct foreign policy, or that the hopes and dreams for peace in the Middle East rested on this one issue.

> Under the Speaker's leadership, and that of Senate majority leader Dole, legislation was introduced which is finally seeing the light of day, and which we fully expect will become law. Original sponsors of H.R. 1595, Speaker Gingrich's legislation, in addition to myself, Mr. Horn, Mr.

---

[245] The 93 Senators voting in favor of the bill were Akaka, Ashcroft, Baucus, Bennett, Biden, Bingaman, Bond, Boxer, Breaux, Brown, Bryan, Bumpers, Burns, Campbell, Coats, Cochran, Cohen, Conrad, Coverdell, Craig, D'Amato, Daschle, DeWine, Dodd, Dole, Domenici, Dorgan, Exon, Faircloth, Feingold, Feinstein, Ford, Frist, Glenn, Gorton, Graham, Gramm, Grams, Grassley, Gregg, Harkin, Hatch, Heflin, Helms, Hollings, Hutchison, Inhofe, Inouye, Johnston, Kassebaum, Kempthorne, Kennedy, Kerrey, Kerry, Kohl, Kyl, Lautenberg, Leahy, Levin, Lieberman, Lott, Lugar, Mack, McCain, McConnell, Mikulski, Moseley-Braun, Moynihan, Murkowski, Murray, Nickles, Nunn, Pell, Pressler, Pryor, Reid, Robb, Rockefeller, Roth, Santorum, Sarbanes, Shelby, Simon, Simpson, Smith, Snowe, Specter, Stevens, Thomas, Thompson, Thurmond, Warner and Wellstone.

[246] The 5 Senators voting against the bill were Abraham, Byrd, Chafee, Hatfield and Jeffords.

[247] The record reflects that Senator Bradley from N.J. was necessarily absent and didn't vote.

[248] JERUSALEM EMBASSY ACT OF 1995; Congressional Record Vol. 141, No. 165(House of Representatives - October 24, 1995), beginning at page H10680 et seq.

Lazio, Mr. Zimmer, Mr. Smith of New Jersey, Mr. Weller, Mr. DeLay, Mr. Paxon, Mr. Solomon, Mr. McIntosh, Ms. Molinari, Mr. Hastert, Mr. Archer, Mrs. Myrick, Mr. Nussle, Mrs. Vucanovich, Mr. Barr, Mr. Torkildsen, and Mr. Burton of Indiana.

This measure, the Jerusalem Embassy Act of 1995, makes a series of findings, concluding with stipulation that it is the policy of the United States that ``Jerusalem should remain an undivided city in which the rights of every ethnic and religious group are protected; Jerusalem should be recognized as the capital of the state of Israel; and the United States Embassy in Israel should be established in Jerusalem no later than May 31, 1999.''

In negotiations with the administration and other opponents on the original bill, this revised measure does contain a 6 month, renewal Presidential waiver based on national security interests. I question this inclusion, since the waiver authority does not end on a date certain, and the standard being employed is inappropriate.

Congress does not intend for the President to utilize this waiver indefinitely, nor should the employment of such a waiver, on national security grounds, be invoked lightly. Frankly, it is preposterous that a national security waiver is being employed. The national security interests of the United States are not threatened because our Embassy is located 40 miles from where Congress and the American people believe it ought to be. The legislation is clear that congressional intent is for our Embassy in Jerusalem to be established no later than May 31, 1999.

This bill is important because it rectifies an imbalance in our relationship with Israel--a nation that has shown itself to be, time and time again, the best friend that the United States has in the world, bar none.

When Saddam Hussein was raining Scud missiles throughout Israel, Israel did not retaliate, abiding by the United States request not to do so. To those cynics who may believe that Israel complied because of United States foreign assistance, I say--no moral nation, especially one that was born out of the ashes of the Holocaust as Israel was, will sacrifice its people for any sum of money.

But, a nation that has proven its friendship and reliability over the decades, as Israel has, often suppressing its own national interests in favor of ours, especially when the very lives of its own citizens is at stake, deserves our particular American brand of loyalty. There is nothing more basic than recognizing the capital of a country, which is why I strongly endorse this bill.

Since 1967, when Israel reunified Jerusalem, access for the three major religions, an American priority, became the norm. It is only under Israel that each religion has had free access to their holy places as well as control over them. In 1969, Secretary of State William Rogers modified United States policy further by stating that Jerusalem should remain a unified city, a point made repeatedly by subsequent administrations.

Administration officials maintain that the United States should not move our Embassy until negotiations have taken place on Jerusalem. This policy infers that such a move would demonstrate a preference for one of the parties, and that the U.S. role as honest broker would be compromised. But, United States policy on Jerusalem changed both before and after the onset of the peace talks in 1991.

In January 1989, the United States signed a 99-year lease with the Government of Israel at $1 per year for a 14-acre site in southwest Jerusalem. The Middle East peace process did not collapse when it was disclosed that the site had been chosen. That action, 6 years ago, did not prevent the Madrid peace talks from convening, did not prevent them from moving forward, and did not prevent the various agreements Israel signed with the PLO or its peace treaty with Jordan.

Another departure from previous U.S. policy took place in March 1994. In prior instances, the United States had supported U.N. resolutions claiming Jerusalem to be ``occupied territory''. That month the United States insisted on voting paragraph by paragraph on U.N. Resolution 904, considered in the aftermath of the Hebron massacre.

On language pertaining to Jerusalem, the United States abstained. United States Ambassador to the United Nations Madeleine Albright explained that Jerusalem was improperly included in the resolution as occupied territory and that the United States would continue to oppose including Jerusalem in this category.

It is not a major departure from existing U.S. policy to support moving the U.S. Embassy from Tel Aviv to Jerusalem by 1999, which is what the legislation being considered today proposes to do. The administration, Israel, Jordan, and the PLO have all stated that the peace process is irreversible.

This past spring, along with other Members of the House, I circulated a letter to Secretary of State Christopher, expressing support for Jerusalem as the undivided capital of Israel, noting that with negotiations on Jerusalem expected to begin in May 1996, discussion should begin in order to move the United States Embassy from Tel Aviv to Jerusalem by May 1999, when the negotiations are expected to end. Two Hundred fifty-seven Members of the

House signed that letter, another resounding measure of support from Congress to move the embassy.

Unfortunately, no response was received from the Secretary of State, and no attempt at outreach to discuss the letter's contents was made by the administration.

Congress today has the opportunity of expressing its support through the adoption of this legislation that would relocate our embassy to Jerusalem no later than 1999. I urge my colleague's strong support for this legislation, despite the inclusion of the waiver language. Moving our embassy in Israel is something the United States should have done in 1948. We have an historic opportunity today to right a wrong, to rectify an imbalance against one of our staunchest allies. Accordingly, I urge strong support of this bill.

Then Congressman, now Senator and Majority Leader, Chuck Schumer also spoke in support of the bill and said:

Mr. Speaker, I thank the gentleman from Indiana [Mr. Hamilton], ranking member, my friend, and someone whom I admire, for this time, but I must disagree with the gentleman and rise in support of this important resolution.

Mr. Speaker, let us not forget something: For any of the time that Israel has had control of any portion of Jerusalem, it has been open.

The world's holy places have been open. When the Arab nations had control of Jerusalem between 1948 and 1967, no Jew was allowed to visit any of those holy places, and many are important to the Jewish religion, as well as the Christian and Islamic religions.

Mr. Speaker, whenever I went to Israel and would have to meet with American officials and leave Jerusalem and go to Tel Aviv, it was embarrassing. It was humiliating. It was wrong.

As has been said before, it is a nation's sovereignty to choose its capital. Israel has chosen Jerusalem. It is about time the United States went along.

Mr. Speaker, I salute the gentleman from New York [Mr. Gilman] for his resolution.

Congressman Peter Deutsch spoke in response to concerns raised by a few of his colleagues about timing and whether passing this law would interfere with the prospects for peace. He made the following heartfelt remarks:

Mr. Speaker, I rise today in support of H.R. 1595, which is a piece of legislation that will facilitate a long overdue movement of the United States Embassy in Israel from Tel Aviv to Jerusalem. This is the only Embassy in the world, American Embassy, that is not in the capital that is designated by the country that the Embassy is in.

It is unprecedented and almost bizarre that it exists at this point in time. It is an anachronism from a misguided policy of really 40 years ago that this country has continued. I really congratulate my colleagues in the leadership of this House for bringing this bill to the floor at this time.

It is a bill that really should not be necessary, but we are here today discussing it and hopefully we will pass it in a few minutes. It is setting the size of the sandbox. Why should this Congress be dictating to another country what their capital is? Obviously Jerusalem is the center of the world for most people on this planet. But still that remains the capital of the state of Israel.

To offer anything else but passage of this resolution today, I think, would be really sending a terrible signal to the world, a terrible signal. In fact, I would argue very strongly that failure to get the two-thirds vote on this bill today would be sending an exactly wrong message because it would be sending a message that there is not resolve in this Congress of support of the peace process and that there is an opening in terms of what could happen in terms of Jerusalem, that the United States Congress has weakened its supports for this peace process.

So I really urge my colleagues, hopefully as close to unanimous as we can be in support of this process, that we will continue an effort, and I hope we have a situation in the Middle East that we will have peace in that region for all time.

Congressman Deutsch made more formal remarks later that day and said:

Mr. Speaker. I rise today to speak in support of S. 1322, a piece of legislation that will facilitate a long overdue movement of the United States Embassy in Israel from Tel Aviv to Jerusalem. As an original cosponsor and strong advocate of relocating our embassy to Jerusalem, I congratulate the leadership in both the House and Senate for making this a priority and moving this legislation.

For 3,000 years Jerusalem has been the capital of the Jewish people, the very heart of its religious, spiritual, cultural, and national life. It is and will forever be the eternal, undivided capital of Israel. Yet for nearly five decades Israel's closest ally--the United States--has failed to acknowledge Jerusalem as the capital. In fact, Israel is the only country in the world that the United States does not recognize the designated capital of the host country.

When you think about it, our position is nothing short of bizarre, illogical, and offensive. For 47 years, the United States has shared an extraordinary friendship with Israel but for 47 years, the United States has been frozen in this state of inconsistency and insensitivity.

But instead of looking back at what may be our mistake let's look ahead at what may be our fortune. As the peace process moves forward, moving the United States embassy to Jerusalem will send a clear message to the world, to the Middle East and most importantly, to the Palestinians that America supports Israel's claim to Jerusalem. We must stand behind Prime Minister Rabin's words to the Knesset:

United Jerusalem will not be open to negotiation. It has been and will forever be the capital of the Jewish people, under Israeli sovereignty, a focus of the dreams and longings of every Jew.

For far too long, the United States has allowed this matter to linger in ambiguity throughout the peace talks. There is absolutely no reason to risk uncertainty about the U.S. Government's commitment to the status and the destiny of Jerusalem.

Tomorrow, Prime Minister Rabin will be here to celebrate the 3,000th anniversary of Jerusalem as the capital of Israel. What better way for the United States to celebrate this occasion with Israel than to begin the process of relocating our embassy to Jerusalem.

Congressman Eliot Engel, a longstanding member of the House Foreign Affairs Committee, also spoke in strong support of the bill, despite mentioning some procedural concerns on how the legislation was brought for a vote in the house. He said:

Mr. Speaker, for almost 45 years only one country has had the dubious distinction of having to send its government officials out of its capital to visit the United States Embassy. This insult was not reserved for Libya, North Korea, Cuba, or any of America's historic detractors. It was reserved for Israel--one of America's closest friends and our most important ally in the turbulent Middle East.

Because the U.S. Embassy in Israel is based in Tel Aviv, not Jerusalem--Israel's declared capital--the United States has managed to reject a general principle of international practice: The placement of a state's embassy in the location of a foreign nation's capital. I, therefore, rise in strong support of S. 1322, the Jerusalem Embassy Relocation Act, which states that an undivided Jerusalem should be recognized as the capital of Israel and that our Embassy should be moved to that city. As the sponsor of the resolution declaring Jerusalem to be the united capital of Israel, which overwhelmingly passed the House in 1990, I strongly support this resolution and urge the House to pass it.

Some have raised concerns with the impact of S. 1322 on the ongoing peace process in the Middle East. According to those opposed to the bill, any decision to move the Embassy before the conclusion of final status talks on Jerusalem would damage the process and set back chances for peace in the Mid East. I would like to take this opportunity to allay those concerns. According to the Oslo agreement signed by Israel and the PLO in 1993, the issue of Jerusalem will be discussed during final status negotiations beginning of 1996. Moving the Embassy by 1999 is not only the principled thing to do, it is fully compatible with the timetable of the peace process. Final status negotiations are to be complete by May 1999.

While I strongly support this bill, I would like to express my opposition to the procedure under which it has been brought to the floor. S. 1322 is authorizing legislation and should rightfully have been referred to the International Relations Committee, of which I am a member, for hearings and a markup. Similar to the procedure--or lack thereof--on the Middle East Peace Facilitation Act, the International Relations Committee has not seen fit to exercise its jurisdiction on this critical issue.

On this 3,000th anniversary of the establishment of Jerusalem, the city of David, however, I am proud to announce my support for this legislation. As Israel's closest ally, the United States must take the lead in supporting the unity of Jerusalem and its permanent status as capital of Israel by moving our Embassy to the holy city.

Congressman Tom Lantos also spoke in strong support of the bill and, among other things, he detailed some of the vagaries of the hypocritical stances taken by the State Department in his remarks, as follows:

Mr. Speaker, I rise today in strong support of the legislation we are considering, S. 1322--the Jerusalem Embassy Relocation Implementation Act of 1995.

Symbolically, this is an important and an appropriate gesture for the United States to make at this particular time. This week we commemorate the anniversary of the date 3,000 years ago when David, the King of Israel, captured the city of Jerusalem and made it his capital. Under David and his successors, Jerusalem became the religious and political and emotional center of Israel, and it remains so to this very day.

Mr. Speaker, almost 12 years ago--in November of 1983--I introduced legislation in the Congress that was identical in purpose to the legislation that we are considering here today. At that time, a majority of the Members of the House cosponsored this legislation, and a majority of the Members of the Senate cosponsored the identical bill which was introduced in the other body by the distinguished Senator from New York, Senator Daniel Patrick Moynihan.

Then--as now--this legislation had broad bipartisan support. Our distinguished colleague, Congressman Benjamin A. Gilman of New York, was the principal cosponsor of our bill in the House, and a broad bipartisan group of our Democratic and Republican colleagues joined us in cosponsoring the bill. I might add that there were fewer Republican cosponsors at that time, in part because there were fewer Republican Members of the House in those days. I might add that 12 years ago, the administration of Republican President Ronald Reagan and his Vice President, George Bush, opposed our legislation.

Mr. Speaker, we have witnessed important changes since 1983 and 1984--changes which now make the adoption of this legislation more timely and appropriate. The peace process has transformed the Middle East. The Government of Israel has taken bold steps in a courageous effort to resolve the conflict with the Palestinians. The end of the cold war has created the fundamental conditions that have permitted this peace process to move forward.

U.S. administrations have played a critical role in encouraging and facilitating this peace process-- administrations of both parties with the bipartisan support of the Congress. The Bush administration played a major role in starting the process following the victory of U.S.-led forces in the gulf war. The Clinton administration continued actively to encourage, cajole, and support the process, culminating in the signing ceremony on the White House lawn in September 1993. With the support of the United States, a peace treaty between Israel and Jordan has been signed, and agreements have been signed regarding Palestinian administration of Palestinian-inhabited territories and arrangements for democratic Palestinian elections.

Although conditions in the region have changed that now permit us to move forward on this legislation, the arguments and reasons for adopting this legislation have not changed over the past 12 years.

Mr. Speaker, the United States maintains diplomatic relations with 184 countries. In virtually all of these countries where we have a resident Embassy, our Embassy is located in the capital city. When the Government of Brazil decided to move its capital from Rio de Janeiro to Brasilia, the United States moved its Embassy to the new capital. When the Government of Saudi Arabia, which until a few years ago indicated that it would like to have Embassies located in Riyadh, the United States Government followed traditional diplomatic practice and constructed an Embassy building in Riyadh. This is as it should be. An Embassy should be in the same city as the Government to which it is accredited.

In one case, however, our Embassy is not located in the capital city--despite the expressed desire of the house country that this be done. Although Jerusalem is the capital of Israel, our Embassy is located in Tel Aviv.

Jerusalem has been the capital of Israel since 1949. Presidents of the United States, Secretaries of State, United States Ambassadors, Members of Congress--all have done business with the Government of Israel at the seat of government in West Jerusalem. When Anwar Sadat of Egypt paid a historic visit to Israel and addressed the Israeli Knesset, he spoke at the Knesset building in West Jerusalem. Moving the U.S. Embassy to West Jerusalem does not affect any of the issues surrounding the peaceful resolution of the Palestinian issue. West Jerusalem has been an integral part of Israel since 1949 and this has been recognized by all nations with whom Israel maintains diplomatic relations.

An analogy with the situation in East Germany prior to the unification of Germany just 4 years ago this month is particularly appropriate in this case. The Government of East Germany claimed that East Berlin was an integral part of its territory. The United States, however, did not recognize this claim and maintained that East Berlin and West Berlin had a unique status guaranteed by the four occupying powers--the Soviet Union, the United States, Britain and France. Nevertheless, when the United States established diplomatic relations with East Germany in 1971, we located our embassy in East Berlin. At that time the State Department affirmed:

The United States Government proceeds on the basis that the locations and functions of an American Embassy in East Berlin, where it will be convenient to the government offices with which it will deal, will not affect the special legal status of the Berlin area.

We were broadminded enough to enunciate and observe this rational principle in dealing with a communist dictatorship which sought to undermine our own treaty obligation for all of Berlin. Why should we not follow the same rational principle in dealing with a democratic ally?

Mr. Speaker, I urge my colleagues to join in supporting the adoption of this legislation. The time has come to end inconvenience, inefficiency, and expense by moving our Embassy to Israel's capital city--Jerusalem.

The bill was resoundingly approved in the House that day, with 374 voting in favor, only 37 against[249], 5 answering present, and 17 not voting[250].

---

[249] Which included then Congressmen, now Senator, Bernie Sanders and Xavier Becerra, now HHS Secretary in the Biden Administration, as well as, Congresswoman Maxine Waters.

[250] Which included, Sherrod Brown, Charlie Rangel, Jose Serrano and Nydia Velasquez.

The law was thus passed by Congress and then sent to President William J. Clinton, who had ten days either to veto or sign the law while Congress was in session or it would automatically pass into law. President Clinton did neither and it became the law of the land on November 8, 1995[251].

---

[251] The Jerusalem Embassy Act had passed with a veto proof majority and, hence, vetoing the bill was not a real alternative. It appears President Clinton, therefore, chose to do nothing and just let it become the law of the land.

V.

THE PRESIDENTIAL WAIVER PROVISION-ITS HISTORY OF USE AND ABUSE

For over twenty years, President after President, until President Trump, formulaically exercised the waiver provision under the Jerusalem Embassy Act of 1995 to delay formal recognition of Jerusalem and moving the embassy there.

Here's an example of the text of one of them:

Presidential Determination No. 2001–06 of December 15, 2000

Suspension of Limitations Under the Jerusalem Embassy Act

Memorandum for the Secretary of State

Pursuant to the authority vested in me as President by the Constitution and the laws of the United States, including section 7(a) of the Jerusalem Embassy Act of 1995 (Public Law 104–45) (the "Act"), I hereby determine that it is necessary to protect the national security interests of the United States to suspend for a period of 6 months the limitations set forth in sections 3(b) and 7(b) of the Act.

You are hereby authorized and directed to transmit this determination to the Congress, accompanied by a report in accordance with section 7(a) of the Act, and to publish the determination in the Federal Register.

This suspension shall take effect after transmission of this determination and report to the Congress.

WILLIAM J. CLINTON

THE WHITE HOUSE,

Washington, December 15, 2000.

The last one signed by President Trump (Presidential Determination No. 2019-06 of December 7, 2018-Suspension of Limitations Under the Jerusalem Embassy Act) used the same format.

The waiver was formally described as a "Suspension of Limitations under the Jerusalem Embassy Act", because absent the exercise of the Presidential waiver every six months, there would have been an automatic reduction in the budget afforded the State Department for the operations of Embassies, under Sections 3(b) and 7(b) of the Act.

Interestingly, President George W. Bush added a clause that "My administration remains committed to the beginning of the process of moving our Embassy to Jerusalem". President Barack H. Obama did so as well for a time, but then removed this sentence. The rest of the form waiver was otherwise standardized.

Well-meaning sentiments aside, the crux of the waiver procedure, as specified by the Act, was embodied in the substantive national security interests condition, expressly provided in Sections 7(a) and 7(a)(3) of the Act. This was the sole basis permitted for the President to exercise the waiver. The Act required that the national security interests, which were the justification for the exercise of the waiver, be described to Congress in a report submitted to Congress, together with the waiver document. Thus, the Act provided, in relevant part, as follows:

The President may suspend such limitation for an additional six month period at the end of any period during which the suspension is in effect under this subsection if the President determines and reports to Congress in advance of the additional suspension that the additional suspension is necessary to protect the national security interests of the United States.

A report...shall include—

(A) a statement of the interests affected by the limitation that the President seeks to suspend; and

(B) a discussion of the manner in which the limitation affects the interests.

This is because, as discussed above, the waiver was not supposed to be a mere perfunctory exercise. It was intended that it be premised on a legitimate concern involving genuine national security interests, which would be negatively affected if the waiver was not invoked. The waiver was not to be exercised for any or no reason, just because the President unilaterally and personally felt like doing so. In this regard, it should be noted that a mere conclusory statement that it was necessary to do so in order to protect the national security interests of the United States was insufficient under the law. An accompanying report (which typically took the form of a written statement or memorandum), complying with the provisions of Section 7(a)(3) above, was required. In essence, providing the justification for the President's waiver was a necessary component of its exercise.

Set forth below is the text of the waiver issued by President George W, Bush, dated June 15, 2006, as well as the accompanying Justification submitted, as published in the Federal Register:

Presidential Determination No. 2006–15 of June 15, 2006

Suspension of Limitations Under the Jerusalem Embassy Act

Memorandum for the Secretary of State

Pursuant to the authority vested in me as President by the Constitution and the laws of the United States, including section 7(a) of the Jerusalem Embassy Act of 1995 (Public Law 104–45) (the "Act"), I hereby determine that it is necessary to protect the national security interests of the United States to suspend for a period of 6 months the limitations set forth in sections 3(b) and 7(b) of the Act. My Administration remains committed to beginning the process of moving our Embassy to Jerusalem.

You are hereby authorized and directed to transmit this determination to the Congress, accompanied by a report in accordance with section 7(a) of the Act, and to publish the determination in the Federal Register.

This suspension shall take effect after transmission of this determination and report to the Congress.

George W. Bush

THE WHITE HOUSE, Washington, June 15, 2006.

JUSTIFICATION

The President has exercised his authority under the Constitution and the laws of the United States, including the waiver authority granted to him by Section 7(a) of P.L. 104-45. This waiver was necessary to protect critical national security interests, most critically in preserving our ability to work with the parties and the key states in the region to bring about an end to the violence and terrorism in Israel, the West Bank and Gaza. The President has also taken this action at this time because, absent the waiver, the Act would have denied to the Department of State further access to funds necessary to protect its personnel and missions worldwide so it can continue to pursue vital U.S. objectives.

A key foreign policy and national security goal of the United States is to help the parties end the current violence in Israel, the West Bank and Gaza. Moving the Embassy now would complicate our ability to play a helpful role in bringing an end to the violence,

Moreover, in this time of substantial terrorist threats to U.S. missions and personnel abroad, the Department of State must also have access to funds necessary to upgrade the security and operations of its missions worldwide. Sections 3(b) and 7(b) of P.L. 104-45 would prohibit the Department of State access to 50 percent of funds appropriated for its missions abroad. There is a real danger that despite the fact that Congress has directed the use of these funds for just such urgent purposes, the absence of those funds would hamper our ongoing efforts to protect our personnel and missions abroad.

The Administration is committed to beginning the process of moving our Embassy to Jerusalem. However, at this time, it is necessary for the President to exercise his waiver authority in order to protect the national security interests of the United States.

The text of the so-called 'Justification' is an illustration of how to skirt actually complying with the intent of the Act and, perhaps, as suggested below, artfully avoiding strict compliance with its precise provisions. While it does use the term national security, it does not actually set forth the precise national security interests affected by the limitation that the President seeks to suspend or discuss the manner in which the limitation affects those national security interests, as required by the Act.

Consider, although the US might have a most virtuous desire to see an end to the violence and terrorism perpetrated by the PA and Hamas, as well as others like PIJ and Hezbollah, in Israel, Judea, Samaria and Gaza, this is a local matter that does not directly affect the national security interests of the US. Furthermore, in point of fact, the reality of recognizing Jerusalem and moving the Embassy there did not cause a materially adverse change in the role the US might play in working with the parties and key states in the region. Indeed, as subsequent events would demonstrate, it had a positive effect in relation to key states in the region. It also did not materially prejudice the US's role with the PA, which was all too willing to accept the US' largesse while consistently rejecting its advice to reform. Delaying formal recognition of Jerusalem and moving the Embassy there was neither legally justified nor effective. The success of the Abraham Accords is a striking rebuttal to the unfounded fears and misguided policies of the past and proof positive that one must dare to do what's just and right.

The argument in the Justification that funding of security for missions worldwide would be affected is a good example of State Department Orwellian double-speak. First of all, this was not a real concern. The limitation of funding provision under the Act definitionally did not impinge on funding of security. Secondly, it ignores the fact that it is a self-inflicted problem caused by the State Department's intentional failure to comply with the law[252]. In essence, just comply with the law, move the Embassy to Jerusalem, and avoid any funding issues at all under the Act.

Moreover, as noted below, based on the State Department's own records, the Embassy location in Tel Aviv lacked sufficient security, and relocating it to another more secure location was desirable. Thus, relocating the Embassy to the site in Arnona, Jerusalem, actually improved security.

---

[252] The premise is all too reminiscent of Abraham Lincoln's definition of a "Hypocrite: The man who murdered his parents, and then pleaded for mercy on the grounds that he was an orphan."

The so-called "key foreign policy and national security goal of the United States to help the parties end the current violence in Israel, the West Bank, and Gaza" and that "Moving the Embassy now would complicate our ability to play a helpful role in bringing an end to the violence" is a study in obfuscation and distraction. It begins with the introduction of the term "goal". In essence, it's not a national security 'interest'; it's merely a national security 'goal'. The added qualifier that it's a 'foreign policy' goal adds nothing in terms of meeting the requirements of the Act. It merely serves to muddle the response by detracting from clearly specifying the particular national security interest at issue. After all, if there were a true 'national security interest' at issue, then the document could just have simply stated what it was and left it at that. In essence, there really wasn't a national security 'interest' at risk, which presented a real and present danger to the US; it was merely a 'goal'.

The assumption that moving the Embassy would complicate the US' ability to play a helpful role in bringing an end to the violence is not only presumptuous; it's baseless. The violence had little, if anything, to do with where the US located its Embassy and everything to do with the stated goal of these terrorist organizations to eliminate the Jewish State of Israel. The assertion that moving the Embassy to Jerusalem now might complicate the US' ability to play a helpful role in bringing an end to the violence begs the questions of precisely how and why was it more complicated to proceed 'now' than at any other time? There was no pending negotiation at the time. As a practical matter, the use of the term 'now' in this context might verily be described as a euphemism for not ever or there's never a good time. Furthermore, as more fully discussed above, the Act rejects this false premise and asserts that recognizing Jerusalem and moving the Embassy might actually improve the prospects for peace in the region. This it did by strengthening the bonds between the US and its friends and allies.

In sum and substance, the Justification is little more than a proforma and conclusory restatement of previous biased formulations of the State Department and the foreign policy establishment designed to frustrate the recognition of Jerusalem and movement of the Embassy there. This was a repetitive theme, which served to prevent or inhibit a new and fresh reasoned analysis of the reality of the situation at hand.

Consider the State Department Reports issued pursuant to Section 5 and then Section 6 of the Jerusalem Embassy Act after it was first enacted. The excuse given for inaction was that the administration would take no action, which would undermine the peace process. However, other than a mere hope that this failed approach would somehow help conclude a genuine peace, there was no actual tangible progress. Even the reference to the Palestinian National Council amending the PLO covenant to revoke the sections that called for the destruction of the State of Israel on April 24, 1996, proved false. The illusion of progress being made and the illusory speculation, at the time, that a real peace agreement was just beyond the horizon was nothing more than a pipe dream.

Jon Kyl called out the State Department for submitting periodic reports under the Jerusalem Embassy Act that were unresponsive and, at times, even hostile to the idea of moving the Embassy to Jerusalem. He noted instead of offering a specific plan for the move, the reports were written as primers on how embassies are established and on the history of the peace process. He declared the generalities offered in the reports fell well short of complying with the intent of the reporting requirements under the Act.

However, other than complaining about the flouting of the Act by the State Department, there was little that Kyl could do to enforce its provisions. This was especially so given the administration's apparent lack of interest in pursuing recognition and the move. It is presumed that a referral to the

Department of Justice to enforce the requirements of the Act would have been futile.

Imagine, though, if a duly authorized and independent counsel could have been enlisted to march into Federal Court to seek an order compelling compliance with the Act. The Court would then have had the job of determining whether there was a cogent national security interest for not moving the Embassy. If it could not make such a finding, then the erstwhile Suspension could be judicially voided, triggering the budgetary limitations provided for under the Act. However, this would have required the Act to have a provision allowing for this remedy of an independent special counsel. Similarly, the Act could also have expressly provided for a private right of action. The same can be said for other laws passed by Congress, like Taylor Force, where the Executive Branch has, as discussed below, seemingly resisted adherence to the spirit and perhaps even avoided strict compliance with the provisions of the law. Absent a truly independent, non-partisan legal mechanism for enforcing the law, it appears that the seriousness of the Executive Branch's efforts to comply with laws it doesn't fully agree with and embrace is sometimes questionable.

The Executive Branch is also not a monolithic structure where the decisions of the President are automatically effectuated. Sometimes, even after an exhaustive decision-making process, with input from all the relevant constituencies within the governmental administration, there can still be resistance by some in an effort to frustrate the implementation of a Presidential directive. There are also corporate cultures within the bureaucracy, which inhibit their ability to process a change in attitudes, direction or policies. Consider the curious obsession by the State Department with unerringly doing the same thing, over and over again, despite repeated failures to accomplish the ostensible goal of establishing true peace between the PA and Hamas, on the one hand, and Israel, on the other hand; it's mystifying. So too, is the compulsive need furtively to excuse failure and disclaim any other alternatives to the repeatedly failed course of action. It all appears so irrational and, frankly speaking, perverse. A dispassionate observer might clinically view this all as symptomatic of some kind of neurotic infatuation or fanatical adherence to an ideological construct divorced from reality. Whatever the source of the problem, the continued insistence on these failed policies has not resulted in positive accomplishments. Is it any wonder that policies premised on appeasement, which reward wrongdoers and don't penalize wrongdoing, have failed to transform the offenders into saints?

There was no real damage to the peace process with the PA and Hamas because there was no actual peace process. On the other hand, as to the other states in the area, continuing the very same failed policies inhibited the possibility of promoting peace in the region. In a sense, the misplaced focus on pursuing peace with villains in the ranks of the PA and Hamas prejudiced any true prospect of the US having a credible role with the leaders of the real nations in the region. The leaders of Arab nations better understood how ridiculous it was for the US to be chasing after, foolishly relying on and even rewarding the criminals heading the PA and Hamas.

Under the Trump administration, there was a refocus on other nations in the region and dealing with the real national security threat posed by Iran and its proxies. A practical and realistic approach that fostered enlightened self-interest to achieve just and right goals and peace through strength were a welcome and refreshing change in US foreign policy. It made it worthwhile to join with the US and Israel to create a circle of peace and a united front against the threats of foes they faced in common. The fact that the Abraham Accords occurred after the US recognized Jerusalem and moved the Embassy there, resulting in a warm peace between Israel and each of the parties that continues to flourish and bring prosperity to the parties, is a striking rebuke to the failed policies of the past.

In a similar vein of realism, the Taylor Force Act was passed, as discussed above. This law of the land also appears to be disregarded by some in the Executive Branch, as noted above and discussed below. However, given the history of lack of compliance with the Jerusalem Embassy Act described above, it should not be surprising. This selective compliance with and enforcement of the law seems to have become a more common phenomenon in recent times. It reaffirms the need for an independent counsel provision to be inserted in these laws, as noted above, so as to avoid this seemingly endemic problem. How else to deal with an apparently pervasive ideological ethic that has taken hold among some exercising the levers of power within the government, which countenances resistance to and even actively violating laws duly enacted by Congress without recourse or consequence? This ideological compulsion to flout the law is an anathema to democracy.

It is nevertheless shocking that the State Department appears to have, in effect, been complicit, by either improperly issuing the required certification, despite the PA's failure to meet the conditions to funding under the Act or not doing so and apparently violating its obligation to report why it was unable to do so, as required under Paragraph (e) of the Act.[253]. Either way,

---

[253] The text of Paragraph (e) is as follows: Report (1) In general: If the Secretary of State is unable to certify in writing to the appropriate congressional committees that the Palestinian Authority, the Palestine Liberation Organization, and any successor or affiliated organizations have met the conditions described in subsection (a), the Secretary shall, not later than 15 days after the date on which the Secretary is unable to make such certification, submit to the appropriate congressional committees a report that contains the following: (A) The reasons why the Secretary was unable to certify in writing that such organizations have met such requirements. (B) The definition of "acts of terrorism" that the Secretary used for purposes of making the determination in subparagraph (B) of subsection (a)(1). (C) The total amount of funds to be withheld.

there appears to be a concerted effort to avoid compliance with the law.

A number of members of the Senate, including Ted Cruz, Marco Rubio, Rick Scott, and Tom Cotton, among others, wrote to Secretary Blinken to address the matter in a letter dated April 8, 2021. They noted, as follows:

> On March 18, the State Department transmitted an unpublicized report to Congress pursuant to its obligations under the TFA, which confirmed that the PA has in recent years funneled hundreds of millions of dollars toward terrorists and their families, and that in 2019 alone the PA expressed its intention to spend approximately $342.6 million on such rewards. It noted that "the PA has not revoked any law, decree, regulation, or document authorizing or implementing" that system of payments. The existence and details of the report were revealed by the Washington Free Beacon, which noted the report said "[t]he Biden-Harris Administration has made clear its intent to restart assistance to the Palestinians" but "[i]t remains unclear how the Biden administration will restart American aid without violating [TFA]."

> On March 19, the Government Accountability Office (GAO) issued a report finding that for the fiscal years 2015-2019, when USAID was distributing Palestinian assistance, USAID "did not consistently ensure" that those grants would not be passed along to terrorist groups and terrorists. The GAO recommended that, should funding resume, USAID should "(1) verify prime awardees have procedures to ensure compliance with requirements before making subawards and (2) conduct post-award compliance reviews in time to make corrections before the awards end." It also noted that "USAID agreed with the recommendations."

On March 26, the General Secretary of Fatah, the party that controls the PA, revealed that Fatah and Hamas were working towards a consensus document for unity control over the PA after upcoming elections. The announcement came after months of talks aimed at such an agreement, including through the exchange of messages outlining the groups' mutual agendas, the negotiation of a plan to establish a fused government, and the setting of spring elections.

The Senators went on to describe an unpublicized submission made by the State Department, which he referred to as a USAID "program narrative" transmitted to Congress on March 26, 2021. It purported to appropriate:

> $75,000,000 in Economic Support Funds (ESF) for "programs that USAID/West Bank and Gaza intends to carry out," with funding able to commence 15 days after the notification was received, i.e. April 10. The notification describes new assistance that would go towards, inter alia, "municipal roads," "internal roads, sidewalks, safe and designated bus parking lots, and driving routes," "reservoirs, pump stations, water distribution and transmission networks," "basic commodities," "emergency preparedness," "community initiatives," "safe spaces to engage in community initiatives," and "building the resilience of the Palestinians to climate change and strengthening their adaptation to climate change.

However, as the Senators pointed out:

> "These activities are the governance responsibility of the PA, and Congress prohibited American assistance to such activities against the backdrop of the PA using its available resources for pay-for-slay programs. In fact, Congress explicitly and narrowly enumerated in TFA what Palestinian governance programs should nevertheless still

receive assistance: wastewater projects, childhood vaccination programs, and payments to East Jerusalem hospitals. The programs described in the March 26 USAID notification do not fit into those exceptions and so likely violate the TFA.

To better appreciate the cogency of these arguments, reference should be made to the findings made under the Act. It provides, in pertinent part, as follows:

(1) The Palestinian Authority's practice of paying salaries to terrorists serving in Israeli prisons, as well as to the families of deceased terrorists, is an incentive to commit acts of terror.

(2) The United States does not provide direct budgetary support to the Palestinian Authority. The United States does pay certain debts held by the Palestinian Authority and funds programs for which the Palestinian Authority would otherwise be responsible.

(3) The United States Government supports community-based programs in the West Bank and Gaza that provide for basic human needs, such as food, water, health, shelter, protection, education, and livelihoods, and that promote peace and development.

(4) Since fiscal year 2015, annual appropriations legislation has mandated the reduction of Economic Support Fund aid for the Palestinian Authority as a result of their payments for acts of terrorism, including, in fiscal year 2017, a reduction 'by an amount the Secretary determines is equivalent to the amount expended by the Palestinian Authority, the Palestine Liberation Organization, and any successor or affiliated organizations with such entities as payments for acts of terrorism by individuals who are imprisoned after being fairly tried and convicted

for acts of terrorism and by individuals who died committing acts of terrorism during the previous calendar year'.

The flouting of the intent and purposes of the Taylor Force Act and even its express provisions makes a mockery of Congress and the law. The concocted artifice and obvious subterfuge promulgated by the State Department in an effort to evade compliance with the plain meaning and express portions of the Act were summarily dismissed by Senators, as described above.

Senator Tom Cotton also reportedly later stated[254]:

Secretary Blinken's promise to send millions in aid to the Palestinians almost certainly violates restrictions in the Taylor Force Act," and adding: "The Biden administration must halt all U.S. aid to the Palestinians until we can be sure that this aid isn't benefitting the Palestinian Authority or terrorist organizations like Hamas that are eager to wipe Israel off the map.

This was in response to what appeared to be yet another and even more flagrant violation of the Taylor Force Law by Secretary Blinken. He met with Mahmoud Abbas on May 25 2021 and announced an overall aid package in excess of $360 million for the Palestinian people[255]. This was done despite the P.A. not terminating payments under its heinous Pay to Slay program or revoking any law, decree, regulation or document authorizing the same.

Abbas has a long history of paying lip service to peace in discussions with US interlocutors and then laughing it off when

[254]See, Is the Biden administration violating the Taylor Force Act?, by Donna R. Edmunds, at JNS, dated 6/15/2021.
[255] See, Secretary Antony J. Blinken and Palestinian Authority President Mahmoud Abbas Statements to the Press, Remarks to the Press, Anthony J. Blinken, Secretary of State, Ramallah, West Bank, May 25, 2021, at state.gov.

addressing another audience. Thus, for example[256], Abbas said in an interview with the London-based Qatari daily Al-Quds Al-Arabi that he would not give in to the American and Israeli demand to stop payments to the families of prisoners and martyrs, calling them "fighters" and underlining his obligation to them. At the July 23 2018 Ramallah ceremony honoring prisoners, Abbas conferred medals on the families of the "martyred prisoners" and on the released prisoners and said:

> We will neither reduce nor prevent [payment] of allowances to the families of martyrs, prisoners, and released prisoners, as some seek, and if we had only a single penny left, we would pay it to families of the martyrs and prisoners.

He went on to stress:

> From our standpoint, the martyrs and prisoners are stars in the firmament of the Palestinian people's struggle, and take priority in every matter. In 1965, a few days after the outbreak of the Palestinian revolution, the first mission undertaken by the martyr late president Yasser Arafat was to establish an institution to care for the families of the martyrs and the mujahideen of Palestine – for they are the pioneers and must be cared for, and we will care for them.

He expressed his deep appreciation for the activity on the prisoners' behalf, and noted that it "paves the way for the liberation of Palestine.

Palestinian Prime Minister Mohammed Shtayyeh, on November 17, 2020[257], said: "We will continue to pay aid to the families of

---

[256] See, Palestinian Authority (PA) President Abbas: 'If We Had Only A Single Penny Left, We Would Pay It To Families Of The Martyrs And Prisoners', dated July 24, 2018, at Memri.org.
[257] See, Palestinian Authority Financing of Terrorism, at Jewish Virtual Library.org and sources noted therein.

martyrs and prisoners to ensure a decent life for their families, and we will not abandon them."

In 2021, the PA was reportedly in dire financial condition; yet, it nevertheless still paid roughly $193 million to prisoners and released terrorists and another $78 million to wounded terrorists and the families of dead terrorists. Due to international pressure and scrutiny, the PA tried to conceal the payments by hiding expenditures to terrorists under different budget categories, integrating released terrorists into PA ministries, developing a new payment system to circumvent the banks that refused to provide services to terrorists and manipulating published PA financial reports to mask the payments[258].

In May of 2022, Abbas yet again reaffirmed his commitment to continue the "Pay-for-Slay" payments[259].

In essence, the administration acted ultra vires by improperly spending money not unqualifiedly authorized by Congress, in flagrant disregard of the conditions Congress attached thereto, which were not truly satisfied. How is this not considered a defalcation and why is the Justice Department not enforcing the law against the offending parties in government?

It is curious that there appears to be no publicly available copy of a certification by the Secretary of State, as required under the Act, to enable the continuation of funding. FOIA requests have reportedly been made and there is even a lawsuit[260] that was filed

---

[258] How much did the PA spend on terrorists' salaries in 2020?, by Maurice Hirsch, Itamar Marcus and Nan Jacques Zilberdik, at Palestinian Media Watch, dated 2/22/2021 and Three ways the PA tried to hide its terror reward payments in 2021, Maurice Hirsch, at Palestinian Media Watch, dated 5/5/2021.

[259] See, On 'Nakba,' Abbas vows to continue payments to prisoners and 'martyrs', by Khaled Abu Toameh, in the Jerusalem Post, dated 5/15/2022 and As Biden meets with Abbas, Abbas raises the salaries of hundreds of terrorists, by Maurice Hirsch, at Palestinian Media Watch, dated 7/12/2022.

[260] Watchdog Files Lawsuit to Obtain Records Supporting State Department's Decision to Fund Palestinian Authority, at protectpublicstrust.org, dated 1/17/2022.

to obtain copies of the relevant documents showing the basis for any such certification.

It is also reported[261] that the State Department had admitted it was unable to certify to Congress that the PA and PLO were complying with the Taylor Force Act because they had not, in fact, terminated payments for acts of terrorism to any individual after being fairly tried, who had been imprisoned for such acts of terrorism and to any individual who died committing such acts of terrorism, including to family members.

The administration reportedly privately confirmed to Congress in March of 2021 that the PA has continued to use international aid money to reward terrorists. The State Department submitted to Congress a March 18, 2021 report (presumably the one referred to in the Senators' April 8, 2021 letter, noted above), which states that the PA continues to fund the Pay to Slay program.

In addition, the State Department reportedly determined that the PA had "not taken proactive steps to counter incitement to violence against Israel" and "incitement to violence and glorification of terrorism occur in public statements and social media posts by PA officials and politicians, in official media broadcasts and social media outlets, and in school textbooks". Is it any wonder that Abbas' deputy chairman at Fatah brazenly admits that the PA security forces fight alongside terrorists against Israel and that they are all one[262].

Yet, rather than publicizing what amounts to a grievous indictment of the sordid activities of the PA and terminating funding, as required under the Taylor Force Act, the administration was undaunted. It irresponsibly committed to

---

[261] See, Palestinians Funneled Hundreds of Millions to Terrorists, State Dept Report Reveals, by Adam Kredo, in the Free Beacon, dated 3/22/2021.
[262] Abbas deputy admits PA security personnel work with terrorists, at JNS.org, dated 10/27/2022.

doing the very opposite by undoing the previous administration's cuts and immorally restarting and even increasing funding[263].

Another law that is seemingly not currently being actively enforced by the administration is the Anti-Boycott Law, discussed in Chapter XIV below.

It is hard not to see a pattern in the lack of enthusiastic compliance with all three of these seminal laws involving Israel, passed by Congress, as well as the Koby Mandell Act, discussed in Chapter VI below and other laws referenced below intended to curb PA abuses and wrongdoing.

Take, for example, the Anti-Terrorism Law-PLO[264], as amended, and the Palestinian Anti-Terrorism Act of 2006[265], which require limitations on aid and provide for other restrictions, unless the President or State Department, as the case may be, furnish certifications every six months that, among other things, the PA is adhering to the Oslo Accords. The fact is the PA has materially breached the Oslo Accords in a number of significant respects that go to the very heart of the agreement. This includes but is not limited to its cynical failure to root out terrorism. As discussed above, not only has it not made any serious effort in this regard, it actually positively promotes terrorist acts against Israel. Presidential waivers have also been routinely issued, which skirt compliance with the Anti-Terrorist Law, as amended. While referencing that important to the national interest of the US, they fail even to address the other condition that must also certify that PLO complying with the Oslo Accords and its other commitments. The failure so to certify is understandable because it is most assuredly not the case. Contemptuously

---

[263] See, Commentary: Has the Biden Administration Violated the Taylor Force Act, by Mike Pompeo, Sander Gerber and Stuart Force, in the Detroit Jewish News, dated 6/17/2021.

[264] 22 USC 5201, et seq., Chapter 61: Anti-Terrorism-PLO originally passed at the end of 1987, as amended by Public Law 103-125, dated 10/28/1993 (107 Stat. 1309) and the clarification, Public Law 115-253, dated 10/3/2018 (132 Stat. 3183).

[265] Palestinian Anti-Terrorism Act of 2006 (120 Stat. 3318).

ignoring this absolute obligation and continuing funding is incomprehensible. In a republic like the US, this kind of disdain for the law by government officials, seemingly without consequence, should be inconceivable; yet, apparently, it is not. The apparent prevalence of this disdain for fully complying with the spirit and sometimes possibly even the letter of the law is appalling. The seeming impotence in the face of what amounts to a tyrannical exercise of executive power cynically flouting laws duly passed by Congress is one of the evils our Constitutional system of government was designed to eradicate. Under the Constitution, there is a separation of powers[266]. The power of the purse was reserved to Congress. The remedy for those in government who may disagree with a law is to seek to change it, not to undermine or evade it. This should be an issue of profound concern to everyone, no matter the party or affiliation.

The insidious gas lighting is palpable and begs the question of why? Perhaps, the answer lies in the transformation of the latent antisemitic traditions, endemic to the ethos of the State Department since before World War II, as described below, into a cultural diffidence when it comes to the Jewish State of Israel. Perhaps, it is because of another ideological imperative currently in vogue, which presumptively demonizes Israel while reflexively treating those that prey upon it as victims instead of as the predators. In essence, those perceived as being stronger must automatically be deemed the wrongdoer and those perceived as being weaker are treated as the victim, no matter what the actual facts and circumstances may be. This ideological principle is an analog derived from the Marxist conception of the class struggle, which has infected the groupthink of many.

Whatever the case, it is patently obvious that there is a problem of selective enforcement of and compliance with the law, which

---

[266] US Constitution, Article I.

is calculated and not haphazard; and it is inexcusable. Reasonable people can disagree on policy and are free to urge Congress to enact a change in the law. However, it is unacceptable for a person or Department in the Executive Branch unilaterally to disregard the sacred responsibility of enforcing and/or complying with a law because of a disagreement with the law or the policies it promotes.

This is particularly galling in light of the magnificent bipartisan effort that crafted these laws, which reflect policies that received overwhelming bipartisan support. In effect, a few people who think they know better than everyone else or are guided by some compulsive commitment to ideological purity that demeans the wisdom of others and the will of the people are unilaterally pursuing their own private policies.

Instead of doing what is just and right, they are promoting an immoral policy condoning and effectively financing the murder of innocent Americans, Israelis and Palestinian Arabs. Whatever virtuous-sounding slogans they may declare about their desire to promote peace, the facts belie their presumptuous and specious assertions, and they bear responsibility for the untoward outcome. By funding evil, peace is not being encouraged; it is only emboldening the wrongdoers. Those acting to effectuate this perversion of the law are, in essence, complicit in the ensuing despicable terrorist actions and the wicked Pay to Slay program of the PA.

VI.

WHY THE RELUCTANCE TO RECOGNIZE JERUSALEM AS THE CAPITAL OF ISRAEL?

The reluctance of the US State Department and successive administrations, from President Truman through and including President Obama, to recognize Jerusalem as the capital of Israel is mystifying.

Why single out the Jewish State of Israel as the only country in which the US did not maintain its Embassy in the host country's chosen capital, as desired by the host? Many have asked this or similar questions. There is no obvious, logical, and supportable answer. After all, Jerusalem is not the only situation in the world where there are competing interests and claims; yet Jerusalem is singled out for unique treatment to the point of seeming absurdity.

Some of the excuses offered may have appeared facially rational at one time or another, but only for a limited period of time; others made little or no sense at all. In this regard, it should be noted that when there is no apparent rational explanation for a policy, then there are often one or more undisclosed insidious reasons which animate the offensive policy. It is suggested that, as summarized below, there existed severe biases that infected many within the ranks of the State Department, which seem to have colored its policies when it came to the matter of Jerusalem. These were reinforced by a not atypical practice in large organizations of perpetuating institutional myths through a culture of conformity and the discipline of groupthink.

Challenging the prevailing wisdom is not considered wise or acceptable in a highly bureaucratic organizational structure. The answer to why a particular practice or policy is followed is often because that's the way we do things here. Instead of a continuous search for truth that invites questions and healthy skepticism, there is an effete attitude, which smugly presumes we know better. It's so persistent that there appears to be almost a callous indifference to new data and facts that emerge, which challenge and even give lie to the assumptions made and positions taken by the keepers of our foreign policy.

As detailed above, there were a number of assumptions made, as disclosed in the reports to Congress required under the Jerusalem Embassy Act of 1995, which were flawed or turned out to be just plain wrong. This Chapter is about the more fundamental biases that seem to have been entrenched and prevalent and may have also contributed to some of the incorrect assumptions summarized above.

Interestingly, the US, like so many other countries, including Great Britain, France, Germany and Russia, established its consulate in Jerusalem during the reign of the Ottoman Empire. Its first location, in 1844, was in the Old City of Jerusalem, near the Jaffa Gate. The US Consulate eventually moved outside the Old City and, from 1912 through March of 2019, it was located on Agron Street.

The US Embassy was located in Tel Aviv until President Trump moved it to Jerusalem. This was so even though Israel moved its seat of government to Jerusalem and declared it as its capital in 1950. The Jerusalem Consulate remained open, but mainly to serve the needs of Arabs residing in Jerusalem and, after the reunification of Jerusalem in 1967, also to serve Arabs residing in Judea and Samaria. There were a whole set of arcane rules developed to negate any appearance of the US recognizing Jerusalem as the capital of Israel. This included not allowing official cars to fly the US flag in Jerusalem and marking the birthplace of Americans born in Jerusalem as Jerusalem, not Israel.

The US Ambassador in Tel Aviv was also reportedly treated somewhat suspiciously and aloofly by his colleagues from other US Embassies in the Middle East and even by the Consul General in Jerusalem[267]. Indeed, the Jerusalem Consulate was known as a longtime bastion of antisemites. Len's brother, Harry, of blessed memory, experienced this firsthand when, as an American citizen living in Efrat, he tried to make use of the consular services there. It is exasperating to realize that an American citizen working and paying taxes in the US and also residing in Israel, with dual citizenship, was callously mistreated and discriminated against by personnel in a US Consulate in Jerusalem simply because he was Jewish. Indeed, he was explicitly told that this consulate was not for him. Len remembers this attitude proved particularly difficult for his mom, who is also a US citizen. As a Holocaust survivor residing in Jerusalem, she needed her signature notarized at the consulate on a Life Certificate (lebensbescheinigung, in the original German) attesting to her being alive and, therefore, still entitled to her regular German Holocaust reparations payments. The undignified and reprehensible treatment she received was particularly distressing.

It took courage for Secretary of State Blinken to acknowledge some of the overt and poisonous antisemitism that characterized the State Department during the Holocaust. It resulted in many Jews, who might have been saved, being murdered by the Nazis and their cohorts. Although his rebuke was focused mainly on Breckenridge Long, an assistant Secretary of State[268], he did note that Long did not act alone. There were others at the State

---

[267] U.S.-Israel Relations: History of the U.S. Consulate in Jerusalem (Online at www.jewishvirtuallibrary.org).
[268] U.S. Holocaust Memorial Museum Days of Remembrance Commemoration speech, By Anthony J. Blinken, Secretary of State, dated April 8, 2021.

Department who helped him, as well as those who just sat silently. Moreover, the problem was not just limited to the State Department; there were also others within the Roosevelt administration[269]who participated in this historic wrong. Unfortunately, the problem still persists at the State Department, as more fully discussed below. This includes the recent disclosures about antisemites who still work at the State Department[270].

Dennis Ross, a veteran diplomat, reflected on the nature of this endemic antisemitism problem at the State Department[271]. It created a toxic atmosphere where Jews were not so subtly falsely presumed to have dual loyalties, but no other identity group was similarly treated. The result was that Jewish experts with real knowledge, who could make genuine and meaningful contributions to the understanding of the true conditions on the ground in the Middle East, were effectively neutered.

Ambassador David Friedman was reportedly[272] warned by a State Department official "not to be so Jewish". This was because of his unabashed and rational advocacy of policies and positions that advanced US interests by standing with US ally Israel instead of automatically embracing the pro-Arab bias and anti-Israel prejudice which permeated the State Department.

Perhaps, there were others who may have agreed with Friedman's analysis, but it appears they were cowered by the

---

[269] See, for example, Blinken's Holocaust Gaffe, by Rafael Medoff, in the Algemeiner, dated 4/12/2021 and Commemorating Holocaust, Blinken knocks State Dept.'s WWII failure to save Jews, by Ron Kampeas, in the Times of Israel, dated 4/9/2021.
[270] See, for example, We Feel His Presence in the Department 'Is Threatening', by Debbie Gramer, in Foreign Policy, dated 8/31/2021 and Biden condemns anti-Semitism after swastika found at State Department, reporting by Doina Chiacu and editing by Mark Heinrich, in Reuters, dated 7/28/2021.
[271] Memories of an Anti-Semitic State Department, op ed by Dennis Ross, in the New York Times, dated 9/26/2017.
[272] See, for example, How can a Jew be 'too' Jewish, by Stewart Weiss, in the Jerusalem Post, dated 2/10/2022. See also Sledgehammer, by David Friedman (Broadside Books, Harper Collins-2022).

pervasive groupthink that seemed to choke off any legitimate dissent. Those who happened to be Jewish were particularly vulnerable when it came to discussions about Israel. It may be that they remained silent because of fear of being labeled as too Jewish or just went along and submitted to the prevailing culture. Like so many others at the State Department, they toed the line so as to fit in. Some may have even agreed with the time-honored, albeit stale, State Department views on the subject of Israel and Jerusalem[273]. After all, there is a diversity of views among Jews, as well as all of humanity. The concept of there being a collective doctrinaire Jewish point of view, shared by all Jews as a bloc on a political issue, is just another antisemitic trope.

It did, though, take heroes like David Friedman, Jason D. Greenblatt, Jared Kushner and Avi Berkowitz, patiently and rationally, to challenge the overwhelming and enduring bias that peremptorily torpedoed any questioning of State Department policy when it came to Israel and Jerusalem. Ivanka Trump also strongly favored the move and tangibly demonstrated her commitment by visibly participating in the Embassy Opening Ceremony and, together with Treasury Secretary Mnuchin, unveiling the new Embassy at the formal opening. She also displayed a copy of her father's speech as President, recognizing Jerusalem, in her office. It was inscribed with the notation, 'To Ivanka, Love Dad'.

Nevertheless, the latent and sometimes patent antisemitic ethic, which typically excluded Jews from having roles with genuine authority over matters relating to Israel, appears to have been a fact of life in the foreign policy establishment and characterize State Department groupthink[274].

---

[273] Farley discusses the position of a number of former officials at the State Department, who were Jewish, on the matter of Jerusalem and even some of their regrets, in his column, Why the US Senate should reject Kahl's appointment, at JNS, dated 3/22/2021.
[274] See Len's posts, The ancient and sordid history of the dual loyalty canard, dated

As Dennis Ross wrote:

> When I began working in the Pentagon during President
> Jimmy Carter's administration, there was an unspoken but
> unmistakable assumption: If you were Jewish, you could
> not work on the Middle East because you would be biased.

> However, if you knew about the Middle East because you
> came from a missionary family or from the oil industry, you
> were an expert. Never mind that having such a background
> might shape a particular view of the region, the United
> States' interests in it, or Israel. People with these
> backgrounds were perceived to be unbiased, while Jews
> could not be objective and would be partial to Israel to the
> exclusion of American interests.

> Sometimes, I would find this view expressed subtly. Other
> times it would be overt, including well after Secretary of
> State George Shultz tried to change the culture of the State
> Department during the early years of the Reagan
> administration. For Mr. Shultz, being Jewish was no longer
> a disqualification from working on Arab-Israeli issues. He
> was more interested in your knowledge than your identity.
> He made me, someone who is Jewish and was working on
> the National Security Council staff at the time, a member
> of the small team working with him on Arab-Israeli
> diplomacy. (Daniel Kurtzer, who is also Jewish and a career
> Foreign Service Officer, was on that team as well.)

> When James Baker[275] became secretary of state in 1989, he
> continued to help remove suspicions about Jews from the
> national security establishment. And yet, I remember well
> the time in 1990, when I was the head of the State

3/19/2019 and Is It Good for the Jews and Why Does the NYT Purport to be the Arbiter?, dated 11/23/2018, at The Times of Israel.
[275] James Baker was reputedly no friend of Israel and reportedly used an infamous expletive when referring to Jews. See, for example, Why J Street loves Jim Baker, by Ron Kampeas, in The Times of Israel, dated 3/25/2015.

Department's policy planning staff, I was visited by a diplomatic security investigator who was doing a background check on someone who had listed me as a reference. This person was being considered for a senior position in the George H. W. Bush administration, not one directly involved with the Middle East.

At one point, the investigator asked me a question that is routine in these background checks: Was this person loyal to the United States? I answered yes, without a doubt. But his follow-up question was if this person had to choose between America's interests and Israel's, whose interests would he put first? There was nothing subtle about this presumption of dual loyalty.

"Why would you ask that question?" I asked, even though I realized I might not be helping the person using me as a reference. He answered, "Because he is Jewish." So I went on: If he was Irish and had to work on problems related to Ireland or if he was Italian and had to work on Italy, would you ask that question? Initially, the investigator did not seem to know how to respond, but then I saw a look of recognition. He suddenly realized that I was Jewish. And, at that point, he changed the subject.

This investigator was not a rookie. And his experience with senior State Department officials led him to believe it was natural to ask this question. Like most mythologies which take on a life of their own, the idea that Jewish Americans might have dual loyalties was not challenged or questioned, it was assumed. That made it all the more insidious.

Dennis Ross' reference to what amounts to the automatic and unqualified acceptance of the expertise of someone from the oil industry in the Middle East, but exclusion of or harboring of suspicions about Jewish experts, is most cogent. It is hard to imagine being productive in a work environment where obvious biases of some are just categorically ignored and the expertise of Jews is reflexively discounted because of unfounded suspicions.

Deceitfully accusing or secretly harboring suspicions about Jews being disloyal or having dual loyalties is an antisemitic canard, which is ancient in origin and has been discredited time and time again. History can help us better understand this unique phenomenon, which has plagued the Jewish people for millennia.

The Bible[276] describes what was likely the original effort cynically to contrive the dual loyalty or more generic disloyalty false narrative. It started with the very inception of Jewish peoplehood in ancient Egypt. The Bible depicts a new king arose over Egypt, who knew not Joseph[277]. He felt insecure in his position[278], possibly because he was not a descendant of the prior king[279]. He gathered together with his advisors, Balaam, Job, and Jethro[280], who were not Egyptians, to deal with the perceived threat of a powerful Jewish presence in Egypt[281].

The meeting was not about fact-finding. As the Bible reports, they had a preconceived notion that the Jewish people were too numerous and strong[282]. Pharoah's concern was really about remaining in power[283] , and his fear was borne of projection. This makes the most sense when viewed through the prism of how the new Pharaoh came to power in the first place. If he could seize power, then so could someone else and replace him.

The object of the cabal of Pharaoh and his advisors was to contrive a shrewd plan to deal with the perceived threat to their

---

[276] Exodus 1:9-10.
[277] Exodus 1:8.
[278] Exodus Rabbah 1:8.
[279] Ibn Ezra commentary on Exodus 1:8.
[280] BT Sota, at page 11a.
[281] Exodus 1:7.
[282] Exodus 1:9.
[283] BT Sota, at page 11a.

remaining in power. They formulated the libel that if a war came, the Jews would join the enemy and fight against the Egyptians. They deceitfully advanced this fabricated excuse for their notorious program against the Jews.

Sound familiar? It should be because it is the same false narrative being advanced today about Jews having allegiance to a foreign country or dual loyalty.

A similar theme is evoked in Megillat Esther[284]. This time the perpetrators are King Achashverosh, a usurper of the Persian throne[285], and Haman, a non-Persian[286], who is his notorious advisor and partner in crime. Achashverosh is insecure in his new position. As the Talmud[287] explains, he sought approval from the elites he invited to his 180-day-long party[288]. He even demanded his royal wife Vashti, a descendant of Nebuchadnezzar[289], appear unclothed on the last day of his subsequent 7-day gathering for the people[290] to please his guests[291].

After disposing of Queen Vashti[292], Haman and Achashverosh hatched a scheme against the Jews. They invoked the ancient canard of disloyalty to target the Jewish people[293]. Haman described the Jews as a certain people who are different and scattered and dispersed throughout the realm. He then slandered them by accusing them of following their own laws and not the King's. In substance, he falsely asserted the Jews were not loyal

---

[284] Megillat Esther 3:8.

[285] BT Megillah, at page 11a.

[286] As noted in Megillat Esther 3:1, Haman was a descendant of Agag, who was an Amalakite. See also Pesikta Rabbati 13:1.

[287] BT Megillah, at page 12a.

[288] Megillat Esther 1:3-4.

[289] BT Megillah, at page 10b and Esther Rabbah, Petichta 12.

[290] Megillat Esther 1:5-11.

[291] BT Megillah, at page 12b and Esther Rabbah 3:13.

[292] Megillat Esther 1:16-19. See also BT Megillah, at page 12b, which identifies Memuchan as Haman.

[293] BT Megillah, at page 13b.

to the King and it was not worth tolerating them. His solution to the perceived threat was wholly to eliminate the Jews.

Whether characterized as outright disloyalty or dual loyalty, the effect is the same; it is about identifying the Jews as enemies. The promoters of this false and notorious conspiracy theory typically have an agenda. Blaming and demonizing the Jews is often viewed as a politically expedient tactic by demagogues. Stoking fear and hatred of an identifiable minority can help establish solidarity within a constituency. The modus operandi is all too familiar. The pattern of branding someone else as an enemy can also divert attention away from any personal character deficiencies or similar disabilities.

It is likely the motivation for promoting this egregious canard today is no different. Like the Biblical headline of yore, the new one could just as well be newly ennobled and insecure political actors seek validation by attacking others. It's calculating and contrived, but it's also reckless. The effect is only temporary because hatred is a vile and poisonous emotion that eats away at the souls of those involved. Historically, it eventually causes their own self-destruction in the orgy of hatred they engendered.

A potent and more recent example of the destructive influence of this poisonous canard is epitomized by the delusional Austrian Hitler, may his name and memory be blotted out. He also invoked the ancient disloyalty canard. Never mind that Jews loyally served in the German army in World War I. Indeed, as loyal citizens of the many countries at war with each other in World War I, they often fought against each other, too. Hitler, though, managed to unify the German people, in no small measure, by falsely labeling the Jews as disloyal and demonizing them as the enemy of the people. This enabled him, as the aggressor, to play the victim. Thus, he proclaimed the German people were the victims of the Allies and the Versailles Treaty, as well as the Jews. He also managed to deflect attention away from himself as an Austrian, who, despite failing at most things in life, became the Fuhrer of Germany. He and his cohorts were the masters of the modern big lie, invoking all sorts of conspiracy theories and fantasies about Jewish power to justify causing World War II and perpetrating the Holocaust.

Stalin, the notorious communist Premier of the Russian Soviet Empire, was also no stranger to anti-Semitism. As a Georgian by birth, he was not readily accepted by polite Russian society. Is it any wonder that he saw conspiracies everywhere? Why not single out the Jews to villainize, as the enemy, to deflect attention from himself? Almost to his last breath, he sought to brand Jewish doctors in the Soviet Union as disloyal and enemies of the state. This was to be the prelude to his new anti-Semitic campaign. Fortunately, he died before he could actually set his plan in motion. However, when leftist antisemitism is allowed to fester and grow, as in the UK Labor Party under Corbyn[294], and members of the far-left in the US continue to spout their deceitful hate of Jews[295], is it any wonder that we feel unease at the specter of renewed antisemitism in our wonderful United States of America?

The Talmud[296] analyzes the problem of projection and concludes that anyone who habitually claims others are flawed should themselves be examined because they likely possess those same flaws. This is a powerful critique of those who regularly accuse others of disloyalty or dual loyalty. Consider the misplaced focus on and denunciation of the legitimate domestic lobbying efforts of proponents of a strong US-Israel relationship. Is this perhaps an effort to divert attention from the outsized role of foreign

---

[294] See, for example, Jeremy Corbyn barred from rejoining UK Labour Party, by Ben Zion Gad, in the Jerusalem Post, dated 1/26/2022.
[295] See, for example, Did US Jews wake up on the wrong side of 'woke' progressive politics?, by Luke Tress, in The Times of Israel, dated 12/28/2022 and Some 2022 Left-Wing Candidates Espouse Troubling Rhetoric on Israel, at ADL.org, dated 4/5/2022.
[296] BT Kiddushin, at pages 70a-b.

money from Gulf States like Qatar[297] and identification with terrorist-linked groups[298]?

The reaction of some is to treat the accusation as if it were a rational one. However, it is most assuredly not. Efforts to explain, educate and discuss are misplaced; they often only embolden the perpetrators of the canard. This is because the entire issue is cunningly contrived just to generate this kind of response. It is designed to enable the victimizer falsely to claim the status of a victim because of his or her inability to respond coherently to any factual or logical arguments and, most especially, to any irrefutable defenses. In essence, the vigorousness and unassailability of the defense is used to support the very conspiracy theory he or she is falsely promoting in the first place.

We can't afford to be naïve, and it is reckless to ignore the connivance the Bible warned about in its introduction to its report of this canard. It uses the expression 'Havei NisChachma Lo', which is loosely translated as let's deal shrewdly with them. Should we expect any less of the Jew-haters of today? Don't be taken in by the appearance of youth and inexperience of some of the spokespeople spouting this calumny. While some are just ignorant dupes, others are an integral part of the propaganda apparatus created to foment Jew-hatred and undermine the legitimacy of Israel. It's all part of a contrived charade designed to mislead and obfuscate the malicious and callous intent hidden

---

[297] See, for example, What about 'the Benjamins' coming from the Gulf States?, by Barbara Boland, dated 3/13/19, in the Spectator and Former U.S. ambassador points finger in Qatar lobbying probe by Alan Suderman and Jim Mustian, at AP, dated 6/3/2022.

[298] See Ilhan Omar to Speak at Banquet for Group Known for Terrorist Group Support, by Ilanit Chernick, in the Jerusalem Post, dated 2/19/19, ; Ilhan Omar to Speak Alongside Man Who Praised Killing Jews, Report Says, by Ryan Saavedra, in the Daily Caller, dated 2/11/19, ; and CAMERA Op-Ed: Stop Whitewashing Ilhan Omar's Antisemitism, by Sean Durns, dated February 18, 2019. See also, Qatar, Money, and Terror, Doha's Dangerous Policies, at Counter Extremism Project 2021 Report, at counterextremism.com.

in the evil heart of those promoting this libelous slander against Jews.

Is it any wonder that the US' Middle East policies have often been dysfunctional, and efforts to formulate better and more meaningful US policies to foster peace and advance its interests in the Middle East were impeded?

Besides the overt variety of antisemites, there are also many more, who share the abhorrent sentiment, but in the more insidious form, sometimes referred to as being a closet antisemite. The covert form can be every bit as dangerous, especially because it animates a bias that is often denied, which infects and distorts the thinking process of the bearer and, by extension, those who trustingly and unknowingly come in contact with the person possessing the incipient and notorious bias. The result of this biased and clouded thinking is usually bad policy. Over time, biased assumptions are often assumed to be true and can result in profoundly bad decisions. They become so embedded that they are accepted as a part of the ethos of the organization and many may not even be aware of the source of their misguided assumptions. It is suggested that this occurred in the State Department. Its misconceived and erroneous conceptualization of the matter of Jerusalem and enforced corporate memory based thereon became fixed and nearly immutable. The result was a cascade of errors, over the years, based on the original sin of blind acceptance of agenda-driven and biased assumptions.

To put this in perspective, consider that the US established an embassy in East Berlin and recognized the German Democratic Republic of East Germany in 1974[299]. This despite the fact that the US had previously stated that the East German Government was 'without any legal validity' and the US would 'continue to

---

[299] A Guide to the United States' History of Recognition, Diplomatic, and Consular Relations, by Country, since 1776: East Germany (German Democratic Republic), Office of the Historian, US Department of State.

give full support to the Government of the German Federal Republic at Bonn in its efforts to restore a truly free and Democratic Germany'. The East German government was a Soviet creation and as later events proved after the fall of the Soviet Union, in 1990, Germany reunified. So-called East Germany had no right to sovereignty over East Berlin.

In stark contrast, not only did the US deny recognition of Israeli sovereignty over an undivided Jerusalem before the Jerusalem Embassy Act of 1995 and President Trump's actions, it didn't even recognize Israeli sovereignty over West Jerusalem. It is frankly illogical to treat Israel's actual legal right to sovereignty over West Jerusalem worse than the illegitimate assertion of control over East Berlin, by a puppet of the Soviet Union, based on temporary occupation zones created in the aftermath of World War II. Indeed, there is every reason to believe Israel should morally have been treated more favorably and yet, it wasn't. This begs the question of why Israel was treated so shabbily by the US. This historical wrong is not explainable in terms of precedent and it did not arise in a vacuum. There's a history to this abusive treatment of the sovereign State of Israel and it's not pretty. Some of it is motivated by antisemitism, as noted above, but that's not the whole answer. There were other intervening and perverse influences that manipulated the US into taking this inappropriate course of action.

Indeed, the specious issues raised by the doyens at the State Department regarding the recognition of Jerusalem are eerily reminiscent of similar concerns raised by the State Department when President Truman made the momentous decision to recognize Israel. It appears that even after all these years, the persistent failures of their misguided policies, the debunking of their biased and prejudiced presumptions and, in many cases, being proven to be profoundly wrong, they remain unrepentant.

Clark Clifford was the White House Counsel to President Truman at the time[300] and intimately involved in the matter of recognition of Israel. His descriptions[301] of the State Department's machinations are gripping and most informative. This includes the attempts by the State Department to subvert President Truman's desire to recognize Israel and even preempt recognition. As discussed below, the State Department sought to scuttle the UN General Assembly's Partition Resolution 181 and substitute a new UN Trusteeship in place of the expiring League of Nations Mandate.

Clifford reported that officials in the State Department had done everything in their power to prevent, thwart or delay President Truman's efforts to enable the reestablishment of the Jewish State and recognize it.

Among other things, the so-called 'Wise Men'[302] of the State Department reputedly charged that the President was motivated by purely domestic political concerns about the Jewish vote. This was not only a low blow; it was untrue. As Clark Clifford so well noted, President Truman's policy was premised on America's national interests, the realities of the situation in the region, America's moral, ethical and humanitarian values and the costs and risks inherent in any course of action other than recognizing the then nascent reestablished State of Israel.

Secretary of State Marshall and this effete crew also marshaled other arguments, which proved to be misguided. These included

---

[300] He also served as Secretary of Defense in the Johnson administration and in other official positions, as well as, being an advisor to a number of Presidents.

[301] See Chapter 1 (entitled: Showdown in the Oval Office) of his memoirs, Counsel to the President: A Memoir (1991), which he wrote with Richard Holbrooke (who served as an Assistant Secretary of State, as well as, Ambassador to Germany and US Ambassador to the UN).

[302] Robert Lovett, Undersecretary of State; Lovett's predecessor, Dean Acheson; Charles Bohlen, number three in the leadership of the State Department; George F. Kennan, Chief of the Policy and Planning Staff; and Dean Rusk, then the Director of the Office of the United Nations Affairs and later Secretary of State. Also included in this brain trust was James V. Forrestal, the Secretary of Defense.

the numerical premise of thirty million Arabs versus six hundred thousand Jews at the time. It was asserted that it was inconceivable the Jews would not be overwhelmed by sheer numbers. As Clifford Clark noted, this attitude was typical of the foreign policy establishment, especially the pro-Arab professionals at the State Department, who, deeply influenced by the huge oil reserves in the Mideast, supported the side they thought would be the likely winner in the struggle between the Arabs and the Jews. Like so many assumptions, this one, thank G-d, was proved to be conclusively wrong; and Israel triumphed.

There was also misplaced reliance on the British, who were viewed as experts on the region, despite their numerous failures in Egypt, Iraq and Israel itself under the Mandate. It boggles the imagination that Loy Henderson, Director of Near Eastern and African Affairs at the State Department, who was known to be strongly pro-Arab and heavily influenced by the British, as well as widely regarded as antisemitic[303], considered American policy in the Middle East his personal domain. He had no use for what he considered White House interference in his affairs. Is it any wonder that this kind of endemic bias and prejudice at the State Department infected their policy considerations?

It is all the more amazing that State Department leaders like Lovett resented Israel for its successes instead of celebrating them, as would a good friend and ally. He actually criticized what he termed signs of Israel's 'assertiveness' because of some recent military successes and the prospect of what he termed a 'behind the barn' deal with King Abdullah of Jordan. What a cynical comment and arrogant view. It seems as if his commitment to his own narrative was so strong and his prejudices so pronounced that he even had to dismiss progress made by Israel on the peace

---

[303] See, for example, President Truman's Decision to Recognize Israel, by Ambassador Holbrooke, at JCPA.org, dated 5/1/2008.

front as antithetical to US interests, as he perceived them. His worldview and those of others at the State Department seems to have been hopelessly mired in self-interest bias. In essence, they viewed what was good for them as being in the US' national interest, without qualification. Therefore, if a policy option were adverse to their own interests, then they would discount it. If a policy prescription or the underlying assumption they had made proved flawed and might be personally embarrassing, then they would not re-evaluate. Rather, they would just declare even more forcefully that any other alternative couldn't be in the US' best interests. This myopic and distorted view of US national interests, as necessarily having to coincide with the personal self-interests of the decision-maker, is an example of a fundamental flaw in how our foreign policy is promulgated.

Marshall also informed President Truman that he had bluntly informed Moshe Shertok, the future Foreign Minister of Israel, that Israel could expect no help from the US. He averred that the US should support the proposed UN trusteeship resolution and defer any recognition of Israel. The efforts to convince President Truman just to defer any decision on recognition appear to have been little more than a subterfuge. As Clifford realized, the delay was, in fact, just a euphemism for deny.

As shocking as it may seem, the State Department was actively lobbying UN members to support abrogating the previously approved Partition Resolution 181, which the US had supported, and instead establish a trusteeship to replace the expiring Mandate. This perfidious conduct could hardly be justified morally or on the basis of the actual facts and circumstances as they unfolded. Partition already was happening on the ground, as Arab armies and Arab residents fought Jews for control of territory. There was no going back and besides, a one-state solution, as envisioned by the trusteeship proposal, was neither practical nor fair to either side of the dispute. Furthermore, the State Department had put the President in an untenable position. President Truman had assured Chaim Weitzman, the future President of Israel, of the US' continuing commitment to partition and here was the State Department undermining the President and causing the US delegation to the UN to reverse its support for partition. As President Truman wrote on his calendar for March 19, 1948:

> "The State Dept. pulled the rug from under me today....The first I know about it is what I see in the papers! Isn't that hell? I am now in the position of a liar and a double-crosser. I've never felt so low in my life. There are people on the third and fourth level of the State Dept. who have always wanted to cut my throat. They've succeeded in doing it."

President Truman was deeply moved by the plight of the Jews who alone, unlike the other homeless of World War II, had no homeland of their own to which they could return. He was horrified by the Holocaust and denounced it vehemently. He also believed that the US and Great Britain shared a certain global responsibility and commitment to the re-creation of the Jewish State in its historical homeland.

President Truman was a student and believer in the Bible since his youth. From his reading of the Old Testament, he felt the Jews derived a legitimate historical right to Palestine, and he sometimes cited such biblical lines as Deuteronomy 1:8: 'Behold, I have given up the land before you; go in and take possession of the land which the Lord hath sworn unto your fathers, to Abraham, to Isaac, and to Jacob.'

President Truman was a realist and appreciated that turning back the matter to the UN would only serve to embolden the Arab states to combine aggressive military action with diplomatic diversions in order to throttle the Jewish State at its birth.

A seminal meeting was scheduled in the Oval Office on the subject of recognizing Israel and on May 12, 1948, General

Marshall and his deputy Robert Lovett met with President Truman, together with Clark Clifford, among others. Marshall and Lovett presented first, arguing in favor of trusteeship and against recognition.

When it was Clark Clifford's turn, he argued in favor of recognition and urged that it not be delayed. He offered that it should occur immediately after the expiration of the British Mandate on May 14, 1948. The effect would be to restore honor to the office of the Presidency, which had been tarnished by the State Department's abrupt about-face on the matter of US support for partition. It was also critical to beat out the Russians, who were planning to recognize Israel too. Clifford also asserted the US had a great moral obligation to oppose discrimination such as that inflicted on the Jewish people. The Holocaust had only just ended, and antisemitism was already reappearing in communist-controlled Eastern Europe. It was critical for the Jewish people to have a haven in their own homeland, like all other people who have their own country. This was an opportunity to end these ancient injustices. He offered, 'And perhaps these steps would help atone, in some small way, for the atrocities so vast as to stupefy the human mind that occurred in the Holocaust'. In this regard, it is important to note the active and direct participation of notorious Grand Mufti Haj Amin al-Husseini[304] and his cohorts in the Holocaust, alongside the Nazis[305], as well as their revolt against the British[306] and massacres of Jews[307], which caused so many needless deaths,

---

[304] See, for example, Full official record: What the mufti said to Hitler, in the Times of Israel, dated 10/21/2015.
[305] See, for example, Photographic Evidence Shows Palestinian Leader Amin al-Husseini at a Nazi Concentration Camp (An analysis of photographs sold at a Jerusalem auction house offers new insight into the role of foreign accomplices in Hitler's Final Solution), by Wolfgang G. Schwanitz, in Tablet Magazine, dated 4/7/2021, as well as, Revealed: SS Chief Heinrich Himmler's Warm Wishes to Mufti Haj Amin al-Husseini, by Chen Mallul, at National Library of Israel, dated 11/6/2017.
[306] See, for example, Who was Mufti Haj Amin al-Husseini, by Ben Sales, in the Times of Israel, dated 10/23/2015.
[307] Haj Amin al-Husseini's murderous history includes being an Ottoman officer, who

both before and during in the Holocaust, including by denying Jews safe haven in their ancient homeland of Israel.

Clark Clifford's final point could have been made today and it would be every bit as cogent and objectively persuasive. He explained:

> In an area as unstable as the Middle East, where there is not now and never has been any tradition of democratic government, it is important for the long-range security of our country, and indeed the world, that a nation committed to the democratic system be established there, one on which we can rely. The new Jewish state can be such a place. We should strengthen it in its infancy by prompt recognition.

Marshall and Lovett didn't actually counter Clifford's arguments; they really couldn't dispute his reasoning and logic. Instead, they employed typical diversionary tactics to avoid dealing with the substance of Clifford's remarks and instead to refocus the discussions solely on their own agenda. Thus, Marshall's immediate retort was to attack the bona fides of the spokesman and ask why Clifford was even there; he was a domestic advisor, not a foreign policy expert. President Truman's answer was vintage Truman. He responded characteristically, in a straightforward matter-of-fact manner, 'Well, General, he's here because I asked him to be here.' Marshall responded by invoking the specter of domestic political

---

participated in the Armenian Genocide. He orchestrated a number of massacres of Jews, including the infamous Hebron Massacre in 1929. See, for example, Amin al-Husseini: From The Armenian Genocide to the Hijacking of the Muslim World, by Deborah Sharavi, at the Narkive Newsgroup Archive online (narkive.com); The Hebron Massacre, at jewishunpacked.com; Hitler's Palestinian Ally: Grand Mufti Amin Al-Husseini, by Akiva Van Koningsveld, dated 2/10/2021, at honestreporting.com; and Haj Amin al-Husseini, the Nazis and the Holocaust: The Origin, Nature and Aftereffects of Collaboration, by Jeffrey Herf, dated 1/5/2016, at Jerusalem Center for Public Affairs (jcpa.org).

considerations, notwithstanding that they played no part in Clifford's presentation. As Clifford reports:

> 'Marshall, scarcely concealing his ire, shot back, 'These considerations have nothing to do with the issue. I fear that the only reason Clifford is here is that he is pressing a political consideration with regard to this issue. I don't think politics should play any part in this.'

It is important to understand that the domestic political consideration he was referring to was the so-called Jewish vote, a classical antisemitic trope. The implication was that a disloyal group was lobbying the President to do something that Marshall perceived was in their own personal interests. The fact that Marshall and his State Department team were so utterly wrong in offering this specious and defamatory assertion did not diminish their ardor or irrational belief in their assumption about Jewish influence over the President. Their prejudice seems to have limited their ability even to consider, let alone analyze, the substance of the arguments Clifford made. As far as the State Department was concerned, their minds were closed on the subject.

Clifford noted that Lovett then joined the attack and said:

> 'It would be highly injurious to the United Nations to announce the recognition of the Jewish state even before it had come into existence and while the General Assembly is still considering the question. Furthermore, such a move would be injurious to the prestige of the President. It is obviously designed to win the Jewish vote, but in my opinion, it would lose more votes than it would gain.'

As Clifford reports in his memoirs:

> 'Lovett had finally brought to the surface the root cause of Marshall's fury – his view that the position I presented was

dictated by domestic political considerations, specifically a quest for Jewish votes.'

Clifford handily disposed of this specious presumption by simply rebutting it. This was solely about acting in the US' national interest, which, as he had cogently explained, was favored by recognizing Israel.

It is stunning to realize that neither Marshall nor Lovett were actually talking about what were the national interests of the US and explaining how their proposal better served those interests than the one proposed by Clifford. Instead, they engaged in an ad hominem attack on Clifford and, by extension, the President.

Curiously, Lovett also argued recognizing Israel would somehow have a negative effect on the UN. Yet, he did not explain why or how nor how this might injure the US. Moreover, he also neglected to mention that the pending trusteeship question was a self-inflicted problem because the State Department had gone behind the back of the President to lobby for it and thereby undermine the President's policies. Ironically, the State Department's own folly and hubris was used to support its categorical and unsubstantiated pronouncement from on high that the President must not recognize Israel.

The use of the UN excuse was a repetitive theme[308] in the State Department's playbook when it came to Israel. This was despite the absurdity of the excuse. After all, why would any sensible person rely on a UN populated by rogue actors and dictatorships and controlled by nefarious forces that were anti-American and

---

[308] As more fully discussed below, the UN excuse would be invoked again and again to forestall recognition of Jerusalem as the capital of Israel, by arguing the UN (non-binding) resolution called for the internationalization of Jerusalem, using the rubric of corpus separatum. Astonishingly, Secretary Tillerson raised this lame excuse, as late as 2017, in the meeting with President Trump, summarized below in Chapter XII. This despite the fact that the State Department had concluded it was an impractical idea, by 1949 and the entire matter had been tabled by the mid-1950's, at the latest; but more on this below.

anti-Israel[309]? It would appear that the important lessons of the Biblical Tower of Babel[310] were lost on the diffident pseudo-pundits making these banal pronouncements.

Whether it is the United Nations or other global initiatives, there are those still trying to unify the world. But to what end? Is unity a worthwhile goal in and of itself or is there something more important?

Unity is not an appropriate end if it serves no useful purpose. If people unite in order to do harm, then what good is that? UNESCO[311] is just one of the most recent examples of misusing the banner of unity in order to pursue the nefarious purpose of erasing the Jewish connection to the Western Wall and Temple Mount[312]. History is replete with attempts to unify the world. From the ancient Assyrian, Egyptian and Babylonian empires to the Greek and Roman empires and, most recently, the Nazi Reich, many have tried forcibly to unite the world. However, their intent was not to improve the world; it was to dominate their fellow man and satisfy their own selfish needs and desires.

On another level, a group may ostensibly seek to achieve beneficial goals. It is assumed that, generally, the means used by

---

[309] Such as the USSR, at the time, and China and Iran today, as well as, the member nations within their orbits.

[310] Genesis 11:1-9.

[311] An acronym for the United Nations Educational, Scientific and Cultural Organization.

[312] See, for example, Conference of Presidents Leaders Call on UNESCO Executive Board to Reject Highly Politicized Anti-Israel Resolution on Jerusalem, at Conference of Presidents.org, dated 5/1/2017 and UNESCO Decisions on Jerusalem Spark Wave of Anti-Semitic Cartoons in Arab Press, at the ADL.org, dated 5/3/2022. UNESCO has also had to deal with its own antisemitism problem, as well as, the failure to enforce its own rules prohibiting antisemitic content in Palestinian textbooks. See, for example, European Parliament Hearing on Palestinian Textbooks that Violate UNESCO Standards, at AJC Transatlantic Institute and 2021 EU Study Confirms Incitement in Palestinian Textbooks (in violation of UNESCO standards), at Jewish Virtual Library.org. See also, United Nations Body Accused of Anti-Israel Bias Launches Teacher Trainings on Antisemitism, by Dion J. Pierre, at the Algemeiner, dated 12/29/2022 and Issue 331: UNESCO funded pro-Hitler Palestinian magazine - UN Watch.org, dated 12/25/2011.

group members to achieve these goals will also be good, consistent with their pure intent. If, however, inappropriate means are used to accomplish their goals, then it is hard not to view their expressions of pure intent with suspicion.

It is suggested that this was one of the inherent flaws in the Biblical Tower of Babel project. Even if the ostensible purpose was, assuming arguendo, a good one, there were insidious problems with the manner in which it was executed that raised genuine ethical concerns about the nature of the entire project. As a threshold matter, consider the means used to construct the Tower.

The Midrash [313] describes how arduous the building process was in constructing the Tower. It was not easy to fashion the bricks and bring them up to the top of the Tower as it was being built. Intense focus on the task at hand was required, and this resulted in a callous indifference to anything outside of building the structure. Thus, a worker might fall and die during the construction process, and the people would pay no heed to him. However, if a brick fell, then they sat down and wept about its loss because another brick would have to be fashioned and brought up in its stead[314].

---

[313] Pirke D'Rabbi Eliezer 24:6.

[314] The Abarbanel (in his commentary on Genesis 11:2) discusses how the very construction process was problematical. It began with mankind divorcing itself from the pristine order of the world. Instead of locating the project in an area where there were sufficient natural resources to accomplish the task, they sought out one where they had to create the building materials, artificially. This did prompt technological innovation, including creating bricks that were fired in an oven, instead of using natural stones, and also the need to fashion a new type of mortar. Nevertheless, why unnecessarily seek these kinds of artificial devices in order to satisfy their cravings? This focus on technology for its own sake diverted mankind's attention. It separated them from their traditions and they were no longer grounded in the natural order of the world. They didn't focus on knowing and acting in accordance with divine truths. Instead, they were focused on bricks and mortar not the health, safety and welfare of their fellow human beings.

This is reminiscent of the analogous slavish devotion to process, which characterizes so many insular bureaucracies like the UN and even our own State Department. As bureaucrats mindlessly pursue their sacrosanct procedures, they are often indifferent to the harm they may be causing. Purity of motives does not convert bad policies, callously enforced, into virtuous ones. The inviolability of process cannot be an end in and of itself, nor is it appropriate to pursue a process directed at achieving an inappropriate or misguided goal. It's why both the process, as well as the intended goals to be achieved, must constantly be re-evaluated for flaws and unintended consequences. The key is initially to set noble goals and then effectively monitor the process to see that appropriate means are being used to achieve those desirable ends. Even avowedly noble goals can be distorted when inappropriate means are used to achieve the desired ends. At the same time, the goals set must also be re-evaluated on a regular basis to confirm whether the intended results are still right and just in practice.

Unifying to accomplish a good deed can be incredibly useful as a means of aiding in the achievement of that righteous goal. However, both the goal and means must be ones that benefit mankind. Unity for the sake of demonstrating our prowess and achieving an evil or misguided goal is a nefarious exercise, not a good one. We must seek to align appropriate means to good and desirable goals. The end usually does not justify the means. If the means are wrong, then the end should be re-examined. This is because if the means are inappropriate, then the end is usually wrong, as well.

When viewed against the backdrop of history, it is indisputable that the cabal that continued unequivocally to support a UN, which was a virtual Tower of Babel, was causing more harm than good. Moreover, the failure to do what was just and proper in reliance on some mythical fascination with the possibility that the UN might finally do the right thing has been proven time and again to be delusional or, worse, some form of artifice, deceptively used to delay and frustrate the US doing what was right and just.

Was this part of the strategy of those in the State Department who continued to promote this kind of misdirected effort to abort the birth of the State of Israel? It would appear so and the charade is continued by their successors in their furtive attempts to wield similar tools directed at diminishing the legitimacy of Israel. This kind of duplicity seems to have been standard operating practice at the State Department, as more fully discussed below. These same tactics appear to have been enlisted by those opposing recognition of Jerusalem.

Lovett then invoked another antisemitic trope about Jews and communism:

> How do we know what kind of Jewish state will be set up? We have many reports from British and American intelligence agents that Soviets are sending Jews and communist agents into Palestine from the Black Sea area.

Clifford reported:

> Lovett read some of these intelligence reports to the group. I found them ridiculous, and no evidence ever turned up to support them; in fact, Jews were fleeing communism throughout Eastern Europe at that very moment.

Clifford recorded that the charge that domestic politics determined President Truman's policy on Israel angered President Truman for the rest of his life. Clifford shared his ire at the implication that the President and those Americans who supported the Zionists were somehow acting in opposition to our nation's interests. As Clifford noted:

> In fact, though, the President's policy rested on the realities of the situation in the region, on America's moral, ethical, and humanitarian values, on the costs and risks

inherent in any other course, and – of course – on America's national interests.

The history of the State Department's insouciance and plainly arrogant wrongheadedness, when it came to matters of Israel, is troubling. It reflexively colored the thought process of many and clouded their judgment. Here's just one example. Walt Rostow, then the National Security Advisor to President Lyndon Johnson, reported[315] his recollections of a meeting on June 5, 1967, concerning what would later be known as the Six-Day War. Among others, Dean Acheson attended the meeting and Rostow reports as follows:

> There was an interesting moment, as I remember it. Mr. Acheson looked back on the whole history of Israeli independence and, in effect, said that it was a mistake to ever create the State of Israel.

This ethos seems to have been endemic at the State Department and helps explain many of the untoward actions taken over the years that were antithetical to the national interests of the US and its common and shared values and interests with Israel. Len remembers well being asked to prepare a draft position paper by a former State Department official who was his professor in college. The professor had taken a liking to Len and appeared to be grooming him for a possible future position there. Whatever the case, Len had to sift through all sorts of data and prepare a reasoned analysis in the required format and present his conclusion. This he did and the professor appreciated the depth of his analysis and clarity of his presentation. He didn't, however, agree with the conclusion proffered. In discussing it, the professor casually noted to Len, wouldn't it be better if Israel didn't exist? The remark appeared to be made in all innocence and without malice in an attempt to share genuine candor with

---

[315] 149. Memorandum of Record, dated November 17, 1968, Office of the Historian, Foreign Relations of the United States 1964-1968, Volume XIX, Arab-Israeli Crises and War, 1967.

Len and he had no reason to doubt it over the years. At the same time, in reflecting on the declassified State Department records and in researching documents and other source materials for this book, it is clear that there was a bias and, indeed, prejudice against the Jewish State of Israel, which infected many at the State Department and evolved into what appears to be a department-wide ethos.

This kind of syndrome might be referred to as groupthink today, which also tends to be self-reinforcing. However, as noted above, the sources are more insidious and varied. Given that the collective consciousness results from people with variable backgrounds and different sources of biased thinking that coalesced around the topic of Israel, makes it exceedingly more difficult to confront and overcome than ordinary groupthink with a common source. Perhaps, this helps explain why it has endured and even morphed into the anti-Jewish Jerusalem syndrome analyzed in this book. It is suggested that the irrational view taken by the State Department, even in regard to the Western part of Jerusalem, let alone an undivided Jerusalem, as the capital of Israel, is a manifestation of this collective prejudice.

The age of prophecy ended millennia ago. Ever since then, the Sages[316] counsel, be deliberate in judgment. Said another way, a person should not be so presumptuous about the validity of his or her assumptions, opinions, or judgments. Take a moment to reflect and, better yet, do a thorough investigation of the facts and circumstances before reaching a conclusion. Assumptions may not prove accurate, or circumstances may have changed. There may also be biases and agendas that have to be accounted for so as not to yield a prejudiced or foreordained result.

---

[316] Avot 1:1.

The Bible[317] provides a profound insight into the nature of this societal malady. It begins by enjoining those occupying positions of presumptive moral or legal authority from receiving gifts or other remuneration. It deems it axiomatic that under those circumstances there perforce exists a situation of incipient bias. Interestingly, bribing someone to do what he or she would otherwise have done anyway is also proscribed[318].

The bias may manifest itself in a variety of manners. It may just be viewing a person more favorably and, therefore, presumptively accepting the validity of their statements. The result, though, is a suspension of the critical function of healthy skepticism, which is so important to making an informed and well-reasoned decision.

The Bible uses the term 'Shochad' to describe the animating cause of the problem. It is typically translated as a bribe, but its meaning is much more nuanced. As Rava in the Talmud[319] explains, the term is a contraction formed by the words "Shehu' and 'Chad'; meaning that he (i.e., the beneficiary) becomes as one (i.e., of one mind with the benefactor). Rava then goes on to discuss the psychological mechanics of how this occurs in practice. In essence, the beneficiary so identifies with the benefactor that an identity of interests is created. Thus, the beneficiary tends not to find fault in the benefactor because that is perceived as finding fault in his or her self. This is so even when he or she wants to do the right thing[320].

It is not only money that triggers this kind of response. As the Talmudic text goes on to point out, the bias can also result from friendship or mere words[321]. This is a critical observation. Who

---

[317] Deuteronomy 16:19.

[318] See BT Ketubot, at page 105a and Sifre Devarim 144:10

[319] BT Ketubot, at page 106b.

[320] Ibid, Rashi commentary thereon.

[321] See also Rif, Sanhedrin 2b; Maimonides, Mishne Torah, The Sanhedrin and Their Penalties 23:3; and the Vilna Gaon's Aderet Eliyahu commentary on Deuteronomy 16:19.

among us has not felt pressured to conform to the thinking of a social or other group to which we belong? We identify with the members of the group or we wouldn't have joined the group in the first place. However, why does that require we share the same point of view on everything and all hew the party line or face expulsion?

The response to any dissent within the ranks is often punishing, whether a person chooses to remain in the group or, voluntarily or involuntarily, leave. Suffering in silence offers very little solace. What's the point, if no one will debate and offer any other perspective? With everyone feeling pressured just dogmatically to recount the party line, effectively, it stifles any other perspective.

This prejudiced view regarding the existence of Israel, generally, was magnified on the subject of Jerusalem. This was not just a function of cognitive dissonance, triggered by dogmatic adherence to the party line and narrative. It appears there were also sinister forces at work relating to Jerusalem, beyond the usual biases and prejudices, as disclosed in declassified State Department documents and records, summarized in this book.

Consider, for example, the role of the Vatican[322] in the deliberations of the State Department. The Vatican and its representatives, including Cardinal Spellman, the Archbishop of New York, at the time, lobbied the State Department to internationalize Jerusalem[323]. They also lobbied other nations,

---

[322] Pope Pius XII, who signed the Concordat with Nazi Germany, in 1933, when he was Cardinal Secretary of State Eugenio Pacelli, issued Encyclicals Multiplicibus Curis (October 24, 1948) and Redemptoris Nostre Cruciatus (April 15, 1949), calling for the internationalization of Jerusalem and its environs..

[323] See, for example, draft letter prepared by the State Department for President Truman to respond to Letter, dated April 29, 1949, from Cardinal Spellman, the Archbishop of New York to Truman, on the subject of the internationalization of Jerusalem. As noted in the State Department files, the draft letter was transmitted to President Truman on May 17, 1949 and presumably sent out on May 19, 1949 (copy in the State Department files, under title: Draft Letter From the President to Francis Cardinal Spellman, Roman Catholic Archbishop of New York, 867N.01/5-449, Foreign Relations of the United

like Brazil, which in turn also lobbied the US[324]. Interestingly, by October of 1953, it would appear that the Vatican's position had moderated somewhat from the insistence on strict and full territorial internationalization of Jerusalem. This was communicated by the Minister of Brazil in Tel Aviv, Jose Fabrino de Oliveira Baiao, to the State Department, after he had reportedly consulted with Monsignor Tardini, the Vatican Secretary of State to Pope Pious XII, in Rome, on his way back to Rio de Janeiro. The Vatican proposed, through the Brazilian Minister, that, as a provisional matter, Jerusalem and a surrounding zone, with a radius of fifty kilometers, be demilitarized. If this concept worked, in practice, to achieve the goal of internationalization, which was protection of the Holy Sites, then it could become the actual definitive agreement; in essence, in place of internationalization. The Minister went on to say that the Vatican would support Brazil initiating a movement among the Catholic nations, especially in Latin America, for the solution of the problem along these lines, thereby safeguarding the treasure of Christianity situated in the proposed Jerusalem Zone, including Bethlehem[325]. Nevertheless,

---

States, 1949, The Near East, South Asia and Africa, Vol. VI, at history.state.gov). There was reportedly also additional follow up correspondence on the matter, including a Letter, dated July 13, 1949, from Cardinal Spellman, said to be in response to a Letter, dated June 22, 1949, from President Truman, which answered a Letter from Spellman, dated June 10, 1949. None of those Letters are printed in the State Department records online. Secretary Acheson answered the Spellman Letter, which he said was at the request of President Truman, by Letter dated August 11, 1949 (copy in the State Department Files, under title: The Secretary of State to Francis Cardinal Spellman, Roman Catholic Archbishop of New York, Washington, August 11, 1949, 867N.01/7–1349, Foreign Relations of the United States, 1949, The Near East, South Asia and Africa, Vol. VI, at history.state.gov).

[324] See, for example, No. 702, The Brazilian Embassy to the Department of State, Confidential Memorandum SN/920.(55a) (51), dated Washington, October 22, 1953, at Foreign Relations of the United States, 1952-1954, The Near and Middle East, Vol. IX, Part 1, at history.state.gov.

[325] The Brazilian Minister added that if the provisional arrangement succeeded, then he proposed a peace conference could be held that would include Jordan, Israel, the US and UK, as well as, the Catholic countries. The Peace Treaty, he suggested would include not only the countries directly concerned, like Israel and Jordan, but also the Christian

the Vatican recognized that for a movement of this magnitude to be successful, the support of the US was imperative.

It is understandable that these concerns were taken seriously, however, what is most shocking is that they were blithely assumed to be dispositive and representative of the views of a bloc of Christian nations at the UN or the Christian world[326]. Even the Brazilian/Vatican lobbying effort noted above, recognized that without the active support of the US, it was fruitless. Indeed, far from having a bloc, the Vatican, through Brazil, was trying to inveigle the US into helping create one.

It is frankly hard to imagine that a seasoned foreign affairs expert would actually believe in the existence of such a bloc of nations, with purely Christian religiocentric concerns, unrelated to their national interests, let alone that the territorial status of Jerusalem was a vital issue of national interest to each and every one of them. Indeed, it would appear that almost from the very outset, the ill-fated internationalization recommendation of the UNGA was stillborn. There was neither an appetite to implement it by military force nor to pay for such an action or the substantial ongoing cost of maintaining a governmental apparatus and defensive security force[327]. It was nothing more than an

---

nations would participate and the Treaty would contain a provision guaranteeing the protection of the Holy Places, not only in the Zone of Jerusalem, but also throughout the area formerly known as Palestine, under the mandate.

[326] See, for example, Footnote 7 to Memorandum by the Secretary of State (Acheson) to the President (Truman), dated December 20, 1949, 501 BB Palestine/12-2049, at Foreign Relations of the United States, 1949, The Near East, South Asia, and Africa, Volume VI, at history.state.gov.

[327] See, for example, the draft letter prepared by the State Department for President Truman to respond to Cardinal Spellman's Letter, dated April 29, 1949, regarding internationalization of Jerusalem, noted above. See also Memorandum of Dean Acheson, in Foreign Relations of the United States, 1949, the Near East, South Asia, and Africa, Volume VI, at page 1499, as well as footnote 2 thereto, referring to Acheson's conversation with President Truman on November 21, 1949 approving the Memorandum. It contained the proposed instructions to the US delegation to the UN. This included a number of qualifications to the internationalization proposal under consideration by the UN. Of critical importance is the fact that the objective was no longer territorial internationalization of Jerusalem and its environs. Rather, it focused

on the status of Jerusalem as the center of three great world religions and providing for the necessary protection of and access to Holy Places under UN supervision. In addition it must contribute to peace and stability in the area, as well as, be workable and take into account the interests of the principal communities in Jerusalem and the views of Israel and Jordan. In essence, both Israel and Jordan were, effectively, given a veto over any such arrangement. The fact of the matter is that the notion of a corpus separatum for Jerusalem, from its very inception, was ill-conceived and unrealistic. It never really evolved into a practical plan and even the attempt to pass a Jerusalem Statute was stillborn.

In 1950, in a position paper prepared by the State Department, the State Department recognized the futility of this endeavor. [See, Foreign Relations of the United States, 1950, The Near East, South Asia, and Africa, Volume V-Position Paper Prepared in the Department of State for the Seventh Session of the Trusteeship Council- confidential SD/T/157 [Washington,] May 19, 1950, Item 10: Question of an International Regime for the Jerusalem Area and Protection of the Holy Places (General Assembly Resolution 303 (IV) of December 9, 1949)]. It recommended that the US Delegation oppose any proposals directed to the imposed implementation of the Statute against the wishes of the parties, on the ground that an imposed implementation would contribute neither to a viable solution of the problem nor to the peace and stability of the area.

This position is consistent with a prior position paper on the matter (Position Paper Prepared in the Department of State-Foreign Relations of the United States, 1949, The Near East, South Asia, and Africa, Volume VI, IO Files, Lot 71 D 440, SD/A/C.1/273, confidential, [Washington ,] September 14, 1949, titled-Jerusalem), which noted that in addition to heavy financial requirements such commitments would also include an obligation to maintain peace and order in a City which, if legally separated from the adjacent states, might very soon be faced with serious threats either internally or from outside.

A later State Department Memorandum (281. Memorandum From the Department of State Executive Secretary (Battle) to the President's Special Assistant for National Security Affairs (Bundy), Washington, May 31, 1962, Foreign Relations of the United States, 1961–1963, Volume XVII, Near East, 1961–1962, Subject- United States Position on Jerusalem) provides a good précis of the history of what occurred. It notes that the 1947 UN Partition Resolution could not be carried out since hostilities broke out in May 1948 between Arab states and Israel. It states, "The hostilities were terminated by a series of armistice agreements in 1949. The armistice agreement between Israel and Jordan of April 3, 1949, established armistice demarcation lines which divided Jerusalem into sectors under Israel and Jordan control with a no-man's-land between the two sectors. The United Nations General Assembly on December 9, 1949, reaffirmed its recommendation that a corpus separatum be established, and requested the Trusteeship Council to proceed with formulating a Statute for a Corpus Separatum for Jerusalem. The United States and certain other interested powers did not support this resolution, which was, nevertheless, passed by the Assembly... The Trusteeship Council failed to produce an acceptable draft statute as did the United Nations General Assembly that same year (1950)".

Astoundingly, eventhough there was no legal requirement to do so, the Memorandum notes: "The United States undertook, however, to give due recognition to the formal acts of the General Assembly and the Trusteeship Council relating to Jerusalem and has

241

aspirational idea, albeit vacuous and impractical, in light of existing conditions, specifically, and the reality of world affairs, generally.

In this regard, it is important to appreciate that no UN Security Council Resolution was ever passed to enforce implementation of the UNGA recommendation. In essence, it was and would remain merely a non-binding recommendation and the votes in favor were just expressions of political or ideological views, without force of international law or otherwise. Thus, for example, the UNGA formed a Palestine Conciliation Commission (PCC) and tasked it with drafting a statute for the governance of Jerusalem. The PCC prepared a draft but the UNGA never adopted it. The UNGA then assigned the task of drafting a statute for Jerusalem to its Trusteeship Council. Once again a draft was prepared and it too failed to be adopted[328].

As the records of the State Department and behind the scenes debate at the UN clearly reveal, protection of rights of worship at the Holy sites was the real underlying matter of concern to Christians, Muslims and Jews and not who had actual territorial sovereignty over Jerusalem. It should also be noted that President Truman, in his letter responding to Cardinal Spellman, as drafted by the State Department, described what amounts to the US' hybrid position on the subject. It veered away from full internationalization and, in place thereof, substituted a proposal

since maintained its position that the Holy Places in the Jerusalem area are of international interest to a degree which transcends ordinary considerations of sovereignty."

The Memorandum went on to state that the US' position was: "the status of Jerusalem is a matter of United Nations concern and no member of the United Nations should take any action to prejudice the United Nations interest in this question. Our objective has been to keep the Jerusalem question an open one... " In essence, the US was exercising deference to what the Memorandum referred to as a 'United Nations attitudes towards Jerusalem'.. It did this eventhough there was no binding resolution or legal compulsion to do so. It was just keeping its options open at the expense of an ally and friend, with no demonstrable benefit and as the Abraham Accords would demonstrate at great cost to the standing and reputation of the US as a reliable friend and ally.
[328] Ibid.

dealing with control of the Holy Sites and protection of access thereto.

Secretary Of State Acheson provided a status report to President Truman on the matter of Jerusalem at the UN and how it was evolving into something short of full and actual internationalization, in a memorandum, dated December 20, 1949[329]. Among other things, he noted:

> In the General Assembly this year Australia introduced a resolution incorporating the first of these extreme positions—i.e., the principle of full internationalization under complete United Nations control. This resolution immediately attracted the votes of the Catholic countries, (strongly urged by the Vatican), of the Arab States (except Jordan), and of the Soviet bloc. With minor modifications, it was adopted by 39 votes to 14, with 5 abstentions. The United States, United Kingdom and other states opposed the resolution on the grounds that it was unrealistic as it could not be implemented by the United Nations against the wishes of Israel and Jordan without the use of substantial forces. The United States delegation also pointed out that to set up a new City-State in Palestine would cost the United Nations large sums of money even on the assumption of willing cooperation by Israel and Jordan.

Acheson went on to list his conclusions, which included the following:

> 1. Our underlying objective is to achieve a solution of the Jerusalem problem which will meet with a considerable degree of concurrence by the world

---

[329] Memorandum by the Secretary of State to the President, Washington, December 20, 1949, 501.BB Palestine/12–2049, in Foreign Relations of the United States, 1949, The Near East, South Asia, and Africa, Volume VI, at history.state.gov.

community and be acceptable to the two nations which are most directly involved.

2. We do not believe that this objective can be achieved under the terms of the General Assembly resolution because neither Israel nor Jordan will ever willingly agree to the establishment of Jerusalem as a corpus separatum divorced from their respective control.

....

5. To assist affirmatively in the settlement of the problem, the United States should privately encourage informal conversations between Israel and Jordan and the Vatican, but the United States should not take any part in such conversations. We might suggest that a single individual, such as Dr. Ralph Bunche, but not a representative of the United States, conduct quiet consultations with the parties and with the Vatican with a view to exploring the possibilities of an agreed solution.

....

7. We continue to believe, as we did as a member of the Palestine Conciliation Commission, that a reasonable solution should contain certain underlying principles, such as protection of and free access to the Holy Places under appropriate United Nations auspices, progressive demilitarization of the Jerusalem area, administration by Israel and Jordan of their respective parts of the City, and the maintenance of human rights and freedoms. However, it is our view that any solution agreed upon by the Christian world and by Israel and Jordan could be supported by us.

Notice the emphasis Acheson placed on the views of the Vatican, in item 5 above, and the reference to the Christian world, in item 7. To appreciate how myopic this perspective was, it is important to view it in the context of the opposing positions expressed by other religious leaders and authorities, at the time. Thus, a fact-finding mission of Christian leaders and spokesmen had been sent to Israel, under the auspices of the American Christian Palestine Committee, which sponsored the investigatory commission. Their charge was to investigate the feasibility of the internationalization plan for Jerusalem. The group made public their findings at a press conference, in January of 1950. It is reported[330] they unanimously concluded:

> the (United Nations) plan to internationalize the Jerusalem area is dangerous and unnecessary.

Having rejected the internationalization plan, the group recommended that a United Nation's Commission "with no territorial sovereignty" be established in order to assure the free accessibility of the Christian world to the Holy Places of Jerusalem. They reportedly went on to say:

> Guarantees should be given to such a commission by both Jordan and Israel assuring the freedom and sanctity of the sacred places within their territories. This is all that the Christian world has a right to require of two sovereign states, which we believe will in time compose their differences.

The group went on to emphasize that the making of peace would be accomplished all the more speedily if Israel and Jordan were encouraged in their negotiations by the Western powers.

---

[330] See, U.S. Mission of Christian Leaders Rejects Internalization of Jerusalem, in JTA, dated January 20, 1950, as well as, a similar article entitled, Christian Group Rejects UN Plan for Jerusalem, in The Jewish News of Northern California, Vol. 102, Num. 6, dated February 3, 1950.

Members of the investigation commission were said to occupy leading positions in the Presbyterian, Methodist, Baptist and Congregational denominations. Their report was transmitted to Secretary of State Dean Acheson, Roger Garreau, the President of the United Nations Trusteeship Council and Francis B. Sayre, the US Delegate to the Council.

The State Department's view on the status of Jerusalem was the subject of a secret internal Policy Statement memorandum dated February 6, 1951[331]. It concludes that the concept of establishing Jerusalem as a corpus separatum under an international regime has been unsuccessful. It goes on to state:

> In view of the evident impracticability of complete internationalization, the United States has and should continue to support the establishment of a less comprehensive arrangement for an international regime which would still provide for the protection of the legitimate rights of the world community in Jerusalem. While the United States would support any arrangement in Jerusalem which was agreed to by Israel and Jordan and a majority of the international community, it is assumed that such an arrangement would generally conform to one which the United States would consider desirable for the area.

The fantasy of having an International regime with sole territorial sovereignty over Jerusalem and its environs, to the exclusion of Israel and in disregard of the will of the majority of the local population as expressed by their duly elected leaders, was effectively ended. It is astounding that in the post-colonial era, any serious consideration could be given to establishing what amounts to a colonial outpost in the midst of a sovereign

---

[331] Department of State Policy Statement-Israel, in Foreign Relations of the United States, 1951, The Near East and Africa, Vol. V, 611.84A/2–651, marked secret and since declassified, dated, [Washington] February 6, 1951, at history.state.gov.

state. Frankly, how was this misguided conception any different from the short-lived crusader kingdom of yore? Imagine the outcry today if the US even considered unilaterally sending US armed forces to a foreign country in order brutally to impose and enforce, by force of arms, a so-called international regime, in the midst of that country, against the will of the people living there. Thankfully, cooler heads prevailed and the ill-conceived project was abandoned.

The US did continue to pay some lip service to creating some sort of international establishment to protect access to the Holy Places, but this too proved impractical. In the end, it was Israel and only Israel[332], which provided for access to members of all faiths to their Holy Places, as embodied in its law.

The Policy Statement then went on to express profound truth regarding the paucity of legal support for the UNGA's opposition to Israel declaring Jerusalem as its capital, as follows:

> A special policy problem has developed as a result of the United Nations concern with Jerusalem. The Israel Government has proclaimed Jerusalem to be the capital of Israel, an act... not specifically prohibited by the United Nations[333].

What the Policy Statement concludes in light of the foregoing analysis is a striking rebuttal to the specious arguments made by the State Department over the next approximately sixty-six

---

[332] Jordan did provide some limited access to Christians to their Holy Places, but barred Jews from accessing their Holy Places and even the Jewish Cemetery on the Mount of Olives. In addition, Jordan destroyed synagogues in the Old City of Jerusalem, despoiled and ransacked other Holy Sites and desecrated the Jewish Cemetery on the Mount of Olives, including smashing thousands of tombstones and using them as building materials, paving stones and latrines. The area of the Western Wall was turned into a slum. See, Jerusalem, 1948-1967: Jordanian Occupation of Eastern Jerusalem, at Committee for Accuracy in Middle East Reporting in America (CAMERA), at sixdaywar.org.

[333] The Policy Statement went on to say that while not prohibited, it was in violation of the spirit of the special status recommended for the city by the General Assembly.

years, asserting that the UN's nebulous concept of corpus separatum somehow barred the US from recognizing Jerusalem as the capital of Israel and moving the Embassy there. Here's the State Department's position, in February of 1951, as reflected in the Policy Statement:

> There is thus created the problem of whether the establishment of the capital in this city should be recognized by moving the United States Embassy, which has remained in Tel Aviv, to Jerusalem. Since the UN General Assembly has reach no definite decision on Jerusalem, consideration should be given to moving the Embassy to Jerusalem after consultation with other appropriate nations.

There is also an internal Memorandum from the Office of the Legal Advisor, dated January 13, 1950, on the subject[334]. It summarized the history and predicate asserted by the UN for the internationalization proposal, as follows:

> The General Assembly resolution of December 9, 1949, providing for a special international régime for Jerusalem, was based implicitly on the theory that the Assembly had the right to determine the status and future government of Jerusalem. The chain of reasoning would run somewhat as follows:
>
> (a) In the World War I settlements Turkey renounced all rights and title to certain areas including Palestine, "the future of those territories and islands being settled or to be settled by the parties concerned."

---

[334] Memorandum by Mr. Leonard C. Meeker of the Office of the Legal Advisor to the Officer in Charge of Palestine-Israel-Jordan affairs (Wilkins) 784.00/1-1350, dated January 13, 1950, at Foreign Relations of the United States, 1950, The Near East, South Asia, and Africa, Volume V, at history.state.gov.

(b) Prior to the Treaty of Lausanne, in which this renunciation was made, the Supreme Council of the Allied Powers had met at San Remo and allocated Palestine to be placed under mandate (Class A), pursuant to Article 22 of the Covenant of the League of Nations, with Great Britain as the mandatory power.

(c) Under the mandate instrument approved by the Council of the League of Nations, the mandate was subject to modification with the consent of the League Council and could be terminated by the mandatory power.

(d) At the request of the mandatory power made early in 1947, the United Nations General Assembly made a recommendation concerning the future government of Palestine in the Assembly's resolution of November 29, 1947. This recommendation, "accepted" by the mandatory power, contained provisions for an internationalized City of Jerusalem under United Nations control, apart from the Jewish and Arab States to be created in Palestine.

(e) Although the Statute for Jerusalem which the United Nations Trusteeship Council drafted pursuant to the November 29 resolution was not placed in operation upon the termination of the British mandate for Palestine (May 14, 1949), Jerusalem remained at the disposition of the United Nations.

(f) Through its resolutions of May 6, 1948 and December 11, 1948, the General Assembly has perpetuated its interest and authority with respect to the future of Jerusalem.

There are serious flaws with the UN's legal and factual presentation and its conclusion is erroneous. For example, the

UK famously abstained and did not vote in favor of UNGA Resolution 181 containing the internalization of Jerusalem proposal, which puts into question whether it, as the mandatory actually "accepted" the recommendation. Moreover, the assertion that the UN had any authority over the disposition of Jerusalem, in violation of San Remo and League of Nations Resolutions, is specious, as discussed in Chapter III above. Resolution 181 was and is nothing more than a recommendation, as more fully discussed in Chapter VIII below.

It should, therefore, be no surprise that the Memorandum went on to note, as follows:

> It is evident that the chain of reasoning just referred to is a complicated one, certainly not free from serious doubts and difficulties. It is noteworthy, for example, that the Israeli Delegation at the Fourth Session of the General Assembly took the position that "Jewish Jerusalem" had become integrated with the State of Israel.

The Memorandum then referred to a memorandum submitted to the General Assembly on November 15, 1949 by the Israeli Delegation and set forth the Israeli legal position, as follows:

> "The Mandate unmistakably came to an end in the absence of a 'specific link of any kind between the United Nations and Jerusalem.'" The memorandum went on to assert that no events after May 14, 1948 operated to confer legal authority on the United Nations with respect to Jerusalem. The memorandum concluded:

> "Moreover, it would be misleading to think of the present political relationship between Israel and Jerusalem as a provisional connection which could still be loosened. History knows no precedent of a

population, having once achieved union with its own natural and kindred government, voluntarily turning back to mere semi-autonomy under outside control. The Charter provides for no contingency whereby an area of independence can become a non-self-governing territory."

The State Department Memorandum did not dispute these legal arguments and conclusions.

In this regard, it should be noted that in oral argument before the Supreme Court of the United States[335], the Solicitor General of the US, arguing on behalf of the US, in response to a question by Justice Alito about the legal right of Israel to exercise sovereign power over Jerusalem, answered, as set forth below:

Justice Alito:

...What exactly is the position of the executive regarding Israel's exercise of sovereign power in Jerusalem? Is it the case that it is the position of the executive that Israel cannot lawfully exercise any sovereign powers within Jerusalem?

Solicitor General Verrilli:

The position of the executive is that we recognize, as a practical matter, the authority of Israel over West Jerusalem...

Neither the US Solicitor General nor State Department Legal Advisor could dispute Israel's legal right to exercise sovereign power over Jerusalem. Unfortunately, the State Department felt it appropriate publicly to deal in what it perceived to be political expediencies and remain silent about Israel's legal rights. It did this despite the confusion that it engendered and prejudice it

---

[335] Transcript of Oral Argument in the Supreme Court of the Unites States, in Zivotofsky v Kerry (13-628), on November 3, 2014.

caused to Israel. Thus, the State Department Memorandum merely offered that the US should respect the GA's recommendation and refrain from inconsistent action. It concluded the US and Israel might agree to keeping consular officials in Jerusalem, who would exercise their functions. However, the US should not apply for the issuance of formal consular exequaturs covering the Jerusalem area unless clearly understood that did not involve recognition of sovereignty over Jerusalem.

This is the kind of inane diplomatic gamesmanship that serves no salutary purpose. The subtlety is not appreciated by many and the artifice is usually disdained by most. It only confuses the issue by sending mixed messages that detract from the leadership role the US might otherwise play. This was particularly evident when, as a lame-duck, President Obama, after Donald J. Trump was elected President, did not veto a UNSC Resolution wrongly condemning building in the so-called West Bank, including in the Jewish Quarter of the Old City of Jerusalem, where the renowned prayer plaza of the Western Wall is located. This was a serious break with US tradition, policy and prior practice[336], which had previously vetoed other similar such resolutions[337], especially when it came to Jerusalem and the Holy Places, like the Western Wall. The intemperate decision merely to abstain and not veto the one-sided anti-Israel UN resolution was resoundingly denounced on a bipartisan basis[338].

---

[336] Obama Said to Break With Decades of U.S. Policy to Declare Western Wall 'Occupied Territory' at the UN, by Lee Smith, in Tablet, dated 12/23/2016.

[337] U.N. Security Council: U.S. Vetoes of Resolutions Critical to Israel (1972 - Present), at Jewish Virtual Library.org.

[338] See, for example, Democrats scorch Obama over UN vote condemning Israeli settlements, by Jeremy Berke, in the Business Insider, dated 12/23/2016 and Obama faces widespread backlash after abstaining from UN vote, by Rebecca Kheel, in the Hill, dated 12/23/2016. A number of prominent Democrats and Republicans are quoted in the articles. This includes incoming Democratic Senate Majority Leader Chuck Schumer, who said it was "extremely frustrating, disappointing and confounding" and Democratic Senator Blumenthal, who said it was "unconscionable". Republican Senator John

As US recognition of Jerusalem demonstrated, taking a position with moral clarity could make a fundamental difference, as evidenced by the ensuing Abraham Accords.

Interestingly, in 1989, then Senator Joe Biden, as a member of the Senate Foreign Affairs Committee, at a confirmation hearing for Thomas Melady, who was nominated to be the Ambassador to the Holy See, took up the matter of the Vatican's position on Israel[339]. Remember that the matter of the status of Jerusalem had long been an apparent sticking point for the Vatican. Ambassador Melady reported[340]:

> 'Senator Joseph Biden of Delaware presided at the meeting of the Senate Foreign Affairs Committee where I was to be interrogated. My two Democratic Senators from Connecticut, Chris Dodd and Joe Lieberman, had endorsed my nomination before the hearing with enthusiasm. A Roman Catholic, Senator Biden, delicately raised the issue of the perception of an anti-Semitic bias on the part of the Vatican for not recognizing Israel. He strongly urged me to influence the Holy See to establish diplomatic relations with Israel. Concerned about how the media would report this exchange, I nonetheless responded that I agreed with the sentiment that Israel should be recognized.'

McCain said, "Today's passage of an ill-conceived resolution on Israeli settlements marks another shameful chapter in the bizarre anti-Israel history of the United Nations." He went on in his statement to point out, "The abstention of the United States has made us complicit in this outrageous attack...". Republican Senator Lindsey Graham said the Obama administration's abstention "empowers evil". Republican House Speaker Paul Ryan called the vote "shameful".

[339] Bush Nominee 'cautiously Optimistic' That Pope Will Recognize Israel Soon, at JTA, dated 7/28/1989.

[340] United States-Vatican Diplomatic Relations and the Recognition of the State of Israel, by Thomas Melady, in the Spring 2013 issue of Council of American Ambassadors.

Melady also noted that he had visited with Cardinal O'Connor, the Archbishop of New York in 1989, who advised him to meet directly and confidentially with the Pope, who would be the one to make the decision to recognize Israel. However, he cautioned him to proceed with care and patience and avoid media leaks. The Cardinal also counseled that many Jewish leaders felt there had been some residual antisemitism at play in the Vatican's failure formally to accord diplomatic recognition to the State of Israel. However, it was not just Jewish leaders who were becoming increasingly impatient; there was also a push by President Bush, who met with Pope John Paul II, after the Gulf War and following the Madrid Conference on the Middle East, in October of 1991. President Bush urged the Pope to begin the process of normalizing Israeli-Holy See diplomatic relations.

Cardinal O'Connor visited the Middle East, including Israel, in late December of 1992 through the beginning of January 1992. On January 8, 1992, he met with Pope John Paul II and recommended steps be taken to establish diplomatic relations with Israel. To appreciate the magnitude of these overtures, they must be viewed in context.

The Vatican's discomfort with recognizing a resurgent Jewish State of Israel was likely rooted in what was then classical Church theological doctrine, sometimes referred to as 'supersessionism' or 'replacement theology'. In essence, the Jewish people and Judaism were viewed as obsolete and superseded by the Church. As recently as 1943, Pope Pius XII asserted in an encyclical[341] that the New Testament took the place of the Old Testament and Judaism, which had been abolished.

The Diaspora was viewed as proof this was the case. Thus, the return of the Jewish people to their homeland of Israel was a challenge to this fundamental doctrine of faith. This might also

---

[341] Mystici Corporus Christi, issued on June 29, 1943, during World War II and the Holocaust.

explain why some find a compelling need to demonize Israel. It is difficult for them to accept the reality of a strong and vibrant State of Israel. It is antithetical to the teachings that Jews must be stateless, weak and vulnerable, because they didn't embrace the Christian faith, which is held by some to have replaced Judaism.

After the horrors of the Holocaust, some perceived there was a need for things to change. At the initiative of Pope John XXIII, the Second Vatican Council (known as 'Vatican II') was called together in 1962. It was continued after his death in 1963, under the stewardship of his replacement, Pope Paul VI and closed in 1965. Among other things, a declaration known as Nostra Aetate, proclaimed by Pope Paul VI on October 28, 1965, was overwhelmingly adopted by the Bishops present. It dealt with the relations between the Catholic Church and other religions and specifically the Jews. It affirmed the ancient covenant G-d made with the Jewish people and that it had not been revoked or superseded and remained valid and irrevocable, citing the Apostle Paul in Roman 11:28-29. Thus began the long journey of mutual respect and understanding, which resulted, among other things, in the Vatican recognizing the State of Israel and entering into the Vatican-Israel Accord of 1993.

As noted above, even the Vatican had, in effect, abandoned the concept of territorial internationalization of Jerusalem in favor of assurances of free access to the Christian holy sites. As a matter of fact and law and unlike its predecessors, Israel does assure free access to the holy sites. This was embodied in the Protection of Holy Places Law of 1967, passed on June 27, 1967, shortly after Israel liberated Jerusalem, in the Six Day War.

On June 27, 1967, Prime Minister Eshkol addressed the spiritual leaders of all communities and assured them of Israel's determination to protect the Holy Places. He said:

It is my pleasure to inform you that the Holy Places in Jerusalem are now open to all who wish to worship at them - members of all faiths, without discrimination. The Government of Israel has made it a cardinal principle of its policy to preserve the Holy Places, to ensure their religious and universal character, and to guarantee free access. Through regular consultation with you, heads of the communities, and with those designated by you, at the appropriate levels, for this purpose, we will continue to maintain this policy and to see that it is most faithfully carried out. In these consultations, I hope that you will feel free to put forward your proposals, since the aims that I have mentioned are, I am certain, aims that we share in common. Every such proposal will be given full and sympathetic consideration. It is our intention to entrust the internal administration and arrangements of the Holy Places to the religious leaders of the Communities to which they respectively belong; the task of carrying out all necessary procedures is in the hands of the Minister of Religious Affairs.

On behalf of the religious dignitaries present, His Beatitude Benedictos, the Greek Orthodox Patriarch, replied:

We have heard with pleasure of the free access to the holy sites and we deeply appreciate your kind wish... I believe that I speak on behalf of all my brothers and fellow leaders here tonight if I say that we are pleased with the behaviour of the Israeli army. All of its men have shown us kindness and a willingness to serve us. Everybody has displayed respect for the Holy Places and churches...

The Law provides in the first section, as follows:

> The Holy Places shall be protected from desecration and any other violation and from anything likely to violate the freedom of access of the members of the different religions to the places sacred to them or their feelings with regard to those places.

Yet, the State Department persisted in opposing Israeli sovereignty over Jerusalem even after the Vatican no longer insisted that the territory of Jerusalem be international and despite the Vatican finally recognizing Israel.

Moreover, putting the question of sovereignty over Jerusalem aside, the State Department continued to promote the apparent canard that Israel could not locate its capital in Jerusalem, because of the UN non-binding General Assembly Resolution 181, calling for the internationalization of Jerusalem. However, nowhere in Resolution 181 does it expressly exclude Israel having its capital there or prohibit the US from maintaining an Embassy there. Furthermore, this objection continued even after the entire matter of internationalizing the territory of Jerusalem had, effectively, been superseded and abandoned, as discussed above. Beyond that there is UN Security Council Resolution 242, which effectively supersedes UNGA Resolution 181. There is no longer any consideration of internationalization of Jerusalem under Resolution 242 and the entire concept was, in substance, entirely superseded[342]. Frankly, it appears that the State Department's erstwhile policy of not recognizing Jerusalem or any part thereof, including West Jerusalem, as sovereign

---

[342] It is interesting to note that the even the reference to the UN is deceiving. In the internal Policy Statement on Jordan, referenced below, the State Department recognized that neither Jordan nor Israel was willing to accept internationalization of Jerusalem.. It went on candidly to note: " It is the US hope that these two states can come to an agreed solution which will be acceptable to the Christian world." In this context, apparently the State Department meant the Christian world.

territory of Israel, because of the UN, was nothing more than a convenient and frankly, contrived, artifice.

State Department and UN records also reveal the implicit duplicity of the positions taken by the State department in relation to Jerusalem, as well as, sovereignty over Judea and Samaria. There is the public position and then there is the private or secret position.

Thus, in connection with Jordan's annexation of Judea and Samaria[343], the US went further than just tacitly accepting Jordan's illegal occupation. Astoundingly, it actually approved; but did not wish it to be publicized, as disclosed in a footnote to an internal Policy Statement, dated April 17, 1950 [344], as follows:

> The policy of the Department, as stated in a paper on this subject prepared for the Foreign Ministers meetings in London in May was in favor of the incorporation of Central Palestine into Jordan but desired that it be done gradually and not by sudden proclamation.

However, the footnote to the Policy Statement did not end there, it went on to say, as follows:

> Once the annexation took place, the Department approved of the action "in the sense that it represents a logical development of the situation which took place as a result of a free expression of the will of the

---

[343] The State Department records show that at least by October 22, 1949, they had learned that King Abdullah and the Jordanian Government had decided to proclaim annexation of what they referred to as Arab Palestine by Jordan. See declassified Top Secret Telegram from Acting US Representative at the UN, Jessup, to the Secretary of State, dated October 22, 1949, Foreign Relations of the United States, 1949, The Near East, South Asia, and Africa, Vol. VI, 501.BB Palestine/10-2249 Telegram, at history.state.gov.

[344] Policy Statement Prepared in the Department of State, Washington, April 17, 1950, regarding Jordan (811.85/4-1750), marked secret (that was declassified and is available online at Foreign
Relations of the United States, 1950, The Near East, South Asia, and Africa, Vol. V., at history.state.gov).

people.... The United States continues to wish to avoid a public expression of approval of the union."

Is it any wonder that on April 24, 1950, the Jordanian Parliament granted approval to the complete unity between the portions Jordan had conquered on the west bank of the Jordan and those on the east bank it occupied and their amalgamation into one single state, the Hashemite Kingdom of Jordan. The annexation included the eastern portion of Jerusalem that Jordan had conquered and occupied. It also included Bethlehem and the other portions of the area that the UNGA had desired to be internationalized (as originally configured in UNGA Resolution 181 as the international territory of Jerusalem, i.e.: the Corpus Separatum, as more fully discussed below). The US only had reservations as to the eastern portions of Jerusalem. However, even then, as the internal US State Department internal Policy Statement referenced above noted, " It is the US hope that these two states can come to an agreed solution which will be acceptable to the Christian world". But even so, it appears the US State Department still did not object publicly to Jordan's annexation of the eastern portion of Jerusalem it occupied at the time. Thus, when Acheson was asked about the Jordanian annexation in a news conference of the Secretary of State, on April 26, 1950, The State Department records[345] he responded, as follows:

> Mr. Acheson remarked that our American attitude was that normally we had no objection whatever to the union of people who were mutually desirous of this new relationship.

---

[345] See, Memorandum by the Special Assistant to the Secretary of State for Press Relations (McDermott) of the Press and Radio News Conference of the Secretary of State on April 26, 1950, ON Files: Lot 60 D 641, in Foreign Relations of the United States, 1950, The Near East, South Asia, and Africa, Vol. V, at history.state.gov.

He continued that in this case it had a bearing on the efforts we had made through the United Nations to solve the Palestine matter. He said that we were studying it from that point of view, adding that he thought that was all he could say about it at the present time.

Astonishingly, given the State Department's obsession with the status of Jerusalem, especially when it comes to Israel, there was no express objection to Jordan's annexation of the eastern portions of Jerusalem it occupied or the other areas the UNGA desired to be internationalized under Resolution 181.

The inconsistency of the State Department's position regarding Jordan's conquest of Judea and Samaria and its treatment[346] of Israel's retaking of Judea and Samaria in a defensive war with Jordan is baffling, to say the least. The baseless insistence on labeling Judea and Samaria with the controversial term 'occupied' territories was finally dispensed with by the State Department, under Secretary of State Mike Pompeo, in the Trump administration[347]. Secretary Pompeo also declared[348] that

---

[346] Prior to the Trump administration State Department, under Secretary Pompeo, recognizing Israeli sovereignty; although the new Biden administration State Department appears to be espousing yet again a view, mistakenly believed to be politically expedient, that ignores salient legal and historical facts and precedent, which clearly support Israeli sovereignty. Moreover, given the acceptance of Jordanian sovereignty between 1950 and 1967, it is illogical to assert that Israel, post the Peace Treaty with Jordan, has any lesser claim to sovereignty, as discussed below.

[347] See, for example, State Dept. drops 'occupied' reference to Palestinian territories in report, by Michael Wilner, in the Jerusalem Post, dated 4/22/2018 and Judea/Samaria not 'occupied', in Heritage Florida Jewish News, by World Israel News, dated 5/4/2018.

[348] On November 18, 2019. See, for example, Full text of Pompeo statement on settlements, by TOI Staff, in the Times of Israel, dated 11/19/2019 and Pompeo is right, the settlements are not illegal, by Yigal Dilmoni, in the Jerusalem Post, dated 11/25/2019.

Israeli communities in Judea and Samaria were not per se illegal under international law, as follows:

> Turning now to Israel, the Trump administration is reversing the Obama administration's approach towards Israeli settlements.
>
> US public statements on settlement activities in the West Bank have been inconsistent over decades. In 1978, the Carter administration[349] categorically

---

[349] Interestingly, this was inconsistent with President Carter's expressed view at the time. See, for example, Foreign Relations of the United States, 1977–1980, Volume IX, Arab-Israeli Dispute, August 1978–December 1980, Second, Revised Edition 345. Editorial Note. It explains the comedy of errors that occurred with regard to a UNSC Resolution 465 (1980), passed on March 1, 1980. It notes that, on March 3, 1980, President Carter issued a public statement clarifying the U.S. vote, stating that it "does not represent a change in our position regarding the Israeli settlements in the occupied areas nor regarding the status of Jerusalem." Carter explained: "While our opposition to the establishment of the Israeli settlements is longstanding and well-known, we made strenuous efforts to eliminate the language with reference to the dismantling of settlements in the resolution. This call for dismantling was neither proper nor practical. We believe that the future disposition of existing settlements must be determined during the current Autonomy Negotiations."
This language is a far cry from inappropriate assertions that the so-called settlements are illegal, which they are most assuredly not. It's a political question not a legal one. President Carter also sent a handwritten note to Vance on March 20, in which he wrote, "Had I studied the UN resolution carefully, my concerns would not have been confined merely to Jerusalem references and to 'dismantling'. It would have also dealt with, among other things, refuting any implication of 'sanctions' against Israel under Chapter 7 and not prejudging the permanent status of the West Bank by using words like 'Palestinian and other Arab territories' without qualification or explanation, eventhough recognized this kind of language had been used before." (Carter Library, Plains File, President's Personal Foreign Affairs File, Box 2, Israel, 4/79–11/81).
Is this yet another example of some at the State Department running amok, pursuing their own biased and flawed path and rendering yet another fundamentally wrong opinion?
It would appear that then Secretary of State Cyrus Vance had similar thoughts based on his testimony before the Senate Foreign Relations Committee on March 20, 1980 (See, Hearing Before the Committee on Foreign Relations, 96th Congress, second session, on The Examination of the Current Status of US Policy with regard to the Middle East, March 20, 1980).
For example, Senator Javits referred to the fact that in UNSC Resolution 242, there is no mention of Palestinian and then asked in reference to UNSC 465, "Are you signaling to us that the administration thinks that Palestinians whoever they may be-and you still

concluded that Israel's establishment of civilian settlements was inconsistent with international law. However, in 1981, President Reagan disagreed with that

---

have not defined them as distinguished from "Arab inhabitants"-have some some title, some sovereignty over the territory? Are you denying sovereignty and what goes with sovereignty to Israel but recognizing or signaling the recognition of some other sovereignty?" Vance responded: "The answer is clearly no, we are not."

When pressed on the issue, Vance explained: "It is merely a demographic description. It has been used before both ways in numerous resolutions in the United Nations. Sometimes it has been used with "Palestinian" and other times with just the word "Arab". It does not do anything more than describe in a demographic way. It is not supposed to signal anything with respect to sovereignty." At the Hearing, Vance also noted that the UNSC Resolution was merely recommendatory and not binding.

It should also be noted that On March 21, 1978, at a meeting among President Carter, Prime Minister Begin and others, President Carter said: "We've seen recently, in talks with Sadat, with the Jordanians, with the Saudis, and even with the Shah, a willingness to modify previous views. The Arabs have dropped the idea of a fully independent Palestinian state, and they have abandoned the demand for full Israeli withdrawal from all of the territory occupied in 1967. The PLO, because of its opposition to peace, has excluded itself from the negotiations."

President Carter also told Begin: "There are two points that you keep insisting on: That Sadat calls for full withdrawal; and that he calls for a Palestinian state. This is not true. Not one of the Arab leaders demands this. When you raise this it is not accurate. Neither Jordan nor Sadat want this, nor do we, nor do you."(See, Foreign Relations of the United States, 1977–1980, Volume VIII, Arab-Israeli Dispute, January 1977–August 1978, 232. Memorandum of Conversation1, Washington, March 21, 1978.)

At another meeting with PM Begin and others, President Carter said: "We have not thought a separate Palestinian state would be advisable, and we prefer that a homeland be tied to Jordan, but we have no plan to put forward. We have discussed this in the same way with all of the leaders." (See, Foreign Relations of the United States, 1977–1980, Volume VIII, Arab-Israeli Dispute, January 1977–August 1978, 52. Memorandum of Conversation1, Washington, July 19, 1977.)

President Carter, Menachem Begin and others also met on July 19, 1977 and the issue of refugees was discussed. President Carter acknowledged: "There is no way to avoid the larger question of the refugees, both Palestinians and the Jews from Arab countries. On that issue, the two nations negotiating together might not be enough. Refugees have come from many countries, and on that subject, perhaps all four nations would have to meet?" (See, Memorandum of Conversation between Israeli Prime Minister Menachem Begin and US President Jimmy Carter(19 July 1977)National Security Affairs, Staff Material, Middle East File, Subject File, Box 66, Middle East: Peace Negotiations 1977 Volume I. The Jimmy Carter Presidential Library, Atlanta GA. November 16, 2017, at Center for Jewish Education, at Israeled.org.)

conclusion and stated that he didn't believe that the settlements were inherently illegal.

Subsequent administrations recognized that unrestrained settlement activity could be an obstacle to peace, but they wisely and prudently recognized that dwelling on legal positions didn't advance peace. However, in December 2016, at the very end of the previous administration, Secretary Kerry changed decades of this careful, bipartisan approach by publicly reaffirming the supposed illegality of settlements.

After carefully studying all sides of the legal debate, this administration agrees with President Reagan. The establishment of Israeli civilian settlements in the West Bank is not per se inconsistent with international law.

In line with the foregoing, efforts were made by the Trump administration through Secretary Pompeo and Ambassador Friedman to eliminate territorial restrictions for bilateral agreements[350]. Thus, for example, Ambassador Friedman signed a new protocol that eliminated the broad restrictions on funding of scientific projects in the areas beyond the so-called Green Line, which were modified to permit such funding in the Israeli areas noted above[351]. Secretary Pompeo also initiated new guidelines[352] that were consistent with this new reality based foreign policy approach. Thus all producers within areas where Israel exercises the relevant authorities-most notably Area C under the Oslo Accords- would be marked as 'Israel, 'Product of Israel' or 'Made in Israel', when exporting to the US. Goods in areas of the West Bank where the PA maintains relevant

---

[350] See, US to extend bilateral agreements with Israel into Judea and Samaria, Golan, at JNS, dated 10/27/2020.
[351] See, PM fetes 'important victory' as US okays funding science projects in settlements, by Raphael Ahren, at the Times of Israel, dated 10/28/2020.
[352] Statement of Secretary Pompeo, dated November 19, 2020-Markings of Country of Origin.

authorities would be marked as products of 'West Bank' and goods produced in Gaza would be marked as 'Gaza'. The combined label of 'West Bank/Gaza' or similar markings was no longer acceptable, because these were politically and administratively separate areas and should be treated accordingly.

It is also important to note that the territory of Jerusalem described in UNGA Resolution 181 is far greater than Jerusalem, as we know it today. It included an area bounded by Abu Dis to the east, Bethlehem to the south, as well as, other contiguous areas, where Holy sites were located. Yet, the State Department had no problem recognizing Bethlehem and Abu Dis as a part of Jordan.

There were also those who doctrinairely asserted the primacy of what they understood to be the best interests of the Arab States in the region. The adherence to this nebulous concept had real world ramifications for Israel and Arab States entertaining the possibility of peaceful relations. Thus, for example, Jordan evinced an interest in concluding a separate peace deal with Israel in 1949[353], despite the intransigent insistence of most other Arab States that Israel not be accorded any legitimacy. It is important to recognize that this was the position of most, if not all of the Arab States, in 1947, 1948, 1949, and beyond. This was well before 1967 and the Arab League's pronouncement of the so-called Three No's (No peace, No recognition and No negotiations with Israel[354]).

It is incomprehensible that the State Department didn't publicly and demonstrably urge and support the Jordanian-Israel peace

[353] The Consul at Jerusalem (Burdett) to the Secretary of State, confidential, Jerusalem, December 27, 1949-Foreign Relations of the United States, 1949, The Near East, South Asia, and Africa, Volume VI, 767N.901/12–2749: Telegram.
[354] The Khartoum Resolution of September 1, 1967, issued at the end of the Arab League summit in Sudan. Amazingly, Israel and the Sudan concluded a normalization agreement on October 23, 2020. It appears establishment of full diplomatic relations still awaits endorsement by the Biden administration.

initiative in 1949. There were private messages[355]; but none of the grand gestures like an invitation to Camp David for peace talks, as later occurred with President Sadat of Egypt, when he had an interest in making peace with Israel. The prestige of the US might have made a difference. It also would have provided a shield from the mischievous interlopers at the UN, who continued to frustrate Jordan and Israel from concluding an arrangement on Jerusalem[356]. However, this would have required the US to take an actual, firm (not equivocal) and public position ending the charade that there was any real prospect for territorial internationalization of Jerusalem. Why shouldn't a negotiated arrangement between the real parties in interest, Israel and Jordan, seeking a peaceful resolution between them prevail; especially when protection of and free access to Holy Places was an integral part of the proposed agreement.

Yet, the US did not pursue such a course of action in 1949. There appears to have been overriding concerns about preserving what amounts to a wholly fictional state of Arab unity. It was, therefore, inopportune to do anything that might conceivably offend the presumed sensibilities of other Arab nations by outwardly favoring Israel and Jordan in pursuit of their making a so-called 'separate' peace; an awkward and demeaning term that denigrates the meaning of peace. The primary US focus was on the oil producing states. There was also the related concern about forming a bulwark against any incursions by the Soviet Union in the Middle East, which might interfere with the supply of oil to the US and, hence, prejudice US security interests[357].

---

[355] The Secretary of State to the Legation in Jordan, secret, Washington, March 9, 1950-Foreign Relations of the United States, 1950, The Near East, South Asia, and Africa, Volume V, 684A.85/3–550: Telegram.

[356] The Consul at Jerusalem (Burdett) to the Secretary of State, confidential, Jerusalem, November 21, 1949-Foreign Relations of the United States, 1949, The Near East, South Asia, and Africa, Volume VI, 867N.00/11–2149: Telegram.

[357] 35. Paper Prepared by the National Security Council Planning Board, Washington, July 29, 1958, Issues Arising Out of the Situation in the Near East, Foreign Relations of

As events would later conclusively demonstrate, in practice, these supposed concerns about making separate peace agreements proved groundless. If anything, it was the continuing state of war and especially the 1973 Yom Kippur War that caused an issue; not the subsequent (separate) 1978 Peace Agreement between Egypt and Israel, sponsored by the US. Rather than diminish American prestige, it enhanced it.

Who knows how events might have actually played out had the ice been broken and the benefits of peace allowed to flourish? Perhaps, as we witnessed in our times, it would have been a catalyst for other Arab states to come to the peace table? Yet, the theme of maintaining Arab unity predominated. This despite the fact that it was a fictional construct, which bore no resemblance to the reality of relations among Arab States, which had disparate interests, including being at war with each other, for reasons having nothing to do with Israel.

As more fully discussed below, this false narrative, which dominated the groupthink mentality at the State Department, that the preeminent and over-weaning problem in the Middle East was the existence of Israel, has been debunked by the actual facts and circumstances at play in so many intra-Arab conflicts. Even the storied Brookings Institute, a traditional haven for former State Department personnel, like Martin Indyk, who served as a US Ambassador to Israel and Assistant Secretary of State for Near Eastern Affairs during the Clinton administration, only a few years ago finally issued a report[358] concluding that this myopic and singular focus on Israel as the problem was an erroneous stance.

---

the United States, 1958–1960, Near East Region; Iraq; Iran; Arabian Peninsula, Volume XII.

[358] Building "Situations of Strength" A National Security Strategy for the United States, dated February 2017, a multi-year study and report issued by a bi-partisan group of foreign policy experts, known as the Brookings Order from Chaos Task Force, at the Brookings Institute, which included, among others Martin Indyk and Jake Sullivan (pages 47-51).

As they so well noted, the Middle East that President Trump encountered upon assuming office, required:

Developing a strategy to deal with the collapsing order in the greater Middle East is handicapped by a combination of adverse circumstances:

* Six simultaneous crises across the region (Libya, Syria, Iraq, Yemen, Israel-Palestinians, and Afghanistan).

* Failed states and ungoverned areas in the heartland and on the periphery inhabited by ISIS, al-Qaida, and affiliates.

* Shiite Iran exploiting the cracks and upheavals in the Sunni Arab world to pursue its hegemonic ambitions.

* Depressed oil prices that have dramatically reduced the revenues available to Arab governments to buy off dissent or, better yet, reform their economies.

* A Russian military presence in Syria, which has made it a competitor and potential spoiler of any U.S. reengagement.

They went on to analyze and report:

Despite President Obama's determination to end America's involvement in wars in the Middle East, American forces are still deployed in Afghanistan, have returned to Iraq, and even slipped into Syria. The U.S. military is engaged in daily kinetic military action against ISIS and al-Qaida in both arenas. Notwithstanding that reengagement, the United States now suffers from a widespread regional perception that it lacks the will to maintain the American-led order that it established over the last four decades. President Obama left office at loggerheads with all our traditional allies and partners in the region—Israel, Turkey, Egypt, Saudi Arabia, and the UAE. A wise strategist would conclude that it is better not to begin from this starting point. Unfortunately, President Trump does not have the luxury of choosing to avoid the challenge. While changing circumstances have modified U.S. interests over recent years, they still require a strategy of greater American engagement in the region to:

* Combat ISIS and al-Qaida terrorists who have declared war on the United States and the West and whose destruction the president has set as his primary foreign policy objective.

* Contain Iran's hegemonic ambitions, its stoking of sectarian warfare, and its nuclear weapons ambitions.

* Ensure the security and well-being of our ally Israel and our traditional Arab partners in the region: Egypt, Jordan, Morocco, Saudi Arabia, and the GCC[359] states.

* Prevent the spread of disorder from the Middle East to Europe and Africa via refugee flows and terrorist cadres.

* Maintain the free flow of oil at reasonable prices to our allies in Europe and Asia, and our major trading partners in India and China.

* Encourage economic and political reform to provide improved governance, increased prosperity, and ultimate stability in the region.

---

[359] The Gulf Cooperation Council (GCC) for the Arab States of the Gulf, a regional organization, with six members: The Kingdom of Bahrain, the State of Kuwait, the Sultanate of Oman, the State of Qatar, the Kingdom of Saudi Arabia and the United Arab Emirates.

However, none of those interests requires the launching of another American land war in the region. For example, because of the introduction of hydraulic fracturing technology, the United States is no longer dependent on Middle Eastern oil, which may also allow us to share the security burden in the Middle East with countries that need that oil, especially the major Asian economies. Accordingly, our interests can be preserved by the continued deployment of military forces in the Gulf—increasingly by others—to keep the oil flowing. Similarly, combating ISIS and al-Qaida requires continued military efforts to suppress and defeat them in Iraq, Syria, Yemen, and Libya, but with the region doing more and the U.S. role limited to special operations forces, air power, and other enablers, rather than major ground combat forces. The challenge of reengagement, therefore, is to chart a more cost-effective middle course between the over-commitment of President George W. Bush's efforts to effect a democratic transformation in the region, and the detachment of President Obama's pivot away from the region to avoid involvement in its problems.

It's truly amazing, how refreshingly honest and objective these seemingly new insights are and, by the same token, how allied they are to the positions President Trump actually took and policies he pursued in his administration, in striking contrast to the efforts of those who came before him. This is not to say he did not encounter some of the same intransigent positions that seem to continue to haunt the State Department, but more on this below.

The experts at Brookings, who served in the State Department or foreign policy establishment, don't seem to have accepted any responsibility for the misconceptions that animated State Department policy, while they were in government, prior to the

Trump administration or since. Instead, they appear just to have blamed it all on the new younger leadership that emerged since their tenure in government had ended. Thus, they offered this was a new situation that President Trump inherited:

> President Trump will need to rely more on partners in the region to shoulder their share of the burden, partly because indigenous allies will know better how to do it and partly because the challenge of restoring order is so great; as well as the fact that our interests are not vital enough to justify attempting to do it on our own. Nor would the American people, now wary of engagement in Middle East wars, support such a heavy-footprint course if President Trump sought to do so. Therefore, to achieve the objective of restoring order in a now chaotic environment, the first requirement of an effective strategy is to reset relations with America's traditional allies and partners, all of whom have capabilities of their own to wield in this common cause.

> This should prove to be easier than it appears. Our traditional Arab collaborates—Egypt, Jordan, Saudi Arabia, and the GCC—are now painfully aware of the dangers of leaving a vacuum which American power once filled. They have watched while a host of bad actors in the form of ISIS, al-Qaida, Iran, and Russia sought to take our place. Their own efforts have tended to contribute to the prevailing disorder: in Libya and Syria, they supported competing proxies; in Yemen, Saudi Arabia dragged most of its Gulf allies into what could turn out to be a quagmire, and their competition with Iran fueled sectarian tensions. Egypt needs our economic assistance and technical advice to help it dig its economy out of the deep hole in which it finds itself. All are now hungry for U.S. reengagement and leadership. Each should be more amenable to doing

more for themselves if we insist on it, and if we assure them that we are committed to their security and success and that we are in it for the long haul.

They even went so far as to argue:

In all these countries there is new, often younger, leadership that is more energetic and more cognizant that the ways of the older generation of Arab leaders are no longer viable in the post-Arab Spring and the new social media environments. And instead of using hostility toward Israel as a means of diverting their peoples' attention from their own failings—a favorite technique of the old guard—they all view Israel as a highly capable partner in the common cause of combatting terrorism, Islamist extremism, and Iranian hegemonic ambitions.

They went on to make a most compelling observation, which could have changed the entire tenor of Middle East relations had it been applied in 1967:

Some of them also hope that by drawing closer to Israel, they can use its influence in Washington to secure greater support for their causes. Thus, the old bromide of distancing the United States from Israel to curry favor with the Arabs is no longer relevant.

Why this could not have been done before, is really not explained. It is a convenient assertion of changed circumstances to explain away the possibility of what might have been had they bothered or been able to view the Middle East more objectively over almost seventy years of Israel's existence at the time. Be that as it may, at least now they seem finally to have honed in on the real threats that actually matter to Israel's Arab neighbors and forthcoming peace partners. They even go on to note:

As our Arab partners focus more on the threats in their immediate neighborhoods, they also have less bandwidth for the Palestinian cause.

But then they can't shake their training and endemic biases and prejudices. Once again they resort to the reflexive positions that the Trump administration proved to be faulty and unjustified, with the Abraham Accords. In their own words, they artfully repeat the tired old presumption about the centrality of the so-called Palestinian conflict as being an insurmountable impediment to peace between Israel and other Arab countries. The argument is garbed in some new phrasing, but the message is the same one reverently chanted by many at the State Department as a mantra for so many years to no useful end other than to bedevil themselves. This tired old excuse for their lack of initiative and creativity, lackluster performance and absence of real progress in promoting and sponsoring peace agreements between Israel and other Arab countries is invoked yet again to caution President Trump against recognizing Jerusalem as Israel's capital, as follows:

Nevertheless, they are sensitive to the resonance the Palestinian issue still has for their people, and are therefore cautious about giving their opponents (the Muslim Brotherhood, ISIS, al-Qaida, and Iran) a stick with which to beat them. Egypt and Jordan are more confident about overt engagement because of their peace treaties with Israel. The other Arab states remain skittish, unwilling to take their relations with Israel out of the closet until there is meaningful movement on the Palestinian issue—and they will be even more reluctant to do so if President Trump fulfills his campaign pledge to recognize Jerusalem as Israel's capital by moving the U.S. embassy there.

Their incredulous use of what amounts to a non-sequitur to torpedo what became a central part of President Trumps' successful strategy to bring a realistic approach to the negotiating table is mystifying. Perhaps, the answers that Martin Indyk provided for the record on the subject, at or in connection with his confirmation hearing[360], can shed some light on the matter.

Senator Kyl asked Indyk about whether he would carry out US policy, as stated in the Jerusalem Embassy Act of 1995, that Jerusalem is the capital of Israel and move the Embassy there. Indyk's answers were evasive to say the least. Instead of directly answering the questions, Indyk diverted attention, by substituting a new invented standard for delaying relocation of the Embassy to Jerusalem, as well as, imposing this consideration as a threshold requirement for the President formally recognizing Jerusalem as the capital of Israel. He offered that the President would take no action that would undermine the peace process. While he said it would be his duty to uphold the Jerusalem Embassy Act and that he would do so; he went on to misstate the requirements under the Act and further to qualify his commitment by conditioning it with the proviso, should that be the President's decision.

The Presidential waiver provision under the Jerusalem Embassy Act permitted the President to delay the Embassy move to Jerusalem and avoid the budget limitations set forth in the Act, based on a determination that it "is necessary to protect the national security interests of the United States". The lack of a final peace agreement adhered to by the PA may be a local problem for Israel; but, it does not appear to rise to the level of it being a threat to US national security interests. It is not even

---

[360] Confirmation Hearing for Martin Indyk, conducted by the Senate Foreign Relations Committee, chaired by Senator Sam Brownback, on September 18, 1997. Senator Jon Kyl also submitted written questions for the record to Indyk, which he answered as discussed below.

listed as a threat to national security, by the Director of National Intelligence, in the Annual Threat Assessment of the U.S. Intelligence Community either within the period of four years before or more than four years since the public announcement of recognition of Jerusalem and the decision to move Embassy there[361].

Nowhere does the Act define the lack of a final peace agreement between the PA and Israel as a basis for not recognizing Jerusalem as the capital of Israel or for suspending the Embassy move there. Indeed, the legislative history of the Act suggests that this was a wholly inappropriate basis for delaying recognition of Jerusalem as the capital of Israel and the Embassy move there. The fact of the matter is that recognizing Jerusalem was not a peace deal killer. As the Abraham Accords proved in practice, it was a genuine impetus to Arab States to normalize relations with Israel, under the sponsorship of the US.

Moreover, there were no ongoing talks with the PA to disrupt. The final status talks had stalled as a result of the depraved and illegal acts of terrorism that should have been prevented by the PA; not encouraged, honored and even rewarded by the PA. In this sense, Indyk's answer was also misleading. Indyk neglected to disclose the stark reality that the much talked about ephemeral peace talks were non-existent. This is especially so given that he was being tasked with the seemingly impossible job of reviving the dead peace negotiations, which he ultimately admitted had actually been killed by Arafat. This was due in no

---

[361] See for example, the February 2022, April 9, 2021, January 9, 2019, February 13, 2018, May 23, 2017, February 9, 2016, February 26, 2015, January 29, 2014 and February 2, 2006 (the earliest report available online at intelligence.gov). There are references to Israel in the context of the threats posed by Iran and its proxies, Hezbollah, as well as, Hamas and protégé Syria; but in the reports reviewed, there is no specific National Security threat cited by reason of a lack of a final peace agreement between Israel and the PA. Interestingly, Israel is not even mentioned in the 2015, 2016 or 2017 Worldwide Threat Assessment of the US Intelligence Community delivered by the Director of Intelligence to the Senate Armed Services Committee, noted above.

small measure to the outbreak of terrorism in the aftermath of the Oslo Accords, known as the Second Intifada.

Arafat not only did not stop the violence, he actually surreptitiously orchestrated it, all while facetiously proclaiming his innocence. As Indyk reportedly[362] noted in an interview years later:

The reason he [Arafat] was invited into the White House [to sign the Oslo peace accord] on September 13, 1993, is that he renounced violence, but in the end he has not renounced violence.

> The United States, he said, failed to press Arafat hard enough to stick to his commitments to shun violence and reach a solution with Israel. There were too many carrots for Arafat, including visits to the Oval Office, and too few sticks, he said. Now, he said, the United States should consider whether to put the Palestinian gunmen most closely linked to Arafat-known as the Tanzim-on the State Department's list of terrorist groups.

It is hard to reconcile the approach advocated by Indyk in the interview noted above, with the positions he took at his confirmation hearing and the actual policies he pursued while at the State Department. The State Department's unqualified and doctrinaire focus on resuming final status talks, rather than first assuring the good faith strict performance of existing agreements failed.

The delay in implementing the operative provisions of the Jerusalem Embassy Act, by recognizing Jerusalem and moving the Embassy there, served no useful purpose. The continued insistence on providing rewards to the PA, which only served to

---

[362] U.S. Diplomat's Dream Deferred, by Lee Hockstader, in the Washington Post, dated 7/15/2001.

reinforce bad behavior, instead of insisting on genuine accountability and consequences for wrongdoing, is inexplicable. Not only did the State Department fail to penalize the PA for condoning and even rewarding terrorism or its other willful defaults under its agreements, it appears to have contrived with or at the very least condoned the PA's efforts to evade compliance with the Taylor Force Act.

It is unfathomable why the State Department continues to enable the full and even increased funding of the PA, as it flagrantly fosters terrorism and boosts its Pay to Slay program. Instead of denouncing and stopping the funding of the PA, the State Department enables and even promotes continued funding, which only serves correspondingly to promote terrorism[363]. This includes not rejecting the artifices the PA employs ruthlessly to continue to pay rewards to or on behalf of murderous terrorists, who slaughter or maim Americans and Israelis. The State Department has also for years blithely and cooperatively provided form certifications to Congress needed to avoid mandatory reductions in funding required under the Taylor Force Act, even though arguably the certifications were not fully compliant.

Furthermore, what national security interest would be served by enabling the creation of yet another terrorist state? Wouldn't it be better and more rational to insist that terrorism be eliminated and the PA perform its obligations under existing agreements and only once that was assured proceed to the next phase?

In the real world, excusing misbehavior only enables it. Worse still, rewarding miscreant behavior only serves to reinforce it and assures it will likely be repeated. In this regard, it should be noted that when Indyk was questioned about whether the Palestinian National Charter had actually been formally

---

[363] See, for example, Palestinians see US aid as 'opportunity to promote terrorism', by Ariel Kahana, at JNS, dated 3/15/2023.

amended to remove those provisions that are inconsistent with the Oslo Accords, such as calling for the destruction of Israel, he should have correctly answered in the negative. Instead, he gave a meandering answer about how it was being worked on.

Consider, it's now almost thirty years since Oslo and the Charter has still not been formally amended and this misfeasance seemingly continues to be excused. Is it any wonder that mere entreaties to the PA about meeting its obligations, without the credible implication of tangible and meaningful consequences ensuing for failure to comply, are just casually ignored?

Whether it was the Jerusalem Embassy Act or the Taylor Force Act, it almost seems that rather than feeling empowered to act as contemplated by the Laws, so as to further and protect the US's national security interests as defined by the Laws, the State Department sought to resist the will of Congress and unilaterally impose its own judgment, in disregard of the Laws. Under the circumstances, why would any foreign nation take the US seriously? This kind of dysfunctionality offers malign parties the opportunity to manipulate the system to their advantage.

Senator Kyl noted how he had been very disturbed by Indyk's public comments on the matter of moving the Embassy to Jerusalem. He mentioned that Indyk had said moving the Embassy would "explode the peace process" and also that it was a final status issue and "the President decided it does not make sense to act now". Senator Kyl also explained that although the final status of Jerusalem is mentioned in the Oslo Accords, the late Prime Minister of Israel, Yitzchak Rabin and other Israelis have been emphatic that the sovereignty of Jerusalem is not negotiable. He went on to say that it was his view, "the riots by the Palestinian Authority over Israel's different actions in Jerusalem revolve around the belief that Jerusalem may, some day, be theirs. I believe that administration's failure to comply with the Jerusalem Embassy Act and its insistence on pursuing an 'evenhanded' approach in the Middle East has encouraged the

Palestinian Authority to believe that Jerusalem is negotiable and leads to the riots we all condemn"[364].

While Indyk offered that it was not correct to say he was deeply, personally opposed to moving the embassy to Jerusalem, he nevertheless went on to say he was, however, deeply personally committed to achieving a secure peace for Israel and its Palestinian and Arab neighbors. After this non-answer, he noted that the administration had to walk a fine line between the understandable desire of the Senate to see concrete actions under the Act and the President's strongly held view that nothing should be done to disrupt the effort to put the peace process back on track.

Senator Kyl also asked Indyk "Would not the peace process be better served if all the parties clearly understood that the sovereignty of Jerusalem is not negotiable?"[365]. It was a yes or no question, but Indyk's non-responsive answer was a statement that "The peace process is in a particularly delicate phase because of the crises in confidence between Israel and the Palestinians...the President and the Secretary are determined that we should not do anything to make the conclusion of a permanent status arrangement more difficult..."[366]. It is suggested this non-answer was merely misdirection. In point of fact, the correct answer to Senator Kyl's question was, yes; and, if Indyk had been more candid and forthcoming, instead of doctrinairely repeating the party line, he might have admitted that:

---

[364] See, record of Questions for the Record Submitted to Ambassador Martin Indyk by Senator Jon Kyl, Senate Foreign Relations Committee, dated September 18, 1997, and Martin Indyk's Answers.
[365] Ibid
[366] Ibid.

a) The peace talks were functionally nonexistent, even as some paid virtuous sounding lip service to reviving them.

b) The PA was to blame for the breakdown.

c) There was a crisis in confidence, because as a result of the PA's malfeasance, Israel correctly couldn't trust the PA. The PA had to honor the Agreements already made by stopping terrorism, not promoting, honoring and rewarding it; and remedying their defaults, by actually performing the obligations they had already committed to accomplish.

d) This was not truly a national security matter for the US, but it suited the personal public posture of the President and State Department to say that they we're still working on achieving a peace agreement between Israel and its Arab neighbors and the Palestinians. Therefore, it was averred that deferring, indefinitely, any action on formal recognition of Jerusalem and moving the Embassy there was desirable.

The sentiments expressed by Senator Kyl in his question proved prescient. Recognizing Jerusalem did not spoil the opportunity for Israel to establish peace with Arab States, as many in the State Department predicted. Rather, to the contrary, it can be confidently stated that it was the recognition of Jerusalem and moving the Embassy there, which prompted and enabled the Abraham Accords between Israel and a number of Arab States. Indeed, it might fairly be said that the US's willingness and ability tangibly to demonstrate its loyalty to a good friend and ally, like Israel, by recognizing Jerusalem as the capital of Israel and ending the charade of illegitimacy by moving the Embassy there, was in the national security interests of the US. Moreover, not doing so detracted from the US' image in the world as a worthy ally and friend.

It appears that the State Department bias prejudiced any serious analysis of the matter of recognition of Jerusalem as the capital of Israel and moving the Embassy there, in line with the pronouncements of the ex-State Department wags in the Brookings study group on the subject. The groupthink knee-jerk responses of it's just not the right time, it will undermine the so-called ongoing peace talks (which might better have been described as nonexistent) and the hyperbolic assumption that it would cause explosive violence to occur across the Arab world, were all so predictable. The treatment of the subject of Jerusalem and the conclusion summarily reached by the Brookings group is presumptuous and wholly at variance with the consideration of the other issues covered by the report. This is all the more striking given the Brookings group's apparent understanding of the actual stakes at play for the Arab states, which needed US involvement. Thus, their report goes on to note:

> ...Saudi Arabia sees the Assad regime in Syria as a proxy for Iran, Egypt sees a secular government fighting Islamist extremists. Where Saudi Arabia sees Turkey as a potential ally against Iran, Egypt sees Turkey's President Erdoğan as a leading member of the Muslim Brotherhood. The UAE is closer to Egypt's worldview but seeks to bridge the differences with Saudi Arabia.

This appreciation of the reality of the Middle East is further amplified by their analysis of the threats of Iran and other forces at play threatening the very existence of many of the Arab states:

> Similarly, in seeking to rebuild a relationship of trust with each one of these states, President Trump will need to strike a new balance between the pursuit of stability and the promotion of economic and political reform. Past American efforts that placed too great an emphasis on promoting stability at the expense of meaningful reforms in these Arab societies contributed

to the profound instability of the Arab revolutions. On the other hand, too much emphasis on reform in the current environment of profound instability could prove equally counterproductive.

Each of these regional leaders is scarred by the experience of seeing President Obama, in the face of massive Egyptian demonstrations, demand that Hosni Mubarak leave office immediately. They fear that the next president might repeat that rug-pulling exercise should they find themselves in trouble with their people. That makes them suspicious of American intentions when its diplomats speak of the need for greater inclusiveness or openness in their political systems. This puts a premium on building personal trust between President Trump and the leaders of these Arab countries before the sensitive issue of reform is raised. Nevertheless, it will need to be part of the new compact between the United States and these countries if past mistakes are not to be repeated and truly stable foundations for the renewed order are to be laid.

The Trump administration needs a tough-minded, clear-eyed approach to Iran. The administration should strictly enforce the provisions of the nuclear agreement with Iran (the Joint Comprehensive Plan of Action, or JCPOA), while pushing back against Iran's ballistic missile program, support for terrorism, and destabilizing activities throughout the region. Any moves will need to be closely coordinated with Israel and the Gulf Arabs, whose direct interests are involved. President Trump will need to ensure that the Iranian leadership understands that the international community will never accept an Iran with a nuclear weapons capability.

Israel is that bastion of stability and democracy in the Middle East. It boasts a diverse society, democratically elected government and shared values and interests with the United Stated. It is an ideal partner and fulcrum upon which to leverage the creation of alliances with other nations in the area. The glaring mistreatment of Israel when it came to recognizing Jerusalem as the capital of Israel was interpreted, by regional players, as a tangible sign that America could not be relied upon to be a loyal and trustworthy ally. Rectifying the deficiency was a clarion call to the ambivalent that now was the time to join with Israel and the US in a genuine bulwark against the terrorist Iranian regime and its proxies.

It is frustrating to realize that there were and still are naysayers, who, to this day, belittle the Abraham Accords and continue to maintain, despite all evidence to the contrary, that the heart of the problems in the Middle East is the so-called Palestinian conflict with Israel. How that explains the turmoil in Iraq, the civil war in Afghanistan and recent takeover by the Taliban, the Houthi/Yemen war with Saudi Arabia, the implosion of Libya, the Saharan conflict, Iran, Hamas, Hezbollah, Isis and Al Qaeda is unfathomable.

This kind of agenda driven or biased approach may help explain some of the otherwise irrational positions taken by the State Department, which were demonstrably against the national interests of the United States, when it came to Israel. Whether the origin is derived from plain old antisemitism; evolved from a pro-Arab attitude; is an outgrowth of an ideological imperative; or is the result of a pro-oil interests consciousness; the effect is the same, an inability to view the US' relationship with Israel objectively and a consummate failure to appreciate how Israel benefits the US and its national interests.

Amazingly, little has truly changed in the area, in now more than seventy years. Israel is still the only truly democratic country in the region. It boasts a genuinely diverse society with freedom of speech, religion and press, as well as, equal protection under the law. Besides shared values and interests with the US, it has proven itself to be a reliable ally and good friend to the US.

It is frustrating to realize that even after the Trump administration recognized Jerusalem as the capital of Israel and moved the Embassy there, the Biden administration State Department is still flirting with the concept of locating what amounts to a symbolic Consulate to the PA in Jerusalem. This misguided effort is being pursued despite all the progress made since and as a result of the recognition of Israeli sovereignty over Jerusalem, including the momentous Abraham Accords. Moreover, it would also violate the express provisions of Article IX, Section 5a of the Oslo II Agreement[367].

As more fully discussed in Chapter XVI below, this new attempt to infringe on the sovereign status of Jerusalem as an integral part of Israel and thereby diminish its legitimacy is baffling. It's now indisputably US law that undivided Jerusalem is the capital of Israel. Why engage in frivolous machinations like setting up a symbolic Consulate in Jerusalem to service a foreign non-state? Besides being an absurd and irresponsible way of making this kind of a point, it's also illegal under US and International Law. Yet, the State Department doyens insist on these kinds of backhanded gestures and that's the point. It appears to be a manifestation of the kind of passive-aggressive behavior that is so destructive in managing the affairs of a company let alone a country. If the State Department had pursued a frontal assault and called for the reversal of US policy on the recognition of Jerusalem, then they would likely have failed because both the Senate (overwhelmingly by a vote of 97 to 3)[368] and the

---

[367] Israeli-Palestinian Interim Agreement on the West Bank and Gaza Strip, signed in Washington DC, on September 28, 1995 and witnessed by President Clinton, among others.
[368] US Senate votes 97-3 to keep US Embassy in Jerusalem, Israel Hayom, dated 2/5/2021.

President[369] reaffirmed that Jerusalem is the capital of Israel. Hence, they persist in their game-playing and resort to cunning ploys as a means of expressing their continued adherence to the failed policy they advanced denying the reality of Jerusalem as the capital of Israel.

This kind of an abiding and endemic problem is not easily cured. It is continually promoted and reinforced by the near reverence of the legendary figures of the past originating these myths and the presence of their protégées mentoring yet another generation of operatives. Even though, like so many myths they have proven false and the prejudices of their originators and perpetuators have been uncovered, nevertheless they persist. Perhaps, it's the result of cognitive dissonance or the culture of institutional groupthink; but, whatever the cause, it exercises a pernicious influence on the conduct of a coherent and effective US foreign policy. In the world of hostile corporate takeovers, the answer would have been to clean house and bring in a completely new and fresh leadership team unburdened by the corporate myths of the past. This may be the only solution to deal with the prejudices so ingrained in the corporate culture at the State Department.

The die has been cast. Under US Law, undivided Jerusalem is the recognized capital of Israel and the US Embassy is properly located there. This legal and factual reality cannot be changed by fiat or because of some personal ideology or perspective.

As King David declared in Psalms[370], "Jerusalem built up, a city knit (unified[371]) together". Let no one seek to rend it asunder.

---

[369] White House confirms Biden will keep embassy in Jerusalem, by Niels Lesniewski, in Roll Call, dated 2/9/2021.
[370] Psalms 122:3.
[371] BT Taanit 5a, unified together, both spiritually and physically.

VII.

JERUSALEM IN FIRST PLACE, NOT THIRD PLACE OR JUST A PARTICIPATION TROPHY

The Jewish Religion is unique in its attachment to Jerusalem. The Old Testament mentions Jerusalem more than six hundred and fifty times[372]. The New Testament mentions it more than one hundred and fifty times. The Quran, on the other hand, mentions it not at all. Who can forget the stirring declaration in Psalms[373], 'If I forget you, O Jerusalem, let my right hand lose its skill'. There is no comparable expression of this sentiment in non-Jewish scripture.

In Judaism, Jerusalem is a living focus of prayer and mourning rituals. Thus, when praying, it is required that orient heart towards Jerusalem[374]. It is, therefore, virtually a universal practice in classic Judaism to face Jerusalem when praying. Neither Christian nor Muslim rituals and practice require this orientation in prayer. Indeed, Muslim custom is to face Mecca, not Jerusalem[375].

---

[372] In addition, the synonymous term 'Zion' is used more than one hundred and fifty times.
[373] Psalms 137:5.
[374] BT Brachot 30a, which records that when praying outside of Israel, direct heart towards Israel and by extension Jerusalem. In Israel, orient heart directly towards Jerusalem. Within Jerusalem direct heart towards the Temple Mount. See Shulchan Aruch, Orach Chayim 94:1. See also Daniel 6:11 and I Kings 8:35, 44 and 48.
[375] Historically, facing eastward does have some significance in Christian prayer rituals. This is said to be based either on the fact that the Garden of Eden is located in the East

Mourning rituals are also uniquely associated with Jerusalem. Thus, the traditional formulaic condolence recited to mourners is: 'May you be comforted among the other mourners of Zion and Jerusalem'. There is no such custom in Muslim or Christian practice.

Another unique feature of classic Judaism is the requirement to rip clothing upon approaching Jerusalem and the place where the Temple stood, much like is the case when mourning for a parent. The requirement is first to rend garments, in the place covering the heart, for the Temple, and then extend the rip for Jerusalem[376]. There is no comparable custom in Christian or Muslim rituals.

Even the traditional wedding ceremony is not complete until ashes are placed on the forehead of the groom, a glass is shattered by the groom and the verses from Psalms[377] expressing our integral attachment to Jerusalem are sung. These are done to memorialize our grieving for the destruction of the Holy Temple, even in moments of extreme joy like a wedding and so as to remember Jerusalem[378].

The classic Jewish prayer service is replete with references to Jerusalem. Thus, for example, the quintessential prayer, known as Shemoneh Esrei (Eighteen), because it was originally composed of eighteen blessings[379], has one of its blessings

---

(Genesis 2:8) or because at the end of time, it is believed the Messiah would approach from that direction. However, praying towards or within Jerusalem itself is not required (John 4:21).

[376] BT Moed Katan 26a; JT Moed Katan 3:7; Maimonides Mishne Torah, Laws of Fasts 5:16-18 and Laws of Mourning 9:10; and Shulchan Aruch, Orach Chaim 561:1

[377] Psalm 137:5-6, which declare: 'If I forget you, O Jerusalem, let my right hand wither. Let my tongue stick to my palate if I cease to think of you, if I do not keep Jerusalem in memory even at my happiest hour.'

[378] Aruch HaShulchan Even HaEzer 65:5. See also, Maimonides, Mishne Torah, Laws of Fasts 5:13.

[379] A nineteenth blessing was later added, as discussed in BT Brachot 28b-29a. The prayer is also known as the Amida (a Hebrew term meaning, standing), because it is usually recited while standing.

expressly devoted to the rebuilding of Jerusalem. The prayer is recited three times daily, morning, afternoon and evening. It was reportedly composed in the time of the Great Assembly, which included the Prophets Chaggai, Zechariah and Malachi, at the advent of the Second Temple period[380], approximately two thousand five hundred years ago. Many other prayers reference Jerusalem, including a special blessing in the Grace after Meals[381].

There are also four fast days devoted to remembering Jerusalem[382]. The most onerous is the twenty-five-hour period of rigorous fasting and acute mourning of Tisha B'Av (the 9th day of the month of Av), associated with the destruction of the First and Second Temples in Jerusalem. There are also the seventeenth day of Tammuz when the Romans breached the walls of Jerusalem; the tenth of Tevet, when Jerusalem was besieged by the Babylonians; and the Fast of Gedaliah (third day of Tishre), when the Babylonian appointed Jewish governor was assassinated, ending self-rule in Judea, including Jerusalem.

On the holiest day of the year, Yom Kippur, the climactic and reinvigorating moment at the end of the service each year, after a grueling day of fasting and prayer, is the heartfelt declaration of 'L'Shana HaBa'ah B'Yerushlayim HaBenuyah' (next year in rebuilt Jerusalem). Many break out in dance while singing this prayerful refrain. It's an exhilarating moment that unifies all present in hope and prayer. Similarly, at the end of the Passover Seder, everyone participating in the Seder makes the same declaration. We also break out in singing this refrain and usually dancing, as well. Thus, on the two most well-attended rituals in the Jewish world, Yom Kippur and the Passover Service, the focus and climax of the service is Jerusalem.

---

[380] Megillah 17b-18a.
[381] Known in Hebrew as the Bircat HaMazon.
[382] See, Zechariah 8: 1-19, as well as, JT Ta'anit 4:5, BT Rosh HaShanah 18b and Aruch HaShulchan, Orach Chaim 549:4.

These Jewish rituals and practices are living examples of the unique, profound and vital attachment that the Jewish people have to Jerusalem, the eternal capital of their ancient and ancestral homeland of Israel, as well as the place where the First and Second Temples stood and the prophesized Third Temple is to be built.

It should also be noted that pilgrimages were required to be made to Jerusalem during the First and Second Temple periods[383], three times a year to celebrate the holidays of Passover, Shavuot and Sukkot in Jerusalem[384]. There is also a separate commandment for men, women, and children to assemble in Jerusalem[385]after the conclusion of the seventh year in the Shemitah[386] cycle, on the Holiday of Sukkot, and hear a reading of portions of the Torah[387]. The first formal system of public schools was also established in Jerusalem[388].

Those making the journey were miraculously assured a comfortable place and stay in Jerusalem[389] and that their homes would be protected from any harm while they were away in

---

[383] There is evidence that there were those who continued to make pilgrimages to Jerusalem even after the destruction of the Temple. See Mishna Ta'anit 1:3, as well as, Ran (page 2a of Rif pages on BT Ta'anit, s.v. Ika LeMeidak). See also 15th century Rav Shimon ben Tzemach Duran (in his Sefer HaTashbetz 3:201), who notes the continuing custom of making pilgrimages to Jerusalem and describes how he was witness to one of the miracles of Jerusalem in the time of the Holy Temple, on the Holiday of Shavuot, that despite being in a tightly packed synagogue filled cheek to cheek with pilgrims, no one complained that didn't have enough space.

[304] Exodus 23:14-18 and 34:23-24, as well as Deuteronomy 16:16-17. See also Mishna Chagigah 1:1

[385] Deuteronomy 31:10-13.

[386] The last year of a reoccurring seven-year cycle, when the land is to lie fallow and not be worked and there is to be a release of indebtedness (Leviticus 25:3-6 and Deuteronomy 15:1-2).

[387] Mishna Sotah 7:8.

[388] BT Bava Batra 21a.

[389] Mishna Avot 5:5, which records among the ten miracles performed for our ancestors in the Holy Temple was the fact that it was so crowded people would stand pressed together and nevertheless they had enough room to bow and also no one complained it was too congested to lodge overnight in Jerusalem..

Jerusalem[390]. In addition, there was an obligation, in every first, second, fourth and fifth year of the reoccurring seven-year Shemitah cycle, to set aside a second Tithe[391] of the agricultural produce, which was to be consumed in Jerusalem.

It should, therefore, be no surprise that ancient pilgrimage roads have been unearthed in Israel, which attest to this practice[392]. The recent discovery of the two-thousand-year-old pilgrimage road in the City of David, Jerusalem, leading to the Temple Mount[393], is especially exciting[394].

Rabbi Dr. Meir Soloveitchik[395], who wrote about the new discovery, recorded Ambassador David Friedman's observation that the excavated path was only a part of the mountain of archaeological evidence reflecting the Jewish connection to Jerusalem. As Ambassador Friedman put it, the discoveries made in Jerusalem, 'in most cases by secular archaeologists, bring an end to the baseless efforts to deny the historical fact of Jerusalem's ancient connection to the Jewish people.' Friedman also noted, 'denials of history are part of what prevents resolution of the conflict'.

---

[390] Exodus 34:34, which states that no one will covet the person's land when going up to appear before G-d, in a pilgrimage to Jerusalem, three times a year. See also JT Peah 3:7, as well as, BT Pesachim 8b.

[391] Leviticus 27:30-31 and Deuteronomy 14:22-29 and 26:13. See also Avot 5:9 and Maimonides, Mishne Torah and Sefer HaMitzvot, Positive Mitzva (Commandment) 128.

[392] See, for example, To Jerusalem: Pilgrimage Road Identified?, by Robin Ngo, in Biblical Archeological Review, dated March 3, 2018.

[393] See, for example, New discovery in Jerusalem's City of David: 2,000-year-old pilgrimage road, by Yaakov Katz, in the Jerusalem Post, dated June 30, 2019.

[394] In the Summer of 2019, Farley went on a tour of the Pilgrimage Road with, among others, former Arkansas Governor Mike Huckabee, then candidates and now Congresswomen Nicole Malliotakis and Claudia Tenney and Congressman Nick Langworthy.

[395] Pilgrimage Road and Palestinian Memory, by Meir Soloveichik, in the Wall Street Journal, dated July 4, 2019.

Rabbi Soloveichik also reported how William Seward, who served as Abraham Lincoln's Secretary of State, wrote of his visit to the Holy Land:

> 'Our last day at Jerusalem has been spent, as it ought to have been, among and with the Jews, who were the builders and founders of the city, and who cling the closer to it for its disasters and desolation.'

He noted Seward described watching the throngs of Jews who came to the Western Wall to mourn Jerusalem's destruction:

> 'For many hours they pour forth their complaints, reading and reciting the poetic language of the prophet, beating their hands against the wall, and bathing the stones with their kisses and tears.'

Rabbi Soloveichik concluded by reflecting on how:

> 'Seward's words refute the idea that American Christians only recently have embraced Jews and their connection to the Holy Land.
>
> Millions of Jews and non-Jews ardently pray for peace in Jerusalem. Yet in an age where actual facts are all too often eschewed for "personal narrative," the Pilgrimage Road is another reminder that peace can only be attained through the recognition of historical truth. The ambassador and the administration he represents deserve credit for recognizing the facts on the ground— or, rather, underneath it.'

Christian dogma and scripture are linked to Jerusalem, but it is in the nature of a historical connection and, more specifically, to a time when Jesus and his disciples were and would have considered themselves to be Jews. It was only later that there was a directional shift away from Judaism and Jews, in a process beginning in the time of Paul and culminating at the Council of

Nicaea in the 4th century, when the Sabbath day was formerly changed, for Christians[396], to Sunday from Saturday, observed by Jews. In addition, the holiday of Easter was delinked from Passover by no longer basing the date set for its annual occurrence on the Jewish calendar. In essence, the mission changed from being a parochial one of attracting adherents from within Judaism to a more universal one of establishing a new religion, separated from its Jewish origins. Christianity became primarily focused on attracting erstwhile pagan worshippers from all over the Roman Empire.

This was also a time when the Byzantine center of power in the ancient world sought to dominate Christianity with its authorized version of the faith, which, among other things, ascribed divinity to Jesus and espoused the concept of the Trinity. The Byzantine Church's mission included stamping out so-called heresies within Christianity, like Arianism, which rejected many of these church doctrines, as well as Judaism and Islam. In a sense, because the Byzantine Church doctrine viewed itself as having superseded Judaism, becoming the new Children of Israel and, thereby, wholly replacing the original Jewish people, the very continuing existence of Judaism posed a theological dilemma. If Judaism, the mother faith that bore Christianity, continued to be practiced by Jews, who did not merge their identity out of existence by joining the Byzantine Church and accepting its doctrines, then how could it have replaced Judaism? Moreover, given the existence of Islam, another monotheistic religion that also sprung from Judaism, the matter became even more complicated. Islam was not only a competing religion; it was also vying for temporal dominance within the domain of the Byzantine Empire.

The powerful combined forces of religion, temporal power, and geopolitics, embodied in Byzantine, on the one hand, and Islam,

---

[396] Seventh Day Adventists, as their name implies, do not accept this change.

on the other hand, met and clashed at the crossroads of the world in the Land of Israel.

In the 7th century, Islam conquered Israel from its Byzantine overlords. In essence, the nomadic Arab tribes comprising Omar's army became the masters of the Land of Israel, and the Bedouin occupiers ruled over a population that was primarily Christian and Jewish at the time[397]. Eventually, a number of centuries later, under the leadership of the Ottomans, Islam overran the Byzantine Empire and captured its capital of Constantinople in the mid-15th century.

The Roman Empire had originated in Rome. Its tentacles reached out in all directions, including to the east. The Roman Empire conquered much of what had been the prior Greek Empire. It was Constantine who had moved the capital east to what he referred to as the New Rome and which was eventually named Constantinople. However, despite the fall of the Western Roman Empire in the 5th century, Christendom, centered in Rome, continued to survive and expand into Western Europe. Its central religious authority was the Catholic Church, headed by the Pope and operated by the various organs of the Catholic Church, which was and is still headquartered in Rome. The Catholic Church espoused most of the fundamental church doctrines adopted at the Council of Nicaea. Interestingly, though, in the early 8th century, the Byzantine-centered version of Christianity did differ from the Roman-centered Catholic Church on the matter of the creation and veneration of religious images, known as icons. The Byzantine Emperors were iconoclasts who forbade the creation and veneration of icons as violations of the Ten Commandments. Thus the Byzantine Emperor Leo III ordered that an image of Jesus prominently placed over the ceremonial entrance to the Great Palace of Constantinople be removed and replaced with a cross. Similar orders were subsequently issued

---

[397] A History of Palestine 634-1099, by Moshe Gil (Cambridge University Press-1992).

banning the pictorial representation of Mary, Christian saints, and biblical scenes. Was this perhaps an effort at outreach to the people in the Byzantine realm subscribing to the other major monotheistic religions of Judaism and Islam, which had similar prohibitions? Nevertheless, Pope Gregory III vehemently disagreed. It was Empress Irene, who siding with the pope, called for an Ecumenical Council between the Byzantine and Catholic Churches. In 787, the Second Council of Nicaea was held, and the Pope's position in favor of icons was adopted.

Christianity comprises a variety of different doctrines, practices, disciplines, denominations and sects, including, among others, Roman Catholic, Greek and Russian Orthodox, Protestant, Baptist and Evangelical.

The role of Jerusalem varies, depending on the nature of the church doctrine and how it evolved over time. Thus, for example, Catholicism, for ages, was subsumed with what is referred to as a supersessionist or replacement theology that viewed Judaism as being superseded by Christianity. In this context, Jerusalem had little practical utility other than as a place to be revered because of its historical connection to Jesus, a Judean Jew, who preached and was crucified by Pontius Pilate, the Roman Official ruling Jerusalem at the time. It wasn't long thereafter that Rome had supplanted Jerusalem as the center of worship in Christianity. Although Martin Luther and John Calvin challenged the primacy of the Pope and supremacy of Rome in the Protestant Reformation, they were still, nevertheless, avowed supersessionists[398].

Others, though, like the Anglo-American Pilgrims, felt otherwise and believed that the Jews would be restored to Jerusalem and

---

[398] See, for example, Various Forms of Replacement Theology, by Dr. Michael J. Vlach, in The Masters Seminary Journal 20/1 (Spring 2009), beginning at page 57.

rebuild Jerusalem[399]. The more decentralized structure of the Protestant movement permitted a diversity of opinions on these subjects.

Whatever their position on replacement theology, none of these Christian movements contemplated relocating their central seat of authority to Jerusalem. While Jerusalem was regarded as a Holy Place, it did not have a prominent place in day-to-day Christian rituals. For example, to a Catholic visiting the Vatican and perceiving its centrality, majesty and grandeur in Catholicism, Jerusalem might well be viewed as just another holy place. Besides its historical significance, it did not play a vital and living part in how the Christian Church functioned.

The reestablishment of the modern State of Israel in 1948 presented the traditional Vatican establishment and others espousing replacement theology with a theological conundrum. If their brand of Christianity had, as they then believed, superseded Judaism and, in effect, they were the replacement Chosen People of Israel, then how could Jews have survived and gone on to reestablish the State of Israel, with a capital in Jerusalem? It was antithetical to their particular creed and profession of faith[400].

Rabbi Joseph B. Soloveitchik, of blessed memory, the great 20th century thinker and towering intellect, philosopher, and Halachic authority, discussed how the re-emergence of the State of Israel was a direct challenge to the legitimacy of replacement theology. As he expressed it[401]:

---

[399] See, for example, The Reformed Tradition on Israel is Diverse, by Gerald R. McDermott, at the Gospel Coalition (US Edition): Bible & Theology, dated January 24, 2018.
[400] It should be noted that the Old Testament records numerous assurances that the covenant between G-d and the Jewish people is eternal. This includes Genesis 17:7-8, Psalms 105:10-11, Jeremiah 32:27-40, I Chronicles 16:17-18. The New Testament also confirms the foregoing in Romans 11:28-29.
[401] Kol Dodi Dofek, by Rabbi Joseph B. Soloveitchik, Six Knocks, Third, (1956), as translated by David Z. Gordon (2006) available online at Sefaria.org

Third, the Beloved[402] also began to knock on the door of the tent of theology, and possibly this is the strongest beckoning. I have, on several occasions, emphasized in my remarks concerning the Land of Israel that the theological arguments of Christian theologians to the effect that the Holy One has taken away from the Community of Israel its rights to the Land of Israel, and that all of the biblical promises relating to Zion and Jerusalem now refer in an allegorical sense to Christianity and the Christian Church, were all publicly shown to be false, baseless contentions by the establishment of the State of Israel... We should pay careful attention to the learned explanation of our Secretary of State, Mr. Dulles (who served as the deacon of an Episcopalian Church), to a Committee of the United States Senate that the Arabs hate the Jews because they killed the founder of their religion. This "explanation" possesses hidden and deep symbolic significance. I am not a psychiatrist and surely not a psychoanalyst, but I know how to study Talmud, and I remember well what our Rabbis of blessed memory said about Balaam: "from his blessings ... you may learn what was in his heart" (TB <u>Sanhedrin 105b</u>). Sometimes, when a person speaks too much, something of the truth slips out. When one of the Senators asked the Secretary of State, "Why do the Arabs hate the Jews?" he really wanted to answer, "Personally, I too, as a Christian, have no great love for them, because they [invoking the horrible and historically false antisemitic libel that the Jews, not Roman Pontius Pilate] killed our messiah and consequently forfeited their portion of Abraham's heritage." An angel sat in the throat of the Secretary, or a hook was put into it (as in the exegesis of the Rabbis

---

[402] An English translation of the Hebrew term 'Dodi', used in this context as a term of art symbolizing the Divine Presence.

of blessed memory on the phrase "and God put a word in Balaam's mouth" [Numbers 23:5, TB Sotah 10a], "[i.e.] he put a hook in his mouth"), and instead of saying, "Our Lord" and "for myself," he let other words slip out, the "Arabs" and "Mohammed." In his subconscious he was terrified of the "awful" fact that the Community of Israel rules over Zion and Jerusalem. I find satisfaction in reading about the State of Israel in the Catholic and Protestant newspapers[403]...I always have a special sense of satisfaction when I read in the paper that Israel's reaction is not as yet known because today is Saturday and government offices are closed or when I read, on the eve of Passover, an item from the United Press that "Jews will sit down tonight to the seder table in the hope that the miracles of Egypt will return and recur today." Listen! My Beloved Knocks!

It also appeared to be an obstacle to how they believed the end of the days would unfold, as more fully discussed below. After all, they professed to be the new Chosen People and their centers of worship purported to be the new Jerusalem. The old Jerusalem was viewed as an obsolete construct intimately tied to the Jewish people and their experience, which they purported to supersede. The Vatican, though, did eventually modify this position, as discussed above.

The Protestant denominations within the World Council of Churches (WCC), which coincidentally was founded in 1948, have a similar discomfort with the existence of a renascent Jewish State of Israel. It appears they do not graciously accept the continuing covenantal relationship G-d has with the Jewish people, as confirmed even by New Testament scripture[404]. This may help explain their opposition to the existence of a Jewish

---

[403] He went on to note: "Despite themselves they must mention the name of Israel when they report the news of Zion and Jerusalem, which we possess."
[404] Romans 11:28-29.

State in Israel and their support for BDS. It should be noted that Senator Kyl strongly disagrees with anti-Israel positions taken by the Presbyterian Church USA, with which his local church is currently affiliated.

It is important to recognize that the WCC does not speak for all Christians, many of whom are Christian Zionists. However, members, sub-groups and chapters of the WCC[405], with at least the tacit support of the WCC, effectively deny the Jewish people the right to self-determination in the State of Israel, which is classified as antisemitism under the IHRA[406] definition.

The IHRA definition of antisemitism has been adopted by the US State Department, as well as thirty-eight countries and twenty-eight US States. The State Department website[407] sets forth the definition as follows:

> The Department of State has used a working definition, along with examples, of antisemitism since 2010. On May 26, 2016, the 31 member states of the International Holocaust Remembrance Alliance (IHRA), of which the United States is a member, adopted a non-legally binding "working definition" of antisemitism at its plenary in Bucharest. This definition is consistent with and builds upon the information contained in the 2010 State Department definition. As a member of IHRA, the United States now uses this working definition and has encouraged other governments and international organizations to use it as well.
>
> **Bucharest, 26 May 2016**
>
> In the spirit of the Stockholm Declaration that states: "With humanity still scarred by ...antisemitism and

---

[405] See NGO Monitor, World Council of Churches (WCC) February 15, 2021.
[406] International Holocaust Remembrance Alliance.
[407] Defining Antisemitism, at state.gov.

xenophobia the international community shares a solemn responsibility to fight those evils" the committee on Antisemitism and Holocaust Denial called the IHRA Plenary in Budapest 2015 to adopt the following working definition of antisemitism.

On 26 May 2016, the Plenary in Bucharest decided to:

Adopt the following non-legally binding working definition of antisemitism :

"Antisemitism is a certain perception of Jews, which may be expressed as hatred toward Jews. Rhetorical and physical manifestations of antisemitism are directed toward Jewish or non-Jewish individuals and/or their property, toward Jewish community institutions and religious facilities."

To guide IHRA in its work, the following examples may serve as illustrations:

Manifestations might include the targeting of the state of Israel, conceived as a Jewish collectivity. However, criticism of Israel similar to that leveled against any other country cannot be regarded as antisemitic. Antisemitism frequently charges Jews with conspiring to harm humanity, and it is often used to blame Jews for "why things go wrong." It is expressed in speech, writing, visual forms and action, and employs sinister stereotypes and negative character traits.

Contemporary examples of antisemitism in public life, the media, schools, the workplace, and in the religious sphere could, taking into account the overall context, include, but are not limited to:

Calling for, aiding, or justifying the killing or harming of Jews in the name of a radical ideology or an extremist view of religion.

Making mendacious, dehumanizing, demonizing, or stereotypical allegations about Jews as such or the power of Jews as collective - such as, especially but not exclusively, the myth about a world Jewish conspiracy or of Jews controlling the media, economy, government or other societal institutions.

Accusing Jews as a people of being responsible for real or imagined wrongdoing committed by a single Jewish person or group, or even for acts committed by non-Jews.

Denying the fact, scope, mechanisms (e.g. gas chambers) or intentionality of the genocide of the Jewish people at the hands of National Socialist Germany and its supporters and accomplices during World War II (the Holocaust).

Accusing the Jews as a people, or Israel as a state, of inventing or exaggerating the Holocaust.

Accusing Jewish citizens of being more loyal to Israel, or to the alleged priorities of Jews worldwide, than to the interests of their own nations.

Denying the Jewish people their right to self-determination, e.g., by claiming that the existence of a State of Israel is a racist endeavor.

Applying double standards by requiring of it a behavior not expected or demanded of any other democratic nation.

Using the symbols and images associated with classic antisemitism (e.g., claims of Jews killing Jesus or blood libel) to characterize Israel or Israelis.

Drawing comparisons of contemporary Israeli policy to that of the Nazis.

Holding Jews collectively responsible for actions of the state of Israel.

Holocaust denial, demonizing Israel, claiming it's a racist endeavor or the new libel of apartheid, applying double standards to Israel, labeling Israeli policy as Nazi are just some examples of the despicable practices of antisemites. They try to hide behind the euphemisms of anti-Israel/anti-Zionism, but, as the IHRA working definition of antisemitism makes clear, it's just another form of classic Jew-hatred.

In this regard, it should be noted that the contrived use of the defamatory accusation of apartheid leveled against Israel is calculated. Why not use the more common term of discrimination? But that is the nub of it; most people well understand the meaning of the word discrimination and appreciate it's not applicable to Israel. On the other hand, few can explain what the term apartheid really means. Moreover, despite not specifying how the obnoxious term apartheid applies to Israel, merely invoking the spurious label typically causes a spontaneous negative reaction, evoking the image of an evil regime, and that is precisely what is intended[408]. It's a perfect,

---

[408] See, for example, Mohammed El-Kurd Destroys His Own Credibility With 'Apartheid Israel' Confession, at Honest Reporting.com. It reports that in a virtual appearance live streamed from New York to the Adelaide Writers Week Festival in Australia, on March 5, 2023, Mohammed El-Kurd (who's said to be a correspondent for The Nation (See ADL backgrounder on him), who appears on CNN and MSNBC, admitted that, "I think what the word itself as a word — I'm not even talking about the legal definition of the word 'apartheid'; I'm not talking about the crime against humanity — but the negative word that is 'apartheid' and the negative connotation it carries in the psyche of the public. I think it's capable, and it has been, engineering and establishing a cultural shift in the way people approach and talk about Palestine. But I'm less concerned with the accuracy

albeit depraved, propaganda device which enables minions and followers mindlessly to repeat and propagate the libel. A cooperative media and other useful dupes amplify the coverage, spreading the libel to masses of people. The fact that the charge is false makes little difference to the biased and receptive audience, all too ready to vilify Israel and Jews.

Defending Israel against this spurious and evil accusation requires first defining the meaning of the legal term apartheid and then explaining how it categorically doesn't apply to Israel, as more fully discussed in Chapter XIV below. This kind of presentation requires an attentive audience, willing to listen with an open mind. However, this kind of approach is not readily adaptable to the context of social media, given its constraints. As media advisors are likely to counsel, if you have to explain, then have already lost. Therefore, the propagandists have a clear advantage because they can just coin a provocative slogan or brazenly make a false accusation, without having to justify it at all. Nevertheless, we must continue to try to spread the message of truth.

Interestingly, when challenged by those who truly know what the term means, as well as by those who actually lived in South Africa when it was governed by a real apartheid regime, they hem and haw. Eventually, they are usually forced to admit that Israel does not meet the legal criteria of being an apartheid state; but then they casually assume an attitude that it just doesn't matter because they can use the term any way they want to, even inaccurately, without any real consequences to themselves. In

---

of the word. You know, me and my friends have these arguments about like, 'it's settler colonialism,' 'it's apartheid,' 'it's police brutality,' 'it's ethnic cleansing, 'it's this, it's that.' I don't care. As long as there is a conversation happening in which the villain is portrayed clearly, I think that's good." The video is also available under the title, Mohammed El-Kurd as Vile as You'd Expect at Adelaide Festival, by David Lange, dated 3/8/2023, at IsraellyCool.com

essence, they have reinvented the term when it comes to Israel, redefining it to suit their need to have an explosive label with which to vilify Israel, even if classic definition is wholly inapplicable. It channels the Nazi propaganda technique of using the big lie because if you tell a lie big enough and keep repeating it, people will eventually come to believe it. However, that does not detract from the fact that the despicable accusation of apartheid is false[409]. The BDS movement, which is premised on this evil and specious assertion, is at its heart just another antisemitic ploy, like the one practiced by its Nazi forbearers[410].

While the WCC reportedly denies active involvement as a member of any alliance that is generally promoting BDS or as a member of the so-called BDS movement, these words appear carefully chosen to mask its actual role. As the NGO Monitor reports[411], the WCC plays a key role in mobilizing churches worldwide to support international BDS campaigns against Israel

---

[409] See, for example, 'Absurd': US rejects Amnesty accusation of Israeli apartheid against Palestinians, at the Times of Israel, dated 2/1/2022; State Department rejects Amnesty International's 'apartheid' Israel report, by Joel Gehrke, at the Washington Examiner, dated 2/1/2022; Scholz rejects use of 'apartheid to describe Israel, in DW, dated 8/16/2022; At Abbas' side German leader rejects his use of 'apartheid' in reference to Israel, in The Times of Israel, dated 8/16/2022; and Biden dismisses Democrats critical of Israel, saying they're 'wrong', by Brett Samuels, in the Hill, dated 7/13/2022
[410] See, for example, Herzog: Comparing Israel to apartheid South Africa is a 'blood libel', at JTA, dated 12/15/2022, in which Israel President Isaac Herzog is quoted as saying, "The comparison between the State of Israel and the apartheid regime is not a legitimate criticism—it is a blood libel". He goes on to say, "It is a dangerous and intensifying terrorism, since the legitimacy of the State of Israel and the justification of its existence is directly related to its ability to protect itself and hence they are trying to undermine this ability". The article also notes that Herzog described the BDS movement as a "brutal campaign" spearheaded by organizations "spreading lies and false facts and seeking to build a long-term policy that will undermine the existence of the state." He continued: "Let's make no mistake, this is not a peace-seeking campaign, it is a campaign promoting hatred and incitement."
[411] See, for example, A Manifesto of Lies, by Jacob Puder, at Front Page Magazine, dated 6/16/2010 and Key Issue: Kairos Palestine Document, at NGO-Monitor.org. Jacob Prouder is a freelance journalist and the Founder and Executive Director of the Interfaith Taskforce for America and Israel. He notes 'The Kairos Palestine Document, dated December 11, 2009, is essentially a copy of Hamas and Fatah "talking points" wrapped in religious packaging'..

and calls on churches to be more active agents, including supporting appropriate economic and other measures.

The WCC also promotes the notorious Kairos Palestine Document of 2009[412], which among other things, excuses terrorist acts as legal resistance, mischaracterizes and defames Israel by comparing it with the South African apartheid regime and denies the Jewish connection to Israel in theological terms. Its attack on Christian Zionism is illuminating. It explains that traditional Christian Zionists maintain that the Jewish possession of the Holy Land presages the end of times. Thus, the reestablishment of the State of Israel in 1948 was viewed as the next step toward the fulfillment of God's plan, as foretold in the Bible. Indeed, belief in the Jewish people's special tie to the land can be found across the Christian theological spectrum. Many Roman Catholic and Protestant theologians today grant the Jewish people a special claim to the Land of Israel, linked to their election by God for a special role in history.

However, not content to rely on scripture and authoritative Christian theologians, the authors of the Kairos Palestine Document and their promoters promulgated a new pseudo-theology to suit their insidious purposes. It is not premised on scripture and, despite protestations to the contrary, it is virulently antisemitic. In its ruminations on the matter, it does not deny that the Jewish people had a special tie to the Land of Israel; it just dismisses it as old news. It then adopts a contrived rubric asserting that the Land of Israel now has a universal mission, no longer tied to the Jewish people. Rather, it proposes that it encompasses all of mankind, not primarily the Jews. This dilution of the connection of the Jews to the Land of Israel to the point of relative insignificance is just another form of replacement theology. The object is the same, and it's hardly distinguishable from the original version. Instead of outright

---

[412] It's even featured on the WCC website (oikoumene.org) under the heading, Kairos Palestine Document.

declaring the Jewish people no longer belong in Israel, it just substitutes everyone belongs there. The net effect is the same.

Indeed, to put this in perspective, the view of those who point to the return of the Jewish people to Israel and the reestablishment of the Jewish State of Israel as evidence of G-d's enduring love for the Jewish people is rejected. Thus, the actual and unqualified repudiation of the infamous replacement theological doctrine is dismissed. Instead, a pseudo-replacement doctrine is adopted, which demands everyone, including Muslims and Christians, be placed in Israel in place of Jews, without any scriptural support. It is not a matter of prophecy or theology; it's nothing more than a subterfuge, masking a political or other more insidious attitude that is antisemitic. It seeks to deny legitimacy to the Jewish State of Israel and the right of the Jewish people to self-determination in the Land of Israel.

Lest there be any misconception about how rabidly antisemitic this perspective is, consider the WCC's mistreatment of Israel, as compared to Pakistan. Both emerged at about the same time; the Islamic Republic of Pakistan, on August 14, 1947, in the partition of India, by the UK, within the British Commonwealth, and the Jewish State of Israel on November 29, 1947, in the Partition Resolution 181, at the UN. Pakistan had and continues to have a Muslim majority, and Israel a Jewish one. Pakistan actually oppresses its Christian minority of approximately 15 million people[413], and Israel doesn't.

Israel is a modern, pluralistic society and a genuine democracy, affording equal rights and protections to all of its citizens. It does not discriminate based on sex, race, religion, national origin, or sexual preference. Thus, men and women, whether Jewish, Muslim, Christian or professing other religions or none, have succeeded in Israel in a way that is unimaginable in Pakistan,

---

[413] See, for example, WCC report of pastoral team visit to Pakistan is unbalanced and substandard, in Pakistan Christian Post, dated December 10, 2002.

rising to high positions in government, commerce, and a variety of educational and other institutions.

Pakistan, on the other hand, is an autocratic state that does discriminate against women and minorities. It is reported[414] that many of its pre-state Hindu and Sikh populations either left, were forcibly converted to Islam, or massacred. It is estimated that by 1948, more than 15 million were uprooted. Indeed, the Hindu population reportedly[415] went from 15% of the population within the borders of present-day Pakistan (i.e., after the breakaway of formerly East Pakistan, which became Bangladesh) to less than 1.6 % by 1998. Yet, despite it all, there is no agency like UNRWA devoted only to refugees from Pakistan, calls for a right of return or BDS movement directed at Pakistan, nor does the WCC dispute the legitimacy of Pakistan.

This is just one patent and glaring example of the double standard applied by the WCC and others to Israel. Even more appalling is the brazen spreading of falsehoods by NGOs with misleading names and insidious missions, like Amnesty International, as well as countries with guileful and pernicious agendas. They and their state or other sponsors are often focused on misdirecting attention from their own nefarious misdeeds. They also enlist useful dupes in their duplicitous cause, often with the allure of compensation or the promise of some connection to them or the glitterati they also attract by similar means to magnify the effect of their false narrative.

Israel's not an apartheid state, nor is it committing genocide or ethnic cleansing. This abhorrent contrived libel is absurd, as more fully discussed below. Indeed, coincidently, a few weeks after the notorious and apocryphal screed by Amnesty International was unveiled, the Democracy Index was published

---

[414] See, for example, The Great Divide, by William Dalrymple, in The New Yorker, dated June 22, 2015.
[415] See, for example, The Vanishing Hindus of Pakistan-a Demographic Study, by Anand Ranganathan, at newslaundry.com, dated January 9, 2015.

by the prestigious Economic Intelligence Unit of the Economist[416]. It is a stunning rebuttal to Amnesty's claims. Israel is ranked 23rd in the world and rated 7.97, above the United States at 7.85 in this global index of democratic values and just behind France at 7.99. To put this in perspective, China is rated 2.21 (148th in the world), and Iran is below that at 1.95.

Propagandists misuse words to obfuscate and dissemble, and the above is just one example of this type of abuse. The selective focus on Israel, applying a double standard, and false accusations leveled at the one and only Jewish State is one of the modern forms of antisemitism that are correctly covered by the IHRA definition. Don't be misled; this is just another form of Jew hatred and every bit as harmful as the more prosaic variety of antisemitic tropes, caricatures and vulgar epitaphs hurled at passing Jews in the streets.

It is gratifying to note that the Roman Catholic Church, which is not a member of the WCC, did formally change its position on Jews and Israel, as discussed above. The Vatican eventually entered into a treaty with Israel, which recognized Israel.

It is even more heartening to recognize the movements within Christianity which espouse Zionism as a part of their credo.

Dr. John Hagee, an American Evangelical pastor and founder of Christians United for Israel (CUFI), summed it all up in an interview he gave in March of 2006[417] upon announcing plans to form CUFI. He noted:

> a growing majority of evangelical leaders do not preach "replacement theology, which teaches that the Church has replaced Israel" and the Jews "have no future in the plan of God." The vast majority of evangelicals, rather,

---

[416] See, Israel ranks above Spain, Italy and US for democracy in new global index, by David Rose, in the Jewish Chronicle, dated February 17, 2022.
[417] Evangelicals seeing the error of 'replacement theology', by David Horovitz, in the Jerusalem Post, dated March 20, 2006.

teach that "the Christians have a Bible mandate to be supportive of Israel and the Jewish people without a hidden agenda".

He went on to explain how twenty-five years earlier, he had formulated his conception of Christian support of Israel, as follows:

We began to actively support Israel 25 years ago when the American media responded hatefully toward Israel when the IDF blew up the nuclear reactor in Iraq. The media in America was extremely fierce against Israel, and I felt that Israel had done the world a great favor. I proposed to my congregation and the pastors of San Antonio that we gather all the Christians of our city and go down town to the city auditorium and have a "Night to Honor Israel" to show support for the nation of Israel and the Jewish people. I had a meeting with [members of] the local Jewish Federation, who were very concerned about hidden agendas. It took four lengthy committee meetings to convince them there was no hidden agenda or ulterior purpose. On the night of the event the auditorium was packed. We had our choir, our orchestra, and our television cameras so that we could show the event across the nation. It was a wonderful celebration of unity between Christians and Jews. Just at the end of the celebration there was a threat on the building, to blow it up. While [San Antonio] Rabbi [Aryeh] Sheinberg was praying, the security came to me and said "this building is supposed to blow up in about five minutes." I went to the microphone when the rabbi finished and said, "I hate to end such a wonderful night on a negative note, but we have a threat on this building." And the Christians left that building instantly, because they had never experienced such a threat. The Jewish people flipped their hands and just kept on talking. On the way home, I told my wife that "if the anti-Semites think they can silence us with a threat, they are mistaken. I'm going to do this until they get used to it.

So 25 years later, we're continuing to do 'A Night to Honor Israel', only now we're doing it over live national television so the world can experience it as it goes across America and into 126 countries.

The "Night to Honor Israel" is a non-conversionary event. As Pastor Hagee noted:

We do not target Jewish people for conversion. If a Jewish person comes to me and asks me about my faith, I am under a Bible mandate to tell him about my faith. If he accepts or rejects my faith, it does not enhance nor depreciate that person in my view. From that point we agree to go forward in mutual esteem working on behalf of Israel. All Christians are under a Bible mandate to be supportive of Israel and to be supportive of the Jewish people.

As Pastor Hagee well notes, his position is firmly supported by scripture expressly on point. It's a stunning rebuttal to those still insidiously asserting replacement theology, in whatever disguised form or repackaging to suit the sensibilities of the modern antisemite. His view of the end of the times is also refreshingly honest and balanced, unlike the fanatical meanderings of those less well-schooled in scripture. Pastor Hagee explains:

This is the biblical teaching of St. Paul. St. Paul in Romans 9, 10 and 11 presents what I call in my latest book, *Jerusalem Countdown*, "God's position-paper on the Jewish people." In Romans 9, Paul states that this three-chapter section is exclusively about the Jewish people. He continues that theme in the 10th chapter, and in Chapter 11 writes in the first verse that "God has not cast away Israel." This statement by St. Paul is the absolute death knell of "replacement theology." Something that is cast away disappears forever. Israel is alive. Israel is thriving. Israel is growing. Israel and the Jewish people have not been cast away by God! Paul makes the statement that "God has not cast away Israel" twice. Romans is a post-Calvary document in which St. Paul states, in 11:5, "even so at this present time there is a remnant [a surviving group of Jewish people] according to the election of grace." That means very simply that there are Jewish people right now who have favor with God by the election of grace. What is going to happen when Jesus comes back? Every Christian believes that Jesus Christ is the messiah. The Jewish people do not believe that. In that regard we have to agree to disagree. I say to my rabbi friends: You don't believe it; I do believe it. When we're standing in Jerusalem, and the messiah is coming down the street, one of us is going to have a very major theological adjustment to make. But until that time, let's walk together in support of Israel and in defense of the Jewish people, because Israel needs our help.

He went on to describe how:

Replacement theology teaches that the Church has replaced Israel. In replacement theology, you [the Jews] have no future in the economy of God. Replacement theology falsely teaches that the Church has taken the place of the Jewish people. The Jewish people are no longer in the economy of God, according to this teaching, which places the Church as God's centerpiece. There are fewer and fewer [evangelical leaders who subscribe to replacement theology] as time goes along.

They are seeing, finally, the error of replacement theology. The vast majority of evangelicals do not believe in replacement theology. Evangelicals believe that Israel has a Bible mandate to the land, a divine covenant for the land of Israel, forever. That the Jewish people are chosen of God and are the apple of God's eye. That Christians have a Bible mandate to be supportive of Israel and the Jewish people, to demonstrate to the Jewish people what they have not experienced from Christianity for 2,000 years... the love of God.

It appears that the Christian, Muslim, and Jewish religions all have eschatological traditions about the gathering of the nations on the Day of Judgment, just prior to the ultimate redemption. They may predict a difference in the outcome, but all three agree the Jewish people are in Israel at the time when the gathering occurs[418]. In Jewish tradition, all righteous people[419], whether Jewish or non-Jewish[420], have a portion in the world to come. The definition of righteousness is very important. It is most certainly not self-righteousness or some positivistic morality that suits the tastes and preferences of an individual, like the flavor of the week. As Maimonides notes[421], the universal standard of righteousness for the nations of the world is acceptance of the seven commandments of Noah and careful observance of them.

---

[418] In this regard, it is noteworthy that the Talmudic traditions (BT Avodah Zara 2a-3b) are, frankly speaking, more tolerant and forgiving. After all the polemics and arguments made by the nations before G-d that they, not the Jewish people, are more deserving, G-d rejects their assertions and proclaims the Jewish people worthy. However, G-d then affords the nations a second chance. Here's a hint worth remembering, when the sun is piercing through the Sukkah and it becomes unbearably hot, don't under any circumstances kick it down.

[419] BT Rosh Hashanah 17a.

[420] Maimonides, Mishne Torah, Laws of Repentance 3:5, and Meiri commentary on BT Sanhedrin 57. See also BT Sanhedrin 105a and Rashi commentary thereon, as well as, Tosefta Sanhedrin, Chapter 13.

[421] Maimonides, Mishne Torah, Laws of Kings 8:11.

It appears that some ostensible adherents of Islam, especially the neo-Marxists and new breed of pseudo-Islamists, who commit terrorist acts and disrespect the sanctity of their own Mosques in furtherance of some political or ideological agenda, have gone through a process of what amounts to Quran and classic Islam denial. In effect, they scorn the explicit statements in the Quran about the right of the Jewish people to the Land of Israel[422] and brazenly deny the historical presence of the Jewish people in the Land of Israel, as noted in the Quran. Furthermore, nowhere in the Quran is there any mention of Palestine or a so-called Palestinian people[423]. However, instead of adhering to the express provisions of the Quran, the PA and Hamas instead invented a new false narrative and clothed it in religious garb.

It is astonishing to realize how many are taken in by this canard. Consider, for more than a thousand years of Muslim scholarly history and literature; no one recorded the existence of a so-called Palestinian people. It was only with the advent of the PLO in the nineteen-sixties that the myth first began to be conceived and, even then, only fitfully, until after the 1967 Six Day War, as more fully discussed below. The singular lack of any recorded history would seem to be a glaring anomaly. This is especially so given the panoply of Muslim and other sources, which in striking contrast, evidence the Jewish presence in Israel while making no mention of any Palestinian people. However, in the super-

---

[422] Quran 5:21, 17:104, 7:137, 26:59 and 10:93.

[423] See, for example, Fundamentally Freund: Palestine, Bigfoot and other fairy tales-- Sheikh Ahmad Adwan: There is no such thing as 'Palestine' in the Koran, by Michael Freund, in the Jerusalem Post, dated 2/24/2014. The article reports that in a post on his Facebook page, Sheikh Ahmad Adwan of Jordan unabashedly declared that Palestine is a fabrication, and that the Land of Israel belongs to the Jewish people, as follows: "I say to those who distort the Koran: from where did you bring the name Palestine, you liars, you accursed, when Allah has already named it 'the Holy Land' and bequeathed it to the Children of Israel until the Day of Judgment?" "There is no such thing as 'Palestine' in the Koran. Your demand for the Land of Israel is a falsehood and it constitutes an attack on the Koran, on the Jews and their land," Adwan declares Israel was given as an inheritance to the Jewish people and not to anyone else and cites Quran 5:21 and 26:59 (noted above) in support thereof.

heated, ideologically driven atmosphere that is often generated to prevent or undermine any legitimate debate on the issues, critical thinking is often the first casualty.

It is important to appreciate that while each of the Muslim and Christian religions believe they will triumph in the end, until then and as a presage to the final days, the Jewish people are vested with title to the Land of Israel. The Quran also references Kings David and Solomon[424] of Israel and the Temple[425]. Indeed, the reference to 'al-quds' is short for 'al-Bayt al-Muqaddas' or 'Bayt al-Maqdis', which is just an Arabized version of the Hebrew term 'Beit HaMikdash' (i.e., the Jewish Holy Temple).

The propaganda effort, by what amount to the neo-Marxist pseudo-Islamic cults of Hamas and the PA (as successor to the PLO), to appropriate Jewish identity and dissociate Jews from Israel is absurd. The ignorance of scripture and history, whether real or contrived, is appalling. How else to explain the ludicrous claim made by some[426] unqualifiedly asserting that Biblical King David was a Muslim. The fact that the Quran[427] very clearly identifies David as the King of the Jews and historically, King David preceded Muhammad and Islam by more than one thousand five hundred years is just ignored. The attempt by a Muslim political activist in the US[428] to label Jesus a Muslim is equally ludicrous. As Christian scripture explicitly notes, Jesus

---

[424] See, for example, Quran 2:246-51, 27:15-17 and 21:78.
[425] Quran 17:7 and description of construction by King Solomon in Quran 34:13. Reference is also made to King David's place of prayer (mihrab Dawud) in Quran 38:21. See, The Jewish Temples: The Temples of Jerusalem in Islam, by Martin Kramer, at Washington Institute of Near East Policy, Peacewatch, dated 9/18/2000 and reprinted at jewishvirtuallibrary.org.
[426] See, 'King David Was a Muslim,' Says Linda Sarsour Video, at YouTube, posted by United with Israel.org, in which Amin Aaser appearing with her asserts that King David was a Muslim. Also posted with the same title, dated 6/3/2021, on the United with Israel.org website.
[427] Quran 2:246-51.
[428] See, Linda Sarsour's 'Jesus was Palestinian' comment ignores Jewish history, by Seth J. Frantzman, in the Jerusalem Post, dated 7/8/2019.

was a descendant of King David through his mother, Mary[429], and historically he preceded Muhammad and Islam by more than five hundred years.

These politically driven theological machinations and intrigue are strikingly rebutted by the existence & extraordinary achievements of Israel. Is it any wonder that absent cogent evidence of any kind to support their specious claim to having a superior right to title to Israel, Hamas, the PA and their cohorts resort to ridiculous assertions denying Jewish history and the undeniable connection of the Jewish people to Israel including Jerusalem, the Jewish identity of historical figures, archeological evidence, the existence of the Temple on the Temple Mount, the Holocaust and even that Jews are Jews.

Jews are considered 'Ahl al-Kitab' in the Quran, meaning 'People of the Book' and the choice to remain on their own path of submission to divine will was respected under the Quran[430]. Under the Sharia, Judaism was accorded a legally protected status, even if it is a second-class one, known as 'dhimmi. The term is derived from the phrase 'Ahl ad- Dimmah', meaning the 'People of the Covenant'.

Notwithstanding these designations, which implicitly recognize the continued existence of these monotheistic religions, side by side with Islam, there were some Muslim theorists who also espoused a form of supersessionism or replacement theology. It is respectfully submitted that supersessionism within Islam is, in essence, a political doctrine, not a theological one.

Indeed, given that the Quran makes a number of statements that contradict the very tenets of replacement theology, as noted above, it is submitted that denying the Jewish connection to Israel and the Temple Mount in Jerusalem is tantamount to a perversion of classic Islam. This especially so in the case of the

---

[429] Mathew I.
[430] Quran 3:113-114 and 60:8.

more recent breed of Marxist-trained jihadists, who seek to prey on Jews and other believers in G-d, ostensibly in the name of Islam. However, in reality, they are just disguising their belief in Marxist principles that deny G-d by the artifice and misdirection of disdaining other believers in G-d, including Muslims, who do not share their fanatical ideological beliefs. Marxism disdains religion, marriage, family, and the private ownership of property, as well as considering children, in effect, the property of the state, all of which are contrary to the tenets of the Quran and classic Islam. As an aside, this may help explain their profoundly wicked use of children (including mere infants) as human shields, as well as child soldiers, terrorists, and suicide/homicide bombers. The feigned attachment of pseudo-Muslim jihadists, like members of Hamas and the PLO (including their various factions, affiliates, and front organizations) to Jerusalem (including the Temple Mount, which they rarely, if ever, visit, let alone for prayers) and dedication to barring Jews from it is antithetical to classic Islamic traditions.

Many Muslims living in Jerusalem today do feel an attachment to the Al-Aqsa Mosque and this discussion is not intended to detract from those genuine feelings. Indeed, Israel is not denying the right of Muslims to pray there or seeking to take over the Al-Aqsa Mosque. In striking contrast, though, the PA and Hamas are seeking to redivide Jerusalem and take it away from Israel, including the entire Old City of Jerusalem (containing the Western Wall and Temple Mount), to prevent Jews from living and praying there. Their purported claim is not only baseless, it denies the immeasurably greater historic importance of Jerusalem to the Jewish people. It also denies the reality that Israel legally, factually and historically has an overwhelming right to retain sovereignty over Jerusalem.

To put this in perspective, Jerusalem is not mentioned by name anywhere in the Quran. It was the Muslim Caliph Omar who first conquered Jerusalem from its then-Byzantine overlords and occupied it in the 7th century. He was reportedly guided to the area of the Temple Mount by Jews[431] within his cortege and army when he asked to see the site[432]. The area was used by the Byzantines as a garbage dump, and it was covered in refuse. This would seem to be an outward manifestation of their supersessionist creed; in effect, to bury the old religion of Judaism from which Christianity was spawned and instead tout only the new one, centered in Constantinople.

Omar was at war with the Byzantines and sought to conquer the Byzantine Empire. Undermining the religious philosophy that supported the Byzantines' hold on the population was a well-calculated strategy. Today, we might refer to this effort as winning the hearts and minds of the people.

Consider then the opportunity Omar saw in uncovering the site of the Jewish Temple and publicly displaying its provenance as a rebuke to the arrogance of Byzantine replacement theology. Under the Byzantines, Jews had been banned from living in Jerusalem. Omar, though, permitted the Jews to live and thrive in Jerusalem, as noted below. If this did not pose enough of a theological conundrum for the Byzantines, Omar also provided for the site of the Jewish Holy Temple to become a visible monument to the absurdity that they had been totally replaced as G-d's Chosen People by the Byzantine overlords, as more fully discussed below. This masterstroke put into stark focus the question of by what divine right did the Byzantines govern the

---

[431] Including reportedly one who ostensibly had converted to Islam, by the name of Ka'ab al-Ahbar. Interestingly, when he arrived at the site of the Temple, he removed his shoes as is required by Jewish law (Mishna Brachot 9:5; BT Brachot 54a and 62b and Yevamot 6b; and JT Brachot 9:5 and Pesachim 7:12; as well as, Sefer HaMitzvot, Positive Commandments 21). It is said that when Omar saw him do so, he remarked that Ka'ab was still following Judaism, as more fully discussed below.
[432] The History of al-Tabari, Volume XII, The Battle of al Qadisiyyah and the Conquest of Syria and Palestine. See also Diagnosis Historical Amnesia-Is the Dome of the Rock a Mosque? By Dr. Judith Mendelsohn Rood, in Sacred History Magazine, January/February 2006, beginning at page 40 and A History of Palestine 634-1099, by Moshe Gil (Cambridge University Press-1992).

people in the Middle East, including Muslims, Jews, Christians (who did not share their creed), and those worshipping other religions?

It was Omar's successor Umayyad Caliph Abd al-Malik, and his son who built the Al-Aqsa Mosque. It was completed at the beginning of the 8th century and was located on the southern portion of the platform Herod constructed as an extension of the original Temple Mount plateau (outside of the precincts where the Holy Temple originally stood)[433]. It is believed to have been constructed on what was previously the site of a Byzantine Church[434]. This is consistent with the Islamic practice of demonstrating dominance by building over or converting what had previously been a church or other house of worship into a mosque in conquered lands.

Consider too the profound nature of the struggle between the Byzantine Empire, which under Constantine had converted to Christianity, and the Arab nations, under the banner of Islam, vying for dominance in the area. The explosive situation was intensified because there was no concept of separation of church and state. The mixture of religion and state made for an intoxicating and noxious brew, where the spiritual was used to buttress the temporal. In essence, conquest was justified in the name of spreading religion. Moreover, Byzantine Christian dogma not only outright rejected Islam, as well as Judaism; it did not even offer a modicum of respect for other monotheistic faiths. Indeed, as noted above, one of the fundamental aspects of Byzantine Christian theology is that they were the new Chosen People, having supplanted the Jewish people; and were,

---

[433] The Temple Mount in the Herodian Period (37 BC–70 A.D.), by Leen Ritmeyer, in Biblical History Daily of the Biblical Archeology Society, dated February 01, 2022. See also Mishna, Tractate Midot.
[434] See, for example, Was the Aksa Mosque built over the remains of a Byzantine Church? by Etgar Lefkovits, in the Jerusalem Post, dated November 16, 2008.

therefore, superior to and immune from the charms of the new religion of Islam, spawned from Judaism.

The reaction to this state of affairs might help explain the mystery of why Omar and his successors built the Dome of the Rock in the 7th century on a site within the Holy precincts of the Temple itself. Interestingly, it appears that the Byzantines did not build a church on the site of the actual Temple and instead used it as a garbage dump in what seems to be an attempt to erase its significance[435]. In a sense, this might be one of the original attempts at Temple denial. The disassociation of Jews from Jerusalem and the obliteration of any remnant of the Jewish Temple that stood there was an integral part of the replacement theology that buttressed and reinforced the political doctrine of the Byzantines. In essence, they asserted the Jews were no longer the elect of G-d and that the Byzantines were now the Chosen People.

Hence, no replacement structure was erected on the site so as not to draw attention to it and spark interest as to its historical and religious significance. Instead, the focus of Christian worship in Jerusalem was intentionally shifted away from the Temple site and its Jewish origins to the Church of the Holy Sepulchre[436]. It should also be noted that the church erected on the southern portion of the extended Temple Mount platform constructed by Herod[437] was outside the Temple precincts[438]. Similarly, the Al-Aqsa Mosque, which replaced it.

---

[435] See, for example, A History of Palestine 634-1099, by Moshe Gil (Cambridge University Press-1992), at page 69.

[436] This is consistent with the political nature of replacement theology.

[437] See, for example, The Temple Mount in the Herodian Period, by Leen Ritmeyer, in Bible History Daily, of the Biblical Archeology Review, dated February 1, 2022.

[438] See, for example, Was the Aksa Mosque built over the remains of a Byzantine church? by Etgar Lefkovits, in the Jerusalem Post, dated November 16, 2008; and (Not) Finding Byzantine Churches on the Temple Mount: A Short History, by Dr. Michael D. Press, at Textual Cultures.blogspot.com, dated June 12, 2017.

It's almost as if there was an implicit and perhaps secret recognition that no other religion belonged worshipping in the sacred precincts of the holiest of holies of Judaism. Could it be that there was awe and even fear of what amounts to bad ju ju if the site were desecrated with a foreign form of worship? There were early reports of attempts to build non-Jewish religious structures on the site, which collapsed[439]. While non-Jews could make offerings in the First and Second Temples, this was only through the priestly agency of Kohanim, who conducted the actual sacrificial service. The fate of Titus speaks volumes about why the Temple's sanctity should be respected[440].

Not desecrating the primary holy site of the Jewish religion might help explain why the Dome of the Rock was not constructed as a mosque. The question, though, is what was its purpose and function and why this particular location?

In this regard, it is important to recognize, as noted above, that Omar did not have a political or theological reason for demeaning the Jews. Indeed, as discussed above, they were political allies in the fight against Byzantine domination. Jewish prophets like Moses, as well as Kings David and Solomon, were viewed as seminal figures in the Quran and venerated by Islam. The Quran speaks of Solomon and the Jewish Holy Temple he built with supernatural help[441]. It would be sacrilegious to desecrate the site and devote it to another lesser purpose. Better to venerate it and build a shrine[442] to memorialize its existence. This is especially so, given the Byzantines' efforts to cover it up ignominiously.

---

[439] See, for example, A History of Palestine 634-1099, by Moshe Gil (Cambridge University Press-1992), footnote 76 on page 74, as well as, page 72.
[440] BT Gittin 56b.
[441] Quran 21:78-79, 27:15-16, 34:12-13, and 38:34-35, among others.. See also Quran 17:7, referencing both the First Temple (built by Solomon) and the Second Temple and its destruction.
[442] It is a shrine, not a mosque. See, for example, Shape of the Holy, by Moshe Sharon, Studia Orientalia Electronica 107 (2009) at pages 283-310 and at academia.edu.

Under Byzantine rule, Jews had also been barred from living in Jerusalem[443]. There was a short respite when the Persians succeeded temporarily in conquering Jerusalem with the aid of Jews. However, that was short-lived and the Byzantines came back and treated the Jews even more poorly than before.

Omar, on the other hand, had reason to treat the Jews fairly and even reward them for their support. In his peace agreement with Sophronius, Bishop of Jerusalem, he insisted the Jews be allowed once again to live in Jerusalem, and provision was made for seventy families to live there. He also allowed the Jews to clean up the Temple Mount[444], and it is reported he even erected a structure of some sort there for their use. It's said that the building was a Synagogue[445]. However, it is submitted that while the Jews were cleaning up the site and had genuine reason to be there, it was appropriate to pray there as well. Nevertheless, once the work was done, it is likely the Jews no longer used the prayer house on the actual site of the Temple. They did, however, construct a synagogue on the southern portion of the platform near the Al-Asqa Mosque (i.e., outside the Temple precincts), which was in use for many years until its continued use was prohibited. Jews were also reportedly employed to light the

---

[443] Although, it is reported they continued to visit the site on occasions such as Tisha B'Av (9th of Av) to mourn the destruction of the Temple. See, A History of Palestine 634-1099, by Moshe Gil (Cambridge University Press-1992), at page 69 (and footnote 71 thereon), as well as, pages 71-72 (and footnote 75 thereon).

[444] See, A History of Palestine 634-1099, by Moshe Gil (Cambridge University Press-1992), at pages 71-72.

[445] A Synagogue on Har Habayit in the 7th Century: Dream or Historical Fact, by F.M. Loewenberg, in Hakirah (2016), at page 261; A House of Prayer and Study for Jews on the Temple Mount in the Period of the Arabs, by B.Z. (Ben Zion) Dinur (Dinaburg), in Zion, a Jewish Historical Quarterly (1929); and In Ishmael's House, by Martin Gilbert (McCleland & Stewart-2011), at page 30. See also, Jerusalem Pilgrims before the Crusades, by John Wilkinson (Aris & Philips-1977), at page 153, which cites an account by Bernhard the Monk, who referred to the site of Solomon's Temple on the Temple Mount and that a synagogue was located there, when he visited Jerusalem around the year 870.

lamps[446] and anoint the Foundation Stone with perfumed water[447] and rewarded for their service with exemption from poll taxes.

It is important to note that Omar intentionally did not place a mosque on the site of the Jewish Temple and chose instead to locate the Al-Aqsa Mosque outside of the Temple precincts, on the southern extension of the platform Herod constructed on the Temple Mount. Ninth-century Muslim historian Al-Tabari provides an intimate and detailed account of this and what occurred when Omar came to Jerusalem to accept the surrender of the City[448].

Al-Tabari describes how when Omar came from al-Jabiya to Aelia[449] (Jerusalem), he asked for Ka'ab[450] to be brought to him. Ka'ab was a 7th century Yemenite Jew who had converted to Islam. Ka'ab, together with a number of Jews, were a part of Omar's retinue, and they acted as his guides to show him the place where the Second Temple had been located. Omar then asked Ka'ab where he thought Omar should establish a place of prayer. Ka'ab answered by the Rock, known as the Even Shetiyah (the Foundation Stone[451]). Omar remarked Ka'ab was still following Judaism and that he noticed Ka'ab had removed his

---

[446] See, Palestine Under the Moslems, by Guy Le Strange (1890), at pages 142-143 and Jerusalem, by F.E. Peters (Princeton University Press-1985), at page 149 and Shape of the Holy, by Moshe Sharon, Studia Orientalia Electronica 107 (2009) and at academia.edu, at page 296.

[447] See, The Crescent on the Temple, by Pamela Berger (Brill-2013), at pages 47-50 and Shape of the Holy, by Moshe Sharon, Studia Orientalia Electronica 107 (2009) and at academia.edu.

[448] The History of al-Tabari, Volume XII, The Battle of al Qadisiyyah and the Conquest of Syria and Palestine. See also Diagnosis Historical Amnesia-Is the Dome of the Rock a Mosque? By Dr. Judith Mendelsohn Rood, in Sacred History Magazine, January/February 2006, beginning at page 40.

[449] Aelia Capitolina (the name Hadrian gave to Jerusalem, after he plowed under the site of the Second Temple, established Jerusalem as a Roman colony and built there a temple dedicated to himself and the worship of Jupiter).

[450] Ka'ab al-Ahbar

[451] Mishna Yoma 5:2 (also appearing on BT Yoma 53b and see Maharsha commentary thereon), BT Sanhedrin 26b and Yoma 54b, as well as, JT Yoma 5:3.

shoes when they entered the area of the Temple Mount. Omar said he would not establish a Mosque by the Rock; but rather would do so outside of this area, facing[452] towards Mecca and the Ka'aba[453].

Muthir al-Ghiram, the fourteenth-century Arab historian of Islamic traditions, also recorded[454] that when Omar visited Jerusalem, he was accompanied by Ka'ab. He reports Omar asked Ka'ab whether he knew the position of the Rock and Ka'ab answered in the affirmative. He then provided a set of measurements, presumably based on the Mishna[455], for the purpose of locating the site. It was not visible because, as noted above, this area of the Temple Mount was used as a garbage dump and dung heap by the Byzantines. They dug where Ka'ab indicated and the Foundation Stone was laid bare. Then, Omar asked Ka'ab where he advised the Mosque Omar intended to build should be placed. Ka'ab answered that should lay out a place for the Mosque behind the Foundation Stone, whereby worshipers would be orientated to satisfy praying both in the direction (quibla) of Moses (i.e., the Jewish religion) towards the Holy of Holies, said to be located on the Foundation Stone, and that of Muhammad towards Mecca. Omar rejected this proposal and even quipped about Ka'ab still having Jewish leanings. He instead determined to locate the Mosque on the Southern extension of the Temple Mount platform constructed by Herod, outside the Temple precincts, in the direction of Mecca only and with its back towards the Foundation Stone.

---

[452] The Quibla (direction of prayer) would therefore not be towards the Holy of Holies of the Beit HaMikdash (Holy Temple of the Jews); but rather towards Mecca, and, thus, those praying would in effect have their backs towards the Jewish site.

[453] See also, The History of Jerusalem, by Moshe Gil (NYU Press-1996), at page 66.

[454] See also, Palestine Under the Moslems, by Guy Le Strange (1890), at pages 142-143 and Jerusalem, by F.E. Peters (Princeton University Press-1985), at pages 189, 191 and 196.

[455] Mishna, Tractate Midot. See also BT Yoma 52a, 16b, 19a and 21b,

The parallel accounts are strikingly similar, although each presents some interesting details not contained in the other. However, both resoundingly report Omar's intent and decision not to locate a Mosque on the Foundation Stone. Accordingly, Omar ordered that a Mosque be built on the southern extension of the platform of the Temple Mount that Herod had constructed. The result was those praying in the Mosque towards Mecca would have their backs to the Foundation Stone and the place where the Jewish Holy Temple had been located.

These accounts emphasize Omar's intention to separate the Muslim prayer site and rituals from those holy to the Jews. Thus, Mohammed had fixed the Quibla (direction of prayer) towards Mecca and the Ka'aba, as recorded in the Quran[456], and definitively ended the prior custom of praying in the Jewish prayer direction towards Jerusalem and, by extension, the Foundation Stone. This practice is reflected in accounts of Muslim scholars like Abd al-Rahman from the eighth century and Ibn Taymiyya and Ibn Qayyim al-Jawziyya from the thirteenth-fourteenth centuries[457]. It is important to appreciate that these scholars refuted any holiness attributable to these sites as a matter of Islamic tradition. Indeed, as reported by Professor Moshe Gil[458], Ibn Taymiyya wrote all the alleged traditions dealing with the footsteps of Mohammad (i.e., on the Foundation Stone) are merely deceptions. Professor Gil goes on to report that al-Jawziyya also denied absolutely the holiness in Islamic tradition of the Sakhrah (Foundation Stone) and he asserts all traditions to the contrary are lies and inventions. The Foundation Stone is merely the Quibla (direction of prayer) of the Jews and it is holy to them like Shabbat (i.e., as opposed to Friday for the Muslims). In essence, as noted above, efforts were made to distinguish these sites that were holy to Jews from those

---

[456] Quran 2:143-144.
[457] See, A History of Palestine 634-1099, by Moshe Gil (Cambridge University Press-1992), at pages 102-103,
[458] Ibid, at page 103.

holy to Muslims. Hence, it can well be understood, as the accounts noted above demonstrate, why Omar and his successors did not build a mosque on the actual site of the Jewish Holy Temple. Instead, the Al-Aqsa Mosque, located outside the holy precincts of the Jewish Temple, was set aside for Muslim devotions.

Gil posits that "Among the learned Muslims in the Middle Ages, there was a cognizance of the fact that the extensive publicizing of the tradition about the sanctity of Jerusalem could be ascribed to the war with the Crusaders when the whole Muslim world was trying to awaken the sympathies of people towards Jerusalem." It appears little has changed since the propagandists of old tried artificially to gin up the people's emotions to covet Jerusalem. Islamic theology did not really consider it holy to Muslims; that status was reserved for Jews. Yet, despite the fact that there was no actual, rational or religious connection of Islam to Jerusalem, it belonged to someone else and, therefore, it had to be taken; never-mind, the injunction of the Tenth Commandment enjoining such misconduct.

It was Omar's successor Abd al-Malik and his son who actually constructed the basic configurations of both the Al-Aqsa Mosque and Dome of the Rock. Over time they were both reconstructed, due primarily to earthquakes and other damage[459], into the versions that exist today, in the locations selected by Omar.

It is interesting to note that Arcluf I, a seventh-century Frankish Bishop, records visiting Jerusalem and the Temple Mount in 680. His account verifies the location of an oblong house of worship (forerunner of the Al-Aqsa Mosque) as being at the southern end of Herod's platform[460]. He notes it was pieced together with

---

[459] See, for example, Secrets under the Al-Aqsa Mosque, by Lenny Ben David, at Israel National News, dated 7/5/2016.
[460] See, Jerusalem: The Holy City in the Eyes of Chroniclers, Visitors, Pilgrims and Prophets from the Days of Abraham to the Beginnings of Modern Times, by F.E. Peters (Princeton University Press-1995), at pages 195-196 (citing Arculf I, 1).

upright planks and large beams over some ruined remains and can hold three thousand people[461]. This is consistent with the report of the Byzantine Basilica of the Blessed Mary, which had occupied this location and accommodated at least three thousand hospital beds, as described below.

It is submitted that Omar and his successors had a cogent rationale for building a monument known as the Dome of the Rock, venerating the sacred nature of the site[462], as the location of the Jewish Temple that stood there and above the rock[463], known as the Foundation Stone[464], on the site. It figuratively was a striking rebuke to Byzantine theology, inasmuch as it demonstrated in tangible fashion the veneration of the site and the Jewish connection to it, as well as the continuing existence of the Jewish people. Indeed, as noted above, Omar delegated the responsibility for cleaning up the site specifically to Jews. His successors continued this practice by entrusting to Jews the continuing upkeep of the site. It thus challenged Byzantine claims to theological supremacy as the chosen ones in replacement of the Jewish people.

---

[461] This description accords with another account recorded by Bede (673-735), in his The Book Of Holy Places, Chapter III.

[462] See Midrash Nistarot of Rabbi Shimon bar Yochai, reportedly an 8th century work, which appears to describe Omar, the second Caliph. It records that he was a friend of the Jews and caused the Temple Mount to be cleaned up and set in good order. It also reports that he built a structure over the Foundation Stone (Even Shetiyah) that venerated the site, as more fully discussed below. More incredible is the Midrashic work known as Pirke D'Rabbi Eliezer (Chapters of Rabbi Eliezer ben Hyrcanus, a 1rst to 2nd century Tanna during the period of the Mishna), which presciently states that the Children of Ishmael will build a building in the place where the Heichal (Holy Sanctuary of the Beit HaMikdash) of the Jewish Second Temple stood. Interestingly, it also notes, much like the Talmud (Bt Sota 49b and Sanhedrin 97a) that in the period prior to the coming of the Messiah, falsehoods will multiply and truth will be hidden. The propaganda efforts of Temple denial seem to be an example of this notorious affectation of the PA and Hamas.

[463] See, Responsa of 15-16th century Rabbi David ben Solomon Ibn Abi Zimra, in his Teshuvat HaRadbaz (Volume 2, No. 691), where he notes the Even Shetiyah is under the Dome.

[464] Known, in Hebrew, as the 'Even Shetiyah'.

The decorative mosaic, consisting of well-chosen stylized verses of the Quran and other sayings, add to the force of this message. The content of the artistic stylized writing presentation on the Dome of the Rock reads like a polemic. Among other things, it quotes the Quran as to G-d being one and not the trinity and Jesus not being divine but mortal, albeit a prophet. The placement of the Dome structure above the Rock (Foundation Stone) that was so long hidden by the Byzantines and covered in refuse is a powerful statement that the Byzantines were wrong and, as demonstrated by the very visible monument of the Dome, can and were actually beaten.

Omar had already demonstrated that the Byzantines were not invincible by beating their greater force with his lesser numbers at the battle of Yarmouk in 636, which resulted in his capture of Syria and the Holy Land of Israel. The re-emergence of the Jewish people as a part of his forces and the success in battle of the counterforce of Islam to Byzantine theology was a potent psychological weapon. It could be wielded to win the hearts and minds of the people in the Byzantine Empire and undermine the religious hold Byzantine had on them. After all, the Byzantine Empire was comprised of numerous Christian sects, which did not necessarily believe in all or parts of the Byzantine creed. Many of these sects, like the Arians, named after Bishop Arius, who rejected the concept of the trinity, as adopted at the Council of Nicaea, were denounced and branded heretics. In this regard, consider some of the verses of the Quran[465] chosen by Abd al-Malik and his son, which decorate the Dome, include polemical challenges to Nicaean theological principles espoused by the Byzantines, as noted above. These are tangible displays of the Islamic rivalry with the Byzantines[466]. The Dome, built on a platform so that it was visible and towered over the Old City of

---

[465] Quran 4:171 and 19:34-37
[466] The Historical Background of the Erection of the Dome of the Rock, by S.D. Goitein, in the Journal of American Oriental Studies, Vol. 70, Vol. 2 (April-June 1950), at pages 104-108.

Jerusalem, in effect, acted as a billboard, projecting these messages to the Christians of Jerusalem[467].

Moreover, there were also Muslims, Jews and others who resided in the Byzantine Empire. Yet, Islam had now conquered the place where the Christian religion started and the Church of the Holy Sepulchre, which was meant to replace the Jews and their Holy Temple, was located. Instead of being replaced, Omar was building a monument on the site of the Jew's Holy Temple, announcing to the world the resurgence of the Jews and proclaiming the fallacious underpinnings of the Byzantine theology and political apparatus. The Byzantines were vulnerable and their religious claim to and hold on power was challenged by Omar and his successors.

Context is also important. The struggle between Islam and the Byzantine Empire had not ended with Islam's conquest and occupation of Israel. A key element in the esprit de corps of Byzantium was their belief that they were fighting to extend the territory of the Christian world and to defend themselves as G-d's Chosen People. In their world-view, the mantle of the Chosen People had been transferred to them[468]. This political ideology purported to link the exercise of temporal power with heavenly support so that all warfare was about defending Christianity and the Christian empire of Byzantium.

However, the population of the Byzantine Empire did not uniformly embrace this ideology. There were Muslims, Jews and other minorities, including other Christian sects living in Byzantium, who did not accept that the Byzantine Emperor was what amounts to an infallible agent of G-d or that the Byzantine Christians were the Chosen People.

---

[467] Ibid and see the excellent summary discussion, by S.D. Gotein, of the nature and purpose of the Dome of the Rock therein.
[468] See, Byzantium at War, by John Haldon, beginning at page 72.

Consider then how a canny enemy of Byzantium might seek to reinforce the dissension within the populace and undermine the cohesiveness of Byzantine fighting strength by attacking the belief system that powered it. As noted above, Byzantium asserted it was the Chosen People because they replaced the Jewish people. However, if the Jewish people continued to exist in the Land of Israel and Jerusalem was being rebuilt as prophesized, then Byzantine could not have replaced them as the Chosen People. Thus, Byzantium could not be invincible because, perforce, they would not have heavenly support as G-d's Chosen People. This simple syllogism was most compelling.

Omar revered the site of the Foundation Stone and its environs as the place of the Jewish Holy Temple. He specifically asked the Jews who had accompanied him whether they were interested in cleaning up the whole site[469] and they answered in the affirmative. Indeed, as noted above, Jews were enlisted to maintain the area for many years after and were also afforded tax exemption for their services[470].

The revelation of the site of the Holy Temple on the Temple Mount had both political and religious significance to Omar. His successors constructed a monument there, consistent with his vision for venerating the site, as discussed above, known, in English, as the Dome of the Rock. However, the term 'Rock' is too generic a reference. The actual Arabic name of Qubbat al-Sakhrah is much more precise. It refers to a dome over the 'Foundation Stone'; hence, the translation of the name would more properly read Dome of the Foundation Stone. This accords with Jewish tradition, which refers to this stone as the Even Shetiyah or, in English, the Foundation Stone.

---

[469] See, for example, The History of Jerusalem, by Moshe Gil (NYU Press-1996), at page 71-72 and Chapter 5, at page 163.
[470] Ibid and see also, Palestine under the Moslems, by Guy Le Strange (1890), at page 149, based on Muthir and others, as noted on page 148.

The Arabic term for a rock or stone is Hajar (not Al-Sakhrah), a distinction that is helpful in better understanding some later Islamic traditions, originating many years after the death of Mohammad, regarding what is known as Al-Isra (the Night Journey) and wal-Miraj (the Ascension to Heaven). Among other things, they seek to conflate the Night Journey and Ascension in order to create a contrived narrative that Mohammad went on a night journey from Mecca to the Foundation Stone in the Temple of Solomon on the Temple Mount in Jerusalem (Beit HaMikdash or Bayt Al-Maqdis), that is presently covered by the Dome of the Rock. There are significant problems with this conflated account. These include the following:

> The Quran does not make express mention of the Ascension.

> The reference to the Night Ride in the Quran (17:1) does not expressly mention the Jewish Holy Temple or Jerusalem. Indeed nowhere in the Quran is Jerusalem actually mentioned. Furthermore, in a later verse in the same section (17:7), reference is made to a place of prayer (masjid), which in the context speaks of the Jewish Temple that was destroyed. However, it is not in any way linked to the reference to Masjid Al-Aqsa, the (Farther Mosque[471]). Indeed, the usual rules of construction would dictate that the two could not be the same thing, because otherwise why use two separate terms of art to depict the same place. To the contrary, the typical interpretation is that they perforce must be two distinct places or a common term of art would have been employed to signify the identical place reference.

---

[471] It is plausible to suggest that this Mosque was the one located in Medina, to which Muhammad escaped to in order to avoid capture by his enemies in Mecca. See, The Muslim Claim to Jerusalem, by Daniel Pipes, in Middle East Quarterly, Fall 2001, at pages 49-66, as well as, online at meforum.org.

There is no mention of the Foundation Stone in the Quran or the Hadith[472] in either the discussion of the Al-Isra (Night Journey) or wal-Miraj (Ascension)[473].

Few of the Hadith that describe the Ascension conflate it with the Night Journey[474]. Rather most are separate accounts that don't link the two events.

It should, therefore, be no surprise that the Dome of the Rock, which is decorated with verses from the Quran and other anti-Byzantine polemics, makes no reference at all to the Night Journey or the Ascension. Indeed, it is only a separate domed structure, known as the Qubbat al-Miraj (Dome of the Ascension), located approximately fifty yards away[475] that makes reference thereto. If the Ascension occurred from the Foundation Stone, as some later traditions assert then why would this seminal occurrence not be mentioned on the Dome? Similarly if the

---

[472] A collection of stories of traditions, supposed sayings and accounts of the practices of Mohammad, gathered well after his death, in various versions, which lack the authority of the Quran.

[473] Many believe this is a mythical tale, metaphorical journey or dream-like experience, because but for the story, there is no record of Mohammad ever visiting Jerusalem, nor is Jerusalem mentioned in the more authoritative Quran. In Quran 17:1, known as Surah Al-Isra (Night Journey), the only destination reference is to Majid Al-Aqsa, the farther mosque, which many believe was the mosque in Medina. Historically, he traveled to Medina at night in order to escape his enemies trying to detain him in Mecca. It is the less authoritative stories collected in the Hadith (Muslim oral traditions, of words or deeds ascribed to Mohammad) which make mention of the Beit HaMikdash in Jerusalem as the destination and introduce the concept of ascending to heaven, etc. However, Jerusalem is not mentioned in the Quran and the Hadith report that an approximately 900 mile journey, which in Mohammad's time would usually take approximately a month's time to travel just one way, was miraculously accomplished both ways (from Mecca to Jerusalem and back), with a stop and meeting in heaven with assorted figures of the Old Testament and New, all during the course of one night.

[474] Based on a search of the online resource of Hadith at ahadith.co.uk, with key words to identify Hadith relating to the Night Journey and Ascension, which are summarized below.

[475] See page 12 of A Brief Guide to Al-Haram Al-Sharif, Jerusalem, published by the Supreme Moslem Council (1925), in the section under the heading, The Mosque of Al-Asqa. The Guide is more fully discussed below.

destination of the Night Ride was the Foundation Stone then why not record it on the Dome. The only logical conclusion is that these events are truly unrelated to the site of the Dome of the Rock.

It should also be noted that whether the Hadith describes a physical, spiritual, or dream-like journey to the Land of Israel and Jerusalem, the common theme is a spiritual encounter with Moses and Abraham, or in some cases Jesus in his place of birth, Bethlehem. Interestingly, he does not encounter Ishmael in Jerusalem or elsewhere in the Land of Israel. At the end of the spiritual meeting, Mohammad returns home to Mecca.

Mohammad then conquers and unites the Saudi Arabian Peninsula, including Mecca and Medina. He does not conquer Israel, nor does he urge his followers to do so. If anything, his apparent model is to visit Israel, talk to some outstanding Jews and return home. Yet, in modern times, this otherwise innocent story of a transcendental spiritual journey, uplifting educational experience and ennobling return home has been misappropriated and weaponized into an ignominious quest to steal the holy places and cultural heritage of the Jewish people and purloin their patrimony, the Land of Israel; it's stupefying. Can anyone imagine visiting a holy place around the world and actually claiming title to it because an ancestor had a transcendental experience that's somehow linked to it?

Omar had no such pretensions or illusions. Consider the significance of the decision Omar made, as summarized above. It was a tangible testament to the fact that the Jewish people, the original and actual Chosen People, were still in existence, and the site of their ancient Holy Temple had been reclaimed. This was a striking rebuttal to the Byzantine Patriarch of Jerusalem, Sophronius, who reportedly rode with Omar to the site. Sophronius is said to have remarked to Omar about the desolation of the site, which the Byzantines maintained as a desolate, undeveloped, and forlorn dumpsite to honor the words of Jesus in the verse in Matthew[476] that no stone should remain on top of each other. However, the Jewish people were still alive and well. Indeed, they had joined forces with Islam and successfully conquered and returned to the Land of Israel and Jerusalem. Moreover, a structure was built on the site that directly contradicts the Byzantine interpretation of their scripture. Whatever upheaval occurred was a temporary situation. The Jews were back and the site was being cleared in anticipation of new construction, where stones would visibly be placed on top of each other. Moreover, notwithstanding Sophornius' insistence that no Jews be allowed to settle in Jerusalem, Omar's answer was to deny this so-called nonnegotiable requirement. Sophronius nevertheless surrendered and implicitly waived this obnoxious condition.

The monument attests to the continuing vitality of the Jewish people as the Chosen People and their connection to the Divine. Why else build a monument marking the space, as opposed to a mosque?

In this regard, it is important to distinguish the Foundation Stone, covered by the Dome of the Rock, from other rocks and stones found on the Temple Mount, especially in the area of the Al-Aqsa Mosque. As summarized below, the Al-Aqsa Mosque was built on what had previously been a Byzantine complex.

A Sixth century account[477] reports that, on the site, situated on the southern extension of the Temple platform erected by Herod, outside of the actual holy precincts of the Jewish Temple, was the large Basilica of Saint Mary, which reportedly accommodated a considerable congregation of monks, as well as, hostel facilities

---

[476] Matthew 24:2.

[477] The report and description summarized below is taken from the 6th century written account, of an anonymous Christian pilgrim from the town of Piancenza, Italy, known as The Piancenza Pilgrim, sometimes referred to as the work of Antoninus the martyr, because he is referred to in the first line of the book, as having made a similar pilgrimage to the holy places.

for men and women and three thousand beds for the sick. There was also a smaller Basilica on the site, known as Saint Sophia, which encompassed a raised four-cornered stone, with a set of footprints imprinted as a niche on the top surface of the rock, upon which Jesus was said to have stood, as he was tried by the Roman Governor Pontius Pilate. The Basilica was located outside of the area known as Solomon's Porch.

The Al-Aqsa Mosque was constructed in this area formerly occupied by the Basilica on the site[478]. Besides the documentary evidence referred to above, there is also physical evidence, including the Byzantine mosaic found on the site, below the Al-Aqsa Mosque, when it was being reconstructed during the period 1938-42, after earthquakes in 1927 and 1937 that had severely damaged the Mosque[479]. Interestingly, there was also a Jewish Mikvah (ritual bath) located beneath the mosaic, which yet again attests to the Jewish origin of the site.

It is improbable that the Foundation Stone under the Dome of the Rock is the rock associated with the so-called Night Ride and Ascension, which became mythically associated with Jerusalem, approximately a century later[480]. The Quran does not expressly state that Jerusalem was the destination of the Night Ride; rather, it refers only to the far mosque as the terminus[481]. This was most likely a mosque in Medina, where Mohammad sought refuge after escaping Mecca, where he was in danger of being

---

[478] Charles Wilson, in his work, Ordnance Survey of Jerusalem (1886), records the existence of a Mirab (prayer niche) known as Kadam Aisa (Footprint of Jesus) in the Al-Aqsa Mosque.

[479] See, Treasures in the British Mandate Archives, at the Temple Mount Sifting Project, online at tmsifting.org, as well as, Was the Aksa Mosque built over the remains of a Byzantine church?, by Etgar Lefkovitz, in the Jerusalem Post, dated November 16, 2008.

[480] See, for example, Isra' and the Mi'raj - A Scientific Perspective, by Mahmood Jawaid, dated April 14, 2021, at Academia.edu, Muhammad's Alleged Night Journey in Isra 17.

[481] See, for example, The Muslim Claim to Jerusalem, by Daniel Pipes, Middle East Quarterly, Fall 2001, pp. 49-66.

apprehended by his enemies[482]. Remember, too, that there was neither an Al-Aqsa Mosque nor a Dome of the Rock in existence at the time.

The later attempt to link the Foundation Stone on the Temple Mount in Jerusalem to the Night Ride and conflate it with the Ascension might better be explained as cultural appropriation and a clever artifice of political theology. As noted above, a night ride from Mecca to the Foundation Stone in Jerusalem was physically impossible. Neither the Quran nor any contemporary accounts make explicit mention of it and it does not comport with the nature of the site at the time or the actual monuments built on the site. The fact that it continues to be wielded only as a tactical weapon by those seeking to undermine the undeniable Jewish connection to the site is indicative. It is not being used as a shield to preserve the right to pray in the Al-Aqsa Mosque because that is not a real issue. The Muslim right to pray in the Al-Aqsa Mosque is not only unchallenged, it is also protected by Israel. The whole controversy is about the site of the Jewish Holy Temple, where the Foundation Stone is located and that is the nub of it. The religious overtones are contrived; at its heart, it is merely a political matter.

Consider, if the Foundation Stone under the Dome was Mohammad's destination and from where, as the stories recorded well after his death mythically report, he went to heaven to receive prophetic inspiration, then why not actually build a mosque there? Indeed, why build the Al-Aqsa Mosque in a location where those praying would have their back to the Dome of the Rock? Why not have accepted the suggestion made by Ka'ab, noted above, to locate the Mosque on the northern side of the Dome of the Rock, within the actual Temple precincts,

---

[482] See, for example, Saudi Lawyer claims Al-Aqsa Mosque's true location 'is not in Jerusalem', at I 24 News, dated 11/15/2020 and Saudi Media exposes Palestinian Lie: Al Aqsa Mosque isn't on Temple Mount, by Adam Eliyahu Berkowitz, at Israel 365 News, dated 11/16/2020,

which would have enabled the prayer direction to accommodate both the Foundation Stone and Mecca? Why build the Mosque called Al-Aqsa on the southern portion of the Temple Mount platform, outside the Temple precincts and as remote as possible on the Temple Mount from the rock under the Dome? It is inexplicable if the Foundation Stone was the actual spot where Mohammad was said to ascend to heaven. Moreover, the niche in the Foundation Stone does not resemble footprints at all. It is too large and is actually a rectangular rock-cutting, consistent with it being a niche where the Holy Ark was located within the Holy of Holies of the Jewish Temple[483].

It is also important to consider that the actual Foundation Stone, now under the Dome of the Rock, and the surrounding area comprising the site under the Beit HaMikdash was buried under muck and garbage in Mohammad's time. It wouldn't have been proper for Mohammad even to pray there at the time under those circumstances[484]. Moreover, as noted above, it had to be dug up after identifying its location, which required Ka'ab's knowledge and precise measurements. It was just not otherwise visible according to the accounts noted above and not available to stand on. Furthermore, no mosque or other house of worship stood on this site at the time. On the other hand, there was a place of worship existing at the time, on the southern extension of the Temple Mount platform constructed by Herod that was outside the precincts of the Jewish Temple. This was the Byzantine Christian structures referred to above.

Constructing a Mosque on the site of a Christian Church is consistent with Muslim conquest practices, as was the case with the conversion of Hagia Sophia Church into a Mosque when Constantinople (now Istanbul) was conquered by the Ottomans

---

[483] The Ark of the Covenant: Where It Stood in Solomon's Temple, by Leen Ritmeyer, in Biblical Archeology Review 22:1, January/February 1996.
[484] See, for example, Quran 5:6.

in the 15th Century[485]. Coincidently, there is also a rock that was venerated, as noted above, which resembles the Hajar (rock) referred to in some Islamic traditions that reportedly had indentions consistent with footprints[486]. Perhaps, then this is the rock mythically associated with the Night-Ride and Ascension legend. While still cultural appropriation, it makes more sense to attach the story to this rock. After all, it reportedly had actual footprint markings, as noted above, and even today, it is said, at least partially[487], to be located in the Al-Aqsa Mosque. In this regard, it also answers the question of why the need for this particular detail of the rock in the story. It adds little to the thrust of the theme. None of the Jewish prophets used the Foundation Stone as a means of ascension. However, consider the irony of using a venerated rock reportedly associated with Jesus, which ultimately was instrumental in the tale of his ascension, to meet him. Could this have been a subliminal attempt to link to Christian traditions as a means of winning over adherents or at least partners in the ongoing war with the Byzantine Empire? If so, then, like the Dome of the Rock, it would appear that Omar was a chess-master at the game of political theology.

This would also further support Omar's decision to locate the Al-Aqsa there and not over the Foundation Stone within the Temple precincts. Thus, consistent with the legend in Islamic tradition, Mohammed's ascent would have been from the actual location of the Al-Aqsa Mosque.

It should also be noted that the Dome of the Rock itself is decorated with verses of the Quran, but there is no reference to

---

[485] See, for example, Hagia Sophia has been converted back into a mosque, but the veiling of its figural icons is not a Muslim tradition, by Christiane Gruber and Paroma Chatterjee, at The Conversation, dated 8/18/2020 and The Hagia Sophia Case, in the Harvard Law Review, dated 1/11/2021 (134 Harv. L. Rev. 1278).

[486] See, for example, A little chapel with a footprint, by Patricia Kasten, at The Compass, dated May 19, 2017.

[487] Ibid. The article notes an indented rock with a right footprint is located at the site of a Mosque, formerly a Chapel, on the Mount of Olives. It also notes a similar indented rock, with a left footprint, is located in the Al-Aqsa Mosque.

the Surah Al-Isra 17:1. If this were the destination of the Night Ride, wouldn't that be, first and foremost, the banner decoration of the Dome? However, it's not and the only reference to the wal Miraj (Ascension) is the name of one of the outbuildings of the Al-Aqsa Mosque complex, described below. Indeed, if the Ascension occurred on the Foundation Stone, then why not call the Dome structure the Mosque of the Ascension and not the Dome of the Rock? Wouldn't this be a grander statement for Islam? Why reserve this name for a small, otherwise nondescript structure near the Al-Aqsa Mosque? Furthermore, why not have constructed the Dome as an actual mosque? The fact is it neither looks like nor is it functionally constructed as a mosque. After all, there is no distinctive minaret for the muezzin to call the faithful to prayers. The unusual octagonal shape of the building is also not typical for a mosque, nor is the configuration consistent with or conducive to the functional requirements of the typical mosque, which requires a large central prayer hall. Instead, it is centered on and constructed around the prominently featured Foundation Stone, which is the focus of the structure. The Foundation Stone is encircled by two ambulatories (aisles between it and the exterior walls)[488] that serve as little more than a viewing passage. It is obvious that the building was not intended, nor does it really serve the function of a mosque.

The fact is that it's not a mosque[489] , and its purpose is not about Islam, per se, except to attest to its connection to Judaism, the progenitor of the monotheistic faith. In that sense, it is a rebuke to the inappropriate jeering of the Byzantines that Muslims were just infidels. The legitimacy of Islam and Christianity, for that matter, is premised on the existence of their predecessor, Judaism. Absent the Old Testament, there is no New one or

---

[488] The Dome of the Rock, by Dr. Elizabeth Macaulay, in Smarthistory, dated 8/8/2015.
[489] See, for example, Palestine Under The Moslems, by Guy le Strange (1890), at page 96.

Quran. Omar understood this, and the Byzantines denied it in their supersessionist fantasies of replacement theology.

In answer to the question, a monument to what; it is respectfully submitted it is a monument to Judaism and a testament to its ties to the First and Second Temples that occupied this sacred space. This conclusion makes eminent sense in the context of the times and ever since. This conclusion is further buttressed by Omar's enlisting of his Jewish advisors, including a Jewish convert to Islam, to guide him to the location where the Temple had stood, which was otherwise hidden by the Byzantines. The details of this visit are fascinating, as discussed above. Furthermore, Omar especially requested whether the Jews in his retinue wished to clean up the site and even exempted them from the poll tax as a reward for their services, as noted above[490]. Why would he do this unless he wanted to make a clear and convincing point about the indisputable link the Jews had to the site and as an unambiguous manifestation that they were maintaining the site so holy to them.

In terms of the Byzantines, the Dome of the Rock, towering over the skyline of Jerusalem, including the Church of the Holy Sepulchre, functioned as what might be termed in modern vernacular as a prominent billboard or flashing neon sign. It announced that the Byzantines' political theology proclaiming themselves as the Chosen People, in replacement of the Jewish people, was flawed. Witness the continuing existence of the Jewish people, the uncovering of the site of the Jewish Temple in Jerusalem, and the possibility of it being rebuilt again, as presaged by the Dome. Omar had already demonstrated, in practice, the assumed invincibility of the Byzantines was just a myth at the battle of Yarmouk. The Byzantine Empire's superior numbers were no match for Omar's army, which triumphed in

---

[490] See, for example, The History of Jerusalem: The Early Muslim Period (638-1099), by Joshua Prower and Haggai Ben-Shammai (NYU Press-1969), at page 169 and The History of Jerusalem, by Moshe Gil (NYU Press-1996), at page 72.

the battle, leading to Omar's occupation of Jerusalem. The Dome of the Rock was a tangible rebuttal to the political theology that underpinned the Byzantines' claims of invincibility as the new replacement Chosen People. Indeed, the Jewish people were allies of Omar[491] and, as noted above, were even given some responsibilities for the upkeep of the site of their ancient Temple[492], as represented by the Dome.

In line with the foregoing, it is submitted that the Dome of the Rock, on the site of the Jewish Holy Temple, is a monument to the legitimate and historical claims of the Jewish people to the site. Else, why choose this particular location over other suitable sites? To claim that Jews have no historical ties to Jerusalem, as some in recent times have falsely asserted, is absurd. Even the Waqf and notoriously antisemitic Mufti Haj Amin Husseini acknowledged the indisputable fact that it belonged to the Jewish people, as discussed below.

The reality is the opposition to the existence of Israel and undivided Jerusalem, as its capital, is not based on any genuine fervent desire to posses it or legitimate competing doctrine that assigns the primacy of Jerusalem to some other religion or group than the Jewish people. The unassailable fact is classical Judaism venerates Jerusalem and the Temple Mount; supersessionist Christian sects avoid the Temple Mount, choosing instead to venerate only the Church of the Holy Sepulchre and dismissing the Temple Mount and Judaism as, at best, an anachronism in spite of scripture to the contrary; and Islamist fanatics, in a perversion of classic Islam and scripture, trample on the site of the Holy Temple on the Temple Mount, flagrantly and falsely denying it has any connection to Judaism, at all. There is nothing

---

[491] See, for example, The History of Jerusalem, by Moshe Gil (NYU Press-1996), at page 59, as well as, page 73.

[492] Ibid, at pages 73-74.

positive about it[493]; rather, it's all about denying Jerusalem and Israel to the Jewish people.

This is so among both the Christian and Muslim sects that vehemently oppose the existence of Israel as a Jewish State and seek to demonize it with libelous contrived labels and delegitimize it through BDS and other means. None of them have any plan for what happens next. They don't actually want to live there; they just want to take it away from Jewish control.

The Temple denial calumnies by the PA[494] and Hamas are particularly loathsome. They are inconsistent with the Quran and classical Islam, as noted above. Ironically, it might fairly be said that these false, fanatically obtuse pronouncements, which deny history[495] and scripture, are byzantine in both the historical and modern colloquial sense of the term. It is impossible to deny the existence of the Temple built by Solomon and profess to believe in the Quran[496]. Hence, the subterfuge that it is located elsewhere, like Nablus, as Arafat urged when pressed on the ludicrousness of his Temple denial[497]. He later even denied that the site of the Jewish Temple was located anywhere in Israel and

---

[493] Pictures are worth a thousand words. Just view photographs of the Temple Mount in the 19th century, showing an abandoned site with the Dome of the Rock and other structures in disrepair. They do not depict what might be expected if this were indeed a highly venerated site, important to the Muslim religion, which, after all, was the official and dominant religion of the Ottoman Empire that occupied and was in firm control of Jerusalem and the Temple Mount, at the time.

[494] See, for example, Abbas' Temple Denial, by Dore Gold, in Israel Hayom, dated 3/2/2012.

[495] See, for example, Muslim historians consistently confirm Jewish ties to Jerusalem, by Nadav Shragai, at JNS, dated 5/10/2021 and Islam Itself Recognizes the Jewish History of Jerusalem, also by Nadav Shragai, in Israel Hayom and at JNS, dated 11/6/2016, as well as, the discussion below.

[496] Quran 17:7 and 34:13.

[497] See, for example, The Mounting Problem of Temple Denial, by David Barnett, in the Middle East Review of International Affairs, Vol. 15, No. 2, (June 2011); and Camp David and After: An Exchange (1. An Interview with Ehud Barak), by Benny Morris, 6/13/2002 issue, as published in the New York Review, 8/9/2001.

pontificated that the actual location of the Temple was in Yemen, another facially absurd statement[498].

The archeological, documentary and historical evidence that the Temple stood on the Temple Mount in Jerusalem is overwhelming. It includes scriptural references in the Old Testament[499], as well as the New Testament[500]. It also includes the Midrash[501], Mishna[502], Talmud[503] and historical records, including those summarized below.

Islamic documentary and historical sources also attest to the Temple being on the Temple Mount in Jerusalem. This includes the 9th or 10th century inscription[504], known as the Nuba Inscription, in a mosque south of Jerusalem, near Hebron, which references the Rock of the Bayt al- Maqdis, as well as the Al-Aqsa

---

[498] See, King Solomon's Vanishing Temple, by Yitzhak Reiter, in The American Interest, dated 3/1/2011. See also, Camp David and After: An Exchange (1. An Interview with Ehud Barak), by Benny Morris, in the New York Review of Books, dated June 13, 2002.

[499] See, for example, I Kings, Chapters 5-9; I Chronicles, Chapters 6 and 28 and II Chronicles, Chapters 3, 4, 23, 26, 27, 29, 35, and 36; II Kings, Chapters 18, 23 and 24; Ezra, Chapters 1, 3-6; Nehemiah 6; Psalms 5 and 18; Hagai, Chapters 1 and 2; and Zechariah, Chapters 1 and 8; Malachi Chapter 3 and the Book of Lamentations.

[500] See, for example, Acts, Chapters 6 and 21; Matthew, Chapters 21, 24 and 26; Mark, Chapter 13; Luke, Chapters 2, 4, 18, 21; and John, Chapter 10.

[501] There are thousands of references in the Midrash. Here are just a few examples: Mechilta D'Rabbi Yishmael 15-20, 31 and 35; Sifre Numbers 10, 35, 116, 119, 134, 160 and 161, as well as, Deuteronomy 10, 28, 29, 31, 36, 37, 43, the famous 152 (regarding the Beit HaMikdash being the highest spiritual place), 301, 309, 317, 352 and 357; Sifra Bechukotai, 32 and 52; Pesikta D'Rav Kahana 5, 8, 13, 16, 18, 21, 24, 26 and 27; Midrash Tanchuma Lech Lecha 15, Vayera 3, Shemot 2 and 29, Vaera 7, Mishpatim 3 and 9 and Teruma 9 and 11; Genesis Rabbah 22, 36, 37, 39, 42, 55, 56, 64, 69, 79 and 93; Exodus Rabbah 2:2, Eicha Rabbah, Petichta 24; Seder Olam Zuta 7; Pesikta Rabbati 2, 12, 14, 21 and 26; and Pirke D'Rabbi Eliezer 17, 30, 34 and 49.

[502] See, for example, Mishna Kelim 1:8; Sota 9:12; Sukkah 3:12 and Chapter 5; Middot 1:1; Tamid 1:1-2; Rosh Hashana 4:3; Eduyot 8:6; and Ta'anit 4:6.

[503] See, for example, BT Gittin 56b; Yoma 2a, 9a, 12a, 16b, 19a, 25a, 39b, 51b, 52a, 54a and 77b; Sotah 37b and 48b; Zevachim 116b; Brachot 3a and 30a; Eruvin 2a; Bava Batra 3a and 60b; Yevamot 6a; Sanhedrin 20b and 104b; Makkot 10a; Pesachim 5a, 26a, 86a and 92a; Tamid 25b and 30a; Sukkah 41a, 49a and 51b; Chullin 90b; Kiddushin 66a; Rosh Hashana 18b and 30a; Shabbat 21b; Arachin 10b; Zevachm 40a; and Gittin 56a-57b.

[504] See, for example, Centuries before trying to deny it, Muslims carved Jewish link to Jerusalem into mosque, by Ilan Ben Zion, in the Times of Israel, dated October 31, 2016.

Mosque, as dedicated by the Caliph Omar. The distinction between the site of the Dome of the Rock and the Al-Aqsa Mosque is cogent. The term Bayt al-Maqdis (i.e., the Beit HaMikdash in Hebrew) refers to the Jewish First Temple built by Solomon and then the Second Temple, originally constructed by Ezra and Nehemiah and then rebuilt by Herod. As noted above, the Al-Aqsa Mosque is not located on the site of the Temple; rather, it is located on the southern extension of the Temple Mount platform, outside the Temple precincts. This, as well as the fact that the site of the Foundation Stone covered by the Dome of the Rock was not used as a mosque, is recorded in a number of historical accounts, including Muhammad ibn Jariri al-Tabari, a 9th century respected historian in the Muslim religious world[505]; Abu Bakr Muhammad ibn Ahmad al Wasiti, an 11th century preacher in the Al-Aqsa Mosque[506]; as well as, a number of others noted by S.D. Gotein[507].

The documentary evidence attesting to the existence of the Jewish Temple, whether the First Temple or Second Temple, known in Hebrew as the Beit HaMikdash and in Arabic as the Bayt al-Maqdis[508], is overwhelming. The sources include Old Testament and New, as noted above, as well as the Quran[509]. Jewish documentary sources from the period include those compiled in the Mishna and Midrash, as noted above, as well as

---

[505] The History of al-Tabari, Volume 3, The Children of Israel, at pages 150-151 and 174, of the 1991 SUNY press edition, translated by William M. Brinner.
[506] See, Muslim historians consistently confirm Jewish ties to Jerusalem, by Nadav Shragai, in Israel HaYom, dated 5/10/2021 and Current: Ancient Muslim Texts Confirm the Jewish Temple in Jerusalem, by JCPA-Jerusalem Center for Public Affairs, in the Jewish Press, dated 8/17/2020.
[507] See, The Historical Background of the Erection of the Dome of the Rock, by S.D. Goitein, in the Journal of American Oriental Studies, Vol. 70, Vol. 2 (April-June 1950), at pages 106-7.
[508] The term 'masjid' may also sometimes be translated as Temple or place of worship, depending on the context, as noted below. Similarly, 'mihrab', a sanctuary or prayer niche, in the context of 'mihrab Dawid', may also refer to the site King David identified (and purchased) and on which his son, King Solomon, built the Jewish First Temple, as noted below.
[509] Quran 17:7 and 34:13.

First Century historian Josephus. There are also a variety of non-Jewish historical writings in addition to those summarized above. Some cogent examples, including those that may be critical of the Jews and yet, nevertheless acknowledge the existence of the Jewish Temple in Jerusalem, are set forth below. Others noted below corroborate Biblical accounts or confirm the existence of the dynasty founded by King David. For the most part, they are listed in chronological order:

9th Century B.C.E. Tel Dan Inscription, which references the House of David[510].

9th Century Mesha Stele, which references the House of David[511].

6th Century B.C.E., Cyrus Cylinder[512], which echoes and corroborates the Biblical account in Ezra 1:2-4.

4th century B.C.E., Menander, a Greek historian[513].

4th century, Hecataeus of Abdera, a Greek historian[514].

3rd century B.C.E., Berossus, of Babylon[515].

3rd-2nd century B.C.E, Aristeas, a Greek official in the court of Ptolemy II, in Egypt[516].

1st century B.C.E., Cicero, a Roman statesman[517].

---

[510] The Tel Dan Inscription, The First Historical Evidence of King David from the Bible, in Biblical Archeological Review, dated June 14, 2022.

[511] The Mesha Stele and King David of the Bible, by Megan Stouter, at Biblical Archeology.org, Bible History Daily, dated January 11, 2023. See also, Mesha Stele Mystery solved: King David was real, researchers say, by Adam Eliyahu Berkowitz, at Israel 365news.com, dated 1/17/2023.

[512] The Cyrus Cylinder, edited by Irving Finkel (I.B. Taurus & Co. Ltd.-2013).

[513] See, Menander of Ephesus at Livius.org.

[514] See, The Jewish Temple, A Non-Biblical Sourcebook, by Robert Hayward (Routledge-1996), Chapter 1.

[515] See, Berossus, at Livius.org.

[516] See, the Letter of Aristeas.

[517] See, for example, Marcus Tullius Cicero, For Flacus, Speech of Cicero in defense of Flacus 58 B.C.E.

1st century B.C.E., Edict of Augustus[518].

1st century, Strabo, a Greek geographer[519].

1st century Tacitus, a Roman historian[520].

1st century, Arch of Titus[521].

1st century, Plutarch, a Greek Historian[522].

2nd century, Cassius Dio, a Roman Historian[523].

3rd century Eusebius, a Greek Christian Historian and Bishop of Caesarea[524].

More than a dozen Islamic Hadiths[525].

9th century Muhammad ibn Jair Al-Tabari[526].

---

[518] See, Ancient History Sourcebook, Roman Sources on the Jews and Judaism, 1 B.C.E.-110 C.E., Edict of Augustus on Jewish Rights 1 BCE, online at fordham.edu.

[519] Ibid, Strabo, The Geography (Book XVI. II. 34-38, 40, 46, c. 22 CE) and Strabo 15 AD (Greek Geographer), at bible.ca/archeology.

[520] The Histories of Tacitus, Volume III, Book V, Chapters 8-9, at page 189 et seq. (Loeb Classical Library ed.-1931), online at uchicago.edu. (Also available online at classics.mit.edu.)

[521] See Arch of Titus, at Rome Reborn, Institute for Advanced Technology in the Humanities, archive 1.village.virginia.edu.

[522] See, for example, Plutarch: Quaestiones Convivales IV, 6: 2.

[523] Cassius Dios, Roman History, Book LXIX, Hadrian's Destruction of Jerusalem in 135 C.E. (Loeb series, Macmillan-1914-27).

[524] The Church History of Eusebius, including, Vol. 1, Chapter 6, at page 90; Vol. 2, Chapters 5 (at page 109) and 19 (at page 122); Vol. 3, Chapters 5 (at page 138) and 8 (at pages 142-143); and Vol. 10, Chapter 4, at pages 370-371.

[525] See, for example, Hadith (Hadith Library at ahadith.co.uk)- No. 147, No. 151 from Sahih Bukhari, Chapters 4 (Ablutions) and No. 40, Chapter 2 (Belief); No. 23, from Sunan An-Nasai, Chapter 1, (The Book of Purification) and No. 451, Chapter 5 (The Book of Salah); No. 12, from Sunan Abu Dawood, Chapter 1 (Purification) and No. 457 Chapter 2 (Prayer); No. 4301, from Sunan ibn Majah, Chapter 40 (Ascetism), No. 322, Chapter 2 (Purification and its Sunnah), No. 753, Chapter 6 (Mosques and the Congregations), No. 1010, Chapter 7 (Establishing the Prayer and the Sunnah Regarding Them), No. 4042, Chapter 39 (Tribulations); and No. 17, from Imam Malik's Muwatta, Chapter 5 (Jumua).

[526] In his The History of the Prophets and Kings, Part 1, Volume 1. See also, Islam, Jews and the Temple Mount, by Yitzhak Rieter and Dvir Dimant (Routledge-2020).

The 9th or 10th century Nuba inscription noted above[527].

10th century geographer and Jerusalem resident, Muhammad ibn Ahmad Shams al-Din al-Muqaddasi[528].

11th century Abu Bakr Muhammad Ahmad al-Wasiti[529].

12th century geographer Muhamad al-Idrisi[530].

12th century geographer Yaqut al Hamawi[531].

13th century theologian, Ahmad ibn Taymiyyah[532].

14th century historian, Abd al Rahman ibn Khaldun[533].

15th century historian Mujir al-Din[534].

15th century Jalal al-Din al-Suyuti[535].

Interestingly, 13th century Ahmad ibn Taymiyya, noted above[536], declared with respect to the site of Dome of the Rock as follows:

'Men of Knowledge who were companions or followers of the Prophet chose the best path and did not exalt the Rock, because it is a quibla mansukha, like the Sabbath...so too, the Rock is exalted only by Jews and some Christians.'

---

[527] See also, for example, Ancient Mosque Inscription Referring to Jewish Temple Undermines Palestinian Revisionism, by staff, at the Tower, dated 11/1/2016.
[528] See, Islam, Jews and the Temple Mount, by Yitzhak Rieter and Dvir Dimant (Routledge-2020), at page 51.
[529] In his The Praises of Jerusalem. See also, Islam, Jews and the Temple Mount, by Yitzhak Rieter and Dvir Dimant (Routledge-2020).
[530] See, Islam, Jews and the Temple Mount, by Yitzhak Rieter and Dvir Dimant (Routledge-2020), at page 52.
[531]Ibid at page 53.
[532] Ibid, at pages 53-54.
[533] In his Lessons in the Science of History, Volume 1. See also, Islam, Jews and the Temple Mount, by Yitzhak Rieter and Dvir Dimant (Routledge-2020).
[534] See Islam, Jews and the Temple Mount, by Yitzhak Rieter and Dvir Dimant (Routledge-2020) at pages 27 and 29-32.
[535] In his The History of The Temple in Jerusalem. See also, Islam, Jews and the Temple Mount, by Yitzhak Rieter and Dvir Dimant (Routledge-2020).
[536] See, Islam, Jews and the Temple Mount, by Yitzhak Rieter and Dvir Dimant (Routledge-2020), at page 54 and footnotes 153 and 154 thereon.

It is astonishing that the words of this noted Sunni scholar and important inspirational source of the Salafi and other radical Islamic movements, including, for example, Hamas, is just callously ignored in favor of the dictates of political ideology. The specious claim that the entire Temple Mount is exclusively a Muslim holy site to the exclusion of all other religions and the spurious denial that the Jewish Temple ever stood there is yet another example of the pseudo-Islamist creed of the PA and Hamas[537].

Unfortunately, there are academics who echo or actively promote the false narrative propagated by the PA and Hamas. The atmosphere in academia, when it comes to Israel, is often toxic[538]. Some are entranced by the colorful pronouncements of victimhood; others are attracted because they share the pernicious Jew hatred that animates the BDS[539] movement[540] and some are operatives of or receive some form of compensation, directly or indirectly, from organizations affiliated with or allies of the PA and Hamas. Some misguided souls are even motivated to echo the virulent denunciations so as not to stand out and possibly endure public shaming or worse. There also appears to be a chilling effect that has taken hold, even in the academic

---

[537] Even Aref al-Aref, a journalist and historian, who served as the Mayor of Jerusalem in the 1950's during the Jordanian occupation, acknowledged the existence of the Jewish First and Second Temples on the Temple Mount in Jerusalem, like the Islamic scholars of old. See, his History of Jerusalem, Ta'rikh al-Quds (and Al-Mufassal fi Ta'rikh al Quds), as described in Islam, Jews and the Temple Mount, by Yitzhak Reiter and Dvir Dimant (Rutledge-2020), at pages 107-110.

[538] See, for example, Revive light and truth; eschew night and fog, by Leonard Grunstein, in the Times of Israel blogs, dated 7/8/2021 and Why academics boycott Israel, by Martin Kramer, published online at martinkramer.org, on 7/7/2021.

[539] An acronym, meaning Boycott, Divestment and Sanctions, reminiscent of the infamous Nazi boycott of Jewish establishments, as a prelude to the Holocaust, and a derivative of the Arab boycott of Israel, which inspired the Anti-Boycott Act of 2018, Part II of the Export Control Reform Act of 2018 (50 USC Chapter 58), and the anti-boycott provisions set forth in Part 760 of the Export Administration Regulations, 15 CFR parts 730-774 (EAR).

[540] See, for example, The legal pitfalls facing Ben and Jerry's and their parent company, by Leonard Grunstein, at Israel National News, dated 4/8/2021.

establishment among professors and administrators, which stifles any serious discussion. Hence, some are silent because, unfortunately, in this world of intersectional alliances, they may fear voicing truths that are contrary to the prevailing perverted political ethic[541].

Nevertheless, there are also heroes who voice the truth. This, despite the overwhelming pressure to toe the ideological line and not speak out. One such individual was Dr. Khaleel Mohammed[542], a professor of religious studies at San Diego State University. He asserted, as noted above that the Quran unambiguously stated that the Holy Land of Israel belonged to the Jews. He cites Quran 5:21 and 2:40, as well as, Medieval Islamic scholars[543], in support of his position. Other modern Islamic scholars asserting this truth include Maulana Muhammad Khan Sherani[544], head of the Council of Islamic Ideology of Pakistan, Sheikh Dr. Muhammad Al-Hussaini[545] and Sheikh Abdul Hadi Palazzi, Secretary General of the Italian General Assembly[546].

There is also a substantial and growing body of compelling archeological evidence[547] of the presence of the Jewish Holy

---

[541] See, for example, Intersectional rhapsody, by Leonard Grunstein, in the Times of Israel blogs, dated 7/3/2019.
[542] See, The dissenting Muslim, by Judd Handler, in the San Diego Jewish Journal, dated August 2004 and What the Koran says about the land of Israel, by Simon Rocker, in the Jewish Chronicle, dated 3/19/2019.
[543] Ibn Khatir Tafsir and Al-Tabari
[544] See, Pakistan; Top Cleric Says Israel Belongs to Jews, by Shireen Qudosi, at Clarion Project, dated 12/29/2020.
[545] See, What the Koran says about the land of Israel, by Simon Rocker, in the Jewish Chronicle, dated 3/19/2019.
[546] Allah is a Zionist, by Sheikh Abdul Hadi Palazzi, in Tablet Magazine, dated 3/18/2010.
[547] As an aside, it should be noted that there is also a substantial body of evidence, which confirms the ancient Jewish presence in the Land of Israel. This includes the Egyptian Merneptah Stele, which attests to Israel being in the Land more than 3,200 years ago. There are other such sources, such as the Mesha Stele, Tel Dan Stele and Kurkh Monoliths, from the 9th century B.C.E. However, the Merneptah Stele is one the earliest indisputable extra-Biblical source. See, for example, Merneptah Stele: Proving

Temples on the Temple Mount that is undeniable, including the following:

8th Century B.C.E. Hezekiah stone tablet inscription[548].

8th Century B.C.E. Isaiah Seal[549].

8th Century B.C.E. King Hezekiah Seal[550].

Temple Warning Inscriptions (one of the two found[551]) discovered by French archeologist, Charles Simon Clermont-Ganneau, in 1871; it warns gentiles not to enter further into the Temple compound. Josephus reports that slabs were found at regular intervals along the balustrade, in Greek and Latin, warning of the law of purification and that no foreigner was permitted to enter the holy place[552].

Beit HaTekia Inscription found by archeologist Prof. Dr. Benjamin Mazar, in 1972, which, in Hebrew, said, "lebeit hatekia lehachriz', which means, to the house of blowing (of the trumpets) to announce. The Mishna[553] and Talmud[554] record the custom of sounding trumpet blasts from the Temple Mount to announce, among other things,

Israel's 3,200-Year Existence, by Warren Reinsch, at the Armstrong Institute of Biblical Archeology (Armstroninsitute.org), dated 10/26/2018. See also, Does the Merneptah Stele Contain the First Mention of Israel, by Manfred Görg, Peter van der Veen and Christoffer, in The Biblical Archeological Society, Bible History Daily, dated 6/2/2022, which describes even earlier Egyptian sources that have been discovered.

[548] Israel deciphers 8th century BC Hezekiah inscription after a decade of research, by Noa Fisher, at YNet News, dated 10/27/2022.

[549] In find of biblical proportions, seal of Prophet Isaiah said found in Jerusalem, by Amanda Borschel-Dan, dated 2/22/2018, at The Times of Israel. See also, Is This the Prophet Isaiah's Signature?, by Eilat Mazar, in the Biblical Archaeology Review 44:2, March/April May/June 2018 and On View: Seals of Isaiah and King Hezekiah Discovered, by Robin Ngo, dated 6/12/2018, at Bible History Daily.

[550] Ibid and see also, King Hezekiah in the Bible: Royal Seal of Hezekiah Comes to Light, by Robin Ngo, dated 3/12/2022, at Bible History Daily.

[551] Another fragment of a similar Temple warning inscription was found in 1936.

[552] Flavius Josephus, Jewish War 5, v, 2 and Antiquities 15, xi, 5.

[553] Mishna Sukkah 5:5.

[554] BT Shabbat 35b; Sukkah 53b-54a and 55a; Rosh Hashana 32a; and JT Brachot 1:1 and Pesachim 4:1.

the Sabbath (to alert people to stop work), Holidays and certain sacrificial and other rituals[555].

The lower course of the Eastern Wall of the Temple Mount, north and south of the Golden Gates, which are from the First Temple period (i.e.: Solomon's Temple)[556].

High Priest's (Kohen Gadol's) golden bell, found by Archeologist Eli Shukron[557], in 2011. It is dated from the Second Temple period and is believed to be one of the bells described in the Bible[558], which were sewn into the bottom hem of the High Priest's robe (Me'il).

The Herodian Stones, comprising the retaining wall of the Temple Mount, including the extensive portions below the present grade level, which can be seen in the Museum of the Western Wall, adjacent to the Western Wall. Similarly, the Herodian architecture and art, including in the entry halls of the Double Gate, under the Al-Aqsa Mosque structure, which was a part of the two sets of southern gates, known as the Hulda Gates and referenced in the Mishna[559].

A water cistern at the southeast corner of the Temple Mount platform, near Robinson's Arch, dated back to the First Temple Period[560].

Seals and pottery shards, dating back to the time of King Solomon (10th to 9th centuries B.C.E.), as well as, those from

---

[555] See also Numbers 10:10; and BT Sukkah 51a-b and Arachin 11b.

[556] See, The Quest, Revealing the Temple Mount in Jerusalem, by Leen Ritmeyer (2006) and The Eastern Wall of the Temple Mount in Jerusalem, by Leen Ritmeyer, dated 10/24/2015, at ritmeyer.com.

[557] Ancient Bell Found in Jerusalem Rings Again, by AP, dated 1/8/2015 and 2000-year old golden bell discovered in Jerusalem, by Melanie Lidman, dated 7/22/2011, in the Jerusalem Post..

[558] Exodus 28:33-34.

[559] Mishna Midot 1:3.

[560] Archeologists find 1rst Temple-era cistern in J'lem, in the Jerusalem Post, dated, 9/6/2012.

the First Temple period generally, including seals inscribed as belonging to the Immer family[561], a well known priestly family from the First and beginning of the Second Temple period[562], found by the Temple Mount Sifting Project[563].

Also found by the Temple Mount Sifting Project are silver half shekel coins from the Second Temple period, many of which seem to be burnt, presumably, from the fire that led to the destruction of the Second Temple[564].

Stone tiles, dated to the late Second Temple period, based on parallels to Herodian palaces of the period, found by the Temple Mount Sifting Project.

Wooden beams dating back to the First and Second Temple periods were found repurposed as beams and as bond timbers in the Al-Aqsa Mosque, when it was seriously damaged in earthquakes and rebuilt[565].

---

[561] Clay Seals Give Clues to Wealth of Biblical Jerusalem, by Nathan Steinmeyer, in Bible History Daily, of the Biblical Archeology Society, dated 1/10/2022 and Clay Seals from the Temple Mount and their Use in the Temple and Royal Treasuries, by Zachi Dvira and Gabriel Barkay, in the 2022 Jerusalem Journal of Archeology.

[562] I Chronicles 24:14 and 9:12; Ezra 2:37 and 10:20; and Nehemiah 7:40 and 11:13.

[563] The Sifting Project began in 1999 when the Northern Branch of the Islamic Movement conducted illegal renovations on the Temple Mount and disposed of over 9,000 tons of dirt mixed with invaluable archaeological artifacts. Though Israeli antiquities law requires a salvage excavation before construction at archaeological sites, this illegal bulldozing destroyed innumerable artifacts: veritable treasures that would have provided a rare glimpse of the region's rich history. The earth and the artifacts within were dumped as garbage in the nearby Kidron Valley. In a bold move, archaeologists Dr. Gabriel Barkay and Zachi Dvira retrieved the matter from the dump, and in 2004, they started sifting it. Their initiative became the Temple Mount Sifting Project (TMSP) with the goal of rescuing ancient artifacts and conducting research to enhance our understanding of the archeology and history of the Temple Mount. See their website at tmsifting.org/en.

[564] Flavius Josephus, The Wars of the Jews 6:1:1 (William Whiston edition). See also BT Gittin 55a, which makes reference to the destruction of the Second Temple, including the burning of the Heichal (its Sanctuary, whose innermost sanctum was the Holy of Holies).

[565] Herod's Temple Mount Revealed in Al-Aqsa Mosque Restoration, by Noah Wiener, in Biblical Archeology Review, dated 9/2/2016.

A Second Temple era Mikvah (Ritual Bath) was found under the Al-Aqsa Mosque, when it was being rebuilt after the earthquake that seriously damaged it in 1927. This is in addition to the two others previously identified on the Temple Mount[566].

Remains of a defensive wall, dating back approximately 3,000 years ago, to King Solomon's reign[567], situated on the edge of Jerusalem, between the Temple Mount and the City of David.

Pilgrimage Road, built by King Herod to ascend from the Pool of Siloam, where would ritually purify themselves on route, to the Second Temple on the Temple Mount[568].

The evidence of the existence of the Jewish First Temple and Second Temple (Beit HaMikdash in Hebrew and Beit al-Maqdis in Arabic) on the Temple Mount is overwhelming. The fact that the Qubbat al-Sakrah (more accurately translated as Dome of the Foundation Stone) is situated there is a further testament to this indisputable fact, as referenced in the Waqf's own Guide, as more fully discussed in Chapter X below. The Dome honors and venerates the site, which is holy to the Jewish people. To deny this is to deny history.

Israel is a democratic and diverse State where Muslims, Christians, Jews and so many others are afforded equal rights and protections, as well as access to the Holy sites. It is important to remember that Jordan had barred access to the Holy sites by Jews

---

[566] Third Jewish Mikveh and a Byzantine Mosaic floor discovered on the Temple Mount, by Leen Ritmeyer, dated 11/17/2008, at ritmeyer.com.
[567] The Discovery of King Solomon's Wall-A Personal Account, by Eilat Mazar (Jerusalem Shoham Academic Research and Publication-2011); King Solomon's Wall Found-Proof of Bible's Tale?, by Mati Milstein, in National Geographic, dated 2/27/2010; and Surviving Section of Solomon's 'Torn Down' Temple Wall Found Intact, by Peter Barker, in Newsweek, dated 7/29/2021.
[568] Israeli and American dignitaries unveil Pilgrimage Road, by Doron Spielman, in the Times of Israel, dated 6/30/2019 and Ancient Pilgrim's Road Up To The Temple Mount Uncovered, by Steve Law, at Patterns of Evidence, dated 8/16/2019.

and restricted access by Christians during the years when it controlled them[569]. It was during that period that many dozens of Synagogues were demolished, closed or otherwise plundered in the Old City of Jerusalem and the Mount of Olives Jewish Cemetery, which has existed for millennia, was despoiled.

It is also interesting to note that Jerusalem was never the capital of any nation other than the Jewish nation of antiquity and the reestablished Jewish State of Israel in modern times. Think about it; Jordan, in all the years it occupied parts of Jerusalem, never moved its capital there. The PLO Charter doesn't even make mention of Jerusalem. How can something proclaimed to be so essential go wholly unmentioned? Pictures of Jerusalem from the end of the 18th century and the beginning of the 19th century show a barren and forlorn landscape. Remember, it was the Jews who primarily developed the neighborhoods outside of the walls of the Old City that represent what most people view as modern Jerusalem, east, west, north and south. The pictures of the Temple Mount are also desolate. It just was not a destination location for most Arab dignitaries and their entourages. Even today, there are hardly any State visits by Arab notables. There appears to be a disproportionate relationship between the amount of verbiage devoted by PA spokesmen sanctimoniously proclaiming the importance of Jerusalem to the Arab world and denying its link to Jews, as compared to its actual significance to the PA and the Arab world in practice.

Yet, all this doesn't seem to matter to these disreputable parties. It's all about destroying the Jewish State and undermining its control over Jerusalem.

The sovereign State of Israel liberated all of Jerusalem and the beneficiaries include the world. Denying it to Israel does not

---

[569] Indeed, to this day, Jordan restricts Jews from praying at the Tomb of Aaron. See, for example, Time to Hold Jordan Accountable, by Farley Weiss, at JNS, dated 8/23/2020 and Jordanian police threaten to jail Israeli pilgrims for praying, by Raphael Ahren, at the Times of Israel, dated 7/24/2017.

serve the world; it only allows forces intent on doing evil to ruin it for everyone. Israel's continued stewardship of Jerusalem assures it will remain a spiritual home of all the religions that revere it. As the Bible[570] declares, those who bless Israel will be blessed. The Psalms[571] also provides that those who pray for the wellbeing of and love Jerusalem, as the Jewish people do, will enjoy repose and security.

---

[570] Number 24:9.
[571] Psalms 122:6.

VIII.

UN GENERAL ASSEMBLY RESOLUTION 181 (1947)

The United Nations (UN) was established by the United States and fifty other countries, in 1945, following the end of World War II.

It is critical to appreciate that the UN Charter explicitly provides in Article 80 as follows:

> ...nothing in this Chapter shall be construed in or of itself to alter in any manner the rights whatsoever of any states or any peoples or the terms of existing international instruments to which Members of the United Nations may respectively be parties.

Thus, the rights of the Jewish people to Israel under the San Remo Resolution discussed above took precedence over any UN resolution, including Resolution 181.

It must also be recognized that, in point of fact, United Nations General Assembly (UNGA) Resolution 181, generally known as the Partition Plan, was never implemented. By its express terms, it was merely a recommendation[572]. While it requested that the UN Security Council take measures to implement it, this never occurred.

The Partition Plan was unequivocally rejected by the Arab world, which sought by force of arms to eliminate any possibility of a Jewish state in any part of Israel (then referred to as the Mandate

---

[572] See the preamble to UNGA Resolution 181, dated November 29, 1947.

of Palestine). There was no real appetite by the permanent members of the Security Council to intervene militarily to effectuate the recommended Partition Plan in the face of Arab militant intransigence or to prevent the existing Arab nations from invading and overrunning the country. The Jews in Israel were left on their own to deal with the onslaught and invasion.

It is important to note that there is no reference in Resolution 181 to a so-called Palestinian people. The label was invented more than a decade and a half later, as more fully discussed below[573]. There was also no reference to a so-called West Bank. This was also an artificial construct by Jordan, which illegally annexed it to distinguish it from Jordan proper on the eastern side of the Jordan River, as discussed above. Resolution 181 just referred to the area as the hill country of Samaria and Judea[574]. The name given to the proposed partitioned area intended to house Arab residents of Israel was the "Arab State', not the Palestinian State.

At the time and historically, Arab residents in Israel were viewed and, indeed, viewed themselves as a part of the Arab people. As Anwar Nusseibeh[575] explained[576], Arabs, who happened to reside in the area assigned to the reestablished Jewish State of Israel, saw themselves as a part of the Arab nation, generally, and specifically as a part of Syria. There was no concept of a separate so-called Palestinian people, nor was there any distinct identity beyond being a part of pan-Arabism.

To put this in perspective, the same San Remo conference, which legally recognized the reestablishment of a Jewish State in its ancient homeland of Israel, also granted legal recognition to the

---

[573] Even UN Security Council Resolution 242 of 1967 does not refer to any Palestinian people, as more fully discussed below.
[574] UNGA Resolution 181, Part II-Boundaries.
[575] A leading Palestinian leader at the time and then later in the Jordanian government.
[576] See, How Arab Leader Faisal Supported the Creation of Israel, on YouTube and interview of Anwar Nussebeh, beginning at 4:30, as well as, Why You Should Know San Remo, by Dan Adler, at israelforever.org.

establishment of Arab States. These were carved out of other parts of the former Ottoman Empire, situated outside of Israel (then referred to as Palestine). The area denominated Palestine at the time was reserved solely for the reestablishment of the Jewish state.

San Remo did not recognize any nationalistic claim for the Arabs residing in Israel to establish a separate Arab state in Israel. Rather, it provided only for the Jewish state to respect the civil and religious rights of non-Jewish residents in Israel. In this sense, the legitimacy of the many new Arab states carved out of the former Ottoman Empire at San Remo, and their progeny (which did not exist prior thereto and were merely otherwise legally indistinguishable parts of the former Ottoman Empire) is dependent on and inextricably linked to the carving out of that same Empire of the one Jewish state in its ancient homeland and its reestablishment as the State of Israel. Denying the legitimacy of one ipso facto denies the legitimacy of all. There are now twenty-one separate Arab states as compared to the one and only Jewish state.

Arab representatives[577] participated in the San Remo conference and some accepted the reestablishment of the Jewish State in Israel[578]. Thus, Emir Faisal and Chaim Weitzman signed an agreement confirming the foregoing. Weitzman, on behalf of the Zionist Organization, correspondingly accepted the Arab State Faisal urged be created outside the borders of Israel that would eventually become many separate Arab states[579].

---

[577] Ibid, interview with Nobel Peace Prize winner Philip Noel Baker (who was a part of the British delegation at the Paris Peace conference in 1918-19 and helped form the League of Nations, as well as, the United Nations), beginning 9:20, on how the Emir Faisal and T.E. Lawrence (Lawrence of Arabia) convinced him to support the reestablishment of a Jewish state in Israel (then referred to as Palestine).

[578] Called Palestine at the time and, hence, the Mandate for Palestine granted to Great Britain to effectuate the San Remo Resolution to re-create the Jewish state there.

[579] Agreement between Feisal and Weitzman, dated January 3, 1919.

Among other things, the Faisal-Weitzman Agreement provided, as follows:

ARTICLE III. In the establishment of the Constitution and Administration of Palestine [i.e.: Israel] all such measures shall be adopted as will afford the fullest guarantee for carrying into effect the British Government's Declaration of the 2nd of November, 1917 [the Balfour Declaration].

ARTICLE IV. All necessary measures shall be taken to encourage and stimulate immigration of Jews into Palestine on a large scale, and as quickly as possible to settle Jewish immigrants upon the land through closer settlement and intensive cultivation of the soil. In taking such measures the Arab peasant and tenant farms shall be protected in their rights and shall be assisted in forwarding their economic development.

ARTICLE V. No regulation nor law shall be made prohibiting or interfering in any way with the free exercise of religion; and further the free exercise and enjoyment of religious profession and worship without discrimination or preference shall forever be allowed. No religious test shall ever be required for the exercise of civil or political rights.

Notice the express understanding regarding Jewish immigration. This theme is similarly embodied in the Balfour Declaration, which was incorporated by reference in both the San Remo Resolution and the League of Nations Mandate for Palestine (Israel), as well as the Faisal-Weitzman Agreement. It provides as follows:

Foreign Office
November 2nd, 1917

Dear Lord Rothschild,

I have much pleasure in conveying to you, on behalf of His Majesty's Government, the following declaration of sympathy with Jewish Zionist aspirations which has been submitted to, and approved by, the Cabinet

His Majesty's Government view with favour the establishment in Palestine of a national home for the Jewish people, and will use their best endeavors to facilitate the achievement of this object, it being clearly understood that nothing shall be done which may prejudice the civil and religious rights of existing non-Jewish communities in Palestine or the rights and political status enjoyed by Jews in any other country.

I should be grateful if you would bring this declaration to the knowledge of the Zionist Federation.

Yours,

Arthur James Balfour

As more fully discussed above, San Remo provided for 'national' rights for the Jewish people in Palestine (Israel), as noted in the Balfour Declaration. It is also interesting to note that Emir Faisal separately confirmed the foregoing in a Letter[580] to Felix Frankfurter, an American Zionist, who later helped found the ACLU and went on to become a Supreme Court Justice. He wrote to him from the 1919 Paris peace conference, where he and the Arab delegation and Weitzman and the Jewish delegation were presenting their respective positions to the Allies. Faisal wrote as follows:

We feel that the Arabs and Jews are cousins in having suffered similar oppressions at the hands of powers stronger than themselves, and by a happy coincidence have been able to take the first step towards the attainment of their national ideals together.

---

[580] Letter from Emir Feisal (of the DELEGATION HEDJAZIENNE at the Paris Peace Conference) to Felix Frankfurter, dated March 3, 1919.

The Arabs, especially the educated among us, look with the deepest sympathy on the Zionist movement. Our deputation here in Paris is fully acquainted with the proposals submitted yesterday by the Zionist Organization to the Peace Conference, and we regard them as moderate and proper. We will do our best, in so far as we are concerned, to help them through: we will wish the Jews a most hearty welcome home.

With the chiefs of your movement, especially with Dr. Weizmann, we have had and continue to have the closest relations. He has been a great helper of our cause, and I hope the Arabs may soon be in a position to make the Jews some return for their kindness. We are working together for a reformed and revived Near East, and our two movements complete one another. The Jewish movement is national and not imperialist. Our movement is national and not imperialist, and there is room in Syria for us both. Indeed I think that neither can be a real success without the other.

Felix Frankfurter replied[581] to Emir Faisal and stated:

Allow me, on behalf of the Zionist Organization, to acknowledge your recent letter with deep appreciation.

Those of us who come from the United States have already been gratified by the friendly relations and the active cooperation maintained between you and the Zionist leaders, particularly Dr. Weizmann. We knew it could not be otherwise; we knew that the aspirations of the Arab and the Jewish peoples were parallel, that each aspired to re-establish its nationality in its own homeland, each making its own distinctive contribution to civilization, each seeking its own peaceful mode of life...

---

[581] In a Letter dated March 5, 1919.

We knew from your acts and your past utterances that the Zionist movement -- in other words the national aim of the Jewish people -- had your support and the support of the Arab people for whom you speak. These aims are now before the Peace Conference as definite proposals by the Zionist Organization. We are happy indeed that you consider these proposals "moderate and proper," and that we have in you a staunch supporter for their realization.

The Secretary General of the French Foreign Ministry, Jules Cambon, also confirmed agreement with the national aspirations of the Jewish People in Israel in a Letter[582] to the World Zionist Organization Director Nachum Sokolow, as follows:

You were good enough to present the project to which you are devoting your efforts, which has for its object the development of Jewish colonization in Palestine. You consider that, circumstances permitting, and the independence of the Holy Places being safeguarded on the other hand, it would be a deed of justice and of reparation to assist, by the protection of the Allied Powers, in the renaissance of the Jewish nationality [nationalité juive] in that land from which the people of Israel were exiled so many centuries ago.

The French government, which entered this present war to defend a people wrongly attacked, and which continues the struggle to assure the victory of right over might, can but feel sympathy for your cause, the triumph of which is bound up with that of the Allies.

I am happy to give you herewith such assurance.

---

[582] Dated June 4, 1917.

Nachum Sokolow went on to obtain sign-on from the Italian government and even Pope Benedict XV on May 4, 1917[583]. US President Woodrow Wilson also assented on October 6, 1917[584].

The Congress of the United States adopted a joint resolution of the Senate and the House of Representatives on June 30, 1922, known as the Lodge-Fish Resolution, as follows:

> Resolved by the Senate and House of Representatives of the United States of America in Congress assembled. That the United States of America favors the establishment in Palestine of a national home for the Jewish people, it being clearly understood that nothing shall be done which should prejudice the civil and religious rights of Christian and all other non--Jewish communities in Palestine, and that the holy places and religious buildings and sites in Palestine shall be adequately protected.

On September 21, 1922, President Warren G. Harding signed the Lodge-Fish Resolution, endorsing the Balfour Declaration and the reestablishment of a Jewish homeland in Palestine.

President Wilson also reportedly made the following statement on March 2, 1919:

> I am, moreover, persuaded that the Allied nations, with the fullest concurrence of our own Government and people, are agreed that in Palestine shall be laid the foundation of a Jewish Commonwealth[585].

---

[583] The Forgotten Truth About the Balfour Declaration, by Martin Kramer, in Mosaic Magazine, dated 6/5/2017.

[584] Woodrow Wilson and the Balfour Declaration, by Richard Ned Lebow, in the Journal of Modern History, Volume 40, No.4, December 1968.

[585] See, America and Palestine: the attitude of official America and of the American people toward the rebuilding of Palestine as a free and democratic Jewish commonwealth, prepared and edited by Reuben Fink, New York: American Zionist Emergency Council (1944), at page 35.

This concept was reflected in a Report and Recommendations of the Intelligence Section of the American Delegation to the Paris Peace Conference, dated January 21, 1919, for the use of President Wilson and the delegation. In discussing the recommendation 'to recognize Palestine as a Jewish State, the Report stated as follows:

> It is right that Palestine should become a Jewish State, if the Jews, being given the full opportunity, make it such. It was the cradle and home of their vital race, which has made large spiritual contributions to mankind, and is their only land in which they can hope to find a home of their own; they being in this respect unique among significant peoples.[586]

The Intelligence Section also recommended[587] to the President and the American Delegation that the Jewish State should be separate and distinct from Syria, rejecting, in effect, the Syrian Delegation's demand. The Intelligence Section noted:

> The separation of the Palestinian area from Syria finds justification in the religious experience of mankind. The Jewish and Christian churches were born in Palestine, and Jerusalem was for long years at different periods the capital of each. And while the relation of the Mohammedans to Palestine is not so intimate, from the beginning they have regarded Jerusalem as a holy place. Only by establishing Palestine as a separate state can justice be done to these great facts.

> As drawn upon the map, the state would control its own source of power and irrigation, on Mount Hermon in the

---

[586] See, the Legal Foundation and Borders of Israel under International Law, by Howard Grief, at page 91 and footnote 33 thereon.
[587] See, America and Palestine: the attitude of official America and of the American people toward the rebuilding of Palestine as a free and democratic Jewish commonwealth, prepared and edited by Reuben Fink, New York: American Zionist Emergency Council (1944), at pages 34-35.

east to the Jordan; a feature of great importance since the success of the new state would depend on the possibilities of agricultural development.

It is recommended that the Jews be invited to return to Palestine and settle there, being assured by the Conference of all proper assistance in so doing that may be consistent with the protection of the personal (especially the religious) and the property rights of the non-Jewish population and being assured that it will be the policy of the League of Nations to recognize Palestine as a Jewish State, as it is a Jewish State in fact.

The San Remo Resolution, unanimously adopted by the League of Nations, and the Anglo-American Treaty attest to the validity of these recommendations.

It is also important to recognize that there have been a number of unfounded myths circulated by biased sources promoting a false narrative and ideologically motivated revisionist history in order to undermine the legitimacy of the Jewish State of Israel. As a matter of fact and law, the nations of the world in the League of Nations and the United States unanimously confirmed the legal right of the Jewish people to the Land of Israel, then called Palestine.

In summary, under international law, well before there was a United Nations and recommendation by the UNGA in Resolution 181 of 1947, the Jewish people's right to return to it's homeland of Israel (then called Palestine), join fellow brethren there and reconstitute the Jewish State there[588] was recognized. This includes[589] the following:

1. Faisal-Weitzman Agreement entered into at the 1919 Paris peace conference.

2. Faisal-Frankfurter exchange of correspondence in 1919, which was originated by Faisal, from the 1919 Paris peace conference, which he was attending.

3. President Woodrow Wilson's statement on March 2, 1919.

4. San Remo Resolution of 1920.

5. Council of the League of Nations, which unanimously adopted the San Remo Resolution in 1922.

6. Treaty of Sevres[590] with the Ottoman Empire of 1920.

7. Lodge-Fish Resolution of 1922, a joint resolution of both the Senate and House of Representatives, which was signed by President Warren G. Harding.

8. Anglo-American Treaty of 1924.

---

[588] Those who claim Israel was created solely as a result of the Holocaust are perpetuating a false myth, which is absolutely refuted by these documents and events and as discussed in this book. It might better be asked, if the British Government led by Neville Chamberlain, in response to the 1936-1939 Arab revolt, had not illegally imposed the White Paper of 1939, would the Holocaust have been averted? In any event, all the member nations of the League of Nations and the US recognized the legal right of the Jewish people to reconstitute a Jewish state in Israel and in summary the reason was because it was just and right..

[589] See, Zionism, Post-Zionism & The Arab Problem, by Yosef Mazur, Edited by Mike Cohen, PhD (Professors for a Safe Israel Press-2012).

[590] Article 95.

9. President Calvin Coolidge approval of the Anglo-American Treaty on March 2, 1925.

As Winston Churchill[591] stated, in 1922, the Jews had returned to Palestine "as of right and not by sufferance, and that this was based on their ancient historical connection." Speaking before the Peel Commission years later, in 1937, Churchill snapped at a Commission member who referred to the Jews in Palestine as a "foreign race" and said[592], "The Jews had Palestine before that indigenous population [the Arabs] came in and inhabited it". He was not the only voice who recognized these fundamental truths, as discussed in this book, the nations of the world did.

Thus, terms like colonialist enterprise or the like are unfounded and inapplicable. As discussed below, Omar occupied Palestine (Israel) in the 7th century and hence, it was the Arabs who colonized Israel, not the Jews returning home. Furthermore, consider the statements made by Malcom MacDonald, noted below. MacDonald was the British Colonial Secretary in the Chamberlain Government, which adopted the White Paper and certainly was not prejudiced in favor of the Jews; but rather biased in favor of the Arabs. Remarkably, MacDonald absolutely refuted the allegation that Jews imposed hardships on the Arabs. In a speech before the House of Commons, on November 24, 1938, he said[593]:

> The Arabs cannot say that the Jews are driving them out of their country. If not a single Jew had come to Palestine after 1918, I believe that the Arab population of Palestine today would still have been around about the 600,000

---

[591] See, for example, Churchill's Promised Land: Zionism and Statecraft by Michael Makovsky (Yale University Press-2007), at page 118.

[592] Ibid, at page 49.

[593] See, Hansard, 1803-2005, 1938, Commons Sitting, Palestine, *HC Deb 24 November 1938 vol 341 cc1987-2107*. *See also*, America and Palestine: the attitude of official America and of the American people toward the rebuilding of Palestine as a free and democratic Jewish commonwealth, prepared and edited by Reuben Fink, New York: American Zionist Emergency Council (1944), at pages 119-120 & 224.

figure---instead of over 1,000,000 as at present---at which it had been stable under the Turkish rule. It is because the Jews who have come to Palestine bring modern health services and other advantages that the Arab men and women who would have been dead are alive today, that Arab children who would never have drawn breath have been born and grow strong. It is not only the Jews who have benefited from the Balfour Declaration. They can deny it as much as they like, but materially the Arabs in Palestine have gained very greatly from the Balfour Declaration.

MacDonald also noted:

Since 1922 more than 250,000 Jews have entered Palestine and settled there. Their achievement has been remarkable. They have turned sand dunes into orange groves. They have pushed ever further into waste land the frontiers of cultivation and settlement. They have created a new city, housing to-day 140,000 souls, where before there was only bare seashore. There is no knowing where their achievement might end if Palestine were empty of all other population and could be handed over to them in full ownership.

MacDonald went on to say:

The Jews are in Palestine not on sufferance but by right.

Another debunked myth is that Palestine was twice promised by the British, once to the Jews in the 1917 Balfour Declaration and also to the Arabs, as described below. This is another baseless myth. The document cited to support this false allegation is the Letter[594], dated October 24, 1915, from Sir Henry McMahon, His Majesty's High Commissioner at Cairo, to the Sharif Hussein of

---

[594] See, Appendix 18 in America and Palestine: the attitude of official America and of the American people toward the rebuilding of Palestine as a free and democratic Jewish commonwealth, prepared and edited by Reuben Fink, New York: American Zionist Emergency Council (1944), at pages 452-461.

Mecca. However, that letter dealing with what would become Arab states, such as Saudi Arabia and Syria, expressly excluded the portions of Syria lying to the west of the districts of Damascus, Homs, Hama and Aleppo, which McMahon noted could not be said to be purely Arab. These excluded areas of Ottoman Syria, a grouping of provinces within the Ottoman Empire, included what would ultimately become Lebanon, as well as the area that would comprise the Palestine Mandate.

McMahon, in a Letter dated July 22, 1937, to the Times of London, in response to those referring to the "McMahon Pledge" as including Palestine, explicitly and emphatically denied this was the case. He went on to note that he had every reason to believe that King Hussein well understood that Palestine was excluded[595].

The British Government, in its Statement of British Policy in Palestine, dated June 3, 1922, confirmed in no uncertain terms that the whole of Palestine west of the Jordan was excluded from the McMahon Pledge[596].

---

[595] Ibid and see, Colonel C. E. Vickery's Letter, dated February 21, 1939, to the Times of London, wherein he wrote that he personally met with Sharif Hussein who showed him the McMahon Letter and acknowledged that he did not concern himself at all with Palestine and had no desire to have suzerainty over it for himself or his successors. See also, Secretary's Notes of a Conversation Held in M. Pichon's Room at the Quai d'Orsay, Paris, dated February 6, 1919, in Papers Relating to the Foreign Relations of the United States, The Paris Peace Conference, 1919, Volume III, Paris Peace Conf. 180.03101/31, at the Office of the Historian, at history.state.gov.

[596] Ibid and see also, Statement of British Policy in Palestine, June 3, 1922 (Cmd. 1700, 1022, at pages 19- 20), reproduced in Palestine Correspondence with the Palestine Arab Delegation and the Zionist Organization (Cmd. 1700) (White Paper of 1922), at Center of Online Jewish Studies (COJS.org). It noted: "In the first place, it is not the case, as has been represented by the Arab Delegation, that during the war His Majesty's Government gave an undertaking that an independent national government should be at once established in Palestine. This representation mainly rests upon a letter dated the 24th of October, 1915, from Sir Henry McMahon...to the Sherif of Mecca...That letter is quoted as conveying the promise to the Sherif of Mecca to recognize and support the independence of the Arabs within the territories proposed by him. But this promise was given subject to a reservation made in the same letter, which excluded from its scope, among other territories, the portions of Syria lying to the west of the

As noted above, the 'existing non-Jewish communities' in Palestine (Israel) were not afforded 'national' rights. Rather, they were provided only protections as to their civil and religious rights that were not to be prejudiced, which are fully protected as a matter of law in Israel, as outlined below. Ironically, it is the PA and Hamas that don't respect the civil and religious rights of either non-Muslims or even their own Muslim constituents, as summarized below.

Resolution 181 also contained express provisions for the protection of civil and religious rights, as follows:

Chapter 2: Religious and Minority Rights

Freedom of conscience and the free exercise of all forms of worship, subject only to the maintenance of public order and morals, shall be ensured to all.

No discrimination of any kind shall be made between the inhabitants on the ground of race, religion, language or sex.

All persons within the jurisdiction of the State shall be entitled to equal protection of the laws.

The family law and personal status of the various minorities and their religious interests, including endowments, shall be respected.

Except as may be required for the maintenance of public order and good government, no measure shall be taken to obstruct or interfere with the enterprise of religious or charitable bodies of all faiths or to discriminate against any representative or member of

district of Damascus. This reservation has always been regarded by His Majesty's Government as covering the vilayet of Beirut and the independent Sanjak of Jerusalem. The whole of Palestine west of the Jordan was thus excluded from Sir H. McMahon's pledge."

these bodies on the ground of his religion or nationality.

The State shall ensure adequate primary and secondary education for the Arab and Jewish minority, respectively, in its own language and its cultural traditions.

The right of each community to maintain its own schools for the education of its own members in its own language, while conforming to such educational requirements of a general nature as the State may impose, shall not be denied or impaired. Foreign educational establishments shall continue their activity on the basis of their existing rights.

No restriction shall be imposed on the free use by any citizen of the State of any language in private intercourse, in commerce, in religion, in the Press or in publications of any kind, or at public meetings.

No expropriation of land owned by an Arab in the Jewish State (by a Jew in the Arab State) shall be allowed except for public purposes. In all cases of expropriation full compensation as fixed by the Supreme Court shall be said previous to dispossession.

Israel, in its very Declaration of Independence, states, in no uncertain terms, its dedication to these principles as follows:

The State of Israel...will promote the development of the country for the benefit of all its inhabitants; will be based on the precepts of liberty, justice, and peace taught by the Hebrew Prophets; will uphold the full social and political equality of all its citizens, without distinction of race, creed, or sex; will guarantee full freedom of conscience, worship, education, and culture; will safeguard the sanctity and inviolability of the shrines and Holy Places of all religions; and will dedicate itself to the principles of the Charter of the United Nations.

This is in striking contrast to the situation in the Hamas and PA controlled areas. Astonishingly, the lack of these essential human rights is a typical part of the life of an ordinary member of a non-Muslim minority community under the control of the PA or Hamas, as more fully discussed below. Even under Jordanian control, Jews were expelled and their properties were seized without compensation. Jews were not allowed to visit the Holy Places under Jordanian control. This was despite the express provisions of Resolution 181 and the terms of the Armistice Agreement between Israel and Jordan signed in Rhodes on April 3, 1949. Under Article VII, Section 2 of the Agreement, arrangements were required to be made for Israel to have free access to the Holy Places and cultural institutions, the resumption of normal functioning of Israel's cultural and humanitarian institutions on Mount Scopus (i.e., Hebrew University and Hadassah Hospital) and the use of the cemetery on the Mount of Olives, all as previously agreed to by the parties. However, Jordan never implemented any of the foregoing. In fact, as summarized below, it barred Jews and beyond that, it actually desecrated many of these sites.

Even today, Jews are outright barred from owning land in PA and Hamas controlled areas, restricted from or harassed when visiting religious sites there (such as, for example, the Tomb of Joseph[597]in Nablus) and even warned against entering these areas. The Christian Arab minority residing in the areas under the control of the disreputable PA and Hamas regimes are also

---

[597] See, for example, Palestinian teen killed as gunman attack MK's pilgrimage to Joseph's Tomb in Nablus, by Emanuel Fabian, in The Times of Israel, dated 11/9/2022. The teen was killed by his own IED, when it prematurely exploded.

being discriminated against, harassed and persecuted, but more on this below.

It is also critically important to note that Resolution 181 expressly excluded Jerusalem and its surrounding areas, including Bethlehem (as specified in the Resolution), from any part of any Arab state, as well as the Jewish state. The UNGA preferred to establish it as a separate entity (corpus separatum) under a special international regime administered by the UN. In this regard, it is important to understand the valid concerns about the lack of free access to and ill-treatment of Holy Places under Arab stewardship. Thus, for example, the Holy Sites located in Jordanian-occupied portions of Jerusalem until 1967 were barred to Jews. Indeed, all the remaining Jewish inhabitants of Jordanian-occupied Jerusalem, many of whom traced their family history of residence in Jerusalem back centuries prior to 1949, were expelled. Many synagogues, including the famous Churva Synagogue, were destroyed, Torah Scrolls and holy books were plundered, burnt or otherwise defiled and the ancient Jewish cemetery on the Mount of Olives was desecrated and ravaged, with gravestones being toppled over, broken and used to pave roads and build latrines[598]. Is it any wonder that the world did not trust their Holy Places to the tender mercies of any Arab state? Over time, though, Christian institutions, like the Catholic Church, began to trust the Jewish State and its express commitment to freedom of worship and access to the Holy Places, as discussed above. The drive for internationalization of Jerusalem lost steam in the face of the practical inability to achieve the same and the fact that it was patently unnecessary, given Israel's proven track record of respect and legal protections for all religions.

---

[598] See, History of Jerusalem: Jordan's Desecration of Jerusalem (1948-1967), at Jewish Virtual Library.org. and Cabinet Report Says Jordan Destroyed 56 Old City Synagogues, Desecrated Cemetery, in JTA archive, dated 11/2/1967.

This is unlike the PA and Hamas, which to this day, as a matter of law and practice, bar Jews from areas under their control and land sales to Jews are prohibited under penalty of death[599]. Holy Places are regularly desecrated, including, for example, the Tomb of Joseph[600] , and Jewish[601] and Christian[602] worshippers are harassed.

Islam is the official religion of the PA and Hamas controlled areas. In addition, the principles of the Sharia[603] are the main source of legislation under PA law. Hamas imposes its own misguided standards of morality on its subjugated populace. Despite paying lip service to freedom of belief (which typically would include atheism) and worship, the law is expressly qualified by the subjective standard that they not violate public order or morality. Lest there be any misunderstanding about how restricted, these so-called freedoms are, in practice, consider the fact that blasphemy is a criminal offense. Equal protection of the law for non-Muslims is also not assured. Who can forget the takeover of the Church of the Nativity in Bethlehem by PA forces in April of 2002, when Christian clergy and nuns were taken hostage? Not only were the perpetrators not held accountable for their miscreant actions, they were, instead, hailed as heroes[604].

---

[599] PA: Death penalty for those who sell land to Jews, by Khaled Abu Toameh, in the Jerusalem Post, dated 4/1/2009 and Palestinian Authority: You're a "traitor" if you sell land to the Jews, by Carmel Madadshahi, in the Jerusalem Post, dated 3/1/2020.

[600] See, for example, a recent incident of vandalism, described in: Palestinians attack biblical figure Joseph's tomb in West Bank, in BBC News, dated 4/11/2022 and Palestinian rioters vandalize Joseph's Tomb amid clashes with IDF, by Anna Ahronheim and Tovah Lazaroff, in the Jerusalem Post, dated 4/10/2022.

[601] See, for example, Jewish worshippers attacked in Jerusalem's Old City, by Jerusalem Post Staff, in the Jerusalem Post, dated 4/17/2022.

[602] See, for example, The Beleaguered Christians of Palestinian-Controlled Areas, by David Raab, at jcpa.org, dated 1/15/2003 and What Happens When a Palestinian Doesn't Hate Israel Enough?, by Luke Moon, in the Federalist, dated 5/1/2014.

[603] The Sharia is an Arabic term used to describe Islamic law and practice. It literally means 'the way'.

[604] See, for example, Palestinian gunmen turn heroes in UK production of 'The Siege', by Jenni Frazer, in the Times of Israel, dated 5/2/2015.

All too often, the plight of the Christian minority in PA and Hamas controlled areas is just ignored[605] or distorted by agenda-driven ideologues and contorted to conform to the false narrative they promote as paid agents or useful dupes of those in control of the PA and Hamas apparatus. Their intersectional cohorts in the international community, including in ostensibly Christian-majority nations and at Christian sponsored NGOs, are content to embrace and foster these false narratives rather than focusing on the human rights needs of their brethren, who are actually suffering under the heel of the Muslim majority dominated by these nefarious forces[606].

It is reported[607] that many Christian Arabs living under the PA or Hamas do not trust their religious or lay leaders. In essence, whether out of fear, in consideration of special privileges, or because they want to be identified with the Muslim majority governing authorities, they have been co-opted by the PA. Thus, no matter how radical or corrupt the PA and its cohorts may be, they cover-up the problems or perpetuate the false narratives about everything being copacetic. Many are reluctant openly to express their feelings because of fear of retribution against themselves or their family. Even when Church leaders speak up, the response is usually muted. Thus, when an Orthodox Church near Bethlehem (in the small town of Beit Sahur that is predominantly Christian) was attacked by dozens of Muslim men

---

[605] See, for example, Palestinians: Why Are Attacks on Christians Being Ignored?, by Khaled Abu Toameh, at the Gatestone Institute, dated 10/31/2022. See also, Palestinians: The Nightmare of Christians, by Khaled Abu Toameh, at the Gatestone Institute, dated 12/24/2016.

[606] See, for example, Human Rights of Christians in Palestinian Society, by Justus Reid Weiner, at Jerusalem Center for Public Affairs (jcpa.org-2005).

[607] See, for example, Bethlehem's Beleaguered Christians, by Linda Burkle, Ph.D, at Persecution.org, dated 1/14/2020; A Christian crises in Gaza and the West Bank, in the Jerusalem Post, dated 12/25/2019; Where Christian Persecution Exists in the Holy Land This Christmas, by Barry Shawn, at thej.ca, dated 1/5/2022; and Middle Eastern Christmas Battered, Violated, and Abused, Do They Have Any Chance of Survival (2014), as well as, Human Rights of Christians in Palestinian Society (2005), both by Justus Reid Weiner, at the Jerusalem Center for Public Affairs (jcpa.org).

hurling stones and worshippers were injured, Archbishop
Atallah Hanna of the Greek Orthodox Patriarchate of Jerusalem
did condemn the attack; but, merely impotently demanded that
the PA bring the attackers to trial as soon as possible[608]. However,
as might have been expected, even days later, and despite there
being videos of the incident posted on social media, there are no
reported arrests of any of the wrongdoers[609]. There has also been
no reported public outcry in the corporate media or by the US or
EU. This kind of gaslighting prevents the issue from resonating
throughout the world. This is just one example that is
symptomatic of the problem[610]. Is it any wonder that the false
narrative of the PA and Hamas, which proclaims victimhood,
despite being the terrorist predators, often goes unchallenged?

Bassam Tawil, an Arab Middle East scholar at the Gatestone
Institute, writes[611], "By turning a blind eye to Palestinian lies,

---

[608] Christian leaders condemn attack on church near Bethlehem, by Khaled Abu
Toameh, in the Jerusalem Post, dated 10/29/2022.
[609] Church Attacked by Muslims in Christian Town Near Bethlehem, by All Arab News,
at foreigndesknews.com, dated 10/31/2022.
[610] Israel is also subjected to the same kind of gaslighting. Thus, on October 29, 2022,
there was another horrific terrorist incident that occurred, in which an Israeli was
murdered and others wounded, in Kiryat Arba, by an Arab terrorist from the PA, linked
to Hamas (See, Israeli killed in Kiryat Arba terror attack identified as Ronen Hanania, at
JNS, dated 10/30/2022). It was also not widely reported in the corporate media.
[611] See, for example, European Union, Biden Administration Embrace Palestinian Lies,
by Bassam Tawil, at Gatestone Institute. Org, dated 2/16/2023. Bassam Tawil also
decries how the EU nations and US are ignoring Abbas' ongoing campaign to deny
Jewish history and rights to Israel and the Western Wall. He also reports that the EU has
even been working with the Palestinians to seize land in "Area C" that officially belongs
to Israel under Oslo II. He goes on to note how absurd it is to condemn Jews building
housing arguing it would "exacerbate tensions between Israelis and Palestinians and
undermine efforts to achieve a negotiated two-state solution". He writes that the EU
nations and US know that the Arab-Israel conflict started long before the construction
of even one house on the so-called west bank. As Abbas himself said in Cairo, the Arab
problem with Israel started in 1917. He urges the EU and Biden administration to wake
up and recognize that the Palestinian leaders are not interested in peace with Israel;
they want peace without the existence of Israel. There is no difference to them whether
a Jew resides in the so-called west bank, Jerusalem or Tel Aviv; they want it all and
denuded of any Jews. See also, Europe's Proxy War against Israel-How the EU Ignores
Hamas' Crimes, by Bassam Tawil, at the Gatestone Institute.org, dated 2/13/2023.

fabrications, and antisemitism, the Biden administration and EU are sending a message to the Palestinians that it is perfectly fine to continue demonizing Israel and Jews". It appears that the EU and Biden administration have pursued a similar apathetic and myopic approach in the case of the plight of Christians under the heel of the PA and Hamas, and the results are also extremely disturbing.

PA corruption and ideological imperatives are also to blame for the poverty, unemployment, and difficult conditions encountered by Christians and others. However, Christians have borne the brunt of it, treated as second-class by the Muslim majority and beholden to an ostensibly Islamic government that is peopled by persons who reject or despise them. Christian-owned businesses suffer from boycotts and extortion,, and Christians are restricted from buying or selling land to other Christians. Christian women are particularly targeted for verbal and physical abuse. There are also many other incidents in which Christians are physically attacked and churches are vandalized, desecrated and robbed, all without consequence by an uninterested PA. The fact is Christians are often afraid to go to public places visibly identifying their religious affiliation as non-Muslims, including by wearing crosses.

The undeniable objective proof of the deteriorating conditions for Christians under the PA and Hamas is the emigration of Christians from these areas and manifest decline in the Christian population. Thus, while the Muslim population has grown, the Christian population has precipitously declined since the takeover by the PA. Consider Bethlehem, which was the most populous Christian town in 1994, when the PA took control. For centuries, Christians were the overwhelming majority of the population of Bethlehem. Since then, the Christian population has dwindled to only approximately 12% by 2016[612].

Many of the civil rights taken for granted in Israel, the US, the UK, Canada, Australia, EU and other Western Nations, such as no discrimination by reason of race, creed, color, religion, sex or sexual orientation and equal protection under the law are absent in the areas controlled by the PA and Hamas. Indeed, as a matter of fact, and law, there is actual discrimination against and a lack of equal rights for women. It is reported[613] that, in the PA and Hamas controlled areas, domestic physical and mental abuse against women in the home is rampant; honor killings regularly occur; there is systemic discrimination against women, both civilly and criminally; women are blatantly mistreated and exploited, including in matters of economic access and inheritance; and there is no equal protection for women under the law.

There is also invidious discrimination practiced against Christians, the most prevalent non-Muslim minority, in the areas under PA and Hamas control. They are singled out for mistreatment by the overwhelmingly dominant Muslim majority and the kleptocracies that govern the affairs of the PA and Hamas. This includes reports[614] of the following:

> Violence and other crimes committed against Christians and no accountability or enforcement of the law by police or the judiciary;

---

[612] See, for example, Bethlehem's Beleaguered Christians, by Linda Burkle, Ph.D, at Persecution.org, dated 1/14/2020

[613] See Facts and Figures UN Women-Palestine: Ending Violence Against Women and Jerusalem Institute of Justice, April 2016 Report on the Implementation of the Convention on the Elimination of All Forms of Discrimination Against Women under the PA and Hamas.

[614] See, for example, Human Rights of Christians in Palestinian Society (2005), by Justus Reid Weiner, at the Jerusalem Center for Public Affairs (jcpa.org), as well as, the other sources noted above.

A school system that teaches hate of non-Muslims and glorifies homicide bombers, as well as, training to kill Jews and Americans;

A growing influence of Islamic fanaticism and support for Islamic Jihad and Hamas, which targets non-Muslims and are understandably not typically supported by Christian Arabs.

A perception by some Muslims that Christian Arabs are just stooges of the West. In a sense, they are viewed as enemies, just like the Jews. In Gaza, there is graffiti on the walls to the effect that when they are through with the Saturday people (i.e.: those observing the Jewish Sabbath), they will start with the Sunday people (i.e.: those observing the Christian Sabbath). The Muslim Sabbath is observed on Friday;

Christian women are often forced to wear headscarves;

In the month of Ramadan, anyone caught smoking or eating on the streets before sundown are often arrested, even if Christian.

Christians are forced to pay protection money to stay in business;

Government representatives brazenly rob Christians of their valuables;

Refusing to pay extortion money to members of the Kleptocracy can be deadly;

Christian businesses are boycotted;

Land sales to non-Muslims are discouraged;

Christian women are verbally abused, intimidated, sexually harassed and assaulted, usually without consequence;

Discrimination against Christians is a fact of life. This includes job opportunities, medical care, receipt of government aid and even in the distribution of food or charitable donations from abroad. Imagine, Christian organizations are collecting funds; but Christian Arabs under the PA and Hamas are denied these benefits. There is also effectively no equal protection under the law. Given that Sharia law governs, these practices are, in effect, institutionalized, because Christian are legally treated as second class citizens;

Christians are often targeted as traitors or Israeli collaborators;

Converts to Christianity are sometimes killed with impunity;

The Judicial system is not independent and often functions as just another arm of the kleptocracy;

Churches are often selected by PA and Hamas forces as the cover of choice when engaging Israeli forces militarily, in essence, holding them hostage, using them as a shield or otherwise to create international incidents, if Israel fires back; and

Christians are harassed on the way to and from Church services.

The disinterest by the US State Department, EU and NGOs in investigating, shining light on and denouncing these abhorrent offenses, as well as holding the violators accountable and visiting actual punishment on them, only serves to embolden the predators and dishearten the victims. Consider the effort by the US Congress in 1998[615] to pass a law addressing the problem of

---

[615] International Religious Freedom Act of 1998, Public Law 105-292, dated October 27, 1998, 112 Stat.2787, 22 USC Ch. 73: International Religious Freedom (22 USC 6401, et seq.).

Christian persecution abroad. The Clinton administration opposed the passage of the law and the watered-down version that ultimately passed enabled the President to waive enforcement of its provisions[616]. Sound familiar? Is it any wonder that the problem persists? Why doesn't the US stop funding amounts that directly or indirectly benefit the offending PA and Hamas[617]? Indeed, why does the US effectively continue to fund 'Pay to Slay', despite the express provisions of the Taylor Force Act?

It should be noted that Farley worked with Congressman Matt Salmon's office through his legislative director and eventual Chief of Staff Glenn Hamer concerning the issue of why Palestinian Arab terrorists who murdered Americans were not extradited to face American justice.

A resolution, initiated by Congressman Salmon, was passed by the House of Representatives on May 5, 1998[618], which states as follows:

Whereas the traditional policy of the United States, reiterated by this Administration, has been to vigorously pursue and apprehend terrorists who have killed American citizens in other countries;

Whereas numerous American citizens have been killed by Palestinian terrorists, most of them in Israel or the Israeli administered territories, including 9 since the signing of the Oslo Accords in 1993, namely Nachshon Wachsman (New York), Alisa Flatow (New Jersey), Sara Duker (New

[616] Subchapter III-Presidential Actions (22 USC 6447).
[617] Some in Congress are trying to end this abuse. See, for example, Republican Senators Introduce Bill to Halt Aid to Gaza, by Andrew Bernard, in the Algemeiner, dated 2/22/2023.
[618] The resolution was concurrently passed in the Senate on May 6, 1998. See text at Congressional Bills 105th Congress, H. Con. Res. 220, in the Senate of the United States, May 6, 1998, Concurrent Resolution-Regarding American victims of terrorism at govinfo.gov.

Jersey), Matthew Eisenfeld (Connecticut), Joan Davenny (Connecticut), David Boim (New York), Yaron Ungar (New York), Leah Stern (New Jersey), and Yael Botwin (California);

Whereas at least 20 of the terrorists suspected in the killings of American citizens in Israel or the Israeli administered territories during 1993-1997 have been identified by Israel as Mohammed Dief, Nabil Sharihi, Nafez Sabih, Imjad Hinawi, Abd al-Maid Dudin, Adel Awadallah, Ibrahim Ghneimat, and Mahmoud Abu Hanudeh, Abd al-Rahman Ghanelmat, Jamal al-Hur, Raid Abu Hamadayah, Mohammad Abu Wardah, Hassan Salamah, Abd Rabu Shaykh 'Id, Hamdallah Tzramah, Abd Al-Nasser Atallah Issa, Hataham Ibrahim Ismail, Jihad Mohammad Shaker Yamur, and Mohammad Abbasm;

Whereas, according to the Israeli Government, 10 of those 20 terrorist suspects are currently believed to be free men;

Whereas the Anti-Terrorism Act of 1987 permits the prosecution, in the United States, of individuals who murder American citizens abroad; and

Whereas the United States has previously acted to bring to justice those responsible for the deaths of American citizens and has established a precedence of United States intervention by demanding that Libyan leader Muammar Qadaffi transfer to the United States the Libyan terrorists suspected of bombing Pan Am flight 103:

Now, therefore, be it Resolved by the House of Representatives (the Senate concurring), That it is the sense of the Congress that—

(1) the United States should demand the prosecution of all suspected perpetrators of these attacks against United States citizens;

(2) the United States should seek the cooperation of the Palestinian Authority and all other appropriate authorities in the prosecution of these cases; and

(3) the suspects should be tried in the United States unless it is determined that such action is contrary to effective prosecution.

Congressman Salmon traveled to Israel and met with Prime Minister Netanyahu and Justice Minister Hanegbi to promote cooperation with U.S. Justice officials to ensure the U.S. indicts such terrorists. He also met with Palestinian Authority President Arafat in Gaza and discussed how Palestinian Arab terrorists involved in murdering or wounding Americans should be transferred to the U.S. to face justice.

Farley was also on a Conference Call in December of 1997 with then Secretary of State Madeleine Albright. He asked Secretary Albright the following question:

Madam Secretary, the U.S. has a policy concerning terrorists who murder Americans which is you can run but you cannot hide. Why has the U.S. changed its policy on such terrorists when it concerns Palestinian Arab terrorists who murdered Americans like Mohammed Deif who resides in a safe haven in Gaza under Palestinian Authority control?

Albright responded:

The U.S. has not changed our policy concerning terrorists who murdered Americans and I do not know who you are talking about or anything else about this issue.

Following the call, Farley worked with Congressman Salmon's office on a letter that over 30 Congressmen and 4 Senators signed, including Senator Jon Kyl, calling for Deif and other Palestinian Arab terrorists who murdered or wounded Americans to be brought to America to face justice.

After the letter was sent, Farley was able to be on another conference call with Secretary Albright after she had met with Arafat. Farley asked the following question:

"Madam Secretary in the Spring of 1996 in a grave side visit President Clinton promised the Wachsman family that the United States would go after Mohammed Deif for orchestrating the murder of their American son Nachshon. Did you raise the issue of Deif with Arafat, did President Clinton raise this issue and what was Arafat's response?"

Albright responded:

I raised the issue of Deif with Chairman Arafat as did President Clinton and Deif is a fugitive and we are actively pursuing the matter.

While the Palestinian Authority eventually briefly detained Deif, there seems to have been no public calls by the administration for his extradition. It would appear that whatever the administration was actually doing to pursue the matter, the result was yet another appalling failure. Deif was eventually released, and he became the military leader of Hamas in Gaza, responsible for hundreds of deaths of Israelis and many Americans[619].

In December of 2004, a bill passed by Congress, known as the Koby Mandell Act, was signed into law by President George W. Bush[620]. The law was named after Israeli-American citizen Koby Mandell, who was brutally murdered by a Palestinian Arab terrorist on May 8, 2001. Congress found as follows:

(1) Numerous American citizens have been murdered or maimed by terrorists around the world, including more

---

[619] See, Statement of Farley Weiss, President, National Council of Young Israel, at the Hearing "Seeking Justice for Victims of Palestinian Terrorism in Israel", House Oversight and Government Reform Subcommittee on National Security, dated February 2, 2016. The Hearing is more fully discussed below.
[620] Text - S.684 - 108th Congress (2003-2004): Koby Mandell Act of 2003, at Congress.gov .

than 100 murdered since 1968 in terrorist attacks occurring in Israel or in territories administered by Israel or in territories administered by the Palestinian Authority.

(2) Some American citizens who have been victims of terrorism overseas, especially those harmed by terrorists operating from areas administered by the Palestinian Authority, have not received from the United States Government services equal to those received by other such victims of overseas terrorism.

(3) The United States Government has not devoted adequate efforts or resources to the apprehension of terrorists who have harmed American citizens overseas, particularly in cases involving terrorists operating from areas administered by the Palestinian Authority. Monetary rewards for information leading to the capture of terrorists overseas, which the Government advertises in regions where the terrorists are believed to be hiding, have not been advertised in areas administered by the Palestinian Authority.

(4) This situation is especially grave in the areas administered by the Palestinian Authority, because many terrorists involved in the murders of Americans are walking free there; some of these terrorists have been given positions in the Palestinian Authority security forces or other official Palestinian Authority agencies; and a number of schools, streets, and other public sites have been named in honor of terrorists who were involved in the murders of Americans.

(5) To remedy these and related problems, an office should be established within the Department of Justice for the purpose of ensuring equally vigorous efforts to capture all terrorists who have harmed American citizens overseas

and equal treatment for all American victims of overseas terrorism.

The operative provisions of the Act (Section 3) include setting up a special office within the Justice Department tasked with carrying out the following activities:

1.   Offering rewards for the capture all terrorists involved in harming American citizens overseas, regardless of the terrorists' country of origin or residence.

2.   Working with other United States Government agencies to expand legal restrictions on the ability of murderers to reap profits from books or movies concerning their crimes so as to ensure that terrorists who harm American citizens overseas are unable to profit from book or movie sales in the United States.

3.   Determining if terrorists who have harmed American citizens overseas are serving in their local police or security forces; and if so, then to alert those United States Government agencies involved in providing assistance, directly or indirectly, to those forces; and request that all such assistance be halted until the terrorists are removed from their positions.

4.   Undertaking a comprehensive assessment of the pattern of United States indictments and prosecution of terrorists who have harmed American citizens overseas, in order to determine the reasons for the absence of indictments of terrorists residing in some regions, such as the territories controlled by the Palestinian Authority.

5.   Monitoring public actions by governments and regimes overseas pertaining to terrorists who have harmed American citizens, such as the naming of schools, streets, or other public institutions or sites after such terrorists; and in such instances, encourage other United States

Government agencies to halt their provision of assistance, directly or indirectly, to those institutions.

6.   Securing appropriate financial compensation for American citizens, or the families of such citizens, who were harmed by organizations that claim responsibility for acts of terrorism against Americans overseas and that subsequently become part of a governing regime with which the United States Government maintains diplomatic or other official contacts, such as the Palestinian Authority.

7.   Monitoring the incarceration abroad of terrorists who harmed Americans overseas, to ensure that their conditions of incarceration are reasonably similar to conditions of incarceration in the United States.

8.   In cases where terrorists who have harmed Americans overseas, and are subsequently released from incarceration abroad, are eligible for further prosecution in the United States, to coordinate with other   Government agencies to seek the transfer of those terrorists to the United States for further prosecution.

On February 2, 2016, then-Congressman (now Governor) Ron DeSantis, as Chairman of the Subcommittee on National Security of the House Committee on Oversight and Government Reform, held a Hearing[621] on the matter of "Seeking Justice For Victims Of Palestinian Terrorism In Israel". In his opening statement, he said the following:

Since the signing of the Oslo Accords in 1993, more than 64 Americans, including two unborn children, have been murdered by Palestinian terrorists in Israel and the

---

[621] Hearing before the Subcommittee on National Security of the Committee of Oversight and Government Reform, House of Representative, 114th Congress, second session, February 2, 2016, Serial No. 114-64. Farley made a written submission as President of the National Council of Young Israel.

disputed territories. Some of them were tourists, some were students, some were living and working in Israel. Many were Jewish, but some were not. The stories of these American victims are heart wrenching. In 1996, Matthew Eisenfeld was a young graduate of Yale University who was studying abroad in Israel. He and his girlfriend, Sara Duker from New Jersey, had the misfortune to ride the number 18 bus that was blown up by Palestinian terrorists. Matthew's mother, Vicki, later bemoaned the quote, ``lack of justice. It makes me feel like my son's blood is less American,'' unquote.

In 2002, Americans Dina Carter, Benjamin Blutstein, Marla Bennett, Janis Coulter, and David Gritz were studying at Hebrew University in Jerusalem. They were eating in the school cafeteria when Palestinian terrorists detonated a bomb inside the cafeteria, killing them all.

Malki Roth was a beautiful and talented 15-year-old girl, who was eating at the Sbarro Pizza Restaurant on Jaffa Road in Jerusalem on August 9th, 2001, when a Palestinian suicide bomber blew himself up. He took 15 civilians[622] with him, including Malki and another American, Judith Greenbaum, who was pregnant at the time. The person responsible for planning and executing this dastardly attack, Ahlam Tamimi, has boasted about this many times on video, yet, she resides in Jordan and hosts a television show for Hamas. We are honored to have Mr. Arnold Roth with us at today's hearing. He has traveled from Jerusalem, and we are looking forward to hearing his testimony.

So thank you for joining us, sir.

---

[622] Now 16, since Chana Nachenberg Z"L passed away after being in a coma for 22 years (see, Israeli Sbarro bombing victim dies after 22 years in coma, by Lahav Harkov, in the Jerusalem Post, dated 5/31/2023.

In 2001, Koby Mandell was a 13-year-old American boy who went on a hike with an Israeli friend, Yosef Ishran. They didn't come home, and their parents were worried. Their bodies were later found in a cave. They were so brutally bludgeoned that dental records were needed to positively identify the bodies. More than 10 years ago, the memories of American victims of terrorism, such as Koby and others, provide an inspiration for a bill bearing Koby's name, which became the legislative source for the opening of the Office of Justice for Victims of Overseas Terrorism within the Department of Justice.

The American people overwhelmingly believe that terrorists who kill Americans abroad must face justice. To this end, the office was designed with a purpose of ensuring, quote, ``that the investigation and prosecution of terrorist deaths of American citizens overseas are a high priority within the Department of Justice.

The families of the victims of terrorism and their advocates celebrated the creation of the office in the hope that justice would be sought and achieved for the victims of terrorist attacks. Indeed, when commemorating the establishment of the new office, then-Attorney General Alberto Gonzalez remarked that it would guarantee, quote, ``A voice for the victims and their families in the investigation and prosecution of terrorists who prey on American overseas," end quote.

Yet, DOJ has not been able to cite one example for this committee of even a single terrorist that has been prosecuted in the United States for any of the 64 attacks against Americans in Israel. Indeed, many of these terrorists roam free as a result of prisoner exchanges or evasions. This is not what Congress intended. This is not what the American people want. And this does not provide the justice to the victims' families that has been so tragically elusive.

In fact, the mother of Koby Mandell called the office, quote, ``an affront to her son's name." The case of Ahlam Tamimi is a good example of the DOJ's failure. She is a terrorist who helped orchestrate the bombing that killed Malki Roth and Judith Greenbaum. She was released from an Israeli prison in 2011 as part of a prisoner exchange with the Palestine authority, but she's bragged about her conduct and has maintained a consistent presence on a Hamas television station, and, yet, this malignant woman continues to roam free, sowing the seeds of hate.

When the committee questioned the DOJ about this case, the Department declined to comment. If, in fact, bringing to justice the perpetrators of terrorism against Americans in Israel is a high priority for the DOJ, then, surely, people of this nature should be prosecuted for their crimes.

This afternoon, we will hear from those who might have been harmed in terrorist attacks or have lost loved ones. I thank them for their courage to speak out on this important issue. I also ask unanimous consent to insert into the record statements from individuals who have been impacted by terrorism. We have received testimony from Sherri Mandell, mother of Koby Mandell; Alan Bauer, a victim and father of a victim; and Mark Sokolow, whose family was in a terrorist attack in 2002, as well as the National Council of Young Israel. Israel is a magnet for terrorist attacks because it is a pro-Western Democratic nation of biblical significance. When Americans are the victims of terrorist attacks in Israel, they are, in a sense, being attacked for the shared values that bind our two nations, values that drive the jihadists to consume themselves in a culture of hate. We cannot allow the lives of our own American citizens to be devalued as merely pawns on a diplomatic chessboard. This effectively excuses the terrorist, invites more attacks, and leaves lasting scars on our own citizens due to justice being denied.

I look forward to today's testimony and eagerly await progress on bringing justice to the American victims of terrorism in Israel.

After Ranking Member, Congressman Stephen Lynch, made his opening remarks, Brad Wiegmann, the Deputy Assistant Attorney General of the National Security Division at the Department of Justice, began to testify and made his opening statement. Peter Schwartz, the uncle of Ezra Schwartz, of blessed memory, who was murdered by Palestinian terrorists on November 19, 2015, also made an oral statement. He spoke about how the terrorists had been intent on murdering as many Jews as possible and killed three people, including American Ezra Schwartz, before being apprehended.

Arnold Roth is the father of Malki Roth, of blessed memory. Fifteen people, including 15-year-old American Malki Roth, were brutally murdered in the infamous Sbarro Restaurant attack, on August 9, 2001, by a Palestinian terrorist homicide bomber when he blew himself up in the Restaurant. Yet to this day, Ahlam Tamimi, who helped plan and orchestrate the attack (even accompanying the terrorist to the site of his murderous mission in order to ensure it would be carried out and not be prevented), remains free in Jordan. Unrepentant, she even brags about her heinous crimes. She is also on the FBI's most wanted list[623], but nevertheless, she has yet to face American justice.

Chairman DeSantis then questioned Wiegmann. Here are some of the questions and answers:

Mr. DeSantis: Mr. Wiegmann, the committee has counted that since '93, at least 64 Americans have been killed, as

---

[623] See, wanted_terrorists/ahlam-ahmad-al-tamimi, at fbi.gov.

well as two unborn children, and 91 have been wounded by terrorists in Israel in disputed territories.

How many terrorists who have killed or wounded Americans in Israel or disputed territories has the United States indicted, extradited, or prosecuted during this time period?

Mr. Wiegmann. I think the answer is--is none.

Mr. DeSantis. Okay. How many terrorists who have killed or wounded Americans anywhere else overseas has the United States indicted, extradited, or prosecuted?

Mr. Wiegmann. I don't have an exact figure for you.

Mr. DeSantis. But it would be a decent size number, though, correct?

Mr. Wiegmann. It would be a significant number, yes.

It's now been years since the Hearing, and the answer is there are still no actual prosecutions, trials and convictions against Palestinian terrorists killing or wounding Americans in Israel or Judea and Samaria. As Congressman Mark Meadows pointed out at the Hearing:

...my concern, Winston Churchill has one of my favorite quotes, and it is, 'No matter how beautiful the strategy, we must occasionally look at the results'. And the results are not encouraging.

In point of fact, the results are stunningly disappointing. Sadly, it would appear that no noticeable changes have been made since the hearing and the abysmal record of failure continues.

It might have been expected that with the passage of the Taylor Force Law, efforts would have been redoubled to root out terrorism and bring the perpetrators to justice. At the very least, it might have reasonably been expected that the provisions of the Law requiring funding of the PA and Hamas be reduced would be enforced. This is especially so given the parallel requirement to reduce funding under the Taylor Force Act to cause the despicable Pay to Slay program to be ended. Yet, even as American citizens continue to be murdered or maimed and terrorists continue to be rewarded, not only has funding not been reduced, it has been increased. The State Department's formulaic and frankly disingenuous certifications keep on rolling out on demand, and apparently, the DOJ is not acting either to curtail the State Department abuses or to bring murdering terrorists to justice.

Unlike the PA and Hamas, Israel offers equal rights to all its citizens, including, without limitation, its Arab citizens residing in Israel, as well as to live in peace with its neighbors. Its Declaration of Independence expressly embodies these very principles, as set forth below:

> WE APPEAL - in the very midst of the onslaught launched against us now for months - to the Arab inhabitants of the State of Israel to preserve peace and participate in the upbuilding of the State on the basis of full and equal citizenship and due representation in all its provisional and permanent institutions.

> WE EXTEND our hand to all neighboring states and their peoples in an offer of peace and good neighborliness, and appeal to them to establish bonds of cooperation and mutual help with the sovereign Jewish people settled in its own land. The State of Israel is prepared to do its share in a common effort for the advancement of the entire Middle East.

However, instead of heeding these calls and honoring the recommendations of Resolution 181, many Arab residents of Israel, in coordination with the armed forces of four neighboring and some more distant Arab states, attacked the Jews in Israel, seeking, as they stridently declared, to force them into the sea[624]. It is astounding that so many years later, even after the resounding victory in the 1967 War, the PLO and later Hamas still have[625] as their express goals the elimination of the Jewish State of Israel. It is foolhardy not to take these terrorist entities at their word. Similarly, it is foolish to disregard all of the educational, indoctrination, training, and propaganda efforts and financial resources devoted to terrorism, malicious maiming of people and destruction of property, and outright murder. Substantial resources are also devoted to rewarding the wrongdoers and inventing and perpetuating false myths of victimhood or otherwise excusing or masking these misdeeds.

The enduring, albeit mostly cold, peace treaties with Egypt and Jordan and the new warm ones with the growing adherents to the Abraham Accords all begin with one immutable principle, to wit: recognition of the existence and legitimacy of each party by the other. Absent this fundamental existential fact, there is no genuine peace agreement.

Thus, all of the calls for continuing negotiations and compromises with the PA and Hamas, using so-called land-for-peace formulations, have little chance of success and, perhaps, even promote continuing failures to achieve real peace. After all, why take that fateful step at all when the kleptocracies in control of the PA and Hamas areas continue to make an extraordinary living out of continuing the farce of negotiations without end and playing hard to get without accountability or consequence?

---

[624] See, for example, AIM TO OUST JEWS PLEDGED BY SHEIKH; Head of Moslem Brotherhood Says U.S., British 'Politics' Has Hurt Palestine Solution, by Dana Adams Schmidt, in New York Times, dated August 1, 1948, which reports Sheikh Hassan el-Bana, head of the Moslem Brotherhood, largest of the extremist Arab nationalist organizations, declared in an interview in Cairo that day: "If the Jewish state becomes a fact, and this is realized by the Arab peoples, they will drive the Jews who live in their midst into the sea."

[625] As noted above, despite assurances that the PLO Charter would be amended to recognize the existence and legitimacy of the State of Israel, this never in fact occurred.

There is also the internecine warfare among the various factions that inhabit the PA and Hamas controlled areas that are vying with each other for power and their share of the corruption pie.

Khaled Abu Toameh, a noted and award-winning Israeli Arab journalist, who covers Palestinian affairs for the Jerusalem Post and is also a distinguished fellow at the Gatestone Institute, analyzed and wrote[626] about the dysfunction of the PA, as follows:

- The truth, however, is that neither the Palestinian Authority leadership nor the Palestinian people is ready for statehood. And the responsibility for that fact lies squarely with the ruthless and failed Palestinian leaders.

- The Palestinian bid to obtain UN recognition of a Palestinian state comes at a time when the PA appears to be losing control over some parts of the West Bank, where gunmen belonging to several groups have replaced the Palestinian security forces... [and] are responsible not only for terrorist attacks against Israel, but also the growing scenes of anarchy and lawlessness....

- Abbas himself has long been praising and glorifying Palestinians who carry out terrorist attacks....

- Abbas, who is unable (and unwilling) to rein in a few hundred gunmen in two major Palestinian cities in the West Bank, wants the United Nations, its member states and the rest of the world to believe that he is ready to run a state of his own.

- If Abbas cannot send his officers to confiscate an M-16 rifle from an unruly gunman in Jenin or Nablus, how

[626] The Palestinians and the World Do Not Need Another Corrupt, Failed Terrorist Arab State, Khaled Abu Toameh, at the Gatestone Institute, dated September 13, 2022.

can he be trusted to prevent the future Palestinian state from turning into a launching pad for regional terrorism?

- Abbas wants the UN to grant the Palestinians the status of full member state, but cannot provide any guarantees that the aspired-for state would not be turned into a terror entity that is armed and funded by Iran's regime[627] and its proxies.

- Abbas wants the UN to recognize "Palestine" as a state when he literally has no control over half of the Palestinians... If Abbas dares to go to the Gaza Strip, Hamas will hang him at the entrance to the area on charges of "collaboration" with Israel.

- Abbas is seeking full UN recognition at a time when he continues to block general elections for the PA, arrests and intimidates his political opponents, refuses to share power with other Palestinians and muzzles freedom of expression.

- More than they need a state, the Palestinians need good leadership. They need to rid themselves of the corrupt leaders who have deprived them of international aid and led them from one disaster after the other since the early 1970s, when the PLO was expelled from Jordan for undermining the kingdom's sovereignty.

- The Palestinians' biggest tragedy by far has been failed leadership and more failed leadership. It radicalizes them toward Islamic fundamentalism and deprives them of elections, freedom of expression and international aid. The UN member states would be

---

[627] Indeed, this already occurring, as proclaimed by the supreme leader of the Iranian terrorist regime, Khamenei. See, Iran's Khamenei praises arms supplies to Palestinians against 'tumor' Israel, at Al Arabiya, dated 5/23/2020.

doing a great service to the Palestinians if they asked Abbas about the absence of freedom of speech and a functioning parliament under his regime.

- They would also be doing the Palestinian people a huge service if they asked Abbas about torture in Palestinian Authority prisons and the continuing crackdown by his security forces on human rights activists and journalists. And they should definitely ask him what measures he has taken to end financial and administrative corruption in the PA.

- These issues are more pressing for the Palestinians than another worthless document by the UN recognizing a fictitious Palestinian state that is already marked by the intrusion of other brutal radical Islamist dictatorships.

In addition to these glaring deficiencies, there is also the culture of Jew hatred that has been promoted and reinforced with rewards designed to inculcate the people from a very young age with Jew hatred and foster terrorism against Israel. The offensive indoctrination of young children, requiring them to pledge themselves, including giving up their own lives, to harm Jews is nothing less than child abuse. Is it any wonder that 93% of the Palestinian Arabs polled hold antisemitic views[628]?

The indoctrination of young and old continues, despite commitments to purge textbooks of antisemitism and to stop demonizing Israel. The Pay to Slay program, honoring of terrorist murderers (including by naming schools, streets and buildings in their memory), and celebrations and handing out of candies when Jews, including children, are murdered are abominable. These odious practices that are promoted and

[628] Poll: 93% of Palestinians hold anti-Jewish beliefs, by Rebecca Shimoni Stoil, at The Times of Israel, dated 5/13/2014.

extolled by the PA should shock the conscience of everyone, including those in the US and EU who support the PA and Hamas. Yet, instead of denouncing them and imposing severe consequences for this kind of reprehensible conduct, there is condonation through silence or even the offering of excuses; all while, in effect, continuing to fund the miscreant behavior.

Contrast this with the UAE and the genuine affirmative measures it has taken to eliminate antisemitic materials from school texts and to reorient the curricula so that Israel is no longer demonized. Other signatories are doing so as well. This may help explain the growing tourism, investments and business relations that are tangible results of the Abraham Accords. Egypt and Jordan have not dedicated themselves to this kind of deprogramming to undo the harmful indoctrination of their people. While the Egyptian and Jordanian peace agreements have yielded peace and security cooperation (especially under President Abdel Fattah el-Sisi, of Egypt), the kind of positive derivative developments, resulting from an in-depth, all-embracing and warm peace arrangement that is not just at the leadership level, are as yet missing under these peace agreements, unlike the Abraham Accords.

We hope and pray that, one day soon, responsible parties in the PA controlled areas and Gaza will genuinely seek peace. Until then, the threats to peace must be identified and dealt with in a rational and resolute manner.

IX.

UN SECURITY COUNCIL RESOLUTION 242 (1967) AND 338 (1973)

UN Security Council Resolution 242[629] is often cited in support of specious claims that Israel must unconditionally surrender all areas lying beyond the 1949 Armistice Demarcation Line[630], popularly known as the Green Line, in Judea and Samaria, including the eastern part of Jerusalem.

Like so many pronouncements that are stridently declared with righteous certainty, this, too, is a false and baseless claim. While there are some nuances that must be understood before drawing any conclusions about what Resolution 242 does or does not stand for, it is indisputable that it neither requires all such areas be surrendered nor that it be done unconditionally.

The text of 242 is not lengthy. It is introduced by three short paragraphs of precatory language that are much like whereas clauses in a preamble to the operative portions of a resolution. The first expresses the Security Council's continuing concern with the grave situation in the Middle East. It appears to be a virtuous attitude, but unfortunately, not one backed up by salutary actions that might have prevented the 1967 war from erupting. After all, where was the UN when it came time to enforcing Israel's right to freedom of navigation in the Gulf of Aqaba and through the Straits of Tiran? Egypt had committed a recognized Casus Belli by illegally blocking Israel's transit of

---

[629] Resolution 242 (1967), dated November 22, 1967, which was adopted unanimously by the UN Security Council.
[630] Israel-Jordan Armistice Agreement, dated April 3, 1949.

ships through the Gulf. Moreover, when Egypt unilaterally demanded withdrawal of the UN peacekeeping force on the border between Egypt and Israel, the UN Secretary-General just complied, precipitating the 1967 War.

Be that as it may, the next paragraph emphasizes the inadmissibility of the acquisition of territory by war and the need to work for a just and lasting peace in which every State in the area can live in peace. These are noble sentiments, and expressing them in the abstract, as the resolution purports to do, has little probative value. In this regard, it should be noted that the provision does not reference Israel or any other particular State in this general and frankly simplified statement of principle, which lacks any explanation or nuance. To better understand the actual principle, reference should be made to Article 2 (4) of the UN Charter, which provides:

> All Members shall refrain in their international relations from the threat or use of force against the territorial integrity or political independence of any state, or in any other manner inconsistent with the Purposes of the United Nations.

It must also be recognized that this principle cannot be read in isolation from the other provisions of the UN Charter, including, most importantly, Article 51, which provides:

> Nothing in the present Charter shall impair the inherent right of individual or collective self-defense if an armed attack occurs against a Member of the United Nations, until the Security Council has taken measures necessary to maintain international peace and security.

In essence, self-defense is an exception to the general principle against the use of force, and there is no absolute prohibition, under International Law, against its use under any and all circumstances.

Thus, as the operative provisions of the resolution demonstrate, the stated principle of no acquisition of territory by war really has no applicability to Israel in the circumstances at issue. Indeed, if it were so, then the Security Council would have ordered an unconditional return to the pre-war lines, as it did in other resolutions relating to other conflicts[631]. It didn't do so here because the principle, as properly applied to the circumstances at issue, was not actually violated by Israel.

Interestingly, it was applicable to two of the other states which caused the 1967 war, Egypt and Jordan. Egypt had conquered Gaza in 1948, and Jordan had conquered Judea and Samaria, including the eastern part of Jerusalem. As discussed above, Jordan then illegally annexed the area and made it a part of what was formerly known as Trans-Jordan because prior to this time, in the Mandatory period, it was only located in the area across the Jordan from Israel. As constituted from 1948 through 1967, it occupied both sides of the Jordan, and it called its illegal conquests of eastern and other parts of Jerusalem, as well as Judea and Samaria, the West Bank of its unified State.

Israel's retaking of the area of Judea and Samaria, including the eastern and other parts of Jerusalem, is not a violation of the principle against the acquisition of territory by war for a number of cogent reasons[632]. First of all, the 1967 war was a defensive war by Israel, not an offensive war for the purpose of conquest. Hence, it is not the sort of prohibited use of force covered by the principle. Since the underlying use of force was not prohibited (it was legal and justifiable self-defense), the principle, therefore,

---

[631] See Resolution 242 Revisited: New Evidence on the Required Scope of Israeli Withdrawal, by Eugene Kontorovich, in the Chicago Journal of International Law, Volume 16, Number 1, dated June 1, 2015 and the examples cited therein. See, for example, General Assembly Resolution 62/243 (March 14, 2008) calling for the immediate, complete and unconditional withdrawal of all Armenian forces from all the occupied territories in Azerbaijan.

[632] Ibid. See also The Acquisition of Territory in International Law, by Robert Y. Jennings (Manchester University Press-1963), at pages 52-56.

doesn't apply. Secondly, the area retaken belongs to Israel, as discussed above. Thus, it was merely retaking its own land, not conquering it from others. Indeed, as noted above, the aggressor state, Jordan, which precipitated the war in which Israel was required to defend itself, had actually been the one that illegally conquered the area, as noted above. It would be absurd to suggest that the robber State, which stole the land by force, should be rewarded for starting another war to conquer additional territory with the return of the land it originally stole. In point of fact, 242 does not do so, as more fully discussed below. Thirdly, the use of force by a State to take control of a claimed territory does not, in and of itself, invalidate that State's title to that territory. In essence, it's not the conquest that establishes the title; rather, it is the validity of the pre-existing right to the title. Furthermore, when dealing with a claim to title to a State's own territory, even if it's being governed by another State at the time, the use of force, as a matter of self-help, to reclaim it is not a matter of international law; rather, it may be viewed as an internal matter.

There are then set forth two sets of affirmations that are the substance of the resolution. This is the operative part of the resolution. The first affirms the need for a just and lasting peace in the Middle East, consistent with the UN Charter. This is said to include the following:

(i) Withdrawal of Israel armed forces from territories occupied in the recent conflict; and

(ii) Termination of all claims or states of belligerency and respect and acknowledgement of the sovereignty, territorial integrity and political independence of every State in the area and their right to live in peace within secure boundaries free from threats or acts of force.

The precise language of each provision was negotiated and has genuine meaning as attested to by the parties who were involved. This is not just a matter of interpretation or nuance. It goes to the heart of the agreement that was achieved and resulted in the passage of 242, which cannot be ignored if 242 is to have any legitimate meaning and import. With respect to clause (i) above, the drafters of 242 have left a marvelous record of their intent in drafting 242 as they did, which is summarized below.

1. Lord Caradon (Hugh M. Foot), the UK's representative to the UN and chief drafter of 242, explained:

> Much play has been made of the fact that we didn't say "the" territories or "all the" territories. But that was deliberate. I myself knew very well the 1967 boundaries and if we had put in the "the" or "all the" that could only have meant that we wished to see the 1967 boundaries perpetuated in the form of a permanent frontier. This I was certainly not prepared to recommend[633].

In an interview on the subject, Caradon said the following[634]:

> Q. The basis for any settlement will be United Nations Security Council Resolution 242, of which you were the architect. Would you say there is a contradiction between the part of the resolution that stresses the inadmissibility of the acquisition of territory by war and that which calls for Israeli withdrawal from "occupied territories," but not from "the occupied territories"?
>
> A. I defend the resolution as it stands. What it states, as you know, is first the general principle of inadmissibility of the acquisition of territory by war. That means that you can't justify holding onto territory merely because you

---

[633] Institute for the Study of Diplomacy, *U.N. Security Council Resolution 242*, pg. 13, qtd. in *Egypt's Struggle for Peace: Continuity and Change, 1967-1977*, Yoram Meital, pg. 49.
[634] *Journal of Palestine Studies*, "An Interview with Lord Caradon," Spring - Summer 1976, pgs 144-45

conquered it. We could have said: well, you go back to the 1967 line. But I know the 1967 line, and it's a rotten line. You couldn't have a worse line for a permanent international boundary. It's where the troops happened to be on a certain night in 1948. It's got no relation to the needs of the situation.

Had we said that you must go back to the 1967 line, which would have resulted if we had specified a retreat from all the occupied territories, we would have been wrong. In New York, what did we know about Tayyibe and Qalqilya? If we had attempted in New York to draw a new line, we would have been rather vague. So what we stated was the principle that you couldn't hold territory because you conquered it, therefore there must be a withdrawal to – let's read the words carefully – "secure and recognized boundaries." The can only be secure if they are recognized. The boundaries have to be agreed; it's only when you get agreement that you get security. I think that now people begin to realize what we had in mind – that security doesn't come from arms, it doesn't come from territory, it doesn't come from geography, it doesn't come from one side domination the other, it can only come from agreement and mutual respect and understanding.

Therefore, what we did, I think, was right; what the resolution said was right and I would stand by it. It needs to be added to now, of course. ... We didn't attempt to deal with [the questions of the Palestinians and of Jerusalem] then, but merely to state the general principles of the inadmissibility of the acquisition of territory by war. We meant that the occupied territories could not be held merely because they were occupied, but we deliberately did not say that the old line, where the troops happened to be on that particular night many years ago, was an ideal demarcation line.

401

In an interview on the MacNeil/Lehrer Report, Caradon said[635]:

> We didn't say there should be a withdrawal to the '67 line; we did not put the "the" in, we did not say "all the territories" deliberately. We all knew that the boundaries of '67 were not drawn as permanent frontiers, they were a cease-fire line of a couple of decades earlier... We did not say that the '67 boundaries must be forever.

Caradon is also quoted as saying[636]:

> It would have been wrong to demand that Israel return to its positions of 4 June 1967 because those positions were undesirable and artificial. After all, they were just the places the soldiers of each side happened to be the day the fighting stopped in 1948. They were just armistice lines. That's why we didn't demand that the Israelis return to them and I think we were right not to ...

In an interview on Kol Israel radio, Caradon said[637]:

> Q. This matter of the (definite) article which is there in French and is missing in English, is that really significant?
>
> A. The purposes are perfectly clear, the principle is stated in the preamble, the necessity for withdrawal is stated in the operative section. And then the essential phrase which is not sufficiently recognized is that withdrawal should take place to secure and recognized boundaries, and these words were very carefully chosen: they have to be secure and they have to be recognized. They will not be secure unless they are recognized. And that is why one has to work for agreement. This is essential. I would defend absolutely what we did. It was not for us to lay down exactly where the border should be. I know the 1967 border very well. It

---

[635] MacNeil/Lehrer Report, March 30, 1978.

[636] *Daily Star* (Beirut), June 12, 1974. Qtd. in *Myths and Facts*, Leonard J. Davis, pg. 48:

[637] Kol Israel radio, February 1973, qtd. on Web site of Israeli Ministry of Foreign Affairs:

is not a satisfactory border, it is where troops had to stop in 1947, just where they happened to be that night, that is not a permanent boundary...

2. Eugene Rostow, a legal scholar and former dean of Yale Law School, was the US Undersecretary of State for Political Affairs, who helped draft 242. In a Telegram[638] from the Department of State to the U.S. Interests Section of the Spanish Embassy in the United Arab Republic, his conversations with Soviet Ambassador Anatoly Dobrynin are summarized as follows:

> Rostow said ... resolution required agreement on "secure and recognized" boundaries, which, as practical matter, and as matter of interpreting resolution, had to precede withdrawals. Two principles were basic to Article I of resolution. Paragraph from which Dobrynin quoted was linked to others, and he did not see how anyone could seriously argue, in light of history of resolution in Security Council, withdrawal to borders of June 4th was contemplated. These words had been pressed on Council by Indians and others, and had not been accepted.
>
> ... the question remained, "To what boundaries should Israel withdraw?" On this issue, the American position was sharply drawn, and rested on a critical provision of the Armistice Agreements of 1949. Those agreements provided in each case that the Armistice Demarcation Line "is not to be construed in any sense as a political or territorial boundary, and is delineated without prejudice to rights, claims or positions of either party to the Armistice as regards ultimate settlement of the Palestine question." ... These paragraphs, which were put into the agreements at Arab insistence, were the legal foundation for the

---

[638] Proceedings of the 64th annual meeting of the American Society of International Law, 1970, pgs 894-9.

controversies over the wording of paragraphs 1 and 3 of Security Council Resolution 242, of November 22, 1967. ...

The agreement required by paragraph 3 of the resolution, the Security Council said, should establish "secure and recognized boundaries" between Israel and its neighbors "free from threats or acts of force," to replace the Armistice Demarcation Lines established in 1949, and the cease-fire lines of June, 1967. The Israeli armed forces should withdraw to such lines, as part of a comprehensive agreement, settling all the issues mentioned in the resolution, and in a condition of peace.

On this point, the American position has been the same under both the Johnson and the Nixon Administrations. The new and definitive political boundaries should not represent "the weight of conquest," both Administrations have said; on the other hand, under the policy and language of the Armistice Agreements of 1949, and of the Security Council Resolution of November 22, 1967, they need not be the same as the Armistice Demarcation Lines.

...

This is the legal significance of the omission of the word "the" from paragraph 1 (I) of the resolution, which calls for the withdrawal of Israeli armed forces "from territories occupied in the recent conflict," and not "from the territories occupied in the recent conflict." Repeated attempts to amend this sentence by inserting the word "the" failed in the Security Council. It is therefore not legally possible to assert that the provision requires Israeli withdrawal from all the territories now occupied under the Cease-Fire Resolutions to the Armistice Demarcation Lines.

Rostow wrote in the Jerusalem Post as follows[639]:

> Security Council Resolutions 242 and 338 ... rest on two principles, Israel may administer the territory until its Arab neighbors make peace; and when peace is made, Israel should withdraw to "secure and recognized borders," which need not be the same as the Armistice Demarcation Lines of 1949. ...

> The omission of the word "the" from the territorial clause of the Resolution was one of its most hotly-debated and fundamental features. The U.S., Great Britain, the Netherlands, and many other countries worked hard for five and a half months in 1967 to keep the word "the" and the idea it represents out of the resolution. Motions to require the withdrawal of Israel from "the" territories or "all the territories" occupied in the course of the Six Day War were put forward many times with great linguistic ingenuity. They were all defeated both in the General Assembly and in the Security Council. ...

> Those who claim that Resolution 242 is ambiguous on the point are either ignorant of the history of its negotiation or simply taking a convenient tactical position.

Rostow also wrote in The New Republic[640] as follows:

> Five-and-a-half months of vehement public diplomacy in 1967 made it perfectly clear what the missing definite article in Resolution 242 means. Ingeniously drafted resolutions calling for withdrawals from "all" the territories were defeated in the Security Council and the General Assembly. Speaker after speaker made it explicit that Israel was not to be forced back to the "fragile" and "vulnerable" Armistice Demarcation Lines, but should

---

[639] *Jerusalem Post*, "The truth about 242," Nov. 5, 1990.
[640] *The New Republic*, "Resolved: are the settlements legal? Israeli West Bank policies," Oct. 21, 1991.

retire once peace was made to what Resolution 242 called "secure and recognized" boundaries, agreed to by the parties. In negotiating such agreements, the parties should take into account, among other factors, security considerations, access to the international waterways of the region, and, of course, their respective legal claims.

Rostow further wrote in the New York Times[641] as follows:

Security Council Resolution 242, approved after the 1967 war, stipulates not only that Israel and its neighboring states should make peace with each other but should establish "a just and lasting peace in the Middle East." Until that condition is met, Israel is entitled to administer the territories it captured – the West Bank, East Jerusalem and Gaza Strip – and then withdraw from some but not necessarily all of the land to "secure and recognized boundaries free of threats or acts of force."

Rostow was prolific on the subject and also wrote in the Wall Street Journal[642] as follows:

... Resolution 242 establishes three principles about the territorial aspect of the peace-making process:

1) Israel can occupy and administer the territories it occupied during the Six-Day War until the Arabs make peace.

2) When peace agreements are reached, they should delineate "secure and recognized" boundaries to which Israel would withdraw.

3) Those boundaries could differ from the Armistice Demarcation Lines of 1949.

[641] *The New York Times*, "Don't strong-arm Israel," Feb. 19, 1991.
[642] *The Wall Street Journal*, "Peace still depends on the two Palestines," April 27, 1988

In an article appearing in the Institute for National Strategic Studies[643], Rostow wrote as follows:

> The second territorial provision of Resolution 242 is that while Israel should agree to withdraw from some of the territories it occupied in 1967, it need not withdraw from all those territories. The Resolution states that there should be "withdrawal of Israeli's armed forces from territories occupied in the recent conflict." Five and a half months of vigorous diplomacy, public and private, make it very clear why the wording of the sentence took the form it did. Motion after motion proposed to insert the words "the" or "all the" before the word "territories." They were all defeated, until finally the Soviet Union and the Arab states accepted the language as the best they could get.

3. Arthur J. Goldberg, the United States representative to the United Nations at the time, also helped draft Resolution 242. In the course of the discussions, which preceded the adoption of Resolution 242, he said the following[644]:

> To seek withdrawal without secure and recognized boundaries ... would be just as fruitless as to seek secure and recognized boundaries without withdrawal. Historically, there have never been secure or recognized boundaries in the area. Neither the armistice lines of 1949 nor the cease-fire lines of 1967 have answered that description... such boundaries have yet to be agreed upon. An agreement on that point is an absolute essential to a just and lasting peace just as withdrawal is...

Goldberg wrote in American Policy Interests[645] as follows:

---

[643] Institute for National Strategic Studies, "The Future of Palestine," November 1993.
[644] S/PV. 1377, p. 37, of November 15, 1967.
[645] American Foreign Policy Interests-1988.

The resolution does not explicitly require that Israel withdraw to the lines that it occupied on June 5, 1967, before the outbreak of the war. The Arab states urged such language; the Soviet Union proposed such a resolution to the Security Council in June 1967, and Yugoslavia and other nations made a similar proposal to the special session of the General Assembly that followed the adjournment of the Security Council. But those views were rejected. Instead, Resolution 242 endorses the principle of the "withdrawal of Israeli armed forces from territories occupied in the recent conflict" and juxtaposes the principle that every state in the area is entitled to live in peace within "secure and recognized boundaries." ...

The notable omissions in language used to refer to withdrawal are the words the, all, and the June 5, 1967, lines. I refer to the English text of the resolution. The French and Soviet texts differ from the English in this respect, but the English text was voted on by the Security Council, and thus it is determinative. In other words, there is lacking a declaration requiring Israel to withdraw from the (or all the) territories occupied by it on and after June 5, 1967. Instead, the resolution stipulates withdrawal from occupied territories without defining the extent of withdrawal. And it can be inferred from the incorporation of the words secure and recognized boundaries that the territorial adjustments to be made by the parties in their peace settlements could encompass less than a complete withdrawal of Israeli forces from occupied territories.

Goldberg also wrote in the *Christian Science Monitor*[646] as follows:

... all parties are apparently in agreement that the basis for negotiations would be Resolutions 242 and 338 adopted by the UN Security Council. These resolutions, although often

---

[646] *Christian Science Monitor*, "Middle East peace prospects," July 9, 1985.

referred to in the news media, are inadequately analyzed or explained. I shall attempt to provide a measure of enlightenment.

Does Resolution 242 as unanimously adopted by the UN Security Council require the withdrawal of Israeli armed forces from all of the territories occupied by Israel during the 1967 war? The answer is no. In the resolution, the words the and all are omitted. Resolution 242 calls for the withdrawal of Israeli armed forces from territories occupied in the 1967 conflict, without specifying the extent of the withdrawal. The resolution, therefore, neither commands nor prohibits total withdrawal.

If the resolution is ambiguous, and purposely so, on this crucial issue, how is the withdrawal issue to be settled? By direct negotiations between the concerned parties. Resolution 242 calls for agreement between them to achieve a peaceful and accepted settlement. Agreement and acceptance necessarily require negotiations.

Any ambiguity in this regard has been resolved by Resolution 338, unanimously adopted by the Security Council on Oct. 22, 1973. Resolution 338 reaffirms Resolution 242 in all its parts and requires negotiations between the parties concerned aimed at establishing a just and durable peace in the Middle East.

Is Resolution 242 self-executing? The answer is no. Negotiations are necessary to put flesh on the bones of the resolution, as Resolution 338 acknowledges.

Is Israel's withdrawal confined to "minor" border rectifications? No. Resolution 242 reaffirms the right of every area state 'to live in peace within secure and recognized boundaries free from threats or acts of force.'

How are secure and recognized boundaries to be achieved to enable every state to live in peace free from threats or acts of force? By negotiation, agreement, and accepted settlement.

As to the specific matter of Jerusalem, Goldberg wrote in a letter to the New York Times[647], as follows:

Resolution 242 in no way refers to Jerusalem, and this omission was deliberate. I wanted to make clear that Jerusalem was a discrete matter, not linked to the West Bank.

In a number of speeches at the U.N. in 1967, I repeatedly stated that the armistice lines fixed after 1948 were intended to be temporary. This, of course, was particularly true of Jerusalem. At no time in these many speeches did I refer to East Jerusalem as occupied territory.

4. Baron George-Brown (George A. Brown) was the British Foreign Secretary at the time and also helped draft 242. He said the following:

[Resolution 242] does not call for Israeli withdrawal from "the" territories recently occupied, nor does it use the word "all". It would have been impossible to get the resolution through if either of these words had been included, but it does set out the lines on which negotiations for a settlement must take place. Each side must be prepared to give up something: the resolution doesn't attempt to say precisely what, because that is what negotiations for a peace-treaty must be about.

Brown noted in the Jerusalem Post[648] as follows:

I have been asked over and over again to clarify, modify or improve the wording, but I do not intend to do that. The phrasing of the Resolution was very carefully worked out,

[647] New York Times, "What Goldberg didn't say," letters, March 12, 1980:
[648] *Jerusalem Post*, Jan. 23, 1970, qtd. on Web site of Israeli Ministry of Foreign Affairs

and it was a difficult and complicated exercise to get it accepted by the UN Security Council.

I formulated the Security Council Resolution. Before we submitted it to the Council, we showed it to Arab leaders. The proposal said "Israel will withdraw from territories that were occupied," and not from "the" territories, which means that Israel will not withdraw from all the territories

5. J. L. Hargrove was the Senior Adviser on International Law to the United States Mission to the United Nations at the time. Appearing before a hearing *on the Middle East before the Subcommittee of the House Committee on Foreign Affairs*, he is quoted as saying[649] the following:

The provision of Resolution 242 which bears most directly on the question which you raised, Congressman, is subparagraph (1) of paragraph 1 of the resolution, which envisages "withdrawal of Israeli armed forces from territories occupied in the recent conflict."

The language "from territories" was regarded at the time of the adoption of the resolution as of high consequence because the proposal put forward by those espousing the Egyptian case was withdrawal from "the territories." In the somewhat minute debate which frequently characterizes the period before the adoption of a United Nations resolution, the article "the" was regarded of considerable significance because its inclusion would seem to imply withdrawal from all territories which Israel had not occupied prior to the June war, but was at the present time occupying.

---

[649] *Hearings on the Middle East before the Subcommittee of the House Committee on Foreign Affairs*, 92nd Congress, 1st Session 187 (1971), qtd. in "The illegality of the Arab attack on Israel of October 6, 1973," by Eugene Rostow in the *American Journal of International Law*.

Consequently, the omission of "the" was intended on our part, as I understood it at the time and was understood on all sides, to leave open the possibility of modifications in the lines which were occupied as of June 4, 1967, in the final settlement.

6. Mr. Michael Stewart, Secretary of State for Foreign and Commonwealth Affairs, in reply to a question in Parliament[650] on November 17th, 1969, said as follows:

Viscount Lambton: "What is the British interpretation of the wording of the 1967 Resolution? Does the Right Honourable Gentleman understand it to mean that the Israelis should withdraw from all territories taken in the late war?"

Mr. Stewart: "No, Sir. That is not the phrase used in the Resolution. The Resolution speaks of secure and recognized boundaries. These words must be read concurrently with the statement on withdrawal."

On December 9th, 1969, Stewart replied to a question on the subject as follows[651]:

As I have explained before, there is a reference, in the vital United Nations Security Council Resolution, both to withdrawal from territories and to secure and recognized boundaries. As I have told the House previously, we believe that these two things should be read concurrently and that the omission of the word 'all' before the word 'territories' is deliberate."

7. Mr. Joseph Sisco, Assistant Secretary of State, in an interview on Meet the Press[652], said the following:

---

[650] Arab-Israeli Dispute, HC Deb 17 November 1969, vol 791 cc843-6
[651] Foreign Affairs, Hansard, Volume 793, debated on December 9, 1969. Column 261
[652] NBC "Meet the Press", on July 12, 1970.

That Resolution did not say 'withdrawal to the pre-June 5 lines'. The Resolution said that the parties must negotiate to achieve agreement on the so-called final secure and recognized borders. In other words, the question of the final borders is a matter of negotiations between the parties.

8. Mr. Vasily Kuznetsov, the USSR representative to the UN, in the debate that preceded the adoption of Resolution 242, said the following[653]:

> ... Phrases such as 'secure and recognized boundaries'. What does that mean? What boundaries are these? Secure, recognized – by whom, for what? Who is going to judge how secure they are? Who must recognize them? ... There is certainly much leeway for different interpretations which retain for Israel the right to establish new boundaries and to withdraw its troops only as far as the lines which it judges convenient.

9. Mr. Geraldo de Carvalho Silos, the Brazilian representative to the UN, speaking in the Security Council after the adoption of Resolution 242, said the following[654]:

> We keep constantly in mind that a just and lasting peace in the Middle East has necessarily to be based on secure, permanent boundaries freely agreed upon and negotiated by the neighboring States."

Turning now to the second affirmation in 242, it deals with:

(a) Guaranteeing freedom of navigation through international waterways in the area;

(b) Achieving a just settlement of the refugee problem; and

---

[653] S/PV. 1373, p. 112, of November 9, 1967.
[654] S/PV. 1382, p. 66, of November 22, 1967.

(c) Guaranteeing the territorial inviolability and political independence of every State in the area.

Subparagraph (b) is another provision that must be closely read and understood. Notice it does not refer only to Arab refugees. The USSR had attempted to limit 242 only to Palestinian refugees[655], but it was unsuccessful.

As Arthur Goldberg, the US ambassador to the UN, who was directly involved in negotiating 242, said[656]:

> The Resolution addresses the objective of 'achieving a just settlement of the refugee problem.' This language presumably refers both to Arab and Jewish refugees, for about an equal number of each abandoned their homes as a result of the several wars...

242 would thus include a just settlement of the problem of all refugees, including the Jewish ones. Notice, too, there is no qualifier that relates the problem to Israel only and premises the problem on the nature of its creation. Rather, it is a neutral and universal reference to the refugee problem.

There have been resolutions introduced in Congress which sought to address the problem of Jewish as well as Arab refugees. One example is House Resolution 838[657], expressing the sense of the House of Representatives regarding the creation of refugee populations in the Middle East, North Africa, and the Persian Gulf region as a result of Human Rights violations. It notes:

1. Jews and other ethnic groups have lived mostly as minorities in the Middle East, North Africa, and the

---

[655] S/PV. 1382 p. 117 of November 22,1967.
[656] Goldberg, Arthur J., "Resolution 242: After 20 Years." The Middle East: Islamic Law and Peace (U.S. Resolution 242: Origin, Meaning and Significance.) National Committee on American Foreign Policy; April 2002. (Originally written by Arthur J. Goldberg for the American Foreign Policy Interests on the occasion of its twentieth anniversary in 1988).
[657] H. Res. 838, dated October 7, 2004, introduced at the 108th Congress.

Persian Gulf region for more than 2,500 years, more than 1,000 years before the advent of Islam;

2. A comprehensive peace in the region will require the resolution of all outstanding issues through bilateral and multilateral negotiations involving all concerned parties;

3. While the discussion of refugees in the Middle East generally centers on Palestinian refugees, nevertheless, the estimates indicate that, as a result of the 1948 war in which numerous Arab armies attacked the newly-founded State of Israel, more Jews (approximately 850,000) were displaced from Arab countries than were Palestinians (approximately 726,000) from Israel;

4. The United States is concerned about the mistreatment, violation of rights, forced expulsion, and expropriation of assets of minority populations in general, and in particular, former Jewish refugees displaced from Arab countries;

5. A Memorandum of Understanding signed by President Jimmy Carter and Israeli Foreign Minister Moshe Dayan on October 4, 1977, refers to the need for a solution to the problem of Arab refugees and Jewish refugees;

6. After negotiating the Camp David Accords, the Framework for Peace in the Middle East, President Jimmy Carter stated in a press conference on October 27, 1977 that Palestinians have rights . . . obviously there are Jewish refugees . . . they have the same rights as others do;

7. In an interview with Israeli television immediately after the issue of the rights of Jews displaced from Arab lands was discussed at Camp David II in July 2000, President Clinton stated clearly that [t]here will have to be some sort of international fund set up for the refugees. There is, I think, some interest, interestingly enough, on both sides, in also having a fund which compensates the Israelis who

415

were made refugees by the war, which occurred after the birth of the State of Israel. Israel is full of people, Jewish people, who lived in predominantly Arab countries who came to Israel because they were made refugees in their own land.

8. The Senate, in a Senate Resolution 76, 85th Congress, agreed to January 29, 1957, noted that individuals in Egypt who are tied by race, religion, or national origin with Israel, France, or the United Kingdom have been subjected to arrest, forced exile, confiscation of property, and other punishments although not charged with any crime;

9. The House, in a Concurrent Resolution 158, 85th Congress, noted that the Government of Egypt had initiated a series of measures against the Jewish community, that many Jews were arrested as a result of such measures, that, beginning in November 1956, many Jews were expelled from Egypt, and that the Jews of Egypt faced sequestration of their goods and assets and denial or revocation of Egyptian citizenship, and resolves that the treatment of Jews in Egypt constituted persecution on account of race, religious beliefs, or political opinions, further resolving that these issues should be raised by the United States either in the United Nations or by other appropriate means; and

10. Congress, in Section 620 of H.R. 3100, 100th Congress, found that with the notable exceptions of Morocco and Tunisia, those Jews remaining in Arab countries continue to suffer deprivations, degradations, and hardships, and continue to live in peril and that Congress calls upon the governments of those Arab countries where Jews still maintain a presence to guarantee their Jewish citizens full civil and human rights, including the right to lead full Jewish lives free of fear and to emigrate if they so choose.

The Congressional resolution went on to say that the seminal United Nations resolution on the Arab-Israeli conflict and other international initiatives refer generally to the plight of refugees and do not make any distinction between Palestinian and Jewish refugees, including the following:

(a) United Nations Security Council Resolution 242 of November 22, 1967, calls for a just settlement of the refugee problem without distinction between Palestinian and Jewish refugees. Justice Arthur Goldberg, the United States delegate to the United Nations at that time, has pointed out that a notable omission in 242 is any reference to Palestinians, a Palestinian state on the West Bank or the PLO. The resolution addresses the objective of achieving a just settlement of the refugee problem. This language presumably refers both to Arab and Jewish refugees, for about an equal number of each abandoned their homes as a result of the several wars;

(b) The Madrid Conference, which was first convened in October 1991 and was co-chaired by United States President George H.W. Bush and President of the U.S.S.R. Mikhail Gorbachev, included delegations from Spain, the European Community, the Netherlands, Egypt, Syria, and Lebanon, as well as a joint Jordanian-Palestinian delegation. In his opening remarks before the January 28, 1992, organizational meeting for multilateral negotiations on the Middle East in Moscow, United States Secretary of State James Baker made no distinction between Palestinian refugees and Jewish refugees in articulating the mission of the Refugee Working Group, stating that [t]he refugee group will consider practical ways of improving the lot of people throughout the region who have been displaced from their homes; and

(c) The Roadmap to a Permanent Two-State Solution to the Israeli-Palestinian Conflict, in referring to an agreed, just, fair, and realistic solution to the refugee issue, uses language that is equally applicable to all persons displaced as a result of the conflict in the Middle East.

The Resolution also declares that Egypt, Jordan, and the Palestinians have affirmed that a comprehensive solution to the Middle East conflict will require a just solution to the plight of all refugees, as evidenced by the following:

(1) The 1978 Camp David Accords, the Framework for Peace in the Middle East, includes a commitment by Egypt and Israel to work with each other and with other interested parties to establish agreed procedures for a prompt, just and permanent resolution of the implementation of the refugee problem. The Treaty of Peace between Israel and Egypt, signed at Washington, D.C. March 26, 1979, in addition to general references to United Nations Security Council Resolution 242 as the basis for comprehensive peace in the region, provides in Article 8 that the Parties agree to establish a claims commission for the mutual settlement of all financial claims, including those of former Christian and Jewish refugees displaced from Egypt; and

(2) Article 8 of the Treaty of Peace Between the State of Israel and the Hashemite Kingdom of Jordan, done at Arava/Araba Crossing Point October 26, 1994, entitled Refugees and Displaced Persons recognizes the massive human problems caused to both Parties by the conflict in the Middle East. The reference to massive human problems in a broad manner suggests that the plight of all refugees of the conflict in the Middle East includes Jewish refugees from Arab countries.

The Resolution concludes by expressing the sense of the House of Representatives, including as follows:

(1) the United States deplores the past and continuing violation of the human rights and religious freedoms of minority populations in Arab countries; and

(2) with respect to Jews and Christians displaced from Arab countries, for any comprehensive Middle East peace agreement to be credible, durable, and enduring, constitute an end to conflict in the Middle East, and provide for finality of all claims, the agreement must address and resolve all outstanding issues, including the legitimate rights of all peoples displaced from Arab countries; and

The House of Representatives also urges the President to:

(1) instruct the United States Representative to the United Nations and all United States representatives in bilateral and multilateral fora that, when the United States considers or addresses resolutions that allude to the issue of Middle East refugees, the United States delegation should ensure that—

(A) the relevant text refers to the fact that multiple refugee populations have been caused by the Arab-Israeli conflict; and

(B) any explicit reference to the required resolution of the Palestinian refugee issue is matched by a similar explicit reference to the resolution of the issue of Jewish refugees from Arab countries.

(2) make clear that the United States Government supports the position that, as an integral part of any comprehensive peace, the issue of refugees and the mass violations of

human rights of minorities in Arab countries must be resolved in a manner that includes:

(A) redress for the legitimate rights of all refugees displaced from Arab countries; and

(B) recognition of the fact that Jewish and Christian property, schools, and community property was lost as a result of the Arab-Israeli conflict.

There is a later similar Senate Resolution[658], as well. It adds some additional details, which are cogent and summarized below:

1. It notes that the international definition of a refugee clearly applies to Jews who fled the persecution of Arab regimes, where a refugee is a person who "owing to a well-founded fear of being persecuted for reasons of race, religion, nationality, membership of a particular social group, or political opinion, is outside the country of his nationality, and is unable to or, owing to such fear, is unwilling to avail himself of the protection of that country" (Convention relating to the Status of Refugees, done at Geneva July 28, 1951, and entered into force April 22, 1954 (189 UNTS 150)).

2. It reports the United Nations High Commissioner for Refugees (UNHCR) determined that Jews fleeing from Arab countries were refugees that fell within the mandate of the UNHCR. Thus, in his first statement as newly elected High Commissioner, Mr. Auguste Lindt, at the January 29, 1957, meeting of the United Nations Refugee Fund (UNREF) Executive Committee in Geneva, stated, "There is already now another emergency problem arising. Refugees from Egypt. And there is no doubt in my mind that those of those

[658] S. Res. 85, dated February 16, 2017, 110th Congress.

refugee who are not able or not willing to avail themselves of the protection of the Government of their nationality, they might have no nationality or they may have lost this nationality, or, for reasons of prosecution may not be willing to avail themselves of this protection, fall under the mandate of the High Commissioner." (United Nations High Commissioner for Refugees, Report of the UNREF Executive Committee, Fourth Session–Geneva 29 January to 4 February, 1957); and Dr. E. Jahn, on behalf of the United Nations High Commissioner for Refugees, wrote to Daniel Lack, Legal Adviser to the American Joint Distribution Committee, stating, "I refer to our recent discussion concerning Jews from Middle Eastern and North African countries in consequence of recent events. I am now able to inform you that such persons may be considered prima facie within the mandate of this Office." (United Nations High Commissioner for Refugees Document No. 7/2/3/Libya);

3. Like the House Resolution noted above, it states that the seminal United Nations resolution on the Arab-Israeli conflict and other international initiatives refer generally to the plight of "refugees" and do not make any distinction between Palestinian and Jewish refugees, such as United Nations Security Council Resolution 242 of November 22, 1967, calls for a "just settlement of the refugee problem" without distinction between Palestinian and Jewish refugees. It goes on to say that this is evidenced by the failed attempt by the United Nations delegation of the Soviet Union to restrict the "just settlement" mentioned in Resolution 242 solely to Palestinian refugees (S/8236, discussed by the Security Council at its 1382nd meeting on November 22, 1967, notably at paragraph 117, in the words of Ambassador Kouznetsov of the Soviet Union),

which signified the international community's intention of having the resolution address the rights of all Middle East refugees. It also records the statement by Justice Arthur Goldberg, the Chief Delegate of the United States to the United Nations at that time, who was instrumental in drafting the unanimously adopted United Nations Resolution 242, where he observed, "The resolution addresses the objective of 'achieving a just settlement of the refugee problem'. This language presumably refers both to Arab and Jewish refugees, for about an equal number of each abandoned their homes as a result of the several wars.".

It should be noted that 242 also does not expressly reference any right of return at all, let alone an absolute one. Indeed, 242 did not even mention so-called Palestinians or use the term West Bank. In point of fact, the language calls for a just settlement of the refugee problem. This could take many forms, including a financial settlement or resettlement in situ or elsewhere[659].

Resolution 242 concludes with two requests. One is for the UN Secretary-General to designate a Special Representative to facilitate the States' achieving a peaceful and accepted settlement in accordance with the provisions and principles in the resolution. The other is for the Secretary-General to report to the Security Council on the progress of the efforts made by the Special Representative as soon as possible.

242 did not succeed primarily because, while Israel accepted it, the Arab States and PLO rejected it. The leaders of thirteen Arab

---

[659] In this regard, it should be noted that the Jericho Resolutions discussed below, which was a prelude to Jordan's annexation of the so-called West Bank and granting of Jordanian citizenship and voting rights to the Arab residents of the area, contains an expression of thanks to the Arab states for their efforts in connection with the attempted so-called liberation (i.e.: conquest) of Palestine (meaning, Israel; it was named Palestine in Mandatory times and hence the reference to Palestinian Arab refugees hereinafter noted) and generous assistance and support to Palestinian Arab refugees.

States gathered at a meeting in Khartoum, Sudan, from August 29 to September 1, 1967, and issued the infamous '3 No's', to wit: No peace with Israel, No negotiations with Israel, and No recognition of Israel.

The PLO issued its own statement on November 23, 1967[660], which in detail rejected the right of Israel to exist and to have permanent, recognized, safe, and secure borders. It recognized that 242 didn't require withdrawal from all territories and rejected it. Indeed, as noted above, it flat-out rejects Israel entirely, no matter the borders. In essence, it claims all of Israel, which it demands, must fundamentally have an Arab character and be the homeland for the so-called Palestinian people. It also demands a mythical right of return. It correctly views 242 as permitting some other resolution, such as resettlement in Arab countries. It denies Israel freedom of navigation in international waterways like the Gulf of Aqaba. It also notes 242 does not reference the existence of a Palestinian people or provide them with a right to self-determination. However, there is no concomitant demand for statehood in the so-called West Bank. This is not a glaring omission. Rather, it is consistent with the PLO Charter, which is just against Israel's existence. It views Arabs residing in the former Mandatory Palestine area merely as the vanguard of the pan-Arab movement and not as a separate and independent people.

It is important to recognize that the fundamental issue is Israel's existence, which vitiates any attempts at a meaningful negotiation. Unless Israel's existence is unconditionally accepted, there is no basis for constructive talks leading to a real and enduring peace agreement. Don't be misled by the PA, Hamas and their allied propaganda organs, which seek to obfuscate the problem. It's just that simple; each side must accept and recognize the existence of the other. Israel has done

---

[660] A copy of the text is reproduced at israeled.org, under the title: 1967.11.23-PLO Rejection UNSC 242.

so, as demonstrated by the Oslo Accords. However, the PA and Hamas have not actually reciprocated. Despite solemn undertakings to do so, the PA has never actually amended its founding document to remove the abhorrent provisions that are antithetical to genuine recognition of Israel's right even to exist; and, for that matter, neither has Hamas. Moreover, in practice, they advocate the elimination of Israel and promote terrorism against Israel. Their inability, in word and deed, unqualifiedly to agree to Israel's right to exist was and remains the single greatest impediment to peace between Israel and them.

On one of the holiest days of the Jewish calendar, Yom Kippur, October 6th, in 1973, Egypt and Syria attacked Israel. After Israel successfully defended itself and turned the battle around, including crossing the Suez Canal on the Egyptian front and threatening Damascus on the Syrian front, in an almost anti-climactic exercise, the Security Council adopted Resolution 338 (338) on October 22, 1973.

The succinct text of 338 was all of three paragraphs. The first called for a ceasefire in place. The second called on the parties, immediately after the ceasefire, to negotiate the implementation of 242 in all of its parts. The third decided that immediately and concurrently with the ceasefire, negotiations start between the parties, under appropriate auspices, aimed at establishing a just and durable peace in the Middle East. It was adopted by fourteen votes (including the US and USSR) to none, with China not participating in the voting.

338 did nothing of substance other than call for a ceasefire in place. It did not call upon the parties to withdraw to pre-war lines. It did not change 242; it merely referenced it and called upon the parties to negotiate its implementation. In this regard, it should be noted that the use of force to retake one's own territory is not per se a violation of the UN Charter, as discussed above.

However, it is important to remember that Israel's presence in the Sinai did not occur in a vacuum. It was within the context of a legally permitted defensive war. In 1967, Egypt had illegally closed the Straits of Tiran, an international waterway (connecting the Gulf of Aqaba with the Red Sea), massed troops on the border with Israel and, with its allied Arab nations, besieged Israel, as a prelude to unleashing a war aimed at the destruction of Israel and conquest of its sovereign territory[661]. This precipitated the Six Day War, which was miraculously won by Israel and resulted in Israel's legal conquest of the Sinai.

Therefore, Israel was well within its legal rights to defend against the Egyptian onslaught in 1973. In this sense, Egypt and, by extension, Israel were accorded the same treatment of not being ordered to pre-war lines. It was within their rights, as sovereign States, to use self-help, even if that meant the use of force, to assert their sovereign rights. Thus, if Egypt's rights were respected by the UN, then a fortiori Israel's rights must be respected.

Israel certainly had the right to defend itself when attacked by Jordan in the Six Day War and, in the process, retake and liberate all of Jerusalem and Judea and Samaria. Jordan had illegally conquered these areas in an aggressive war of conquest in 1948 and then illegally annexed them, as more fully discussed below.

---

[661] See, for example, Arab Threats Against Israel, at Six Day War.org, (CAMERA).

X.

THE JERICHO RESOLUTIONS OF 1948, PLO ORIGINAL NATIONAL CHARTER OF 1964, AND ISRAEL-JORDAN PEACE TREATY OF 1994

After Jordan illegally conquered Judea and Samaria, including the eastern portion of Jerusalem, in 1948, it sought to legitimize its conquest of these areas, which it proceeded to rename the West Bank of Jordan.

On December 1, 1948, it organized a conference in Jericho that was attended by representatives of numerous constituencies within these areas. In attendance were the Mayors of Hebron, Bethlehem and Ramallah and they, together with the other attendees, adopted what became known as the Jericho Resolutions. Among other things, the Jericho Resolutions confirmed the desire of the Arab residents of the so-called West Bank to be immediately annexed to Jordan. Subsequent conferences occurred in Ramallah and then Nablus, which declared their support for the Jericho Resolutions.

Thus, instead of seeking to have an independent state in these areas Jordan conquered and occupied, they ceded any rights they may have had to Jordan. The Arab (not Jewish[662]) residents of these areas were granted Jordanian citizenship (including voting rights) in December of 1949. Indeed, Jews were forcibly expelled form the areas conquered by Jordan and their homes were seized and synagogues demolished.

---

[662] See Article 3, subsection (2), of Jordanian Law No. 6 of 1954 on Nationality.

The Arab residents of the so-called West Bank participated in the Jordanian Parliamentary elections of April 1950 and were equally represented in the Jordanian Parliament. On April 24, 1950, the newly elected Parliament, noting it represented both the eastern bank of the Jordan as well as the western one (i.e., the so-called West Bank), formally approved annexation of the areas of Judea and Samaria conquered by Jordan, including the eastern part of Jerusalem. It unified them into the single state of Jordan, as confirmed by the King of Jordan.

The Palestinian Liberation Organization (PLO) recognized Jordan's sovereignty over the so-called West Bank. It expressly provided in Article 24 of its original Charter of 1964 that it exercised no sovereignty over the West Bank that belonged to Jordan. Interestingly, it also expressly declared it exercised no sovereignty over Gaza. Its professed twin goals were Arab unity and the destruction of Israel.

Therefore, whatever rights the Arab residents of Judea and Samaria, including the eastern part of Jerusalem, may have had to assert any claim to sovereignty over these areas were fully vested in Jordan. Even the PLO acknowledged they were ceded to Jordan[663].

---

[663] As discussed above, the PLO and by extension the PA make no genuine claim to the so-called West Bank and Gaza. Their sole professed goal is to act as a tool of the Arab people to destroy Israel; not to create a separate Palestinian Arab state for themselves in the area of the so-called West Bank and Gaza. It is obvious, based on their own admissions, why the PA has rejected all the peace initiatives that would have resulted in their recognizing Israel's right to exist within secure borders. It's not their goal and, with malice aforethought, they renounced any claim to the West Bank and Gaza; and ceded the West Bank to Jordan. The conceptual fantasies of land for peace are a projection of some well-meaning and some less than well-meaning impractical thinkers, who can't get past their fixation with their own logic, as opposed to taking their interlocutors at their word, no matter how irrational it may seem to them. Farley encountered David Aaron Miller, a State Department Middle East expert, when he was in law school. Farley asked him about the PLO's stated goal of destroying Israel and how did that jive with the State Department's advocating land for peace, which they kept on rejecting. He was stunned when Miller agreed with his understanding of the conundrum and yet, nevertheless, went on to say that the status quo was unacceptable. That may be

Like any other sovereign state, Jordan could negotiate and barter away sovereignty over any of its land. Thus, when it entered into a Treaty of Peace, dated October 26, 1994, with the State of Israel and, in Article 3, demarcated the international boundary between Israel and Jordan as the Jordan River, it effectively ceded sovereignty over its former West Bank to Israel. In this regard, the provisions of Article 2, Section 1, requiring that, in particular, each party recognize and respect each other's sovereign territorial integrity and political independence, are cogent. Jordan recognized Israel's sovereignty over the land within its borders as demarcated by the Treaty. Section 2 of Article 3 of the Treaty declares the boundary noted above is the

---

so, but as turned out, life under the PA is worse than it was prior to the PA. It must also be recognized that there is presently one actual Palestinian Arab state in existence, known as Jordan. There are also two more self-governing putative states; one in Gaza, governed by Hamas and another located in portions of Judea and Samaria, governed by the PA.. In addition, there are 20 other Arab States. Consider, how obnoxious the PA/Hamas program truly is in theory and practice: (1) pursue the goal of wiping out the only Jewish state, while mouthing euphemisms in English to disguise the Jew hatred and dropping the mask when addressing Arab audiences in the vernacular; (2) teach Jew hatred in schools and educate the children to murder Jews without mercy; (3) pay money to those who slay Jews or to their families and honor the predators; (4) pander to western audiences and secure funding in what amounts to an extortion scheme; (5) continue to blame the victimized Jews and falsely call them the aggressor; (6) invoke all sorts of antisemitic tropes and canards taken from the Nazi and Soviet propaganda playbooks that promote spreading the big lie; and (7) murder or maim Americans with impunity and engage with enemies of the US and Israel, including the terrorist Iranian regime and their proxies, Russia and China. Yet, despite it all, the US, in effect, condones and rewards the PA and indirectly even Hamas, by providing funding to the areas, people and entities that are effectively under their control (which is often siphoned off at least in part by members of the PA and Hamas or their affiliates) or to meet obligations they would otherwise have, as more fully discussed in this book. In the case of Hamas, in addition to all the other concerns outlined above, there is also the legal prohibition against providing funding to Hamas, as a US designated terrorist organization. Nevertheless, members of Hamas reportedly receive benefits from the development funds the US provides for Gaza, as well as, being on the payroll of UNRWA or the schools it maintains in Gaza, which is funded in no small measure by the US. Some members of Congress are seeking to stop this abuse, as noted below. The law of unintended consequences must be honored and much like the medical ethic, the first order of business should be to do no harm. Change that is driven by ideological imperatives is usually not mindful of these practical lessons and it is unfortunately not atypical to cause catastrophic failure.

permanent secure, and recognized international border between Israel and Jordan[664]. There is no explicit carveout for any claim of sovereignty by so-called Palestinians to the West Bank. The Treaty, in Section 3 of Article 3, goes on to say the parties recognize the international boundary, as well as each other's territory, territorial waters, and airspace, as inviolable and will respect and comply with them. Furthermore, Section 6 of Article 3 provides each party is to deploy on its side of the international boundary upon exchange of the instruments of ratification of the Treaty, which occurred during King Hussein's first official visit to Israel on November 1, 1994 (after approval by Israel Knesset and ratification by Jordan's Chamber of Deputies). These sovereign rights are not made subject to or otherwise expressly qualified by any claims of so-called Palestinians.

The purpose of this analysis is not to assert that Israel's claim to sovereignty over Jerusalem is established on this basis. As described above in this book, Israel's historical and legal right to sovereignty over Jerusalem is unchallengeable. Rather, it is intended to bring to light the lack of any objectively sound foundation for the myriad of false and baseless assertions that have been made by the propaganda organs of Hamas, the PA and their allies.

In this regard, the propaganda efforts made to disassociate Jews from Israel (including Jerusalem, Judea and Samaria) and promote a false narrative about members of the Arab nation residing in Israel being the so-called indigenous people of Palestine are ludicrous. This is little more than brazen and obnoxious cultural appropriation of Jewish history in order to foster a false image of victimhood. The menu of propaganda devices includes:

---

[664] The provison continues, without prejudice to the status of any territories that came under Israel military government control in 1967.

1. Impudent and false assertions of Temple denial and claims that the Dome of the Rock is a mosque, eventhough the existence of the Jewish Holy Temple on the site of the Dome of the Rock, on the Temple Mount, is indisputable. In this regard, it should be noted that even the Waqf[665] under the control of the notorious antisemite Haj Amin Husseini, in charge of the Temple Mount under the British Mandate, including when the brochure entitled, 'A Brief Guide to Al-Haram Al-Sharif' was published in 1925, not only didn't deny the existence of the Jewish Holy Temple on the site of the Dome of the Rock, it confirmed it; but more on this below.

2. Cruel assertions of Holocaust denial and inappropriate use of Holocaust terminology, including calling Jews, Nazis and fatuous claims of genocide. This is a part of a crafty and wicked attempt to hijack Jewish history and, like classic predators, project a false image of victimhood, in order to conceal their aggressive intent and defend their terrorist acts, violence and murders. Thus, they hide behind a charming and deceptive facade and ruthlessly use others to get what they want. Besides Jew hatred, it's also about an insatiable desire for power and need to begrudge it to others, no matter how much suffering is caused, including to their proclaimed ostensible constituency. Like classic predators, they must feel dominant, winning and in control and they use a variety of tactics to gratify their drive for power. As a part of their tools of deception, they claim to be victims, usually of the people they're in fact victimizing; they fake sincerity and make emotional appeals. Fake photos of children suffering are often used as a part of these emotional displays. It is not unusual for the photos to be photo-shopped, out of context or lifted from other conflicts, unrelated to Israel, such as Syria or elsewhere. These tools are used to

---

[665] The Religious Muslim Trust, known in English as, the Supreme Moslem Council, in charge of the Temple Mount.

manipulate, influence, charm, disarm and seduce others. The promoters of these frauds pretend to be innocent and ignorant. *An integral* part of their tactics is to isolate and gaslight their target, Jews. They also seek to elicit in the target unmerited guilt and doubt about the target's own sanity. Ignoring rules when that suits their purposes is the rule. By the same token demanding that others punctiliously follow their contrived rules is also a part of their hypocritical creed. Make no mistake about it, they will say or do anything to get what they want. Relentlessly managing their public image to appear as the victim is also a critical part of their scheme. This is aided by a compliant media and intersectional relationships that have been nurtured, greased with funding and enforced by cancellation (a weapon wielded by the cancel culture of the intersectional clique to enforce party discipline) that brooks no independent thinking or scrutiny and requires ideological purity. This is so, no matter what the actual facts and circumstances may be; even if the narrative to be repeated and reinforced is patently false. Remember, a propagandist's bag of tricks include omitting relevant facts or just flat out propagating untruths.

3. Absurd claims about being the indigenous people of Israel, going back as far as the Canaanites (which is ironic, inasmuch as the Canaanites were themselves illegal occupiers, as noted above).

4. Falsely claiming that Old Testament and New Testament figures are Muslim and Palestinians, as they mischaracterize the term (see below); despite scriptural evidence, including in the Quran, to the contrary.

5. Identifying themselves as the indigenous people of the Land of Israel, predating the Jews, despite the fact that they are not and coining the term Palestinians as a part of this canard. In this regard it should be noted that:

(a) The Jewish people inhabited the Land of Israel for well more than 1,400 years prior to the time when Hadrian sought to erase them from history, after the Bar Kochba revolt. Hadrian plowed over the remains of the Jewish Holy Second Temple on the Temple Mount, erecting a pagan temple to worship himself and Jupiter and renaming Jerusalem Aelia Capitalina. He also renamed the ancient Land of Israel, Palestine, harking back to the Philistines (in Hebrew Plishtim, which ironically means invaders). As an aside, the Philistines, by Hadrian's time had long ceased to have a presence in the Land of Israel.

(b) It was the Jewish people who were actually referred to as Palestinians, during the period of the British Mandate, until the Jewish State of Israel was reestablished and they became known as Israelis.

(c) As summarized below, the history of the Arab presence in Israel began with their invading the Land in approximately 627-628 and occupying it, as even their own historical documents admit, as detailed below.

The appellation 'Palestinian' was adopted in the 1960s, in an attempt culturally to acquire the Jewish people's indigenous attachment to the land.

Historically, neither Muslim nor pre-Muslim Arabs have an entrenched attachment to the Land of Israel prior to Omar's invading and occupying it in the Seventh Century C.E. While there were itinerant Arab traders and nomadic Bedouins, who

432

visited Israel, there was no real and significant permanent settlement, prior to that time.

The Roman name Palestine (Syria Palaestina was the original Latin term used) is not mentioned in the Quran or the Bible.

Furthermore, the Arabic language does not have the letter 'p'. Thus, Arabs living in Israel, Judea, and Samaria typically pronounce the word Palestine as 'Falastin'. This anomaly exemplifies the absurdity of the myth promulgated by the KGB-inspired PLO that the Arabs residing in Judea, Samaria and the rest of Israel were the indigenous Palestinian people.

The PLO's 1964 Charter[666] actually contradicts this false narrative. It adopts a more prosaic application of the term Palestinian to refer not to the Palestinian people; but rather to the 'Arab' people residing in the geographic area of Palestine. Thus, the preamble to the PLO Charter begins:

We, the Palestinian 'Arab' people.

It goes on to provide, as follows:

Article 1.

Palestine is an Arab homeland bound by strong national ties to the rest of the Arab Countries and which together form the large Arab homeland.

Article 2.

Palestine with its boundaries at the time of the British Mandate is a regional indivisible unit.

Article 3.

---

[666] See, for example, Soviet Russia, The Creator of the PLO and the Palestinian People, by Wallace Edward Brand, dated 1/28/2014, at ssrn.com, The Soviet-Palestinian Lie, by Judith Bergman, at the Gatestone Institute.org, dated 10/16/2016 and The KGB and Anti-Israel Propaganda Operations, by Eli Cohen and Elizabeth Boyd, in Informing Science, the International Journal of Emerging Transdiscipline, Volume 22 (2019).

> The Palestinian Arab people has the legitimate right to its homeland and is an inseparable part of the Arab Nation. It shares the sufferings and aspirations of the Arab Nation and its struggle for freedom, sovereignty, progress and unity.

Notice that the actual term used is 'Arab' Palestinian people, not simply Palestinian people. This theme is continued in Article 3 of the Charter, which refers to the 'Palestinian Arab people'. The need for the qualifier was obvious then because there were also Jewish people who lived in the geographic area it defined as Palestine, as noted in Article 7.

Article 6 is even more definitive about the lack of distinctiveness of the Arabs living in Palestine. It provides, as follows:

> Article 6.

> The Palestinians are those Arab citizens who were living normally in Palestine up to 1947, whether they remained or were expelled. Every child who was born to a Palestinian parent after this date whether in Palestine or outside is a Palestinian.

Lest there be any misunderstanding about the PLO's goals in relation to Judea and Samaria (including east Jerusalem), then held by Jordan, or Gaza, then held by Egypt, the Charter makes it absolutely clear that it has no claim thereto, as follows:

> Article 24.

> This Organization does not exercise any regional sovereignty over the West Bank in the Hashemite Kingdom of Jordan, on the Gaza Strip or the Himmah Area. Its activities will be on the national popular level in the liberational, organizational, political and financial fields.

In essence, the terms Filastin or Falastin in Arabic and Palestinian in English were artificially contrived by the PLO and their KGB handlers, and they just simply declared it as a label for the group of Arabs they purported to represent.

As an aside, the Romanized name Palestine, which was derived from the Hebrew word, Pelishtim, means invader, an apt name for the Greek tribes that invaded the Land of Israel in Biblical times. The same can be said for the more recent Arab invaders, as well.

The place name given by Hadrian to the Land of Israel did not create a new people; Jews continued to live there. Indeed, until the Jewish State of Israel was reestablished in 1948, the Jews in Israel were the ones usually referred to as Palestinians, and the Arab residents referred to themselves as Arabs. Until the Six Day War in 1967, the Arab residents of the so-called West Bank of Jordan were more likely to refer to themselves either as Jordanian or Arabs. The propaganda myth of the so-called Palestinian people began to take hold in earnest post 1967 Six Day War in response to Israel's liberation of these areas. At its essence, the PLO is a movement defined by its goal of eliminating the State of Israel; it is not about creating one of its own.

6. Proclaiming Palestinian peoplehood, despite the fact that until 1967, Arabs residing in the portions of Judea and Samaria conquered by Jordan in 1949 referred to themselves as Arabs and were Jordanian citizens. Prior to that time, there was no assertion of separate people-hood; rather, the emphasis was on being a part of the Arab people, as noted above.

7. Disingenuous claims of an ancient so-called Palestinian (Arab) settlement in Israel that constituted the majority from time immemorial and which was displaced by the Jewish so-

called settlers or colonialists have long been debunked[667].
This is nothing more than an invented myth that is contrary
to the truth. For example, in 1714, Hadriana Relandi, a
mapmaker and scholar from Utrecht, published Palestina ex
monumentis veteribus illustrata. The book documents
Relandi's trip to Palestine in 1695-96, in which he surveyed
around 2,500 places that were mentioned in the Tanakh
and/or Mishna. He also carried out a census of the people
living in these places, discovering that not a single
settlement in Palestine had an Arabic name. In fact, the place
names were derived from the Hebrew, Roman, and Greek
languages. There were, of course, no signs of any definable,
sizable sub-group of Arabs called Palestinians in 1714.
Relandi found that most of the inhabitants of Palestine were
Jews, along with some Christians and a few Bedouins.
Nazareth was home to fewer than a thousand Christians,
while Jerusalem held 5,000 people, mostly Jews. Gaza was
home to around 250 Jews and about the same number of
Christians. The only exception was Nablus, where around 120
Muslims lived, along with a handful of Samaritans whose
ancestors belonged to the northern tribes of Israel.

---

[667] See, for example, Debunking the claim that "Palestinians" are the indigenous people
of Israel, by Daniel Grynglas, in the Jerusalem Post, dated 5/12/2015 and Were the Arabs
Indigenous to Mandatory Palestine, by Sheree Roth, in Middle East Quarterly, Fall-
2016, at meforum.org. See also, From Time Immemorial, by Joan Peters (HarperCollins-
1984); The Year the Arabs Discovered Palestine, by Daniel Pipes, in Middle East Review,
dated Summer 1989; From Time Immemorial, by Joan Peters, by Daniel Pipes, in
Commentary, dated July 1984; and The Rape of Palestine, by William B. Ziff (originally
published by Longmans, Green and Co.-1938 and in paperback by Martino Publishing-
2009).

This, as well as other historical data[668], controvert the claim that there was a huge indigenous population of so-called Palestinians, which had been there from time immemorial, a fallacious myth[669]. Remember, too, that the Arab conquest and occupation of the land only first occurred in the 7th century. Before then, there was no significant Arab or Muslim presence. As an aside, the Peel Commission reported in 1937[670] that a "shortage of land" was "due less to the amount of land acquired by Jews than to the increase in the Arab population". To put this in perspective, from the 16th century through most of the 19th century, prior to the improvement in the economy due to Jewish capital investments and the upsurge in Jews returning to Israel, the total population of the area of the Mandate hovered around

---

[668] Including, for example, the demographic history of Jerusalem, which confirms that ever since the end of the 19th century, Jews constituted the majority of the population of Jerusalem. See, for example, Jerusalem: The City's Development from a Historical Perspective, at embassies.gov.il, dated 2/3/1997 and The Population Of Palestine prior to 1948, at mideastweb.org.

[669] See, for example, Arab immigration into pre-State Israel: 1922-1931, by Fred M. Gottheil (College of Commerce and Business Administration, University of Illinois at Urbana-Champaign-1971), From Time Immemorial, by Joan Peters (HarperCollins-1984), Whose Palestine, by Rael Isaac, in Commentary Magazine, dated July 1986 and The Rape of Palestine, by William B. Ziff (originally published by Longmans, Green and Co.-1938 and in paperback by Martino Publishing-2009).

[670] The Palestine Royal Commission Report, July 1937, known as the Peel Report, at page 254. It also reports the objective reality that: "The Arab population shows a remarkable increase since 1920, and it has had some share in the increased prosperity of Palestine. Many Arab landowners have benefited from the sale of land and the profitable investment of the purchase money. The fellaheen are better off on the whole than they were in 1920. This Arab progress has been partly due to the import of Jewish capital into Palestine and other factors associated with the growth of the National Home. In particular, the Arabs have benefited from social services which could not have been provided on the existing scale without the revenue obtained from the Jews." Ascribing the "remarkable increase" in the Arab population only to birthrate and not considering the real likelihood of, at the very least, the likely material effect of immigration in producing this otherwise miraculous result, is indicative of the underlying bias. While the Peel Commission couldn't help but view this increase as remarkable, the objective of the British and its Commission was to defeat the purpose of the Mandate, the reestablishment of a Jewish State..

only approximately a few hundred thousand people, including Jews, Christians, and Muslims[671].

As to Jerusalem, the venerable 1906 Baedeker Travel Guide to Palestine and Syria[672] notes the population of Jerusalem was estimated to be approximately 60,000. The Guide went on to report that this consisted of about 7,000 Muslims, 40,000 Jews and 13,000 Christians. Thus, an approximately two-thirds majority of the population of Jerusalem was Jewish at the time.

The source of this sudden increase in the population of Mandatory Palestine has been a subject of dispute. Some argue it was virtually all due to natural increase. However, available demographic statistics[673] belie this ideological or politically driven conclusion. Consider, from 1914-1922, the Muslim population in the area of the Palestine Mandate reportedly increased by 12% or approximately 1.5% per year. This rate of increase was significantly higher than the US rate of increase at the time. The rate of increase reported for the period 1922-1931 is 29% or approximately 3.2% per year, more than double the prior rate and almost triple the US rate at the time. Lest there be any misunderstanding, the US population growth statistics include both natural increase due to births and immigration. The reported rate of increase for Muslims in the Mandate area from 1931-1947 was even higher, at 55% or approximately 3.4% per year. By way of comparison, the US annual rate of increase in population averaged 1% or less per annum during the same period.

It is just hard to imagine and nearly impossible to justify a doubling of the Muslim population during this short period of

---

[671] See, Jewish and Non-Jewish Population of Israel/Palestine (1517-Present), at Jewish Virtual Library.org.

[672] Baedeker's Palestine and Syria, Handbook for Travelers, by Karl Baedeker (1906), at page 24.

[673] See, for example, Overview of Palestine's demographics from the 1rst century to the Mandate Era, by Sergio Della Pergole (2001) and Jewish and Non-Jewish Population of Israel/Palestine (1517-Present), at jewishvirtuallibrary.org..

time[674] due only to natural increase. Thus, some amount must be factored in for immigration. The problem is that the British statistics on immigration only considered legal immigration. Moreover, the Peel Commission Report admits that there was no actual census conducted since 1931[675]. Thus, the statement about the source of the increase in population is just mere speculation. Given the institutional bias against factoring in illegal Arab immigration, which likely dwarfed the legal variety, it is no surprise that the Commission would make such an agenda-driven conclusory statement. Hence, there is no absolutely reliable measure of the actual number of Muslim immigrants to the area of the Palestinian Mandate administered by the British. However, to insist that the entire population of so-called Palestinian Muslims was there from time immemorial is patently absurd.

Robert F. Kennedy, a keen and astute observer, reporting, in the Boston Post[676], on his visit to Israel in 1948, wrote:

> From a small village of a few thousand inhabitants, Tel Aviv has grown into a most impressive modern metropolis of over 200,000. They have truly done much with what all agree was very little.

> The Jews point with pride to the fact that over 500,000 Arabs, in the 12 years between 1932 and 1944, came into Palestine to take advantage of living conditions existing in

---

[674] The span of time between one generation and the next is typically a period of 20- 30 years.
[675] Indeed, as William Ziff notes in his book, The Rape of Palestine (Martino Publishing-2009), at page 179, "The [British] Government itself says in relation to its population estimates, 'the precision of these figures is not great'." He cites in footnote 3, the Report by the British Government to the Council of League of Nations on the Administration of Palestine and Transjordan for the Year 1936, at page 236, as the source of this quoted admission. Ziff also notes an understatement of the Jewish population in the reported figures..
[676] See, British Hated by Both Sides, by Robert Kennedy, in the Boston Post.

no other Arab state. This is the only country in the Near and Middle East where an Arab middle class is in existence.

While anecdotal, these impressions are fresh and compelling. This is especially so given the obvious; an attractive locale with favorable economic and living conditions far better than those of neighboring countries and a demonstrable need for employees. There was no rational basis to presume the veracity of the outlandish and biased claim of a monumental increase in the birth rate, which historically would be incredible and anything but natural. As Occam's razor suggests, logically, if there are two competing ideas to explain the same phenomenon, then prefer the simpler one.

Fred Gottheil and others make a most persuasive presentation in support of the conclusion that a significant portion of the increase in the Arab population during the Mandatory period was due to immigration, which was often of the illegal variety[677].

William Ziff[678] provides a detailed account of British malfeasance in executing its duties under the Mandate. It was required to promote the reestablishment of a Jewish State in the area covered by the Mandate. Instead, it frustrated it, including by severely limiting Jewish immigration. It also turned a blind eye to and even encouraged Arab illegal entry by affirmatively prioritizing hiring of Arab employees (even illegal ones) over Jewish employees. The artificial limiting of Jewish immigration also assured that vacant employment slots in the burgeoning economy, financed by Jewish capital investment and energized by new and more productive technology and expertise, had to be filled by Arabs from neighboring countries, attracted to Israel by the opportunities for higher wages, better working conditions

---

[677] The Smoking Gun: Arab Immigration into Palestine, 1922-1931, by Fred M. Gottheil, in the Middle East Quarterly, Winter 2003, pp. 53-64, See also, The Population of Israel, by Roberto Bachi (1974).

[678] The Rape of Palestine, by William B. Ziff (originally published by Longmans, Green and Co.-1938 and in paperback by Martino Publishing-2009).

and higher standard of living. They were able to access the newly created job opportunities because of British misfeasance permitting them to cross the borders into Israel from their home countries. This same *laissez-faire* policy did not apply to Jews, who were either intercepted or later arrested and deported, which was antithetical to the intent and purposes of the Mandate. Indeed, it also violated express provisions of the Mandatory documents, including the 1924 Anglo-American Treaty, in connection therewith, as more fully discussed above[679].

To put this in perspective, the modern metropolis of Tel Aviv was first created by Jews on vacant sand dunes miles out from Jaffa. No one lived there before and yet, so-called Palestinians purport to claim it as their own. Even Jaffa, which had a significant prior existing Jewish presence, was colonized by Arabs and others, as described below.

Ziff also describes many of the incursions and other identifiable occupations by foreigners over the years, which account for most of the non-Jewish residents of the area of Mandatory Palestine, now Israel. These include the following[680]:

1. The 9th century Tulinids brought Turk and African soldiers with them.

---

[679] See discussion of the 1924 Anglo-American Treaty and its applicable provisions in Chapter II above. It is interesting to consider that the approximately 60,000 or more US citizens reportedly residing in Judea and Samaria (see, for example, 15% of settlers are US citizens new research claims, by JTA, in The Times of Israel, dated 8/28/2015 and In 2021 American immigrants again moved to settlements far more than other arrivals, by Judah Ari Gross, in The Times of Israel, dated 8/13/2022). In addition, there are also US citizens residing in Jerusalem on the other side of the so-called green line. They have the legal right to be there as discussed in this book. It is respectfully submitted that this may also be a right protected under US Law. In essence, the Treaty is deemed US Law and the rights thereunder survive, as discussed above.

[680] See, The Rape of Palestine, by William B. Ziff (Martino Publishing-2009), including at pages 368-369 and as noted below.

2. The 10th century Fatamids introduced Berbers, Slavs, Greeks, Kurds and other mercenaries from other locales.

3. 12th century Saladin had Persian conscripts, who he rewarded by settling them in Israel.

4. The 13th century Mamelukes imported Georgian and Circassian troops.

5. In the 14th century, Tartars, Ashiri, Mongols, Kaisaite and Yeminis occupied parts of Israel.

6. In the 19th century, Albanian conqueror Mehmet Ali colonized Jaffa and Nablus with Egyptian and Sudanese soldiers and his son, Ibraham Pasha, also brought in Ethiopians.

7. In the 20th century, tribes from the Hejaz and southern Transjordan immigrated to the Beersheba area[681] and groups of Numidians and Abyssinians, as well as, unaccounted others from Transjordan and from Syria[682] moved to Israel.

In this regard, it should be noted that many of the surnames commonly found among the Arab residents of the PA and Hamas controlled areas refer to or can be traced to places of origin in one of the surrounding Arab countries, including Egypt, Syria, Jordan and Lebanon, as well as, Saudi Arabia, Iraq, Yemen and the Maghreb (North African Arab countries). For example, Yasser

---

[681] A fact that is acknowledged by the British in their Report and General Abstracts of the Census of 1922, at page 4, which reports that don't know how many actually immigrated. The British also admit that whole tribes illegally immigrated but are unaccounted for in the census figures. The British census is, therefore, inherently flawed when it comes to distinguishing between population growth by reason of natural increase and immigration.

[682] See, The Rape of Palestine, by William B. Ziff (Martino Publishing-2009), at pages 247-248.

Arafat was born in Egypt[683]. Hence names like Masri (Egyptian), Tibi (Syrian), Chamys (Bahrainis), Al - Farocki (Iraq), Al - Arge (Morocco), Al - Lubnan (Lebanon), Al – Mogravi (Mugrave = Morocco), Al - G'zir (Algerian), Al – Yemenite (Yemen), Al - Afgani (Afghanistan), Hamati (Hamat, Syria), Autman (Turkey) and Allawi (Syria). It would appear that surnames involving the use of the name al-Palestini or al-Falastin are not listed among those commonly used[684]. Given the pretentious assertions of indigeneity, this would otherwise be extremely surprising, except for the fact that the claim to be the indigenous people of Israel is truly just another unfounded element in the mythical Palestinian false narrative. Indeed, as the surnames in common use evidence and as history indisputably confirms, the roots of most Arab residents are from outside Israel, which is consistent with the history of Israel.

It should also be noted that one of the significant indicia of indigeneity is the existence of ancient graveyards identified with the group claiming indigenous status. Thus, consistent with the ancient Jewish presence in Jerusalem, there is the more than 3,000-year-old Jewish cemetery on the Mount of Olives, with approximately 150,000 or more gravesites[685]. It is reputed to be the most ancient Jewish cemetery in the world. If the so-called Palestinian people existed in Jerusalem prior to the Jewish people, then there should be at least one such major cemetery that is comparable and significantly older[686]. However, there is no such ancient Palestinian graveyard that is older than the Jewish one on the Mount of Olives. The lack of such tangible

---

[683] See, for example, A Brief History of Yaser Arafat, by David Brooks, in The Atlantic, July/August 2002 issue.
[684] See, for example, Most Common Last Names In Palestine, at forebears.io. and Palestinian Surnames, at surnames.es.
[685] See, for example, Israel Mapping Every Grave in 3,000-Year-Old Mount of Olives Necropolis, Associated Press (at Fox News.com), dated1/8/2015 and The Mount of Olives, at jewishvirtuallibrary.org.
[686] While a few older graves (or burial caves) have been found elsewhere in Israel, there is no comparable cemetery that has been identified in Jerusalem that is older.

evidence of a more ancient habitation of the land of Israel is telling.

The myth of the so-called Palestinians was invented and weaponized as a means of undermining the legitimacy of the Jewish people's right to live and have sovereignty over Israel, nothing else. It was not about having a separate state side by side with Israel. It is solely about destroying the Jewish State. Else, why would the PLO cede any claim to the so-called West Bank, including Jerusalem, to Jordan? Why was there no movement to have a separate state of Palestine between 1948 and 1967? Indeed, why did the Arabs located in the portions of Judea and Samaria (including Jerusalem) illegally conquered by Jordan in 1948 and illegally annexed by Jordan in 1949 opt for Jordanian citizenship, as noted above, and not insist on their own state?

Zuheir Mohsen, who was a member of the PLO executive council and head of the as-Sa'qa military wing, explained why as follows[687]:

> The Palestinian people does not exist. The creation of a Palestinian state is only a means for continuing our struggle against the state of Israel for our Arab unity. In reality today there is no difference between Jordanians, Palestinians, Syrians and Lebanese. Only for political and tactical reasons do we speak today about the existence of a Palestinian people, since Arab national interests demand that we posit the existence of a distinct "Palestinian people" to oppose Zionism. Yes, the existence of a separate Palestinian identity exists only for tactical reasons, Jordan, which is a sovereign state with defined borders, cannot raise claims to Haifa and Jaffa, while as a Palestinian, I can undoubtedly demand Haifa, Jaffa, Beer-Sheva and Jerusalem. However, the moment we reclaim our right to

---

[687] In an interview with James Dorsey, which he reported on in the Dutch newspaper Trouw, on March 31, 1977.

all of Palestine, we will not wait even a minute to unite
Palestine and Jordan.

The false narrative of being a separate people that is
conveniently divorced from the rest of the Arab people, as
needed (despite unqualified statements to the contrary, as
discussed above), is also used to divest any responsibility for the
expulsions of Jews from Arab nations in the aftermath of the
1948 War. This is despite the fact that Palestinian Arabs
participated in the war as an integral part of the Arab nations,
seeking to kill the Jewish State at its re-birth and to eliminate the
Jewish people in Israel. Over 850,000 Jews in Arab countries
became refugees, which exceeded the estimated 700,000 Arab
refugees from Israel in 1948[688]. It should also be noted that many
of the Arab refugees from Israel originated from those same Arab
countries where Jews were forced out. This would, of course,
include the Jews forced out of Jerusalem. As discussed above,
Resolution 242 was intended to cover the resolution of all
refugee matters, including both Jewish and Arab refugees. It is
also submitted that the fate of Christians and others forced out
by the PA and Hamas should also be considered as a part of any
overall settlement.

The international community has been silent for too long when
it comes to injustices and human rights violations perpetrated by
the PA and Hamas. Unfortunately, in this world of intersectional
alliances, many fear voicing truths that are contrary to the
prevailing perverted political ethic[689]. Thus, the calculated and
false myths propagated by the PA and Hamas are now a part of

---

[688] See, for example, The Jewish Refugees from Arab Countries: An Examination of Legal
Rights - A Case Study of the Human Rights Violations of Iraqi Jews, by Carole Basri, in
the Fordham International Law Journal, Vol. 26, Issue 3 (2002) and Why Jews Fled the
Arab Countries, by Ya'akov Meron, in the Middle East Quarterly, September 1995, at
pages 47-55. See also, Jewish Refugees from Arab Countries, Arab League Draft Law
regarding Jews in Arab Countries, 1947, by Ami Isserhoff (2007), at zionism-israel.com.
[689] See, for example, Intersectional rhapsody, by Leonard Grunstein, in the Times of
Israel, dated 7/3/2019.

the accepted jargon in most of the media when discussing the so-called Palestinian-Israel conflict.

At the same time, it should be noted that gone is the rubric that framed the conflict as an Arab-Israeli one. This is because there really no longer is a general Arab-Israeli conflict. With the advent of the Abraham Accords and the warm ties that have developed with an expanding group of Sunni Arab countries, in addition to the peace agreements with the neighboring states of Egypt and Jordan, the term is trite and nearly obsolete. These supervening achievements have eclipsed the so-called Palestinian-Israel conflict, which continues to survive on life support, provided, knowingly or unknowingly, by the EU[690], US, and NGOs (many with virtuous-sounding names but obnoxious agendas that promote Jew hatred).

The subtle rhetorical shift from what was termed an 'Arab-Israeli conflict' to one labeled 'Palestinian', which is said to be at the heart of the problems in the Middle East, not only distorts the reality of what drives the conflicts in the region, as discussed above, it also promotes a false narrative that is intended to erase the origin of the conflict. It also ignores the fact that it is a non-Arab Shia nation, Iran, which is at the heart of the existing threats to Israel, the US, and the world, including through its proxies Hezbollah in Lebanon and Hamas in Gaza, as well as its protégé Syria.

How quickly many forget the declared Arab goal of wiping out the Jewish State, in which many Arabs living in Palestine pre-1948 participated as members of the Arab people. The conflict was never about creating an Arab state in what had been called

---

[690] See, for example, The EU's Lethal Obsession with Israel, by Bassam Tawil, at the Gatestone Institute.org, dated 3/9/2023. Among other things, Bassam Tawil describes how the EU helps the PA flout the Oslo Accords, including encouraging illegal land grabs and funding the illegal construction of more than 80,000 housing and other structures in Area C (as of 2022), in disregard of the Oslo Accords, which provide that Area C is under Israeli jurisdiction.

Palestine alongside the Jewish State. It was and, with regard to the PA and Hamas, remains about undermining the legitimacy of Israel and the right of Jews to self-determination in their ancient homeland.

Consider the myth of Temple denial and the nature of the Dome of the Rock. The Dome of the Rock is more fully discussed above. However, set forth below are excerpts taken from the Waqf's own A Brief Guide to Al-Haram Al-Sharif Jerusalem, published in English in 1925, relevant to this subject and a summary analysis thereof. The Guide notes:

> The two principal edifices are the Dome of the Rock, on a raised platform in the middle, and the mosque of al-Aqsa against the south wall.

Notice the Dome of the Rock is not described as a mosque. It is only the Al-Aqsa Mosque that is designated a mosque in the Guide. Notice, too, the location of the Al- Aqsa is described as against the 'south wall', whereas the Dome of the Rock is in the middle of the Temple Mount platform. As detailed above and summarized in the Guide, this is a critical difference because locating the mosque outside of the actual Temple precincts is precisely what Omar intended and his successors more fully effectuated.

The Guide continues as follows:

> Other buildings, which we shall consider later lie dotted about here and there. On the left, along the east wall, the double portals of the Golden Gate appear. On every side, trees break the prospect, which lend a particular charm to the scene. The site is one of the oldest in the world. Its sanctity dates from the earliest (perhaps from pre historic) times.

Some of these buildings have some interesting names and perhaps significance in terms of Islamic traditions regarding the site, as discussed above.

The Guide then expressly and in no uncertain terms rebuts the myth of Temple denial on the Temple Mount, as follows:

'Its identity with the site of Solomon's Temple is beyond dispute'

The brazen lie, asserted by Arafat at Camp David, denying the Jewish Holy Temple was located on the Temple Mount, on the site of the Dome of the Rock, was even disputed by then President Clinton[691]. His successor Mahmoud Abbas, like Arafat, also denied the Jewish connection to the Temple Mount[692]. So too, the Mufti he appointed[693]. Arafat and Abbas are both reputed to be KGB operatives[694]. It is any wonder that neo-Marxist KGB agents, spouting the party's antisemitic line, would have the temerity to spread such outrageous falsehoods. They may clothe themselves in Islam, but their actions betray their lack of commitment to or understanding of classic Islam. Otherwise, they would be ashamed to make such outlandish statements so contrary to indisputable facts and Islamic traditions. In this regard, it should be noted that for all the hype about the centrality of the Temple Mount to Islam, few, if any, of the PA leaders regularly pray there, nor have many leaders of Arab nations actually visited there.

---

[691] See, The Missing Peace, by Dennis Ross (Farrar, Straus and Giroux-2004) at page 694 and Brit Hume interview of Dennis Ross, Fox News Sunday, on April 21, 2002. See also, Books Stones and Ancient Jewish History: A View from Camp David, by David Goodblatt, at page 311 in Historical and Biblical Archeology and the Future, edited by Thomas E. Levy (Routledge-2010)

[692] See, Abbas' Temple Denial, by Dore Gold, dated March 2, 2012, originally published in Israel Hayom and republished at Jerusalem Center for Public affairs and Abbas, Temple Denial and the Distortion of History, by Richard L. Cravatts, in the American Thinker, dated 9/9/2012.

[693] See, Jerusalem Mufti: Temple Mount never housed Jewish Temple, by Ilan Ben Zion, in the Times of Israel, dated 10/25/2015.

[694] See, for example, The KGB's Middle East Files: Palestinians in the service of Mother Russia, by Ronen Bergman, at Ynet news.com, dated 11/4/2016, The KGB's Man, by Ion Mihai Pacepa, in the Wall Street Journal, dated 9/22/2003 and Palestinian President Mahmoud Abbas 'was KGB agent', BBC News, dated 9/8/2016.

This is not intended to disparage the precious souls who choose to pray at the Al-Aqsa Mosque and feel a spiritual connection there, nor is this about infringing on the right of Muslims to pray there. As an aside, it should be noted that non-Muslims are not allowed to visit inside the Al-Aqsa Mosque, which is a Muslim house of worship. Muslims are free to pray at the Al-Aqsa Mosque and everyone's religious freedom is actually protected by law in Israel, unlike in the areas controlled by the PA and Hamas.

It is suggested that much of the uproar and machinations regarding the Temple Mount are inspired by pseudo-Muslims (not pious ones), with political and ideological driven agendas, unrelated to prayer at the Al-Aqsa Mosque. Instead it appears they callously tread in the Al-Aqsa Mosque, clad in shoes, despite the Islamic prohibition against doing so, dressed in inappropriate apparel, like shorts and tee shirts and without head covering. They also play soccer and conduct other non-prayer activities on the Temple Mount, without regard to its sanctity. This includes despoiling the Al-Aqsa Mosque, throwing rocks, setting off explosive devices, breaking windows, arson and other despicable acts. This abusive behavior by fellow Muslims should offend the Muslim authorities in charge of the site. Yet, they don't seem to have taken any actions to prevent a reoccurrence; nor does there appear to be a public outcry against the perpetrators or the laxness of the Muslim authorities. At the same time, there are all sorts of negative reactions, protests and rancor when non-Muslims quietly and reverently pray elsewhere on the Temple Mount. This is wholly inconsistent with the usual religious sensibilities and kindness practiced by those treasuring the sanctity of a site, be it a synagogue, church, mosque, ashram, Buddhist temple or other place of worship, almost anywhere else in the world. In this regard, it is interesting to note that the Ottoman Empire agreed, pursuant to the Treaty of Paris of 1856, the peace agreement entered into at the end of the Crimean War, that Christians and Jews were legally permitted to pray on the

Temple Mount and this practice continued until it was unilaterally ended by the British, during the Mandatory period for purely political reasons[695].

The Guide then goes on to refer to a seminal Jewish link to the Temple Mount, citing Old Testament scripture[696]:

> This, too, is the spot, according to the universal belief, on which "David built there an Altar unto the Lord, and offered burnt offerings and peace offerings".

The pseudo-Islamist Temple deniers should be universally reviled for their impudent rejection of their own religious traditions and beliefs in favor of neo-Marxist propaganda.

The Guide then focuses on Muslim history and its first encounter with the Temple Mount, as follows:

> But, for the purposes of this Guide, which confines itself to the Moslem period, the starting point is the year 637 A.D. In that year the Caliph Omar occupied Jerusalem and one of his first acts was to repair to this site, which had already become sacred in the eyes of the Moslems as the place to which the Prophet was one night miraculously translated.

Notice the reference to that being the year when "Caliph Omar occupied Jerusalem". This was the beginning of the Arab occupation of Jerusalem. This is a striking rebuke to those who falsely assert they, as Arab Muslims, were indigenous to Jerusalem. As the Waqf's own Guide recognizes, the Jews and their Holy Temple on the Temple Mount were there first. This was more than one and one-half millennia before the Arabs arrived and began their occupation of Jerusalem.

---

[695] See Article IX of Treaty of Paris, dated March 30, 1856, as well as, How Great Britain Lost Control of the Temple Mount, by Prof. Meir Loewenberg, Bar –Ilan University, presented at the International Conference on the British White Paper of 1922 on Palestine and the Beginning of the British Mandate-a Century Anniversary, Western Galilee College, Akko, Israel, 6/2/2022, available online at Academia.edu.
[696] II Samuel 24:25.

The Guide then continues:

> The site had long since been neglected. The Caliph and his
> 4,000 followers found little more than desolation and
> rubbish. There were the ruined walls of the Herodian and
> Roman periods, the remains of an early basilica (probably
> on the present site of al-Aqsa), and the bare Rock. Yet from
> this rock had the Prophet, according to tradition, ascended
> to heaven on his steed. So the Caliph ordered a mosque to
> be erected by its side. His orders were executed, and the
> building was seen and described by Bishop Arculf who
> visited Jerusalem about 670 A.D. But no vestige of it
> remains to day, save for the name, "Mosque of Omar"
> which is still, but quite wrongly, sometimes used for the
> Dome of the Rock.

Notice the reference to the remains of Herodian walls. There is
no mention of the wall of buraq. The basilica is probably the
Byzantine one discussed above and, similarly, the mosque on the
site of the Al-Aqsa Mosque visited by Arculf.

Lest there be any doubt about the Dome of the Rock not being a
mosque, the Guide even notes the mischaracterization of the
Dome of the Rock as the Mosque of Omar and puts the matter to
rest by labeling this notion quite wrong. It is interesting to note
that the reference to this "rock" from which Mohammad
mythically ascended to heaven is cited as a matter of tradition
and not expressly sourced in the Quran or Hadith, as discussed
above. The textual reference to this "rock" is also in lowercase
type, not in initial cap, as it is when referring to the "Rock" that
is under the Dome of the Rock in the prior sentence. This may
indeed allude to a rock other than the "Rock" (i.e., the
Foundation Stone)[697]. This is especially so given the description
of Omar erecting a mosque by its side (i.e., the lowercase "rock"),

---

[697] At the very least, it creates an ambiguity as to which rock it is actually referring to,
"the bare Rock" (i.e.: the Foundation Stone) or another "rock"..

inasmuch as the Al-Aqsa Mosque is located quite a ways from the Foundation Stone under the Dome of the Rock. Perhaps, the reference is indeed to another rock. Consider the Dome of the Ascension[698], which was so named specifically to commemorate the tradition of Mohammad's ascent to Heaven, is located near the Al-Aqsa Mosque. There is also the niche marking the footprints associated with Jesus on a rock within the Al-Aqsa Mosque, as discussed above. Whatever the case, the Guide correctly does not source this myth as being premised on the Quran or even Hadiths but merely recites it "according to tradition".

It should also be noted that the Muslim historian, Al-Tabari, does not mention the Night Ride or Ascension in relation to Omar and the Foundation Stone, nor does the Quran. Some of the Hadith do speak of Mohammad either spiritually or physically traveling to Jerusalem, but they do not expressly make mention of an ascension from the Foundation Stone, as more fully discussed above. It would appear that the Guide is ambivalent as to the veracity and provenance of this tradition and any connection to the actual Foundation Stone and, therefore, it does not expressly link the ascension to the "Rock", (i.e., al-Sakhrah-Foundation Stone), but to a lower case, generic "rock"[699].

The political ideology of the PA and Hamas, denying any connection of the Jewish people to the Land of Israel and promoting a false narrative that so-called Palestinian Muslim Arabs are the indigenous people of Israel, is untethered to reality. It is also inconsistent with classic Islam, as embodied in the Quran, as discussed above. Much like the horrendous practice of suicide/homicide bombers targeting innocent civilians, despite the express prohibitions against suicide in the

---

[698] Qubbat al-Miraj.

[699] As noted above, a 'rock' in Arabic is referred to as a 'hijar', in contradistinction to the 'Foundation Stone, which is referred to as 'al-Sakhrah'.

Quran[700], as well as the abhorrent use of children and others as human shields, another transgression of the Quran[701], this new political ideology is borne of another ethic[702].

It would appear that the godless positivistic morality of neo-Marxist ideological doctrines espoused by the KGB infected Arafat, Abbas and their minions. Marxist ideologues disdain religion and belief in G-d, marriage, family, children & private property[703]. They believe children are the property of the state

---

[700] Quran 2:195 and 4:29.

[701] Quran 2:190.

[702] See, for example, The Use of Force under Islamic Law, by Niaz A. Shah, in the European Journal of International Law, Volume 24, Issue 1, February 2013, at pages 343-365.

[703] See, for example, The Communist Manifesto, by Karl Marx and Friedrich Engels (1848). New terms may be used by so-called Democratic Socialists, but the essence of the socialist ideology has not changed. Thus, they preached elimination of private property, disdain for marriage and family, viewing children, in effect, as property of the state, and mockery of religion and belief in G-d. There is an extraordinary rebuttal to the Marxist view of G-d and religion by Rabbi Dr. Joseph b. Soloveitchik ZT"L, in footnote 4 from his work, Halachic Man. It is not as Marx suggested a so-called opiate for the masses. To the contrary, Rabbi Soloveitchik posits:
The consciousness of homo religiosus flings bitter accusations against itself and immediately is filled with regret, judges its desires and yearnings with excessive severity, and at the same time steeps itself in them, casts derogatory aspersions on its own attributes, flails away at them, but also subjugates itself to them. It is in a condition of spiritual crisis, of psychic ascent and descent, of contradiction arising from affirmation and negation, self-abnegation and self-appreciation. The ideas of temporality and eternity, knowledge and choice (necessity and freedom), love and fear (the yearning for God and the flight from His glorious splendor), incredible, overbold daring, and an extreme sense of humility, transcendence and God's closeness, the profane and the holy, etc., etc., struggle within his religious consciousness, wrestle and grapple with each other. This one ascends and this one descends, this falls and this rises.
Religion is not, at the outset, a refuge of grace and mercy for the despondent and desperate, an enchanted stream for crushed spirits, but a raging clamorous torrent of man's consciousness with all its crises, pangs, and torments. Yes, it is true that during the third Sabbath meal at dusk, as the day of rest declines and man's soul yearns for its Creator and is afraid to depart from that realm of holiness whose name is Sabbath, into the dark and frightening, secular workaday week, we sing the psalm, "The Lord is my shepherd; I shall not want. He maketh me to lie down in green pastures; He leadeth me beside the still waters" (Ps. 23), etc., etc., and we believe with our entire hearts in the ultimate destination of homo religiosus, not the path leading to that destination. For the path that eventually will lead to the "green pastures" and to the "still waters" is not

and don't respect the sanctity of marriage, the family[704] or private ownership of property.

Abbas and the other kleptocrats[705] who run the PA and Hamas are a part of the Orwellian clique of more equal than others[706]. Is it any wonder that they are willing to sacrifice children of others on the altar of their idolatrous pursuit of power and personal wealth? They think nothing of taking the property of others and embezzling aid monies and other public funds[707]. Coveting other

---

the royal road, but a narrow, twisting footway that threads its course along the steep mountain slope, as the terrible abyss yawns at the traveler's feet. Many see "the Lord passing by; and a great and strong wind rending mountains and shattering rocks . . . and after the wind an earthquake . . . and after the earthquake a fire" but only a few prove worthy of hearing "the still small voice" (1 Kings 19:11-12). Out of the straits of inner oppositions and incongruities, spiritual doubts and uncertainties, out of the depths of a psyche rent with antinomies and contradictions, out of the bottomless pit of a soul that struggles with its own torments I have called, I have called unto Thee, O Lord. Interestingly, much like so many preachers of neo-Marxist ideology today, neither the personal life of Marx nor Engels comported with their philosophical pronouncements. They were both Christians (Marx's parents had converted to Christianity) and scions of wealthy families. Marx was also a virulent antisemite. Marx married and had a family. Engels had a life partner; but he ultimately did formally marry her to please her on her deathbed. Hardly an example of the free love they preached or disdain for family ties and loyalty between parents and children. They also enjoyed the benefits derived from ownership of private property despite urging others to forgo these emoluments. George Orwell captured this hypocritical perspective in his book, Animal Farm, where he depicts how all the animals are equal, except that some are more equal than others. The kleptocracy governing the PA and Hamas controlled Gaza are good examples of this perverted ethic.

[704] See also, for example, Americans Buy Into Marxist Family Planning, by Paul Kengor, in the Federalist, dated 6/29/2015.

[705] See, for example, CHRONIC KLEPTOCRACY: CORRUPTION WITHIN THE PALESTINIAN POLITICAL ESTABLISHMENT, Hearing before the Subcommittee on the Middle East and South Asia of the Committee on Foreign Affairs, House of Representatives, 112th Congress, Second Session, July 10, 2012, Serial No. 112-167; Palestinian kleptocracy: West accepts corruption, people suffer the consequences, by Ziva Dahl, at The Hill, dated 11/15/2016; Terrorists & Kleptocrats: How Corruption is Eating the Palestinians Alive, by Aaron Menenberg, at the Tower Magazine (Issue 15- June 2014); and Mahmoud Abbas: The perpetual dictator and the missing peace, by Bassem Eid, in the Times of Israel blogs, dated 1/10/2023..

[706] See, Animal Farm, by George Orwell (1945).

[707] See, for example, Gaza's Millionaires and Billionaires-How Hamas' Leaders Got Rich quick, by Deborah Danan, in the Algemeiner, dated 7/28/2014; The Businesses of Mahmoud Abbas and His Sons, by Yoni ben Menachem, at Jerusalem Center for Public

people's property and taking it from them in violation of the Biblical Tenth Commandment[708] seems to be a part of their standard modus operandi.

However, they seem to have elevated this obnoxious ethic to a national desire and obsession to take away from or otherwise begrudge and deny Israel and its Jewish citizens any property or success. This poisonous attitude is inculcated in the masses through the propaganda organs of the PA and Hamas and their educational systems, which are dedicated to propagating Jew hatred and training people of all ages habitually to blame the Jews for their failures. People are robbed of the ability to exercise their free will, freedom of choice, and opportunity to act independently. Instead it is the collective will, as dictated by the elite and self-serving leadership, which governs and immorally seeks to prevent individuals from actually enjoying good relations and doing business with Jewish neighbors in Israel. Jews are also prohibited from living in the PA-controlled areas and Hamas dominated Gaza. Denied opportunities to gain from meaningful relationships with Jews and even punished under obscene anti-Jewish laws or extra-judicially by the PA for daring to try, as well as being bombarded by propaganda and educational training devoted to demonizing Jews, is it any wonder that peace has proved so elusive. Blaming someone else also distracts from the leadership's own malfeasance and corruption. It creates a culture of victimhood and dependency.

This abhorrent ethic also robs many people of their positive desire to achieve similar success to their neighbors in their own enlightened self-interest. It also leads to malevolent jealousy, which not only begrudges others for their success, it promotes the negative, destructive instinct of seeking to abscond with the

---

Affairs, dated 9/14/2016; For Palestinian Leaders, a legacy of corruption, by David Bedein, dated 10/25/2019; and The Brother Abbas, by Jonathan Schanzer, at Foreign Policy, dated 6/5/2012.

[708] Exodus 20:17 and Deuteronomy 5:18.

rewards of others or otherwise undermine their achievements. The result is to create a toxic atmosphere where opportunities for success are denied to the people or otherwise sabotaged. Hence, the absurd and pernicious focus on denying Israel, including Jerusalem, to the Jewish people, instead of concentrating on building a vibrant state of their own side by side with the Jewish state of Israel[709].

Imagine if all that negative energy was sublimated and channeled so as to inspire and reinforce the innate positive desire of people to succeed like their neighbors by emulating them. This is one of the most elegant aspects of the Abraham Accords, which overcomes the psychological barriers to peace by generating shared prosperity and mutual respect among the members of the Circle of Peace it created. It tangibly demonstrates how success is not a zero-sum game, where someone wins only because another loses. Rather, by partnering with each other and embracing the free-market, mutual success

---

[709] This kind of gratuitous animus against the Jewish people of Israel channels the conduct of infamous villains of the Bible like Balak (Numbers, Chapters 22-24). Indeed, Balak's ethos bears a striking resemblance to that of Israel's modern-day antagonists. They are not content to live side by side with Israel in peace. It appears that Israel's outsized success, both spiritually and materially, as a democratic, inclusive and innovative society, lies at the heart of the issue. Like Balak and his notorious cabal of ancient Moav and Midian, they find it hard to compete with the glorious reality of Israel. They may even feel that by comparison it mocks their own failures. Rather than partnering with Israel to spread its blessings throughout the Middle East and the world, they seem to be doing their best to frustrate any progress. BDS and the rejection of any solution that allows for a secure and prosperous Jewish State of Israel to exist are just example of this cynical attitude. Rabbi Shmuel Bornsztain of Sochatchov, in his early 20th century commentary the Shem MiShmuel on Balak, Chapter 1, analyzes Balak's disturbing reasoning. He was quite amenable to the Jewish people pursuing a spiritual path while sequestered in the confines of the wilderness. However, he was most concerned that when they entered the Land of Israel, they would demonstrate how that spiritual quality could successfully be integrated into the everyday life of a farmer. It was a model of life that he disdained and until now he didn't have to compete with it in practice. He, therefore, wanted this almost utopian vision of a life, antagonistic to his own weltanschauung, to be eliminated before it had a chance to take root and flourish.

and prosperity can be achieved at a level that was previously unimaginable[710].

Terrorism is a tool the leadership of the PA and Hamas wield to achieve their disreputable goals. It has also proved to be a source of great wealth in what amounts to a worldwide protection racket led by the leaders of the PA (formerly PLO and its affiliates) and Hamas. In a sense, it might be said that Abbas is making a living out of the situation where there is no peace with Israel. Thus, many believe they must court him and subsidize the PA and its leadership to prevent its nefarious program of terrorism from spilling over into their domains. If the PA made peace with Israel, then the aid money it receives might dry up, as the international community would rightly expect the PA to make its own way and get along with its neighbors, like any other polity. Absent the availability of the outside bonanza of virtually free aid money being showered on the PA, it would likely be significantly more difficult for the leadership cavalierly to steal the money. When taxpayers pay for government services, they usually expect accountability. They usually don't submissively tolerate corruption at the level reportedly committed by Abbas and his sons, as noted below. This might help explain why Abbas reportedly rejected a multi-billion dollar offer from Saudi Arabia to accept the Trump peace plan. As he explained, if he made peace with Israel, then perforce, he would lose his job or said another way, he would forfeit his extremely lucrative gig, as well as the outlandish benefits his sons enjoy in the PA under his leadership[711].

---

[710] See, for example, Democratic Socialism May Sound Noble But It's Not Virtuous in Practice, by Leonard Grunstein, at Newsmax, dated 4/16/2019. See also American Marxism, by Mark R. Levin (Threshold Editions of Simon and Schuster-2021), which discusses how many of the so-called progressive doctrines can be traced to classic Marxist ideology. As King Solomon taught: 'What has been will be again, what has been done will be done again; there is nothing new under the sun' (Ecclesiastes 1:9).
[711] See, Saudi Arabia offered Abbas $10 Billion to accept Trump's peace plan-report, by Khaled Abu Toameh, in the Jerusalem Post, dated 5/2/2019.

Consider how the European Union and European countries continue to fund the PA and Hamas, despite their ongoing acts of murderous terrorism, funding of Pay to Slay, human rights violations committed against their own people[712] and rejection of peace with Israel[713]. Perhaps, though, the continued funding is part of an overall tacit, if not express, arrangement dating back to Arafat and the PLO in the era of terrorist acts committed by the PLO in Europe. Secret deals were reportedly made by European governments like Italy, Germany, France, and Switzerland to turn a blind eye to Palestinian terrorist actions elsewhere, so long as they were not committed on their national soil[714].

It would appear that this kind of international extortion is a very lucrative business. Arafat is reported to have amassed a fortune worth in excess of a billion dollars[715]. Abbas and his sons have reportedly collectively accumulated hundreds of millions of

---

[712] See, for example, Palestine: Impunity for Arbitrary Arrests, Torture, at Human Rights Watch, dated 6/30/2022; Palestinians protest arrests, torture by PA security forces, by Khaled Abu Toameh, in the Jerusalem Post, dated 7/31/2022; Rights Group Exposes Palestinian Torture Ahead of First UN Review, at UN Watch, dated 7/14/2022; Israel NGO urges the Hague to investigate PA over torture allegations, by Tamir Morag, at Israel Hayom, dated 7/20/2022; and Israeli group levels torture accusations against the Palestinian Authority, group submits claim to ICC, by Louis Casiano, at Yahoo Finance, dated 7/19/2022.

[713] See, for example, Abbas admits he rejected 2008 peace offer from Olmert, by Josef Federman, in The Times of Israel, dated 11/19/2015 and Abbas Admits He Said No to Israel's Peace Offer, by Elliot Abrams, at the Council of Foreign Relations, dated 11/18/2015. Astonishingly, Abbas admitted he declined the Olmert peace proposal, which included near-total withdrawal from West Bank and relinquishing Israeli control of Jerusalem's Old City.

[714] See, for example, Secret diaries of Arafat come to light, confirming PLO pact with Italians, in the Times of Israel, dated 2/4/2016; The story of Germany's capitulation to Palestinian terrorism, by Eldad Beck, in Israel Hayom, dated 6/17/2020; French intelligence made secret deal with Palestinian militants, ex-spy chief claims, by Joseph Fitsanakis, in Intel News, dated 8/12/2019; and Switzerland 'made secret deal with PLO' after bomb attacks, by Imagen Foulkes, at BBC News, dated 1/22/2016.

[715] See, for example, He's Billion Dollar Arafat; Got Rich on Aid for Palestinians, Israel General Says, by Uri Dan, in the New York Post, dated 8/14/2002 and Arafat's Billions, by Tricia McDermott, at 60 Minutes, CBS News, dated 11/7/2003.

dollars, and some say upwards of a billion dollars[716]. Hamas leaders like Mashaal and Marzouk are reportedly multibillionaires, and many more are multimillionaires[717].

It is interesting to note that the emergence of terrorist bands, like the PLO and Hamas, is adumbrated in an abstruse Biblical verse[718] in the prophetic speech of Moses recorded in poetic form in Deuteronomy[719]. The verse begins by noting how people will incense G-d by their belief in no G-d and vex G-d with their vanities. It is respectfully submitted that this refers to a time like ours, where there is a resurgence of neo-Marxist ideology that disdains G-d, marriage and family and disincentivizes individual achievement and success. Denying there's a spiritual component to life, including belief in G-d, demeaning the bonds of marriage and family, and making individual achievement unrewarding reduces life to a banal and mundane existence, bereft of true meaning, which might fairly be viewed as futile.

The Biblical verse goes on to predict that the corresponding, tit for tat, response will be that G-d will incense them with a non-nation and vex them with groups of scoundrels. An authoritative medieval commentary on the Bible[720] explains that the 'non-nation' refers to bands of terrorists who will invade the Land of Israel, leaving destruction in their wake. It goes on to say that the terrorists will be universally despised because they will also harm others, not just the Jewish people in the Land of Israel. It's

---

[716] See, for example, The Brothers Abbas, by Jonathan Schanzer, in Foreign Policy, dated 6/5/2012; For Palestinian leaders, a legacy of corruption, by David Bedein, in the Jewish Journal, dated 10/25/2019; and The Business of Mahmoud Abbas and His Sons, by Yoni Ben Menachem, at the Jerusalem Center for Public Affairs, dated, 9/14/2016.

[717] See, for example, Meet the Hamas billionaires, by Ella Levy-Weinrib, in Globes, dated 7/24/2014 and Gaza's Millionaires and Billionaires-How Hamas' Leaders Got Rich Quick, by Deborah Danan, in Algemeiner, dated 7/28/2014.

[718] Deuteronomy 32:21.

[719] In the Parsha (the sequential section of the Torah read each week on the Sabbath in Synagogue so as to complete the reading of the entire 5 Books of Moses annually) denominated HaAzinu, beginning with Deuteronomy 32:1.

[720] Da'at Zekeinim M'Ba'alei HaTosafot. a 12th-13th Century commentary on the Torah.

chilling to appreciate that this ancient description, from the 12th – 13th century, could just as well have been ripped from the headlines of modern newspapers.

Terrorist acts are rampant and plague humanity. They are directed by pompous charlatans, who clothe themselves in pseudo-Islamic piety, as they smugly urge others, like their sycophants, mindless followers (including children) and useful dupes, to sacrifice themselves, while committing terrorist acts and then callously financially reward it. Their disreputable pronouncements of Temple denial are calculated to delegitimize any connection between the Jewish people and Israel in order to promote a toxic environment where Islamic extremists believe they can function with impunity.

Ironically, neither Mahmoud Abbas, President of the PA, nor Khalid Mashaal, a founder and former Chairman of Hamas, are recorded as having publicly visited the Temple Mount and prayed at the Al-Aqsa Mosque. Yet, they, the PA and Hamas purport to insist that what they call East Jerusalem, including the Old City of Jerusalem, encompassing the Temple Mount, Western Wall (Kotel), and Jewish Quarter, as well as the City of David, must be ceded to their putative Palestinian state, which they insist would have Jerusalem as its capital, as a condition to any peace agreement. Of course, this is notwithstanding the fact that they also want Israel to disappear.

Nevertheless, in polite diplomatic settings, Jerusalem, including the Temple Mount, is avowed to be the intractable issue that prevents any peaceful solution. Of course, there's also the matter of claiming an unlimited and mythical right of return, which is tantamount to the destruction of Israel as a Jewish State, as discussed above. Presumably, if these matters could be solved, there would be other insurmountable issues. Indeed, no rational person could believe that these matters could not somehow be offset, compromised, and subsumed by the give and take of a negotiated settlement for those genuinely desiring peace.

Hence, the dilemma faced by so many participants in these endless negotiations, who hoped in good faith to make progress. Again and again, they are frustrated by the roadblocks put up by representatives of the PA and Hamas, who sometimes actually acknowledge that they are in no position to conclude a peace deal. In this regard, it must be recognized that some of the issues, like Jerusalem and the Temple Mount, are not truly insurmountable religious issues for all the reasons discussed above. Instead, they are often just politically motivated pretexts or subterfuges designed to obfuscate or seemingly rationalize a hidden agenda that is the very essence of the problem.

As Charles Krauthammer, of blessed memory, so wisely and succinctly summarized it[721]:

> ...Israel evacuated Gaza completely. It declared the border between Israel and Gaza an international frontier. Gaza became the first independent Palestinian territory in history. Yet Gazans continued the war...Why? Because occupation was a mere excuse to persuade gullible and historically ignorant Westerners to support the Arab cause against Israel. The issue is, and has always been, Israel's existence. That is what is at stake.

It is in this context that the vitriolic and hyperbolic pseudo-Islamist creed that the PA, Hamas, and others like them invented, which condones and even celebrates murderous terrorism and the other obnoxious practices summarized above, must properly be viewed. This kind of loathsome behavior is inimical to the traditions of universal morality of the Old Testament and, by extension, the New Testament and Quran. Nevertheless, the politically motivated demagogues will use any means to achieve their goals, even if antithetical to classic Islam. Criticism of these abhorrent practices is not Islamophobia;

---

[721] See, Why They Fight, by Charles Krauthammer, of blessed memory, in the Washington Post, on July 14, 2006.

rather, it is respect for the tenets of classic Islam that detest this type of misbehavior. As the Arab nations which have made peace with Israel recognize, Israel's existence is not a catastrophe[722], as urged by the PA and Hamas; but to the contrary, it's a blessing.

---

[722] Nakba, in Arabic.

XI.

THE TIMELY ROLE PLAYED BY THEN CONGRESSMAN RON DESANTIS IN PROMOTING THE RECOGNITION OF JERUSALEM AS THE CAPITAL OF ISRAEL

On Wednesday, November 8, 2017, then-Congressman Ron DeSantis, as Chairman of the Subcommittee on National Security of the House Oversight and Government Reform Committee, presided over a hearing on moving the American Embassy in Israel to Jerusalem[723]. In his opening statement, he noted, as follows:

> In 1995, Congress passed the Jerusalem Embassy Relocation Act, which states that Jerusalem is the capital of Israel, that it should remain an undivided city, and that the American Embassy should be relocated from Tel Aviv to Jerusalem. Yet, for more than 20 years, U.S. Presidents have signed waivers for stalling the Embassy move.

> To this day, 50 years after the liberation and reunification of Jerusalem, the State of Israel, one of America's strongest allies, is the only nation in the world in which the American Government refuses to locate its Embassy in the host nation's chosen capital.

---

[723] Moving the American Embassy in Israel to Jerusalem: Challenges and Opportunities- Hearing Before the Subcommittee on National Security of the Committee on Oversight and Government Reform, House of Representatives, 115th Congress, First Session, November 8, 2017, Serial No. 115-44.

Now, as a candidate for President, Donald Trump promised to move the Embassy to Jerusalem, and he has reaffirmed that commitment since taking office. And there are good reasons why the President will follow through with his commitment.

For one thing, U.S. policy should recognize Jerusalem as Israel's capital because Jerusalem has been the capital of the Jewish people for thousands of years and is the beating heart of modern Israel. Why should we reject the chosen capital city of a close ally?

Second, Israel's stewardship of Jerusalem's holy sites has been tremendous, especially regarding religious freedom. During the Arab occupation of the Old City of Jerusalem, between 1949 and 1967, Jews were systematically discriminated against and Christians were treated as second-class citizens. Most of the Old City's synagogues were destroyed or desecrated. Under Israeli sovereignty, religious freedom is the rule, and the holy sites, Christian, Jewish, and Muslim, are treated with care and respect. The disrepair that plagued Jerusalem under Arab occupation has given way to a flourishing city that is one of the world's crown jewels.

Third, following through with the commitment to move the Embassy will demonstrate American leadership. Leaders in the Middle East respect the strong horse, and acting with decisiveness to defend American interests and to stand by a close ally is far more preferable to defaulting on a key promise like past leaders have done.

Fourth, the Embassy can be relocated to one of the sites in Jerusalem that the U.S. already controls. This can be as simple as changing the sign on one of the existing consulates. For example, the consulate annex in Arnona combined eventually with the adjacent Diplomat Hotel can be a sizeable complex that provides adequate security. That the annex in Arnona straddles the 1949 armistice line also counsels in its favor as a potential site.

The Trump administration has delayed moving the Embassy in light of its efforts to pursue a peace deal between Israel and the Palestinian Arabs, but there are incremental steps that the Trump administration could take in the meantime.

The State Department should allow Americans born in Jerusalem to list Jerusalem/Israel on their passports. The U.S. Ambassador should make a point to conduct at least part of his workweek from Jerusalem, and the American consulates in Jerusalem should report to the American Embassy in Israel, not directly to the State Department.

Now some say the U.S. can't move its Embassy to Jerusalem because that enrage elements of the so-called Arab street and provide a pretext for acts of terrorism. And who knows? That may be true, but does it make sense to shirk from doing what is right for fear of what our enemies might do?

With the advent of the Trump administration, the U.S.-Israel relationship is probably stronger than it has ever been. Our countries have shared security interests, common cultural ties, and mutually beneficial economic relationships. Relocating the Embassy to Jerusalem, especially if done in 2017, the 50th year anniversary of Jerusalem Day, will make the relationship that much stronger.

Of course, there were the usual perfunctory warnings about timing and to proceed with caution because of preconceived notions that Egypt, Jordan, and other regional Arab nation partners would reflexively react in an exaggeratedly negative manner, which might prove detrimental to US, Israeli, and regional security interests in the near term. As we all now know, these concerns proved spurious, and, in fact, the opposite was true. It was the recognition by the US of undivided Jerusalem as the capital of Israel and moving the US Embassy there that solidified the relationship among the US, Israel and regional Arab nation partners and yielded the Abraham Accords. The State Department's establishment of naysayers notwithstanding, unilaterally recognizing Jerusalem as the capital of Israel and moving the Embassy there did not upset the US's relationship with its Arab partners. Indeed, it liberated them to pursue their own formal and public normalization arrangements with Israel under the sponsorship of the US.

The Abraham Accords and the growing circle of Arab nations embracing normalization with Israel and regional security arrangements are a striking rebuttal to the old duplicitous way the State Department functioned, with its mixed signals, disloyalty, and courting of enemies at the expense of friends. Alas, the doyens and old hands at the State Department and their spiritual successors, who have drunk the proverbial Kool-aid, have learned little from the failure of their policies. They can't seem to wrap their minds around the successful policies promoted by President Trump and his team, including Ambassador David Friedman, Vice President Mike Pence, Secretary of State Mike Pompeo, and Ambassador to the UN Nikki Haley, as well as his advisors like Jason D. Greenblatt, Jared Kushner, Avi Berkowitz and his astute daughter, Ivanka Trump.

John Bolton, a former US Ambassador to the UN and later, in 2018, a National Security Advisor to President Trump, appeared at the Hearing in support of recognizing Jerusalem as the capital of Israel and moving the US Embassy there. In businesslike fashion, he rebutted the prevailing wisdom or lack thereof, which automatically ascribed dire and negative consequences to any such action, as follows:

I believe that recognizing Jerusalem is Israel's capital city and relocating our Embassy there on incontestably Israel sovereign territory would be sensible, prudent, and efficient for the United States Government.

Indeed, fully regularizing the American diplomatic presence in Israel will benefit both countries, which is why, worldwide, the U.S. Embassy in virtually every other country we recognize is the host country's capital city.

Relocating the Embassy would not adversely affect negotiations over Jerusalem's final status or the broader Middle East peace process, nor would it impair our diplomatic relations among predominantly Arab or Muslim nations.

In fact, by its honest recognition of reality, shifting the Embassy would have an overall positive impact for U.S. diplomatic efforts.

Over the years, as with so many other aspects of Middle Eastern geopolitics, a near theological and totally arid to scholasticism has developed here and abroad about the impact of moving the Embassy. Now is, in fact, the ideal time to sweep this detritus aside and initiate the long overdue transfer.

Bolton addressed the specific arguments usually raised[724], as set forth below:

So, while I think the overwhelming diplomatic and managerial advantages to the United States argue for relocation, there are obviously a number of political arguments to the contrary. I think there are three, basically.

---

[724] John Bolton also submitted a fuller written statement, which is a part of the record of the Subcommittee Hearing.

And I think it's important to take these arguments seriously, because many are made in good faith, but let's be honest, many are argued for precisely the opposite reason, to continue to deny to Israel the acknowledgment that it is a legitimate state with a legitimate capital.

The three arguments basically are that moving the Embassy, even to West Jerusalem, would somehow affect final status negotiations about that city. I think this stems from U.N. General Assembly Resolution 181, which contemplated an international status for Jerusalem. That resolution was rejected by the Arab State shortly after it was passed. And let's face it, 181 is a complete dead letter today. Jerusalem will never be an international city, and we need to move on from it, as indeed the Russian Federation acknowledged earlier this year.

The second argument is that it will break the broader Middle East peace process. And I have to say, if the peace process is such a delicate snowflake that moving our Embassy would destroy it, you have to ask what its viability is to begin with. And it's also to mistake pretext for cause. If somebody wants to demonstrate against the United States or Israel, can pick a lot of other pretexts as well, not just moving the Embassy.

And, finally, to conclude, Mr. Chairman, we hear over and over again that we want to move the Embassy but the time is just not right. As they say in the Near East Bureau of the State Department, they only have to press one key on their computers to spit out the phrase ``at this particularly delicate point in the Middle East peace process.''

In diplomatic circles, Mr. Chairman, ``not now'' too often means ``not ever.'' We should reject that counsel and move the American Embassy to Israel's capital city. Thank you.

Ambassador Dore Gold of Israel also appeared[725]. He focused in on the matter of western recognition of Jerusalem as the capital of Israel, which was an explicit part of the Embassy move to Jerusalem. In this regard, he discussed the international interest in protection of the holy sites and assuring free access to them. He noted that religious freedom and pluralism were core values shared by the US and Israel. He went on to discuss how it was only since Israel reunited Jerusalem after the 1967 Six Day War that free access to the holy sites was protected for all people and faiths. Prior to then, access by the Jewish people, including to the Western Wall (Kotel), was barred. Israel also found many holy sites destroyed or otherwise despoiled during the Jordanian occupation. He also noted that in the Second Intifada of 2000, religious sites were specifically targeted. There were also the assault on Rachel's Tomb in December of 2000, the armed forcible entry into the Church of the Nativity in Bethlehem two years later and the violent attacks on Joseph's Tomb in Nablus during that period. As a matter of fact and in practice, it is only free and democratic Israel that can be counted on to protect the holy sites of all the great faiths in Jerusalem.

Mort Klein, the President of ZOA, spoke next and, in his plainspoken manner, eloquently explained why it was so important to move the Embassy to Jerusalem as soon as possible[726]. He discussed how not doing so sent the wrong message and only served to frustrate peace efforts by rewarding wrongdoing, as follows:

> The U.S. should move the Embassy to Jerusalem, not only because it's the just and moral thing to do, but because it's a law, passed with bipartisan, almost unanimous support, almost 22 years ago. Delaying implementation sends the

---

[725] Dore Gold also submitted a fuller written statement, which is a part of the record of the Subcommittee Hearing.

[726] Mort Klein also made a fuller written statement, which is a part of the record of the Subcommittee Hearing.

message that Islamist threats and terrorism work, but moving the Embassy will strengthen American security and enhance worldwide respect for America by demonstrating the U.S. can be counted on to keep her commitments to her allies and will not, dare not, be intimidated by appeasing radical Islamic threats.

If we allow U.S. policy to be determined by terror threats, we have only encouraged more such threats, more such terror, and undermined the U.S. campaign to eradicate radical Islamic terror. And Israeli control of Jerusalem is critical to security in all of Jerusalem and its surroundings.

And moving the Embassy will not cause further Mideastern instability. Israel's relationship with Egypt and Jordan and Saudi Arabia are strong today because of strong mutual concerns and interests and threats from Iran. Moving the Embassy will not change this.

The Jerusalem Embassy Acts waiver provision has been inappropriately used for 22 years. The act's drafters made it clear that the waiver was not intended to be invoked repeatedly or for policy disagreements, but only for a serious security emergency. Senate Majority Leader Bob Doyle said then: The President cannot lawfully invoke this waiver because he thinks it's better to move it at a later date. The President dare not infinitely push off the establishment of the American Embassy in Jerusalem.

``If a waiver were to be repeatedly and routinely exercised by a President, I would expect," said Dole, ``that Congress should remove the waiver authority."

And by the way, Dole and Kyl, who I spoke to at the time, told me the President should never use it, once or twice at the most.

We haven't moved the Embassy for 22 years, yet we're further from peace today than we were 22 years ago. Not moving the Embassy did not help. Peace is impossible solely because of the Palestinian Arabs' refusal to accept Israel within any border, their refusals to even negotiate and outlaw terrorist groups, and refusal to end the promotion of hatred and murder and violence in their speeches, schools, and media. They are continuing to pay Arabs to murder Jewish people. It's an outrage...

We have to tell them the jig is up, that the only way for peace is if we hold them accountable and say there will be no more money, no more support to the Palestinian Authority, no more American money, unless they change... And under Jordanian control, 70 percent of the Christians left because of oppression, and under Palestinian control, 80 percent of the Christians left Bethlehem. Mahmoud Abbas, the President of the PA, made it clear that he would cut off access to religious sites by regularly making the astonishing racist statement, and I quote: In a final solution, we will never see a single Israeli civilian or soldier in our land. Jews and Christians have suffered greatly. Now their sites are under PA control. Jerusalem has been the capital only of Israel throughout history, never any other regime, country, or entity.

I now turn to a rarely mentioned fact. Jerusalem is not very holy to Muslims. They have not treated Jerusalem as holy to them when they controlled it. During Arab Muslim control of Eastern Jerusalem, they allowed it to become a slum. There was virtually no water, electricity, or plumbing. Jordan built its royal residence and universities in Amman, not Jerusalem. They broadcast their Friday prayers from a mosque in Amman, not the Al-Aqsa in Jerusalem. In the Holy Koran, Jerusalem is never mentioned. In the Jerusalem Holy Books, it's mentioned 700 times...

When Jerusalem was under Arab control, not a single Arab leader, other than King Hussein and his father, visited. If it's so holy, why didn't others visit it? It belies their claim of holy status.

Chuck Schumer, the Democratic minority leader, has recently stated: Move the Embassy to Jerusalem now, an undivided Jerusalem.

Senator Joe Biden, at the time future Vice President, said, quote: ``Moving the U.S. Embassy to Jerusalem will send the right signal, not a destructive signal. To do less would be to play into the hands of those who will try the hardest to deny Israel full attributes of statehood.''

``The only way,'' Biden said, ``there will be peace in the Mideast is for the Arabs to know there is no division between the U.S. and Israel.'' None, zero, none. Thank you very much.

Dr. Michael J. Koplow also spoke at the hearing. While recognizing that moving the Embassy to Jerusalem would rectify the historical wrong of locating it in a city that is not the declared capital of Israel and that Israel's controlling rights to the modern city of Jerusalem are not in dispute, he nevertheless was concerned about an explosion of violence following the move. He also suggested it would cause unrest in other countries that are US allies, which would somehow compromise their ability to cooperate with the US on other regional issues. He also argued it could negatively affect the nebulous, virtually non-existent peace process. Of course, there was the ever-present issue of timing; historically, it was never the right time.

Former Ambassador Daniel C. Kurtzer submitted a written statement[727] that similarly advised the President to invoke the waiver yet again. Curiously, he voiced his concern that the Tel

---

[727] Which is a part of the record of the Subcommittee Hearing

Aviv location may not be the most secure one and that the State Department should be permitted to move it within Tel Aviv, just not to Jerusalem. In this regard, it should be noted he also made a striking admission that, in the weeks prior to the 1993 signing of the Oslo Accord, he had proposed moving the Embassy to West Jerusalem while simultaneously establishing a second mission in East Jerusalem to represent US interests vis a vis the PA. He expressed his regret that no action was taken. Then, it seems, was the right time, in his judgment, but just not now.

Next up was Professor Eugene Kontorovich[728], a noted expert on International Law. He responded to the concerns noted above as follows:

> ...I'm going to...focus on the objections to moving the Embassy because it seems, in a kind of diplomatic version of Augustine's prayer, everybody agrees that the Embassy should be moved, just not yet. And so I'm going to focus on those ``not yets," ``not right nows."

> The arguments focus on certain practical concerns, whose existence or realism can't really be proven while the waiver is issued, and so they are, in a sense, unfalsifiable. But one interesting thing about the arguments for not moving the Embassy, security arguments essentially is that they have not changed in the 20-some years since the act's passage, despite the radical change in the security and political, geopolitical, situation in the region. In a sense, they are entirely unresponsive and invariant to political development.

> They can be summarized like this: Don't move the Embassy until the Palestinians, and maybe the Jordanians and the Egyptians, say it's okay. Don't move the Embassy until they agree. This holds American policy, this holds a statute

---

[728] Eugene Kontorovich also made a fuller written statement, which is a part of the record of the Subcommittee Hearing.

subject to veto and waiver by third countries. In no geopolitical conflict, in no geopolitical dispute do we give parties, do we give neighbors, a waiver on where the U.S. Embassy should be. That is to say, maybe Pakistan and India would like the U.S. Embassies to those countries to be somewhere else, but we don't ask them.

Now, it's not surprising that supporters of the Palestinians come and couch their arguments in national security terms, that is to say, implied threats of violence. Under the terms of the statute, the only reason for not implementing it is national security. The only permissible waiver is national security.

Not surprisingly, we commonly hear national security threats from the Jordanians and the Palestinians, that they're in a sense shoehorning their foreign policy and political concerns into this justification. It's not surprising that such threats continue to be made because the Palestinian Authority finds that such threats work. They continue to keep the U.S. Embassy from being moved. This means that waiving the act based on such threats, in fact, invites further threats. Waiver creates its own predicate.

I should point out that the security arguments have been significantly undermined by recent developments in the region. The security arguments were first made when the act was passed over 20 years ago, and they continue to be recited as if nothing has changed.

One, the Sunni States, in particular Saudi Arabia, are--as of now--literally at war with Iran. They cannot afford a rift with the United States. The notion that Saudi Arabia would endanger itself--it just shot down yesterday an Iranian-provided missile with a Patriot missile battery--the notion that it would endanger the air security of Riyadh over the Embassy issue is preposterous. The notion that Jordan would expose itself to ISIS threat because of the Jerusalem Embassy issue is preposterous.

So there has been a fundamental realignment in the Arab world. Twenty years ago, when people said that the Arab street is going to explode, that meant one thing. Now, I would point out, the Arab street has already exploded, principally internally. We need not fear riots against the U.S. in Damascus. The U.S. no longer has diplomatic representation there. Benghazi happened, not because of the Jerusalem Embassy. In other words, the people committed to keeping America out of the Middle East already, they are fully incentivized. U.S. Embassies in the area are constantly under threat. There was a threat this year to the Embassy in Cairo. Indeed, in 1998, two U.S. Embassies in Africa were blown up, in Tanzania and Kenya.

The response of the United States was not to cut and run and say: Wow, there are people who threaten violence to our presence here; we might as well leave.

The response by Congress was to appropriate nearly $1 billion for embassy security and, of the executive, to hunt down the perpetrators and ensure that they come to justice. That's the American response.

There is no other situation in which threats to embassies, especially to a major ally, are a reason for not having diplomatic representation in a country's capital.

In particular, this has a very bad consequence for the peace process because it puts Israel in a special unique category where its existence, its sovereignty over its capital, is only provisionally recognized. It's recognized with a question mark. Israel is a country in a class of one. That undermines the peace process.

Moreover, the Palestinians base their claims to a state to the Jordanian and Egyptian conquest of areas of the British mandate in 1949. Large parts of Jerusalem, including potential locations for the Embassy, are not in those areas illegally conquered by Jordan and Egypt, and the Palestinians have no conceivable claim to them. Waiting for a--tying this to the peace process makes the Palestinians' eyes bigger than their plate and gives them an appetite for that which they could not potentially have and fundamentally undermines the peace process.

Set forth below are excerpts of some of the questions posed, answers given, and comments made at the Hearing (including by Congressmen Ron DeSantis, James Comer, Peter Welch, Glenn Grothman, and Mark Meadows). They are most illuminating.

Mr. DeSantis.

Ambassador Gold, sometimes in America, people will say: Yeah, yeah, yeah, we want to move the Embassy, but the Israelis really don't want the Embassy in Jerusalem.

I've been to Israel recently. Left, right, center, they all said to move it. Is that accurate that Israel would welcome it? Not that Israel is dictating what President Trump does, but would it be welcome in Israel.

Mr. Gold.

A, I believe it would be welcome. B, this sounds like Act II of something we went through earlier in the year called the Taylor Force Act, where people were saying Israel doesn't really want it. Really? Is that true? Somebody went to Tel Aviv and had coffee in a coffee shop and came back as an expert on Israel?

So let me reassure you: Our Prime Ministers have all sought, if we're asked, that the U.S. Embassy be moved. Yitzhak Rabin, who was the father of the Oslo Agreements in the 1990s, spoke about Jerusalem remaining united under the sovereignty of Israel. And our public opinion polls indicate support for that. That is not the same as the Embassy, but it's all part of the same complex. Support for Jerusalem, the U.S. position in Jerusalem is at an all-time high.

Mr. DeSantis.

Ambassador Bolton, the point was made by Professor Kontorovich that the Gulf States, these Arab states, they are worried about Iran; they have a President now in America who believes Iran is a threat, who thinks the nuclear deal was a bad deal. Are they all of a sudden not going to work with us and Israel simply because we move our Embassy to Jerusalem?

Mr. Bolton.

No, I think it would have no material effect at all either on the broader geostrategic in the Middle East or on the Middle East peace process involving Israel or really on anything significant. You know, there's a lot of rhetoric in public in diplomatic matters that suits the political needs of the people who are uttering the words, when behind the scenes you're hearing something completely different, which is, ``We understand.''

The issue for me is, what's in the best interest of the United States? How are our interests best served? How can our diplomats be most effective? And I think the argument there is incontestable. What hurts us is when we give in to unfounded pressure and intimidation because it says something about the United States that we won't do what's purely common sense. It's harmful to us. It's harmful to Israel. It's harmful to the stability in the region.

Mr. Comer.

Ambassador Bolton, the Trump administration has clearly stated that it intends to move the U.S. Embassy to

Jerusalem and, quote, ``the question is not if that move happens, but only when," end quote.

Ambassador Bolton, when is the appropriate time to make this move and why?

Mr. Bolton.

Well, I think the appropriate time to make the announcement is today. And let me just say, in respect of the comments that have been made about the strategic implications of a move, as I said in my prepared statement, I think we should take very seriously the concerns of countries like Jordan and Egypt. But I don't think that means they have a veto. I think it means we do what diplomats do. We consult with them in advance. We explain our reasons. We work with them to facilitate their ability to explain to their own citizens why it's happening.

And let's be realistic; the construction of a new embassy is not something that happens in 24 hours. First, you have to announce it. Then you have to break the ground. I suppose you have to design the Embassy first. You have to build it. You have to dedicate it. You have to--this is going to take place over years. And so there's a long period of time involved. And if the decision to go forward floor by floor of the Embassy varied with the temperature of the Middle East peace process, this building could take forever to build.

I think it's very important that we understand that the country in the world most sensitive to the regime in Jordan, most aware of the implications for security, is Israel. And it defies credulity to think that Israel would advocate a step that could cause King Abdullah to be overthrown and a terrorist regime to take power there. They're not going to do it, and neither are we.

Mr. Comer.

Thank you, Ambassador. With the stalled peace process and deteriorating security situation in the Middle East, what do you think the U.S. could do to best support Israel and stand by our ally? Obviously, you touched on moving the embassy, but what are some other things?

Mr. Bolton.

Well, beyond the embassy, I think the greatest threat to peace and security in the Middle East remains the Iranian nuclear weapons program, which has not paused, has not slowed down, has been camouflaged by the Iran nuclear deal. I have disagreed with the administration on the handling of that deal. I would break it immediately and establish a new reality.

But I think specifically in terms of Gaza and the West Bank, I really think that the United States is taking advantage of a potential for a reopening of the peace process. I think it's significant that the Trump administration is moving at the beginning of its term, not at the end as happens so often in the past. And I don't know whether the chances for success are any better or any worse. But when it comes to the embassy issue, the administration's effort is going to have its ups and downs, like all peace processes. And if you said after a step forward in the peace process, well, we don't want to risk that by moving the embassy, or at a downturn in the peace process, well, we don't want to tank it entirely by moving the embassy, this is how not now becomes not ever. And I think that's a mistake.

I think when the United States acts in a realistic way, recognizing a reality in a particular region, it enhances our credibility, it demonstrates that we are prepared to act on the basis of reality. That makes our efforts I think more likely to succeed, not less likely.

Mr. Comer.

Right. One of my colleagues had mentioned that when they were in Israel everyone that they had talked to, or the majority of the people in Israel supported moving the embassy. When I was in Israel this summer, that was my impression too, speaking to a vast array of Israelis there in Jerusalem and Tel Aviv. Getting back to the embassy, opponents of moving the embassy, opponents here in Congress, have cautioned that it could hinder the peace process. Do you believe peace negotiations between Israel and the Palestinians, do you think that that would impede that in any way? And why or why not?

Mr. Bolton.

No, I don't think it would affect the overall Middle East peace process. I think the embassy move has been given a symbolic significance well in excess of its practical effects. If you believe, and some do, that the United States is fundamentally biased against the Arab side, that it's so much in the tank for Israel that we can't be an honest broker, and they cite the billions of dollars of military and economic assistance we have given to Israel since Camp David--and quite properly, in my view--they look at the world historical events that have affected the Middle East since the 1967 war at least, what possible effect can moving the embassy have in comparison to all of that? I mean this has taken a pebble and made it into a mountain.

And the way to break through that, and I do think it is scholasticism, as I said in my testimony, is to move forward with actually relocating the embassy, acknowledging the reality that Jerusalem is the capital of Israel. It's going to be in an area west of the green line that nobody except a proponent of eradicating Israel entirely would ever say would be in a Palestinian state. So putting it in a place that nobody's disputing cannot affect either final status or the broader peace process.

Mr. Welch.

Let me ask you this. There is a question on the holy sites. And all of us want them to be secure. Will they be more secure, in your view, if the embassy is moved to Jerusalem?

Mr. Bolton.

It will have absolutely no effect on the security of the holy sites.

Mr. Welch.

Ambassador Gold?

...

Mr. Gold.

If anyone thinks that Israel may under certain circumstances or pressures withdraw from the core of Jerusalem and withdraw from the holy sites, you will have an explosion of violence, not reduced violence.

Mr. Grothman.

...You know, I think we move the embassy, it would put some realism into some discussions over there. I will bring up another matter, though. Since we are talking about where the Israeli Embassy is, we just spent a second here on where as a practical matter the American Embassy to the Palestinians is.

Do you think it would introduce a dose of reality if we moved that embassy or representative, whatever you want to call it, to Ramallah, rather than put it in Jerusalem? Does that also, the fact that that building is in Jerusalem, does that also kind of encourage this lack of common sense or lack of reality in the region?

Mr. Bolton.

I think others will want to comment on this, but I think we need to revisit the entire concept of having a kind of permanent de facto embassy to a Palestinian state that doesn't exist yet. I mean that person, at least the last time I was in the State Department, the consul general in Jerusalem is instructed not to have contact with officials of the Government of Israel, that their job is to talk to the Palestinians. That's one reason why the consulate there has the authority, which a few other consulates do, to send cables back to Washington without the approval of the Ambassador in Israel, the country in which it's located.

And I just think this has been in aid of perpetuating the myth that if you think about it hard enough, a Palestinian state will appear out of nowhere. I think that's a mistake from the U.S. point of view. It's not realistic.

...

Mr. DeSantis.

We have one of our strongest allies, only democracy in the Mideast, and yet we act like Jerusalem's not their capital, Tel Aviv. But then you have Palestinian Arabs who have rejected states, have gone to war with Israel for years and years, and we have something in Jerusalem for them. I mean it really is maddening. Good questions.

The chair now recognizes Mark Meadows for 5 minutes.

Mr. Meadows.

Thank you, Mr. Chairman. Thank you for your leadership on this issue. Obviously, as being members of the Republican Conference, there is always a very willing partner on behalf of the gentleman from Florida on issues that are pro- Jewish and pro-Israel, and I thank you for your leadership.

Ambassador Bolton, let me come to you. Would you suggest that there are a number of people in the State Department that are vehemently opposed to moving the embassy to Jerusalem?

Mr. Bolton.

Absolutely. And look, this is a problem at the State Department. I wrote about it in my book that I wrote after I was at the U.N., that there are elements in the Department who are excellent civil servants who follow the direction of new Presidents. There are others who think they should run American foreign policy. And they have been running this issue for as long as anyone can remember.

Mr. Meadows.

So to your knowledge were any of those people at the State Department elected on November 8th?

Mr. Bolton.

No, strangely, and they are not mentioned in the Constitution either.

Mr. Meadows.

And to your knowledge, when the President ran on this particular issue, do you believe that there were a number of people who felt like there was a reset in terms of our relationship with the Jewish community, and finally the United States of America?

Mr. Bolton.

Yes. And I think it's a campaign promise that a lot of people paid a lot of attention to. I think it's very important.

Mr. Meadows.

So would you characterize this as a campaign promise that if the President failed to follow through on that would be a major disappointment to the Jewish community?

Mr. Bolton.

Well, I will just speak as a Lutheran, it would be a major disappointment to me.

Mr. Meadows.

As an Evangelical, it will be a major disappointment to me. And I can tell you that it is something that not only have we brought up with the President directly, I can tell you that he understands the commitment that he has made on this particular issue.

Dr. Koplow, I am going to come to you. There is always one skunk at the party. And so as we look at this, obviously you don't believe that we should be moving the embassy to Jerusalem. Is that correct?

Mr. Koplow.

I believe that national security considerations at this time dictate that we should probably leave it in Tel Aviv at least for another 6 months.

Mr. Meadows.

All right. So what has changed over the last 20 years in terms of our national security interests? I mean because we continue to debate this over and over. Do you know who Erekat is?

Mr. Koplow.

I am sorry?

Mr. Meadows.

Do you know who Erekat is? Or Erekat?

Mr. Koplow.

Oh, Saeb Erekat, of course

Mr. Meadows.

So you know who he is. So how long has he had his job?

Mr. Koplow.

Certainly as long as I can remember.

Mr. Meadows.

Yeah. Well, the closest thing to eternal life here is an eternal job of being able to negotiate a peace agreement between the Palestinians and the Israelis. Wouldn't you agree?

Mr. Koplow.

Yes.

Mr. Meadows.

All right. So since he has not been successful in over 21 years, and the embassy has not been in Jerusalem, how could moving the embassy to Jerusalem have affected his track record? I mean so if we move it do you think he will be any less successful?

Mr. Koplow.

Do I think Erekat will be any less successful?

Mr. Meadows.

Yes.

Mr. Koplow.

I can't imagine that he personally will be less successful.

Mr. Meadows.

I agree. So from a national security standpoint, is the Knesset fairly secure?

Mr. Koplow.

Yes.

Mr. Meadows.

I have been there. It's very secure. So are you saying that we couldn't secure our embassy in Jerusalem? Is that what you are saying or you are just saying that geopolitically it makes national security less viable?

Mr. Koplow.

I have no doubt that we would be able to secure our embassy in Jerusalem the same way that we secure our embassy in Tel Aviv.

Mr. Meadows.

I agree. So what empirical data do you have that would suggest that this would create a national security incident? Because you were just talking, because I find your logic fascinating, you were just talking about how the Palestinians were pushing back against the security agreement, and yet the embassy is in Tel Aviv. So why would--I mean there is something to the logic that doesn't seem to mesh.

Mr. Koplow.

I think that there are a number of issues regarding Jerusalem that affect national security both for us and for Israel. The embassy is one of them. It's not the only one. But in general, as I note in my testimony, things that occur in Jerusalem tend to be the spark for----

Mr. Meadows.

So you are saying the very presence of a building in Jerusalem is going to create a national security issue?

Mr. Koplow.

I think it very well may.

Mr. Meadows.

Okay. And you don't have any empirical data to support that. That's just your feeling being a doctor from Georgetown in political science, right?

Mr. Koplow.

Based on the fact that other violent incidents in Israel are generally sparked by changes in Jerusalem, I think that one can assume that this is----

Mr. Meadows.

Could you possibly be wrong?

Mr. Koplow.

Absolutely.

Mr. Meadows.

Okay. Ambassador Bolton.

Mr. Bolton.

Just one quick point. On this question of physical security for American diplomats, I think anybody, probably many people on the committee, have been to Tel Aviv. You have seen our embassy. I can only imagine the heartburn that it causes in what we call OBO at the State Department, the Overseas Building Operations Bureau, the Diplomatic Security Bureau. It's very close to a main street. In contemporary terms, we would never build an embassy like that again.

Obviously, building a new embassy in Jerusalem would give us ample opportunity to include the most advanced security techniques that we could. And I think our personnel would be safer in a new facility than in the embassy that they currently occupy in Tel Aviv. And we don't need to be reminded of the risks to our people overseas. None of us want to see those risks continued.

So from that perspective, which involves American lives right on the front end, I think every consideration argues for moving the bulk of our personnel to Jerusalem.

Mr. Meadows.

Well, I agree. December 1st is a critical date because we have another waiver. It would be a great message that this President could send on the 50th anniversary of reunification that we go ahead and finally move the embassy to the eternal capital of Israel, Jerusalem.

In concluding the Hearing, Chairman Ron DeSantis made some final remarks summarizing his own impressions as follows:

I thank the gentleman. I just wanted to thank the witnesses for your testimony. I think we have gotten a lot of very good information. I think it was presented very crisply. And I just come away from the hearing more convinced than ever that we need to follow this 1995 law.

I would love to do it before the end of the year to coincide with the 50th anniversary of Jerusalem's reunification during the Six-Day War. But I think from a security perspective it makes sense. I think from the religious freedom perspective, the endorsement of Israeli stewardship over those religious sites is something that is very important both here, there, and I think throughout the world. And I think geopolitically, people will see that America is standing with a close ally. And that's exactly what we need to be doing at this point in time.

It was shortly after this seminal Hearing, on December 6, 2017, that President Donald J. Trump announced that the US recognized Jerusalem as the capital of Israel and would move its Embassy there.

On May 14, 2018, the US Embassy was opened in Jerusalem, Israel, coinciding with the date seventy years prior, when David Ben-Gurion, the first Prime Minister of the reestablished modern State of Israel, declared independence and, on that same date, President Truman, acting on behalf of the US was the first to recognize it.

XII.

PRESIDENT TRUMP RECOGNIZES JERUSALEM AS THE CAPITAL OF ISRAEL AND CAUSES THE US EMBASSY TO BE MOVED TO JERUSALEM

The scene was set for what would be a pivotal moment in the modern history of Jerusalem. It occurred in the Situation Room, in the White House, on November 27, 2017, beginning at three p.m., as depicted by Ambassador David Friedman[729].

Attending this seminal meeting were President Donald Trump at the head of the table, Vice-President Mike Pence, Secretary of State Rex Tillerson, Secretary of Defense Jim Mattis, National Security Advisor H.R. McMaster, Chief of Staff John Kelly, UN Ambassador Nikki Haley (on the video screen[730]) and Ambassador David Friedman.

The meeting, though, was not the first on the topic of recognizing Jerusalem as the capital of Israel and moving the Embassy there. It was the culmination of an effort that followed up a prior discussion in the Oval Office of President Trump on November 15, 2017. At that time, President Trump sat with Ambassador David Friedman, National Security Advisor H.R. McMaster, Chief of Staff John Kelly, Jared Kushner and Jason D. Greenblatt.

Ambassador Friedman, in response to President Trump's appreciation that he was there to move the Embassy to Jerusalem, advocated for a two-phased approach since there was

---

[729] Sledgehammer, by David Friedman (Broadside Books, Harper Collins-2022), Chapter 8, pages 95 et seq.
[730] Friedman reports that Tillerson had objected to her attending in person.

as yet no building to move into at the time. He proposed first formally recognizing Jerusalem as the capital of Israel and issuing a directive to begin the process of moving the Embassy there.

The President characteristically asked whether this two-step process was in keeping with his campaign pledge and Friedman answered in the affirmative. The President indicated approval of Friedman's approach and turned to McMaster for his input. McMaster responded the approach was creative and said he would run a so-called interagency process on the matter. The President agreed, and when Friedman requested he be closely involved in every aspect of the interagency process, the President wholeheartedly agreed, as well.

After the Oval Office Meeting, John Kelly pulled Friedman aside and urged him to remain in Washington D.C. until the matter was resolved. Kelly advised him that he was secretly in favor of the recognition; but could not personally advocate for it. It was Friedman who had to carry the ball, but Kelly would make sure that Friedman was in attendance at every meeting that discussed the subject. He offered that Friedman had the President's ear and was not intimidated by Secretary of State Tillerson, National Security Advisor McMaster, or Secretary of Defense Mattis.

As might be expected, given the sordid history of the State Department and foreign policy establishment, when it came to Israel and recognition of Jerusalem, attempts were made to rig the process. It began with a proposed paper intended to present the risks and opportunities presented by recognizing Jerusalem as the capital of Israel. Not unsurprisingly, it contained a detailed listing and description of risks; but when it came to opportunities, the section was blank. Friedman volunteered to write the opportunities section on the understanding that it would be presented as written and in unedited form as a part of the memo. Of course, the fact that it was wholly prepared by Friedman could be footnoted, as well as any disagreement with the substance of the points made. McMaster accepted the suggestion.

Summarized below are the points Friedman recorded listing as 'opportunities':

1. Recognition would strengthen the presidency and highlight that President Trump (unlike so many before him on the matter of Jerusalem) kept his promise and fulfilled the will of the American people. It would also demonstrate that the US stands with its allies, as well as, inspire the tens of millions of Americans who love Jerusalem.

2. Recognition would demonstrate that the US does not flinch when threatened by rogue regimes and terrorists.

3. Recognition would advance the cause of peace, by signaling that the Palestinians no longer hold a veto on significant matters and America is no longer bound to failed past practices.

4. The bifurcation of recognition, an intangible act, and the actual embassy move, a tangible one, mitigates some of the perceived risks. So would the coupled announcement that will leave open the prospects for a two-state solution.

5. The timing was propitious, and it might not last in the volatile region of the Middle East, where unforeseen events can overtake policy considerations.

Friedman reports that to his credit, McMaster included his points as written and even acknowledged that they were reasonable. He was reportedly under significant pressure from Tillerson and Mattis but wouldn't yield to their position against recognition of Jerusalem and the moving of the Embassy there. McMaster may not have personally been in favor of recognizing Jerusalem;

nevertheless, Friedman felt McMaster honored his commitment to provide Friedman a fair opportunity to present the case in favor of recognition to the President. In this regard, it should also be noted that Israeli Ambassador to the US Ron Dermer reports that then CIA Director Mike Pompeo also neutrally presented the CIA's concerns about potential terrorism and, therefore, in opposition to recognition of Jerusalem, even though he personally supported recognition. Friedman similarly confirmed to Farley that Pompeo presented the CIA's potential concerns about the Embassy move at the meeting, as was his responsibility, but he did not expressly oppose the move. Indeed, later as Secretary of State, Pompeo championed the strengthening of the US-Israel relationship and instituted policies that unabashedly favored Israel, a valued friend and trusted ally of the US, for the benefit of the US; something that prior administration had often irrationally shied away from, for fear of upsetting enemies of the US.

The interagency process then first began in earnest, with many agencies and parties becoming involved, including Homeland Security, intelligence agencies, and US Embassies. The results of all this diligence in evaluating the possibility of Jerusalem recognition were, unfortunately, entirely predictable. As Friedman reports, everyone thought it was risky because it had always been thought to be risky. However, this was nothing more than mere speculation about hypothetical threats. There was no actionable intelligence, nor could anyone identify any specific threat that would become reality as a result of the recognition of Jerusalem as the capital of Israel.

Friedman records an exchange with Tillerson that is illustrative of the problem. Tillerson argued the proposed recognition would not make the US or even Israel any safer or secure. He offered the relationship between Israel and the US was fine and didn't need to improve it. He warned recognition would pour gasoline on the fire.

This is the kind of irresolute thinking that has prejudiced the interests of the US and its allies throughout the world. In essence, why take any chances; it was much easier for the US to take advantage of its friends and allies. After all, there was little likelihood they would dare to complain, and the State Department has been doing it for ages. Better for the US to try to ingratiate itself with enemies at the expense of allies.

The problem was that this kind of reckless and demeaning thinking had failed miserably to advance US interests. Thus, for example, as the US sought to court enemies like the Iranian regime, it actually abandoned the good people of Iran, who were seeking freedom from the tyrannical and human rights abusing regime, as well as the US' Sunni allies in the region. As should have been expected, the administration prior to President Trump not only failed with Iran; it also sorely disappointed its allies, who rightly felt dejected.

Consider, too, that during the period prior to the new Trump administration's change in policies, there were no further peace treaties made since the ones between Israel and Egypt and Israel and Jordan, respectively. Iraq, Syria, Yemen, and Lebanon were failed states and under the influence of Iranian terrorist proxies. Gaza was controlled by Iranian proxy Hamas, and the PA had its own internal strife with Hamas. China and Russia were also infiltrating the Middle East.

In the midst of this maelstrom of anti-American activities stood one ally and friend of the US, the only true democracy in the region. Yet, here was Tillerson being callously dismissive of why it was fundamentally important to strengthen that relationship as a model worthy of emulation by Saudi Arabia and the Emirates, as well as other Arab nations. Is it any wonder that he and his cohorts were clueless as to the potential for extraordinary accomplishments like the Abraham Accords, which ensued as a result of recognition of Jerusalem as the capital of Israel and moving the Embassy there?

In response to Tillerson's droll and effete sentiments, Friedman said:

> Mr. Secretary, America will be stronger and safer because it will be led by a president who can be trusted to stand with an ally and keep a promise. And that alone will resonate throughout American foreign policy.

Friedman's answer was spot on and proved true, as evidenced by the subsequent Abraham Accords. Nations began to recognize once again that being an ally and friend of the US meant something. In terms of enemies, the discredited policy of appeasement was eschewed. Instead, there was accountability for malign activities, as everyone witnessed with the imposition and enforcement of strict sanctions against the terrorist Iranian regime[731].

Friedman recognized that each side had staked out their positions and minds wouldn't be changed; a decision had to be made by the President. As noted above, a meeting was, therefore, scheduled by the President, for November 27, 2017, in the White House Situation Room to resolve the matter.

The meeting bore an uncanny resemblance to the one President Truman conducted in advance of his recognizing Israel, summarized above. Friedman[732] was cast in the role of Clifford,

---

[731] See, for example, Snapback Sanctions; Reprising the Sordid History of the So-Called Iran Deal, by Leonard Grunstein, in The Times of Israel, dated 9/4/2020.

[732] Interestingly, there is another uncanny parallel shared by both practical, plain spoken and good-hearted Truman and Trump. They were each advised by a Jewish individual, who was both a genuine mensch and helped solve creditor issues arising out of an insolvent business. In the case of Truman, both he and Eddie Jacobson had been partners together in a haberdashery business, which failed in the depression. Eddie Jacobson went personally bankrupt and hence had no further liability for the debts of the business. However, Truman refused to do so and was hounded by creditors of the failed business. Despite being released in bankruptcy, as noted above, Eddie Jacobson nevertheless privately, in confidence, made payments to cover his own share of the joint debt to Truman so that Truman could pay off the debt over time. As noted above, this was despite Jacobson no longer having any personal liability. Nevertheless, he felt a moral obligation to his friend and former partner Truman. This is a little known fact

the celebrated Presidential advisor, and, well, Tillerson played the part of Secretary of State, like Marshall before him.

The meeting began with the President's charge that they proceed to get the matter of Jerusalem resolved now. He wanted to hear any objections one at a time and called on Friedman to respond after each one. He asked Tillerson to start with his concerns. The process was eerily similar to the one that occurred in Truman's office, and thank G-d, the conclusion the President reached was also affirmatively in favor of recognition. It appears that divine providence scripted the proceedings to perfection, given what reportedly occurred next.

Friedman records Tillerson began by reading a prepared statement from his briefing loose-leaf binder. He began by saying Jerusalem, since its capture by Israel in 1996 (sic), had been viewed as a corpus separatum by the US because of its sensitivity within the Middle East and the competing claims. He went on to say that the US had never taken a side on Jerusalem.

It is astounding how patently erroneous these purported statements of facts casually uttered by Tillerson are and how profoundly misinformed he must have been about Jerusalem.

Trump called upon Friedman to respond and this he did with aplomb. He kindly noted that the 1996 date was just wrong. Israel reconquered Jerusalem in 1967, not 1996. He also referenced the 1995 Jerusalem Embassy Act, which was passed with an overwhelming bi-partisan majority, and negated the statement that the US had never taken a position on Jerusalem. It most

reported by Michael J. Cohen, in his book, Truman and Israel (University of California Press-1990), at page 16. It was as a result of Jacobson's reasoned entreaties that Truman met Chaim Weitzman, which set in motion the course of events that eventually resulted in Truman's recognition of Israel, over the strong objection of Secretary of State Marshall. In the case of Trump, it was David Friedman, Esq., an expert, gifted and extremely talented bankruptcy attorney, who had helped resolve Trump's own business bankruptcy issues and now advised President Trump on the matter of Jerusalem. As noted above, he too by reasoned argument enabled Trump to recognize Jerusalem as the capital of Israel, over the strong objection of Secretary of State Tillerson.

assuredly had, and as the law expressly provides, Jerusalem is the undivided capital of Israel.

The effect of the revelation of these stunning mistakes must have been electrifying. Friedman reports Tillerson looked him in the eye, slammed his loose-leaf binder closed and said he'd said his piece and was done.

It should also be noted that Tillerson's vapid remark about Jerusalem, since its capture by Israel, being viewed by the US as a corpus separatum is not only incorrect, as discussed above, it is asinine. First of all, as more fully discussed above, the inane and impractical concept of establishing Jerusalem as a corpus separatum under UN control and administration, a part of the recommendations of the UNGA under its Resolution 181 of 1947, had by the mid-1950s, at the latest, effectively been treated as moot and no longer taken seriously. It also had nothing to do with the liberation of all of Jerusalem by Israel in the 1967 Six Day War. Moreover, it had been superseded by UNSC Resolution 242.

The concept of turning over sovereignty over Jerusalem and its environs to the UN, as a corpus separatum, to the exclusion of Israel and, at the time, Jordan as to the eastern portion, had been firmly rejected by both of them. Moreover, the origin of the concept was not in the Middle East but in the halls of the Vatican and at the State Department. It had nothing to do with competing claims between the parties. Rather, it was about imposing a superseding regime over Jerusalem, for the benefit of outside parties, with no real actual benefit to those advocating for it or anyone else involved and only risks, liabilities, and costs for those assuming any such burden and responsibility.

By the time of UN Security Council Resolution 242, it was little more than a footnote in history. Indeed, the Vatican itself, once one of the primary proponents of the idea, had concluded a treaty with Israel in 1993, in which the notion of the internationalization of Jerusalem was not even mentioned, as noted above. Furthermore, there are the US-sponsored Oslo Agreements, which nowhere reference this entirely superseded Western fantasy and expressly treat Jerusalem as a matter of local concern. Otherwise, how else would Ambassador Kurtzer have seriously proposed moving the Embassy to Jerusalem at the time, as noted above. Who would have imagined re-raising the absurd proposition of creating a corpus separatum for Jerusalem in the 1993 talks? It not only would have been a non-starter, it likely would have been perceived as tantamount to igniting a bomb to abort any chance at signing an accord and undermined any bonafide associated with the American role in the process.

It was ludicrous for Tillerson to bring up this topic at all, let alone present it in the fashion he did. Was he just being facetious, or were he and his State Department handlers truly that fatuous?

Mattis argued that he almost never went to Jerusalem because the Israeli defense establishment was in Tel Aviv. The President asked Friedman to respond to the point. Friedman asked why isn't the capital of the US in Virginia, given that it is where the Pentagon is located. In essence, it's because the President, Congress, and the Supreme Court are located in Washington, D.C. This is similarly the case with Jerusalem. Mattis replied fair point.

Pence and Haley weighed in, noting they favored recognition of Jerusalem. President Trump then asked Friedman to sum up with the single best reason why Jerusalem should be recognized. Friedman records he said:

> Mr. President, the world is watching. What they are watching for is whether you are truly the courageous leader you claim to be, or just another politician who gets cold feet and breaks a promise. The choice here couldn't be more stark; stand with an ally and fulfill the will of the American people, or cower in fear to rogue actors and

Islamic terrorists. How you decide this issue will reverberate in Iran, North Korea, and anywhere else that America is challenged, and your message of peace through strength is all on the line, right here.

No one interjected or said anything more after Friedman's summation. After a few moments of awkward silence, President Trump reportedly said:

Of course that's right. Let's do it.

Decision made, the President then left the meeting.

The rest of the group stayed behind for a short while. Tillerson plaintively remarked, how was he going to keep his embassies safe around the world? General Mattis chimed in that while he didn't agree with the President's decision, nevertheless, it had been made and it was their job to execute that policy. He added that the Defense Department knew how to protect US embassies and staff abroad and none would be at risk.

The seemingly inevitable leaks began to occur about this momentous decision. The President began to receive calls from leaders around the world seeking to change his mind, but the President was steadfast and determined to proceed with recognizing Jerusalem.

Nikki Haley[733] reports most who opposed the move didn't make reasoned arguments against it; they merely issued dire warnings of massive violence or threats. Hamas called the move a declaration of war. Al-Qaeda leader Ayman al-Zawahiri, an unrepentant enemy of the US, who the US eventually eliminated, called on his followers to escalate jihad against the US. These entirely predictable statements from the usual suspects were ever ready, just looking for a pretext to be issued yet again.

---

[733] With All Due Respect, by Nikki R. Haley (St, Martin's Press-2019).

Some Western leaders expressed their opposition in less hyperbolic terms. For example, Haley reports UN Secretary-General Antonio Guterres felt President Trump's decision resulted in a moment of great anxiety; German Chancellor Angela Merkel stated she didn't support the move; French President Emmanuel Macron called the decision regrettable; and British Prime Minister Theresa May said the decision was unhelpful in terms of the prospects for peace in the region.

The common unifying theme of those opposed to the recognition of Jerusalem is how categorically wrong they were and, unlike President Trump, their unwillingness to take any risk to do what was just and right. Many were not even willing publicly to support President Trump's decision after he made the historic announcement. However, some did, whether by voting against or tacitly by abstaining, when the UN General Assembly notoriously sought to undermine the recognition[734].

As Haley famously said, she was taking names and her staff compiled data on how often countries voted with the US at the UN as compared to how much foreign aid the US provided them. While, as she noted, this should not be the only factor determining the allocation of foreign aid, she reported the disparity found was shocking. What is most surprising is that this kind of analysis was not regularly done in the past. It would take President Trump and his administration to usher in a foreign policy derived from an analysis of reality, not ideological pretensions, to enable peace treaties like the Abraham Accords, based on peace through strength.

There was no third intifada, explosion of violence on the streets of Arab nations or disruption of relations with the US. All the dire predictions and handwringing turned out to be baseless. It was President Trump who resisted the State Department's

---

[734] UN General Assembly, Emergency Special Session, on 12/21/2017, GA/11995.

importunities, including the formulaic pious declarations of assumed insurmountable challenges and risks that proved meritless. The cool, rational and good instincts of President Trump and some of his team, as well as their desire to promote what was just and right, had triumphed over the hyperbolic knee-jerk reactions and biases of those influenced by the failed ideologically driven policies of the past.

This was no mean achievement. Consider how many Presidential candidates and Presidents, prior to President Trump, had said they would recognize Jerusalem as the capital of Israel; but, in the end, didn't.

Even before the 1995 Jerusalem Embassy Act, Senator Hubert Humphrey[735], who was then running for President, in 1972, declared:

> ...the American Government betrays a shocking lack of awareness of 3,000 years of Jewish history in our continued refusal to recognize a single united city of Jerusalem as the capital of Israel.
>
> We were wrong when we were silent in the fact of Jordanian forced annexation of the Old City in 1948. We were wrong when we were silent in the face of the atrocities perpetrated upon the City's sacred places by the Jordanian Arab Legion from 1948 to 1967. And we compound these wrongs: now when we dare to condemn the reunification and rebuilding which has shown respect and honor to the traditions and Holy Places of all great faiths.
>
> Jerusalem the golden must be united and be recognized as the capital of Israel. We must not turn back the clock by advocating redivision or internationalization.

---

[735] In a speech he gave, on May 24, 1972, at the NCSY Regional Annual Banquet, in Beverly Hills, California.

Then Senator Barack Obama, after he secured the Democratic nomination to run for President, in a speech at the AIPAC Policy Conference[736], stated:

Now, let me be clear: Israel's security is sacrosanct. It is nonnegotiable.

The Palestinians need a state -- the Palestinians need a state that is contiguous and cohesive and that allows them to prosper. But any agreement with the Palestinian people must preserve Israel's identity as a Jewish state, with secure, recognized, defensible borders.

And Jerusalem will remain the capital of Israel, and it must remain undivided.

I have no illusions that any of this will be easy. It will require difficult decisions on both sides. But Israel is strong enough to achieve peace, if it has partners who are committed to the goal.

Most Israelis and Palestinians want peace, and we must strengthen their hand. The United States must be a strong and consistent partner in this process, not to force concessions, but to help committed partners avoid stalemate and the kind of vacuums that are filled by violence.

And that's what I commit to do as president of the United States.

Presidential candidate Obama soon thereafter backtracked on this commitment[737]. He, like George W. Bush and Bill Clinton,

---

[736] The American Israel Public Affairs Committee annual Policy Conference, in Washington D.C., on June 2, 2008 (see, Transcript: Obama's Speech at AIPAC, at NPR.org, dated 6/4/2008.)
[737] See, for example, Obama Clarifies Remarks on Jerusalem, by Glenn Kessler, in the Washington Post, dated 6/5/2008 and Obama backtracks on an undivided J'lem, in the Jerusalem Post, dated 7/14/2008.

before him, almost perfunctorily issued waivers and never took the decisive step of recognizing Jerusalem as the capital of Israel.

The distinction and honor of recognizing Jerusalem as the capital of Israel and actually moving the Embassy was reserved to President Trump[738] and, by all accounts, he courageously earned it. He made the formal announcement[739], beginning at 1:07 pm, on December 6, 2017, in the Diplomatic Reception Room, at the White House, as follows:

> When I came into office, I promised to look at the world's challenges with open eyes and very fresh thinking. We cannot solve our problems by making the same failed assumptions and repeating the same failed strategies of the past. Old challenges demand new approaches.
>
> My announcement today marks the beginning of a new approach to conflict between Israel and the Palestinians.
>
> In 1995, Congress adopted the Jerusalem Embassy Act, urging the federal government to relocate the American embassy to Jerusalem and to recognize that that city — and so importantly — is Israel's capital. This act passed Congress by an overwhelming bipartisan majority and was reaffirmed by a unanimous vote of the Senate only six months ago.
>
> Yet, for over 20 years, every previous American president has exercised the law's waiver, refusing to move the U.S.

---

[738] Farley recollects that just before the election, he attended an event at the Bayit, a Chabad synagogue in Miami, at which Ivanka Trump answered a question on the issue. She said 100% that her father would recognize Jerusalem as Israel's capital. President Trump had personally made that commitment when he spoke at AIPAC in the spring of 2016 and again in September of 2016 when he met Prime Minister Netanyahu. During the week before Trump made the formal announcement, Farley publicly organized a White House call from members of the Young Israel Synagogues nationally to urge President Trump to go forward with recognizing Jerusalem as Israel's capital.

[739] Statement of President Trump on Jerusalem, December 6, 2017, at usembassy.gov.

embassy to Jerusalem or to recognize Jerusalem as Israel's capital city.

Presidents issued these waivers under the belief that delaying the recognition of Jerusalem would advance the cause of peace. Some say they lacked courage, but they made their best judgments based on facts as they understood them at the time. Nevertheless, the record is in. After more than two decades of waivers, we are no closer to a lasting peace agreement between Israel and the Palestinians. It would be folly to assume that repeating the exact same formula would now produce a different or better result.

Therefore, I have determined that it is time to officially recognize Jerusalem as the capital of Israel.

While previous presidents have made this a major campaign promise, they failed to deliver. Today, I am delivering.

I've judged this course of action to be in the best interests of the United States of America and the pursuit of peace between Israel and the Palestinians. This is a long-overdue step to advance the peace process and to work towards a lasting agreement.

Israel is a sovereign nation with the right like every other sovereign nation to determine its own capital. Acknowledging this as a fact is a necessary condition for achieving peace.

It was 70 years ago that the United States, under President Truman, recognized the State of Israel. Ever since then, Israel has made its capital in the city of Jerusalem — the capital the Jewish people established in ancient times. Today, Jerusalem is the seat of the modern Israeli government. It is the home of the Israeli parliament, the Knesset, as well as the Israeli Supreme Court. It is the location of the official residence of the Prime Minister and the President. It is the headquarters of many government ministries.

For decades, visiting American presidents, secretaries of state, and military leaders have met their Israeli counterparts in Jerusalem, as I did on my trip to Israel earlier this year.

Jerusalem is not just the heart of three great religions, but it is now also the heart of one of the most successful democracies in the world. Over the past seven decades, the Israeli people have built a country where Jews, Muslims, and Christians, and people of all faiths are free to live and worship according to their conscience and according to their beliefs.

Jerusalem is today, and must remain, a place where Jews pray at the Western Wall, where Christians walk the Stations of the Cross, and where Muslims worship at Al-Aqsa Mosque.

However, through all of these years, presidents representing the United States have declined to officially recognize Jerusalem as Israel's capital. In fact, we have declined to acknowledge any Israeli capital at all.

But today, we finally acknowledge the obvious: that Jerusalem is Israel's capital. This is nothing more, or less, than a recognition of reality. It is also the right thing to do. It's something that has to be done.

That is why, consistent with the Jerusalem Embassy Act, I am also directing the State Department to begin preparation to move the American embassy from Tel Aviv to Jerusalem. This will immediately begin the process of hiring architects, engineers, and planners, so that a new embassy, when completed, will be a magnificent tribute to peace.

In making these announcements, I also want to make one point very clear: This decision is not intended, in any way, to reflect a departure from our strong commitment to facilitate a lasting peace agreement. We want an agreement that is a great deal for the Israelis and a great deal for the Palestinians. We are not taking a position of any final status issues, including the specific boundaries of the Israeli sovereignty in Jerusalem, or the resolution of contested borders. Those questions are up to the parties involved.

The United States remains deeply committed to helping facilitate a peace agreement that is acceptable to both sides. I intend to do everything in my power to help forge such an agreement. Without question, Jerusalem is one of the most sensitive issues in those talks. The United States would support a two-state solution if agreed to by both sides.

In the meantime, I call on all parties to maintain the status quo at Jerusalem's holy sites, including the Temple Mount, also known as Haram al-Sharif.

Above all, our greatest hope is for peace, the universal yearning in every human soul. With today's action, I reaffirm my administration's longstanding commitment to a future of peace and security for the region.

There will, of course, be disagreement and dissent regarding this announcement. But we are confident that ultimately, as we work through these disagreements, we will arrive at a peace and a place far greater in understanding and cooperation.

This sacred city should call forth the best in humanity, lifting our sights to what it is possible; not pulling us back and down to the old fights that have become so totally predictable. Peace is never beyond the grasp of those willing to reach.

So today, we call for calm, for moderation, and for the voices of tolerance to prevail over the purveyors of hate. Our children should inherit our love, not our conflicts.

I repeat the message I delivered at the historic and extraordinary summit in Saudi Arabia earlier this year: The Middle East is a region rich with culture, spirit, and history. Its people are brilliant, proud, and diverse, vibrant and strong. But the incredible future awaiting this region is held at bay by bloodshed, ignorance, and terror.

Vice President Pence will travel to the region in the coming days to reaffirm our commitment to work with partners throughout the Middle East to defeat radicalism that threatens the hopes and dreams of future generations.

It is time for the many who desire peace to expel the extremists from their midst. It is time for all civilized nations, and people, to respond to disagreement with reasoned debate –- not violence.

And it is time for young and moderate voices all across the Middle East to claim for themselves a bright and beautiful future.

So today, let us rededicate ourselves to a path of mutual understanding and respect. Let us rethink old assumptions and open our hearts and minds to possible and possibilities. And finally, I ask the leaders of the region — political and religious; Israeli and Palestinian; Jewish and Christian and Muslim — to join us in the noble quest for lasting peace.

Thank you. God bless you. God bless Israel. God bless the Palestinians. And God bless the United States. Thank you very much. Thank you.

The day after President Trump gave this speech and publicly recognized Jerusalem as the capital of Israel, with VP Pence standing behind him, there was a Chanukah party in the White House. Farley was in attendance and had the opportunity to speak to Vice President Pence to thank him for his support for recognizing Jerusalem as Israel's capital. In his humble manner, Vice President Pence appreciated the kind words and credited the President for the decision.

Even after the announcement was made, there were still those who tried to frustrate it, including at the UN Security Council, which the US vetoed[740] and at the UN General Assembly, as noted above. Undaunted, President Trump pushed forward, and the next step was moving the Embassy to Jerusalem. Not unexpectedly, the location of the Embassy in Jerusalem now became a point of contention. As Jason D. Greenblatt[741] reports, some countries tried to convince the US to locate the Embassy in West Jerusalem, not the eastern portion that had been occupied by Jordan, prior to the Six-Day War in 1967. However, the Trump administration did not accept that argument, inasmuch as Jerusalem was a city that should not be divided, as the 1995 Jerusalem Embassy expressly provided.

Greenblatt records that he asked one of the most knowledgeable members of the career staff at the State Department to locate any document that 'recognized' East Jerusalem as Palestinian. Of course, the answer was there was no such document; it was just something that people at the State Department and elsewhere mindlessly said. It appears the baseless and pernicious rhetoric of anti-Israel sentiment had so infected and biased the minds of many at the State Department that critical and incisive thinking

---

[740] Explanation of Vote following the Veto of a Draft UN Security Council Resolution on Jerusalem, by Ambassador Nikki Haley, U.S. Permanent Representative to the United Nations, U.S. Mission to the United Nations New York City, dated December 18, 2017, at usun.usmission.gov.

[741] In the Path of Abraham, by Jason D. Greenblatt (Post Hill Press-2022), at page 225.

when it came to Jerusalem, was well neigh impossible for them. It was just an accepted part of the ideology within the corporate culture at the State Department and foreign policy establishment.

The actual location of the US Embassy in Jerusalem is a marvelous example of how mankind plans and G-d laughs. There was an existing consular facility in the Arnona section of Jerusalem, which Friedman thought could readily be retrofitted to become the Embassy. Providentially, a part of the Arnona facility was situated in West Jerusalem, but there's also a portion located in what was referred to as 'No Man's Land'[742]. This was the area between the Israeli and Jordanian positions under the 1949 Armistice Agreement.

When Vice President Mike Pence visited Israel in January of 2018, he asked Friedman when the Embassy would be opened in Jerusalem. Friedman responded he hoped within the year, but the State Department was not supporting him and was slow-rolling the process. Pence said he would check with the President, and so he did, informing Friedman at the airport as he was leaving that the President had put Friedman in charge of moving the Embassy.

Friedman reports he conferred with foreign-service officers who had expertise in security, logistics, real estate, land use, management and law. He presented each with the scenario of repositioning the existing Arnona consulate facility campus for the Embassy. By early February of 2018, he was convinced it would work and called Kelly to arrange for a call to report to and discuss the concept with the President. Friedman records that the President mused about Tillerson telling him, with all the detailed requirements, from land acquisition, zoning, design,

---

[742] See, for example, U.S. Jerusalem embassy lies' at the end of the world', by Stephen Farrell and Maayan Lubell, in Reuters, dated 7/17/2018 and US Opening Jerusalem Embassy on Territorial Anomaly, at VOA Middle East News, dated 5/13/2018.

security, protocols, etc., it could take at least ten years and cost a billion dollars. Friedman responded that he could do it in three months for one hundred and fifty thousand dollars. He offered that it already met all the security requirements as a functioning consulate and was also already performing some embassy functions. All that was needed was some money to build a few offices and some new plaques. The President responded that was incredible and when did Friedman want to open it. Friedman suggested May 14, 2018, which corresponded with the seventieth anniversary of Israel's independence. The President said that sounded great and to spend up to five hundred thousand to make it real nice. In response to Friedman's request that the President inform Tillerson, the President told Friedman to do so. He said to email anyone he thought necessary and that Friedman had the President's authorization to proceed as he had outlined. Friedman did so and received no express opposition. A few weeks later, he announced the Jerusalem Embassy would open on May 14, 2018, in Arnona, Jerusalem.

It is interesting to note that then Congressman, now Governor Ron DeSantis, also proposed relocating the Embassy to the Arnona site. He mentioned to Farley that he had conducted his own survey when he visited Israel in March of 2017[743]and confirmed that Arnona was the right site for the Embassy. He said he reported this to President Trump. He also referenced the Arnona site and the possibility of moving the Embassy there, in his introductory remarks[744], on November 8, 2017, at Hearing of the House Subcommittee on National Security he chaired, as follows:

---

[743] See, Congressman Ron DeSantis says Trump will make good on embassy move in promise, at I24 News, dated 3/5/2017; Congressman tours possible embassy sites in Jerusalem, confident Trump will move embassy, by Oren Lieberman, at CNN, dated 3/5/2017; and Florida governor-elect says his first trip abroad will be to Israel, in The Times of Israel, dated 11/8/2018.
[744] See the fuller discussion of this Hearing above, in Chapter XI.

...the Embassy can be relocated to one of the sites in
Jerusalem that the U.S. already controls. This can be as
simple as changing the sign on one of the existing
consulates. For example, the consulate annex in Arnona
combined eventually with the adjacent Diplomat Hotel can
be a sizeable complex that provides adequate security.
That the annex in Arnona straddles the 1949 armistice line
also counsels in its favor as a potential site.

For those who believe in divine providence, this is another
example confirming how there are no coincidences in life. Three
unrelated individuals, Jon Kyl, Ron DeSantis and Donald Trump,
interested in doing what was just and right, played their part in
the flow of history spanning over a period of over twenty-two
years and achieved what most everyone said was impossible. The
story continues to unfold as the Abraham Accords take hold and
expand the circle of peace and prosperity, but more on that
below.

In the meantime, Friedman was hard at work with his team on
the Embassy project and it was not easy to complete it on time.
The State Department has rigorous requirements for the
construction of an embassy, including that the construction
company have a minimum amount of prior experience working
for the State Department. Amazingly, as Friedman records, the
only eligible construction company in the region that could meet
the tight deadline requirements was of Turkish origin. Given that
Turkish President Erdogan was a vocal critic of the Embassy
move, Friedman was more than a little apprehensive that
Erdogan might interfere. It appears, though, either the matter
never crossed his desk or he didn't care to intervene and the
construction proceeded apace.

Friedman reports that even the wording on the plaque became a
heated issue with the State Department bureaucrats because the
top lines of the text correctly stated: United States Embassy,
Jerusalem, Israel. Imagine, staff members of the Near Eastern

Division were lecturing Ambassador Friedman about their strong-held views that because the President had not determined the final boundaries of Jerusalem, they could not be certain that the Embassy was, in fact, located in Israel and, therefore, that reference should be removed. Friedman then cleared the text with President Trump, Vice President Pence and John Bolton, who had by then become the National Security Advisor.

Interestingly, as Friedman records, the plaque names President Trump and Vice President Pence, as well as Ambassador Friedman. Tillerson was no longer the Secretary of State at the time the plaque was ordered, and so his name is not listed. Mike Pompeo is also not named because, although he had been nominated to be the Secretary of State, his appointment had not as yet been confirmed by the Senate at the time. However, once he became Secretary of State, not only did he strongly and publicly support the recognition of Jerusalem and the Embassy move there, but he also corrected many other untoward State Department policies. This included forthrightly and unreservedly confirming that Israeli settlements in Judea and Samaria, as well as, on the Golan Heights, per se, did not violate International Law[745], as outlined above.

The opening ceremony for the Embassy was moving and magnificent, as noted above. The Embassy is not just a building where local State Department administrative work is done. It stands today as a tangible reminder of the shared values and strength of the US-Israel relationship. It has become a place of homage by many visitors, who honor and treasure the relationship. One of the plaques is inscribed with the text of the Jerusalem Embassy Act. It is a fitting tribute to all those, like Jon Kyl, who worked so hard to make recognition of undivided Jerusalem as the capital of Israel and having the US Embassy

---

[745] See, for example, Full text of Pompeo's statement on settlements, in The Times of Israel, dated 11/19/2019.

there a reality. So too, the plaques recognizing that it was President Trump's determination that made it a reality and Ambassador Friedman's work that brought that vision to realization.

It is a testament to the proven wisdom of moving the Embassy to Jerusalem that President Trump's successor, President Biden and his administration confirmed it would remain in Jerusalem. This is unlike so many other policies of the Trump administration that were reversed by the Biden administration.

As Psalms[746] so eloquently declares: Pray for the peace of Jerusalem; they who love you shall prosper.

---

[746] Psalms 122:6.

XIII.

ANALYSIS OF THE SCOTUS DECISION IN ZIVOTOFSKY IN LIGHT OF PRESIDENT TRUMP'S RECOGNITION OF JERUSALEM

On June 8, 2015, the Supreme Court of the United States issued its decision in the case of Zivotofsky v. Kerry[747]. The case arose many years earlier[748] when the Zivotofskys sought to obtain a passport for their son, who was born in the City of Jerusalem, Israel, that correctly reflected the country of birth as Israel.

They made their request pursuant to Section 214 (d) of the Foreign Relations Authorizations Act of 2003. The law required the State Department, upon request, to record the place of birth of a US citizen born in Jerusalem, as Israel, on the US Passport issued to that person. However, the State Department refused to do so and the Zivitofskys brought suit in Federal Court to compel the issuance of the appropriate passport as required under Section 214(d).

While the Supreme Court determined that Section 214(d) was unenforceable at the time, its reasoning is most cogent. This is because the circumstances then existing, which the Court focused on in detail in rendering its decision, no longer exist. In

---

[747] 576 U.S. 1 (2015); 135 S.Ct. 2076 (2015).

[748] Zivotofsky v Secretary of State, 2004 WL 5835212 (D.D.C. 2007), reversed 444 F.3rd 614 (D.C. Circuit 2006), then 511 F.Supp.2nd 97 (D.D.C. 2007), affirmed 571 F.3rd 1227 (D.C. Circuit 2009), reversed under the name Zivotofsky v Clinton, 135 S.Ct. 1421 (2012), then 725 F.3rd 197 (D.C. Circuit 2013), certiorari granted under the name Zivotofsky v Kerry, 134 S. Ct. 1873 (2014) ultimately leading to the decision discussed above. Among other things, the earlier decisions dealt with whether this was a political question that could not be decided by the Court. Once the Supreme Court determined it was not a political question, the stage was set for the Court to rule on whether Section 214(d) was enforceable or not.

this regard, it is critically important to reflect on the conclusion of the Opinion of the Court, as artfully phrased by Justice Kennedy, who delivered the Opinion on behalf of the Court, to wit:

> Congress cannot command the President to contradict an earlier recognition determination in the issuance of passports.

By the same token, the Court also noted:

> But whether the realm is foreign or domestic, it is still the Legislative Branch, not the Executive Branch that makes the law... The Executive is not free from the ordinary controls and checks of Congress merely because foreign affairs are at issue... It is not for the President alone to determine the whole content of the Nation's foreign policy.

In analyzing the import of the Zivotofky decision, it is also necessary to consider what the Court did not do. Thus, while it could have ruled on the constitutionality of the Jerusalem Embassy Act of 1995, which expressly provided that undivided Jerusalem was the capital of Israel, it refrained from doing so[749]. It focused only on the enforceability of Section 214(d) and the issuance of the passport, in light of what it understood to be the President's then longstanding position that did not acknowledge any country's sovereignty over Jerusalem[750].

---

[749] The presidential waiver provision, contained in the Jerusalem Embassy Act of 1995, insulated the law from any serious constitutional challenge, as discussed above. It is interesting that the intent of some who originally proposed the waiver provision was, as a practical matter, to defeat the Law ever becoming effective. Yet, ironically, it was this very provision that assured the law would survive intact for President Trump to implement it. Now that he has done so, it remains effective as the law of the land and a future President may no longer unilaterally revoke recognition of Jerusalem in violation of the law, as more fully discussed below.

[750] As the Court notes, this was reflected in the Foreign Affairs Manual (Section 1383) at issue, which instructed State Department employees to record the place of birth for citizens born in Jerusalem as Jerusalem (i.e.: not Israel), purportedly because the US did

In essence, the Court held that Congress could not force the President to change the long-standing policy of the State Department regarding recognition of Jerusalem, borne of the corpus separatum delusion discussed above, which excluded sovereignty by either Israel or Jordan (and by extension the so-called Palestinians). Congress could legislate, as it did in the 1995 Jerusalem Embassy Act, but not expressly force the Executive Branch to change its existing recognition statement. It is suggested that had the administration never taken any position at all and been wholly silent on the issue of recognition and sovereignty over Jerusalem, then the Supreme Court might have reached a different result in Zivotofsky. This is especially so given the spirited and erudite dissenting opinion of Chief Justice Roberts, in which Justice Alito joined. As Chief Justice Roberts noted:

---

not recognize any country as having sovereignty over Jerusalem. This has since been changed, as more fully discussed above. As noted in Chapter II above, the Government in the Zivotofsky case argued it was pursuing the more than 60 year old policy of not recognizing any state's sovereignty over Jerusalem because of the unique sensitivity surrounding the issue (page 41 of Brief for the Respondent, on the Writ of Certiorari to the Supreme Court of the United States-no. 10-699, submitted by Donald B. Verrilli, Jr. Solicitor-General, et al, dated September 2011). In essence, the State Department was artificially preserving the internationalization (corpus separatum) scheme for Jerusalem, hatched by the UN in 1948 (which, in point of fact and law, was nothing more that a suggestion that was not legally binding), to negate any formal Israeli status for those born in Jerusalem. However, the Government's presentation ignored the even longer standing Presidential policy originated at San Remo and embodied in the 1924 Anglo-American Treaty and by virtue thereof US Law. Moreover, it appears that this later policy urged by the State Department contravened the substantive import of this prior existing US Law, as well as, the President's prior stated position. Furthermore, the Governmental assurances regarding the history of Presidential policy regarding Jerusalem should, at the very least, have been seriously qualified by virtue of the Treaty and the rights it granted, which survive and have the force of US Law. It should also be noted, as discussed in Chapter II, that Solicitor General Verrilli stated: "The position of the executive is that we recognize, as a practical matter, the authority of Israel over West Jerusalem...". In essence, as the Solicitor General admitted, the matter of recognition was much more nuanced, and it could not be unqualifiedly argued that there had been no Executive Branch recognition at all.

Never before has this Court accepted a President's direct defiance of an Act of Congress in the field of foreign affairs...

The first principles in this area are firmly established. The Constitution allocates some foreign policy powers to the Executive, grants some to the Legislature, and enjoins the President to "take Care that the Laws be faithfully executed." Art. II, §3. The Executive may disregard "the expressed or implied will of Congress" only if the Constitution grants him a power "at once so conclusive and preclusive" as to "disabl[e] the Congress from acting upon the subject." Youngstown, 343 U. S., at 637–638 (Jackson, J., concurring)...

The majority attempts to reconcile its position by reconceiving §214(d) as a "mandate that the Executive contradict his prior recognition determination in an official document issued by the Secretary of State." Ante, at 27...

As Chief Justice Roberts pointed out, ultimately, the Government's position is based on the supposition that the President has the exclusive authority to conduct diplomatic relations, which was rejected by the majority opinion, as well. The Government's reliance on the Supreme Court decision in United States v. Curtiss-Wright Export Corp.[751] was misplaced. As the majority rightly acknowledged, Curtiss Wright did not involve a claim that the Executive Branch could contravene a statute; it held only that the President could act pursuant to a legislative delegation. As Chief Justice Roberts went on to state:

But our precedents have never accepted such a sweeping understanding of executive power. See Hamdan, 548 U. S., at 591–592; Dames & Moore, 453 U. S., at 661–662; Youngstown, 343 U. S., at 587 (majority opinion); id., at

---

[751] 299 U. S. 304, 319–320 (1936).

635, n. 2 (Jackson, J., concurring); cf. Little, 2 Cranch, at 179 (Marshall, C. J.)...

Just a few Terms ago, this Court rejected the President's argument that a broad foreign relations power allowed him to override a state court decision that contradicted U. S. international law obligations. Medellín, 552 U. S., at 523–532. If the President's so-called general foreign relations authority does not permit him to countermand a State's lawful action, it surely does not authorize him to disregard an express statutory directive enacted by Congress, which—unlike the States—has extensive foreign relations powers of its own.

In any event, the precise concern cited by the majority as the basis of its opinion was mooted when President Trump, on December 6, 2017, recognized Jerusalem as the capital of Israel.

The Biden administration reconfirmed that the US Embassy would remain in Jerusalem, which is recognized as the capital of Israel[752].

The State Departments Foreign Affairs Manual[753] was also amended to provide that for those born after May 14, 1948 (i.e., when the reestablished State of Israel was declared and recognized by President Truman), in Jerusalem, if the applicant lists Israel, the POB (place of birth) must be Israel on the US passport.

Interestingly, the State Department Foreign Affairs Manual notes:

As stated in the President's December 6, 2017 Jerusalem Proclamation, the United States recognizes Jerusalem as the capital of Israel and its seat of government but

---

[752] White House Confirms Biden will keep embassy in Jerusalem, by Niels Lesniewski, in Roll Call, dated 2/9/2021.
[753] 8 FAM 403.4

continues to take no position on the boundaries of Israeli sovereignty in Jerusalem. The final boundaries of sovereignty in Jerusalem remain subject to final status negotiation between the two Parties.

However, in practice, it correctly does not distinguish between the existing borders of Jerusalem and those prior to 1967. Thus, unless and until the parties agree otherwise, Israel is the sovereign authority over Jerusalem. Indeed, even in the case of those born prior to May 14, 1947, the distinction made is concerning the borders of Jerusalem at the time, not since.

It should also be noted that the actual language in the President's recognition text is somewhat different than that recorded in the Foreign Affairs Manual. It states:

This decision is not intended, in any way, to reflect a departure from our strong commitment to facilitate a lasting peace agreement. We want an agreement that is a great deal for the Israelis and a great deal for the Palestinians. We are not taking a position of any final status issues, including the specific boundaries of the Israeli sovereignty in Jerusalem, or the resolution of contested borders. Those questions are up to the parties involved.

The President's statement is more nuanced than the Foreign Affairs Manual. It is only in the context of the resolution of the final status issues by the parties that the President is not taking a position on the specific boundaries of Israeli sovereignty in Jerusalem. However, unless and until that occurs, undivided Jerusalem, as it exists today, as specified in the 1995 Jerusalem Embassy Act, is recognized as the capital of Israel. Indeed, as a practical matter, the State Department Foreign Affairs Manual also does not specify otherwise in terms of recording Israel as the place of birth for applicants born in present-day Jerusalem requesting the same, as noted above. In effect, the results yielded in any final status agreement are in the nature of conditions subsequent, not conditions precedent.

It is now undeniable that the 1995 Jerusalem Embassy Act is the law of the land and the President has no more right to violate this law than any other law. Thus, the President can no longer unilaterally retract recognition, impinge on, dilute or otherwise act with impunity regarding the matter of recognition of undivided Jerusalem, as expressly provided in the law.

It is most gratifying to note that the Zivotofsky case had a wonderful conclusion. Approximately eighteen years after his birth in the City of Jerusalem, Israel, US Ambassador David Friedman issued Menachem Zivotofsky a US passport recording that he was born in Israel[754]. It was reputedly the first such passport so issued[755].

The issuance of the passport to Zivotofsky in Jerusalem is especially poignant. As Psalms[756] states, just like Jerusalem is enfolded with hills, so too will G-d enfold the Jewish people, now and forever. Psalms[757] also records G-d's blessings will emanate from Zion and how will be blessed to share in the prosperity of Jerusalem and live to see children's children; peace be upon Israel[758].

---

[754] Which Jerusalemite was first to put 'Israel' as birthplace on passport?, by Tovah Lazaroff, in the Jerusalem Post, dated 11/1/2020.

[755] Even after President Trump had recognized Jerusalem as Israel's capital and even after the Embassy had been moved to Jerusalem, the State Department had still not agreed to put Israel on U.S. Passports for Americans who were born in Israel. Farley had the opportunity on a conference call with Secretary Pompeo to ask him to correct the Passport situation and Pompeo responded that he was working on it and hoped to have a decision soon. True to his word, within a few months after the conference call, Secretary Pompeo approved putting Israel on U.S. Passports as a place of birth for U.S. citizens born in Jerusalem.

[756] Psalms 125:2.

[757] Psalms 128:5.

[758] Psalms 128:6.

Let's continue to strengthen the US-Israel relationship and build on that solid foundation to bring peace and prosperity to the region and beyond.

XIV.

MALIGN ACTIVITIES OF HAMAS AND THE WAR OF WORDS

Gaza is occupied by Gazans. Neither Egypt nor Israel, its territorial neighbors, occupy Gaza, as a matter of fact or law.

Yet, the provocative terms "occupation" and "occupier" are casually used, by many in the news media and others, to describe the relationship between Gaza and Israel. The words project an explosive image of Israel as a so-called occupier, which is assumed to be oppressing an otherwise innocent and peaceful Gaza. The portrayal is expressed with such certainty as if the occupation were an obvious truth, but it is a categorically false pronouncement. Gaza is not occupied by Israel, and Gaza's problems are self-inflicted[759].

The foundational definition of the term occupation under International Law is embodied in the Hague Convention[760]. It provides that a territory is only considered occupied when it is actually placed under the authority of a hostile army. The occupation extends only to the territory where such authority has been established and can be exercised. There have been a number of cases over the years that have analyzed whether an occupation existed under International Law and the nature of its

---

[759] See, Gaza's Miseries Have Palestinian Authors, an opinion piece by Brett Stephens, in the New York Times, dated May 16, 2018.
[760] Convention IV, Annex to the Convention Regulations Respecting the Laws and Customs of War on Land, Section III: Military Authority over the Territory of the Hostile State, Article 42.

essential constituent elements, to wit: (1) a military presence in the occupied territory; and (2) effective control of the territory.

One of the lead decisions is a judgment by the United States Military Tribunal in Nuremberg[761], in 1948, in the aftermath of World War II. The Tribunal held that an occupation was more than an armed conflict, which destroyed any organized resistance. It also required maintaining a military presence and exercising governmental authority over the area conquered, to the exclusion of the established civil government.

In 2003, an International Tribunal[762] dealing with claims of human rights violations in the aftermath of the breakup of Yugoslavia further refined the standards for determining when an occupation existed under International Law. It focused on the degree of control necessary to support such a finding. The Tribunal held that control meant actual and effective overall control over a territory and listed the indicia to be considered in making such a determination, as outlined below.

As a threshold matter, the military forces of the conquered territory must have surrendered, been defeated or withdrawn[763]. The putative occupier must have established its own temporary governmental administration over the territory, which it substituted for the displaced original government that it had rendered incapable of functioning publicly. The occupier had to be in a position to issue and enforce directions to the civilian

---

[761] United States v. List, United Nations War Crimes Commission, Law Reports of Trials of War Criminals, Volume VIII, 1949, CASE No. 47, THE HOSTAGES TRIAL, TRIAL OF WILHELM LIST AND OTHERS, UNITED STATES MILITARY TRIBUNAL, NUREMBERG, Part I, beginning at page 38.

[762] Judgment, by the International Tribunal for the Prosecution of Persons Responsible for Serious Violations of International Humanitarian Law Committed in the Territory of Former Yugoslavia, in Prosecutor v. Naletic and Martinovic (Case No. IT-98-34-T), dated March 31, 2003.

[763] The Tribunal noted that areas where battles were still being fought were not to be considered occupied territory; although, this did not include sporadic resistance in areas already conquered.

population of the conquered territory. In addition, it had to maintain a military presence, on the ground, in the territory. The military force present either had to be sufficient, on its own, to make its occupying power felt, or there had to be a capacity to send additional troops within a reasonable period of time to do so.

Unless all of these criteria were satisfied, there was no occupation, as a matter of law. The Tribunal went on to say the law of occupation applied only to those areas actually so controlled by the occupying power. The occupation ceased when the occupying power no longer forcibly exercised this degree of actual and effective control.

In 2005, an International Tribunal[764]dealing with the conflict between Uganda and the Congo focused on the requirement of a continuing military presence as a condition to finding there was an occupation. Its analysis is cogent. It held that merely having the potential to invade and control a territory, not coupled with an actual presence and effective control, was insufficient.

The requirement that all these tests be met in order to establish the existence of an occupation makes eminent sense. Otherwise, it might well be argued that the United States occupies Canada and Mexico, not because it does, but because it could. The United States also has security arrangements with and military bases in such far-flung places as Germany, South Korea, the Philippines and elsewhere. Yet it would be nonsensical to suggest that it was, therefore, an occupying power in those countries. This is because it does not, in fact, exercise effective control. Moreover, a security arrangement or military presence, pursuant to an agreement with the host country, like those noted above, is neither hostile nor forcibly imposed.

---

[764] Armed Activities on the Territory of the Congo (Democratic Republic of the Congo v. Uganda), I.C.J. Reports 2005, beginning at page 168.

How, then, could the terms "occupation" and "occupier" be so cavalierly, albeit inappropriately, applied to Israel's present relationship with Gaza? How is it that so many are taken in by this canard? It may help to outline some of the modern history of Gaza to better understand how ludicrous it is to continue to mislabel Israel as an occupier of Gaza.

The European Court of Human Rights[765], in 2015, also ruled on whether control of the airspace above a territory and the adjacent sea was sufficient to constitute an occupation under International Law. The Court held that an occupation did not exist unless the alleged occupier had its military troops on the ground in the subject territory, in addition to being in a position to exercise effective control, without the consent of the sovereign. The Court found that the presence of foreign troops was a sine qua non (essential condition) for there to be an occupation. As the Court noted, an occupation is inconceivable without "boots on the ground". It went on to say, therefore, forces exercising naval or air control did not suffice.

Gaza has borders with Israel and Egypt. Both Israel and Egypt, like so many other countries, have a security presence on their own side of the border, but not in Gaza. They also have the general right to control their own borders and close them to non-citizens[766]. Our own US Supreme Court[767] recognized this as a sovereign right of all countries. It held it was an established principle of International Law that every sovereign nation has the power, as inherent in sovereignty and essential to self-preservation, to forbid the entrance of foreigners within its

---

[765] Sargsyan v Azerbaijan (Application no. 40167/06), Judgment dated June 16, 2015 and Chiragove and others v Armenia (Application no. 13216/05), Judgment dated June 16, 2015.
[766] There are limited exceptions under International Law for asylum seekers and refugees.
[767] Ekiu v US, 142 US 651, 659 (1892).

dominions or to admit them only in such cases and upon such conditions as it may see fit to prescribe.

Gaza also has a security presence on its side of the borders with Egypt and Israel. It controls who and what enters and leaves[768] Gaza.

The Egyptian border crossing with Gaza is not controlled by Israel; it is controlled by Gaza and Egypt. Gaza also has use of its own adjacent territorial waters, but not for the purpose of importing weapons and other such materials, which are proscribed under the Oslo II Agreement[769] and the Disengagement Agreement of 2005[770]. As discussed in Chapter III, under these Agreements, Israel has certain rights to patrol Gaza's coastal waters and air space in order to enable Israel to interdict the delivery of any illegal weapons or other expressly prohibited contraband to Gaza. These agreed-upon rights do not constitute effective governmental control[771] over Gaza.

Notwithstanding the foregoing, Hamas has managed to smuggle in rockets, other prohibited weapons and war-making materials in flagrant breach of these Agreements, including by sea, over

---

[768] See, for example, As Gaza hospitals suffer shortages, Hamas refuses Israeli medical aid, by Judah Ari Gross and AP, in the Times of Israel, on May 16, 2018; Hamas border guard killed in suicide attack on Gaza-Egypt border, by Jack Khoury, in Haaretz, dated August 17, 2017; Hamas is known for its suicide attacks. Now it's been hit by one for the first time, by Hazem Balousha and Loveday Morris, in the Washington Post, dated August 17, 2017; and Hamas closes Gaza border following assassination, by Elior Levy, on Ynet, on March 26, 2017.

[769] Annex I, Articles XIII and XIV of the Oslo II Agreement.

[770] Israel-Palestinian Authority Agreement on Movement and Access and Agreed Principles for Rafah Crossing, signed on November 15, 2005.

[771] See, Israel and the Struggle over the International Laws of War, by Peter Berkowitz, Hoover Institution Press-2012; Occupation and other forms of Administration of Foreign Territory, Report of Expert Meeting, by Tristan Ferraro, of the ICRC, dated March 2012; and Is Gaza Occupied?: Redefining the Status of Gaza Under International Law, by Elizabeth Samson, in the American University International Law Review, Volume 25, Issue 5, Article 4 (2010). See also the 2015 Judgments of the European Court of Human Rights, discussed below.

land, and through underground tunnels illicitly constructed under the Egyptian border[772].

Alas, Gaza and its people are under the control of Hamas, a terrorist organization[773]. Its avowed goal, enshrined in its Charter, is the destruction of Israel[774]. It also espouses antisemitic and genocidal doctrines[775] directed against the Jews, generally.

Hamas has attacked both its neighbors, Egypt[776] and Israel. This required each to close their borders from time to time. However, despite Hamas's continuing malevolent activities, they have each reopened border crossings to provide humanitarian aid to the people of Gaza[777]. It appears that Israel is more concerned

---

[772] See, for example, Shin Bet: Hamas bringing weapons, rocket-making material into Gaza, by Judah Ari Gross, in the Times of Israel, dated May 16, 2016; and Israel: Rockets Smuggled Into Gaza, by Steven Gutkin, the Associated Press, dated April 28, 2006; and reported in the Washington Post. See also Hamas Firing China-Designed, Syria-Made M-302 Rockets: Israel, on the NBC news site, dated July 10, 2014.

[773] Hamas is designated a terrorist organization by the US. See US State Department Country Reports on Terrorism, dated April 27, 2005, Chapter 6, Terrorist Groups, listing Hamas as a Foreign Terrorist Organization.

[774] See, Articles 6, 11, 13 and 14 of the Covenant of Hamas.

[775] See, Article 7 of the Covenant of Hamas. See also, for example, Hamas in Their Own Words, dated May 2, 2011, on the ADL website; Anti Semitic Hate Speech in the Name of Islam, by Matthias Küntzel, in Der Spiegel online, dated May 16, 2008; Palestinian Nazi flags and Hamas talking points, by Sean Durns, at JNS, dated April 26, 2018; and Hamas co-founder admits 'we are deceiving the public' about peaceful protests, by TOI staff, at the Times of Israel, dated May 17, 2018.

[776] See, Hamas: Increased security along Gaza-Sinai frontier after deadly attack - Arab-Israeli Conflict, by Adam Rasgon, in the Jerusalem Post, on July 9, 2017; Egypt seals last breach in Gaza border, a Reuters report on the Australian Broadcasting Corporation news website, dated February 3, 2008; and Egypt and Palestine: The Hamas Factor - Palestinian Nationalism: Regional Perspectives, by Hamr Hamzawy, dated September 8, 2017, on the Carnegie Endowment for International Peace website;

[777] See, Israel to reopen Gaza crossing after rioters burn it for 3rd time, by Judah Ari Gross, in the Times of Israel, on May 15, 2018; and Egypt opens Gaza border following three-day closure, by Rabie Abu Zamil, on the Anadolu Agency website, dated July 2, 2018.

about the health and welfare of the people of Gaza than Hamas or the PA[778].

Instead of choosing peace[779], Hamas chose to wage an offensive war against Israel, shooting many thousands of rockets and mortar shells into Israel, launching explosive and incendiary devices against Israel and attempting armed incursions of Israel. Hamas uses human shields and creates provocations in order to cause incidents, which, as Hamas intends, are then dutifully reported by the news media. All this is instead of living in peace with its neighbors and devoting itself to the development of Gaza for the benefit of its people[780]. Yet, Hamas remains firmly in control of Gaza and continues, however unwisely, to govern it[781].

Consider, if Hamas were so interested in the health and welfare of the people of Gaza and their ability to travel outside of Gaza, then why is it spending so much treasure on the surreptitious acquisition of missiles and other offensive weapons prohibited under the Oslo II Agreement[782] and building terror tunnels? Why is it not focused, instead, on building infrastructure to improve the lives of the people? Why is it continuing to attack Israel and Egypt? Neither Egypt nor Israel threatens Gaza. Before it proceeded on this reckless belligerent path, Gaza was doing mutually beneficial business with Israel; Gazans regularly worked in Israel and Gaza's GDP was growing, not declining. The issue is not Israel or Egypt; it is Hamas that is the problem.

---

[778] See, The Palestinian Authority Rejects Israeli US Ideas to Help Gaza, by Khaled Abu Toameh, in the Jerusalem Post, dated June 26, 2018, as well as, Israel reopens Gaza crossing, but Palestinians turn back some trucks, by Judah Ari Gross, in the Times of Israel, on May 15, 2018.

[779] See, Hamas could have chosen peace. Instead, it made Gaza suffer, by Dennis Ross, an opinion peace in the Washington Post, on August 8, 2014.

[780] See, Gaza and Hamas, by Elliot Abrams, on the Council on Foreign Relations website, dated May 16, 2018.

[781] See, Hamas co-founder says Gaza-based group 'stronger than it has ever been', I24 News, 12/14/17.

[782] Annex I, Article XIV:4 of the Oslo II Agreement.

Why is the news media not focused on these matters? Why is it instead reinforcing the fiction of a so-called occupation? Why are many people taken in by this con, perpetuated by Hamas, with the active or at least complicit support of the news media? Why does the media continue, repeatedly, to make the same mistake of relying on what amounts to Hamas-generated propaganda? When will they and others learn that there is something wrong afoot? Indeed, something is egregiously wrong when a violent invasion of Israel by Hamas-controlled Gaza is falsely called a peaceful protest[783] and the armed participants, who were shot, are incorrectly referred to as protestors[784]. There is a pattern here; it's not just a one-time innocent mistake that might be casually overlooked.

Perhaps, the answer, in part, lies in how news reports originate in places under the tight control of a terrorist or totalitarian regime like Hamas[785]. Often reporters are, figuratively, parachuted in to cover a conflict or other explosive situation. Their guides are often untrustworthy and more likely to be minders in the employ of the regime's security services. They don't have existing sources, proven to be reliable, or other facilities for independently fact-checking a story. The local press is neither free nor reliable. Hamas has censored, threatened, intimidated, jailed, silenced, and, in effect, co-opted the local press into its service[786]. Indeed, most of the local news media is

---

[783] See, Hamas Leader Admits Gaza Protests are Not Peaceful, in Israel Today, dated May 16, 2018; Senior Hamas Official: This Is Not Peaceful Resistance, It Is Supported by Our Weapons, by Andrew Kugle, in The Washington Free Beacon, dated May 15, 2018; and Media Coverage of Israeli-Palestinian Clash is Built on a Myth, by David Harsanyi, in National Review, dated May 18, 2018.

[784] See, CAMERA Prompts Los Angeles Times Correction on Fatalities Among Gaza 'Protestors', dated June 25, 2018, at camera.org.

[785] See, for example, Hamas' rules for reporters control news, by Clifford D. May, an analysis/opinion piece in the Washington Times, dated, August 5, 2014; and The Palestinians and the Press Hazards for Reporters Working in the West Bank and Gaza, by Dave Gilson, in Frontline/World, at PBS.org, March 2003

[786] See, Gagged in Gaza, in the Economist, dated September 24, 2016; Press freedom group shocked at Hamas ban on Gaza journalists, by Roy Greenslade, in the Guardian,

funded by Hamas. Given the hold Hamas has on the people of Gaza, even seemingly spontaneous interviews of individuals on the street are suspect, as nothing more than Hamas-staged Kabuki Theater.

Foreign journalists on the ground in Gaza are easy prey for the Hamas information/propaganda apparatus. They usually only see what Hamas wants them to see. With pressing deadlines, they often just report the unverified information supplied by inherently unreliable Hamas-linked sources. As a result, the news media often gets it wrong. Just check the articles cited in this book or the online corrections site for a newspaper and see how many times this occurs. Unfortunately, by the time the truth ultimately emerges, it is too late, and it is not afforded the same coverage or interest as the original flawed report.

But this is only a part of the story. It appears there are more insidious reasons for the biased and otherwise less-than-truthful reporting regarding Israel and Gaza. In 2014, Hamas attacked Israel with many thousands of rockets, targeting exclusively civilian areas in Israel. Many of the rocket and mortar attacks were launched from densely populated neighborhoods in the vicinity of hotels and offices (where foreign journalists[787] were located), mosques, hospitals and schools. Yet, somehow, reports or photographs of this activity were not published by the news media at the time. Instead, we were bombarded with provocative images and news reports focused on the tragic consequences of

---

on January 1, 2013; In Gaza and West Bank, Palestinian journalists fear squeeze on free press, by Nidal al-Mughrabi and Ali Sawafta, in Reuters, on September 19, 2016; In Gaza, authorities crack down on freedom of speech, by Victoria Schneider, in the New Arab, dated November 13, 2017; Violations of Freedom of the Press in Gaza, on the IDF.il website; West Bank and Gaza, on the Freedom House website; and Palestine: Dangerous escalation in attacks on freedom of expression, on the Amnesty International website, dated August 23, 2017;

[787] This is not the first time something like this occurred. See Gaza Reporter Caught on Tape Confirming Hamas Fired Rockets Near TV Offices, by Yoav Stern, in Haaretz, on January 1, 2009.

what the media falsely described as indiscriminate or even intentional bombing of civilian targets in Gaza.

The news media just repeated the misinformation received from Hamas-controlled sources as if it were credible[788]. Any counter-narrative, which contradicted the Hamas one, appears to have been suppressed. What happened to the highly touted journalistic standards of integrity and editorial safeguards[789] designed to prevent this kind of abuse? They were nowhere apparent in the often false, misleading, biased[790], or hyperbolic pronouncements[791] of reporters on the ground in Gaza or news anchors at home, seemingly caught up in the moment. It was not serious, thoughtful, and responsible reporting; it was theater. The more gruesome the visuals, the better TV it made. It was a Hamas-orchestrated dramatic presentation right out of its propaganda playbook.

It was only later that we learned about the travesty of this reporting when the Hamas-inspired canard was laid bare. The sites Israel targeted were being used for rocket or mortar attacks against Israel. It was, most assuredly, not intentionally or indiscriminately bombing civilian targets. To the contrary, Israel took precautions to safeguard civilians, including providing advance warning of the sites to be bombed. As a result, the casualty figures for innocent civilians were significantly lower than is typical in comparable conflicts elsewhere in the world[792].

---

[788] See, Hamas Lies and the media believed it, by Oren Kessler, in US News, dated August 12, 2014.

[789] See, What the Media Gets Wrong About Israel, by Matti Friedman, in The Atlantic, dated November 30, 2014.

[790] See, for example, BBC Bias in Gaza, by Simon Plosker, on the Honest Reporting website, dated July 9, 2014; and Reporting from Jerusalem: The astonishing bias of NBC's Ayman Mohyeldin, by Richard Grenell, on Fox News, dated October 16, 2015. See, for example, BBC finds Andrew Marr guilty of rules breach over a 'misleading' claim that Israel killed 'lots of Palestinian kids', by Chris Hastings, in the Daily Mail, on June 24, 2018; and Was it okay for U.K. journalist to make emotional, personal video about Gaza children?, in Haaretz, on September 10, 2014.

[792] See, for example, Stop ignoring the facts about Cast Lead, by Jonathan Sacerdoti, in the New Statesman, dated December 30, 2011.

This was achieved, despite Hamas' urging civilians to stay, become martyrs and not heed Israel's advance warnings to leave the area.

Imagine if Hamas actually cared about its people. It could have avoided any civilian casualties by choosing not to attack Israel. Instead, it elected to start an unprovoked and offensive war against Israel, launching rocket and mortar attacks against civilian areas in Israel and using its own civilian population as human shields. Hamas intentionally and mercilessly put Gazan children and adults in harm's way in order to maximize civilian casualties.

How was it then that the reality of the situation was callously ignored, even as rockets were being fired in the vicinity of news studios and hotels where news people stayed? Could the journalists in Gaza have been so unaware of everything occurring around them? It strains credulity to accept this as the explanation. Didn't good reporting require checking where the rockets were fired from and to confirm whether the Hamas tales about indiscriminate bombing were, in fact, true?

Later, it emerged that journalists were being intimidated, threatened, and acting under duress[793]. They risked bodily harm or being expelled from Gaza if they challenged Hamas and

---

[793] See, Why Everything Reported from Gaza is Crazy Twisted, by Mark Levine, in the Tower Magazine, Issue 17, August 2014; Testimonies from Gaza and Hamas Intimidation of foreign journalists, on the Israel Ministry of Foreign Affairs website, dated August 11, 2014; Foreign press group condemns Hamas intimidation in Gaza, by Stuart Winer, in Times of Israel, dated August 11, 2014; Hamas Admits to Intimidating Foreign Journalists, by Simon Plosker, in Honest Reporting on its website, dated August 17, 2014; BBC interviewee admits intimidation of journalists in Gaza, bbcwatch.org, dated August 16, 2014; Hamas admits intimidating foreign press who reported wrong 'message', by TOI Staff, at the Times of Israel, on August 15, 2014; Foreign journalists reveal Hamas' false front, by Daniel Bettini, in Ynet news.com, dated August 7, 2014; Foreign Press group blasts Hamas' 'thuggish behavior', by TOI Staff, at the Times of Israel, dated May 21, 2016; and Gaza prejudice and perfidy, an opinion piece at the Jerusalem Post, by David Weinberg, dated May 17, 2018.

reported news contradicting its false narrative[794]. Cameras were broken and reporters were prevented from filming anti-Hamas demonstrations, where many Gazans were shot dead by Hamas operatives. Some foreign journalists were even threatened with death. Editors[795] worried about their people on the ground in Gaza and said nothing. Many reporters on the ground in Gaza feared reprisals and, hence, didn't provide a report of what was actually occurring until they were safely out of Gaza. Eventually, the true facts began to leak out[796]. However, it wasn't until well after the fact that the Foreign Press Association condemned Hamas' intimidation tactics and interference with their reporting in Gaza[797].

When will the media recognize that, whether willingly or unwillingly, they have, in effect, become an integral part of the Hamas apparatus intended to spread misinformation? In effect, real-time reporting, under these circumstances, without the benefit of informed, serious, intensive and independent fact-checking, should be qualified by a disclaimer that the reporting is biased, inherently flawed and lacks credibility. This condition must be factored into our own appreciation of what we are hearing or seeing on the news or elsewhere.

---

[794] See, the in-depth analysis of the problem in: The Media Intifada: Bad Math, Ugly Truths About New York Times in Israel-Hamas War, by Richard Behar, in Forbes, dated August 21, 2014

[795] See, An Insiders Guide to the Most Important Story on Earth, by Matti Friedman, in Tablet Magazine, dated August 26, 2014.

[796] See, 'Don't Use Me': Reporter Admits Seeing Rocket Fired from Gaza Hospital, then Blasts Pro-Israel Media for Quoting Her, by Shoshana Schwartz, in the Blaze, on August 3, 2014; Rare Footage Appears to Capture Gaza Rocket Site, by Nick-Robbins Early, dated August 5, 2014; The story Behind NDTV's rocket launch footage, by Uriel Hellman, JTA, August 7, 2014; Hamas admits it did use schools and hospitals in Gaza Strip as 'human shields' to launch rocket attacks on Israel-but claims it was a 'mistake', by Mathew Blake, in the Daily Mail, on September 12. 2014; Gaza rocket launched during CBC interview, CBC News, August 8, 2014; and Why Everything Reported from Gaza is Crazy Twisted, by Mark Levine, in the Tower Magazine, Issue 17, August 2014;

[797] See, Foreign press group condemns Hamas Intimidation in Gaza, by Stuart Winer, in the Times of Israel, on August 11, 2014;

It is important for us not to be so naïve as to believe that everyone in the media is wise or devoted to the truth. History teaches us otherwise. Never underestimate the power of laziness or stupidity; no profession is immune.

Sometimes, though, the motives are more sinister. A reporter can be biased[798] and influenced by deeply held ideological beliefs, including a misplaced sense of virtue too closely identified with the self-proclaimed victimhood of Hamas-controlled Gaza. Some can be callous and cynical about the content of their reporting. They recognize the power of glaring headlines and displaying raw and horrible images, no matter the provenance or whether truthful or accurate. They are only interested in the potential for ratings generated from a viewership addicted, like voyeurs, to savage imagery. They may not intend to be enablers[799], but when dealing with terrorist enterprises like Hamas, this is the net effect of their misguided actions. These are not new phenomena and its masters were and are some of the most disreputable forces in modern history[800].

---

[798] The New York Times had to end a relationship with a reporter who assisted on its Middle East reporting when Honestreporting.com under the leadership of Gil Hoffman discovered that the reporter publicly called for the murder of all Jews, on Facebook.
[799] See, Palestinians in Gaza are Dying for a Photo Op, by Liel Liebowitz, in Tablet Magazine, on May 15, 2018, as well as, Pavlich: Media gives Hamas exactly what they want, by Katie Pavlich, in the Hill, dated May 15, 2018.
[800] Nazi Germany and its use of euphemisms like resettlement, special actions, special handling and the final solution to mask the mass murder of 6 million Jews is just one example. Others include Stalin, who, for example, covered up the reality of the pervasive famine that ensued as a result of his so-called "collectivization" program in the Ukraine and other parts of the former Soviet Union, in the years 1932-33. Many millions of people died from hunger as a result of the forced collectivization. (See The Man-Made Famine of 1932-1933 in Soviet Ukraine, by Bohdan Krawchenko in Conflict Quarterly, Spring 1984: Kazakhstan: The Forgotten Famine, by Bruce Pannier, Radio Free Europe, Radio Liberty, dated December 28, 2007; and How Stalin Hid Ukraine's Famine From the World, by Anne Applebaum, in Atlantic Magazine, dated October 13, 2017.)
The use of the term collectivization is instructive, because it exemplifies how easily a virtuous sounding label can fool people. What could be wrong with working collectively together to accomplish a worthy goal, in furtherance of the common good? Unfortunately, that is not what the term, in fact, described. It was a euphemism for

The major difference between the past and the present are the enhanced modes of communication in today's information age. The evil intent of propaganda has not changed. However, its effect has been enhanced because of the power of this new media to reach and influence people. The propagation of disinformation via social media and other Internet platforms has become a near science[801]. Hamas and the digital propaganda apparatus it controls have become masters of the medium, using social media, bots, trolls and sham or less circumspect news sites

---

forcibly taking away a peasant's crops, seeds, farmland, home, livestock, agricultural tools and most other belongings. Even after one intrepid journalist disclosed the enormity of the crime, the accepted wisdom was there was no famine. Rather, the mantra promoted by many of the remaining foreign journalists in Russia, who supported the false utopian vision of communism, was that the Russians were hungry, but not starving. The wordsmiths might just as well have substituted the word "plenty" for "hunger". After all, those suffering from malnutrition had plenty of problems. Another example is Mao's so-called "Great Leap Forward" program for China, in the years 1958-62. It was nothing of the sort; it was just another exercise in deceit. Overly ambitious goals for food production were established, never met and falsely reported as achieved. Grain needed for subsistence was seized. Instead of feeding the people, it was used to make ethyl alcohol to fuel newly developed missiles and as a cash crop for export to fund the modernization of the military. Mao's effort at central planning and agricultural development was not a great success, as he claimed; it was a spectacular failure. This time, many tens of millions of people died from starvation in the ensuing famine. (See China's Great Famine; the true story, by Tania Branigan, in the Guardian, dated January 1, 2013; After 50 Years of Silence, China Slowly Confronts the 'Great Leap Forward', by Helen Gao, in The Atlantic, dated May 29, 2012; Remembering the Biggest Mass Murder in the History of the World, by Ilya Sonim, in the Washington Post, dated August, 3, 2016; and Mao's Great Leap to Famine, by Frank Dikotter, in the New York Times, dated December 15, 2010.)
These awful, avoidable, man-made tragedies were covered up, at the time. Many willingly or innocently participated in this charade, because they believed they were serving a higher purpose. Some were what the KGB reportedly referred to as UI's or useful idiots. Others were more sinister and had their own self-styled virtuous motives for perpetuating a fraud on the clueless public. Those desiring to tell the whole truth and nothing but the truth were deemed to be lacking in virtue. These failed experiments in scientific socialism and central planning are not generally and intensively studied in school. It's a pity. There are some valuable lessons to be learnt from how socialism actually functioned in practice. It might temper the enthusiasm of some who suggest embracing this bankrupt economic system, yet again.
[801] See, Disinformation Wars, by Chris Meserole and Alina Polyakova, in Foreign Policy, dated May 25, 2018. See also Israel is Losing the Social Media War, by David Patrikarakos, in Tablet Magazine, on June 25, 2018.

to disseminate and repeat provocative and pithy slogans, false information and bogus[802], staged or manufactured images as potent tools to fool us.

Many innocent people are profoundly affected or even overwhelmed by the provocative imagery and seemingly virtuous sentiments expressed. The constant repetition of messages that go viral makes them seem reliable. It is also so easy to succumb to their simplicity and seductive charm, championing the rights of supposed victims. Never mind that the victims may actually be the aggressors. It is exceedingly difficult not to virtue signal acceptance of the apparent popular wisdom; it's all but irresistible. The new media is a gift to propagandists and others seeking to disseminate their agenda-driven messages. This may soon become an even more challenging problem as Artificial Intelligence is adapted to become a player in this black art of disinformation. Consider the prescience of the Talmud[803], more than 1,500 years ago, in predicting that in a future period[804], which may be our time, truth would be absent[805].

We, therefore, must steel ourselves not to be so naïve and trusting. It is a critical lesson that informs how we might engage the new media of the Internet and social media. Indeed, the first clue that a source may be tainted is when it immediately engages

---

[802] Images can be manipulated, including being staged, edited, cropped, photoshopped or composited. The lack of context or provenance can also affect how an image is perceived.

[803] BT Sotah, at page 49b and Sanhedrin, at page 97a.

[804] The Talmud refers to this period as the 'Footsteps of the Messiah', preceding the arrival of the Messiah.

[805] It is noteworthy that the Talmud also describes how the generation will have the face of a dog. Rabbi Aaron Soloveichik, of blessed memory, explained that the face of a generation was its leadership. The reference to a dog is an allusion to how it appears to lead, by walking ahead of its master. However, in reality it is gazing over its shoulder at its master and actually following. In modern parlance, the leaders will not genuinely lead, but rather, in effect, do what polling suggests their constituency desires. The Talmud also describes how there will be a culture of youth where elders defer to minors; those who fear sin will be despised; wisdom will decay; and an atmosphere of disrespect and mistrust, including within the home, will be prevalent. It is hard not to recognize the existence of these conditions in our times.

our emotions and overwhelms us with a sense of injustice and outrage. It is also not easy to challenge proponents of a seemingly virtuous cause or the reliability or truthfulness of the message without seeming to challenge the perceived virtue of the cause expressed. This is because challenging the applicability of noble sentiments is often confused with denying the validity of those sentiments.

Take a breath and wait a moment. We must be skeptical and not act out of an emotional connection to the perceived virtue of a cause.

Consider the apocryphal tale of the tragic death of an 8-month-old baby, who reportedly died from tear gas inhalation at the Gaza border with Israel in one of Hamas' attempts at an armed invasion of Israel. Who could not be moved by the accompanying image of a dead child held in the arms of a grieving mother in the morgue of a hospital.

As it turns out, the whole story was contrived by Hamas, which paid for the parents to lie about the cause of death of the baby. It was not inhalation of tear gas at a border clash; rather, it was a blood disease that caused the baby's death. It was the same deadly disease that felled her sibling earlier in the year[806].

The version of the story Hamas invented and disseminated engendered a great deal of news coverage, with predictable results. As Hamas intended, it created a pall, which prevented any critical public discourse about the Hamas-led armed invasion of Israel and what actually was occurring at the Gazan border with Israel. The true story did not receive much news coverage. It makes one wonder, where's the outrage about this abuse? The news media continues to allow itself to be used as a

---

[806] See, Hamas paid family of 8-month-old to say she died during Gaza border clashes, in JTA, dated June 21, 2018. See also a similar article, by Jacob Magid, in the Times of Israel that same day, as well as, A Dead Baby, by Jerold Auerbach in the Algemeiner, on June 24, 2018.

mere tool by Hamas and other nefarious players to communicate falsehoods in service of their abhorrent agenda to delegitimize Israel.

Consider also the context. Much as we might wish that Hamas were conducting a so-called peaceful protest along the Gaza border, this was not the case.

Let's be clear; it was not peaceful; it was not a protest, and it was not along the Gazan border with Israel. It was a violent armed invasion of Israel itself[807].

As we now know conclusively, 53 of the 60 people reported as fatally shot by Israeli soldiers were Hamas or Islamic Jihad operatives[808]. Hamas' cynical and callous use of the Gazan people to mask, aid and reinforce an armed invasion by Hamas operatives has been acknowledged by Hamas[809]. They were seeking to infiltrate into Israel, concealed in the confusion and surge of thousands of people attempting to breach the border fence[810]. Many were armed with guns, grenades, improvised explosive devices and other weapons. Their intention was ignoble; it was to kill Israeli civilians and commit mayhem within Israel. The Gazans were callously and recklessly urged on by Hamas to invade Israel, despite the many warnings by Israel not to approach the border fence. Hamas wanted to create martyrs.

---

[807] See, The truth about Hamas and Israel, by IDF Brigadier General Ronin Manelis, in the Wall Street Journal, dated May 20, 2018 (and reproduced at www.idf.il/en/), as well as, Misplaced sympathy for the Hamas lynch mob, by Alan Dershowitz, at foxnews.com.
[808] Ibid. See also, Gaza's Miseries Have Palestinian Authors, by Bret Stephens, in the New York Times, on May 16, 2018; The Blood Isn't on Trump's Hands, by Jonathan S. Tobin, in the National Review on May 15, 2018; and What Sparked the latest Palestinian protests, by Thane Rosenbaum, at cnn.com, on May 16, 2018.
[809] Ibid. See also, Hamas official: 50 of the 62 Gazans killed in border violence were our members, by Judah Ari Gross and TOI staff, in the Times of Israel on May 11, 2018;
[810] See, the excellent Opinion piece in the New York Times, by Matti Friedman, entitled: Falling for Hamas' Split Screen fallacy, dated May 16, 2018. See also, Journalists Should Stop Falling for Hamas Deadly PR Efforts Against Israel, by David Harsanyi, in the Federalist, dated May 14, 2018 and another of his articles, entitled: Media Coverage of the Israeli-Palestinian Clash Is Built on a Myth, in the National Review, dated May 18, 2018.

Yet, some in the mainstream media remained obsessed with promoting the false narrative[811] created by Hamas that this armed invasion was somehow a peaceful protest.

The fact that so many attacking Israel were only injured, not killed, speaks volumes. Israel used tear gas and predominately other non-lethal means to turn back the incursion on its sovereign territory. Even when shots were fired, Israeli soldiers sought to wound, not kill. Considering the pogroms that would have ensued had the terrorists and other Gazans been able to break through the border fence and attack the nearby civilian neighborhoods, Israel Defense Forces showed exceptional restraint. The right to self-defense is recognized under International Law and enshrined in the UN Charter[812]. Ambassador Nikki Hailey eloquently supported Israel's right to defend itself against the Gazan onslaught. She noted that no nation would have acted otherwise and glowingly acknowledged the extraordinary restraint shown by Israel in dealing with the situation[813].

Amazingly, even as Israel continues to defend itself against Hamas attacks, it still also has feelings of genuine empathy for the people of Gaza. Unlike many who just emote and vociferously express outrage about the crises in Gaza, Israel is actually doing something constructive to help. For example, Israel has provided thousands of Palestinian children, including from Gaza, with life-saving heart operations[814]. It continues to provide

---

[811] See also, The Media Continues to Lie About Israeli Actions in Gaza, as reported by Alan Levick, in the Algemeiner, on July 2, 2018.

[812] Article 51 of the UN Charter. Israel's actions in self-defense are also consistent with the highest standards of military conduct, including as described in the Talmud (BT Sanhedrin, at pages 74a and 72b) and Maimonides' Code of Jewish Law (Maimonides, Mishne Torah, Laws of Murder and the Preservation of Life 1:7-14).

[813] See video of Nikki Halley speech at UN on the subject, in Real Clear Politics, entitled, Nikki Haley on Gaza: No Country Acts With More "Restraint" Than Israel, posted by Tim Hains, on May 15, 2018.

[814] See, for example, 3000th Palestinian child has heart operation in Israel through Save a Child's Heart, by Jack Mukand, in The Times of Israel, dated 11/22/2022.

humanitarian aid to the people of Gaza, despite all the challenges posed by the terrorist regime of Hamas. The crises in Gaza is not only self-inflicted, it is perpetuated and needlessly deepened by Hamas[815]. Israel is also lending a helping hand and real assistance to the Syrian refugees on its northern border, in spite of all the dangers[816].

Preventing armed terrorists from entering Israel and killing innocent civilians is a sacred mission. Israel has a very diverse society. Its citizens include members of the Jewish, Christian, and Muslim religions, as well as those of many other faiths, creeds, denominations and beliefs. Israeli society is a veritable kaleidoscope of color, orientation and places of origin from throughout the world. This cannot be said about Hamas-controlled Gaza. Hamas is and was the aggressor, and yet it manages to cast itself as the victim in this tragic drama it authored, produced and presented with the help of an accommodating news media.

There appears to be an obsessive need to create victims, even when they don't exist, in order to paint Israel as the villain. Thus, when the US eliminated murderous Al-Qaida terrorist leader Ayman al-Zawahiri, the US was hailed. On the other hand, when Israel eliminated murderous PIJ terrorist leader Taysir al-Jabari, Israel was condemned[817]. Moreover, Israel did this based on actionable intelligence to prevent imminent attacks planned by terrorist PIJ (an Iranian Regime proxy), led by Jabari, on the Israeli population. These libelous smears of Israel, often involving children, channel the craven, tawdry and almost

---

[815] See, for example, As Gaza hospitals suffer shortages, Hamas refuses Israeli medical aid, by Judah Ari Gross, in the Times of Israel, on May 16, 2018.
[816] See, Israeli residents go public with heartfelt aid to Syrians, by Abigail Klein Leichman, on The Israel 21c website, dated July 3, 2018.
[817] See, for example, Gaza: The Usual Suspects Condemn Israel, by Richard Kemp, at the Gatestone Institute, dated 8/7/2022.

obscene obsession with the notorious antisemitic trope of blood libel[818].

Has propaganda, therefore, triumphed? Its object is to spread misinformation and quash any reasoned discussion. It appears that it is succeeding in many quarters. What can we do?

We must demand the unvarnished truth and balanced and unbiased news reporting. We have to challenge myths. How else can we have a constructive discourse? Len visited Gaza. It is not all a large refugee camp or an open-air prison, as some have proclaimed. It has many beautiful buildings and neighborhoods. Check it out yourself by googling: Gaza beautiful pictures. Indeed, check out Gaza Airbnb. Be prepared for a pleasant surprise; it looks very little like the conditions described by many talking heads on television. By the way, similarly, Ramallah, Hebron and other Palestinian cities and towns in Judea and Samaria. They boast luxury buildings that rival those here in the US, and more are being built.

It's time to recognize the reality of the situation, as it exists and not as spuriously promoted by Hamas, its propaganda agents, and knowing or unknowing supporters and dupes.

As a matter of fact and law, there is no occupation of Gaza by anyone other than the Gazans living there. It's time to end the masquerade about Hamas-controlled Gaza wanting peace if only Israel would satisfy some suicidal condition. These artifices and the verbal furor raised in reaction to events occurring in Jerusalem, like the moving of the US Embassy there, are nothing more than cunning pretexts that are intended to conceal Hamas' express goal of destroying Israel.

---

[818] The Blood Libel That Went Viral: Israel Blamed for Palestinian Islamic Jihad Rocket That Killed Children, by Rachel O'Donoghue, in the Algemeiner, dated 8/9/2022.

Peace should have been achieved when Israel fully withdrew from Gaza in 2005. As the wise Charles Krauthammer, of blessed memory, wrote[819] almost a dozen years ago:

> "...Israel evacuated Gaza completely. It declared the border between Israel and Gaza an international frontier. Gaza became the first independent Palestinian territory in history. Yet Gazans continued the war...Why? Because occupation was a mere excuse to persuade gullible and historically ignorant Westerners to support the Arab cause against Israel. The issue is, and has always been, Israel's existence. That is what is at stake."

Not much has changed in all these years. Peace is still available simply by Gaza stopping its attacks on Israel and Egypt and just living in peace. The framework for peace is and has been in place for many years. All that's left to do is for Gaza to honor it.

As Charles Krauthammer cautioned, we can't continue to be gullible and historically ignorant. The issue is and always has been Israel's existence.

It's time for Hamas to stop the charade, recognize Israel and stop attacking it. We should no longer be excusing or funding their misbehavior or giving credence to their pretexts. All Gaza has to do to have peace is stop attacking its neighbors. Let the blessing of peace prevail.

---

[819] See, Why They Fight, by Charles Krauthammer, of blessed memory, in the Washington Post, on July 14, 2006.

XV.

REVIVE LIGHT AND TRUTH, ESCHEW NIGHT AND FOG-DEFEATING BDS AND THE APARTHEID LIBEL

The Yale University emblem is inscribed with the Hebrew words Urim V'Tumim, which it translates into the Latin motto Lux et Veritas (Light and Truth). It's a noble sentiment that appears to have been profaned.

On Sunday, June 27, 2021, Yale's undergraduate student government, the Yale College Council (YCC), by a vote of eight to three, with four abstentions, adopted a statement falsely accusing Israel of being an apartheid state and committing genocide and ethnic cleansing[820]. As if this hyperbolic and bogus statement was not enough of a mockery of truth, the YCC also took a swipe at the US. It baselessly asserted "connections between the US's (sic) domestic racial oppression and its imperial oppression of people of color worldwide". It went on speciously to claim that Israel's military enforces the alleged apartheid system just like the US police enforce the system of white supremacy against Black Americans.

In yet another fatuous display of misplaced piety, it was noted that the condemnation was not political because they felt

---

[820] Yale student council approves statement accusing Israel of 'genocide', by Ron Kampeas in the Times of Israel, dated 6/29.2021 and Yale College Council adopts statement of condemnation against Israel, by Rebecca Salzhauer, in the Forward, dated 6/28/2021.

compelled to call out injustice wherever it may occur[821]. Curiously, there is no similar condemnation of Hamas' attacks on Israel, with over four thousand rockets targeting civilian areas or use of children as human shields. Nor has the YCC passed a resolution condemning the PA's killing of an outspoken critic and violent response to protests, including brutalizing women protestors[822]. Indeed, where was the outcry about the deep-rooted, endemic and rampant problem of physical and mental abuse against women in the home in Hamas and PA controlled areas, including honor killings? Why did they not call out Hamas' and the PA's systemic discrimination against women, both civilly and criminally? Women are blatantly mistreated and exploited, including in matters of economic access and inheritance and there is no equal protection for women under the law in the Hamas and PA controlled areas[823]. Why was there no outrage about the Hamas terrorist training summer camps for children[824]? There also seems not to have been any condemnation of the human rights violations under the regime of the Communist Party of China against the Uyghur people nor by the terrorist Iranian regime. It would appear that the selective

---

[821] Yale Student Gov't Resolution Accuses Israel of "Genocide," "Ethnic Cleansing", by Aaron Bandler in the Jewish Journal, dated 7/1/2021.

[822] UN Human rights chief urges Palestinian Authority to allow protests, in the Times of Israel, dated 7/1/20121; As Palestinians Protest Death of Abbas Opponent, Women are Assaulted in Response, by Amira Hass, in Haaretz, dated 7/3/2021; Palestinian Authority kills and tortures dissenters while the media yawns, by James Sinkinson, at JNS, dated 7/6/2021; and Palestinian frustrations with West Bank government boil over with death of activist, by Steven Hendrix and Sufian Taha, in the Washington Post, dated 6/29/2021.

[823] See, Facts and Figures UN Women-Palestine: Ending Violence Against Women and Jerusalem Institute of Justice, April 2016 Report on the Implementation of the Convention on the Elimination of All Forms of Discrimination Against Women under the PA and Hamas and Intersectional rhapsody, by Leonard Grunstein, in the Times of Israel blogs, dated 7/3/2019, including footnoted sources.

[824] At annual summer camps, Hamas trains kids to fire guns, kidnap soldiers, in the Times of Israel, dated 7/3/2021; Hamas continues recruiting soldiers: Where is the condemnation?, by Seth J. Frantzman, in the Jerusalem Post, dated 6/27/2021; and COUGAT: Hamas summer camp trains kids to 'commit acts of terror', in Jerusalem Post, dated 6/11/20.

focus on Israel and obvious double standard falls plainly within the IHRA definition of antisemitism.

Many might wonder why the YCC did not hold a fact-finding hearing to try to ascertain the truth instead of just cavalierly making such outrageous pronouncements. Where was the healthy skepticism, intellectual curiosity and intensive and independent research, which are the hallmarks of university-level study? Wouldn't it have made sense to visit Israel, Judea, Samaria and Gaza to ascertain the actual situation on the ground first-hand? Had they done so, they would have quickly realized their folly. Indeed, how could such serious and slanderous pronouncements be made solely on the basis of a mere set of talking points, in the form of baseless accusations from a clearly biased source, without any semblance of proof offered? Is our time-honored tradition of not presuming guilt and demanding proof not a part of the YCC proceedings? Furthermore, are serious legal accusations just thrown around, with abandon, like some propaganda exercise, with no thought given as to their applicability to the circumstances at issue? It would appear so, because there was no factual or legal basis for invoking the explosive and chilling terms of apartheid, genocide and ethnic cleansing as to Israel.

Israel is not an apartheid state and it is patently absurd to claim otherwise[825]. The term apartheid was the Afrikaans name given by the Nationalist Party, composed of members of the minority white community then ruling South Africa, to the country's harsh, institutionalized system of racial segregation, in 1948. It

---

[825] See, for example, Israel is not an Apartheid State, by Bassem Eid (a Palestinian human rights activist living in Israel), in the Times of Israel blogs, dated 6/24/2021 and Free Debate must continue, but 'apartheid' causes confusion, by Rabbi Dr. Warren Goldstein (Chief Rabbi of South Africa and PhD in human rights and constitutional law), in the Jerusalem Post, dated 7/1/2021.

came to an end in the early 1990s in a series of steps that led to the formation of a democratic government in 1994[826].

Israel is a democratic and diverse country where all citizens, Jewish, Muslim, Christian and others, have the right to vote. There are no public toilets, benches or other public spaces, buses, trains, hospitals, public schools or universities segregated by race or religion. The professions, businesses and jobs are open to every citizen. There is no racism institutionalized by the Knesset, enforced by the police and legitimized by the courts. Thus, for example, Muslim citizens serve as judges, including as a Justice of the Supreme Court of Israel, in government positions, including recently as a member of the ruling coalition of Government and as attorneys, doctors and other medical personnel, teach as professors or attend as students at universities and patronize restaurants and shop at stores of their choice.

As Mesola Lekota, President of the Congress of the People party, former South African Defense Minister and senior African National Congress official, is quoted as saying, "I tried to find a comparison between how we lived under the apartheid regime and the situation in Israel and I could not find one".

In a post[827] on the subject of apartheid, Bassem Eid, a Palestinian human rights activist, noted: "The new diverse government truly makes a mockery of the absurd 'apartheid' label. A devout Muslim and adherent of an Islamist ideology is now Israel's Joe Manchin- a dealmaker at the center of a 50/50 legislative chamber with enormous clout. Anyone who chooses to look objectively can plainly see Israel as the bastion of diversity and democracy that it is."

---

[826] US Department of State, The End of Apartheid, at state.gov.
[827] Israel is not an Apartheid State, by Bassem Eid, in the Times of Israel blogs, dated 6/24/2021

President Joseph Biden, when asked about those in his own Democratic Party labeling Israel apartheid, responded[828], "There are few of them. I think they're wrong. I think they're making a mistake". He went on to say, "Israel is a democracy. Israel is our ally. Israel is a friend, and I think that I make no apologies".

German Chancellor Olaf Scholz rejected Abbas' use of the term apartheid in relation to Israel[829]. He also condemned Abbas' use of the terms Holocaust and genocide in describing Israel's treatment of Palestinian Arabs. Scholz declared he was "disgusted by the outrageous remarks made by Palestinian President Mahmoud Abbas"[830].

Israel is not committing genocide[831]. That would require Israel to intend to destroy, in whole or in part, a national, ethnic, racial or religious group. There is no such intent and census data belie any such claim. Indeed, the Muslim Arab population of Israel, the PA controlled areas and Gaza has grown, not declined. Consider the population statistics of ethnically diverse Jerusalem, Israel's most populous city, as a pertinent example. Over the years since 1967, when the City was reunified, the population has grown; but the increase in the Muslim population has been proportionately greater[832].

Israel is not ethnic cleansing. Although there is no precise legal definition of ethnic cleansing under International Law, the term was used to describe the abhorrent conduct that occurred in the

---

[828] See, Biden dismisses Democrats critical of Israel, saying they're 'wrong', by Brett Samuels, in the Hill, dated 7/13/2022.

[829] See, for example, Scholz rejects use of 'apartheid to describe Israel, in DW, dated 8/16/2022 and At Abbas' side German leader rejects his use of 'apartheid' in reference to Israel, in The Times of Israel, dated 8/16/2022.

[830] See, German chancellor 'disgusted' by Abbas's 'intolerable' 50 holocausts claim, in The Times of Israel, dated 8/17/2022.

[831] Convention on the Prevention and Punishment of the Crime of Genocide approved by UN General Assembly Resolution 260 A (III) of 12/9/1948 and entered into force on 1/12/1951.

[832] Jerusalem Facts and Trends 2019, by Michal Korach and Maya Chosen at the Jerusalem Institute.

conflict that ensued among the constituent nations that emerged[833] in the aftermath of the dissolution of Yugoslavia. The UN Office on Genocide describes ethnic cleansing as: "a purposeful policy designed by one ethnic or religious group to remove by violent or terror-inspiring means the civilian population of another ethnic or religious group from certain geographic areas". This is yet another example of projection by a predator accusing others of their own disreputable conduct. Thus, the Hamas and PA controlled domains are ethnically cleansed of Jews. Christians are also being oppressed and the number still remaining in Gaza and the PA controlled areas has been severely reduced, as discussed above. The fact is that neither Christians nor Jews are welcome. Israel, in stark contrast, is an ethnically diverse country with growing Muslim[834] and Christian[835] populations, which embraces its diversity, as described above.

A landlord/tenant dispute in a Jerusalem neighborhood, which could be cured by just paying the rent, is not ethnic cleansing by any stretch of the imagination of an objective observer. To put this in perspective, there were two hundred thousand eviction cases pending in New York City in 2020[836]. Employing the term ethnic cleansing in this context is not just preposterous; it's venal and calculatingly designed to evoke unrestrained furor.

Use of these explosive and horrendous terms to vilify Israel in reference to some mythical misdeeds goes beyond merely being inappropriate and slanderous. Indeed, it might be argued that, whether knowingly or unknowingly, the YCC, in validating them, has become nothing more than a propaganda arm of the Hamas

---

[833] UN Office on Genocide Prevention- Definition of Ethnic Cleansing at un.org.

[834] See, for example, The Muslim Population of Israel 2022, at the Israel Central Bureau of Statistics (cbs.gov.il), dated 7/6/2022.

[835] See, for example, Israel's Christian community is growing, 84% satisfied with life here-report, in The Times of Israel, dated 12/22/2021.

[836] Evictions on Hold until October 1, but Pre-Pandemic Housing Court Cases Forge Ahead, by Christine Chung, in The City, dated 8/12/2020.

and PA apparatus. In the days of the USSR, they might have aptly been called useful dupes.

Reference should be made both to the Hamas Covenant and the PA's National Charter, which are available online and are discussed in Chapter III and below. Even a cursory study of these documents reveals the offensive antisemitic nature of these organizations, which should give anyone pause about promoting their agenda of accusing Israel of these horrible crimes. It would appear, like so many propaganda slogans and false narratives, the classic subterfuge of projecting unto others thine own flaws and sins may be at the heart of these meritless claims against Israel.

Consider some of the actual misdeeds and horrifying calls to action by Hamas and the PA[837]. No Jews reside in the PA controlled areas or Hamas controlled Gaza. Jordan ethnically cleansed Judea and Samaria of Jews when it conquered the area in 1948. The Jordanians and other Arabs residing there (now calling themselves Palestinians) massacred or forcibly expelled any remaining Jewish residents and destroyed Jewish synagogues, cemeteries and schools. Anyone who has visited the Kfar Etzion Museum can appreciate the ruthless extermination campaign mounted against the Jews in Israel in 1948. In striking contrast, the Arabs who remained in Israel gained citizenship, equal rights and became an integral part of Israeli society.

To this day, PA law prohibits land sales to Jews. Those breaking the law are subject to harsh penalties that the PA does not shirk from imposing. The PA and Hamas also spew classical antisemitism, incite and glorify terrorism and call for Israel's destruction. This includes promoting hateful antisemitic

---

[837] See Alternative Report of United Nations Watch to the 99th Session of the Committee on the Elimination of Racial Discrimination for its review of the State of Palestine, submitted by Hillel Neuer and Dina Rovner, dated 7/12/19, including the extensive footnoted sources cited.

rhetoric in the media, as well as teaching their children in school to hate Jews.

The Palestinian National Charter describes the entire Land of Israel, including the land within the ceasefire lines of 1948, as belonging to the Arab Palestinian people and calls for liberation through armed struggle. Despite assurances that it would be amended to recognize the State of Israel, this, in fact, never actually occurred. Shocking as this may be, it is even more galling that foreign policy experts in the State Department and elsewhere just gloss over the failure to meet this threshold requirement. Not satisfying this most basic and essential condition is a glaring deficiency. However, like so many failures by the PA and Hamas to comply with their obligations under agreements, they are often just ignored.

The Hamas Covenant is overtly antisemitic. It compares Jews to Nazis, asserts Jews were behind both World War I and World War II, and finds Jewish conspiracies everywhere. It requires an armed Jihad be conducted against Israel to eliminate it.

Hamas and the PA, in their own words and actions, express their professed desire, in no uncertain terms, to commit the very crimes and evil deeds with which the YCC charged Israel. In a typical propagandist fashion, they just contrive to accuse and impute their own criminal intent to Israel in a cynical attempt to distract. How unfortunate that it appears the YCC fell for their ruse and canards.

This is not the first time university students have been in the vanguard of a sinister and abhorrent movement. It is all too reminiscent of 1933 in Germany when students sought to boycott and expel Jewish professors and force out Jewish students from universities. This was before the notorious antisemitic Nuremberg Laws of 1935. Moreover, it was the students, rather than the professors and administrators, who were leading the charge[838]. Amazingly, a rector and law professor at Humboldt University and supporter of the Nazi party telegraphed Hitler following his appointment as German Chancellor in 1933 to complain about the students, who he viewed as 'immature misguided idealists'[839]. He was concerned about the harm they might do to the German Universities as valuable German cultural assets. Among other things, he objected to the targeted shaming of Jewish faculty members and the displaying of anti-Semitic materials on campus.

The Nazis sought to clothe their evil intent to eliminate the Jews in euphemisms like relocation to the East and the Endlosung der Judenfrage (Final Solution to the Jewish Question). It was a calculating, cynical and ruthless canard to lull the Jews and make them more compliant and docile. The Nazis and their local minions facetiously proclaimed Jews were just being relocated to work in the East, not to be eliminated. But, as we all know, it was all just a con job designed to fool the intended victims so as to enable their obedient transport to what turned out to be killing centers. Many rationalized the threat they faced arguing how could Germany seek to kill them when there were labor shortages and they could still be productive. Even at the gates of Auschwitz, the sign at the entrance proclaimed Arbeit Macht Frei (work makes free). But it was all a subterfuge and the ultimate goal was death, either a quick one in the gas chambers for most or a slow agonizing one for some in the forced labor camps. Nacht und Nebel (Night and Fog) was the title of a Holocaust film many viewed in High School, as a part of Holocaust studies. The title is based on the code name for the secret extermination program. The Nazi tactic of employing code words, euphemisms

---

[838] The Role of Antisemitism in the Expulsion of non-Aryan Students, 1933-1945, Bela Bodo, at yadvashem.org.
[839] Telegram regarding the "Action against the Un-German Spirit", at perspectives.ushmm.org.

and other propaganda techniques to mask their true insidiously evil goals is the antithesis of Light and Truth.

We must understand the use of the terms anti-Israel and anti-Zionism in this context. Israel is the only country in the world where Jews are a majority. As a matter of fact, Jews are not more than three percent of the population of any other country in the world and are only approximately two tenths of one percent of the world population. The total population of Jews in the world would constitute only a statistical anomaly in the population of China. There is no reasonable explanation for being against the existence of Israel and no other country in the world. Don't be misled, it's just a ploy to divert attention from the inexplicable animus felt against the Jews who live there or, said another way, antisemitism. Similarly, is the connivance of using the term anti-Zionism. An overwhelming majority of Jews favor the existence of Israel[840]. In this regard, it should be noted that the incomparable Biblical Moses, who led the Jewish People out of Egypt and taught them the Torah, was a Zionist. As the Bible records[841], he even pleaded with G-d that he be allowed to enter the Land of Israel. Thus, to express hatred towards all Zionists is just another way of expressing hatred of Jews. These terms are cleverly devised euphemisms designed to fool the naïve and cruelly give succor to those who somehow delude themselves into believing they are exempt. This was how the Nazis did it and their spiritual successors like terrorist Hamas are no different. The recent spate of murders, violent attacks and hate crimes committed against Jews because they are Jewish, in Europe, the US and Israel speak volumes about the essential nature of the threat we are facing. It's undeniably antisemitism[842].

---

[840] 80% of US Jews say they are pro-Israel, study finds, by Jeremy Sharon, in the Jerusalem Post, dated 2/4/2020.

[841] Deuteronomy 3:23-27.

[842] See, for example, FBI Joins NYPD to Address Rise in Anti-Semitic Crimes in New York City, by Ben Chapman, in the WSJ, dated 5/29/21; US Faces Outbreak of Anti-Semitic Threats and Violence, by Ruth Graham and Liam Stock, in NYT, dated 5/26/21;

As anyone can see, by visiting Israel and objectively viewing life there, it is not an apartheid state, and it is not committing genocide or ethnic cleansing. That is the truth. As to those who would falsely accuse Israel of such unspeakable evil, they might better take stock of themselves. As the Talmud[843] aptly notes, those who accuse others of fundamental flaws should themselves be examined because they likely possess those flaws.

The toxic atmosphere these students are creating on the college campus is pernicious. As noted above, some might even echo the virulent denunciations so as not to stand out or be canceled. At the very least, there is often a chilling effect that stifles any serious discussion[844].

It's time to eschew the darkness of falsehoods and the contrived fog of propaganda slogans and platitudes. Let's revive light and truth.

As to the BDS movement, consider the boycott of Israel, whether in whole or in part, by Ben & Jerry's or anyone else. It's just another obnoxious instance in the sordid history of economic warfare against the Jews. BDS is the latest rhetorical term used to obfuscate its nefarious character. Don't be misled by the attempts to sanitize it as some sort of social awareness program. It's an insidiously malevolent and antisemitic scheme directed at delegitimizing Israel and undermining it as a haven and homeland for Jews.

The connection between the notorious Nazi boycott of Jews and the Arab one in the Middle East dates back at least as early as 1937[845]. In that year, the armed extremist Arab National Youth

---

and British Jews' fear and defiance amid record monthly anti-Semitism reports, by Mary O'Connor, dated 6/29/2021.

[843] BT Kiddushin 70a-b.

[844] Why academics boycott Israel, by Martin Kramer, published online at martinkramer.org on 7/7/2021.

[845] See, Nazis Affiliate with Arabs; To Boycott Palestine Goods, in the Sentinel, dated 12/9/1937.

Organization threatened a boycott of Arab merchants who bought goods produced by Jews in Palestine. This reportedly followed a visit by Baldur von Shirach, head of Hitlerjugend (the Hitler youth organization of Germany), who was accompanied by fifteen Nazi agents. While he was in the Middle East, he also met with other Nazi representatives in the area and decided to establish closer contact with Arab youth groups and increase propaganda.

One of the most infamous Nazi collaborators in the Arab world was Haj Amin al-Husseini, the notorious Grand Mufti of Jerusalem. He first sought contact with the Nazis in March of 1933, only two months after Hitler's appointment as Chancellor[846]. Al-Husseini then met with Heinrich Wolff, the German counsul in Jerusalem, which the counsul reported in a telegram to Berlin, on March 31, 1933[847]. Among other things, the consul recorded that the Mufti, on behalf of Muslims, urged Germany to boycott Jewish goods, which he and other Muslims would enthusiastically join throughout the Muslim world.

Grand Mufti Haj Amin al-Husseini eventually personally met with Hitler in 1941[848] and discussed their common goal of the destruction of the Jews. Al-Husseini helped transmit and propagate the Nazi obsessive Jew hatred to the Middle East, including among the Muslim Brotherhood[849]. Hamas is just one of one of its offshoots[850].

---

[846] See, for example, The Mufti and the Holocaust, by John Rosenthal, dated 3/28/2008, at the Hoover Institution (hoover.org).

[847] Ibid.

[848] See, Full official record: What the mufti said to Hitler, The Times of Israel, 10/21/2015.

[849] See, for example, The Nazi Roots of Islamic Hate, by Jeffrey Herf, in Tablet Magazine, dated 7/6/2022.

[850] The Muslim Brotherhood's Global Threat Hearing before the House Subcommittee on National Security of the Committee on Oversight and Government Reform, 115th Congress, Second Session, on July 11, 2018 (Serial No. 115–90), at docs.house.gov.

The Arab boycott of Jews predates the reestablishment of the State of Israel, in 1948. The newly formed Arab League declared an economic boycott of the Jews in what was then Mandatory Palestine, at the end of 1945[851]. The terms 'Jewish' and 'Zionist' were used interchangeably. Earlier Arab boycotts of Jewish business in Israel occurred in the 1890s, 1909, 1920s and 1930s[852].

BDS seeks only to harm and serves no salutary purpose. It is not about having a state for the so-called Palestinian Arabs. That was not an issue at the time or even thereafter, until the stunning victory of Israel in the 1967 Six-Day War. It was all about hatred of the Jews and then, post 1948, also the elimination of the Jewish State of Israel. Moreover, the creation of a so-called Palestinian state, side by side with Israel, could have been accomplished years ago by merely saying yes to one of the many proposals made by Israel over the years, including those sponsored by the US. Indeed, ever since the Oslo Accords, Gaza and the PA controlled areas have functioned as proto-states, with their own elected governments and security forces. But that is not what BDS wants. As the founder of the BDS movement, Omar Barghouti, explained, the goal of BDS is the elimination of Israel[853].

BDS does not enhance the lives of those living in the PA and Hamas controlled areas. It actually hurts them, because it results

[851] See, Arab League Boycott of Israel, Background & Overview, by Mitchell Bard, at jewishvirtuallibrary.org. See also, Arabs to Boycott Palestinian Goods, in the New York Times, dated 12/4/1945.
[852] See, for example, From Boycott to Economic Cooperation: The Political Economy of the Arab Boycott of Israel, by Gil Feiler (Routledge-2013), Chapter II and The Arab League Boycott and WTO Accession: Can Foreign Policy Excuse Discriminatory Sanctions, by Eugene Kontorovich, 4 Chicago Journal of International Law (2003), at page 286. See also, Nazis Affiliate with Arabs to Boycott Palestine Goods (JTA-Damascus, December 7, 1937) in the Sentinel, dated 12/9/1937.
[853] See, The Boycott, Divestment and Sanctions (BDS) Movement Unmasked, at creativecommunityforpeace.com. and BDS: In Their own Words, at jewishvirtuallibrary.org.

in loss of jobs by the many who are gainfully employed in enterprises that demonstrate peace and harmony is entirely possible[854]. It also ignores the fact that more then half of the goods imported by those in the PA controlled areas reportedly came from Israel[855]. Beyond that there is also a most inconvenient fact that BDS just seems to miss that over ninety percent of all goods exported from the PA controlled areas are reportedly sold to Israel. If the PA chose to boycott Israel the impact on the Israeli economy would be miniscule. However, if Israel responded in kind, the effect on the PA economy would likely be devastating. Consider too the blatant hypocrisy of calling for boycotting Israel, while the PA itself does a great deal of satisfactory business with Israel. The specter of BDS also hampers development, because it disincentivizes those who might otherwise invest in joint enterprises. Why take the chance that outside nefarious forces, like the terrorist Iranian regime and/or its local terrorist partner Hamas, will seek to foster a boycott of the business, in furtherance of their own irrational antisemitic programs to destroy Israel.

There are also many political, business and legal ramifications associated with boycotts of Israel, under US and State laws.

To address this harmful practice, Congress passed the Anti-Boycott Law[856]. It covers a variety of circumstances, including those arising out of the notorious original Arab League boycott of Israel. Indeed, the law was originally enacted in response to this boycott and was designed to protect US ally Israel.

The Law declares it is the policy of the United States to oppose restrictive trade practices or boycotts fostered or imposed by any

---

[854] See, for example, Ben and Jerry's boycott hurts Palestinians, by Bassem Eid, in the Times of Israel blogs, dated 7/21/2021.

[855] See, for example, Another Palestinian BDS fail, by Maurice Hirsch, at Pal Watch.org, dated November 15, 2022.

[856] Section 8 of the Export Administration Act of 1979, which was implemented as Part 760 of the EAR.

foreign country against other countries, like Israel, friendly to the US or against US citizens. The use of the terms 'fostered' and 'foreign country' is cogent. Neither of these terms is precisely defined, unlike, for example, the term 'foreign state' which is expressly defined in the Foreign Sovereign Immunities Act[857].

The legislative history of the Anti-Boycott Law supports a broad interpretation of these words to cover non-government organizations like the Arab League and, hence, the use of these expansive terms[858]. This would, therefore, include Hamas and the PA, which are proto-state organizations that purport to speak for the Arab Muslim residents of the areas they control. It also does not require the foreign source to be in control of the US party promoting the boycott. Thus, for example, the mere fact that Iran is, directly or indirectly, associated with, sponsors or otherwise supports a boycott by US parties of Israel may also be sufficient basis for invoking the provisions of the Law.

Among other things, the Law, as amended[859], prohibits refusing or requiring any other person to refuse to do business with or in a boycotted country, with any business concern organized under the laws of the boycotted country or with any national or resident of the boycotted country. This would perforce include Israeli nationals wherever they may reside. In this regard, it is important to note that the efforts reportedly made by Unilever to limit the boycott to the so-called occupied territories of Judea, Samaria and Jerusalem produced only a distinction without merit. The law expressly covers a national of the boycotted country, without reference to where the person resides and in addition covers all residents of the country. Consider, how

---

[857] 28 USCA 1602-1611 and see 1603 (a)-(b).

[858] See: The BDS Movement: That Which We Call a Foreign Boycott, by Any Other Name, Is Still Illegal, by Marc A. Greendorfer, in the Roger Williams University Law Review, Volume 22, No. 1 (Winter 2017).

[859] Anti-Boycott Act of 2018, Part II of the Export Control Reform Act of 2018 (50 USC Chapter 58), and the anti-boycott provisions set forth in Part 760 of the Export Administration Regulations, 15 CFR parts 730-774 (EAR).

absurd it is to argue that not boycotting a country, but only boycotting some of its people, who happen to be on the other side of a contrived Green Line. What's next, prohibiting Israelis from buying ice cream in US stores? Furthermore, what if they also happen to be US citizens?

The Anti-Boycott Law also provides an express prohibition against discriminating against any United States person on the basis of race, religion, sex or national origin and well it should. A US company should not be able to treat US citizens overseas any differently from in the US. Could anyone condone a US company being permitted to discriminate against any Americans in Latin America, Europe, Asia or Africa? Imagine the outrage if some US company announced that it wouldn't serve any non-white person who dared to move into a particular neighborhood because it believed it should be preserved as a white-only enclave? That's real Jim Crow and fortunately it's against the law in the US and, similarly, it's also prohibited under the Anti-Boycott Law. This includes the approximately sixty thousand (60,000) Americans reportedly living in Judea and Samaria[860].

In essence Jewish American residents of Efrat, like Len's brother Z"L and his family, his Jewish American aunt and cousins, who live in the Jewish Quarter of the Old City of Jerusalem, are targeted by this obnoxious boycott. There's no rationale, other than latent or patent Jew hatred, for the ideological driven gospel of the board of Ben and Jerry's to require places over the so called Green Line to be Judenrein?

How could Ben & Jerry's and its parent Unilever, in effect, support the Hamas and PA policies barring Jews, as described above? The PA and Hamas also spew classical antisemitism, incite and glorify terrorism and call for Israel's destruction. Do BDS'ers appreciate that this is what they are actually supporting?

---

[860] 15% of settlers are American, new research claims, by JTA, Times of Israel, 8/28/2015.

What about the other less than admirable aspects of Hamas and PA controlled society summarized in this book? The reality is BDS is just new packaging for classic antisemitism, channeling the sordid Nazi tactic of targeting and boycotting Jews.

In striking contrast, Arab-Israeli citizens have equal rights and are an integral part of Israeli society. They enjoy freedoms that are unparalleled in most Arab countries, let alone in the Hamas and PA controlled areas. It should be no surprise that ninety-three percent of Arabs in Jerusalem polled prefer Israeli rule over the PA and most of the remaining seven percent would not give up their Israeli identification cards[861]. It should also be no wonder that eighty percent of Gazans blame Hamas and the PA for problems in Gaza, not Israel[862]. Here's another stunning rebuttal to the misguided negative view about Israel's vibrant democracy by the forces of BDS. Israel's rank as a democracy (at 7.97), under the Global Index[863], is above the US (at 7.85), just below France (at 7.99) and well above China (at 2.21) and Iran (1.95).

Why would the BDS movement seek to harm Israel and promote the dystopian nightmare scenario of terrorist Hamas instead? They shouldn't and it's why the Anti-Boycott Law should be enforced to protect Israel, the US and US citizens from these misguided and illegal actions.

Under US law[864], it is the policy of the US that Jerusalem should remain an undivided city in which the rights of every ethnic and religious group are protected and Jerusalem be recognized as the capital of Israel. The President of the US officially recognized

---

[861] See, الإسرائيلي الحكم بقاء يفضلون القدس في العرب من 93% : رأي إستطلاع, at SHFA Palestinian News, dated 12/13/2021. (The title of the article translated by Google translate into English is: An opinion poll: 93% of the Arabs in Jerusalem prefer the continuation of Israeli rule).

[862] Hamas, PA responsible for crises, say Gazans – poll, by Khaled Abu Toameh, in the Jerusalem Post, originally dated 12/23/2021 and updated on 12/24/2021.

[863] See, for example, Israel ranks above Spain, Italy and US for democracy in new global index, by David Rose, at the Jewish Chronicle, dated 2/17/2022.

[864] Jerusalem Embassy Act of 1995.

Jerusalem as the capital of Israel[865]. Do BDS'ers, like the Board of Ben and Jerry's and others actually intend to defy US law and pursue its own foreign policy in conflict with US policy? Are Jews praying at the Western Wall, the Tomb of the Patriarch, Rachel's Tomb or the graves of ancestors at the Mount of Olives to be similarly treated under this toxic policy? Don't they understand that these areas were ethnically cleansed of Jews by the Arabs in 1948, who rejected partition? Do the Oslo Accords and the withdrawal from Gaza mean nothing to these zealous ideologues? Apparently not; their program merely effectuates the malign policies of Iran and Hamas, who support this inimical program of boycotting Israel. This goes to the very essence of why there is a US Anti-Boycott Law.

In 2021, more than sixty groups from the US and Europe teamed up with Iran and Hamas to wage a BDS war against Israel[866]. The Gaza event was called 'Year to Confront Normalization' and the related Iranian event, broadcast simultaneously from Teheran, was called 'Together Against Normalization'. In furtherance of the boycott of Israel by the terrorist Iranian and Hamas regimes, the more than sixty anti-Israel and pro-BDS organizations launched what was called 'Peoples Against Normalization' campaign[867]. The collaborative link to the Iranian regime is probative[868]. It establishes that, at the very least, Iran is fostering these BDS malevolent efforts in the US and, hence, the applicability of the Anti-Boycott Law.

It's hard not to wonder about the ignorance or insensitivity of many of these dilettante boycotters who have joined with abhorrent terrorists in boycotting Israel. Don't they realize they have become the useful dupes of the terrorist Hamas and Iranian

---

[865] Presidential Proclamation 9683 of 12/6/2017.
[866] BDS groups from US and Europe team up with Iran and Hamas against Israel, by Lahav Harkov, in the Jerusalem Post, dated 3/8/2021.
[867] BDS groups partner with terrorists from Gaza, Turkey, Iran to fight normalization, dated 3/9/2021 in the Cleveland Jewish Journal.
[868] When BDS Groups and Iran Meet, in Camera on Campus, dated 5/18/2021.

regime[869] in their efforts to delegitimize and destroy the State of Israel and ethnically cleanse it of Jews?

Unilever did settle with the local licensee in Israel, who claimed violation of the Anti-Boycott Law, by selling it a separate license for Israel[870]. It should be noted that besides the criminal and civil remedies under the Anti-Boycott Law, there are also reporting requirements. This would have put Unilever in the untenable position of likely having to report to the US government the details of its own reported intervention[871] with the board of its subsidiary, as well as its own actions.

Given the penalties that might be incurred under the Anti-Boycott Law, it is mystifying why a company would seek to pursue a boycott and not hold any such decision in abeyance, pending obtaining a ruling from both the US Departments of Commerce and the Treasury, which have jurisdiction over this kind of a violation. In this regard, it should be noted that aside from governmental action, there might also be a private right of action under the Anti-Boycott Law, as discussed in the Abrams v. Baylor case[872]. This would permit the affected US citizens, under certain circumstances, to seek to compel compliance with the Law and also sue for damages.

In addition to the Federal Law Anti-Boycott Law, 35 US States[873] have also adopted Anti-BDS legislation. The Federal Court of

---

[869] It would appear that the uprising against the Iranian regime, by the good people of Iran, have taken a toll on the regime's ability to fund terrorist Hamas and PIJ. See, for example, Iran cuts off funds for Palestinian terror groups-report, at I24 News, dated 12/11/2022.

[870] See, Ben & Jerry's sales to continue in Israel after Unilever sells license, by Yasemin Craggs Mersinoglu, in the Financial Times, dated 6/29/2022.

[871] See, Ben & Jerry's board in dispute with owners Unilever over remaining in Israel, by TOI Staff, in Times of Israel, dated 7/20/2021 and Ben & Jerry's Board Head Says Parent Company Didn't Seek Their Approval To Say They Will Continue in Israel, by Aaron Bandler, in the Jewish Journal, dated 7/20/2021.

[872] Abrams v Baylor College of Medicine, 581 F.Supp.1570 (S.D. Texas-1984).

[873] See, State Anti-BDS Legislation, at jewishvirtuallibrary.org.

Appeals for the Eighth Circuit[874] upheld the constitutionality of the Arkansas Anti-BDS Law, which prohibited state entities from contracting with private companies unless the contract included a certification that the company was not currently engaged in a boycott of Israel and, furthermore, agreed, for the duration of the contract, not to engage in a boycott of Israel. The term 'boycott of Israel' was defined as:

> "engaging in refusals to deal, terminating business activities, or other actions that are intended to limit commercial relations with Israel, or persons or other entities doing business in Israel or in Israel-controlled territories, in a discriminatory manner."

The above-mentioned Federal Court of Appeals held that the statute did not violate the First Amendment, which prohibited the government (applied to States by virtue of the Fourteenth Amendment) from abridging freedom of speech. It was clear that the law did not prohibit the exercise of free speech. It did not limit what a contractor could say nor require them to say anything. Thus, for example, there was no limit on what the Arkansas Times, the plaintiff newspaper, could say about Israel. It was not required publicly to endorse or disseminate a message. The issue was much more nuanced. It was about the nature of "non-verbal conduct that was intended to be, and likely understood as, expressing a particularized message". The basic dispute was about whether the anti-boycott Israel law prohibited conduct that was inherently expressive, as opposed to otherwise generally unexpressive commercial conduct.

As the Supreme Court held in the FAIR case[875], First Amendment protection is only extended to inherently expressive conduct,

---

[874] Arkansas Times LP v. Mark Waldrip, in his official capacity as Trustee of the University of Arkansas, et al, No. 19-1378, (United States Court of Appeals for the 8th Circuit, filed 9/12/2021, filed 6/22/2022).
[875] Rumsfeld v Forum for Academic & Institutional Rights, Inc. (FAIR), 547 U.S. 47 (2006).

say, like a flag burning, which was intended to convey a political message. It did not, however, extend to the requirement to allow military recruiters on campus as a condition to receiving federal funding. This conduct did not inherently mean the University approved of the military and nothing stopped the University from speaking out in disapproval of the military. Indeed, the fact that explanatory speech is necessary to communicate the intended message is strong evidence that the conduct at issue is not inherently expressive. In line with the foregoing principle, consider unless a point was expressly made explaining that not doing business with Israel because of adherence to BDS, no one would have reasonably assumed that this was the case. By the same token, merely doing business with Israel or any country or company does not inherently communicate approval of all its actions and policies. Ponder whether, in the analogous situation of a product made in China, would most conclude that merely buying or not buying a Chinese product inherently communicated approval or disapproval of its mistreatment of the Uyghurs. The answer is likely not. More would have to be said for the average reasonable person to understand that the act of buying or not buying was intended to make a political statement. Hence, the commercial conduct was not protected speech under the First Amendment.

The Court of Appeals found the Arkansas Law targeted the non-communicative aspect of the contractor's conduct. It was about what the contractor did in a commercial context, not said.

Another more insidious source of violation of the Anti-Boycott Law was called out by Senators Ted Cruz and Marsha Blackburn in a letter to Commerce Secretary Gina Raimondo, dated September 28, 2022[876]. They asked her to address the role of so-called Environmental, Social, and Governance (ESG) standards in

---

[876] Text of Letter and press release available at cruz.senate.gov. See also, Biden Admin Pressed to Police Companies That Participate in Israel Boycotts, by Adam Kredo, at the Washington Free Beacon, dated 9/29/2022.

facilitating anti-Semitic boycotts of Israel that would fall under the purview of the Office of Antiboycott Compliance within the Department of Commerce. The letter specifically cites practices by Morningstar Inc., as follows:

> *Advocates of economic warfare against Israel have increasingly sought to use ESG criteria as pretexts for boycott advocacy. Companies that rely on ESG ratings in their business decisions have minimal transparency into the details let alone motivations behind how the ratings were set. The practice introduces exposure to American anti-boycott laws along the entire chain, and most acutely for the firms opaquely designing and setting the ESG criteria.*
>
> ...
>
> *We are concerned that... the Commerce Department is not sufficiently engaging Morningstar and similar companies. The ratings and implicit advocacy from Sustainanalytics come remarkably close to blackletter violations of prohibitions described at the federal level by the EAR and in laws of states such as Texas. The Commerce Department, both generally and as the agency housing the Office of Antiboycott Compliance, is charged with ensuring American companies are aware of these risks and working with them to mitigate and end any exposure. It is also charged with insuring the integrity of those federal prohibitions, as necessary.*

It is also interesting to note the hypocritical approach taken by many who enjoy the marvelous products and services originated by Israel. Indeed, Omar Barghouti[877] himself, who was born in Qatar, lives securely in Israel. Astoundingly, he has called for an academic boycott of Israel eventhough he has a Master's Degree from Tel Aviv University and began pursuing a doctorate there.

---

[877] See, Omar Barghouti, at canarymission.org.

In addition, as noted above, ninety plus percent of the PA's exports are to Israel and fifty-plus percent of its imports. In essence, BDS only causes harm, including to those it purports to benefit, as noted above. Wouldn't it be better to encourage greater constructive cooperation and beneficial business relations instead of discouraging it by penalizing it?

The blatant hypocrisy and absurdity of BDS is risible. Some even feel compelled to virtue signal by invoking BDS as the reason they may not use a particular product, which they likely would not otherwise use in any case. Others piously declare their adherence to BDS while knowingly or unknowingly using products developed in Israel, which are directly or indirectly an integral part of most everyone's daily lives.

Set forth below are a sampling of some of the products and services produced by Israel[878] that so many benefit from:

1. Intel PC and mobile phone chips.

2. USB flash memory device, also known as a thumb-drive.

3. Waze.

4. Proven and commercially viable technology that extracts potable water from air.

5. Desalination plants.

6. Water management, including recycling of wastewater.

7. Iron Dome and Iron Arrow.

---

[878] See, for example, Israel's top 45 greatest inventions of all time, by Abigail Klein Leichman, at Israel21c.org, dated 9/26/2011; Celebrating a decade of life-changing Israeli inventions, by Shoshanna Solon, in The Times of Israel, dated 1/1/2020; and Israeli breakthrough helped cure Jimmy Carter's cancer, by AP and Raoul Wootliff, in The Times of Israel, dated 12/8/2015.

8. Iron Beam, new laser missile defense technology[879].

9. Exoskeleton system enabling paraplegics to walk.

10. Pill cam for GI imaging.

11. Drip irrigation and other incredible breakthroughs in high-tech agricultural enabling high quality and greater yields.

12. Epilady.

13. 3G Solar, a low cost alternative to silicon that generates significantly more electricity.

14. MobileEye.

15. Wind Tulip wind turbines.

16. Flexible stent.

17. Pressure bandage and Quixil, a surgical sealant.

18. A host of life-saving drugs and the promise of more[880].

---

[879] Israel successfully tests new laser missile defense system, by Laurie Kellman, at AP, dated 4/15/2022.

[880] Examples include: Doxil, a chemotherapy for ovarian cancer, developed at the Hadassah Medical Center and sold to J&J; Copaxone, a multiple sclerosis treatment, developed by Teva/Weizmann Institute; Azilect, a Parkinson's Disease therapy, developed by Teva based on research at the Technion; Rebif, a MS treatment, developed by the Weizmann Institute in conjunction with Serono's subsidiary InterPharm; Exelon, a drug for the treatment of Alzheimer's originated at the Hebrew University and developed and marketed by Novartis; Cohen's pioneering peptide therapy for type 1 diabetes; Macrocure, with its potentially revolutionary cell therapy for hard to heal wounds (already on the market in Israel); Protalix, harnessing its plant cell-based protein expression system for biologics; Proteologics, exploiting the ubiquitin system for the discovery and development of novel therapeutics, with an SAB led by Nobel laureates Hershko and Ciechanover, who discovered the ubiquitin system; Quark Pharmaceuticals, one of the pioneers in RNAi therapies; Vaxil Bio Therapeutics, developing T-cell vaccines for tuberculosis and cancer; and Pluristem, heading toward multi-national Phase II/III trials with its proprietary PLX stem cell technology (as reported in: Israel: The 'Start-Up Nation' is now the 'Biotech Nation', by Yaky Yanay, in the Jerusalem Post, dated 8/4/2021).

Israel is known as the 'Start-Up Nation'[881] and today it is also referred to as the 'Biotech Nation'[882]. Here are just a few examples of some extraordinary products Israel is pioneering in the area of biotechnology[883]:

1. Meat grown in the lab (and soon at a commercial production facility), from cells called fibroblasts taken from an animal and nourished in an animal-free cell growth medium. Initially planned is cultured chicken meat and then cultured beef. In August 2022, the company produced its first cultivated lamb prototype.

2. Cancer diagnostics using the blood of patients, also known as liquid biopsy, without tissue biopsies, which are invasive and uncomfortable for patients and do not require outside labs for testing.

3. Producing milk in the lab (and soon a commercial production facility), a sustainable alternative to traditional milk production, which consumes a lot of resources and emits a lot of greenhouse gasses. This is not a plant-based substitute for milk; rather, Israeli technology produces the real thing using genetically modified yeast.

4. Exosome technology to deliver proprietary agents that have the potential to support nerve regeneration.

5. Treating cancer with precision medicine, including using digitized biopsy imaging and real-time molecular analysis and nano-technology or nano-particles to

---

[881] Start-up Nation: The Story of Israel's Economic Miracle, by Dan Senor and Saul Singer (Twelve Hachette Book Group-2009).

[882] Israel: The 'Start-Up Nation' is now the 'Biotech Nation', by Yaky Yanay, in the Jerusalem Post, dated 8/4/2021.

[883] See, for example, The 5 hottest biotech companies making waves in Israel, by Jonathan Smith, at LabioTech.eu, dated 9/21/2022 and Israeli Companies Are Leading the Global BioTech Charge, Here's How And Why, by Max Golderstein, at Entrepreneur, dated 5/2022.

target only cancerous cells and stimulate the patient's own immune system response[884].

Other examples of Israel's achievements that have greatly benefited the world include a world-class academic[885], superb research and reliable testing establishment, as well as cutting-edge computer and cyber security prowess. Thus, for example, the IDF stopped hackers from hitting US power plants[886]. There are many other tangible benefits to the US derived from the US-Israel alliance that go beyond shared values and genuine friendship. This includes sharing of intelligence and technology[887].

Israel's humanitarian efforts throughout the world are renown. It has a long-standing tradition of extending aid to alleviate hunger, disease, and poverty, as well as in the wake of natural disasters and terrorist attacks beyond its borders[888]. Among other things, Israeli doctors have been giving kids from around the world, including from the PA, Iraq, Jordan and other Arab nations, free life-saving heart operations. Thousands of children have been treated (almost half were reportedly from the PA,

---

[884] See, for example, 7 Recent Israeli Breakthroughs In Cancer Research and Detection, at Technion UK, dated 4/20/2018; Breakthrough Israeli treatment bolsters immune system to attack cancer cells, by Assaf Golan, in Israel HaYom, dated 4/15/2022; New Israeli cancer study leads to possible immunotherapy breakthrough, in the Jerusalem Post, dated 10/17/2021; Israeli 2-in-1 cancer drug shows promise in boosting chemo and immunotherapy, by Nathan Jeffay, dated 4/5/2022; and Israel nanotech breakthrough automatically targets tumors with anti-cancer drugs, by Judy Siegel-Itzkovich, dated 10/4/2022.

[885] See, for example, Google sets up high-tech school at Israeli University, at Reuters, dated 10/25/2022; Israel is world leader in number of high tech employees, by Hili Yacobi-Handelsman, in Israel Hayom, dated 5/11/2022; and Hebrew University and Meta launch AI PhD program, at JNS, dated 10/26/2022.

[886] IDF stopped hackers from hitting US power plants-Unit 8200 official, by Yonah Jeremy Bob, in the Jerusalem Post, dated 6/29/2022.

[887] See, for example, Friends with Benefits: Why the US-Israeli Alliance is Good for America, by Michel Eisenstadt and David Pollock, at the WashintonInstitute.org, dated 11/7/2012, as well as, their more extensive report, Asset Test-How the United States Benefits from Its Alliance with Israel, Washington Institute Strategic Report of 2012 Strategic Report 7, of the Washington Institute for Near East Policy.

[888] See, for example, Israel's humanitarian aid, at embassy.gov.il/boston.

Jordan and Iraq). Many around the world have benefited from Israel's timely and capable teams of first responders and experts when facing natural and other disasters, including in the US[889].

BDS is antisemitic and foolish. Israel is not an apartheid state. It's a diverse society with freedom of speech, religion and press, as well as equal protection under law. This is not the case in the areas controlled by Hamas and the PA[890].

Don't be misled by the scurrilous claims generated by the propaganda organs of the Iranian Regime, Hamas or other sources and repeated by their local minions or others in the US and elsewhere.

The Bible[891] declares those who bless Israel are blessed. Israel does so much good; it's a blessing to the world. It's time to unite to defeat BDS.

[889] See, for example, Israeli relief workers fly to Florida in hurricane's wake, by Abigail Klein Leichman at ISRAEL21c.org, dated 10/2/2022 and Israel sends IDF rescue team to Florida disaster site, at JNS, dated 6/27/2021
[890] See, for example, Revive Light and Truth; Eschew Night and Fog, by Leonard Grunstein, in the Times of Israel blogs, dated 7/8/2021.
[891] Numbers 24:9 and Genesis 12:3.

XVI.

PROPOSAL TO OPEN A SYMBOLIC CONSULATE TO THE PA IN JERUSALEM AND EFFECTIVELY CONTINUING TO FUND PAY TO SLAY ARE ABSURD EXAMPLES OF FAILED POLICY OF APPEASEMENT

It is perplexing, to say the least, that even after two successive administrations (those of former President Donald J. Trump and his successor, President Joseph R. Biden) recognized Jerusalem as the capital of Israel and the Trump administration moved the US Embassy from Tel Aviv to Jerusalem, which President Biden confirmed would remain there, the State Department is still seriously flirting with the concept of locating what amounts to a symbolic consulate to the PA in Jerusalem.

This misguided effort is being pursued despite all the progress made since and as a result of the recognition of Israeli sovereignty over Jerusalem, in accordance with US Law, including the momentous Abraham Accords.

Moreover, the Oslo II Agreement, signed in Washington D.C. on September 28, 1995 and witnessed by President Clinton, among others, expressly prohibits establishing a consulate to the PA. Thus, Article IX, Section 5a of the Oslo II Agreement provides that the PA:

> ... will not have powers and responsibilities in the sphere of foreign relations, which sphere includes the establishment abroad of embassies, consulates or other types of foreign missions and posts or permitting their

establishment in the West Bank or the Gaza Strip, the appointment of or admission of diplomatic and consular staff, and the exercise of diplomatic functions.

Why would the State Department seek to induce a breach of the Oslo II Agreement, which is the very basis for the two-state solution for which it so fervently advocates? Furthermore, it is hard to imagine why anyone other than a dilettante would insist on opening a consulate dedicated to serving the PA, in the heart of Jerusalem, in what amounts to a foreign country. As an aside, why not open the proposed consulate in Ramallah, where the PA maintains its government offices and to which Israel was graciously willing to accede, even though it had the absolute right to reject a general consulate to the PA, as noted above?

Incredibly, it would appear that the proposed consulate is intended to serve only the non-Jewish residents that the PA governs in the areas of Judea and Samaria that it controls. The approximately sixty thousand US citizens who live in Judea and Samaria, plus those living in Jerusalem beyond the so-called Green Line, who are Jewish, would effectively be excluded.

Aside from this being invidious discrimination of the most sordid variety, why would the US actually reward the PA for being Judenrein (cleansed of Jews)? Consider the PA even imprisons those violating its noxious laws prohibiting the sale of land to a Jew. Is this Jim Crow-like paradigm the State Department's policy of choice?

Moreover, how can anyone reasonably expect to make a new enforceable agreement that will be respected by the parties if don't insist on scrupulous fulfillment of the terms of prior agreements as a condition to any new ones? The whole purpose of making an interim agreement is to demonstrate reliability and build trust as a prelude to making a final agreement. If a party can't be relied upon to honor their word, why would anyone take any risks in reliance on that word?

The situation becomes even murkier and complicated when instead of punishing misbehavior, it is rewarded, as the US has done in the years prior to the Trump administration and since, by continuing to fund the PA. This is so despite the PA continuing to reward terrorism with its so-called 'pay-to-slay' program of paying bounties and pensions to terrorist murderers (and their families) who kill and maim Israelis and Americans. In spite of the Taylor Force Act prohibiting the US from funding the PA under these nefarious circumstances, the Biden administration continues to fund the PA, as well as UNWRA schools, which teach antisemitism[892]. Is honoring agreements only in the breach the new standard of making progress towards a binding and durable Middle East peace agreement? Condoning breaches of agreements and bad faith is a sure-fire prescription for further bad faith and non-compliance, not inspiring good faith honoring of agreements. It's long past time to hold the PA accountable for its malfeasance and misfeasance. The US must reward only good behavior and positively reinforce it, not just call out negative behavior and, in effect, excuse and even remunerate it.

Consider, too, the anomalous character of this initiative. Congress passed the Tibet Policy and Support Act[893], requiring the US to open a consulate in Tibet[894]. Yet, to this day, there is no consulate in China-occupied Tibet serving Tibetans. Nor, for that matter, is there a consulate in Turkey serving only the

---

[892] See, for example, UNRWA textbooks still include hate, antisemitism despite pledge to remove — watchdog, in The Times of Israel, dated 7/7/2022, Palestinian Schools Have a Problem—and Are Running Out of Time, by Yardena Schwartz, in Foreign Policy, dated 11/5/2021 and UNRWA-produced education materials contain antisemitic content, watchdog group documents, by Marc Rod, in the Jewish Insider, dated 7/11/2022.
[893] Tibet Policy and Support Act (www.congress.gov/bill/116th-congress/house-bill/4331/text)
[894] See, for example, Risch, Rubio, Cardin, Feinstein Welcome Passage of Their Bipartisan Bill in Support of Tibet, dated 12/22/2020, on the Senate Foreign Relations Committee website (at foreign.senate.gov). President Trump signed the Consolidated Appropriations Act-2021, which included the Tibet Policy and Support Act, into law on 12/27/2020.

Kurds, in China serving only the Uyghur Muslims, or in Myanmar serving only the Rohingya Muslims.

This is understandable, given that Article 4 of the Vienna Convention on Consular Relations requires the consent of the receiving State be obtained before any such consulate may be established. Presumably, the receiving States just said no or the request was never made because a negative reaction was expected.

Why, then, the double standard when it comes to Israel? Given that Israel has repeatedly said no[895], shouldn't this end the discussion? Indeed, it is reported[896] Israeli Foreign Minister Lapid told US Secretary of State Blinken that Jerusalem should not be allowed to host diplomatic missions that aren't to Israel. He also argued that reopening the consulate would "send the wrong message" to the Palestinians.

We are celebrating the anniversaries of the historic and inspiring Abraham Accords with a growing number of nations. It was the impetus of having the US as a trusted ally and friend, as a part of a reliable and powerful nexus with Israel and as a deterrent to the Iranian Government's quest for hegemony in the region, which, in no small measure, played a part in promoting these peace treaties. In this regard, the Trump administrations' recognition of Jerusalem as the capital of Israel was tangible proof that the US could be counted on to be a loyal friend and ally. The mixed messaging of prior administrations, which sought to flirt with everyone, had created a perception that it was not a genuine friend to anyone.

The on-again, off-again consular initiative and the substitute special offices within the Embassy reporting directly to the State

---

[895] See, for example, Israeli minister sees no compromise on U.S. Palestinian mission in Jerusalem, in Reuters, dated 10/12/2021
[896] Blinken and Lapid discussed options for Iran not previously on table — official, by Jacob Magid, in the Times of Israel, dated 10/14/2021.

Department and not through the local US Ambassador to Israel, devoid of any practical utility, is all too reminiscent of the misadventures of the past. Let's be clear, despite President Biden's clear and unqualified declaration that the US Embassy would remain in Jerusalem, there suddenly appears to be some ambiguity on the subject of Jerusalem. However, it is suggested that no such equivocation is legally proper or desirable.

In 1995, the US Congress virtually unanimously passed the Jerusalem Embassy Act[897]. It provides[898] that Jerusalem should remain an undivided city, in which the rights of every ethnic and religious group are protected, and Jerusalem should be recognized as the capital of the State of Israel. President Biden (then Senator), in his remarks on the Senate floor[899] urging its passage, reproduced in Chapter III above, explained how "it is unconscionable...to refuse to recognize the right of the Jewish people to choose their own capital... Regardless of what others may think, Jerusalem is the capital of Israel. Moving the U.S. Embassy to Jerusalem will send the right signal, not a destructive signal. To do less would be to play into the hands of those who will try their hardest to deny Israel the full attributes of statehood."

The prescient wisdom embodied in these plainspoken and forthright words requires no further explanation; they have proven true. The extraordinary progress made with the Abraham Accords is a testament to the perspicacity of this policy, as is the exciting prospect of further agreements being made expanding the circle of peace.

It's now indisputably US law that undivided Jerusalem is the capital of Israel. This new attempt to infringe on the sovereign status of Jerusalem as an integral part of Israel and thereby

---

[897] 109 Stat. 398, Public Law 104-45, dated November 8, 1995.
[898] Ibid, Section 3.
[899] Congressional Record Volume 141, Number 165 (Tuesday, October 24, 1995), Senate, Page S15533.

diminish its legitimacy is baffling. Why engage in frivolous machinations like setting up a symbolic consulate in Jerusalem to service a foreign non-state? Besides being an absurd and irresponsible way of making this kind of a point, it's also illegal under US and International Law. It also flies in the face of the President and the Senate by an overwhelming near-unanimous vote (97 to 3), reaffirming that Jerusalem is the capital of Israel. Yet, the State Department doyens insist on this kind of game-playing and resort to cunning ploys as a means of expressing their continued adherence to failed policies that should have been discarded long ago.

Similarly, as discussed above, the Biden administration's determination to restore funding to the PA, despite the failure of the PA to eliminate its loathsome program of paying pensions or other emoluments to those committing terrorist acts against Israel, is irresponsible. It is ludicrous and frankly abhorrent to continue funding the PA so long as it continues to fund terrorism. It not only doesn't disincentivize this evil program of murder, it actually reinforces it. Indeed, it's no coincidence that with the restoration of funding, announced by President Biden on his trip to the Middle East[900], Mahmoud Abbas[901] declared an

---

[900] See, for example, U.S. announces $316M for Palestinians as Biden visits West Bank, by Alexander Ward, in the Hill, dated 7/14/2022.

[901] The misplaced reliance on the bonafides of Abbas is mystifying. Abbas wrote his doctorial thesis at the University of Moscow in Russia, which can fairly be described as a screed in Holocaust denial. Abbas has repeatedly made outrageous comments on the Holocaust, including even as recently as a press conference in Germany, on August 16, 2022, with the German Chancellor Olaf Scholz. See, for example, German chancellor 'disgusted' by Abbas's 'intolerable' 50 Holocausts claim, in The Times of Israel, dated 8/17/2022. Abbas was also one of the architects of the infamous Olympic Munich Massacre. When asked if he apologized for the Olympic Munich Massacre in that same press conference, Abbas refused to do so. Abbas had also previously honored Abu Daoud, a leader of the Munich Massacre, as a hero when he passed away. Outrageously, the Olympics continue to allow a Palestinian Authority team to participate without requiring the Palestinian Authority to apologize for the Olympic Munich Massacre and pay reparations to the victims' families.

increase in the compensation paid to those murdering Jews[902]. This was a predictable consequence of the administration's policy of appeasement and callous indifference to the suffering it causes.

Lest there be any misunderstanding, the consequences of this asinine policy and, frankly, malfeasance by the ideologically driven State Department has not been a decline in terrorism. Rather, there has been a very substantial increase in the number of terrorist incidents perpetrated against Israel[903].

Another example of the misplaced priorities and disloyalty to US ally Israel is the continuing funding of UNHRA[904], despite its abject failure to reform and flagrant violation of its commitment to stop teaching antisemitism. In the face of institutional Jew hatred and an active program of perpetuating and promoting antisemitism in its schools, poisoning the minds of yet another generation, the US continues to fund UNHRA.

---

[902] See, for example, As Biden Meets with Abbas, Abbas Raises Salaries of Hundreds of Terrorists, by Palestinian Media Watch, dated 7/13/2022, at Israel 365 News.

[903] See, for example, Summary Report on Terrorism Against Israel, dated 12/22/2022, at guim.co.uk, which reports over 5,000 terrorist incidents in 2022 (as of 12/21/2022) and Palestinian Terrorism Against Israel, 2022: Methods, Trends and Description, dated 1/29/2023, a publication of the The Meir Amit Intelligence and Terrorism Information Center, at terrorism-info.org.

[904] Some in Congress are trying to stop this travesty. See, for example, Senate and House Republicans move to cut funding to UNRWA, at Israel National News, dated 2/21/2023, which reports the bill sponsors noted UNRWA has a "rampant history of anti-Israel and antisemitic propaganda and activity". It also reports Congressman Chip Roy said,"UNRWA's lengthy and detailed history of promoting antisemitism, violence and terrorism through 'educational' materials, and its continued ties to Hamas, should completely disqualify this corrupt entity from receiving any US taxpayer funding" and "UNRWA has failed to meet previous commitments to stop its hostility towards Israel, and it is an obstacle to peace." It goes on to report that Senator James Risch, the ranking member of the Senate Foreign Relations Committee, noted UNRWA employs people with ties to Hamas, a US designated foreign terrorist organization and its schools have been used to promote antisemitism and store weapons. He concluded that US funding of UNRWA was unacceptable, unless the administration could certify without a doubt that UNRWA has no affiliation with a US designated foreign terrorist organization and does not support antisemitic rhetoric.

Appeasement is a failed policy. It's one thing to facilitate getting to yes in a serious negotiation between two parties, where there is meaningful mutual give and take by both parties. It's another thing to try to seduce a party, even to appear at the negotiating table, by offering gratuitous gifts that actually reinforce bad behavior rather than rewarding good deeds. Appeasement didn't work in 1938 to prevent World War II; it merely delayed it somewhat[905]. Indeed, it likely made it inevitable because it tangibly demonstrated the fecklessness of the erstwhile allies of Czechoslovakia and the lack of accountability by Germany for its wrongdoing. As the Mishna[906] so pithily teaches, performing a good deed engenders more good deeds and sinful conduct begets more sins. We may not condone, let alone reward, wicked conduct.

Israel is a loyal friend and vital strategic ally of the US. Diminishing it or sending mixed signals serves no useful purpose; it only tarnishes the prestige of the US. It's time to end these unrealistic and frankly dangerous ploys. If the goal is to have a diplomatic presence with the PA, then do so in Ramallah. There is no genuinely rational or constructive reason to impinge on the legitimacy of Jerusalem as the capital of Israel. Indeed, as history has demonstrated in no uncertain terms, this kind of ambivalent policy only causes confusion and raises unrealistic expectations that serve to prevent and not enhance the prospects for peace.

It is also not constructive to continue to fund the PA and UNWRA even as they cruelly promote murderous terrorism against Israel and Jew hatred. The Midrash[907] warns that anyone who is

---

[905] The Munich Agreement (surrendering the Sudetenland in Czechoslovakia to Germany, as it demanded) was entered into on September 30, 1938 and World War Two began on September 1, 1939, when Nazi Germany invaded Poland. See, Munich Agreement, at Britanica.com.
[906] Avot 4:2.
[907] Midrash Tanchuma, Metzorah 1 records this statement by Rabbi Eleazar. Midrash Ecclesiastes Rabbah 7:16 in its commentary on the verse, which counsels a person not

merciful to the cruel will end by being cruel to the merciful. This is sobering advice, which should inform how we react to the malevolent hatred and murderous terrorism being promoted by Hamas and the PA and their surrogates. We cannot allow our compassion for those who, unfortunately, are suffering under the oppressive yoke of Hamas and the PA to excuse the funding, directly or indirectly, of their very oppressors, Hamas and the PA. This misplaced compassion only serves to cause more harm, as described above.

The pursuit of peace is a noble endeavor. However, the path to peace does not lie in reinforcing hatred and violence. Psalms[908] records peace emanates from Jerusalem, a city unified together. As has been amply demonstrated by the Abraham Accords, by supporting Israel and a unified Jerusalem, peace can be secured. Let's not stray from this proven path to peace. Instead, let's redouble our efforts to strengthen the US-Israel relationship for the benefit of all parties concerned.

---

to be overly righteous, reports a similar statement made by Resh Lakish that anyone who becomes compassionate when they should be cruel will ultimately become cruel when they should be compassionate.
[908] Psalm 122:3-7.

XVII.

PROSPECTS FOR FUTURE PEACE-THE ABRAHAM ACCORDS ARE THE ANTIDOTE TO ISLAMIST EXTREMISM AND THE TERRORIST IRANIAN REGIME

The miraculous UAE-Israel Agreement brokered by President Trump's administration and signed in Washington was an outstanding achievement. It had been over a quarter of a century since the peace treaty between Israel and Jordan and more than forty years since the peace treaty with Egypt.

It was also the first of a number of agreements that heralded a new age of peace and prosperity in the Middle East. Since then, peace agreements have been made by Israel, under US sponsorship, with Bahrain, Sudan and Morocco. These agreements are collectively aptly named the Abraham Accords. They honor of the memory of the Patriarch Abraham, the father of the Jewish people, as well as the ancestor of the Arab people. It was Abraham who publicly championed the belief in the one true G-d and gave birth to Judaism. He is venerated by all three of the major monotheistic religions, Judaism, Christianity and Islam.

Unfortunately, not everyone shared in the glee. As might have been expected, the Iranian government vehemently decried the peace agreement[909]. The club of nefarious players opposing the

---

[909] See Iran's Khamenei: UAE 'treason' against Palestinians and Islam will not last long, by Agencies and TOI staff, in the Times of Israel, dated 9/1/20; In 1rst response from Iran, official says 'UAE will be engulfed in Zionism fire', by TOI staff, in the Times of

deal also included Hamas[910] and the PA[911]. What animates this hatred? The Iranian regime does not have a common border with Israel, nor did Iran prior to the Islamic terrorist regime of Ayatollah Khomeini and his successors have this kind of animus towards Israel. Indeed, Israel enjoyed a measure of peaceful relations with the more secular regime under Shah Pahlavi. What then changed when he was deposed and the Ayatollahs took over?

The Iranian terrorist regime of the Ayatollahs is virulently anti-Israel[912]. It is also anti-American[913]. While both Israel and the Vatican[914] have reached out to the Muslim community to express their respect for the Muslim religion, this has not been reciprocated by the Iranian regime or others, like the PA and Hamas. Indeed, there are Imams who continue to incite the members of their Mosques with poisonous rhetoric that demonizes Jews and Judaism, as well as Christians.

Unlike the Vatican, there is no central authority of Muslims, which can act to reinterpret or change religious doctrine or practice, generally among its adherents, as it did in Vatican II. Instead, there are varieties of schools of thought in various regions, as well as individual Imams, who are not bound by any religion-wide authoritative precedents. Each can issue their own Fatwas (rulings on Islamic law) and there can be conflicting rulings. Thus, there are Imams who preach respect and admiration for Jews and Christians and those who don't.

Israel, dated 8/14/20; and Iran, Turkey, Ben Rhodes, Tlaib United in Criticism of UAE–Israel Deal, by Seth Frantzman, in the Jerusalem Post, dated 8/15/20.

[910] See At joint Hamas-Fatah rally in West Bank, 2,000 protest Israel-UAE deal, by AFP and TOI staff, at the Times of Israel, dated 8/20/20.

[911] See Palestinians say United Arab Emirates Deal with Israel hinders quest for Mideast peace, Joseph Krauss, AP, dated 8/14/20.

[912] See, for example, When Iran Says 'Death to Israel,' It Means It, By Behnam Ben Taleblu, in The Atlantic, dated 7/15/2022.

[913] See, for example, Anti-Americanism, at UnitedAgainstNuclearIran.com.

[914] See, for example, Nostra Aetate, of Pope Paul VI, dated October 28, 1965, discussed above.

Unfortunately, the Iranian Regime is a particularly extremist one that not only exercises religious authority over the population; it also has overwhelming temporal power over its people. There is no separation of religion and state, which is an intrinsic and fundamental feature of life in the US. Iran is governed by an oppressive, theocratic and terrorist regime which seeks to eliminate the US and Israel because they exist. They don't pose a direct threat to Iran or desire the destruction of Iran or its people. On the contrary, the US and Israel only desire to live in peace with Iran and enjoy mutually beneficial and prosperous relations. However, the Iranian regime's religious ideology prevents this from occurring. In their perverted vision of the world, Islam must be dominant and Jews and Christians subservient (dhimmis) as a prelude ultimately to converting to Islam.

The Iranian regime's desire for hegemony is thus an inflexible religious imperative. This combination of religious fervor and the doctrinal dictated need for temporal dominance makes it nearly impossible to overcome. This is because it does not accept rational compromise even in what we would assume is a non-religious area. Just imagine if you believed that your religion mandated you be the overlord of others. It's difficult because we come from a tradition that everyone is created in the image of G-d and the ideal is to live and let live, not to dominate others.

The mere existence of Israel, let alone its success, is perceived as a direct challenge to the Iranian regime's religious doctrine. By the regime's delusional view of history, Judaism and Christianity should have disappeared and their prominence is an affront to the Muslim religion that should have replaced them.

There is an even more virulent version of this supersessionist philosophy that seeks culturally to appropriate the very history of the Jews. In essence, they consider themselves to be the Jews, and the real ones are viewed as just being impostors. As ridiculous as this false narrative is, it seems to have infected a number of people who are a part of the PA and Hamas apparatus. The syndrome has also manifested itself in the propaganda materials and pronouncements of many in the PA and Hamas and their allies, agents and useful dupes, including in the US. Thus, the propaganda materials circulated by them and their proxies or fellow believers in Hamas and the PA insist it is they who are the indigenous people of the Land of Israel[915] and that they predated the Jews and Christians. They also claim that prophets and other revered figures in Judaism and Christianity were Muslims. The absurdity of these patently false declarations does not deter those who flagrantly invoke them as they shout down anyone suggesting they are baseless and untrue. Reason appears to be suspended. Demonstrating ideological purity and unbridled allegiance to a cause, no matter how nebulous, is the only goal.

So too, is the fallacious claim that the Jewish Temple never existed on the Temple Mount. The ignorance and willingness outright to deny the validity of any factual evidence, including the existence of overwhelming archeological and documentary proof and even corroboration from Muslim texts and other authentic sources, is shocking. Although more fully discussed above, some repetition is appropriate to show how absurd and antithetical to mainstream Islamic traditions this specious claim is and, therefore, set forth below are excerpts[916] from the pamphlet entitled, A Brief Guide to Al-Haram Al-Sharif Jerusalem, published in English, in 1925 (many decades before there was a PA or Hamas), which was published by the Supreme Muslim Council that was in charge of the Temple Mount, at the time:

The HARAM

---

[915] See, for example, the Jews: One of the World's Oldest Indigenous Peoples, by Alan Baker, at Jerusalem Center for Public Affairs, dated 7/30/2017 (jcpa.org)
[916] Page 4 of the pamphlet.

HISTORICAL SKETCH

The site is one of the oldest in the world. Its sanctity dates from the earliest...times. Its identity with the site of Solomon's Temple is beyond dispute. This, too, is the spot, according to the universal belief, on which "David built there an altar unto the Lord, and offered burnt offerings and peace offerings". (1)

(1) 2 Samuel XXIV, 25.

The pamphlet goes on to summarize the history of the site, which it explicitly confines to the Muslim period, as follows:

But, for purposes of this Guide, which confines itself to the Moslem period, the starting point is the year 637 A.D. In that year, the Caliph Omar occupied Jerusalem...There were the ruined walls of the Herodian and Roman periods, the remains of an early basilica (probably on the present site of al-Aqsa), and the bare Rock.

Yet, despite it all, there are still representatives of the PA and Hamas who insist there was no Jewish Temple on the Temple Mount in Jerusalem and the Jewish people have no connection to the site. Whether this is the result of a cynical and contrived propaganda effort designed to divert attention from the reality of the resurgence of a strong and vital Jewish State of Israel or the hysterical delusions of psychopathic ideologues, it is poisonous to the prospects for peace. A concerted effort by the PA or its successors to negate these falsehoods is required to prepare for eventual peace. In essence, Vatican II paved the way for the Catholic Church's recognition of Israel and the equivalent Muslim version should be a threshold condition to providing financial aid or other benefits to the PA and, similarly, Hamas.

The US must demonstrate the seriousness of its position on these fundamental matters by tangible actions, not just impotent rhetoric. The failure to do so has allowed the minds of generations to be poisoned with Jew hatred and malevolent falsehoods. Similarly, UNWRA[917] contributions must be suspended so long as PA schools funded by UNWRA continue to promote antisemitism as a part of the school curriculum and in books used to educate the children[918].

The Biden administration's determination to re-commence this funding serves no salutary purpose. It, in effect, rewards and reinforces misbehavior instead of disincentivizing it. The good intentions and ideologically driven imperatives that animate the State Department in its relations with rogue actors like the PA, Hamas, and Iran are no substitute for meting out a dose of genuine accountability, responsibility and real-world consequences for malign actions. Indeed, it is suggested that when malevolent activities are condoned or otherwise excused, without there being any semblance of real repercussions, the lesson learned is either the world doesn't really care; or, even worse, just pays lip service to calling out the wrongful conduct,

---

[917] It is reported the EU cut funding and during the Trump administration funding was cut as well. See, for example, Trump Is Right to Cut Funding to UNRWA, by Gregg Romat, in the Hill and reproduced at Middle East Forum, dated 1/7/2018; Biden funding decision inflames debate over textbooks for Palestinian refugees, by Laura Kelly, in the Hill, dated, 4/9/2021; and EU Slashes Funding for Antisemitic Palestinian Schoolbooks, by JNS, dated 5/18/2022. See also, Bill that prevents US funds going to antisemitic Gazan textbooks passes cmte. vote, by Omri Nahmais, in the Jerusalem Post, dated 9/17/2022, a bi-partisan bill (H.R. 2374-Peace and Tolerance in Palestinian Education Act) on April 5, 2021 (at congress.gov. 117th Congress, house-bill 2374), sponsored by Congressmen Sherman, Mast, Zeldin, Gottheimer and Trone. In the House of Representatives. Congressman Sherman is quoted as saying, "Instead of envisioning a Palestinian state alongside Israel, textbooks erase Israel from maps, refer to Israel only as 'the enemy,' and ask children to sacrifice their lives to 'liberate' all of the lands between the Jordan River and Mediterranean Sea," He reportedly went on the say "One horrific example includes a 5th grade textbook which encourages students to emulate Dalal Mughrabi, a convicted terrorist who perpetrated the 1978 Coastal Road massacre, which killed 38 Israeli civilians-including 13 children".

[918] See, for example, UNRWA textbooks still include hate, antisemitism despite pledge to remove-watchdog, in The Times of Israel, dated 7/7/2022 and UNRWA chief acknowledges antisemitism and glorification of terrorism in Palestinian textbooks, in the EUReporter, dated 9/3/2021.

but wink, wink, it actually agrees it's not wrong and instead is justified under the circumstances. These kinds of perverted assumptions should be anticipated. They are predictably derived from the kind of mixed messaging and lack of any tangible ramifications resulting from the continuing malign activities of the PA, Hamas, Iran, and its proxies. The need for a practical and realistic approach that fosters enlightened self-interest in achieving just and right US foreign policy goals is compelling. This is an essential part of the new approach that resulted in the Abraham Accords.

It is noteworthy that in connection with a peace agreement brokered by the US between Kosovo and Serbia, Jerusalem was referenced, including a declaration of intent to open an Embassy there. It brings to mind the words of Psalms[919] that those who seek the peace of Jerusalem shall prosper and enjoy tranquility, as well as the Biblical[920] assurance that those who bless Israel will be blessed. The prospects for further peace agreements between Israel and other nations who desire to join the circle of peace is inspirational. May the blessings of peace prevail.

All these wonderful and historical events are occurring against the backdrop of the ominous threats posed by Iran's inimical and autocratic regime. These include the flagrant and egregious violation of its commitments under the JCPOA and obligations under the Nuclear Non-Proliferation Treaty, as well as its other malign activities. However, the response of the US under the Trump administration, in contrast to the prior administration and the ineffectiveness of the EU, may help explain why the Trump administration's efforts at peacemaking were more successful while these others failed.

---

[919] Psalms 122:6.
[920] Numbers 14:9.

It is indisputable that Iran is not in compliance with the JCPOA[921]. Whether the Iranian regime was clandestinely violating it all along[922], including hiding the Uranium metal disk used as a triggering device for a nuclear bomb, or this first occurred later may be a source of debate; but nevertheless, the fact remains it is in non-compliance. As the International Atomic Energy Agency (IAEA) reported, Iran has already exceeded by ten times the enriched uranium limits under the JCPOA.

After the disappointing failure of the Security Council to renew the thirteen-year-old arms embargo against Iran[923] and in response to Iran's violations, Secretary of State Mike Pompeo delivered a notice to the UN Secretary General and president of the Security Council initiating the so-called snapback sanctions procedure[924], under UN Security Council Resolution 2231 of 2015.

By way of background, Resolution 2231 recognized the JCPOA and lifted the nuclear sanctions the UN Security Council previously levied on Iran[925]. It also sets forth a procedure for reinstating those sanctions, known as the snapback. Thus, the UN sanctions are reinstated 30 days after notice from anyone

---

[921] See, UN agency says Iran is violating all restrictions of nuclear deal, by Kiyoko Metzler, David Rising and Edith M. Lederer, AP, dated 6/5/20; Europeans trigger dispute mechanism in urgent bid to save Iranian nuclear deal, by Natash Turak, CNBC, dated 1/14/20; UN reports increasing violations of Iran nuclear deal, by Kiyoko Metzler, David Rising and Jon Gambrell, AP, dated 11/11/19; Iran is Not Complying with the Nuclear Deal, by Fred Fleitz, in National Review, dated 7/14/17; and Iran Nuclear Deal, by Peter Brookes. Brett Schaefer and James Phillips, Heritage Foundation, dated 1/29/20.
[922] See, for example, the matter of the missing uranium disk that could be used to generate neutrons for triggering fission in an atomic bomb's U-235 core, reported in New tensions dim hopes for salvaging Iran nuclear deal, by Richard Stone, in Science Magazine, dated 6/17/20 and The IAEA's nuclear reports on Iran are its harshest rebuke yet, by Samuel M. Hickey, at armscontrolcenter.org, dated 6/16/20.
[923] See, The United Nations failed to renew the arms embargo on Iran. What does that mean?, by Hollie McKay, Fox News, dated 8/18/20.
[924] Secretary of State Michael R. Pompeo-At a Press Availability, Remarks to the Press, on August 20, 2020 (on the State Department website at www.state.gov).
[925] As detailed in Resolution 2231 of 2015.

named in Resolution 2231 as a 'JCPOA participant' that there is believed to be significant non-performance by Iran of its commitments under the JCPOA. The Resolution provides that the only way to stop this automatic reinstatement of the UN sanctions is if, within such 30 days, there's an affirmative vote by the Security Council to continue the sanctions relief provided for in Resolution 2231.

The US is one of those expressly named as a JCPOA participant in the Resolution and, therefore, it's entitled to initiate the snapback, as described above. Since the US, as a Permanent Member of the Security Council, could veto any such Security Council effort to avoid the automatic snapback, the mechanism should have assured the UN sanctions would perforce be reinstated into full force and effect once the snapback was triggered by the US.

Some have raised the issue of whether the US still had the right to trigger the snapback since President Trump announced withdrawal from the JCPOA[926]. However, it is submitted that this misapprehends the nature and import of Resolution 2231, as well as the JCPOA.

First of all, it is important to understand that the term 'JCPOA participant', as noted above, is a defined term under Resolution 2231. This is a typical drafting device that's often employed as an expedient means of referencing a list of names repeatedly used throughout a document. As used in the Resolution, the term includes any of the US, China, France, Germany, Russian Federation, UK, and Iran, as well as the EU. The EU is not an actual party to the JCPOA, yet it is included within the rubric of a JCPOA participant. This reinforces the plain meaning of the Resolution that being a party to the JCPOA is not a precondition to exercising rights under the Resolution.

---

[926] See, Remarks by President Trump on the Joint Comprehensive Plan of Action, issued on May 8, 2018 (on the White House website at www.whitehouse.gov)

It should also be noted that the JCPOA is not an actual legal agreement. It is unsigned and was never approved as a binding legal treaty by the US Congress. It was also likely not appropriately approved by the Iranian Parliament[927] in the form presented to Congress or by Ayatollah Khamenei[928].

The US Department of State of the Obama administration, in a letter to then-Congressman Pompeo[929], admitted the JCPOA was not a legally binding agreement and postured that it was merely a political commitment. The withdrawal from the JCPOA is nothing more than a symbolic act. Even the title JCPOA, an acronym referring to the Joint Comprehensive Plan of Action, describes it as a plan, not an agreement. Interestingly, the letter goes on to acknowledge that the only real deterrent to Iran's violation of its commitments is the US' right to snap back UN sanctions and to impose its own unilateral sanctions against Iran. Legal arguments about the US' status as a party to what amounts to a non-agreement are specious and irrelevant.

The only relevant document is Resolution 2231, and under it, as noted above, the US is definitionally a participant entitled to snapback protection. As a practical matter, this is immutable, given that this provision cannot be changed without amending the Resolution, which the US could veto. The US is, therefore, entitled to enforce the Resolution by its terms.

Consider the absurdity of suggesting Resolution 2231 enforcement is tied to remaining a JCPOA participant. Iran also withdrew[930] from the JCPOA and is no longer a participant. Does that mean it, too, could argue it was no longer subject to the

---

[927] See, MEMRI, The Iranian Majlis Has Not Approved The JCPOA But Iran's Amended Version of it, dated 10/14/15.
[928] See, MEMRI, Iranian Guardian Council Secretary-General Ahmad Jannati: Khamenei Has Not Approved or Signed the JCPOA, dated 10/16/15.
[929] Letter, dated November 19, 2015, from the State Department to the Honorable Mike Pompeo, House of Representatives.
[930] See, Iran is withdrawing from the 2015 nuclear deal after Trump ordered deadly strike on its top general, by John Haltiwanger, in Business Insider, dated 1/5/20.

Resolution and the snapback thereunder; of course not. Indeed, it would make a complete mockery of Resolution 2231 if this were the case. Moreover, the Resolution is clear and it expressly references Iran's commitment thereunder, never, under any circumstances, to seek, develop or acquire any nuclear weapons[931]. It also reaffirms Iran's obligations as a State Party to the Treaty on the Non-Proliferation of Nuclear Weapons. Remember, it was Iran's violation of its legally binding obligations under that Treaty, which was the source of the sanctions originally levied against Iran, in the first place.

It should also be noted that Resolution 2231 does not prevent the US imposing its own sanctions on Iran for non-nuclear matters. Thus, the US was within its rights to sanction Iran for its egregious human rights violations, detention of US citizens on fabricated charges, support of terrorist groups, and ballistic missiles program[932].

Britain, France and Germany also formally accused Iran of violating the terms of the JCPOA and triggered the dispute resolution mechanism, as noted above. In theory, this should have quickly led to their initiating a snapback. Instead, they've acted in concert with Iran to delay the process, despite the egregious violations reported by the IAEA. This reckless behavior and lack of support for the US' effort to snapback sanctions is not only mystifying; it's galling. As allies of the US and ostensibly guardians of non-proliferation under the Treaty, their pandering to the terrorist regime controlling Iran, in the face of its violations of the Treaty and other malign activities, is immoral and inexcusable.

---

[931] See also, Joint Statement of Foreign Ministers of France, Germany and the United Kingdom on the JCPOA, dated 1/14/20, which makes clear that Iran continues to be obligated and has violated those obligations, as well as, noting the triggering of the Dispute Resolution Mechanism, under Section 36 of the JCPOA.

[932] See, Do Recent U.S. Sanctions Against Iran Violate the JCPOA?, by Richard Horowitz, in the National Interest, dated 9/26/17.

Nevertheless, even if the EU, Russia and China balk at the US' right to snapback, the US can still act unilaterally to impose crippling secondary sanctions, including on their banking systems. This would effectively deter most business dealings with the Iranian regime. Thus, European firms have curtailed their business dealings with Iran based solely on the sanctions imposed by the US on Iran, despite the EU urging them to defy the sanctions[933]. The fact that the Iranian regime is already suffering mightily under existing US sanctions is further evidence of its effectiveness. It would also impinge on the ability of Russia and China freely to do business with Iran, given their dependence on exchange currencies like the dollar and euro for trade.

The renewed muscular effort by the US to contain not only the nuclear threat posed by the Iranian regime but also its malign activities has yielded other beneficial results. Thus, we were greeted with the wonderful and unexpected good news that President Trump and his team had successfully brokered a peace agreement between the UAE and Israel[934]. Then a US and Israeli delegation flew to the UAE in a historic flight over Saudi Arabia, which in another breakthrough, granted permanent over-flight rights to Israel[935]. There are also prospects for other countries,

---

[933] See, How the US sanctions are paralyzing the Iranian economy, by Rick Noack, Armand Emamdjomeh and Joe Fox, in the Washington Post, dated 1/10/20. See also, Why Companies around the World are Reversing Course on Iran Business, at Iran Watch, dated 8/11/20.

[934] See, Remarks by President Trump Announcing the Normalization of Relations Between Israel and the United Arab Emirates of 8/13/20, online at www.whitehouse.gov; Stunning Israel-UAE deal upends the 'rules' about peace-making in the Middle East, by Michael Oren, in the Times of Israel blogs, dated 8/14/20; The Israel-U.A.E. Deal and the Beirut Blast Both Box in Iran, by Farnaz Fassihi and David D. Kilpatrick, in the New York Times, dated 8/18/20; and With UAE deal, Israel opens tentative new chapter with Gulf Arabs, by Frank Gardner, BBC, dated 8/18/20.

[935] In boon for Israel, Saudi Arabia gives permanent overfly rights to and from UAE, by Raphael Ahren, in the Times of Israel, dated 9/2/20.

like Saudi Arabia[936] and Indonesia[937], to join in making peace with Israel.

The entering into the UAE peace and normalization agreement was a historical achievement, as were the others that followed. Much had changed in the forty years since the peace treaty with Egypt. Iraq, once a powerful opponent of Iran, was soundly defeated by the United States and its coalition partners and it is no longer a regional power in the Middle East. A civil war broke out in Syria, which has allowed it to become prey to ISIS, Russia, Iran and now Turkey. Lebanon, once a state that balanced the interests of its Christian, Sunni and Shiite citizens, is now held hostage to Hezbollah, an Iranian proxy. Gaza is controlled by Hamas, another Iranian proxy. The autocratic kleptocrats of the PA presume to control and oppress the lives of the people in the PA controlled areas for more than a decade since their last elected terms expired. In the new era of the Abraham Accords, their intransigence has become more of a liability rather than an asset in their relationship with the Arab world around them.

One of the most significant and adverse changes that occurred, though, is the emergence of Iran, under the control of the Ayatollahs and their terrorist Islamic Revolutionary Guards Corps (IRGC) enforcers, as a nefarious force determined to achieve hegemony in the region and wipe out its opponents. The current government of Iran is a Shiite Theocracy and there are few, if any, internal checks on its power. It is a repressive regime and many in Iran don't agree with its policies or appreciate the lack of freedom. Unfortunately, a promising popular massive uprising was brutally suppressed in 2009, while the Obama

---

[936] See, Trump expects Saudi Arabia to join UAE-Israel deal, in Reuters, dated 8/19/20 and Saudi Arabia Cautiously Welcome UAE, Israel Normalization, in AP, dated 8/19/20.
[937] See, for example, Israeli delegation pays rare visit to Indonesia, by Rina Bassist, at Al-Monitor (al-monitor.com), dated 8/17/2022.

administration stood aloof, failing to support the protestors in any meaningful fashion[938].

The autocratic Iranian government views itself as being in a state of war with Israel and the Sunni Arab nations like Saudi Arabia and the Emirates. It seeks to annihilate Israel[939], control Mecca, and dominate the Sunni-controlled countries. It also views the United States as its enemy. Make no mistake about it; despite the so-called Iran deal, the Iranian government still views the US as the great Satan[940].

One of the drivers of the UAE-Israel deal and the success of President Trump's bold new peace initiative is the credibility he established by finally acknowledging the reality that the so-called Iran deal was nothing more than a charade. The Obama administration's overture to Iran that dismissed the very real concerns of allies, like Israel and the Sunni Arab States, left them wondering whether the US was still a reliable and trusted friend. The fact that Iran was able to continue and even accelerate its malign activities and development of its other weapons programs, like ballistic missiles, without any active US countermeasures, only served to embolden Iran's misbehavior and frighten US allies in the region.

Despite the assurances made by the Obama administration that there would be a rigorous inspection regime[941] and, as a result of

---

[938] See, for example, Unrest in Iran forces Obama's hand, by Ben Smith, in Politico, dated 6/15/09 and Why Obama Let Iran's Green Revolution Fail, by Eli Lake, in Bloomberg, dated 8/24/16.

[939] See, Iran's Post Modern Jihad Against the Jews, an excellent analysis by Dr. Reza Parchizadeh, at BESA, dated 7/20/20.

[940] See, for example, U.S. Remains the Great Satan, Hardliner in Iran Say, by Thomas Erdbrink, in the New York Times, dated 9/1/15.

[941] See The Iran Nuclear Deal: What You Need To Know About The JCPOA, at obamawh.archives.gov/iran-deal, under the Title: The JCPOA is Based on Verification, not Trust, which touts that it provides for the most comprehensive and intrusive verification regime ever negotiated.

the JCPOA, Iran would moderate its misbehavior[942], this turned out to be aspirational, not reality. The canard has been exposed and it appears Iran honored the so-called deal only in the breach. There are numerous examples of the Iranian Regime's breaches of the JCPOA, as noted above[943], and its continuing malign activities[944], directly or through its proxies, against the US and its allies, in the region and elsewhere[945]. We also cannot forget that the US State Department has declared Iran a State Sponsor of Terrorism ever since January 19, 1984[946] and the US intelligence community views Iran as an enduring threat to US national interests, despite the JCPOA[947].

The JCPOA neither prevents the Iranian government from securing nuclear weapons nor incentivizes it to become a good neighbor. It merely serves to condone its reckless and nefarious behavior, including the criminal and terrorist activities of its proxies, which was reinforced by the Obama administration's policy of continuing to fund the Iranian regime[948], despite its

---

[942] Statement by the President on the Framework to Prevent Iran from Obtaining a Nuclear Weapon, dated 4/2/15, at obamawh.archives.gov/the- press-office/2015/04/02/statement.

[943] See also, Iran blocking sites access, UN nuclear watchdog says, in BBC news, dated 6/5/20 and Iran rejects US call for UN watchdog to inspect more sites, by Laura Smith-Spark and Sarah El Sirgany, CNN, dated 8/30/17.

[944] See, Iranian Aggression and Bad Actions Since the JCPOA, at Endowment for Middle East Truth, at www.emetonline.org.

[945] See, Overview of State-Sponsored Terrorism by Iran at www.unitedagainstnucleariran.com.

[946] See, State Sponsors of Terrorism-United States Department of State at www.state.gov/state-sponsors-of-terrorism/.

[947] See, Statement for the Record, Worldwide Threat Assessment of the US Intelligence Community, to the Senate Select Committee on Intelligence, by Daniel R. Coates DNI, dated 5/11/17.

[948] See, The secret back-story of how Obama let Hezbollah off the hook, an expose of Iranian backed Hezbollah drug trafficking, weapons smuggling and money laundering, by Josh Meyer in Politico, dated 12/18/17; Yes, Obama Helped Fund the Iranian Regime, by David Harsanyi, in National Review, dated 1/8/20; U.S. wire payments to Iran undercut Obama, by Louis Nelson, in Politico, dated 9/18/16; Secret Obama-era permit let Iran convert funds to dollars, PBS News Hour, dated 6/6/18; and transcript of Senate Hearing before the Subcommittee on National Security and International Trade and Finance, examining the terrorism financing risks of allowing the Islamic Republic of

wrongdoing. This included the notorious delivery of over $1.5 billion in virtually untraceable cash, in a variety of currencies, as a part of the many billions in assets released to Iran[949], which, at least in part, was funneled to Iran-backed terrorists[950]. These misguided policies and actions were viewed as a comprehensive shift in favor of the terrorists governing Iran and away from the US' traditional, loyal friends in the region, including Israel, the Emirates and Saudi Arabia. It was also at the expense of the Iranian people yearning to be free of their autocratic and repressive regime.

To better understand the overwhelming nature of the threat posed by the Iranian regime to US interests in the region, outlined below are just some recent occurrences and those of the not-so-distant past. History is an invaluable tool to deepen our understanding of those who have declared themselves to be our avowed and implacable enemies. It strongly suggests we should believe the threat is real.

CNN[951] reported that the Iranian government was paying bounties to kill US soldiers in Afghanistan. It is also responsible for the death of more than 600 US troops in Iraq[952]. Who can forget how the Iranian regime blatantly attacked US bases in Iraq[953] with ballistic missiles in January of 2020 and then there

---

Iran to gain access to large amounts of hard currency and the US Government's payments of $1.7 billion in foreign cash to Iran, dated 9/21/16.

[949] See, Sorry 'Factchecker,' Nikki Haley is Right-Obama Sent Iran a Planeload of Cash, by David Harsanyi, in National Review, dated 8/25/20 and Obama should apologize for shameful cash payment to Iran, by Douglas MacKinnon, in the Hill, dated 1/1/20.

[950] See, Obama-era cash traced to Iran backed terrorists, by Bill Gertz, in the Washington Times, dated 2/7/18 and How Obama Secretly Gave Iran Access To Billions Of Dollars-And Enabled Terrorism, in Investors Business Daily, dated 6/8/18.

[951] See, US intelligence indicates Iran paid bounties to Taliban for targeting American troops in Afghanistan, by Zachary Cohen, CNN, dated 8/17/20.

[952] See, Iran killed more US troops in Iraq than previously known, Pentagon says, by Kyle Rempfer, in Military Times, dated 4/4/19.

[953] See, American troops had only hours to react to Iranian ballistic missile attack. Here's what they did, by Shawn Snow, in Military Times, dated 4/21/20.

were rocket attacks, by its Hezbollah proxy, in March of 2020[954]. Iran has also repeatedly conducted dangerous and harassing approaches to US Naval forces in the international waters of the Persian Gulf[955].

The flurry of revelations include reports that the explosion in Beirut, which caused so much devastation in 2020, was the result of Hezbollah's bomb-making activities and a new delivery of additional explosives material[956] funded by the Iranian government. There's also the International tribunal determination that Rafiq Hariri, the former president of Lebanon, was killed by Hezbollah, an Iranian proxy, as ordered by Khamenei and planned by Soleimani, as a part of their scheme to exert complete control over Lebanon[957]. The Houthis, another Iranian government proxy, have been firing Iranian-supplied ballistic missiles against Saudi Arabia and they declared their readiness to attack Israel alongside Iranian government-backed Hezbollah[958]. They are also responsible for oppressing and expelling the last few remaining Jews in Yemen[959]. Hamas, yet another Iranian government proxy, is constantly shooting rockets and missiles at Israel and, for a time, it was also launching incendiary devices against Israel[960].

---

[954] See, Iraq base attack: US in retaliatory strikes on Iran backed fighters, BBC news, dated 3/13/20.

[955] See, IRGC Vessels Conduct Unsafe, Unprofessional Interaction with US Naval Forces in Arabian Gulf, by US 5th Fleet Public Affairs, Centcom, dated 4/15/20.

[956] See, Hezbollah purchased explosive material during time of post storage-report, by Benjamin Weinthal, Jerusalem Post, dated 8/19/20.

[957] See, Iran: Rafiq Hariri Was Assassinated by Hezbollah on the Orders of Khamenei and Qassem Soleimani's Plan, ncr-iran.org, dated 8/19/20.

[958] See, Houthis, Hezbollah and Hamas: Israel and Saudi Arabia face similar threats, by Seth Frantzman Jerusalem Post, dated 3/26/18.

[959] See, Houthis are forcing out Yemen's last remaining Jews, by Hanan Greenwood, in Israel Hayom, dated 8/21/20.

[960] See, Israel-Hamas ceasefire deal reached after weeks of Gaza balloon attacks, by Judah Ari Gross and Aaron Boxerman, in the Times of Israel, dated 8/31/20.

The history of Iranian government attacks against the US includes the 1983 bombings of the US Marine Barracks[961] and Embassy in Beirut[962], as well as the 1996 Khobar Towers bombing in Saudi Arabia[963].

It is critical to recognize that the Iranian regime is at war with the United States. Indeed, as Federal District Court Judge Daniels ruled, Iran, including Ayatollah Khomenei, were responsible for the 9/11 attacks on the US[964], one of the most provocative and destructive terrorist acts committed against the US homeland and its people. In his 53 pages of detailed Findings of Facts and Conclusions of Law, Judge Daniels describes the role Iran and its various governmental organs played in this horrible attack on the homeland. Among other things, the Court found: (1) Iran has been waging war against the United States for over 30 years; (2) the Ayatollah Khomeini holds absolute power and can dismiss the president, overrule the parliament and courts and overturn any secular law; (3) the religious division between Sunni and Shi'a did not, in fact, pose an insurmountable barrier to cooperation on terrorist operations and an alliance was formed between Shi'a Iran and Sunni al Qaeda to conduct terrorist attacks against the United States, including 9/11; (4) Iran was behind the Khobar Towers bombing and the attacks on the US Embassies in Nairobi, Kenya and Dar-es-Salaam; and (5) Iran devised plans aimed at breaking the backbone of the American

---

[961] See, Families of Beirut bomb victims mark 30th anniversary of first major terrorist attack on US, by Cristina Corbin, Fox News, dated 11/29/15.
[962] See, Beirut Rules: The Murder of CIA Station Chief and Hezbollah's War Against America, by Fred Burton and Samuel M. Katz (Berkley, 2018), which describes Iran's complicity in the terrorist attack.
[963] Attorney General Ashcroft laid responsibility for this dastardly deed on Iranian backed Hezbollah. See Attorney General Statement, dated 6/21/01.
[964] The historic ruling was entered, on December 22, 2011, in the Havlish case, brought by family members and legal representatives of victims of 9/11, in US District Court, Southern District of New York, 03 MDL 1570 and 03 Civ. 9848 (GBD) (FM). See also, The 9/11 Commission Report, beginning at pages 240-241, which also details Iranian regime contact with al-Qaeda, directly and through proxy Hezbollah, including travel of hijackers through Iran.

economy, crippling or disheartening the United States and its people and disrupting its economic, social, military and political order, including the scheme to crash Boeing jumbo jets, with large fuel capacities, into the World Trade Center, White House and Pentagon that was code named "Shaitan dar Atash" (loosely translated as, Satan in Flames).

Nothing in the purported Iran deal changed this, as the Ayatollah continues to make clear on a regular basis. Hope and spin are no substitute for putting in place genuine safeguards to prevent Iran and its proxies from attacking the US and its allies. It's not just about the nuclear threat. The Court found that Iran has many plans for attacking the US, including (a) using chemical weapons and radioactive dirty bombs; (b) bombing hundreds of electrical power plants, gas stations and oil tankers; (c) using passenger airliners as bombs against US cities; and (d) bombing the railroads.

Isaiah[965] offers some insights into the ineffectiveness of disingenuous agreements. He cautions the scorners and spin doctors. An agreement purporting to establish limits, like red lines not to be crossed or to cheat death, can't be sustained. Mere words can't provide shelter and refuge in the face of an enemy intent on war. It's nothing more than a false hope.

Let's take the lessons of Isaiah to heart. The promise of safety for the homeland, because of some contrived and hopeful strategy to limit Iran from completing a nuclear bomb, for a short period of 10-15 years, is not genuine. It is based on a false premise. We are, as 9/11 demonstrated, vulnerable to terrorist attacks by non-nuclear means.

We cannot afford once again to promote a non-binding impotent agreement like the JCPOA. It is also foolhardy not to address Iran's misbehavior outside of the limited scope of its already illegal quest for a nuclear device. The Trump administration's

---

[965] Isaiah 28:15.

strategy of renewed sanctions against the Iranian regime and bad actors like the IRGC has taken a toll. It's time to ramp them up further and, hence, the initiation of the snapback. An unreformed and reinvigorated Iranian regime, with renewed access to world markets and sanctions relief, is still an avowed and implacable foe of the US and Israel, as well as the Iranian people. It's why many of the freedom-loving people of Iran support the re-imposition of sanctions as a means of ridding themselves of this oppressive regime. We must also support their efforts to free themselves from tyranny.

With the advent of the Trump administration, terrorism by Iran was no longer blindly tolerated. Sanctions were levied against the IRGC and other bad actors in the Iranian regime in response to their malign actions. No longer was Iran's misbehavior just condoned and without consequences. Murderous terrorist leaders like Solimani were surgically targeted and received their just due. The territorial pretensions of ISIS were virtually eliminated. Instead of empty talk of red lines, Assad's gas attack on innocent children and civilians was unequivocally responded to by launching precision missile strikes on three of Assad's chemical weapons facilities[966].

A new reality appeared to have taken hold in the Middle East, where once again, the US was viewed as a force for good, not a callous associate of Iran's ambitions and disloyal to its old friends in the region. There can be little doubt that these measures helped restore confidence in the US as a reliable partner and added new luster to its prestige in the region. It could once again be counted on to intervene in support of its allies against the immoral machinations of the Iranian government and its proxies.

---

[966] Trump Strikes Syria, by Michael Crowley and Andrew Restuccia, in Politico, dated 4/13/2018 and updated on 4/20.

We should all be united in support of the US' efforts to snap back the full weight of the sanctions. Don't be misled by calls by those in the prior Obama and current Biden administrations who condone the Iranian government's wicked activities. The new approach of the Trump administration had already succeeded in yielding a real peace dividend and presented the prospect of continuing to do so. It's time to revert back to the practical and realistic approach that fosters enlightened self-interest to achieve just and right goals. The peace through strength posture of the Trump administration and the tangible manifestation of what it means to be a friend or foe of the US worked in practice.

It is critical, on the one hand, that the US demonstrate, in no uncertain terms, what it means to have the US as a true friend and trusted ally, as well as, on the other hand, how devastating it is to be an enemy of the US. There can be no mixed messages in this regard. Saying what you mean and meaning what you say is a key element in a strategy of deterrence. Bad behavior must not be rewarded or condoned and good behavior should be reinforced. Uncertainty is to be avoided in the extreme and certainty embraced.

It's time to build on the success of the US brokered Abraham Accords and preserve and enhance them by creating a regional alliance for peace and security sponsored by the US. Indeed, why not establish a Middle East Treaty Organization (METO) based on the NATO structure? METO, anchored by Israel, Egypt, the UAE and future peace partners, could be a vehicle to enhance security and preserve peace in the region. Hopefully, one day soon, the good people of Iran, unhampered by the current tyrannical Iranian regime, will be able to join too. Until then, we must unite those interested in peace in containing the threat to peace posed by the existing terrorist Iranian regime and its proxies.

XVIII.

PERSONAL REFLECTIONS

Farley was able to obtain one ticket to the Jerusalem Embassy opening ceremony. He left Saturday night on a non-stop El Al flight from Miami to Israel. Fortuitously, he met Rabbi Efrem Goldberg, the Senior Rabbi of the Boca Raton Synagogue, on line at the ticket counter at the airport.

The El Al Jet was a Boeing Dreamliner, in which the windows were kept darkened throughout most of the flight. This was great for sleeping, but presented some challenges in discerning when it was day or night for purposes of determining when it was time to recite the morning prayers. On a night flight going east, this meant getting up earlier than usual to meet the approaching sunrise. Fortunately, Rabbi Goldberg was there with his handy calendar marked to show the prayer times for the flight, three to four hours after takeoff. This included the time for saying the Shema and Amida prayers. Farley and Rabbi Goldberg managed to get up in time to recite the prayers, including the traditional blessing about returning to and rebuilding Jerusalem.

It was thrilling to realize he was on a mission to be a part of inaugurating the new Embassy in Jerusalem. It was only a dream more than two decades ago, in 1994, when Senator Jon Kyl first indicated that he was determined to make this day happen and here Farley was about to see that vision come to fruition. Like the theme expressed in the blessing about Jerusalem he recited, Farley felt that he was playing the personal role G-d assigned to him in assisting in the process that led to US recognition of Jerusalem as Israel's capital and thereby helping to rebuild

Jerusalem. It was invigorating and he couldn't wait for the festivities to begin and to celebrate with all those present.

Reflecting on how this all came to pass, Farley remembered when he had invited Senator Kyl to be the honoree at the first annual dinner of the Young Israel of Phoenix, where he served as president. It was a small congregation at the time, with just a little over forty members and it was also between Rabbis. Farley was concerned about the turnout for the occasion. He asked the American Israel Public Affairs Committee (AIPAC) to co-sponsor the event, even though it was something AIPAC rarely did at the time. AIPAC graciously acceded, a testament to the well-deserved esteem Senator Kyl was held in by so many who interacted with him.

The dinner was held at the Western entertainment facility in Scottsdale called Rawhide. In the end, one hundred fifty people attended. Farley also solicited letters from major Jewish organizations to thank Senator Kyl for his seminal role in the legislation. The letters poured in and they were effusive in their gratitude and praise, including from the Conference of Presidents of Major Jewish Organizations, Anti-Defamation League (ADL), AIPAC, Orthodox Union (OU), Zionist Organization of America (ZOA) and National Council of Young Israel, as well as, from Ehud Olmert, the Mayor of Jerusalem[967].

---

[967] Farley invited the Mayor of Jerusalem, Ehud Olmert, to Arizona the following year to the second annual Young Israel of Phoenix dinner. He graciously accepted and attended the dinner together with Senator Kyl and Congressmen John Shadegg and Matt Salmon. By then the synagogue membership had grown to 63 and over 250 people attended the dinner, held in the grand ballroom of the Arizona Biltmore. Olmert (who later became Prime Minister) spoke movingly about Senator Kyl and declared his name would be recorded in 'Golden Letters in Jewish History'. Senator Kyl was most appreciative and, as was his custom, he wrote a kind personal note to Farley thanking him. Thereafter, several national Jewish organizations also honored Senator Kyl at dinner events, including the National Council of Young Israel and ZOA and featured him as a speaker.

Farley had worked with Senator Kyl and his office on the Jerusalem Embassy legislation. The letter[968] he received from

---

[968] Glenn Hamer wrote Farley a personal note, on July 24, 2018, after the Embassy opening, acknowledging the indispensable role Farley played. It is a beautiful letter, recounting some of the history of the legislation and Farley's role in the process. Here are some excerpts from the text:

"You, Farley played an indispensable role in advancing this legislation. I believe that before my former boss, Sen. Jon Kyl, was elected to the U.S. Senate in 1994, you had discussed the idea of moving the U.S. Embassy from Tel Aviv to Jerusalem with him. As someone who worked on the successful campaign and then had the great privilege to work for the senator in Washington, DC, it became part of my job to help work on legislation to move the embassy from Tel Aviv to Jerusalem. Sen. Kyl was the true author of the legislation and the Member of Congress most responsible for pushing it through a tricky and difficult legislative process.

Throughout the process, you were a constant source of help in advancing the legislation on all levels and far and away the most important voice in the Senator's home state of Arizona. You assisted in ideas on the language and helped connect dots nationally for us to move the bill forward. Looking back, it is somewhat surprising that Sen. Kyl was able to get this historic measure passed in his first year in the United States Senate! We both know the path was difficult and compromises were necessary. Your skillful work helped navigate the bill through the troubled waters and eventually into law...

A final point to acknowledge your leadership and dedication, After its successful passage, you organized a still talked about dinner in Phoenix honoring Sen. Kyl for his leadership in gaining passage of the law in 1996, which featured the Mayor of Jerusalem as the keynote.

The connection between Jerusalem and the Jewish people has been unbreakable for over 3,000 years. We pray in the direction of Jerusalem and repeat 'next year in Jerusalem' as a common refrain. The Jerusalem Embassy Act is arguably the most important policy statement the United States has made about Israel since supporting its creation of a state.

I want to acknowledge you leadership, Farley, and say... Your role was critical and one that deserves permanent recognition in the history of the United States and Israel."

Farley also received a beautiful letter from Congressman Matt Salmon, dated February 2, 2005, after he left office, thanking him for "valuable political advice in Congress in making a national issue of the need to bring to justice Palestinian Arab terrorists who have murdered Americans. I feel that your idea to pursue this issue of fundamental justice was the right thing to do and I am very proud of the fact that I authored with your help the first Congressional letters on the subject.... Time has shown that we showed great foresight in pursuing this issue as we saw the danger to America of terrorism and the need to aggressively pursue terrorists well before 9/11." This effort eventually resulted in passage of the Koby Mandell Act.

Farley's moving to Florida brought him into contact with another luminary figure, Congressman Ron DeSantis, who would go on to become the Governor of Florida. Farley developed a wonderful relationship with Congressman DeSantis and his staff and he worked with them to propel the move of the US Embassy to Jerusalem.

Glenn Hamer, who was his main contact on Senator Kyl's staff, in appreciation of his efforts, is among Farley's prized possessions. Farley was witness to and well understood the tremendous efforts Senator Kyl had expended to accomplish passage of the Jerusalem Embassy Act of 1995. Nevertheless, Senator Kyl was content to have others take credit for the outstanding achievement. When asked by Farley why he did not better publicize his essential role in authoring and negotiating the bill's passage, he responded that those who need to know do.

This was not the only time that Senator Kyl helped Israel out behind the scenes. There was a time after the horrible attack against the US by terrorists on September 11, 2001, when astoundingly, President George W. Bush's administration seemed to veer somewhat away from his prior pro-Israel policy. The change was discernible and disturbing to Benjamin Netanyahu and he sought an audience with the Senate Foreign Relations Committee to explore the matter. However, the Chairman of the Committee at the time, Senator Joe Biden, refused the request. Netanyahu reached out to Senator Kyl and he coordinated with Senator Joe Lieberman for Netanyahu to speak to a group of Senators. The speech was covered on cable television. Thankfully, after the speech the Bush administration policy towards Israel improved significantly. Netanyahu subsequently called Senator Kyl to thank him for arranging the event and praised him as one of Israel's best friends in the Senate.

Farley was in email contact with Senator Kyl on the day of the Embassy opening. Unfortunately, arrangements were not made for him to be there in person. However, at an event in Washington D.C. that occurred after the Embassy had been opened in Jerusalem, Farley met and spoke to Israeli Ambassador to the US, Ron Dermer. Farley asked Dermer if he could come to Phoenix and personally thank Senator Kyl, with his family present. Dermer immediately agreed and Farley proceeded to help organize the event[969]. Dermer came and brought along a beautiful personal letter from Prime Minister Benjamin Netanyahu thanking John Kyl for being such an extraordinary friend of Israel. Senator Kyl's family was in attendance, including his mother, who was over 100 years of age at the time. Glenn Hamer was also there. There were pictures with the notables, including, of course, the Guest of Honor, Jon Kyl. One of the photographs included Senator Kyl, Glenn Hamer and Farley. They had all worked closely together on the Jerusalem Embassy Act.

Senator Kyl's genuine humility is inspirational. However, Farley felt the American people and the world needed to know about the prominent role Senator Kyl had in achieving US recognition of Jerusalem as the capital of Israel and moving the Embassy there and, hence, he collaborated with Len in order to write and publish this book.

Farley's brother Josh, who lives in Tel Aviv, picked him up at the airport. After moving to Israel, Josh played for the Israel national baseball team. More recently, he completed the Comrades 90 Kilometer race in South Africa. Farley's sport was tennis and, when he was younger, he was a world ranked tennis player[970] and a Division 1 tennis player at Arizona State University and at the University of Pennsylvania. In the summer of 2022, Farley made the US tennis team (age 55 and over), participating in the Maccabiah Games in Israel. One of the important life lessons Farley learned from tennis was that you can be one point from losing and come back and win and therefore to fight to the very end.

---

[969] This was in addition to another Dinner, which Farley had arranged when he was President again of the Young Israel of Phoenix, to thank Senator Jon Kyl when he first retired from the Senate after 18 years. Senator Kyl was later appointed for a few months to the Senate to serve out a part of Senator McCain's term after he passed away.
[970] Ranked 736 in the world in 1986 and 713 in Doubles.

On the Monday morning, May 14, 2018, the day of the formal Jerusalem Embassy Opening Ceremony, Farley attended a breakfast celebration in Jerusalem with his brother Josh and son Benjamin. Florida Governor (now Senator) Rick Scott was there, as well as Members of the Knesset and Pastor John Hagee.

Josh and Benjamin noticed most everyone was sitting outside in the shady area and few were sitting in the sun-drenched area where there were plenty of available chairs. They grabbed three seats in the sun and Farley found himself sitting across from television and radio star Mark Levin and his wife. They were able to chat for about fifteen minutes. Mark Levin told Farley how excited he was to be in Israel for the momentous occasion of the Embassy opening. Farley was much impressed with Mark Levin and how warm, gracious and down-to-earth he and his wife were, as well as how much they truly treasured Israel. This was a common theme among those in attendance. Farley met Mark Levin again at the White House Chanukah party in December of 2020 and was pleasantly surprised that Mark remembered him, despite both sporting Covid masks at the time.

Security was tight at the Embassy Opening Ceremony, with Prime Minister Netanyahu, Treasury Secretary Steve Mnuchin, Jared Kushner and his wife Ivanka Trump, President Trump's daughter in attendance. Everyone was, therefore, advised to arrive early. Farley took the special bus set aside for the event and was transported to the Embassy around two hours before the formal start of the ceremonies.

Like most things in life, there are no coincidences. As Farley sat down, he overheard someone in need of a Minyan (quorum of at least ten men) for the Mincha (afternoon) prayer service. It appeared that the person was having little success in organizing the Minyan because so many were hesitant about leaving their seats. Farley jumped up and assured the man he had experience in rounding up people for a Minyan, having been a synagogue president. He then proceeded to do so and met with success.

Rabbi Efrem Goldberg joined in the prayer service as well. As a result, Farley was able to organize the first Jewish prayer service at the Jerusalem Embassy, which auspiciously took place about an hour before the official dedication ceremony. Someone must have been filming the service because it appeared on YouTube[971]. Many who were not at the Embassy opening reported to Farley how moved they were viewing it.

After the event concluded and all the picture-taking with the assembled dignitaries was done, Farley rejoined his brother Josh and son Benjamin. They first went to the Tomb of King David. Farley felt it was most benefitting, because it was King David who had first established Jerusalem as the capital of Israel more than three thousand years ago. After saying some prayers there, Farley went to the Western Wall to join in the Maariv (evening) prayer service. It was a particularly moving experience for Farley, as he humbly offered his gratitude to G-d for being allowed to participate in this momentous occasion. The next day, Farley flew back to the US.

Like so many in the US, Len watched the Embassy opening ceremony online. As he did, he reflected on how his Father, of blessed memory, would have been thrilled to witness the historic event. His Dad was a Holocaust survivor. He was a slave laborer in Nazi concentration camps, including Auschwitz, where he was indelibly marked with a tattooed number on his arm. He was one of the few who weren't immediately killed in the gas chambers and reduced to ashes in the crematoriums.

The concentration camp regime was intended to cause a slow agonizing death, as he and his fellow slave laborers were worked beyond all endurance. He was also subjected to regular torture and the cruel games the Nazi guards played, designed to purge those who defied all odds and somehow managed to live a few more days. Len's Father told him about a particularly sadistic

---

[971] The prayer service had over 10,000 views on You Tube.

Ukrainian SS guard, with a limp, who viciously and mercilessly beat him and the other young boys in his charge. Those who survived each day were subjected to the notorious selections, where anyone sick or unable to work was sent to the gas chambers and death. Any visible weakness or infraction of the rules meant death. There was no medical care for the plagues of typhus or other illnesses that ravaged the malnourished slave laborers; a visit to the infirmary meant death. As a result, like many concentration camp survivors, Len's Dad had an understandable reticence when it came to seeing a doctor.

However, Len's Dad never gave up. He had an iron will and unshakeable belief in G-d. He miraculously survived. When he emerged from the camps, he weighed barely fifty pounds. Somehow he recovered and went on to marry and build a family. He sacrificed mightily in order to bring up a classical Jewish family devoted to the observance of Jewish traditions and to support Israel. This was his living testament to the survival of the Jewish people.

Len's Father was proud to be a US citizen. He also took pride in Israel and its outstanding achievements. He cherished the shared values and common interests that formed a strong bond between the two countries. This was one of those moments when he would have kvelled (Yiddish, meaning bursting with pride) like he did when Israel won a striking and miraculous victory in the 1967 Six Day War. Unfortunately, he didn't live to see this amazing day, having passed away all too young on Purim in 1995.

Each and every life is precious. As the Mishna (Sanhedrin 4:5) records, causing a single life to perish is effectively destroying the entire world. Correspondingly, saving one life is tantamount to preserving the entire world. It goes on to say that no two people are alike so that everyone can rightly claim the world was created for his or her sake.

We each have our own unique mission in life and it's not to offer excuses based on pretensions of victimhood. Let's embrace our individual humanity and do good deeds. Respect each and every soul; life is precious.

This is a genuine life lesson woven throughout the story of how it came to be that Jerusalem was recognized as the capital of Israel and the US Embassy was moved there.

But the story doesn't end there. History continues to unfold with the success of the Abraham Accords that resulted from the US' recognition of Jerusalem as Israel's capital. We can all do our part and hasten the ultimate redemption. It starts with the first step of doing something constructive in support of a positive project. The experience of being fully engaged with others in the project transcends the individual and elevates personal feelings of satisfaction and accomplishment into a sense of unity, completeness and peace.

The Talmud[972] equates the notion of increasing peace throughout the world to being a builder. Rabbi Dr. Lord Jonathan Sacks Z"L noted[973] the entire nation of Israel was unified and at peace during the time they were building the Tabernacle. It is suggested that being fully engaged in a project with a higher purpose not only has the positive effect of conferring the satisfaction of accomplishment but also infusing a sense of peace.

May we all continue to build on the success of the recognition of Jerusalem as the capital of Israel and relocating the US Embassy to Jerusalem. As Farley and so many others demonstrated in practice, our good deeds do matter.

---

[972] BT Brachot 64a.
[973] Team Building by Rabbi Sacks, on Parshat VaYakel, February 17, 2014, in Covenant and Conversation online at rabbisacks.com.

CONCLUSION

This book is intended to be more than a historical account of how it came to be that the US finally formally recognized Jerusalem as the capital of Israel and moved its embassy there.

As the title implies, it is also an analysis of why it is just and right that this be so. Somehow, in the current environment, where many are bound by strict adherence to ideology, encumbered by its own form of positivistic morality and apparent disinterest in seeking universal truth, this message of truth is sometimes subverted. Instead, each person is encouraged aggressively to embrace only their own ideologically driven truth, no matter how flawed or discordant with reality and honest debate is discouraged[974]. Thus, rather than challenging false narratives, they are often excused with the wave of a hand or just ignored because that is more expedient.

Nevertheless, this quaint affectation of polite discourse can become exceedingly dangerous when it offers succor to and effectively supports a misguided ethic, which condones, justifies or excuses murder, destruction and other evil or criminal acts by terrorists. It's astounding that some otherwise educated and cultured individuals, who should know better, justify or otherwise condone terrorist acts, including by children.

The seemingly obsessive desire of some to court, appease and even reward these terrorist regimes, which are otherwise

---

[974] Frankly, it is nearly impossible to face down an unruly, boisterous and sometimes threatening crowd, employing mob like tactics to swarm and stifle a speaker with another point of view. Slogans or epithets are just mindlessly shouted by those uninterested in reasoned discussion and unwilling to engage in civil discourse. The forums where ideas can be exchanged and debated are becoming more and more limited.

dedicated to destruction of the US and Israel, is irrational. Often, it is motivated by ideological concerns that doctrinairely demand obeisance to this kind of approach. Justifications may be offered, such as this kind of approach will serve to moderate the misbehavior of the offensive regime, even though there is little or no evidence to support this conclusion. Indeed, the opposite is often the case.

Making decisions based on suppositions that prove incorrect or false narratives can lead to catastrophic consequences. It is advisable to keep searching for the truth and this book summarizes what we found as a result of our dedicated efforts to do just that. While only G-d has perfect knowledge and knows absolute truth, we have humbly devoted the skills G-d endowed us with, our knowledge and experience and our unquenchable thirst for truth, to ferret it out and then accurately record it. Our findings are set forth in detail above and may be summarized as follows:

1. The right of the Jewish people to the Land of Israel, including Jerusalem, is superior to the claims of all others, including the so-called Palestinian Arabs governed by the PA or Hamas. The historical connection of the Jewish people to Israel is indisputable and the legal basis of such right is overwhelming. Indeed, the written record of title is reputedly the oldest in the world. Thus, the Jewish people were in and had sovereignty over Israel, including Jerusalem, well more than three thousand years ago and are in and have sovereignty over Israel, including Jerusalem, today. There was a continuing Jewish presence in the land of Israel all those years and more importantly the Jewish people never entered into any treaty surrendering title to Israel. It is also undeniable that those fora, which weighed the evidence and adjudicated competing claims in the past,

have found in favor of the Jewish people and Israel, as summarized above. There are few countries in the world as old and none in Europe and North or South America, which can make a better claim to title and sovereignty over their current borders. Those clamoring to divest Jerusalem from Israel or Israel itself from the Jewish people have no basis in law or fact.

2. Jews have a right to purchase land and reside anywhere in the Land of Israel, including Jerusalem.

3. International Law and US Law support these conclusions.

4. Terrorism and BDS are morally reprehensible and violate applicable law.

5. The claim by the so-called Palestinian people to indigeneity in Israel is unsupported and inconsistent with the historical record. If anything, the opposite conclusion may properly be drawn that they were implanted or arrived in the area primarily populated by Jews and Christians, at the time, as a part of successive invasions by Muslim Arab colonial empires.

6. The denial of Israel's legitimacy, efforts to eliminate it, labeling Israel an apartheid state, singling out of the Jewish State of Israel for calumny, to the exclusion of all other states, which are actually guilty of wrongdoing and applying double standards to Israel, are, as the IHRA definition prescribes, just a modern version of classic antisemitism. Criticism of Israeli government policies is one thing. However, denying the right of Israel to exist is quite another and there should be no misunderstanding that doing so is antisemitism.

7. Holocaust denial and Temple denial are indisputably false narratives and those who utter them are contemptible or willfully ignorant.

8. Corpus Separatum is a misguided proposal that was never actually given the force of law and is violative of applicable International Law as it applies to Jerusalem. Lacking any legal substance, as applied to Jerusalem, to cite it, as a legal issue, is nothing more than posturing, using legal jargon, without substance.

9. Continuing, directly or indirectly, to fund the PA, in the face of its willful failure to eliminate Pay to Slay and Hamas, despite its continuing terrorist attacks on Israel, is not only immoral, it violates the intent and likely the letter of US Law.

10. It is undeniable that the US-Israel relationship benefits both the US and Israel. The military, strategic, economic and other benefits the US derives from the relationship are substantial and meaningful. Israel is still the only truly democratic state, with shared values and common interests with the US, in the Middle East, a very dangerous neighborhood vital to US security interests. The US can genuinely rely on Israel and continuing to deepen and strengthen the US-Israel relationship, which enjoys bi-partisan support, has a proven track record of yielding successful results for both the US and Israel.

As a result of our analysis of the relevant facts and law and for all of the reasons set forth above in this book, it is respectfully submitted that recognizing undivided Jerusalem as the capital of Israel and moving the US Embassy there was and is just and right. We reach this conclusion without reservation or qualification.

Modern propaganda techniques, offering catchy and virtuous sounding albeit empty slogans, delusional messages disguised as pious pronouncements and evocative (often manufactured) attention-grabbing images, are no substitute for critical analysis and substantive truth[975]. Indeed, they were designed to flood our senses and overpower our critical reasoning function so as to eclipse the truth and trigger a wholly emotional and unthinking reaction.

We must be unabashed in our rejection of false narratives designed to distort the truth, no matter how emotionally compelling the story or heart rendering the imagery. It is critical to appreciate that we are just being manipulated by nefarious forces trying to induce a misplaced feeling of guilt and using our own innate goodness against us[976]. The PA and Hamas keep stridently and brazenly repeating their outlandish demand to take Jerusalem away from Israel. This is despite the fact that Jerusalem was never governed by the PA or Hamas regimes, it was never the capital of the PA or Gaza and those regimes have no legal or factual connection to Jerusalem that is remotely comparable to the deep and enduring legal, historical and factual bond of the Jewish people to Jerusalem. Indeed, Jerusalem has only been the capital of Israel and not any other country or empire. Denying Jerusalem to Israel is both unjust and wrong.

---

[975] Consider, for example, the almost childlike fascination with any reference to Palestine prior to 1948, during the Mandatory period, eventhough for the most part, whether it is the Palestine Post, Palestine Bank, Palestine Soccer League, Palestine coins, they really refer to Jewish organizations by this name. In essence, Palestine was the place name given to Israel at the time. Debunking Palestinian mythology is sometimes as easy as pointing out the Hebrew letters on the document, uniform, or currency being offered in support of the specious claim.

[976] In this regard, it is important to appreciate that there are 193 member countries in the UN, as well as, other self-governing and distinctly identified areas such as Taiwan (see, World Atlas.com). Approximately 20 of such countries identify as Arab Muslim Countries. There is only 1 country identified as the Jewish State of Israel. It is the smallest country in the Middle East, about the size of New Jersey in the US, and one of the smallest countries in the world (see, National Geographic.com). Many of the Jews returned home to Israel from Muslim countries, which they were forced to leave (see, The expulsion of Jews from Arab countries and Iran-an untold history, at the World Jewish Congress.org, dated 2/2/2021). Others returned home to Israel from all over the world.

Jon Kyl, Ron DeSantis and Donald Trump understood all this intuitively. Our mission was to endeavor to prove why this is case, in this book. We have, therefore, provided references to the many essential and authoritative primary and other sources we relied on in reaching this conclusion.

Researching and writing this book also provided us with a unique perspective of the extraordinary and seminal events that occurred to make the re-establishment of the modern State of Israel, with Jerusalem as its capital, a reality. It is exceedingly clear that this was no quirk of fate or result of mere chance. Divine providence guided the efforts of so many good people to reach this miraculous outcome.

Maimonides records[977] that in the Messianic age, do not presume that any facet of the world's nature will change or there will be innovations in the work of creation. Rather, the world will continue according to its pattern. He also noted that there was no real difference between the world as he knew it and the Messianic era except for the emancipation of Israel from subjugation to other nations[978]. This appears to have occurred in our times, and we must be forever grateful.

There is a new reality burgeoning in the Middle East, fostered by the US and centered on peace with Israel. It is empowering other nations, as well, which are freely joining with Israel and the US in the growing circle of peace. The new reality is invigorating. Unlike the not-so-distant past, the progress being made by the member nations in the circle of peace engendered by the Abraham Accords is not based on one nation subjugating another. Rather, it is based on mutual respect and cooperation, each pursuing their own enlightened self-interest, based on the recognition that together, everyone can better fulfill their individual destinies. This is not an unrealistic fantasy or purely

---

[977] Maimonides, Mishne Torah, Laws of Kings and Wars, Chapter 12.
[978] See also, BT Brachot 34b, Shabbos151b and Pesachim 68a.

utopian vision. It is being proven in day-to-day activities that are yielding real benefits to the parties involved. It is also not some naïve Pollyannaish construct. The parties recognize they share common enemies, like the terrorist Iranian regime and its proxies, which are determined to destroy them. Nevertheless, they are persevering and succeeding in ways that seemed nearly impossible only a few years ago.

This is one of the real lessons of this book. We cannot keep on pursuing the same failed policies over and over again and expect different results. The new path open before us is truly energizing in terms of the opportunities offered for improving the well-being of humanity in the Middle East and the world. We may not disdain the achievements made because of some inexplicable attachment to ideology or prejudice borne of some biased or misguided corporate ethic of the past, untethered to reality. All too often, as described in this book, these affectations have resulted in immoral outcomes that harm instead of benefit humanity.

Peace through strength and moral policies based on a practical and realistic approach that fosters enlightened self-interest to achieve just and right goals are better suited to achieve useful results, which have proven to benefit humanity in practice.

Israel is a true and reliable ally and friend of the US, with shared values and common interests. Israel is a vibrant democracy with a diverse population and boasting cutting-edge technological achievements. It also fields one of the finest armed forces, possesses world-class health facilities and has a first-rate intelligence establishment that the US can trust and count on in real time. The US-Israel relationship is a real partnership, and the benefits flow both ways. As noted above, Israel makes remarkable contributions to the world, including in times of crisis and under the most difficult of circumstances. It is a genuine blessing to the world.

Psalms[979] declares that those who seek the peace of Jerusalem shall prosper and enjoy tranquility and the Bible[980] assures those who bless Israel will be blessed. We embrace these ethical imperatives and trust others will too. We hope that those who read this book will find a good reason to do so, as well.

May the blessings of peace prevail.

---

[979] Psalms 122:6.
[980] Numbers 24:9.